SOUTH AFRICA: TIME RUNNING OUT

The Report of the Study Commission on U.S. Policy Toward Southern Africa

UNIVERSITY OF CALIFORNIA PRESS

106279

FOREIGN POLICY STUDY FOUNDATION, INC.

University of California Press
Berkeley and Los Angeles, California

University of California Press, Ltd.
London, England

Library of Congress Cataloging in Publication Data

Study Commission on U.S. Policy Toward Southern Africa
South Africa: Time running out

1. United States—Foreign relations—South Africa.
2. South Africa—Foreign relations—Unites States.
I. Title
E182.8.S6S78 1981   327.73068   81-2742
                                          AACR2
cloth ISBN 0-520-04594-1
paper ISBN 0-520-04547-5

Printed in the United States of America

Book design by Samuel N. Antupit

Maps by General Cartography, Inc.

Contents

MAPS

TABLES

PART II. THE WIDER STAGE

PART III. POLICY

The Study Commission on U.S. Policy Toward Southern Africa

COMMISSIONERS

Franklin A. Thomas, Chair
President, the Ford Foundation

Robert C. Good
President, Denison University

Charles V. Hamilton
Wallace S. Sayre Professor of
Government; Columbia University

Ruth Simms Hamilton
Professor of Sociology and
Racial and Ethnic Studies,
Michigan State University

Alexander Heard
Chancellor,
Vanderbilt University

Aileen C. Hernandez
Urban Affairs Consultant

Constance Hilliard
International Director, Booker
T. Washington Foundation

C. Peter McColough
Chairman of the Board,
Xerox Corporation

J. Irwin Miller
Chairman, Executive and
Finance Committee,
Cummins Engine Company, Inc.

Alan Pifer
President, Carnegie
Corporation of New York

Howard D. Samuel
President, Industrial Union
Department, AFL-CIO

COMMISSION STAFF

Marc Fasteau
Staff Director and General Counsel

Milfred C. Fierce
Research Director

Linda Potter
Assistant to the Chair

Paul Lancaster
Senior Writer

John de St. Jorre
Senior Writer

Kenneth Thomas
Deputy General Counsel

Barbara H. Nelson
Research Associate

Stanley B. Greenberg
Research Associate

William N. Raiford
Research Associate

Stella L. Britton
Research Associate

Mark Collins
Research Assistant

Mary J. Keller
Treasurer

Edna Schwartz
Administrative Secretary

Evelyn Dalmeda
Secretary

ADVISERS TO THE COMMISSION

G. A. Costanzo
Vice-Chairman, Citibank N.A.

Donald F. McHenry
*Research Professor of
Diplomacy and International
Affairs, School of Foreign
Service, Georgetown University*

William S. Sneath
*Chairman and Chief Executive
Officer, Union Carbide
Corporation*

CONSULTANTS TO THE COMMISSION

Heribert Adam

David Albright

Millard Arnold

Larry W. Bowman

Gwendolen Carter

Duncan Clarke

Michael A. S. Corke

Chester Crocker

Kevin Danaher

Jorge I. Dominguez

Joyce Dube

John Dugard

C. Clyde Ferguson

William Foltz

Thomas Franck

Lawrence Franko

George M. Fredrickson

Michael George

Hermann Giliomee

Roy Godson

June Goodwin

William B. Gould

Ernest Gross

Ted Robert Gurr

C.R.D. Halisi

Peter Hawthorne

James Hoagland

Dudley Horner

Robert Jaster

Walton Johnson

Willard Johnson

Michael Kamara

Mark N. Kaplan

Thomas Karis

Helen Kitchen

Adam Klein

Eric Lane

Bruce Larkin

Robert Legvold

Tilden LeMelle

William M. Leogrande

Peter Lewin

Richard B. Lillich

Hollis Lynch

Bernard Magubane

John A. Marcum

Anthony Mathews

Congress Mbata

Steven McDonald

John E. Metcalf

Thami Mhlambiso

Ezekiel Mphahlele

Dunbar Moodie

Caryle Murphy

Desaix Myers III

Jill Nattrass

Quentin Peel

Robert M. Price

Richard D. Ralston

James W. Rawlings

Clarence Redekop

Elizabeth Reid

Stephen Ritterbush

Robert I. Rotberg

Robert Schrire

Aaron Segal

Ann W. Seidman

J.H.P. Serfontein

Charles Simkins

Bernard Simon

David Smock

Theodore C. Sorenson

Leonard Thompson

Sylvanus Tiewul

André du Toit

Dunstan M. Wai

Dwight Wait

Gary Walker

Vaughn C. Williams

EDITORIAL AND OTHER CONSULTANTS

Gilda Abramowitz

Ann Banks

Victoria Boughton

Martina D'Alton

Joanne Donelley

Hilary Elliott

Tamar Jacoby

Barbara S. Machtiger

Marjorie Mahle

Sydne Silverstein

Joel Solkoff

Martin Timin

Veronica Windholz

Foreword

My direct contact with South Africa began when I visited the country in 1976. I was struck first by the enormity of its problems and then by the vast potential of the land and its people, black and white. South Africa has the capacity to attract and repel a visitor—that is part of the tension one feels, part of the mystery of that country.

I left with a sense that there ought to be a way to help South Africans walk through the mine field that faced them, to a place where the future of the country could be freely and openly determined by all of its people, where individual freedoms are protected and opportunities to achieve are assured. I felt then that if a chance arose to make even a small contribution to change in South Africa I would take that opportunity. So, when the Rockefeller Foundation asked me to examine the feasibility of forming a study commission on U.S. policy toward that country, I accepted.

Eleven people joined me to form the Study Commission on U.S. Policy Toward Southern Africa. (One had to withdraw later because a new appointment precluded participation.) Our assignment was to determine how the United States can best respond to the problems posed by South Africa and its dismaying system of racial separation and discrimination. I did not know three of the commissioners, and most of them had not met one another. They have diverse backgrounds and strong reputations in a variety of fields: business, labor, universities, foundations, government service. None was a specialist in southern Africa. All of us have served in our individual capacities, not as representatives of the institutions or groups with which we are affiliated.*

From the outset, we made no claim to a dispassionate attitude toward

---

*Biographical sketches of the commissioners appear at the end of the report.

South Africa. We began our work with the firm conviction that apartheid is wrong and the hope that the transition to a more just society in South Africa would not be long delayed. At the same time, we did not come with preformed conclusions as to the relative importance of the different U.S. interests at stake in South Africa or policies for advancing them. We pledged to give a full and fair hearing to all points of view.

We agreed to absorb information for a year, to refrain from talking about policy until we felt reasonably confident of the facts. Only then did we begin to tackle the policy questions. This procedure had the merit of draining some of the emotion out of the issues and allowing us to focus more clearly on the complex realities.

One of our members with extensive experience on other commissions told us: "It usually takes a year to reach a point of maximum disagreement within a commission, and at least another year to put things together again. The danger is that if the second phase is rushed because of arbitrary deadlines, the quality of the analysis will suffer in pursuit of a quick consensus."

The other danger, of course, is that after the nadir is reached, a commission fails to arrive at a consensus of any kind on the difficult issues. We had moments of profound disagreement and debate and, on some key topics, we found ourselves taking different routes to reach what turned out to be the same conclusion. But we did, in the end, achieve a genuine consensus on all the major issues, and we present a unanimous report.

Scholarly and journalistic studies of South Africa have not been lacking in the past, but we found that serious gaps existed. Most conspicuous has been the absence of a carefully thought out and articulated framework relating the full range of U.S. interests to policy. Sometimes when specific proposals have emerged—withdrawal by American business or broad economic sanctions against South Africa, to mention two frequently urged—little effort has been made to think through how they would produce the desired changes. Persuasive analysis of the strategic and economic importance of South Africa to the West has also been missing. The feasibility study for the Commission observed: "The absence of reliable analysis of various policy options has made it easy to take either the 'realpolitik' or the 'high moral' position in a kind of factual vacuum."

The decision to proceed with the project was made by the Rockefeller Foundation in December 1978. I agreed to serve as chair, and the Commission began taking shape the next spring. Funding was provided, and an independent, tax-exempt nonprofit corporation, the Foreign Policy Study Foundation, Inc., with commissioners serving as its board of directors, was established to receive and administer the grant. The original name of the Commission—the Study Commission on U.S. Policy Toward Southern Africa—was retained, even though its main focus has been South Africa.

A staff was hired and a research program mapped. A stream of background reading began flowing to Commission members in the summer of 1979. In the fall we began our formal exploration of the issues through a series of meetings in New York City with a wide range of knowledgeable persons. Among the topics covered were South African history, black and white politics, the law and practice of apartheid, the South African economy, internal forces for change, South African military and internal security capabilities, South Africa's relations with the rest of Africa and with the international community in general, American interests in South Africa, past and present U.S. foreign policy toward South Africa, and the Soviet and Cuban roles in southern Africa.

This was followed by a two-and-a-half-week trip to South Africa in early 1980. Commission members traveled widely—Johannesburg, Cape Town, Durban, Port Elizabeth, Pretoria, Ulundi, the Transkei. We talked with cabinet members, government administrators, leaders of the white parliamentary opposition, businessmen, farmers, union leaders, scholars, and journalists. We visited urban African "townships" and rural resettlement communities occupied by Africans newly evicted from "white" areas. We listened to the views of African leaders and angry young residents of Soweto, the large African township outside Johannesburg. We met with representatives of the Coloured and Indian communities. We gained firsthand experience of the South African legal system when we met one by one with "banned" dissidents, who were forbidden to see more than one person at a time.

In South Africa the Commission sometimes split into smaller groups to cover more ground. We did the same in subsequent travel elsewhere in Africa, visiting Namibia, Botswana, Lesotho, Mozambique, Malawi, Zambia, Tanzania, Kenya, and Nigeria. Commission members talked to, among many others, President Kenneth Kaunda in Lusaka, an African National Congress leader in Dar es Salaam, Nigerian legislators in Lagos, and young South African exiles in Nairobi. Staff members accompanied us and made additional trips of their own to South Africa and Zimbabwe.

Along with continuing research, in the spring of 1980 the Commission held meetings in New York City, Washington, and San Francisco, at which representatives from a wide spectrum of U.S. groups and institutions presented their views on policy toward South Africa. Their recommendations ranged from support for immediate all-out armed struggle against the South African government to what amounted to acceptance of the status quo. Civil rights, antiapartheid, religious, congressional, and student groups were represented, as were university administrations, corporations, research and public policy institutes, and state and local governments.* In the late spring and early summer of 1980, groups of Commission members also held meetings in Eng-

*A full list of the groups and individuals whose views were solicited by the Commission can be found in Appendix A.

land, France, and West Germany with government officials, business leaders, and others involved with South African issues.

Following these meetings, we began to sort out what we had learned and to assess the current course of events in South Africa, the prospects for change, and the range of American policy options. This effort continued into the fall, and then in November we returned to South Africa. Renewing discussions with South Africans encountered on the first trip and eliciting the views of others, we sought reactions to our emerging ideas and tried to gauge the impact of proposals under consideration.

Back home the Commission held a final series of meetings lasting into 1981 to draft its policy recommendations (part III) and to review and edit the background chapters (parts I and II) of the report. With some exceptions, information in the background chapters is drawn from papers written for the Commission by specialists in the particular subject. The Commission also consulted with its advisers and their staffs: G. A. Costanzo, vice-chairman of the board of Citibank; and William Sneath, chairman of the board of Union Carbide Corporation—as well as with three former senior government officials: Henry Kissinger, Donald F. McHenry, and Cyrus Vance. The Commission spent a total of seventy-five days in meetings and fact-finding trips, and many additional days in individual work.

It is understood that the people referred to above are not responsible for the Commission's findings and recommendations, although they may find their viewpoints reflected in sections of the text.

I am deeply grateful to the members of the Commission for the devotion, energy, and wisdom they applied to the task. I am grateful to the staff for its extraordinary skill and zeal in serving the members' needs. My thanks go as well to the many individuals and organizations who gave generously of their time to help educate us. Finally, we all acknowledge not only the generous sponsorship of the Rockefeller Foundation but also its prescience and that of its late president, John Knowles, in focusing on South Africa as an issue destined to come to the fore in the 1980s.

I am aware that we are addressing an audience of great diversity. There is a tendency when dealing with a subject as emotional and complex as South Africa for all of us to grab only a piece of the elephant. The hard thing is to see all the different parts at once, to see that there is indeed a very large and complex object confronting us. Many readers will turn first to the sections of the report that interest them most. Ideally, they will read the others as well.

Our report appears as the new administration settles into office in Washington. There is talk of a shifting emphasis in foreign policy, of less stress on its human rights component and more on strategic and economic "realities." While these realities are both present and important in the problem of policy toward South Africa, the issues of political freedom and civil liberties in that country also have a tangible impact on the United States. We hope that policymakers will carefully weigh all aspects of the South African question before deciding on a course. That is what we have tried to do.

—Franklin A. Thomas
New York City
May 1981

Introduction

For the casual reader the question may arise: Why South Africa? Or for one already familiar with the subject: Why South Africa *again*?

The African continent is the only major area in the world where the United States does not have a history of close involvement. But things are changing. Three African countries—Nigeria, Libya, and Algeria—supply the United States with almost 40 percent of its imported oil. There is increasing strategic interest on the part of the superpowers in the Red Sea and the Indian Ocean. South Africa itself has resources that are valued by the West. The forces of African nationalism, checked for a time on the banks of the Zambezi River, have moved south to the Limpopo. The South African army is fighting African nationalist forces along the Namibia-Angola border. Over recent years, the level of Soviet, Cuban, and other Communist states' involvement in Africa has increased.

We cannot ignore South Africa. What happens in that country affects the United States. The uniqueness of apartheid attracts world attention. "What sets South Africa apart from other countries that have equally oppressive human rights records," a U.S. senator said not long ago, "is that its policies are based on race, made 'legal' through legislation, and justified in the name of defending the West from Communism."

Most Americans, when asked to focus on it, deplore apartheid. But they disagree sharply on what policy the United States should adopt toward South Africa. Some urge a broad assault on apartheid: wide-ranging economic sanctions, perhaps even aid for groups beginning to wage an armed struggle against the South African government. Others back selective pressures but shrink from military involvement of any sort. Some would rely largely on moral suasion. Others argue that however strongly we disapprove of apartheid, South Africa's management of its affairs is its own business.

Those who are wary of acting vigorously against apartheid often reflect the widespread uneasiness about taking on expanded obligations abroad that has characterized the United States since the Vietnam war. Skepticism persists about our ability to influence events beyond our shores and to cure the world's ills—indeed, even to look out for our own vital interests. To many who share this skepticism, the racial practices of the white minority that rules a largely black nation in a remote corner of the globe seem beyond the effective reach of American policy.

Other considerations also affect American thinking about South Africa, further complicating the forging of a consensus on policy. U.S. companies carry on significant trade with South Africa and have sizable investments there. The United States imports from South Africa a number of relatively scarce minerals—including chromium, manganese, platinum, and vanadium—of great industrial and military importance. Some analysts contend that South Africa's active collaboration is required to protect the ocean shipping lanes around the Cape of Good Hope, the path now followed by much of the West's oil. All agree, however, that South Africa's mineral riches and its position on the Cape route are inescapable considerations in shaping a realistic policy. So, too, is the U.S. interest in minimizing Communist influence in southern Africa. Communist support contributed to the end of white rule in Angola, Mozambique, and Rhodesia. In the Angolan civil war, Soviet-backed Cuban troops fought for the present government against forces aided by South African troops. Now there is concern about a Communist threat to South Africa. Some analysts assert that the United States should support the South African government to counter this threat.

Others take the opposite view. They insist that by maintaining friendly ties to the present government of South Africa we will ensure the enmity of the black government that they predict will someday assume power there. The way to block the spread of Communist influence, they argue, is to give strong backing now to the forces for change in South Africa. Moreover, it is suggested, American economic and political relations with the black states that occupy most of the African continent will hinge increasingly on the stand we take on South Africa. If we fail to oppose apartheid at every turn, according to this view, we will lose friends in the rest of Africa. We will also run the risk of losing access to black Africa's resources. Nigeria, a major supplier of oil to the United States, has already hinted that it might use its oil weapon against nations that fail to take firm measures against apartheid.

Whatever the importance of access to resources and other geopolitical calculations, debate over American policy toward South Africa always returns to apartheid. This is inevitable because South Africa's racial system dismays large segments of the American public sensitized by our own history of racial discrimination and the struggle to overcome it.

For all South Africans, but particularly for blacks—using "black" to embrace Africans, those persons of mixed descent known as "Coloureds," and

Asians—racially based laws govern most aspects of life. For blacks, they circumscribe daily life and limit possibilities. They determine residence, job, schooling, and leisure activities. Racial laws also deny South African blacks any significant voice in the government that controls their existence. Whatever explanations and defenses South African whites may offer, such a system could not fail to offend most Americans. The issue also continues to roil corporations, campuses, and churches.

If it is accepted that apartheid is evil, is promoting political freedom and civil liberties abroad a proper concern of U.S. foreign policy? We discuss this in greater detail in chapter 17, but it may be helpful to touch on the issue here. The emphasis given human rights inevitably varies from situation to situation. And, historically, human rights have seldom been the determining factor in shaping foreign policy—other, more concrete interests usually play that role. But over the last two decades the human rights question has become an accepted element of policy formulation, established by law, practice, and common concern. The bedrock for this development is our belief in political freedom and civil liberties. This is the core of the political ideology the United States and its allies have sought to defend against communism, fascism, and other arbitrary and repressive forms of government.

There is another reason for the United States to seek to advance the cause of representative government in South Africa. That is the issue of race. Unlike South Africa's other major trading partners—Britain, France, West Germany, Japan—the United States has a long history of conflict, experiment, and accommodation in racial and ethnic matters. The United States is, in ways these other countries are not, a truly multiracial, multiethnic nation. Although inequalities, grievances, and prejudice remain, significant progress has been made. But race relations in the United States are not immune to events beyond our borders. Sustained racial violence in South Africa would initiate a bitter domestic debate over the appropriate U.S. response, a debate that could erode the consensus favoring progress on race relations here.

The landscape has changed rapidly in southern Africa. The white buffer of Rhodesia and the Portuguese colonies that used to separate South Africa from black-ruled Africa has gone. In its place are the independent black nations of Zimbabwe, Angola, and Mozambique. Namibia, still ruled by South Africa as the territory of South-West Africa, is being fought and argued over but it appears likely that it, too, will join the ranks of independent black-ruled countries. Thus, South Africa faces the future as the last outpost of white supremacy on the continent. There also change is inevitable, though the timetable, the form it will take, and whether it can happen without major violence are open questions.

The pressures for change now building within South Africa are not new. The African National Congress, a major element in black resistance to white domination, dates from 1912. The early 1960s saw a wave of sabotage and demonstrations, beginning with the bloodily repressed Sharpeville protest.

Today blacks appear determined not to continue to submit to apartheid. In what has been viewed as a turning point in black militancy, students in Soweto, the vast segregated African "township" outside Johannesburg, marched and demonstrated in 1976 to register dissatisfaction with their schooling. Their actions and the government's response touched off disturbances around the country. Another wave of student demonstrations occurred in 1980, dominated this time by Coloured youths in Cape Town and Port Elizabeth angry over poorly staffed, poorly equipped schools. In recent years black workers in Durban, Port Elizabeth, Johannesburg, and Cape Town have engaged in major strikes, many of them political in character.

The South African government has met the protesters with an iron hand. During the 1976 student demonstrations the police opened fire on several occasions, killing hundreds. There have been jailings and "bannings," a South African procedure that sometimes amounts to house arrest. Many young people have gone into exile.

At the same time, the government has sought to satisfy at least some black demands. And on the wider scene there are hints that the protests have sharpened a sense among some Afrikaners, the whites of predominantly Dutch descent who control the ruling National party, that apartheid has hit a dead end. There appears to be a growing awareness that the flood tide of history and the reality of black numbers cannot be resisted forever and that change—as yet of a hazy, undefined nature—is inevitable.

Some South African critics of apartheid doubt that significant progress is under way. Commenting on conciliatory statements by Pieter W. Botha, the current prime minister, South African legal scholar John Dugard told us in 1980: "There has been a great deal of talk about change under Botha. What is left of apartheid after all of this change? I would say ninety percent or more. There has been a confusion of rhetoric with real change."

But perhaps the change in rhetoric is not without significance, reflecting a new sensitivity to black concerns. Hendrik Verwoerd, prime minister from 1958 to 1966 and the principal architect of apartheid, could blandly describe the role of African workers as "the service of white people." Now such naked racism has largely disappeared from official pronouncements, and Prime Minister Botha talks of the need to consult with blacks as South Africa charts its course for the future.

Whether or not these changes are merely "cosmetic," as some would insist, an abyss still yawns between the aspirations of blacks and the willingness of whites to share power. "What Afrikaners feel will come the day after tomorrow is what blacks feel should have come yesterday," says a South African newspaperman. That is probably an understatement. "One man, one vote" is the rallying cry of most black leaders. "Never," responds Prime Minister Botha. Thus, the crucial question is whether change can take place fast enough to prevent a confrontation that would almost certainly produce appalling bloodshed.

Although large-scale armed intervention from outside remains a remote possibility, most of those closely concerned with the situation believe the major impetus for change will come from within South Africa. "Only the people inside South Africa can make changes," says President Kenneth Kaunda of Zambia. In South Africa, Percy Qoboza, a leading African editor who was imprisoned in a 1977 crackdown on government critics, declares: "Whatever happens, the solution lies with us."

But none of this means that outside forces are without influence, and the United States must be counted among the most important of these. Both whites and blacks in South Africa tend to look to the United States with hope. It is sometimes said that South African whites respond to external pressures by figuratively withdrawing into the "laager"—the circle of wagons that the Boers trekking into the interior in the nineteenth century relied on for protection—but the visitors to the country quickly learn that outsiders' attitudes do matter to them. A cabinet member told us, "I couldn't care less what conclusions you come to." Then he spent the better part of two hours showing he indeed cared greatly.

As for South African blacks, many have drawn hope from America's concern for human rights. More specifically, some black leaders have borrowed ideas from the civil rights and black power movements in the United States. A prime example was Steve Biko, the young African leader who died in 1977 as a result of injuries received while held in detention by the South African police and who has become a martyr to the antiapartheid cause in South Africa. Blacks now look to the United States to act more forcefully against apartheid. In Ulundi, Chief Gatsha Buthelezi, the Zulu leader, admonished us: "You must do more than cry for us. We can drown in your tears."

Even in the face of such appeals, Americans' acute awareness of the limitations they encounter abroad gives pause. In the case of South Africa, statements by the American government criticizing apartheid over the years have produced little tangible benefit for South African blacks. On the other hand, a significant number of American businesses operating in South Africa—putting aside for now the debate over whether they could strike the strongest blow against the racial system by withdrawing—have lately achieved real, if modest, improvements in the lot of their black workers. And so the question arises whether there are other possibilities, including economic, diplomatic, political, and cultural actions, for the United States to bring its weight to bear against apartheid and to promote change with a minimum of violence.

In parts I and II of the report, those aspects of the South African scene and related international developments on which decisions about U.S policy must be based are examined in detail. In part III, U.S. options are analyzed and policy recommendations are made for both the U.S. government and private institutions. We think we have produced a comprehensive and realistic framework for policy, based on a thorough analysis of U.S. interests and the South African context, that should remain useful whatever happens in South Africa in the years to come. The report is also intended to serve as a basic resource on the subject for both the general reader and the specialist.

There is a risk in studies of this kind of slipping into abstractions, of forgetting the human factor. We have tried to avoid this by asking South Africans of all races to talk about themselves, their lives, their country. The resulting interviews are grouped in three separate sections in the report. They cover a broad range of opinion, experience, and background. By mutual agreement, the people interviewed remain anonymous. The aim of the interviews was to reproduce some of the flavor of South Africans talking, avoiding, if possible, explicitly political matters. Politics, nevertheless, remained pervasive.

The first group of interviews includes a migrant worker, a farmer, an industrial painter, a priest, a manager, and a township teacher; the second group, a clerk, an investment banker, a sculptor, a business family, a builder, a doctor, and an executive; the third group, a lawyer, a civil servant, a homeland teacher, a union leader, and a student.

The last glimpse of South Africa is a short description of a church service in Soweto. This was the Commission's first contact, as a group, with black South Africans. It was a moving experience.

White South Africans often say, in defense of their system or to justify the slow pace of change, that you cannot compare the United States and South Africa. There are too many differences between the two societies, they say, for lessons about race relations in the United States to apply. While that is true in important ways, there are also instructive parallels. Much of the rhetoric from white South Africans is familiar to Americans who remember the justifications offered here for resistance to desegregation and equal political and civil rights for blacks. "If it weren't for outside agitators, blacks would be content. . . . We know our blacks better than anyone else. . . . We are working on the problem but we must do it in our own way and at our own pace."

The formulation of new approaches to the problem is urgent. There is already violence in South Africa. If genuine progress toward meeting the grievances of South Africa's blacks is not made soon, it will intensify and spread. Time is running out.

Summary of Findings and Recommendations

U.S. INTERESTS: WHAT'S AT STAKE FOR THE UNITED STATES IN SOUTH AFRICA?

- **Protecting U.S. military and strategic interests and minimizing Soviet influence in southern Africa.** Unimpeded use of the Cape sea route, along which much of the West's oil passes, is of great strategic importance to the United States. So is curbing Communist influence in the region. The question is how best to go about protecting these interests.

- **Ensuring adequate supplies of key minerals imported from South Africa.** Four groups of minerals exported by South Africa are strategically and economically important to the United States: chromium and ferrochrome, manganese and ferromanganese, platinum, and vanadium.

- **Advancing political freedom and civil liberties for all South Africans.** This concern grows out of our national history and fundamental American moral and philosophical beliefs. The denial of basic freedoms under apartheid also risks sustained racial violence in South Africa that would trigger bitter controversy within the United States, controversy that could erode the consensus favoring progress on race relations in this country. The United States therefore has a strong interest in promoting movement, with a minimum of violence, toward a system in which political power is shared in a manner acceptable to all racial groups and the civil liberties of all South Africans are protected.

- **Maintaining satisfactory diplomatic and commercial relations with other African countries.** The United States has $4.5 billion in direct investment in African countries other than South Africa and $13.7 billion worth of annual trade. Nigeria is particularly significant as the United States' second largest foreign oil supplier and a leading African opponent of apartheid. Diplomatic and political support of the African countries is important to the United States, especially in international organizations, and is linked to a considerable extent to U.S. policies toward South Africa.

- **Maintaining commercial relations with South Africa.** The United States has $2 billion of direct investment in South Africa and trade totaling $3.4 billion a year.

SOUTH AFRICAN REALITIES AND TRENDS AND THE COMMISSION'S FINDINGS

- Whatever the South African government does to reinforce the status quo, black forces inside the country will eventually alter it.

- The final battle lines have not yet been drawn in South Africa. Fundamental political change without sustained, large-scale violence is still possible, although time is running out.

- For blacks and whites, certain positions are nonnegotiable. For blacks, an acceptable solution must give them a genuine share in political power. For whites, an acceptable solution cannot be based on a winner-take-all form of majority rule. This is both the core of the problem and, because the nonnegotiables are not necessarily irreconcilable, the key to its solution.

- Many white leaders appear to accept the need to undertake some real reforms, and many black leaders appear to accept that fundamental changes will not come quickly and that compromises will have to be made. Younger blacks, however, are growing more radical and impatient.

- There is much ferment and many contradictory forces at work in South African society. Continuing government repression coincides with some positive reforms and a great deal of debate among all racial groups. There is no clear pattern for the future.

- Whites are not ready to accept blacks as equals or to share power with them. Some whites talk of the need to do so but have not begun to address the issue in a way satisfactory to blacks. And blacks do not yet possess sufficient leverage to compel whites to share power.

- Black and white South Africans must make their own choices, and whatever system they freely and fairly choose should be respected by the United States and the international community.

- There are no easy solutions for South Africa. The choice is not between "slow peaceful change" and "quick violent change" but between a slow, uneven, sporadically violent evolutionary process and a slow but much more violent descent into civil war.

- Both paths could lead to genuine power sharing. The United States should do what it can to encourage the former course because it promises less bloodshed and economic destruction and a government more responsive to the rights of all groups, and is more likely to protect the full range of U.S. interests.

- The active collaboration of the South African government, whatever its ideology, is *not* an important factor in protecting the Cape sea route. A greater source of danger to the West is the growth of Soviet influence in the region, promoted by white intransigence in South Africa, growing political instability, rising levels of racial violence, and armed conflict.

- Stoppages in the supply of key minerals exported from South Africa, should they occur, are likely to be partial, intermittent, and short term in duration. Medium-term (five-to-ten-year) and long-term (more than ten-year) interruptions are unlikely.

POLICY RECOMMENDATIONS: OBJECTIVES AND ACTIONS

We recommend a policy based on the simultaneous pursuit of five objectives. These are intended to serve as an integrated framework for action by both the U.S. government and U.S. private organizations. Actions supporting the objectives are intended to be put into effect as soon as possible, except for those associated with Objective 2. They should remain in effect until a genuine sharing of political power, acceptable to all races, is implemented in South Africa.

Objective 1

To make clear the fundamental and continuing opposition of the U.S. government and people to the system of apartheid, with particular emphasis on the exclusion of blacks from an effective share in political power.

Actions taken to pursue this objective show black and white South Africans and all those concerned with the issue that the United States' opposition to apartheid is profound and constant. If this point is made clearly and continuously, misunderstanding of U.S. motives in recognizing and encouraging partial progress in South Africa (see Objective 2) and remaining engaged with that country in other ways (see Objective 3) should be minimized.

The actions for this objective fall into two categories. First, those to be implemented by the U.S. government, which include broadening the arms embargo to cover foreign subsidiaries of U.S. companies, broadening the nuclear embargo, and withholding diplomatic recognition and economic aid from the independent homelands.

The second category applies to U.S. corporations. Those in South Africa should not expand their operations, and those not already there should stay out. Those in South Africa should commit a generous proportion of their corporate resources—determined in accordance with a specific "social development expenditure standard"—to improving the lives of black South Africans, and should subscribe to and implement the Sullivan Principles. Compliance with the principles should be effectively monitored. All these measures should be undertaken on a voluntary basis for the moment, and the government should endorse them as important parts of overall U.S. policy.

Disinvestment and other major economic sanctions are not recommended under current circumstances.

Objective 2

To promote genuine political power sharing in South Africa with a minimum of violence by systematically exerting influence on the South African government.

Effective pressure for change in South Africa requires not only a clearly communicated overall posture toward apartheid, but also continuing government-to-government contact to maximize the weight and credibility of the United States' views on particular events in South Africa. The United States has limited leverage. It cannot alter the situation in South Africa radically, but it can encourage positive and discourage negative initiatives by the South African government through the use of inducements and pressures.

Many pressures are already in force, but there are others that could be used if the South African government showed signs of adopting more repressive policies. These include diplomatic moves such as reducing the levels of U.S. representation in South Africa and South African representation in the United States. Barring the export of particular categories of U.S. goods, services, and technology through the Export Administration Act is another avenue for possible action. A case in point is the export of American technology in oil exploration and drilling, on which South Africa relies heavily in its efforts to find the only major energy resource it now lacks.

Inducements tend to be the reverse of pressures. If the South African government showed itself to be serious about genuine change through specific actions, the United States should take commensurate steps toward a closer and more friendly relationship.

Objective 3

To support organizations inside South Africa working for change, assist the development of black leadership, and promote black welfare.

The purpose of this objective is to strengthen the forces for change within South Africa and provide a mandate for constructive action by the U.S. private-sector organizations in the United States. Specific actions are proposed in support of black and multiracial labor unions, educational programs, and public interest, self-help, and other organizations in South Africa.

Objective 4

To assist the economic development of the other states in southern Africa, including reduction of the imbalance in their economic relations with South Africa.

Strengthening the economies of these states and making them less dependent on South Africa serves all U.S. interests. Actions for pursuit of this objective include aid on a regional basis to the newly formed Southern African Development Coordination Conference (SADCC), particularly for the development of agriculture, transport, communications, and energy resources. Increased aid for Zimbabwe is emphasized as well as encouragement to the private sector to expand trade and industrial development in the region.

Objective 5

To reduce the impact of stoppages of imports of key minerals from South Africa.

Actions taken to pursue this objective are not intended to end U.S use of South African minerals, but to minimize the impact of potential stoppages of imports of the four key minerals: chromium and ferrochrome, manganese and ferromanganese, platinum, and vanadium. The recommended actions include increasing stockpiles, particularly of ferrochrome and ferromanganese, developing a national minerals policy and contingency plans, some diversification of sources of supply, and development of the transport systems of the other mineral-supplying states in the region.

GENERAL RECOMMENDATIONS FOR THE U.S. GOVERNMENT

- Encourage the United States' allies to adopt similar policies.
- Issue a white paper defining U.S. interests in South and Southern Africa and describing the overall framework for policy.
- Establish a high-level interdepartmental committee to coordinate policy toward South Africa.

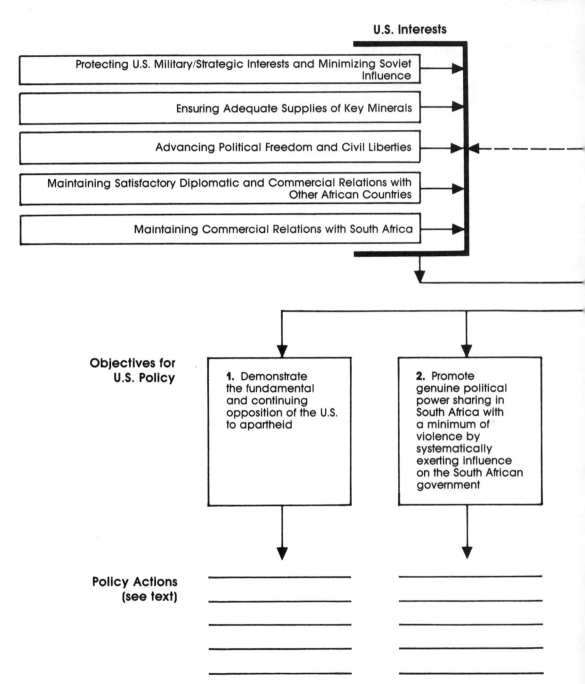

U.S. Interests

Protecting U.S. Military/Strategic Interests and Minimizing Soviet Influence

Ensuring Adequate Supplies of Key Minerals

Advancing Political Freedom and Civil Liberties

Maintaining Satisfactory Diplomatic and Commercial Relations with Other African Countries

Maintaining Commercial Relations with South Africa

Objectives for U.S. Policy

1. Demonstrate the fundamental and continuing opposition of the U.S. to apartheid

2. Promote genuine political power sharing in South Africa with a minimum of violence by systematically exerting influence on the South African government

Policy Actions (see text)

FRAMEWORK

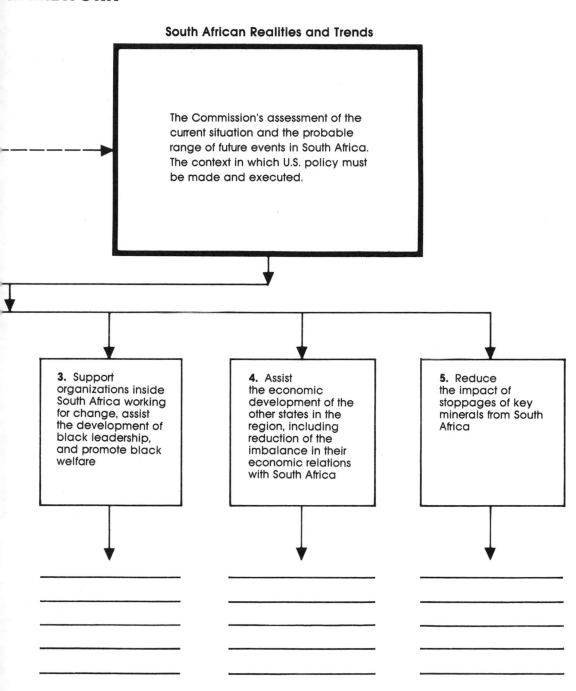

South African Realities and Trends

The Commission's assessment of the current situation and the probable range of future events in South Africa. The context in which U.S. policy must be made and executed.

3. Support organizations inside South Africa working for change, assist the development of black leadership, and promote black welfare

4. Assist the economic development of the other states in the region, including reduction of the imbalance in their economic relations with South Africa

5. Reduce the impact of stoppages of key minerals from South Africa

SOUTH AFRICANS TALKING

A Migrant Worker

At dawn in the Dube hostel in Soweto (an acronym for Johannesburg's African southwest township), in a corner of the long, cold dormitory, a man climbs stiffly from his simple metal-frame bed. He folds the sheets and single blanket carefully. The dormitory is cold: Most of the windows are broken and the door has been kicked in. He lights a Primus stove by his bed and heats a bucket of water for shaving. While he waits for the water to heat, he takes a suitcase from a tall steel locker by the side of his bed. It contains a jacket and trousers and a crisply ironed shirt. As he dresses he listens to an FM radio station broadcasting in his tribal language, Tswana. It competes with the noise of similar broadcasts in other languages—mainly Sotho and Zulu—from other radios in the room. Before he leaves, he puts the suitcase, radio, and stove into the steel cabinet, securing the door with a strong padlock.

The last thing he does is to check that he has his passbook in his jacket pocket. "I was once picked up without my pass," he recalls, "and held in jail overnight before they put me on a train back to Rustenburg," a city neighboring Bophuthatswana, his homeland in the western Transvaal. "When I got to Rustenburg, I walked across to the other side of the railway line and got on another train going back to Johannesburg. I only missed two days of work."

When I first came to Johannesburg, in about 1968, I was

working part-time. I found a man who got me some papers—I paid him some money and didn't ask any questions. I registered for temporary employment because I could not be registered permanently. But even then I couldn't get accommodation in Soweto because I belonged to Bophuthatswana. I did not know the formula for staying legally in Johannesburg, I didn't know what steps to take. So I told my boss the whole thing, and he told a bit of a lie, saying I was a domestic servant staying at his place. That was the only way I could get permission to stay in the city. According to my passbook I was a domestic servant, but I worked in my boss's company as a salesman.

My contract as a migrant worker is for twelve months, and every year I have to return to Rustenburg and renew the contract for another year. Strictly for one year; you cannot extend your contract for more than one year. I have a Bophuthatswana passport. I don't know if it is internationally recognized or not, but it is the only passport they are issuing to us presently in Bophuthatswana. But I never have to show my passport anyway, because I also have a reference book that says whatever person I am, and if I need to I show that.

At present I'm registered as a clerk. I work for an export company. I have been doing this for almost ten years. The people who own my work are very, very nice. There are a few people in the office who are not nice, but my bosses are nice to me, so I will stay with them. I have no option but to stay. There is no point of leaving. I will get a pension when I retire. And if I am disabled at all, those people are responsible for me.

I am happy with this company because I feel that they are giving me an opportunity to slowly learn more. My duties presently are filing and handling office supplies, but I feel that one day I will be doing jobs that some whites are doing and I will be getting the same pay. It's a matter of time and training. They are training me in the company, on the job, and I have been studying on my own—commercial subjects, accounting and so on. I would be happy to stay with this company for a long time.

I live at Dube men's hostel, in the center of Soweto, not far from the railway station. The hostel is like a barracks for soldiers. It's not a nice place for anyone to stay at. I stay there because it's cheap and I want to save money. There is no plaster on the walls and the floors are rough concrete. More than seven hundred people are crammed into it. We have only cold showers, and no canteen or cooking facility. You cook your own food on a Primus stove. You supply your own blankets and mattresses and pillows. The toilets are communal, and we have no privacy.

At night we have electricity. We can read and write letters home. We do our own washing and ironing—heating up the iron on a Primus stove. When I finish ironing I put my shirt and trousers in my suitcase and lock them up in my locker, because if I leave them exposed they get dirty or they get stolen. No one cleans the hostel. We clean it. I don't think anybody cares about anything but getting the rent. They make sure they get their rent. If you don't pay them one day you find that your stuff has been taken away and someone else is in your bed—and they chase you away.

We are not allowed to have women in the hostel. The police raid it frequently and arrest any women they find there. But when the law doesn't see, we get prostitutes and girlfriends in. Many of the women don't get paid by the men, but they stay in the hostel anyway because they have nowhere else to go. Some of them stay there and drink all day. The men are lonely, a long way from home, and they have to have women—there's not much anyone can do about it. I'm lucky because I can get a bus sometimes at weekends to see my wife in Rustenburg.

Sometimes my wife comes to visit me here. She has a Bophuthatswana passport, otherwise she would be arrested for being in Johannesburg without permission. But when she comes here I have to make arrangements for her to stay with my sisters. Of course, if I had a lot of money we could book into the Carlton Hotel over the weekend [he laughs].

If I don't go home over the weekends, I watch soccer matches in the township. And if there is no soccer, I go to bioscopes [the movies]. On Sunday I go to church in Soweto—the Lutheran church. And sometimes on weekends I stay with my two sisters, who are domestic servants—they are also migrant workers—in Johannesburg. I'm not a drinking man, but some of the guys at the hostel drink all weekend. They process their own Bantu beer. They process quite a lot and sell it to others. Then they get drunk and fight among themselves. Me, I keep to myself. I keep out of the way.

The men who live in Dube come from all over the place. They are different nations—Shanganis, Zulus, Tswanas, Pedis—and they seem to get on reasonably well with each other. Only the Zulus are funny; they keep their group separate from the others. Some of these men get home only once every year for a few weeks. I am much better off than people who live so far away. And there are many in the hostel who are earning only 10 rand* a week—people working for the municipality or in laboring jobs that other people won't do. They are from far away and that's the only type of employment they can get.

I get 300 rand a month. Five years ago I was earning half that much. It costs me nearly 5 rand per month to travel by train from the hostel to work. Then I pay 5.50 rand round trip each time I go home to Rustenburg. I budget my wages so that I can go and see my wife and kids once a month. And I live cheaply in the hostel: Rent is 7.45 rand per month. A lot of my friends say, "How can you stay in that terrible place?" But it suits me. I don't spend too much, and I am saving a little money. My wife must have enough money for groceries and to look after my parents and my sister's children—my sister is in Johannesburg, so I help keep her children, put them in school, and clothe them. It's sort of a family affair. I also built my own house, on a plot of land fifty meters by fifty meters. It's just a little four-room house with no electricity, but we have a few goats and fowl.

The worst thing is being away from your family for such a long time. But there is nothing you can do. We just have to accept these conditions. If I stay in Rustenburg, I am not able to earn enough to make a living, especially with a family. But in Johannesburg it is much better. You just have to make the sacrifice. You can achieve your aims here.

I feel that if at some stage we are allowed to live where we want to live, I would bring my family and stay in Johannesburg. I would still be happy to be a Bophuthatswana citizen provided that my wife and family could stay with me. But now they are trying to tighten the law.

---

*One rand: A unit of South African currency equivalent to 1.25 U.S. dollars on March 31, 1980. One South African cent equals U.S. 1.25 cents.

It's much more difficult now. You can't stay where you
want to stay.

And I think things are going to get worse. Let's say
Bophuthatswana gets more developed, more towns, more
employment opportunities. Then I am afraid all the migrants who came from that particular place will have to
go back and find work there. That means they will have
to start from scratch again and make very little money.
But maybe it will not be so bad. I've got it in my mind
that with a bit of luck I might be able to do some business
of my own in Bophuthatswana—open a little shop to sell
vegetables and things, or maybe I could build a big hall
to run a bioscope. I have plans for the future, because I
feel that one day all the Tswanas here and the Zulus and
the Sothos, all those people from the homelands, will have
to go back.

A Farmer

*The wine farmer's house is a classic Dutch-gable, white-
washed and thatched, set among tall ferns and wild fig
and mimosa trees. Part of the old stable has been converted
into a restaurant. The setting is so traditional that the Van
Riebeeck Society holds functions there several times a year,
with Afrikaners dressed in seventeenth-century costumes
for* volkspele *(folk dancing).*

*A sleepy Great Dane is draped across the entrance to
the main house. Inside, the paneling, floors, and beams are
made of local teak and yellowwood. The meal consists of
Cape salmon and lamb casserole cooked with dried raisins
and peaches, followed by a rich syrupy pudding. The old
boer [farmer], whose hair is white now, tastes the wine
before serving his guests around the long gnarled table.
One bottle is not up to scratch and is returned to the kitchen.
A Coloured maid in a green apron and* doek *(turban) serves
at the table. After the meal there is thick sweet coffee and
a fine ten-year-old Cape brandy.*

*"The saying goes that the Huguenots arrived here with
a Bible in one hand and a vine in the other. What we have,
we created for ourselves. We inherited nothing. My ancestors sailed to the Cape in 1688, fleeing religious and political persecution in France. Three hundred years later*

5

it's easy to see their roots. Look at their names: Du Plessis, Joubert, Le Roux, Labuschagne, de Villiers. Some of my family went inland, but most of us stayed here in the wine country."

The Huguenots were good farmers and found the sheltered valleys and climate of the Cape perfect for cultivating the vine. "There's about seven thousand wine growers here now—a $150-million industry." The old man, who is passing on a lot of the work to his son, sips his coffee. "It's funny how history repeats itself. Did you know that a Protestant minority governed France for more than fifty years through the House of Bourbon? Things haven't changed much, have they? We still seem to be in the minority here."

I was a product of the Great Depression of the 1930s: As the English say, I enjoyed bad health. That was exactly what happened to us, we had no choice but to enjoy the very meager situation. We had to work very hard and we saw very little for it. And that was also a time when many farms were subdivided in this area. Since then, luckily, we've been in a position to consolidate many of these farms again. Everybody says what macabre effects inflation has, but I would prefer to live with inflation rather than depression. I find it much easier. That is not to say that inflation is good or that we farmers get away with anything. Every time the wages go up in all other sectors, they have to go up in agriculture as well.

We deal largely with untrained labor, but even at the low end of the scale, you can't expect them to work for nothing. We have roughly one hundred laborers. At harvesting their womenfolk and youngsters come in and work on a piecework basis, and it becomes a sort of family effort. I don't want to create the impression that we are employing children. It's not true. But at one time or another, you know, a child has to learn to work.

I provide housing for all of my farm workers. Some of the families have been on the farm for generations. You know, they also have aspirations, and we always prompt them to attend school. We have a school next door to the farm, run by the provincial administration. And medical care is available through the clinics of the district council. Our laborers can go to Groote Schuur [a hospital in Cape Town] just like everybody else. We have an old-age pen-

sion fund run by the government; I think it's a fair provision, calculated on the cost of living. And once a year
we have a bonus day. After the harvesting, just before
Easter, a bonus is handed out, calculated on years of service and on their present scale of pay, time, merit, and
so on.

The *dop* system [payment in wine instead of money]
was never a widespread practice, you know. It might have
happened in particular cases, but it was abolished by the
farmers themselves many years ago. I don't deny a man
a drink, call it a *dop* if you like. It goes hand in hand with
producing the wine. It's hard work from early in the morning until late at night, and bloody warm sometimes and
very cold other times, but wine isn't forced down anybody's throat. The tradition has been handed down from
my father to me, and I'll hand it down to my son. But
nobody ever works for liquor only, you know. You're never
paid in liquor. I'm not denying there were some malpractices, but not to my knowledge. Now it's evolved into a
system where a man gets a bottle of wine in the evening.
He must take it home. I don't want him to gulp it down
there and then. If we find out that he sells it or something
or drinks it and falls down, then we'll suggest that he not
take it. We suggest a worker take it home and drink it in
a civilized fashion, the way we do.

On the farm here we certainly don't have a large
incidence of delinquency. In fact, I'm always surprised at
the friendliness of blacks and Coloureds, who admittedly
live in very poor circumstances, housing, and so on. In
terms of housing, a large effort has to come from us farmers. One of our number-one priorities today is to provide
good housing for our laborers. About ten percent of the
staff houses on this farm already have electricity and it's
something we have to spend a lot of money on very soon.
Providing we have the money, that is.

The Coloured people have improved terrifically in
my lifetime. Most of them were illiterate, for instance,
which is not the case today. A man has no excuse to be
illiterate. There's terrific potential in human resources
among the Coloureds and the blacks. And it's only a matter of whether they are able to utilize it and make it
productive. It's all-important for the country.

I think the blacks in South Africa are more or less
on friendly terms with us but there's always this political

prodding going on to twist them into going this way or that way. Our everyday contact with them is most friendly. I wouldn't say that everything is fine and dandy, but it doesn't show on the surface provided you treat them with respect, and that we have been taught from our mother's knee.

It's not that blacks shouldn't have a share in the running of this place, but there's the matter of competition, you know. Can they hold their own in most spheres of our economic life? And you know, there's one fallacy. Where were they when we came here? I mean, it's a known fact that the blacks were only halfway down the east coast of Africa when the whites settled here in the Cape. It probably is true that most of the Coloureds today have a fair smack of white blood in them. In that case, they must surely have started some nine months after the whites arrived here, if my logic and my biology are correct. I'm not saying that we should forever be in command or that we should be the owners of what is in Africa. I think we are all willing to share, but we are only willing to share it on a merit basis. We are not prepared to share what are our existing assets.

If one looks around, there is a very good reason for South Africans to say, Let's keep things as they are, because it all works, unlike in other parts of Africa where it doesn't work. We also know we must do justice to so-called human rights, but there must be certain limits to it. My son said a clever thing the other day; he said when it comes to equal rights, or shall I say the division of wealth and so on, it can only happen by starting off equally. You can't divide the riches at the end of the story. You can't expect everyone to win the race. Some of them are going to drop out.

Could I live under a black government? Not any of those that I know of today. They have to prove themselves. If they are good enough no one could have any objections. I don't think it's anything that should scare us, you know. Let's wait and see what happens. [Prime Minister] P. W. Botha seems to be confident that we will rise to the occasion. You loosen the brakes when it's necessary, and when you go too fast you turn on the brakes. That's democracy at its best. And you must also remember that we have also inherited a smack of the French pragmatism. You have to be pragmatic in a situation that is continually changing. We are products of the Reformation, and I am firmly in the belief that the Reformation hasn't stopped yet. We can never accept a situation where we become engulfed in paganism or anything that is anti-Christ. I don't go to church [Dutch Reformed] very often. I don't like the *predikant* [preacher] but the church is my anchor and I still believe very firmly in the Christian creed. We cannot be a party to heathenism.

An Industrial Painter

District Six was once a jumble of shops and houses and shanties and mosques that straggled up the side of Cape Town, following the lower slopes of Table Mountain. It was the home of the city's "in between" people, the Coloureds. In the 1970s it was decided that District Six should be cleared in order to build a fashionable white residential and commercial area.

Among the Coloureds who were removed from the district was a painter who worked for the Cape Town City Council. He is a shop steward in a transport union and the father of seven children. When the removals began, the painter moved to Walmer Estate, a strip of more modern houses adjoining District Six. From there he could look across the ridge and watch the bulldozers tearing down his old house and the neighborhood where he was born.

Now he has been told that a new highway is to be built through a part of Walmer Estate. His house will have to come down. He has been offered another house in Mitchell's Plain, a new Coloured township about twenty miles from Cape Town that will accommodate some 250,000 Coloured people by the end of 1982. "Choice," the painter says. "Choice is the operative word. But what is the point of arguing? I figure if I move to the Coloured homelands now, at least I'll be safe—they won't move me anymore."

My racial background is what the government terms Coloured—of mixed blood. We are evolved from the Hottentots or Bushmen who were here before the white people, before Van Riebeeck landed in the Cape in 1652. I would say I'm a product of African and Hottentot. Not white. There may be some white strain but I'd have to go much further back to get that strain. And I'm not proud if I've got any white strain in me. I'm not proud of it because of the way I've been treated.

I enlisted in the army in 1941, when I was sixteen. We Coloured were allowed to join the Cape Corps, but we were classed as noncombatants—we weren't allowed to fight. And after we came out of the army in 1946, General [Jan] Smuts made us a lot of promises—promises which didn't materialize. The government promised they would look after us. They made such a lot of promises about working conditions and housing and all that, but they never materialized. In 1948 the Nationalist party came to power, and the whole thing changed. That's when we lost the right to vote.

We still have to live with the color issue. We are still struggling. I'm a qualified painter. For the past ten years I've had a steady job working as a painter for the city council. But if a black painter and a white painter show up for the same job, the employer will always choose the white man. I once went with ten other painters to get some extra work at Cape Town University. There was only one white man, but he got the job—without being asked for any qualifications or employment card or anything. That's the thing that really hurts, when a man is not employed on merit but on his color. The same thing happens in our union. It's a mixed union, and we have to make allowances for the minority group—the whites— because they don't want to be swamped. A clause in the union constitution says the treasurer has got to be a white man. The chairman, vice-chairman, and secretary can be of any race, but the treasurer's got to be a white man.

Now I'm waiting to be moved out to Mitchell's Plain. I was born and bred in the heart of the city and now I've got to go twenty miles away. The cost of living is automatically going to rise. I get free fare on the buses because I work for the city council, but my wife and children will have to pay more. Still, what's the point of turning down the house in Mitchell's Plain? If you move to a Coloured homeland now, at least you'll be safe there. You won't be pushed around anymore.

I can't help feeling anger toward white people. They are very dishonest. We can't trust them. Once they see a black skin, they get that superiority complex. It's in them.

They treat you with contempt. They don't treat you on par. I've met very few exceptions to this. I have a few white friends, in a personal sense, some beautiful people, but never in my working experience have I met a white man who has been nice to me. My son has some white friends at Cape Town University [where he studies with special government permission], and at the university level you find that some whites are more liberal. But if you meet a white bus driver or a railway worker or a post office worker or other white working person, that's entirely different. And once whites leave university and go into the mainstream of Afrikanerdom, they take on the part of the oppressors and they behave like oppressors. Where are those freedom fighters who were at university fighting for the rights of blacks? Where are they now? Show them to me.

I'll be honest with you, I prefer to be called a black man. This started in 1960, from the uprising at Sharpeville. That's when they really made us realize what is happening; made us realize that you are either white or black in this country. They term us Coloureds, but we have come to our senses now. The Nationalists are dividing the people to make it easy for them to rule. By giving us these homelands and different states and Coloured cities, it weakens us. There's no such thing as Coloured or Indian or Asiatic. We are blacks.

My kids were involved in the school boycott in 1976. I didn't try to stop them. I was worried sick about them. But the kids are realizing what we went through, and they are showing us the way now. I think they'll go on doing that because they know their education is inferior to the white man's. Even my son at university is having trouble, because the white youngster has got so much better education behind him.

I think we could achieve an integrated society without bloodshed. But it's for the whites to take the lead. The people that are in power. I don't see any signs that this is in their minds, however. So I don't see that it will happen in my short life span. I think it's possible that the buildup of anger and frustration will happen again, like in 1960 and 1976. The frustration is not going to die, just like that.

My point is that what is good for the white man must be good for the black man. There must be no discrimination. We don't want concessions. I don't want to be told that what we've got now is an improvement. I just want to be treated as anybody else would want to be treated—like a human being, that's all. We are all citizens of this country, and a citizen should have the right to choose where he can live. We must have one voters' roll and complete integration in the government. There must be no discrimination in the work force, in education, in sports, in anything. The future must be one race in South Africa. That is the solution.

I used to play a lot of sports and do a lot of swimming. Now I coach rugby. I belong to a nonracial rugby union, which is mostly black, and we oppose the white South African Rugby Board. Sure, they've come to us and said, Let's get together. But somehow they are always pulling strings and making concessions. We don't want concessions. We want to be governed under the same law. I'm a man not only for sports. I'm a man for all walks of life. Because our livelihood doesn't depend on sports.

I don't want to be a black man who runs a mile under four minutes. I don't want to be made a fuss of because I've done this as a black. It may seem that I'm on par with the white man, but once I've finished running that mile, after that I'm still the same old me. When it's all over you leave the sports field and go back to your ghetto. Until the next Saturday when you're playing sports again.

I'm not demanding that I live in a white suburb. I just want the right to choose. Say I take my family for a drive on Sunday and we pass Muizenburg beach, and my kids say, "Daddy, we want to swim here." I want to be able to stop my car right there. I don't want to have to check for notices that say the beach is for whites only. A man must be free to choose. You can be a king in your own home, but the moment you go outside of it, you are a pauper again.

A Priest

The Zulu Anglican priest makes his way over the railroad tracks that run through the Groutville Reserve, an enclave on the north coast of Natal that was named after an American missionary. He passes the house that once be-

*longed to Nobel Peace Prize winner Albert John Luthuli.
Luthuli, who was banned for his role as president-general
of the African National Congress, served as a chief in
Groutville during the last seventeen years of his life. He
was killed in a train accident. The priest remembers seeing
Luthuli reading on his veranda, rocking himself in a rick-
ety cane chair. "I still feel myself searching back for Luthuli's roots," he says. "His message is the same message
that many of our black men—our men of the church—are
saying today. It is what [Bishop Desmond] Tutu is saying."*

*The parish is large. The priest travels in a battered
old car as far as seventy-five miles into the heart of Zululand, into the stony, eroded Tugela basin, which twists
and turns through the Valley of a Thousand Hills. Other
days he drives down into the urban township, where his
cynical parishioners are more concerned with economic
problems like employment and housing than with the
promises of what many of them scorn as "the white man's
religion."*

I decided to join the church when I was young because
of my grandfather's teaching—he was a *dominee* [priest]
in the Dutch Reformed church. But because that church
is segregationist, I switched to the Anglican church. And
when I grew up I found that my fellow man wouldn't keep
me or help me in any other way, so I went out to help
other people. I decided to take on a poor man's job in the
Anglican ministry. And I found that there you are more
than just a preacher; you become a social worker.

I prefer to preach in the hills than in the urban township. In the township people are often not at home. They
work, they come home late, they're tired. And when you
want to sit down to talk with them, they tell you they
haven't got time. Then on Sundays, when they get their
day off, they prefer just to sit and do nothing. They don't
trust you. Besides, the people in the township are scattered, divided by all kinds of petty quarrels. The people
in the hills are more united. And the people in the hills
will survive longer. They have more stability and they
are more dedicated to what they are doing. These people
in the townships are fooling themselves. They've left the
land and gone to work in the city, but they don't know
what they are doing or whether it is right or wrong.

In the village I find people much more receptive to my preaching. Sometimes my wife travels with me on her days off. She works as a full-time nursing sister. I really go way into the sticks—in the *bundu,* as we say. I get up early, at five o'clock. I have my own car and I drive out way off the main road, onto the dirt roads. I call the people together and start with a service. Then I ask all those who have got problems if I can help them.

Many of them are women whose husbands are working away, usually in Durban. They are wives with small children who only see their husband once a month—if they are lucky—and then he's coming home with those few cents he has got from his job. These women come to me and I try to help them solve their problems. It's a very difficult job, but I think it's worthwhile. Because I can see the fruits of my work. Maybe I've found someone a house, or maybe someone has lost a job and I get them working again.

Many of the people who come to me for spiritual help are just on the fence between Christianity and the ancestor worship of their parents. I find that what they're most afraid of is death. They need to be told more about God. But it isn't easy for me, a comparatively young man, to try to explain to an old man, who has lived all his life with certain beliefs, that he is doing things that in a Christian sense are wrong. These people are confused.

Many of them say, "But this religion came with the white man, and maybe the white man was just misleading us because he wanted our land." The problem is that I am presenting them with a white man's concept. I always tell them that Jesus Christ was not white or black. And then they ask, "Why is he white in the pictures we see?" I tell them it's because the picture was painted by a white man—and if he hasn't seen a black man, a white man will paint a white man. I tell them that in fact Christ could be black. And they say, "You are just saying that because you are working for the white man." They want to know why so many positions in the church are held by white men. I tell them we've got a black bishop now in Natal, and it gives some of them encouragement for the future. But others here in the township say I'm just a sellout.

I'm a Zulu, but I'm not a member of Inkatha [a political and cultural organization led by Gatsha Buthelezi, chief minister of KwaZulu]. I haven't joined Inkatha yet because I haven't really seen its aim, and no one has told me what its aim is. Not all Zulus are members of Inkatha, not unless they're working for the KwaZulu government. I think Buthelezi is a clever guy, but I still haven't been able to fathom out what he ultimately wants to do.

The people in my parish have two different kinds of problems: spiritual problems and political problems. And when I sit down and think about it, sometimes I wonder where my work is going to lead me, where I go next. Maybe it will lead me to be a politician instead of a spiritual man—a politician like Desmond Tutu or Albert Luthuli. Right now people here in the townships are aware that if they get involved in politics they might lose their jobs and be sent back to Mozambique or Zambia or wherever they come from. They think what they think, but they don't say it too loud. But if I could unite these people, that would be marvelous.

Of course it's very difficult to reconcile my Christian code with what is happening in this country. Not unless the black man can be brave enough to tell the white man that we are also made in the image of God, that we are just like you. When people come and tell me about their problems with whites, they don't say, "We must do something about it." They always say, "It's the law, we can't run away from it, we must just follow it." They are not brave enough to do what is within them. I worry a lot about that. But I feel that one day, with the help of God, I may be brave enough. I pray a lot to God and I ask him that there must be love in this country. Because I don't think there is anything that is going to help us if there is no love. But then, right now, I can't say that I find much love here.

A Manager

The sea is in his blood. As a boy in Durban he was one of a group of surfers who regularly braved the shark-infested waters of the Indian Ocean. He became an accomplished oceangoing yachtsman, and with his son he has raced two southern Atlantic competitions—from Cape Town to Rio and to Uruguay. He is managing director of a marine services company that specializes in the painting, cleaning, and repair of cargo ships. It is one of a half dozen such companies in Durban, Africa's largest port. He is a South African of British descent.

Our Zulu workers do a fantastic job. Some of the mates from German and Greek and French ships are really amazed by them. The Zulus can't read the name of the ship for you, but they certainly can paint it. They'll paint it in Greek or Japanese. They're quite remarkable.

At times you feel isolated here in Natal, but then the sea brings in our business. If the price is right and the trade is right, the ships come here, there's no doubt about it. For the last three years we've had a fantastic run. This little harbor has really been working overtime.

We employ casual labor. In this country *togt* labor—labor paid by the day—is illegal, but we get a special exemption because of the nature of our business. What it amounts to is that we can employ labor as we need it. Each morning we register the daily guys assigned to us by the Bantu Administration Board. Then if we're busy on a particular day, one of the other company's laborers can come and work for us as well. If the other company happens to get busy, our laborers move to them. We feel this is fair because the laborers get a chance to work all the time.

The laborers here seem to enjoy this arrangement. They like to be able to come when they want to and stay away when they want to. They just show up in the morning and work for the day; one of the rules of the exemption is that you have to pay them within twenty minutes of their finishing work, and it's got to be in cash.

Through the years things have gotten a lot more progressive. We now employ about forty-eight laborers who we pay by the week, and we are teaching them to spray paint, sandblast, and secure cargo. This group is our source of boss-boys, or *indunas*. When we're very busy, we employ three hundred to four hundred boys, and we carry a permanent staff of twenty-four boss-boys. We are bringing them up continuously. If a chap looks as though he'll be a good boss-boy, he's immediately pulled out and set aside for training. As they progress and an *induna* leaves, another is chosen from that gang.

We really don't have much trouble with them. You

know, initially one was able to chase them up quite a bit, but now you have to put up with a little bit of cheek. I always tell the story that when I was a boy and you walked down the street, the old coon—for the sake of the term—would get off the sidewalk and say, *Baas* [boss]. Today if you don't get out of his way he pushes you in the bloody gutter. So how can one say it's not progress?

But the majority of them are very steady. They get paid and they go off to whatever living accommodation they've got. They earn roughly ten rand a day. With overtime included, let's say two nights, they can go away with one hundred rand a week quite easily.

When they've accumulated a little bit of money, they don't have to ask me for permission not to turn up this weekend. It makes them businessmen of their own. Some of them work for a year and then take six or seven months leave. You won't see them, then they'll turn up again. We find this even with our boss-boys. A boss-boy will stay a bit longer, maybe five or six years.

There are no white dockworkers. We have mostly Zulu laborers with a sprinkling of Xhosas. We ask the Bantu Administration Board to stick to the local boys as far as possible. In the early days boys would wander down from Mozambique, but we found that as soon as we registered them, there was not enough here to make them want to stay with us. I mean, you work in all sorts of weather conditions, day and night, and there was nothing to attract them other than the fact that they got their money on the dot.

Every now and then a Coloured boy turns up, but I think it's very unwise to mix the Coloureds or the Indians with the blacks. They're usually degenerate types, and the Zulu is proud of what he's doing. Mixing them can create problems, there's no doubt about that. We remember those riots between the Zulus and the Indians. It was a bad time. The Indians get very scared very quickly. They were scared that time, all right. As I remember it, for many years the Indian dealers—they're a nation of shopkeepers—had been ripping off the blacks. What finally sparked it off was a little *umfaan* [youngster] who went into an Indian shop and got shortchanged while his father happened to be standing outside. The boy complained, and the Indian gave him a belt over the ear and sent him out. Then the father went in and all hell broke loose.

We've periodically had minor wage disputes. Luckily, these invariably seem to happen just before we're about to give the annual increase laid down by the Bantu Administration Board. The workers negotiate and you give them the increase you'd have given them anyway, and so it goes on.

Our biggest problem has been finding them beds, which we're required to do. Accommodations are so limited that, over the course of the year, our labor force gradually decreases until we have to discuss the problem with the Bantu Board. Then they try to help us by allocating beds here or there, or by allowing us to use temporary premises, and so we get going again.

Up to now, thank goodness, we haven't had to deal with black unions, but I'm damn sure that we will eventually. They're going to wake up to the situation and we'll have to deal with somebody. We'll have to find a way around that like everything else. I don't think anybody would object to unions. It's an accepted tendency. But both the unions and the employers have got to be honest with one another. You can't reach these situations where the unions start telling you what the men should be doing or what they should be paid.

I think that what we're proud of is that we provide work for these people, because I'd hate to think what they'd be doing if we didn't provide work. As we very often say to the police and everybody else they get involved with, if they weren't working, where would they end up?

The ships that we work on—British, Swedish, and so on—they're all in sympathy with us because they know the setup firsthand. They're not all looking at the television and accepting everything that everyone tells them. They've actually had experience with these people. I think we all appreciate that things have to move on and conditions have to improve all the time. One would be a fool not to see this. I think it's steadily moving that way.

My wife and I went up to São Paulo, Brazil, to see a friend of mine who married a Brazilian girl. We were out on the streets with these millions of people—all different colors of the rainbow—rubbing shoulders. Quite frankly, I find the way they live there quite exciting. The Brazilians are very proud people as well, and they seem to get around the color bar because they don't mix to any great extent. That could be the situation in this country eventually.

A Township Teacher

She was born in a mining town in the northern Transvaal, where her father worked as a laborer and her mother as a cook. After completing Catholic primary school, she attended teacher training college in Johannesburg. For twenty years she has lived in Soweto. She is married to a leather cutter and has four children, who attend school and live at home. On a Sunday morning after church, she spoke with visitors in the kitchen of her house.

We are luckier than most of the families here in Soweto. We bought our home twenty years ago; we got a loan from the Johannesburg City Council, and now it is all paid off. The housing situation here is difficult. People just recently married cannot find a house. Young couples have no privacy. And you know what it is like to stay with in-laws. Ten or more people often live in the same four-room house. Everything is communal: mealie [maize], sugar. There are bound to be quarrels if one cannot contribute to the upkeep of the house. Things are tight.

We are *ten-one-A'ers,* according to the government. This means that we can legally move from city to city as long as we can find jobs and a place to live. But this is difficult. Housing is almost impossible to find, so we can't really go anywhere.

People get frustrated, so the crime rate is high. Plenty of problems revolve around crime. After dusk, it is not safe to send my daughters to the shops. And if your husband goes out, you are not at ease until you have seen him again; anything can happen. I hear there are sometimes three murders a day.

Together my husband and I make about 780 rand a month. That is considered a good income for Soweto. But we don't have a savings account. The family has never had a vacation together. It's not that we don't want to, but we cannot afford it. I have accounts at two department stores, so I can buy on time. I get some of my best outfits from a rich Jewish lady when she has a sale. These rich ladies don't keep their clothes very long. And we belong to a neighborhood bereavement club. When someone from the neighborhood dies, each family in the club gives money to cover the funeral costs. It's a sort of burial policy.

My husband is a talented artist. If he had the chance, he would be one of the best artists. He's been working for so long in the leather factories, so much so, it's as good as going through a training course. He could start his own factory. If he had the necessary capital, he would open a factory in the homelands. Such wishes show you a person has not achieved what he wanted in life.

During the week I teach at a primary school. It is on the grounds of a tuberculosis sanitarium. I started the school eighteen years ago so that the children could learn while they were being treated. We teach about thirty children reading, math, and science in three languages: English, Afrikaans, and Sotho. It is difficult for us teachers, since our pupils don't stay very long—two or three months, usually.

There have been changes here. When I first came, all the officials were white. Now they're all black except for the warden. I don't think that matters much, just as long as he is good and does his job.

Besides teaching, I have the church. I attend Mass on Sundays at Saint Margaret's, and then sometimes I go to the Anglican church services with one of my friends. I'm interdenominational!

I am not very active in the struggle. I've never had a chance to attend meetings. Except for what I casually read in the papers, I don't think I have enough information about it. From the little I've seen I think that it's a movement to conscientize a black person to be proud of what he is and to uplift himself. For example, not having their hair straightened to be like whites and appearing as God has made them.

I am not used to discussing politics. We grew up at a time when fear was ruling us, and it's difficult to break out of it. Informers are one big thing that makes people keep quiet. You don't know who is who and the next thing you know, there is a knock on the door at night and you are interrogated. During the riots I didn't join any of the black parents' organizations. They were under surveillance all the time.

I was extremely worried. Police were just picking up most of these youngsters. People were engaged as informers and would say such-and-such about so-and-so; they had no evidence. We working parents were the most unhappy because the children didn't tell us. The day they went to storm John Vorster [the central police station in Johannesburg], we woke up to find them gone. Other things happened too. See that [she points to a small hole in the wall]; that was one of what the police call "stray" bullets. You know, those stray ones that kill people.

After the riots, children's attitudes toward their parents changed. They no longer take things at surface value as we did. They say the government is unjust to blacks—for example the education system. It is not standardized or the same as that for whites.

And when Dr. [Pieter] Koornhof [minister of cooperation and development] came to Soweto, was that not something to give us hope? People of my age think of him as one of the best Afrikaner ministers we've ever had. But the children just call him "the Doctor of Promises."

I have always felt that the so-said "homelands independence" is a mockery. It's not independence as such: How can an underdeveloped state afford to be independent? It cannot stand on its own. Take Bophuthatswana—all those spots being spoken of as a state; it's ridiculous.

It's heartbreaking to see how these homeland leaders are "swimming" when the people they rule are living in such poverty. Not that one is jealous, but don't they think that the people they represent feel betrayed when the leaders have such high standards of living?

The mayor of Soweto just recently said he didn't think blacks wanted majority rule in South Africa. I don't agree with him. What are the young people fighting for then? I prefer majority rule for the country.

But I honestly do see things are getting better. I think my children will be living in a different South Africa. What is going on—talking, negotiating, and representations to the government—will bring change. The apartheid gap is going to narrow up. Our children are going to be much nearer to whites than we used to be.

For example, take the Toastmistress Club [a U.S.-based international organization]. I belong to the first all-black chapter in South Africa—all the members live in Soweto. Four years ago, it was started by the Johannesburg chapter. I suppose that every time they went to America, there were questions as to why there were no blacks in the South African branch.

Now when we have meetings you wonder if you are in South Africa. The spirit which prevails is so social, so warm, you even forget you are different colors. We are color-blind there. Before, if I had a white friend and she saw me in the street, she would not talk to me. Now, that's not so.

In much of South Africa, with anybody who is white, we maintain that master-servant relationship. So when you meet someone as a human being, it's such a jubilation.

Johannesburg

Soweto

African miners, Vaal Reef gold mine, near Johannesburg

Coloured children at track meet, Cape Town

African dry-dock worker, Cape Town

New recruits, South African army

Prime Minister P. W. Botha and his cabinet

Village in the Transkei

Studying by candlelight, Soweto

Single men's hostel for migrant workers, Soweto

Crossroads squatter camp

Black Sash demonstration against banning, Cape Town

Part I
SOUTH AFRICA

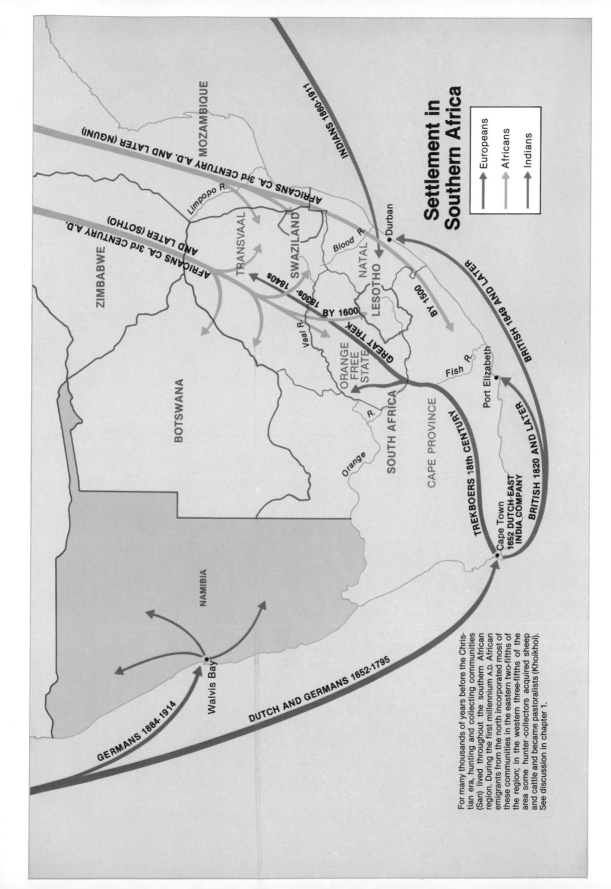

Settlement in Southern Africa

Legend:
- Europeans
- Africans
- Indians

ZIMBABWE

MOZAMBIQUE

AFRICANS CA. 3rd CENTURY A.D. AND LATER (NGUNI)

AFRICANS CA. 3rd CENTURY A.D. AND LATER (SOTHO)

Limpopo R.

TRANSVAAL

SWAZILAND

Blood R.

NATAL

LESOTHO

INDIANS 1860–1911

Durban

BY 1500

BRITISH 1849 AND LATER

1830s–1840s

BY 1600

GREAT TREK

Vaal R.

ORANGE FREE STATE

Fish R.

R.

SOUTH AFRICA

Port Elizabeth

Orange

CAPE PROVINCE

BRITISH 1820 AND LATER

TREKBOERS 18th CENTURY

Cape Town
1652 DUTCH-EAST
INDIA COMPANY

BOTSWANA

NAMIBIA

Walvis Bay

GERMANS 1884-1914

DUTCH AND GERMANS 1652-1795

For many thousands of years before the Christian era, hunting and collecting communities
(San) lived throughout the southern African
region. During the first millennium A.D. African
emigrants from the north incorporated most of
these communities in the eastern two-fifths of
the region; in the western three-fifths of the
area some hunter-collectors acquired sheep
and cattle and became pastoralists (Khoikhoi).
See discussion in chapter 1.

Chapter 1
The Road to Apartheid

Every society has its myths, and South African whites are no exception. One of their principal myths is that the history of South Africa begins in 1652, the year the Dutch East India Company established a refreshment station at the Cape Peninsula for the crews of its fleets plying between the Netherlands and Indonesia. The land that was to become South Africa was almost empty then, runs the myth, and when white farmers later fanned out over it they were settling virgin territory.

The reality differs. People have lived in southern Africa since early in the evolution of the human species. Until about 2,000 years ago the region was isolated and its only inhabitants lived by hunting game and collecting wild plants and insects. But abundant archaeological evidence shows that early in the third century A.D. African farmers, who owned sheep and cattle, cultivated millet and sorghum, and fashioned iron tools, began to migrate across the Limpopo River into the eastern part of the region. This migration process continued over a long period, with peaks in the fourth and eleventh centuries.

The newcomers represented the southernmost extension of a complex migratory movement that started in the first millennium B.C., in the vicinity of the present Nigeria-Cameroon border, and brought the Bantu group of languages to most of Africa south of the equator. By 1652 the Bantu languages and the farming way of life prevailed wherever the environment was suitable in the eastern half of southern Africa. Some of the aboriginal hunters had been killed by the farmers, others had been driven away from the better land, and many others had blended into the farming communities.

The farming peoples lived in settled, largely self-sufficient villages. Wealth took the form of cattle. Most people spoke one of two closely related Bantu languages that have evolved into the dialects spoken by the majority of Africans in South Africa today: Nguni (Xhosa and Zulu are its principal offshoots), in the area between the mountain escarpment and the Indian Ocean, and Sotho (Sesotho and Setswana are its main offshoots), on the interior plateau.

Their political units varied in size, with populations ranging from a few hundred to about 50,000. Chiefs ruled in consultation with kinsmen and councillors, but all the men of a chiefdom took part in making decisions. Men often indulged in cattle raiding, but there is no evidence of large-scale warfare before the early nineteenth century. By then, however, the population had increased sufficiently to touch off acute competition for land and water. This culminated in the rise of a Zulu chief named Shaka (ca. 1787–1828), who organized a disciplined standing army and used it to build a Zulu kingdom. In a series of wars, Zulu regiments equipped with deadly short stabbing spears ranged over large areas of southeastern Africa. So did several splinter groups, including the Ndebele, who carved out a kingdom first in what is today the Transvaal and then across the Limpopo in the western part of present-day Zimbabwe.

Before Europeans arrived in the region, the farming culture did not extend west of a line running northerly from near Port Elizabeth; the land to the immediate west of that line receives less than twenty inches of rain a year and is too arid for growing crops, although, still farther west, the Cape Peninsula and its hinterland have reliable winter rains. However, some of the indigenous inhabitants of the area west of Port Elizabeth acquired sheep and cattle from farming neighbors, and by the seventeenth century pastoralism had become the preferred way of life wherever conditions were suitable, notably in the fertile zone in and near the Cape Peninsula. So, in 1652, when Europeans began to settle at the Cape, pastoralists lived in the Cape Peninsula and its vicinity and hunters and pastoralists overlapped in the adjacent arid territories. Europeans called the pastoralists Hottentots and the hunters Bushmen. Because both names have acquired derogatory overtones, modern scholars use the indigenous words *Khoikhoi* for Hottentot and *San* for Bushman.

The Bantu-speaking farmers—known to Europeans as Kaffirs, another word that in time acquired derogatory overtones—dominated the eastern half of southern Africa in 1652. Of the indigenous communities, these African farmers had the most complex material culture and the most highly developed political systems. They were also the most numerous inhabitants of the region as a whole, as they are today.

In 1657, five years after the Dutch East India Company established a station at the Cape, nine employees were freed from their service contracts and given land at Rondebosch, five miles from the company's fort and garden in the embryonic Cape Town. Others followed, and a white settler community gradually took root in the fertile southwestern tip of southern Africa. It was recruited largely from company employees, who came mainly from the Netherlands and Germany. A French element was added in 1688–89, when the company provided passage and land for 150 Huguenots who had fled France because the Catholic monarchy had revoked religious freedom for Protestants.

The company applied a policy of cultural assimilation to the settlers. The Dutch Reformed church, led by clergy employed by the company, was the only church in the colony. Dutch was the official language, although in the new environment the spoken form gradually developed into a distinct language, Afrikaans, and by the end of the eighteenth century the people were calling themselves Afrikaners. Their numbers grew slowly, reaching 1,000 shortly before 1700 and 20,000 around 1800—small figures compared with North America, where the U.S. population numbered 4 million in 1790. Small as this band was, however, it spread over a steadily widening area. By 1800 fewer than half the Afrikaners lived in Cape Town or on the neighboring arable land. Most had become *trekboers,** seminomadic pastoral farmers, and had acquired control from the indigenous hunters and herders of most of the pastures and water supplies as far north as the Orange River and as far east as the Fish River, where African chiefdoms blocked their further expansion.

For a generation after Great Britain conquered the Cape Colony in 1806, Africans continued to hold the *trekboers* to the west of the twenty-inch rainfall line. Beginning in the second half of the 1830s, however, thousands of Afrikaners, dissatisfied with British rule, took advantage of the fact that the Zulu depredations had partially depopulated some of the most fertile territory in the eastern part of South Africa. In what later became known as the Great Trek, they traveled in organized parties with their wagons, their sheep, and their cattle, and eventually established settlements in upper Natal and on the plateau on either side of the Vaal River.

Meanwhile, the British conquest of the Cape Colony had paved the way for British settlement. In 1820 and again in 1902, the British government provided several thousand English men and women with free passage and land grants. Many times that number paid their own way to South Africa. By 1870 British farming communities had taken root in the eastern Cape Colony and in Natal, and residents of British origin dominated the professions and trades in Cape Town and the other towns and villages throughout the region. Considerable numbers of British and other whites were drawn to South Africa by the discovery of diamonds in Griqualand West in 1867 and gold on the Witwatersrand in 1886.

White immigration has continued. It peaked at 35,000 in 1948, declined for a period, and then rose to an average of about 40,000 a year from 1963 till the mid-1970s. In recent years the flow has slowed markedly. British immigrants have remained a substantial part of the inflow, accounting for nearly half the total in the twentieth century. Other immigrants have come from continental Europe, including a sizable number of Jews fleeing anti-Semitism in nineteenth-century Russia and twentieth-century Germany. More recently there has been an influx of whites from tropical Africa, retreating from decolonized Kenya, Zambia, Zaire, Angola, Mozambique, and Zimbabwe.

Boer is the Afrikaans word for farmer and more generally refers to an Afrikaner.

Despite the steady stream of newcomers, South Africa has never attracted white immigrants on the same scale as the United States. Today the Afrikaner people, descended from the 20,000 Afrikaners of 1800, constitute nearly 60 percent of the white population. The white population as a whole is about 16 percent of the total population of South Africa, including the territories designated as African "homelands."

Despite the sizable indigenous populations, whites brought two other groups to South Africa as laborers. One group came as slaves. The Dutch East India Company imported slaves from Madagascar, tropical Africa, India, Ceylon, and Indonesia, and during the eighteenth century their numbers roughly equaled those of the white colonists. Most slaves were owned by the company itself or by the white residents of the Cape Town area, but many *trekboers* also owned one or two slaves.

In 1834 the British Parliament emancipated the slaves in the colonial empire, including those in the Cape Colony. By that time there had been a great deal of interbreeding among the different groups in the colony—the slaves, the Khoikhoi, and the whites living there or calling at the port. The interbreeding continued, and for a time there was a considerable social and economic overlap between the poorer colonists and the more successful freed slaves. During the latter half of the nineteenth century, however, a fairly rigid color line began to emerge between a dominant caste of Afrikaners and people of British origin, who were white or deemed to be white, and a subordinate caste of people of mixed racial origins. The latter became known as the Cape Coloured people.

The other group brought in by the whites from outside were contract laborers from India, who were put to work on sugar estates in Natal. The Indians arrived between 1860 and 1911. As their ten-year contracts expired, most chose to stay in South Africa. Thus, an Indian community took root in Natal, where it outnumbered the white population by the end of the nineteenth century. It also spilled over into the Transvaal.

If it is a myth that the whites who settled South Africa moved into land that lay empty and idle, so too is it a myth that the South African whites of today are colonialists on the order of those who snatched up large chunks of the globe in the nineteenth century. Their roots run deep. South Africa *is* their land. But it is also the land of many others, some of whom were there long before the whites arrived—and with all of whom they are now inextricably intertwined.

AFRIKANERS VERSUS BRITISH

In the calculations of the businessmen who directed the affairs of the Dutch East India Company, South Africa performed only one useful function: aiding the flow of commerce between Europe and Asia. Consequently, they concentrated their local officials in the Cape Peninsula, where Table Bay provided shelter from the southeast winds that prevail in summer and False Bay offered protection from the winter northwesters. They left the people of the interior to their own resources, with scarcely any protection or control. There, the *trek-boers* improvised their own military force to deal with the indigenous hunting bands. By the last quarter of the eighteenth century, all segments of the Afrikaner population were dissatisfied with a commercial regime that ignored their interests. There was a vigorous reform movement among the farmers near Cape Town and outright rebellion among the *trekboers*.

Initially, the British regime that succeeded the Dutch in 1806 had no more interest in the Cape Colony than had its predecessor. Gradually, however, Great Britain was sucked into the interior. British governors and settlers were generally expansionist, and London found it difficult to disown their aggressive efforts to extend British sway. Many Protestant missionaries, eager for reforms in the treatment of blacks, also favored extending British rule, and they exerted considerable influence over many British politicians in the first half of the nineteenth century.

By the mid-1830s the British had carried out some of these reforms and, in the process, alienated many *trekboers*. By 1845 some 14,000 Afrikaner men, women, and children—revered by later generations of Afrikaners as the *voortrekkers*, or pioneers—had left the Cape Colony on the Great Trek to new homes on the interior plateau and on the coastal side of the mountain escarpment in Natal. The British annexed Natal in 1843, but in the 1850s, after an abortive attempt to exert authority over the southern part of the plateau, they recognized the independence of the Afrikaners in what became two landlocked Boer republics—the Orange Free State and the Transvaal.

In the ensuing years Great Britain kept a fairly loose rein on its South African interests. It stationed troops in the Cape Colony and in Natal to protect the white minorities, and its maritime and mercantile power enabled it to dominate the external trade of the entire southern African region. But, following precedents established in Canada, the British government began to devolve political power on predominantly white electorates in the Cape Colony and in Natal. The two Boer republics were allowed to go their own ways.

Then, later in the nineteenth century, Britain was once more moved to exert a strong hand in southern Africa. The discoveries that were making the South African interior the principal source of the world's fresh supplies of diamonds and gold came at the time when European imperialism was reaching its height in the scramble for African territory. In this heady atmosphere, British agents made several attempts to subjugate the Boer republics. Even before the discovery of the Witwatersrand gold reef, a small British expedition annexed the Transvaal in 1877. The Boers offered no resistance at the time, but four years later they rebelled and won a series of victories against the weak garrison, whereupon the British withdrew.

In 1895 Cecil Rhodes planned a coup against the Transvaal. Rhodes had built a fortune in the diamond and gold industries and had become prime minister of the Cape Colony and head of the British South Africa Company, which colonized Rhodesia. But despite Rhodes's past successes, the coup failed ignominiously.

The British maneuvering for control of the Transvaal and the Orange Free State culminated, in 1899, in the Boer War. Alfred Milner, governor of the Cape Colony and high commissioner for South Africa, in collusion with Joseph Chamberlain, the colonial secretary, manipulated the British mine workers to foment unrest on the Witwatersrand. He also caused the British cabinet to put intense pressure on the Transvaal government of President Paul Kruger to give the vote to the *uitlanders* (immigrants), in the expectation that the Kruger supporters would then be outvoted. In 1899 both the Transvaal and the Orange Free State declared war on Great Britain, hoping to win quick successes and persuade the British to come to terms before sufficient reinforcements reached South Africa to turn the tide. They were unsuccessful. Although many Europeans and Americans sympathized with the Boers, none of their governments became officially involved. After fighting courageously enough to hold the British Empire at bay for nearly three years, the Boers surrendered in 1902.

In the long run, however, the losers triumphed. They were able to negotiate terms that promised them early self-government, and within a few years the South Africa of today began to take shape. In England, the Liberal party, several of whose leaders had opposed the war, won a landslide victory in a general election in 1906. It moved ahead on the pledge of local self-government for the white populations of the former Boer republics and stressed British cooperation in the development of their economies.

By 1909 the Transvaal economy was flourishing under a government led by Louis Botha, the former republican commander in chief, and Jan Christiaan Smuts, one of his chief lieutenants. Botha and Smuts were calling for reconciliation between Boer and Briton, South Africa and the United Kingdom. In 1910 the Transvaal, the Cape, Natal, and the Orange Free State joined to form the Union of South Africa.

Over the next quarter century South Africa virtually completed the decolonization process. In 1910 the Union acquired the same Commonwealth dominion status as Australia, Canada, and New Zealand, and South African politicians then played leading roles in the gradual elimination of British controls over the dominions. During the First World War, South African forces conquered the German colony of South-West Africa (Namibia), and at the end of the war the territory became a South African mandate under the League of Nations.

The 1933 Statute of Westminster, reinforced in Cape Town by the Status of the Union Act in 1934, established once and for all that the ultimate power over all South African affairs lay with the government of South Africa. As a result of these developments, South Africa's entry into World War II on the side of Great Britain was not automatic, as it had been in World War I. Indeed, it entered the war several days after Great Britain and only after a close vote in the Parliament in Cape Town and the formation of a new government committed to the war. Jan Smuts, head of the new government, became an important Allied leader, serving as a confidant of Winston Churchill and later as a principal author of the charter of the United Nations.

Although South Africa won wide acceptance on the international scene during World War II, its foreign policy troubles do not date entirely from the rise to power of the Nationalists in 1948. In 1910 politicians in Great Britain as well as in South Africa assumed that it was the manifest destiny of the Union to absorb Basutoland (Lesotho), Swaziland, and Bechuanaland (Botswana), which were territories inhabited almost entirely by Africans and administered by a British high commissioner. It was also widely expected that South Africa would take over Rhodesia (Zimbabwe), which was administered by the British South Africa Company under a charter from the British government. It was further expected that, after World War I, South Africa would take over South-West Africa, which in fact it did. Jan Smuts, like Cecil Rhodes before him, had grandiose visions of an even vaster country, including the Portuguese territories of Mozambique and Angola and lands as far north as Kenya.

These hopes were disappointed. In response to criticism of South Africa's segregation policy, successive British governments declined to transfer the high commission territories. In a 1922 referendum the white settlers in Rhodesia voted to become a separate self-governing colony rather than join the Union. After the Second World War, the United Nations turned down Smuts's bid to absorb South-West Africa, and even before 1948 the international organization began to pass resolutions denouncing aspects of South Africa's racial policies.

ESTABLISHING WHITE SUPREMACY

Whites established dominance over the indigenous peoples of what is today South Africa in three phases. By 1700 whites occupied the arable territory within fifty miles of Cape Town. A century later they also controlled the usable pastures throughout the entire western half of the region. By the end of the nineteenth century whites dominated the whole area.

The Bantu-speaking farmers in the eastern part of the region resisted white expansion more vigorously than the hunters and herders in the western area. More numerous and less susceptible to European diseases than the hunters and herders, they managed to retain some of their land and to preserve elements of their culture and social organization even after they had been conquered. Whites were fortunate that their initial bridgehead in southern Africa was in the Cape Peninsula, more than four hundred miles from the nearest African chiefdoms. They had learned to cope with the environment

31

and had built up their numbers by the time they confronted the African farmers. The whites also had great technological advantages—notably, superior weapons. Initially, they alone had firearms, and when the Africans did obtain some, the whites had better guns, more ammunition, and more practice in shooting. Their ox-wagon commissariats also enabled them to wage longer campaigns than the Africans.

Despite these handicaps and despite internecine divisions, many of the African communities fought tenaciously for their land and their independence. The Xhosa held their own until 1811, when the British committed sufficient regular troops to start the process of conquest. Even so, the Xhosa fought again and again, until their final battlefield resistance was squelched in 1878. The Zulu opposed white expansion in two successive generations. In 1838 they massacred an advance party of *voortrekkers* and their Coloured servants in an attempt to deter the rest from settling in Natal. Later that year they made repeated attacks on a Boer laager at what became known as Blood River, only to be mowed down by *voortrekker* firepower. In 1879, when the British invaded Zululand, the Zulu annihilated an entire regiment at Isandhlwana before being overwhelmed by a large British army aided by colonial and African allies.

The Basotho, under the leadership of Chief Moshweshwe, defeated the Boers of the Orange Free State in 1858, only to be subdued in 1865. In the 1880s, however, they made things so difficult for the Cape colonial administration that Britain had to assume direct responsibility for Basutoland. Basutoland remained a British colony until 1966, when it became the independent country of Lesotho, even though it was surrounded by South Africa. There were many other cases of active resistance to white power. The last chiefdoms to be conquered in southern Africa were those of the Venda in the northern Transvaal, who turned back the flow of Boer settlement in the 1860s and remained independent until 1898.

The subjugation of the Venda climaxed the whites' drive for control of southern Africa. With few exceptions, the original hunters and herders had lost their land and their ethnic identities, and their descendants had become members of the Cape Coloured community, subservient to whites. On the other hand, though conquered, the Bantu-speaking Africans continued to occupy much of the land in the eastern part of southern Africa: all of Lesotho, most of Botswana, half of Swaziland, and about one-eighth of what is now the Republic of South Africa, including the homelands. But while those landholdings enabled the Bantu-speakers to preserve much of their culture and social cohesion, they were not sufficient for economic autonomy. To survive, the African communities had to export more and more labor to earn wages in the areas occupied by whites.

The Dutch East India Company was responsible for taking the first steps in shaping modern South African society. In the Cape settlement's very first decade, the company generated two classes of persons in the colony besides its own employees: white colonists, former company employees who became land-owners and employers of labor; and slaves, people of African, Malagasy, and Asian origin, imported to provide labor for the government and the colonists.

The decision to import slaves had far-reaching implications. Dark-skinned slaves performed most of the skilled and unskilled labor in the Cape Town area until Great Britain abolished the slave trade in 1807 and emancipated the slaves in 1834. As elsewhere, the presence of slaves differing in appearance from their owners paved the way for a caste-oriented, racially stratified society. The colonists grew to despise manual labor and to equate inferior status with inferior talent—and both with race.

The company showed no interest in helping the colony develop large-scale agriculture for the export of the grain and wine it produced. Moreover, land was readily available in the arable area near Cape Town until about 1700 and in the more distant *trekboer* area until about 1770. These circumstances combined to make the embryonic white society in South Africa more internally egalitarian than other slave-owning societies of the period. In the middle of the eighteenth century half the colonists owned at least one slave and only seven colonists owned more than fifty. As for the blacks, the manumission rate was unusually low in the Cape Colony: in 1770 there were only 352 free blacks, amounting to 4.4 percent of the number of white colonists. Sexual relations between white males—colonists and transients—and slave women were common. The offspring of such unions inherited the status of their mothers, and the slave population increasingly acquired Caucasian genes.

Initially, the company treated the herders, known today as the Khoikhoi, as outsiders—people to trade with for their livestock rather than to incorporate as subjects. However, as Khoikhoi communities gradually disintegrated, most of the survivors found themselves inside the expanding colonial frontiers. The company never defined their status clearly, nor did it pay much heed to their fate. They could not be registered as landowners, and although they were technically free—that is, they were not slaves—white officials and colonists regarded them as culturally inferior to most of the slaves, especially the Asian slaves. The Khoikhoi therefore became dependent on colonists, mostly *trek-boers*, who used them as herders and domestic servants in return for squatting rights and handouts of food, tobacco, and liquor. These relationships were informal, without official constraints, and the treatment of the Khoikhoi varied from benevolent paternalism to callous cruelty. Since there were far more men than women among the *trekboers*, sexual activity between male *trekboers* and Khoikhoi women was common. Most of the offspring, like those of the slave women, were absorbed by their mothers' community. Some, however, passed into the Afrikaner population, while others joined the mixed communities of displaced Khoikhoi, escaped slaves, and renegade whites, known initially as Bastaards and in the nineteenth century as Griquas, that developed beyond the fringes of the *trekboer* frontiers.

The first outside challenge to white domination of colonial society in South

Africa came early in the nineteenth century. Protestant missionaries, mostly British, had begun to work among the Khoikhoi and the Coloureds in the 1790s. They were soon condemning the whites' unbridled power over blacks. Their reports struck responsive chords in influential circles in England, where slavery as practiced in the British Caribbean islands was under persistent attack. Consequently, statutory racial discrimination against free people—nonslaves—was abolished in the Cape Colony in 1828. When slaves were emancipated throughout the British colonial empire six years later the Cape slaves, too, became free people under the law.

White supremacy survived this challenge, as it would survive a similar challenge in the United States for a century after the Civil War. Denouncing the "interfering missionaries," the *voortrekkers* left the Cape Colony for distant lands where they could deal with blacks as they pleased. In the colony, blacks, though technically free and equal before the law, made few economic or social gains. Moreover, although the franchise for the Parliament that was created in 1854 was color-blind, economic qualifications, along with blacks' continued dependent role, prevented them from exerting significant political influence. Another constraint on blacks was a masters and servants law soon passed by the new Cape Parliament; it made breach of an employment contract a criminal offense.

The *voortrekkers* created new societies in the eastern part of South Africa on the old, unreformed Cape colonial model. In their Transvaal republic, they wrote the formula "No equality in church or state" into their constitution. Habituated as they were to the use of servile, dark-skinned labor, they pressed Africans into service. They imposed tight controls on the Africans, prohibiting them from possessing firearms or horses and from being at large in "white areas" without a pass signed by an employer or official. Many Africans, demoralized by the Zulu wars, readily accepted white patronage; in other cases Boers seized black children as "apprentices" or pressured chiefs into supplying laborers. A white farmer was allowed to have four African families living and working on his farm. Africans who were not squatters on white farms were allotted "reserves" or "locations," often vaguely demarcated, where they were ruled by chiefs recognized by the government.

Relationships between Africans and whites were no more equal in Natal. The British settlers there adopted the racial ideas of the *voortrekkers* and applied them more systematically. Theophilus Shepstone, the son of a Cape missionary, had the task of controlling the Natal African communities ravaged by the Zulus. He placed most of the Africans in reserves, where he permitted them to maintain their customs—but with crucial modifications. White officials supervised the chiefs. Magistrates settled Africans' disputes with whites, applying the law of the whites. Africans paid an annual tax for every hut they occupied, while traders and missionaries exposed them to new commodities and new ideas. In this fashion the Africans were drawn into the whites' money economy and, in general, into dependency. Some Natal Africans, like their counterparts in the Boer republics, settled on land that had become white property, paying rent to absentee owners or working several days a week in return for squatting rights and perhaps some remuneration.

Thus, not much more than a hundred years ago South Africa was still an agrarian society. White farmers controlled most of the fertile land. Coloured and African squatters supplied them with labor in return for a place to live, raise crops, and pasture their cattle. Most Africans were still peasants, occupying the blocks of territory left to them after the white conquest, corresponding roughly with the modern homelands, plus Lesotho, Botswana, and Swaziland. This was the matrix from which an industrial society emerged in the years that followed.

In 1867 alluvial diamonds were discovered near the junction of the Vaal and Harts rivers, in arid country north of the Cape Colony. Three years later dry diggings began at nearby Kimberley, and it soon became evident that they were the outcrops of the richest diamond mine ever known. As operations penetrated below the surface, individual diggers were superseded by companies able to use large-scale mechanical equipment, and smaller companies were incorporated into more powerful ones. By the early 1890s, one company, De Beers Consolidated Mines, had acquired a virtual monopoly of diamond production. De Beers also kept the price of diamonds high by controlling their marketing through a London syndicate—a system that continues today.

The discovery of an outcrop of the Witwatersrand gold reef in 1886 ignited an even bigger boom. The gold-mining industry, centered in Johannesburg, soon surpassed the scale of the diamond-mining industry, and year after year to the present South Africa has been responsible for a large part of the world's fresh supply of gold. A succession of new mines have been brought into production in an arc between Heidelberg in the Transvaal and Welkom in the Orange Free State. Technological advances have made it possible to mine as deep as 12,000 feet below the surface, while recent increases in the price of gold have made it profitable to mine previously neglected low-grade ores. Early in its development, the gold-mining industry was organized in a three-tier system: from individual mines, through groups of mines, to the industrywide Chamber of Mines, which eliminates competition in the recruitment of labor and sets uniform conditions of employment.

The mining industries established the precedents for the structure of modern South African industrial society. Initially, it was inevitable that the skilled and supervisory work would be done by immigrants from overseas, since South Africa had no previous experience with large-scale industry. But the blurring of the racial line that probably would have taken place under fair competition did not occur, for in South Africa such conditions were not created. The color line already established in agrarian South Africa was quickly projected into the industrial setting. The whites who worked in mining acquired superior positions and enjoyed high wages and good living standards, while the thou-

35

sands of Africans recruited for the mines were limited to subordinate roles with low wages and meager fringe benefits. In Kimberley, partly to prevent the theft of diamonds, black workers were confined to compounds for the duration of their contracts. Compounds were also introduced on the Witwatersrand, since they had proved an efficient way of controlling labor. These arrangements rapidly became institutionalized, and as time passed they became more rigid. In gold mining, white workers earned more than nine times as much as blacks, and in 1911 they also acquired a legal monopoly of skilled jobs.

De Beers's economic interests were generally compatible with the wage and occupational color bars, the high cost of white labor being offset by the low cost of black labor. On some occasions when management did try to modify the color bars or to reduce the number of white employees, white trade unions struck to protect their privileges. The most dramatic confrontation occurred in 1922. When the Chamber of Mines proposed to increase the proportion of black workers sharply, the white miners staged a rebellion in which more than two hundred people were killed, and although the government suppressed the rebellion, the Chamber of Mines made no further attempts to breach the color bar.

The mining industries engendered rapid growth and profound structural changes in the entire regional economy. For the first time, substantial quantities of capital flowed into South Africa, mostly from Great Britain but also from France and Germany. Starting from scratch in 1886, the population of Johannesburg and the rest of the Witwatersrand cluster of towns reached half a million in 1921, more than a million in 1936, and more than a million and a half in 1948. The older South African towns, especially the seaports, expanded as feeders to the mining industries. Railroads, previously almost nonexistent in South Africa, rapidly pushed inland from the ports to the mining centers. By 1894 the Witwatersrand was linked with Cape Town, Port Elizabeth, East London, Durban, and Lourenço Marques (now Maputo) in Mozambique. Later, the advent of the automobile led to the creation of a national road network. The mining towns, the railroads, and then the highway transportation system stimulated commercial agriculture, transforming the whites still on the land from near-subsistence farmers into producers of specialized commodities for the market. Moreover, during the 1920s the capital and skills generated in mining began to yield significant gains in the previously backward manufacturing sector. It was then that American capital began to enter South Africa on a large scale, with the construction of automobile assembly plants by Ford and General Motors in Port Elizabeth. By 1948, with the further stimulus of restricted shipping space during the Second World War, the South African economy was remarkably buoyant and poised for further spectacular advances.

White South Africans were the major beneficiaries of the country's economic growth. In the early twentieth century poverty among Afrikaners had become a serious problem as a result of the closing of the frontiers and the disruptions caused by the Boer War, but the ranks of poor whites dwindled as Afrikaners flocked to the towns, where they benefited from the discrimination against blacks. Blacks themselves shared the rewards of economic growth only to a limited degree. Wage and occupational differences similar to those in the mining industries permeated the entire economy. Africans were prohibited from owning land outside the reserves. They could not acquire training as artisans, nor could they take part in the statutory system of industrial bargaining. It was a criminal offense for Africans to strike.

There was an official rationale for these differentials. African societies were deemed self-sufficient—able to produce a subsistence by their traditional methods. Hence, Africans who went to work in the towns were visitors, temporarily supplementing their rural livelihoods, whereas white workers had to support their families at "civilized" standards from their wages.

The facts belied this reasoning. The land that remained in African hands after the white conquest became increasingly inadequate even for bare subsistence. It is true that at first some African communities had profited from the rise of Kimberley and Johannesburg by producing a surplus of grain for the market, but in time such surpluses changed into shortages as the African population mounted and African land deteriorated from overuse. Moreover, the monetary needs of the Africans increased because all the governments in the region exacted direct taxes from them and because they became accustomed to manufactured goods sold by white traders, such as clothing, groceries, cooking utensils, tools. So, far from being self-sufficient farmers, the Africans became dependent on the wages provided in the market economy, and they flocked to South African cities in search of work. The Chamber of Mines had an elaborate recruiting organization throughout the region. By the 1940s the mining industry was employing more than 300,000 Africans. It drew them not only from South Africa but also from Mozambique (which was a principal source of South African mine labor from the beginning), Basutoland, and territories as far north as Angola and Tanganyika.

African mine workers were migrants, living in compounds while they served out their contracts for six to eighteen months, then returning to their homes in the reserves. Many village communities rotated their menfolk, so that there were always several wage earners at a time. However, the manufacturing industries, unlike the mining industries, made no attempt to corral their laborers into compounds, and as time went on larger and larger African communities became established in municipal "locations," or "townships," on the fringes of the towns and cities. Their growth spurted during the Second World War as white farmers seeking to modernize operations evicted unneeded African workers and other Africans fled the impoverished reserves. The white authorities were unable to cope with this movement, and by 1948 thousands of Africans—men, women, and children—were squatting in filthy, teeming shantytowns near Johannesburg and other cities, in defiance of the law.

FROM SEGREGATION TO APARTHEID

In the first half of the twentieth century most white South Africans shared the racial assumptions prevalent among whites everywhere, including those in the United States: The human species comprised different races that could be graded on a scale of civilization—with the whites, of course, at the top. Within these assumptions, however, there were considerable variations in attitude. Some white South Africans held that all black people—Coloured and Asian as well as African—were innately inferior. Others thought that blacks were capable of improvement but that it would take them many centuries to become "civilized." A few believed that a significant overlap already existed between the least cultured whites and the most cultured blacks and that the civilizing process might progress quite rapidly.

These variations in white opinion were regional rather than ethnic. Both Afrikaners and English-speakers who lived in the same area tended to have broadly similar racial attitudes and to adopt broadly similar practices. In Cape Town and its vicinity, where most of the blacks were Coloureds, facilities such as buses and trains were unsegregated, there was considerable residential and social intermingling, and sizable numbers of light-skinned Coloureds "passed" into the white community. Elsewhere the taboos against egalitarian relationships across the color line were overwhelmingly strong—in "British" Natal as much as in Afrikaner farming areas. "Providence [has] drawn the line between black and white and we must make that clear to the Natives, not instill into their minds false ideas of equality," Christian de Wet, a Boer War leader from the Orange Free State, told the delegates assembled at a national convention in 1908 to draw up a constitution for the proposed Union of South Africa.

The government that assumed power in 1910 featured an all-white Parliament chosen by an electorate that was white except for a small number of black voters in the Cape Province. (The exclusion of blacks from the franchise in 1910 and later is discussed in detail in chapter 3.) The Afrikaner majority controlled Parliament, and political debate revolved around Afrikaner leaders who took different views of relationships between Afrikaners and English-speakers. Louis Botha (prime minister 1910–21) and Jan Smuts (prime minister 1921–24 and 1939–48) favored merging Boer and Briton into a unified white nation and cooperation with Great Britain to the extent of standing by its side in war. The fundamental objectives of James Barry Munnik Hertzog (prime minister 1924–39) were to preserve Afrikaner identity in a two-culture white nation and to remove all British constraints on South African sovereignty. Botha and Smuts, despite their heroic roles on the republican side in the Boer War, became increasingly identified with the English-speaking voters, as well as with moderate Afrikaners. Hertzog's constituency was almost entirely Afrikaner. By the mid-1930s, Hertzog had achieved his main goals: Afrikaner morale had recovered from the effects of the Boer War and South Africa had acquired all the attributes of a sovereign state.

Even though tensions between the two principal white groups dominated electoral politics, black-white relations were never out of mind. As far back as 1903, Lord Milner, as British high commissioner and governor of the conquered republics, had appointed a South African Native Affairs Commission—composed of white, predominantly English-speaking South Africans—to study the matter. Milner himself had expressed the view that "A political equality of white and black is impossible. The white man must rule, because he is elevated by many, many steps above the black man." Issuing its findings in 1905, the commission accepted that South Africa would always depend on black labor but recommended that whites should be separated from blacks in politics and in land occupation and ownership. The report foreshadowed the shape of things to come.

"Segregation" was the racial slogan of political leaders until the World War II years. Botha, Smuts, and Hertzog lacked clear-cut, comprehensive approaches to the racial question, but their patchwork policies nevertheless had unifying objectives. One was to provide whites with black labor at cheap rates. Another was to ensure that whites continued to dominate blacks politically and economically. Still another was to confine to reserves Africans whose labor whites did not need.

These objectives were furthered by the pass laws, mostly inherited by the Union regime from its predecessors, and the land laws, which were enacted in 1913 and 1936. The land laws laid out the boundaries of the African reserves, the basis of today's homelands. As noted above, they also prohibited Africans from owning land outside the reserves and from living outside the reserves—legally at least—unless employed by whites. In towns Africans were regarded as temporary visitors and were segregated in municipal locations administered by white superintendents. In rural areas the grazing and cultivation rights they had possessed since being subjugated were eroded, and Africans became largely dependent on wages in cash and kind. It was difficult for them to leave a farm without the owner's permission.

Besides pass laws restricting the movements of Africans, the Union inherited masters and servants laws making breach of contract by unskilled workers a criminal offense. These laws, too, remained in force after 1910. Later legislation (described in chapter 5) reinforced the subordinate role of black workers, especially Africans, in industry. Also, in the 1930s the Union government began the process of whittling away the limited black franchise in the Cape Province and of substituting advisory bodies outside the mainstream of political life for black participation in white politics. The first such body, created in 1936, was the Natives' Representative Council, comprising six white officials, four appointed Africans, and twelve elected Africans. It was abolished in 1949.

In 1933 a realignment of South African politics began. His major political objectives achieved, Prime Minister Hertzog found himself confronted by an economic crisis emanating from the world Depression. His response was to form a coalition with Jan Smuts, and in 1934 Hertzog's National party and Smuts's South African party joined to form the United party.

A group of Afrikaner nationalists led by Daniel François Malan refused to follow Hertzog and established a "purified" National party, the forerunner of today's ruling party. At first it seemed that Malan had led the dissidents into a political wilderness, but the Malanites scored a great propaganda victory in 1938. Capturing control of the arrangements for the centennial celebration of the Great Trek, they used it to arouse intense ethnic sentiment among the *volk,* the rank-and-file Afrikaners. The Malanites painted the historic enemies of the *volk* as black savages who made dastardly attacks on heroic, freedom-loving *voortrekkers* and as oppressive imperialists who, in league with English-speaking white South Africans and turncoat Afrikaners, had sought to crush the Boers.

The events of the war years played into their hands. When a Smuts-led government proceeded to prosecute a war in which South African territory was not threatened, the Malanite claim that Smuts and his followers had never cut the imperial apron strings appeared to be vindicated. Moreover, by 1948 the Smuts government seemed to be losing control of the black population and, still worse, to lack the will to restore control. Tens of thousands of Africans had been defying the law by striking and by deserting the reserves and farms for squatter camps on the outskirts of the cities. Some former servicemen were spreading egalitarian ideas among the white population. Prime Minister Smuts himself had publicly expressed uneasiness about segregation, while his part in writing the UN charter, with its stress on human rights, also stirred concern. Moreover, Jan Hofmeyr, his deputy prime minister and heir presumptive, was making equivocal speeches: Had he not said he favored eventual removal of the color bar from the constitution? All this was profoundly disturbing to whites.

In the 1948 election campaign, the Nationalists were able to exploit grievances of the sort that had existed in other countries involved in the Second World War, including demobilization and unemployment problems and shortages of housing and some food items. But the Nationalists also capitalized heavily on the electorate's racial anxieties, and for this purpose they coined a new slogan: "Apartheid"—in English, "apartness."

Ever since breaking with Hertzog in 1934, the Malanites had taken a more exclusive line on the color issue than the government. During the war a group of Afrikaner intellectuals began to promote the radical idea that the South African racial mix should be completely unscrambled. Each race, so the theory went, would then be able to develop along its own lines in its own area (except for the Indians, who should be sent back to India). Several of the Nationalist theorists were steeped in Calvinist fundamentalism. In 1945 one of them, Professor G. A. Cronje of the University of Pretoria, wrote:

The racial policy which we as Afrikaners should promote must be directed to the preservation of racial and cultural variety. This is because it is according to the Will of God, and also because with the knowledge at our disposal it can be justified on practical grounds. . . .

The more consistently the policy of apartheid could be applied, the greater would be the security for the purity of our blood and the surer our unadulterated European racial survival. . . . Total racial separation . . . is the most consistent application of the Afrikaner idea of racial apartheid.

Cronje's program demanded drastic social engineering. Carried to its logical extreme, whites would have to dispense with the black labor on which the economy had been based ever since the days of the Dutch East Africa Company. As the 1948 election approached, the Nationalist politicians sought to appease fears aroused by this program without blunting their attack on the government. In *National News*, addressed to English-speaking voters, the National party explicitly disavowed any intention of stripping white South Africa of its black labor. "Native labour," it said, "is . . . essential to South African industry and agriculture." *National News* also played on the fears raised by the relatively liberal racial views of Deputy Prime Minister Hofmeyr. "Do you want to give the Native a voice in working out your children's future, in making laws for Europeans, in spending your taxes?" it asked. In March 1948 a party commission reported that white South Africa had to choose between "integration and national suicide" on the one hand and "apartheid" and the protection of a "pure white race" on the other. On the hustings J. G. Strijdom, a future prime minister, declared that the result of the Smuts government's policy would be that Africans would "very soon cease to be barbarians," and this would mean they would obtain the vote. Daniel Malan, the Nationalist leader, spelled out the ways in which his government would apply apartheid. It would outlaw interracial marriages, abolish the Natives' Representative Council (which had refused to cooperate with the government) and the limited indirect African representation that still existed in the House of Assembly, treat the reserves as the true African homelands, control the African influx into the cities, protect white workers from African competition, prohibit African trade unions, and generally segregate whites and blacks as much as possible.

The election took place on May 26, 1948. The results surprised almost everyone: Despite obtaining a minority of the popular vote, the Nationalists and their ally, the small, ephemeral Afrikaner party, won a working majority in Parliament. The word *apartheid* would soon become notorious around the globe.

Chapter 2
The People

The central fact about the population of South Africa is that the ruling faction is a small minority that year by year is growing smaller relative to the other groups. From the figures alone, it seems obvious that sometime, somehow, the status quo must change.

Based on official reports, which are generally believed to underestimate the number of Africans, the total population of the country grew from 6 million in 1911, the year after formation of the Union of South Africa, to 27.7 million in 1980.* That comprises some 19.8 million Africans, 4.5 million whites, 2.6 million Coloureds, and almost 800,000 Asians. All racial groups have been increasing, but at significantly different rates. The white proportion of the population has been decreasing—from 21.4 percent in 1911 to 16.2 percent in 1980. In the same period the African segment increased from 67.3 percent to 71.5 percent, the Coloured from 8.8 percent to 9.4 percent, and the Asian from 2.5 percent to 2.9 percent. These trends are expected to continue over the next few decades. According to a government estimate, by the year 2000 whites will have dropped to 13.7 percent of the population while Africans will have risen to 74.2 percent.

Within each major group, of course, there are characteristics other than race that must be taken into account in seeking an understanding of South African society.

---

*The 1980 figures are based on preliminary 1980 census results, plus estimates for the "independent" homelands of the Transkei, Bophuthatswana, and Venda, which were not covered by the census. The figures omit Africans whose presence in "white" areas is illegal under South African laws to be described later.

THE WHITES

The white population of South Africa is still clearly divided into two main components: the Afrikaners, who descend from the seventeenth- and eighteenth-century settlers and constitute 60 percent of the whites, and the English-speakers, who began to settle in the region in the nineteenth century and make up the bulk of the non-Afrikaner whites.

Intermarriage between Afrikaners and members of the other white groups takes place more often now than in the past, but it is still relatively rare. The basic historical division is perpetuated by law as well as custom. English and Afrikaans are both official languages of the Republic, and separate Afrikaans- and English-medium instruction is the rule in public schools. In addition, most white voluntary associations are organized on ethnic lines, from boys' groups (Boy Scouts/Voortrekkers), through student organizations (National Union of South African Students/Afrikaanse Studentebond), to churches and social clubs.

Through the early decades of the twentieth century, there were marked social and economic distinctions between the two white ethnic communities. The Afrikaners were still overwhelmingly rural, the English-speakers predominantly urban. The Afrikaners owned most of the land. The English-speakers dominated industry, commerce, and the upper echelons of the civil service; they were better educated and generally had a far higher standard of living. The Afrikaners remained relatively egalitarian among themselves; the English-speakers had the class divisions of a modern industrial, capitalist society.

The distinctions between the Afrikaners and the English-speakers are now blurring. By 1970 more than three-quarters of the Afrikaners were urban, compared with about 90 percent of the English-speakers. This trend continues. The Afrikaners still constitute a vast majority of the declining white rural population, but they are also at least a substantial minority in every industrial complex—even Durban, in Natal, which was formerly overwhelmingly British. In the towns, there is now a substantial Afrikaner middle class, and the old disparities of education, wealth, and status between the Afrikaners and the English-speakers have been disappearing. This change has accelerated since 1948. The National party has been using its control of the state apparatus to advance the interests of its supporters. Afrikaners now dominate the public service and the parastatals (the corporations controlled and in large measure owned by the government), both of which have burgeoned since 1948. They have also made great gains in the private sector. In 1948 the per capita income of English-speaking white South Africans was more than double that of Afrikaners. By 1976 the ratio had narrowed to 1 to 1.4, and since then the gap has continued to shrink.

THE COLOUREDS

Despite their varied origins, the Coloureds are now virtually a closed population group. Since 1948, few Africans have passed into the Coloured community and few Coloureds have been able to pass for white.

The Coloureds have virtually no links with traditional southern African cultures, the societies of their Khoisan ancestors having disintegrated long ago. Nor do they have strong links with the cultures of their tropical African, Malagasy, or Southeast Asian ancestors, who were brought to the Cape Colony as slaves in the seventeenth and eighteenth centuries. Indeed, a majority of the Coloured people are culturally Afrikaans, for they have always been intimately associated with white Afrikaners. Most speak Afrikaans at home and are members of the Afrikaners' Dutch Reformed church. The principal exception is the subgroup known as the Cape Malays, who make up 6.5 percent of the Coloured population and are Muslim.

Most Coloureds live in the western part of the Cape Province, where they are a majority of the population. Significant numbers of Coloureds also live in the eastern Cape Province and in the southern Transvaal. The Coloureds are now predominantly urban; more than two-thirds live in towns. Most are wage earners employed by whites, but there is a substantial middle class. Status depends in part on educational and economic achievements and in part on skin color, with a light complexion carrying prestige.

It is generally believed that until recently many Coloureds aspired to incorporation in the white population, with whom they are closely identified culturally. Since 1948, however, they have experienced a series of crushing political, social, and economic setbacks as the Nationalist government has pressed ahead with the racial separation demanded by apartheid. As a result, many Coloureds, particularly the young, feel deprived and frustrated and have become alienated from the South African regime.

THE INDIANS

When South Africans speak of Asians, they mean the Indians, even though the Coloured group includes Asian strains and a handful of Chinese live in South Africa. The Indians are now a closed group. They have been since 1911, when the Indian government banned further recruiting of indentured laborers for service in Natal. Two years later the South African government prohibited voluntary Indian immigration. Thus, nearly all the Indians in South Africa today were born there.

The Indians originated in different parts of the Indian subcontinent, practiced different religions, spoke different languages, and belonged to different castes. Today 70 percent are Hindu, 20 percent are Muslim, and 8 percent are Christian. The principal languages are Urdu and Gujarati. There are wide economic differences among the Indians, with a few extremely wealthy businessmen, a large middle class, and a mass of poor. About 85 percent live in Natal, most of the rest in the southern Transvaal. Well over 80 percent are townspeople—half of them in Greater Durban, where they form nearly 40 percent of the population, outnumbering both the Africans and the whites. The Indians have been influenced to varying degrees by the English cultural milieu of Natal and the Witwatersrand. While only 8 percent are Christians, nearly all speak English.

The Indians' position is more uneasy than the Coloureds' in one respect. Unlike the Coloureds, the Indians occupy land previously held by Bantu-speaking Africans, and thus at the same time that they are segregated and dominated by the whites, they are regarded as interlopers by Africans. With their memories of serious anti-Indian rioting by Africans in Durban in 1949 and their knowledge of the fate of Indians in Uganda, South African Indians understandably have ambivalent feelings about eventual black rule in South Africa. But they, too, have endured intensified segregation at the hands of the Nationalist government—especially the loss of residential and business sites under the Group Areas Act—and among them, too, the younger generation is increasingly prone to cast its lot with the African majority.

THE AFRICANS

The African population is increasing more rapidly than the others. Its birth rate is nearly twice that of whites, its death rate somewhat higher but decreasing, and its proportion of younger members far larger. In 1977–78 the African rate of natural increase was estimated at 28 per thousand of population, compared with 8.9 for whites, 16.2 for Coloureds, and 18.7 for Asians. It is virtually certain that the African proportion of the South African population will continue to grow, approaching three-quarters by the end of the century.

The government constantly emphasizes the ethnic or "tribal" differences among the Africans. It treats the African population as though it were composed of ten separate embryonic nations, each with its own "homeland" territory, and tries to confine urban Africans to separate ethnic sections of of the townships. This policy unquestionably has some basis in fact. Africans are divided by language barriers; for example, Sotho-speakers and Nguni-speakers cannot easily communicate. There are also regional differences and folk memories of the internecine wars of the nineteenth century. The persistence of ethnic loyalties is shown in periodic clashes among African mine workers. Inkatha, the formidable African political organization operating aboveground inside South Africa, is primarily, but not exclusively, a Zulu organization.

On the other hand, the traditional patterns of African life have been so disrupted by white settlement and the development of a modern economy that for many Africans other factors loom larger than ethnic differences. To a

45

considerable extent, the government's stress on the existence of ten distinct African nations, with markedly different cultures, is part of the mythology of South African whites, akin to the tales of the *voortrekkers* settling virgin land. In reality, in the South Africa of today the interests and loyalties of Africans depend on their politics, education, economic status, and residence, as well as, in some cases, on their ethnic origins. In urban areas, in particular, ethnic links have diminished in importance.

Roughly half the Africans are in the homelands at any given time.* Most of these suffer from acute poverty, and malnutrition is common. They include a high proportion of women, children, and elderly people.

The other half of the Africans, including a disproportionate number of adult men, live in the "white" areas of South Africa. More than 4 million Africans are in the white rural areas, most as farm laborers. In numerical terms, "white rural areas" is a misnomer—blacks outnumber whites in these areas by about nine to one. Scattered in tiny clusters over vast areas, the African farm laborers are the most culturally deprived of all South Africans. Some are casual laborers, oscillating between the farms and the homelands. Most enjoy neither the traditional benefits of community life that still exist in the homelands nor the amenities of urban living.

The urban African population has increased prodigiously throughout the twentieth century. In the 1970 census 5 million Africans, 2 million Coloureds and Asians, and 3.25 million whites were counted in urban areas. The African figure probably fell far short of the actual number, since Africans are often in towns without legal authority. Many, especially men of working age, migrate at irregular intervals between the homelands and the towns, maintaining a family in the homelands and retiring there when they are no longer employable. As many as 2 million may be in this category, and to these must be added another one-third million migrants from other countries, especially Lesotho. Many migrants in urban areas are mine workers; others work in manufacturing. Despite the South African government's persistent attempt to treat Africans in towns—permanent residents as well as migrants—as temporary visitors, the number who have severed connections with the homelands and regard themselves as urbanized has grown rapidly.

As is true of the Coloureds and the Indians, there are vast differences of wealth and status among Africans. The great majority are extremely poor by any standards. Their lives are dominated by the ceaseless struggle for survival. In the homelands, a few businessmen and artisans boast significantly higher standards of living than the impoverished masses, but the main beneficiaries of the government's efforts to develop the homelands politically seem to be the African politicians and bureaucrats, some of whom have become wealthy. In

*For a closer examination of the distribution of the African population between the homelands and the "white" areas, see chapter 8.

the towns, there is an emerging business and professional class, some of whose members have achieved considerable material success.

Whatever the differences separating the Africans, Coloureds, and Asians and whatever the internal divisions in each group, they all share the heavy burden of apartheid. Increasingly they view themselves not only as Africans or Coloureds or Asians but also as part of a common black cause. And increasingly, for all its multiplicity of racial and ethnic identities, South Africa drifts toward polarization: black versus white.

Chapter 3
The Apparatus of Apartheid

As race became the overriding consideration in organizing South Africa's complex society, a vast apparatus of laws, regulations, and bureaucracies had to be created to carry out the policy. This has been accomplished by the National party since it came to power in 1948. Building on earlier laws and practices, the government has steadily elaborated the structure of apartheid. This chapter examines the legal and administrative framework of the system.

DRAWING RACIAL LINES

In South Africa a person's political, civil, economic, and social rights hinge on membership in a racial group. Thus, the government must fit everyone into a racial slot and guard against racial "crossings."

Rigid racial classifications have always given pause to anthropologists and geneticists, but this has not deterred the Nationalists. Under some statutes and in general usage, the population is divided into four groups: whites, Coloureds, Africans, and Asians. But the central racial classification law, the Population Registration Act of 1950, which is sometimes described as the cornerstone of apartheid, orders the assignment of every person to one of the three groups: white, Coloured, or African. As authorized by the law, the government has further divided the Coloured classification into subgroups that include the Asians as well as persons of mixed racial origin. Under another law the Africans are subdivided into eight major tribal groups.

Sometimes the government may reclassify people. In 1978, for example, 10 whites were reclassified as Coloureds and 150 Coloureds were reclassified as white. Such shifts can cause upheavals in families. "The implementation of the Population Registration Act is strewn with human suffering," says John

Dugard, a leading South African legal authority. "Families are torn apart when husbands and wives, parents and children, brothers and sisters are differently classified, with all the ensuing consequences to their personal, economic, and political lives."

The humiliations endured by the few caught up in such nightmares—probing of family histories and friendships, scrutiny of physical features—are great. But the law's most significant impact is on the daily lives of the masses of South Africans irrevocably consigned to the less-privileged categories. White South Africans sometimes argue that the racial classification law is an example of differentiation rather than discrimination, since both black and white are classified. But this argument fails to take into account that once classified as African, Coloured, or Asian a person is automatically relegated to an inferior social level with lesser rights. The Population Registration Act provides the machinery for unfavorable treatment under other statutes.

To keep racial lines from blurring further, the Nationalists have enacted legal prohibitions against marriage and sexual intercourse between blacks and whites. One of the first laws the Nationalists passed after coming to power was the Prohibition of Mixed Marriages Act of 1949, which forbids marriages between "a European and a non-European." Immorality acts passed in 1950 and 1957 strengthened earlier strictures against interracial sex. The 1957 law outlaws sexual relations between blacks and whites and any "immoral or indecent act" involving a black and a white.

In the 1960s some five hundred to six hundred people were convicted each year under the Immorality Act. Prosecutions have dropped since 1971, when a widely publicized case involving prominent citizens of a small farming community in the Orange Free State led to a new requirement that the attorney general approve all prosecutions. The number is still substantial, however, with 355 persons charged in one recent twelve-month period.

In September 1979, Prime Minister Pieter W. Botha declared that the government was prepared to consider changes in the laws on interracial marriage and sex. His statement was widely welcomed as an indication of a determination to move away from discriminatory laws. Since then, however, Botha has not taken any action, and the 1980 parliamentary session saw no attempt to make changes in this legislation.

THE "HOMELANDS"

The "homelands" policy represents an attempt by white South Africans to come to terms with a basic fact of life: the country's overwhelming African majority. "South Africa's objective is self-determination for *all* its peoples," declares an official explanation of the policy. "The Government's fundamental aim with self-determination for all the country's peoples is the elimination of the domination of one group by another. The very purpose is to facilitate the development of each people into a self-governing national entity, cooperating with others in the political and economic spheres in a manner mutually agreed upon. The principle of self-determination to which the government is committed leaves the way open for each population group eventually to make its own choice regarding its political future."

There is a more plausible explanation. According to this view, by the late 1950s it was becoming clear to South African whites that the traditional policy of *baasskap*—"bossdom," or undisguised white domination of Africans—could not prevail forever because of African restiveness and pressure from abroad. So the Nationalists set out to achieve a fundamental separation of the territorial bases and political destinies of whites and Africans. Under the homelands policy, Africans, even those residing in South Africa, could look forward to achieving political rights only in their own tribal "states," while whites would retain exclusive control over the remainder of the Republic of South Africa, which embraces 87 percent of the original territory. The whites' goal was to avoid sharing political and, ultimately, economic power with Africans in a unitary South Africa but at the same time to retain African labor.

The homelands policy, also known as grand apartheid, separate development, or multinational development, evolved slowly in the early years of National party rule, accelerated in 1959, and reached its peak with the granting of independence to the Transkei in 1976. At that stage, and indeed until the retirement of John Vorster as prime minister in 1978, the final goal was clear: All homelands would become independent states; the entire African population of the Republic would be granted political rights and citizenship in these states; consequently, there would ultimately be no African citizen of the Republic of South Africa requiring accommodation in the political order of South Africa itself.

The ideology of separate development has been diluted by the Botha government. There is now talk of a "constellation" or confederation of states for southern Africa in which Africans would retain the nationality of the proposed confederation while exercising their citizenship rights within black member states. Moreover, the permanency of at least part of the African urban population appears to have been recognized as a political fact. But so far Prime Minister Botha's plans are confined largely to rhetoric, and the institutional structure of 1976 still dominates the statute book.

The homelands scheme was foreshadowed by the Bantu Authorities Act of 1951. It provided for the establishment of tribal, regional, and territorial authorities, and thereby strengthened the power of tribal authorities in the reserves, as the homeland areas were then known. But the homelands policy began to assume its full dimensions only after Hendrik Verwoerd became prime minister in 1958. The thrust of the Promotion of Bantu Self-Government Act, passed the next year, was that Africans could never be full-fledged participants in many areas of life in those parts of South Africa occupied by whites.

The act also asserted that the Africans did not belong to a homogeneous African group but instead comprised a number of separate national units with distinctive languages and cultures and with their own national territories or homelands. In time, these homelands were to become "self-governing Bantu national units."

The Nationalists' hope—never realized—was that eventually the flow of Africans from the rural homelands areas to the white areas would be halted and even reversed. But those Africans who remained in white areas as workers could look to the homelands with which they were linked as repositories of their political rights. A Xhosa-speaking factory hand in Johannesburg, for example, could never vote for a member of the national Parliament sitting in Cape Town but could cast a vote for the legislative assembly in the Transkei.

One criticism of the homelands policy has been that by laying heavy stress on tribal divisions that had appeared to be fading, the government, in effect, pursues a course of divide and rule. Another criticism has been that the homelands—often scattered bits and pieces of land rather than contiguous territory—in most cases are not truly the original tribal lands but instead poor and inadequate substitutes for the large areas of South Africa once held by Africans. The strongest criticism, however, has been that the homelands policy rests on a fiction—namely, that Africans residing in "white" areas are temporary workers rather than a permanent, integral part of South African society. Viewed in this light, the homelands policy becomes a device for assuring a continuing supply of African labor while avoiding the granting of full political, civil, economic, and social rights to the African workers and their families. John Dugard sums up the skeptical view:

> According to the Grand Design of separate development, every African living in the common area will be required to become a citizen of one of the homelands and will therefore become eligible for participation, albeit at a remote distance, in the political process of that homeland (or independent state). They will then be migrant workers (or "guest workers" as they are sometimes euphemistically described) who, so it is contended, will resemble migrant workers from Mediterranean countries employed in Northern European countries. This is an exercise in metaphysics rather than practical politics. Many of the Africans living in the common area have no real link with any homeland and, even where such a link exists, they are as likely to be satisfied with the franchise in a homeland political system as would the English-speaking white South African with a vote in Britain.

African opposition, international skepticism, and other problems have impeded the implementation of the homelands policy. Ten homelands have been designated. Of these, three now are officially classed as independent: the Transkei, Bophuthatswana, and Venda. Five, the Ciskei, Lebowa, Gazankulu, Qwaqwa, and KwaZulu, are classed as self-governing territories. Two, Ka-

Ngwane and Ndebele, are in an early stage, having begun to organize governments only in the late 1970s.

The government has sought to make the Transkei, a large, essentially contiguous area formerly part of eastern Cape Province, the showpiece and pacesetter for its homelands policy. In 1963, when South Africa was trying to convince the International Court of Justice of the sincerity of its intention to grant independence to the African groups under its rule, the Transkei was hurriedly given the legal trappings of self-government. A legislative assembly dominated by traditional tribal authorities was established, and limited powers were transferred to the new government.

Then, in 1976, the South African government took the next step and granted the Transkei independence. By the Status of the Transkei Act, South Africa renounced all authority over the Transkei and declared that henceforth it would be a "sovereign and independent State and shall cease to be part of the Republic of South Africa." At the same time, the Transkei adopted a new constitution that provided for a Parliament evenly balanced between elected members and tribal leaders.

The Transkei provided a model for the development of other homelands. The Bantu Homelands Constitution Act of 1971 empowered the government to grant to other homelands constitutions similar to that granted the Transkei in 1963. Two of the territories given self-government under this act have since become independent: Bophuthatswana in 1977 and Venda in 1979. Other self-governing homelands, most notably KwaZulu, the Zulu homeland in Natal, have resisted government pressure to move toward independence because of fundamental doubts about the policy or dissatisfaction with their territorial allotments or both. Nevertheless, the government's policy until now has been to push ahead with homelands independence, whether or not the areas can be economically self-sustaining.

One of the most intractable conflicts arising from the homelands policy centers on citizenship. The Status of the Transkei Act states that all persons born in the Transkei or directly descended from Transkeians, all who were citizens of the Transkei before independence, and all who have linguistic or cultural ties to the Xhosa or Sotho groups in the Transkei shall no longer be South African citizens. The independence acts for Bophuthatswana and Venda contain comparable provisions. African leaders strongly object to the denial of South African citizenship to Africans living in white areas, asserting that it forecloses any possibility of fair treatment and participation in the political process that governs their lives. Dugard observes:

> The provision in the Status of the Transkei Act seeks to further the fantasy of apartheid by making all Africans in the Republic of South Africa alien citizens attached to some independent homeland who can make no claim to full citizenship in the Republic of South Africa. If all the projected homelands become independent in this way it will then be possible, so it is contended by Government spokesmen,

for South Africa to claim that it accommodates several million foreign workers but has no African citizens itself!

POLITICAL REPRESENTATION

South Africa's political system excludes blacks from any significant role. Various black councils may have their advice solicited on some questions and may oversee certain black affairs. But the advice can be ignored and the governmental powers involve relatively minor matters. When it comes to important decisions at the national and provincial levels, blacks have no authorized voice.

The South African central government operates under a parliamentary system as outlined in a constitution adopted in 1961, the year the country became a republic, and revised in 1980 along lines recommended by an official panel known as the Schlebusch Commission.* Legislative power is vested in the 177-member House of Assembly, chosen by whites and restricted to whites. Executive power is held by the prime minister, the leader of the majority party in the House of Assembly, and the cabinet, whose members are appointed by the prime minister. The state president serves as the titular head of state and performs other functions at the direction of the cabinet.

Parliament is supreme. The House of Assembly may make laws on any subject, and no court may inquire into the validity of any act of Parliament except one that affects the sensitive issue of the equality of the English and Afrikaans languages. Even in such a case the court may consider only whether Parliament has followed the correct procedure. Usually a majority vote passes a bill, but when equal language rights are at issue a two-thirds majority is required.

In a move heralded by the government as opening up a new consultative role to the nation's blacks but whose actual significance is debatable, the constitution was amended in 1980 to abolish the upper house of Parliament, the Senate, and establish a President's Council. The council's sixty-one members are to be appointed by the president acting on the advice of the cabinet. White, Coloured, Indian, and Chinese citizens of South Africa are eligible for membership, but the main concern seems aimed at mollifying the discontented Coloured and Indian populations.

The President's Council, in the words of the amendment, "shall at the request of the State President advise him on any matter referred to it by the State President for its advice and may, in its discretion, advise him on any matter (excluding draft legislation) which, in its opinion, is of public interest." It may also advise on draft legislation if so requested by the House of Assembly. Although the President's Council does not include Africans, the original proposal called for it to consult with a council of Africans to be established by

---

*The commission was headed by Alwyn Schlebusch, formerly minister of justice and now chairman of the President's Council, whose creation was recommended by the commission.

Parliament—limiting the Africans, in effect, to a role as advisers to the advisers. But this plan was withdrawn after major African leaders refused to participate. Partly as a result of the Africans' stand, leaders of the other black groups and of the official white opposition, the Progressive Federal party, also declined to serve. So what the President's Council may come down to in the end is an appointive advisory body composed of whites allied with the government and non-representative Coloureds, Indians, and Chinese.

White control is also entrenched at the provincial level. In each of the four provinces there is a chief administrative officer appointed by the state president, an all-white provincial council elected by white voters, and an executive committee consisting of the provincial administrator and four persons chosen by the provincial council. The provincial councils are limited to making ordinances on provincial taxation, white primary and secondary education, hospitals, municipal institutions, roads, and other local matters.

Blacks have not always been totally excluded from the central political process. In 1910, when the Union was being formed, the four colonies that were to become the four provinces were divided over the part to be played by blacks in political life. While the Cape favored a nonracial, qualified franchise based on individual merit, the other three colonies pressed for the total exclusion of blacks from the franchise. The result was a compromise, with each province retaining its pre-Union franchise and the black vote in the Cape protected by a provision that black voting rights could not be changed without a two-thirds majority vote of both the House of Assembly and the Senate sitting together.

But in the long run the northern philosophy was to prevail. In 1936 African voters in the Cape were removed from the common electoral roll by the required two-thirds majority and placed on a separate roll to elect three white representatives to the House of Assembly. At the same time, provision was made for four white senators, elected by African electoral colleges, to represent Africans throughout the Union.

Coloured males in the Cape were still on the common roll when the National party came to power in 1948 determined to purge all blacks from the political process. But the National party could not command the necessary two-thirds vote, and after its attempts to remove the Coloured voters by a simple majority vote had been ruled unconstitutional by the Appellate Division, South Africa's highest court, the party enlarged the Senate and thus obtained the required majority. So it was that in 1956 the Coloureds, too, were placed on a separate roll to elect four white representatives to the House of Assembly.

Soon the Nationalists found even this unacceptable. In the 1960s, when Coloured voters appeared certain to elect members of the multiracial Progressive party to represent them in Parliament, the government abolished the Coloured representation and in its place created the Coloured Persons' Representative Council, a body made up mainly of elected Coloured representatives but possessing highly circumscribed powers. The elimination of blacks from the central political process was then complete.

Seeking to defuse the resulting black discontent, the government has devised new institutions. The most publicized are the homelands governments, discussed in chapter 8, but whatever rationalizations the theoreticians of apartheid may offer, the homelands obviously do not solve the main problem facing South Africa: the political future of the Africans, Coloureds, and Asians in the "common area" outside the homelands.

In the case of the Africans, the government's only response until now, besides the concept of political rights in the homelands, has been to establish limited forms of local government for urban dwellers. Elected Urban Bantu Councils were authorized in 1961, although none was actually established until 1967. Their powers were limited to minor local matters and to giving advice to white authorities. In 1977, following the Soweto uprising of 1976, Urban Bantu Councils were replaced by Community Councils. These councils, whose members are mostly elected and whose powers are broader than those of the Urban Bantu Councils, oversee such things as rental regulations, land use, building permits, area beautification, recreational facilities, and libraries. African response has varied. In Dobsonville, in the Transvaal, 42 percent of the eligible voters took part in council elections, and in the Vaal Triangle, near Johannesburg, 20 percent of the voters showed up at the polls. But in Soweto, the largest African community in South Africa and a center of antiapartheid militancy, votes of 6 percent or less have been recorded.

Separate political development has also been promoted for the Coloured and Indian peoples, but here the lack of territorial homelands complicates matters. As a result, government policy toward these two groups has been essentially negative. They have been denied participation in white political affairs and restricted to partially representative councils with limited powers over their own peoples.

One such body, the Coloured Persons' Representative Council, faltered from its creation in 1968. It was theoretically empowered to make laws affecting Coloureds on a variety of matters, but its actions were subject to white approval. The elected members opposed all institutions of separate development, including the council itself. They clashed repeatedly with the members appointed by the government, which frequently overrode council actions. Consequently, the council never functioned as envisioned, and in 1980 it was dissolved. A plan to replace it with an all-appointed South African Coloured Persons' Council was shelved after strong Coloured protests. The government has now asked the new President's Council to examine the issue of Coloured political rights and make recommendations.

The government itself appears uncertain about the political future of the Coloured people, and there is wide support among whites—even among Nationalist members of Parliament—for closer political integration with Coloureds. In 1976 a government-appointed commission of inquiry recommended far-reaching social, economic, and political changes that would eliminate many of the hardships of Coloureds under apartheid and bring them closer to the mainstream of political life. But the government quickly indicated it was not prepared to accept the most important political recommendations, which called for some form of direct representation for Coloureds in the institutions of government.

South Africans of Indian extraction have been treated much like the Coloureds. In 1946 they were granted the right to be represented in Parliament by three white members of the House of Assembly and two white senators. But the Indians themselves rejected this token representation by refusing to participate in the election, and in 1948 the National party government withdrew it.

In 1968 the government established the South African Indian Council, consisting of twenty-five Indians appointed by the minister of Indian affairs (whose duties have now been taken over by the new Department of Internal Affairs). In 1974 the council was increased in size to thirty members, with fifteen appointed by the minister of Indian affairs and fifteen elected indirectly through electoral colleges in the provinces, which are composed largely of elected members of Indian local authorities. The council has an executive committee with a chairman appointed by the government from among council members and four members elected by the council itself. While the government may delegate certain executive powers affecting Indian education and community welfare to the executive committee, the council has no legislative powers.

In 1978 a planned enlargement of the council to forty elected and five appointed members was announced, but the change has not taken place and the 1974 arrangement remains in effect. The explanation, according to the government, is that the future form of Indian political representation is uncertain in light of new constitutional developments, including the creation of the President's Council, on which Indians serve.

Despite the exclusion of blacks from the franchise, until 1968 they could join the political parties advocating multiracialism, the Liberal party and the Progressive party. Membership enabled blacks to participate indirectly in the only political process that mattered by influencing the parliamentary policies of these parties. In 1968, however, the Prohibition of Political Interference Act barred racially mixed political parties. The act distinguishes among the African, white, Coloured, and Asian population groups and decrees that no member of one group may join a party enrolling members of another group. As a result of this legislation, the Liberal party dissolved and the Progressive party became exclusively white.

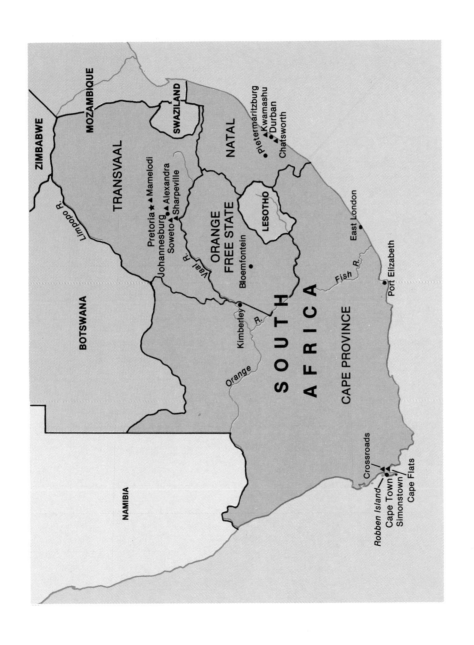

The principal legal underpinning of residential and business segregation in the urban areas of South Africa is the Group Areas Act. The statute was first enacted in 1950, but it is rooted in a number of pre-1948 laws aimed mainly at the ownership and occupation of land by Asians.

Indians were introduced into Natal as contract laborers on the sugar plantations in 1860. After their contracts expired, many elected to stay in South Africa, and discriminatory barriers were soon erected against them. In the Orange Free State Indians were forbidden to own or to occupy land, and in the Transvaal a succession of enactments, dating from 1885, prohibited Indians from owning land and from occupying premises outside "bazaars" set aside for them. Indians sought to circumvent these laws by acquiring land through nominees or Indian-controlled corporations, but the legislature was quick to stop these practices.

In 1924 and 1926 bills were introduced in Parliament requiring separate residential and trading areas for persons "having racial characteristics in common," but these bills were dropped in 1926 when the Indian and South African governments began discussions of the treatment of persons of Indian origin in South Africa. A 1946 law, however, prohibited Indians and other Asians from owning or occupying property not owned or occupied by Asians before 1946 unless an exemption was obtained. The purpose of this measure was to prevent Indian penetration of white areas.

In 1950 the piecemeal attempts to entrench residential and business segregation were replaced by the Group Areas Act, which was revised in 1957 and again in 1966. This act provides for the creation of separate group areas in towns and cities for whites, Africans, and Coloureds. The Coloured group has been further subdivided into Indian, Chinese, Malay, and "other Coloured" groups. Despite widespread de facto segregation, residential intermingling had advanced far enough in many cities to prevent immediate attainment of the final goal of the act: separate "race areas" for residential and business purposes. Consequently, the law allows for phased implementation. Some areas are thus proclaimed "controlled" or "specified" areas within which existing ownership and occupation patterns are fixed. The ultimate aim, however, is separate areas for the exclusive ownership or occupation of the different racial groups. Disqualified persons—those of a racial group other than that for which an area has been designated—may not purchase property there if ownership restrictions have been proclaimed. They must vacate premises by a specified date under threat of criminal penalties if the area has been proclaimed exclusively for occupation by another group. Special permits granting exemptions are the only means to escape the impact of the law, and these are issued at the discretion of white officials.

The law distinguishes between group areas for occupation and for ownership and in practice emphasizes occupation. F. P. Rousseau, a legal adviser on group areas matters, explains: "The clashes and difficulties between persons of different races which other countries have experienced have had their origins almost entirely in undesired occupation. If your neighbor by reason of his race has a way of living different from yours, so that his proximity offends you, you are not likely to worry about the racial group of his landlord."

While *ownership* is a fairly precise term of law, *occupation* is not. The courts have therefore grappled with the meaning to be attached to this term, in particular with the degree of control and the amount of time constituting occupation. In the course of entrenching segregation in the amenities of daily life—"petty apartheid"—the government has contributed to this uncertainty by issuing proclamations that designate forms of intermittent occupation, such as attending a movie or dining at a restaurant, as subject to the Group Areas Act. In 1973 the government declared that the act's prohibition on occupation extended to any person "who is at any time present in or upon any land or premises in the controlled area or group area, as the case may be, for a substantial period of time or for the purpose of attending any place of public entertainment or partaking of any refreshments as a customer at a place where refreshments are served in a licensed restaurant, refreshment or tea room or eating-house where the partaking of refreshments ordinarily involves the use of seating accommodation, or as a member of or guest in any club." This proclamation is extremely vague, but its very vagueness has often intimidated organizations into segregating sporting events and theater performances for fear of prosecution, sometimes in circumstances not obviously contemplated by the law itself.

On its face, the Group Areas Act is not discriminatory. Rousseau comments: "The basis of the new legislation was the eventual territorial segregation of persons belonging to the various groups, but on a nondiscriminatory basis. Propagandists against group areas have had much to say about ghettos, but in theory, at least, the Group Areas Act was, and is, completely undiscriminatory. What is sauce for the goose is sauce for the gander. In practice, it was and is inevitable that the white group should find itself best off in comparison with the other groups. But that is mainly the result of circumstances, not of discrimination."

A number of developments that have occurred under the act, however, expose its discriminatory consequences. By the end of 1979, for example, only 2,234 white families had been moved from their homes and resettled in group areas, compared with 74,909 Coloured families and 35,113 Indian families. By the end of the same year only 21 whites had been moved from business premises, compared with 129 Coloureds and 1,970 Indians. A particularly disruptive upheaval of Coloureds has occurred in a section in the heart of Cape Town known as District Six. The area, occupied by Coloureds since 1834, had a population estimated at 61,000 Coloureds and only 800 whites. But in 1966 it was proclaimed white, and the Coloureds were ordered removed to a bleak tract some ten miles from the center of Cape Town.

South Africa's highest court has acquiesced in the discriminatory implementation of the Group Areas Act. In a case in which a number of Durban Indians alleged unequal treatment under the act, the Appellate Division stated: "The Group Areas Act represents a colossal social experiment and a long-term policy. It necessarily involves the movement out of Group Areas of numbers of people throughout the country. Parliament must have envisaged that compulsory population shifts of persons occupying certain areas would inevitably cause disruption and, within the foreseeable future, substantial inequalities."

Although residential and business segregation rests mainly on the Group Areas Act, other statutes provide for separate townships for Africans and restrict the employment of Africans in certain occupations in African townships and white areas. These statutes achieve substantially the same ends as the Group Areas Act.

In theory, most legislative inroads on freedom of person, speech, and assembly affect all South Africans, regardless of race, despite the fact that in practice the statutes are almost always applied more vigorously against blacks. But Africans are expressly subjected to separate and unequal treatment in one important matter: freedom of movement.

White and Coloured South Africans have virtually unlimited freedom of movement, except that they may not enter an African homeland, township, or location without permission. Before creating the Union, the four colonies restricted Indian travel between colonies, and in 1913 these limitations were converted into restrictions that obliged Indians to obtain permits to travel from one province to another. This requirement remained in force until 1973, when it was dropped and Indians were allowed to travel freely. Until recently, however, Indians were prohibited from remaining for more than a brief period in the Orange Free State and in certain parts of northern Natal without prior permission.

The limitations on Africans' freedom of movement are of an entirely different order. One legal expert sums up the relevant laws this way: "In general the African requires some form of authority or permission for any journey of consequence within the Union. The law of the land regards him as having true freedom of movement only within the circumscribed limits of his own immediate domicile." A web of statutes and regulations confines rural Africans to their tribal homelands and releases them only in the interests of white agriculture and industry. An African who visits a "white area" as a migrant laborer does so on sufferance.

Until very recently, urban Africans were treated as "temporary sojourners" in the "white" cities, but lately there has been a change in this policy. The new policy, largely the product of a body known as the Riekert Commission, whose work is examined more closely in chapter 5, aims at creating stable urban African middle-class communities. It is to be achieved by giving some urban Africans—so-called urban insiders—preferential treatment, relative to other Africans, in employment, housing, and other areas. So far few of the Riekert Commission proposals, including those accepted in principle by the government, have been carried out, and the strict rules governing the movement and residence of Africans—known as influx control—remain largely unchanged. The government has agreed in principle, however, to allow greater mobility for some urban Africans.

The two main statutes restricting the entry of Africans into white areas and requiring them to account for their presence there are the Black Urban Areas Consolidation Act of 1945 and the Black Abolition of Passes and Coordination of Documents Act of 1952. These two statutes are complemented by the Black Labor Act of 1964, which regulates the recruitment of African workers through a network of labor bureaus that seek to balance the supply of labor with the demand.

The Black Urban Areas Consolidation Act is designed to control the influx of Africans into urban areas and their conduct while there. The central provision is Section 10 (1), which accords so-called Section 10 rights to certain "qualified" categories of Africans. This section, dating from a 1952 amendment to the act, makes it an offense for an African to remain longer than seventy-two hours in a prescribed area, as the "white" cities are designated, unless the individual can prove (a) continuous residence in the area since birth; or (b) continuous work in the area for the same employer for ten years or continuous lawful residence in the area for at least fifteen years; or (c) status as the wife, unmarried daughter, or minor son of a male qualifying under (a) or (b); or (d) permission from a labor bureau to remain. In this last case, the African must possess a permit "indicating the purpose for which and the period during which such Black may remain in that area [and] the person by whom and the class of work, if any, in which such Black may be employed."

In criminal prosecutions under Section 10, the accused is presumed to be unlawfully within the urban area until the contrary is proved. A person convicted under Section 10 may be punished by fines up to R100 or imprisonment for as long as three months. Such individuals may also be sent to tribal areas or to one of the resettlement villages where the government is now relocating some "surplus" urban Africans.

The pass system controls the movement of Africans throughout South Africa. Passes for free blacks in South Africa can be traced back to 1809, when the governor of the Cape, Earl Caledon, prohibited Hottentots (Khoikhoi) from moving from one district to another without a pass issued by a magistrate. Pass laws existed in the pre-Union legislation of all the colonies and were retained after establishment of the Union.

In 1952 the existing pass laws were replaced by the statute misleadingly titled the Blacks Abolition of Passes and Coordination of Documents Act. Instead of repealing the pass laws it, in effect, renamed passes "reference books" and for the first time required African women as well as men to possess them. The act requires that every African over the age of sixteen be finger-printed and furnished with a reference book containing the individual's iden-tity card and employment information.

Self-governing homelands may issue identity documents to their citizens to replace reference books, and the independent homelands now issue passports to their citizens. But under South African law these passports are still treated as reference books—in other words, as passes.

A policeman may ask an African to produce his reference book at any time, and failure to produce it on demand is a criminal offense punishable by a fine of up to R50 or imprisonment of up to three months. In 1975 the Appellate Division held that the law does not require an African to carry the reference book at all times and that an individual should be given a reasonable oppor-tunity to get it when it is demanded, under police escort if necessary. The definition of "reasonable opportunity" varies from case to case, however.

PETTY APARTHEID

Whites Only or, in Afrikaans, Slegs Blankes read the signs. A constant re-minder of South Africa's racial policies, they are found at the entrances to public lavatories, elevators, restaurants, railway cars, buses, and many other places. Sometimes there may be a sign nearby denoting a similar amenity for Non-Whites or Nie-Blankes. But this is not necessary, for there is no general legal obligation to provide comparable separate facilities for all racial groups. In South Africa "separate and unequal" treatment is legally acceptable—in-deed, specifically authorized by Parliament.

The whole apparatus of segregation in the routine of daily life—petty apartheid—is now under question in South Africa, and there are indications of change. But, perhaps intentionally, the government's plans are far from clear. Some pronouncements by government officials seem to foreshadow the abandonment of all petty apartheid measures. In 1979 Pieter Koornhof, the minister of cooperation and development, told an American audience: "We will not rest until racial discrimination has disappeared from our statute books and everyday life in South Africa. These are beliefs shared by my government." But just how the government defines discrimination is uncertain. What some consider discrimination it may deem legitimate "differentiation." And in 1979, when Prime Minister Botha announced his twelve-point "total national strat-egy," point six pledged an end only to "unnecessary discriminatory measures." In parliamentary debate on the twelve-point plan, he commented:

What is necessary discrimination? I shall tell you what is necessary   **61**

in my opinion: whatever is necessary to preserve "good neighborli-
ness." If I have a neighbor and there is a dividing line between us,
it does not necessarily mean, although we may be good friends, and
get along well with [one] another, that he can usurp various rights
for himself in my home. I say that we must be in a position to exercise
that necessary discrimination in South Africa. To illustrate this I
want to tell you that I have the right to protect my people and the
community life of my communities in their schools and in their
churches, and I shall not deviate from that; I am prepared to fight
for it.

Political considerations best explain the confused and contradictory rhetoric. The government is well aware that racial discrimination is unacceptable
in the modern world, but it is also well aware that sweeping changes in South
Africa's segregation practices would enrage many of its strongest supporters.
By being vague about what constitutes discrimination, the government slows
the pace of change. At the same time, it leaves latitude for some adjustments
in the system even while retaining the fundamental laws underlying segregated facilities. Modifications have been achieved by exemption permits and
by nonenforcement of laws. Repeal of the laws would be seen by many of the
government's most loyal followers as a serious reversal of National party policy
and might have major political consequences, but nonenforcement of segregation in the major cities can be explained away as special exemptions that in
no way interfere with the fundamental purity of the law.

Legal discrimination in the field of social amenities is founded on the
Reservation of Separate Amenities Act of 1953. The Nationalists enacted the
law after the South African courts held that a number of segregation measures
were invalid because they resulted in unequal treatment. The invocation of
the separate-but-equal doctrine incensed the government and led it to introduce the Reservation of Separate Amenities Act, which allows any person in
control of public premises to reserve separate and *unequal* facilities for different races and abolishes the power of the courts to nullify such actions. This
resulted in separate and substantially unequal amenities for different races in
all spheres of life—buses, trains, restaurants, libraries, and parks among others. In subsequent years, the law's coverage was broadened; thus, in 1960, the
act was amended to cover the sea and seashore, extending apartheid to beaches.

The Reservation of Separate Amenities Act remains the principal foundation of segregation in public facilities. Its passage in 1953 was followed by
provincial ordinances empowering the administrator in each province to direct
local authorities to reserve public premises and vehicles for the exclusive use
of a particular race, and many of the consequent regulations are still in effect.

In recent years, however, the pendulum has begun to swing the other way,
producing a gradual relaxation of segregation in public facilities both under
the control of central and provincial governments and under the control of local
authorities. For example, the rigid separation of races in governmental offices
(including post offices, where there were separate windows for blacks and

whites) has been dispensed with in many cases. Nor is segregation demanded in courts.

In public transportation the picture is uneven, but the trend is toward desegregation. Segregated coaches are still the rule on trains, but there has been a relaxation of railway policy, and conductors may allow blacks into white coaches, particularly when the black coaches are full. Many railway stations have desegregated. Air service has never been segregated. Bus and taxi practices vary considerably, since local transportation boards may require segregation. In the 1960s these boards followed a strict segregationist policy and compelled local authorities to provide separate buses for blacks and for whites. Lately, however, relaxation has occurred here, too, particularly in the case of Coloureds and Indians. For example, Johannesburg has a single bus service for whites, Coloureds, and Indians, and a separate one for Africans. The rules for taxis are also easing. At one time taxis had to confine their clients to one race, but now transportation boards are granting taxis permits to carry members of all groups.

In the early 1950s local authorities were generally permitted to make their own decisions on the use of civic halls and municipal libraries by members of the various racial groups. As with public transportation, practices varied, but in general the Cape favored desegregation while the northern provinces adhered to segregation. The Group Areas Act changed this situation, making it necessary for local authorities to obtain permits from the Department of Community Development for racially integrated functions in their public halls.

Starting in the mid-1970s, however, a number of local authorities decided to abolish some of the racial restrictions on the use of public amenities under their control, acting on their own when possible or obtaining exemptions under the Group Areas Act when necessary. The Johannesburg City Council opened its museums, art gallery, and municipal library to all races and removed White and Non-White signs from benches in its parks. In Cape Town, Durban, Pietermaritzburg, and East London local authorities embarked on similar courses. More recently, several city councils have sought to open civic halls to all races, and some have been granted the requisite permits under the Group Areas Act. The Johannesburg city auditorium has received a blanket permit for public performances, although it still needs separate permits for conferences and meetings.

Racially mixed swimming remains unacceptable. Local authorities have refused to desegregate municipal swimming pools and beach apartheid still prevails in most areas. Beach segregation, imposed on local authorities in the Cape and in Natal under both the Reservation of Separate Amenities and Group Areas acts, has usually resulted in the most developed and accessible beaches being set aside for whites. In recent years some efforts have been made to relax beach apartheid or at least to improve the beaches reserved for blacks. For the most part, however, segregation of beaches is still enforced. In the

63

holiday period in December and January of 1979–80 there were many arrests of blacks on white beaches.

In the case of privately owned premises, the Group Areas Act and a law known as the Liquor Act of 1977 have largely supplanted the Reservation of Separate Amenities Act as the chief bulwark of segregation. The separate-amenities law permits private establishments to segregate but does not force them to do so. As some owners of private facilities open to the public have sought to desegregate, the act has lost much of its importance. But the Group Areas Act and the Liquor Act are sufficient to ensure that most hotels, restaurants, theaters, and clubs remain all white.

The Group Areas Act's application in the enforcement of petty apartheid stems from its ban on blacks occupying premises in areas zoned for white occupation. The 1973 proclamation codifying the proposition that temporary presence, as at a movie or restaurant, constituted occupation has barred blacks from most privately owned establishments serving the public in white areas.

Nevertheless, in line with its policy of relaxing enforcement of segregation without yielding on the principle, the Department of Community Development may grant exemptions to the owners of nonlicensed premises (establishments that do not serve alcoholic beverages). Lately a number of these permits have been issued to restaurants in the central districts of cities. On April 14, 1980, the minister of community development stated that seventy-nine unlicensed restaurants in white areas had received permission to serve black patrons. Ten applications had been refused after due consideration of local circumstances, "including the need for such facilities and possible racial friction." At about the same time, the minister indicated that no such permits had been granted for movie theaters but that some applications were being considered. As far back as 1978, twenty-six legitimate theaters obtained permission to admit patrons of all races, and theaters not given this authorization may still apply for permits for individual performances.

The Liquor Act of 1977 forbids establishments in white areas that are licensed to serve alcoholic drinks from admitting blacks, and thereby continues to buttress petty apartheid. But here, too, exemptions are sometimes available. The Liquor Act ban on serving blacks, together with the Group Areas restrictions, may be waived by a permit granting "international status."

As of mid-1980, fifty-nine hotels had acquired international status. Licensed restaurants not attached to hotels may also be so designated, but such dispensations are handed out sparingly, and by the end of 1979 only eleven restaurants had qualified. Theaters with liquor licenses may also apply for international status, but so far only three have achieved it. Licensed clubs—sports, social, and racing—are also eligible for international status.

64   No law directly forbids racially integrated sports in South Africa. Never-

theless, until recent years the government has been able to keep sports segregated by relying on a wide variety of laws.

Regulations issued under the Group Areas Act prohibit the social aspects of sport—eating, drinking, postgame socializing—and prohibit mixed competition itself unless a permit is obtained for both players and spectators belonging to the racial groups to which the sports ground is out of bounds. The Liquor Act places social restrictions on sportsmen. At a club in a white area that has not achieved international status, black players will not be permitted to drink, even though a permit may have been obtained to integrate the playing field itself. The Reservation of Separate Amenities Act and the various provincial ordinances empowering the administrator to direct local authorities to provide separate amenities account for segregation in stadiums and other facilities under local control.

The Black Urban Areas Consolidation Act, which obliges non-Africans to obtain permits to enter African areas, also obstructs integrated sports. White, Coloured, and Indian players and spectators require permits issued by local administration boards to enter an African area to watch or play sports. A well-known white rugby player, Cheeky Watson, has been prosecuted under this law for entering an African township in Port Elizabeth to play with an African rugby team, and white spectators have been refused permission to enter Soweto to watch a soccer game. A limited easing of these rules occurred in 1980 when Pieter Koornhof, minister of cooperation and development, announced that entrance tickets purchased in advance would suffice as permits for white spectators to enter African urban areas to attend sports events and that club membership cards would serve as permits for white players.

The import of all this is that the central government or the relevant local authorities, which are ultimately subject to the will of the provincial administrators, largely determine whether or not sports will be integrated. This, in turn, means that racially mixed sports depend on the approval of some authority in the form of a permit. And, since permits are granted only in keeping with government policy, the halting movement toward integrated sports in recent years has reflected fluctuating government policy.

As it happens, sports policy is more sensitive to international pressure than policies in any other area of life in South Africa. South Africans love sports and are eager to compete on an international level. Consequently, to combat growing isolation in the international sporting world, the government has been compelled to desegregate sports to a considerable extent. As in other areas, this has been done almost entirely by issuing permits and by not enforcing laws, leaving the laws themselves unchanged.

Government sports policy has gone through a number of phases in the past decade. First, only "multinational" racially integrated sports were allowed. This permitted whites and blacks to compete against each other within the country in "open international" events but disallowed mixed sports at club, provincial, or national levels. Later, in 1976, the government altered its policy to permit sporting contests between teams of different races at club level. It remained opposed to mixed teams and to mixed clubs. In 1978 Pieter Koornhof, then minister of sport, announced that for contests in white, Coloured, and Indian areas no permit was required by any player to use athletic facilities or to join any club, which has led to some mixed teams, particularly in soccer. Koornhof also said that an annual clearance could be obtained by provincial and national bodies for the attendance of racially mixed spectators at sporting events, and that there would be no restrictions on mixed seating. These rulings led to a spate of applications by sports clubs for international status so that sportsmen of all colors might use their facilities and have a drink after the game.

Today, government sports policy is by no means clear. But it is obvious that the government is prepared to tolerate more racial mixing in this field than in other social activities. On the other hand, the government does not interfere with decisions of clubs and local authorities that want to maintain sports segregation, and as a result racial barriers persist in sports. In 1980, for example, the Pretoria City Council refused to allow a long-distance race to finish at the Pretoria Fountains, a park near the city, because blacks were running. It also refused permission to a racially mixed soccer team to use a stadium in Pretoria. Appeals to the central government to intervene were rejected on the ground that it is not government policy to interfere with such local decisions.

Chapter 4
Civil Liberties

Americans visiting South Africa for the first time invariably are struck by the seeming outspokenness of the English-language newspapers. Each day their columns are filled with criticism of apartheid and attacks on Nationalist political leaders. Helen Suzman, a leading member of the opposition Progressive Federal party, is quoted as describing the government's promise of a "new deal" for urban Africans as "blatant nonsense." An African leader warns that a South African raid on alleged African National Congress guerrillas in Mozambique "will stir hatred." A prominent businessman charges that Prime Minister Pieter W. Botha's "authoritarian" ways threaten parliamentary government. An editorial attributes South Africa's troubles to "the reluctance of whites to change a system that discriminates against blacks."

Perhaps, some visiting Americans conclude, the South African government's reputation for restricting political debate is overdrawn. But while the press in South Africa seems relatively free by world standards, serious constraints exist.

"The appearance of a healthy press and liberty of expression is false," says Anthony S. Mathews, a professor of law at the University of Natal in Durban. "While it is frequently argued that there is more freedom of speech than in many Third World and totalitarian societies, this is not a claim that establishes very much. A little freedom is clearly better than none at all, and may even be of some value, but it is dangerous to overrate it."

Commenting on South African newspapers, from Cape Town in February 1981, Anthony Lewis of the *New York Times* wrote: "They are free to criticize government officials and even to portray them in cartoon caricatures—a freedom scarce elsewhere in Africa and most of the world—but the dos and don'ts of reporting are often heavily weighted on the side of the don'ts."

South African newspapers operate under rules that prevent them from printing a word about some of the most important aspects of the South African scene. The press curbs are but one facet of an array of restrictions on civil liberties that are taken for granted in many democratic societies. The clear strategy of the government, according to Mathews, is to stifle any dissent that poses a serious threat to the status quo while at the same time allowing critics in the press and elsewhere limited latitude to speak out when their words are likely to have no significant impact. The regime's tools include vague, sweeping laws that permit it to label almost any activity of which it disapproves illegal, and strong enforcement procedures. There are also severe restrictions on political activities that might lead to effective opposition to white rule. Strengthening the government's hand at every turn is the absence of constitutional restraints that could be used by the courts to block government actions curtailing civil liberties.

THE CATCHALL LAWS

Two key laws, the Internal Security Act and the Terrorism Act, enable the South African government to silence almost anyone who poses a challenge to the regime. Both are so loosely drafted that American courts would almost certainly rule similar statutes unreasonably vague.

The Internal Security Act dates back to 1950. When first enacted it was entitled the Suppression of Communism Act, but, comments South African legal authority John Dugard, "During the following twenty-five years the act was invoked against ardent non-Communists as well as professed Communists, as the definition of communism is wide enough to encompass most radical opponents of the status quo." As a result, in 1976 the Suppression of Communism Act was broadened to cover organizations and individuals who engage in "activities which endanger the security of the State or the maintenance of public order," and renamed the Internal Security Act. Communism was still sweepingly defined, however. In Dugard's words:

> Under the Internal Security Act, "communism" is defined as the doctrine of Marxian socialism expounded by Lenin and Trotsky "or any related form of that doctrine expounded or advocated in the Republic for the promotion of the fundamental principles of that doctrine." It includes any doctrine which "aims at bringing about any political, industrial, social or economic change within the Republic by the promotion of disturbance or disorder, by unlawful acts or omissions" or which "aims at the encouragement of feelings of hostility between the European and non-European races of the Republic" where the consequences are calculated to further the achievement of political, industrial, social, or economic change by the promotion of disorder by unlawful acts.

The language may be convoluted, but the impact is clear. Says Anthony

Mathews: "It is hard to think of any peaceful but effective resistance program that would not be covered."

The Terrorism Act became law in 1967. It is, if anything, more vague and inclusive than the Internal Security Act. Aside from overt acts of violence that might generally be construed as terrorism, the law's definition of the crime, according to Dugard, embraces any acts designed "to further or encourage the achievements of any political aim, including the bringing about of any social or economic change, by violence or forcible means or by the intervention of or in accordance with the direction or under the guidance of or in cooperation with or with the assistance of any foreign government or any foreign or international body or institution"; "to cause substantial financial loss to any person or the State"; "to cause, encourage or further feelings of hostility between the White and other inhabitants of the Republic"; or—most sweeping of all—"to embarrass the administration of the affairs of the State."

The Internal Security Act and the Terrorism Act, along with the loosely drawn Sabotage Act of 1962 (embarrassing the affairs of state is considered sabotage as well as terrorism), are "so widely, vaguely, and unclearly phrased that the task of the prosecutor is greatly reduced," sums up Dugard. "Not only do they offend the certainty-of-law requirement inherent in the notion of legality, but they greatly reduce the burden of the prosecution in proving the guilt of a political offender."

FREEDOM OF PERSON

A person who stands in jeopardy of losing his or her freedom by arbitrary detention or other forms of confinement, because he or she has spoken out against injustice, for example, has, for all practical purposes, no civil rights at all. Thus, a crucial test of the current status of civil rights in any society is the protection accorded personal freedom.

Until the 1960s South Africa would not have come off badly in such a test, despite the use of limited—and court-monitored—pretrial detention at some periods in its history. During the early sixties, however, as overt black resistance to the government's racial policies grew, Parliament responded by enacting a series of tough pretrial and preventive detention laws:

90-day detention. This 1963 law authorized interrogation in solitary confinement for 90 days at a time of persons suspected of certain security offenses or of having information relevant to national security. No court control or intervention was permitted under the law, which was suspended in 1964.

180-day detention. In 1965 the 180-day detention law was introduced as a permanent measure (the 90-day law had required annual renewal). The new law authorized detention in solitary confinement for six months of persons who, in the opinion of the attorney general, were likely to be material witnesses for the state in certain security trials. Again, the courts had no power to control

69

the detention or the conditions under which detainees were held. This law has since been redrawn into two separate laws. One authorizes six months detention in nonsecurity trials with judicial approval, while the other permits detention in security trials for the same period but at the absolute discretion of the attorney general.

Indefinite detention. In 1967 a provision of the Terrorism Act introduced indefinite detention of any person suspected of the catchall crime of terrorism or of having information about terrorism. Such detention is at the sole discretion of a police officer of the rank of lieutenant colonel or above or of the commissioner of police. In such cases solitary confinement is authorized and the courts are expressly precluded from intervening. This measure, along with the 180-day detention law, is still in force.

Preventive detention. This was introduced in 1976 as part of the Internal Security Act. It authorizes the minister of justice to detain persons he suspects are a danger to state security or public order for as long as he desires. Detainees are treated as prisoners awaiting trial and may not challenge their detention in court. The power to impose preventive detention, which must be renewed annually by the state president, is still in force. One of the most notable victims of this law was Percy Qoboza, a prominent African newspaper editor, who was imprisoned in 1977.

The government's overall detention powers have been used extensively in recent years. Through the first eleven months of 1979, according to the South African Institute of Race Relations, an antiapartheid fact-gathering body, 334 persons were detained under the various laws. In 1978 the total was 261 and in 1977 it was about 600. In 1976, the institute found that on May 26, prior to the Soweto riots, 336 persons were in detention. Between June and September, another 2,430 were detained for questioning following the outbreak of violence.

The Internal Security Act authorizes banning as well as detention; and while banning is not as severe a restriction on personal liberty as imprisonment, it can destroy all semblance of a normal existence. A banned person is generally restricted to a certain magisterial district; prevented from entering educational institutions, publishing houses, courts, and other specified places; barred from attending political, social, and other gatherings; and prohibited from communicating with specified persons, usually others who have been banned. A drink with a friend could violate a banning order, as could a family birthday party. Normal employment is impractical. In its most extreme form banning amounts to house arrest, with the individual usually confined to his or her residence for twelve hours a day during the working week and twenty-four hours a day over the weekend, but sometimes prohibited from leaving the house at all.

Banning procedures are totally arbitrary. There is no opportunity to contest the order, the authorities need give no reason for their action, and the courts have no power to intervene. As of mid-1980, more than 150 persons—

mostly blacks—were under banning orders in South Africa, but the number has been much higher in the past and could easily rise again as tensions increase.

The authorities empowered to detain and ban operate without restraint or independent checks on their actions. Thus, anyone who engages in activities frowned on by the government lives in constant danger of losing his or her personal freedom. Although some people refuse to be cowed by this threat, many others are sufficiently intimidated to shrink from activity likely to be offensive to the government.

FREEDOM OF EXPRESSION AND INFORMATION

The Internal Security Act and the Terrorism Act, with their loose definitions of crimes and their severe enforcement procedures, have inevitably dampened free speech in South Africa. For example, statements construed as inciting racial hostility have been held by the courts to be a form of terrorism punishable by a minimum sentence of five years and a maximum sentence of death. Moreover, the Internal Security Act forbids publications from quoting anything a banned person has ever said or written. This prohibition also applies to quotations from specified members of organizations outlawed under the act, such as the African National Congress, the Pan-Africanist Congress, the South African Communist party, several black students' organizations, black writers' groups, and a black women's organization.

Besides these broad laws, there are several censorship measures. One is the Publications Act of 1974, which tightened up a system of censorship that had been institutionalized in 1963. Designed primarily to screen books, periodicals, films, plays, and records (newspapers are covered by other laws), the act authorizes an array of censorship committees and caps them with a board that considers appeals of the committees' decisions. Within guidelines so broad as to make rulings totally arbitrary, committees may declare any material undesirable. Once such a decision has been made, it becomes a criminal offense to produce or distribute such material. Committees may also declare that the possession of material ruled undesirable is prohibited, and it then becomes a crime to possess such material.

Censorship under the Publications Act is applied increasingly to political ideas and information, and it has become a powerful instrument of political control. In 1979 1,326 items (excluding films and plays) were declared "undesirable," about half of which were political publications. Among the books banned for political reasons have been standard works on Marxism and many political analyses of South Africa. Allegations of obscenity are also a frequent cause of banning. A number of books by prominent American authors, including Mary McCarthy, John Updike, Henry Miller, and Erica Jong, have been proscribed on this ground.

Other censorship laws affect all forms of publication, including daily and weekly newspapers. South Africa has a British-style Official Secrets Act that makes unauthorized publication of government papers and documents a crime, especially when they deal with operations paid for out of secret accounts or with "national security activities." As in Great Britain, this stricture severely hampers journalistic investigations of government. The Defense Act of 1957, coupled with the Official Secrets Act, forbids unauthorized disclosure of all but the most innocuous information about South Africa's armed forces. Under this law South African newspapers were prevented from publishing stories about South Africa's invasion of Angola in 1975, even though it was widely reported in the rest of the world.

The government also imposes restrictions on reporting about prisons and the police. The Prison Act of 1959 has been interpreted by the courts as forbidding publication of all critical articles about prison conditions or the treatment of prisoners. Similarly, the Police Act of 1958 and a 1979 amendment effectively bar articles criticizing police behavior, such as allegations of brutality or torture. "This suppression is serious," says Professor Mathews, "since the hard realities of the racial policies of the government . . . are encountered by hundreds of thousands of black people each year in prisons and police stations."

The ultimate step in newspaper censorship, the closing of a paper, has been given sanction in South Africa under the Internal Security Act. A number of newspapers have been proscribed over the years, one of the most recent instances being the banning in October 1977 of the mass-circulation *World,* a Johannesburg newspaper edited by Percy Qoboza and addressed to an African audience.* A publication that is banned loses the R20,000 deposit required by law as a condition of registration. This deposit requirement in itself has been sufficient to prevent many newspaper publishing ventures from ever getting off the ground.

For journalists who persist in voicing strong criticism of the government despite the many constraints, the price can be heavy: detention, banning, loss of passport. At the same time, the government often displays considerable subtlety in applying press curbs. Mathews comments: "Suppression of ideas and information tends to be selective and the authorities are skilled in eliminating discussion which would be a real threat to their policies. By permitting relatively harmless but forceful criticism, they create the illusion of a free public debate. Moreover, because freedom of association is virtually nonexistent for blacks, the mobilization of opinion against the government is rigidly and effectively controlled."

---

*The *World* was succeeded by the *Post* and *Sunday Post,* but these were also banned, in effect, in January 1981, when the government refused to grant the required permission to resume publishing after a shutdown caused by a strike. A new daily addressed to Africans, the *Sowetan,* promptly began rolling off the presses. All these newspapers have been published by the white-owned Argus group.

FREEDOM OF ASSOCIATION

Political participation and representative government require freedom of association. That right does not exist in South Africa, particularly for blacks.

When the Suppression of Communism Act (now called the Internal Security Act) was introduced in 1950, it outlawed the Communist party and authorized the dissolution of other organizations. In 1960 a new measure, known as the Unlawful Organizations Act, provided yet another tool for banning organizations. The combined effect of these two laws is that any organization may be outlawed by an executive decree not subject to judicial or any other independent control. An organization slated for banning is not entitled to advance notice or to a hearing. Once an organization is proscribed, its assets are disposed of by a government-appointed official, its members may be placed on a special list that makes them liable to many statutory disabilities, and it becomes a criminal offense for anyone to carry on the activities of the organization or even to pursue objectives similar to those of the banned group.

Many organizations, principally but not exclusively African in membership, have been suppressed under these laws. The African National Congress and the Pan-Africanist Congress were banned in 1960. On October 19, 1977, eighteen other organizations were proscribed with a single stroke of the executive pen. Today, apart from the Inkatha movement (see chapter 9), not one significant African political organization exists openly in South Africa.

Two other laws also curtail freedom of association. One is the Prohibition of Political Interference Act, described in chapter 3, which bans multiracial political parties. The other is the Affected Organizations Act of 1974, which authorizes the state president to declare an organization "affected" if, in his opinion, it engages in politics with the aid of a foreign organization or person. Such was the case with the National Union of South African Students. Once an organization is declared affected, no one may solicit foreign funds on its behalf. Penalties for violations are stiff—a fine of as much as R10,000 or imprisonment for up to five years for a first offense.

FREEDOM OF ASSEMBLY

The right to assemble for lawful purposes—to hold meetings, gatherings, and processions to express their views and grievances and to formulate policies and plans of action—has a precarious status in South African law.

The broadest inroad into freedom of assembly has been carved by the Riotous Assemblies Act. At its enactment in 1956 it provided for control of public meetings of twelve or more persons, but a 1974 amendment extended control to all meetings, public or private, of two or more persons. Acting under the law, the minister of justice, in 1976, banned all outdoor meetings and processions except sports events and gatherings for which a permit is specifically granted. The prohibition is still in force. Often the authorities have used the power to ban specific kinds of meetings or meetings organized by specific groups. The Riotous Assemblies Act also grants the police wide powers to disperse unlawful meetings.

The sweeping nature of the justice minister's power to prohibit meetings is illustrated by an order that appeared in the *Government Gazette* of June 30, 1980. It was designed to clamp down on political discussion during the 1980 school boycotts by black youths. Here is the text of the order, followed by a list of the areas to which it applied:

GOVERNMENT NOTICE

DEPARTMENT OF JUSTICE

No. 1405

30 June 1980

PROHIBITION OF GATHERINGS.
SECTION 2 (3)(b) OF ACT 17 OF 1956

Whereas I, Alwyn Louis Schlebusch, Minister of Justice, deem it necessary for the maintenance of the public peace, I hereby prohibit, in terms of section 2 (3)(b) of the Riotous Assemblies Act, 1956 (Act 17 of 1956), any gathering of a political nature at which any form of state or any principle or policy or action of a government of state or of a political party or political group is propagated, defended, attacked, criticised or discussed, or at which any protest or boycott or strike is encouraged or discussed or which is held in protest against or in support of or in commemoration of anything, in the magisterial districts mentioned in the Schedule hereto from 1 July 1980 until 31 August 1980 except for such gatherings which I or the magistrate of the magisterial district concerned expressly authorise.

This prohibition shall not apply to any gathering of 10 persons or less.

Dated at Pretoria this 27th day of June 1980.
A. L. SCHLEBUSCH, Minister of Justice.

SCHEDULE
Durban, Pietermaritzburg, Pinetown, Inanda, Lower Tugela, Ndwedwe, Port Shepstone, Umzinto, The Cape, Paarl, Stellenbosch, Somerset West, Strand, Worcester, Wynberg, Bellville, Goodwood, Simonstown, Kuils River, Port Elizabeth, Uitenhage, Albany, Cradock, Kirkwood, Graaff-Reinet, Fort Beaufort, East London, King William's Town, Victoria East, Quenstown, Aliwal North, Johannesburg, Pretoria, Vereeniging, Vanderbijlpark, Roodenpoort, Springs, Benoni, Brakpan, Germiston, Krugersdorp, Randfontein, Westonaria, Bloemfontein, Kroonstad.

Similarly broad powers to prohibit meetings are also conferred on the
minister of justice by the Internal Security Act. Under this law he may ban

either a specific gathering or gatherings of a particular nature "at any place or any area during any period."

Meetings of Africans come under special curbs. The Black Urban Areas Consolidation Act of 1945 empowers the minister in charge of African affairs to prohibit meetings of Africans in an urban area outside an African residential area. The Black Administration Act of 1927 authorizes control of meetings in rural areas, and a 1968 proclamation bars gatherings of more than ten Africans in such areas without a permit except for religious, sports, and a few other types of activities.

For other groups as well as for Africans, processions or gatherings in public places and built-up areas are regulated by laws requiring the approval of local authorities. Even here, however, the central government has stepped in. In 1970 it adopted a rule that, besides local authority approval, the organizers of processions need the consent of the local magistrate, an official acting under the Department of Justice. The magistrate may refuse permission for a procession if he believes it threatens law and order.

FREEDOM OF MOVEMENT

The restrictions on travel within South Africa, which mainly affect Africans, were described in the preceding chapter, but freedom of movement also includes the right to travel abroad. In South Africa the grant or refusal of a passport is at the discretion of authorities whose decisions may not be appealed. Persons denied passports sometimes are granted "exit permits"—but only if they agree to leave the country permanently. Acceptance of an exit permit entails loss of citizenship, plus criminal penalties if the person returns to South Africa. In 1979, 379 passport applications were rejected, 17 passports were withdrawn, and 4 exit permits were granted. But in some years the total of exit permits granted had been much higher—for example, in 1965, 37 exit permits were granted.

The link between antigovernment or antiapartheid activity and the denial of passports is unmistakable, and political dissent is unquestionably inhibited by this arbitrary power. For some, even the cruel alternative of an exit permit is denied. And then there is the peculiar case of the late Robert Sobukwe, the banned president of the Pan-Africanist Congress, who was granted an exit permit but denied permission to leave the magisterial district to which he was restricted. Thus, he was never able to use the permit.

Just as local critics of the government are frequently prevented from traveling abroad, so foreign critics have often been denied visas for visits to South Africa. This situation seems to be changing, however, with recent government actions suggesting a relaxation in the official attitude. In 1979, for example, visas were granted to a number of prominent critics of apartheid to enable them to attend a human rights conference in Cape Town.

CIVIL DISOBEDIENCE

Passive resistance, boycotts, and wildcat strikes have been used in the past to dramatize black grievances, and similar sorts of protests are again occurring. (For an examination of recent events see chapter 9.) But the government possesses effective weapons for dealing with such actions.

One of the strongest was devised following a passive resistance campaign against apartheid by Africans in the early 1950s. Most of the offenses committed in the course of the campaign were minor ones—using park benches or station waiting rooms reserved for whites, for example—carrying minimal penalties. With the passage of the Criminal Law Amendment Act of 1953, the government greatly strengthened its hand. The measure authorized severe penalties (a substantial fine or imprisonment for up to three years and/or a whipping of as many as ten strokes) for persons who committed any offense as part of a campaign of protest against the law. It provided for similar penalties for persons who incited others to take part in a protest. Not surprisingly, this law put an end to the passive resistance campaign of the 1950s and, indeed, has virtually eliminated passive resistance as a protest weapon in South Africa.

Boycotts, such as those by Coloured schoolchildren in 1980, are not specifically outlawed, but the Riotous Assemblies Act could be used to punish those who organize or encourage them. It makes it a crime to accost others "offensively" in a public place to persuade them to join in a boycott or a similar activity. The same law also makes it a crime to trespass on business premises to encourage workmen to stop work, a deterrent to wildcat protest strikes. Another law makes it a crime, in many cases, for workers employed in basic utilities to walk off the job.

ILLEGAL CONSTRAINTS ON CIVIL RIGHTS

Along with the drastic legal restrictions on their civil rights, critics of the regime in South Africa have often had to contend with illegal pressures: threats, harassment, sabotage, and personal violence. While these are difficult to prove, reports abound of threats and harassment from government officials, including reported loss of jobs following a visit to their employers by the security police.

Frequently the pressures are cruder. Members of opposition groups have had their car tires slashed, their houses gasoline-bombed, and shots fired through their doors and windows. A recent form of terror against unpopular groups has been the burning of offices. Arsonists caused extensive damage to the Cape Town offices of the South African Institute of Race Relations in 1979, and in 1980 fire damaged the institute's headquarters in Johannesburg. The most serious incident of all was the unsolved 1978 killing of Richard Turner, a banned political scientist and former lecturer at the University of Natal.

Clandestine right-wing groups, such as the Scorpio Movement, are believed to have perpetrated some of the tire slashings and bombings. The police record in bringing those guilty to book does not dispel suspicions voiced by some that these groups have had a degree of official tolerance. In 1978 it was calculated that since 1964 there had been 1,600 instances of right-wing terrorism but only two successful prosecutions.

A glimmer of change in the government's attitude toward right-wing terrorism was seen by some in the successful prosecution under the Terrorism Act of persons who fired shots into the Cape Town apartment of Colin Eglin, leader of the Progressive Federal party, in 1979. In general, however, the National party's record in dealing with terrorism and other illegal actions against its opponents has not been reassuring to government critics.

THE ROLE OF THE COURTS

The formal constraints on the South African courts as defenders of civil liberties are not limited to the curbs placed on them by the laws affecting rights. The constraints also include the courts' lack of constitutional standing as protectors of rights in South Africa. The principle of parliamentary sovereignty and the absence of a bill of rights enforceable by the courts put the South African judiciary at a marked disadvantage compared with American courts.

Nevertheless, this does not mean (as many South African judges seem to assume) that the South African courts are entirely impotent in the protection of civil rights. At least to some extent, the courts' power and influence depend on their own belief in civil rights and on their assertiveness in the face of legislative and executive encroachments. In recent decades judicial assertiveness has been rare, and the courts have largely abdicated responsibility in the field of civil rights.

One explanation of why the courts have not taken a stronger libertarian stand is that some judges regard the infringements of civil rights as necessary for state security. Allen Drury, in his book *A Very Strange Society,* records an interview with judges who evinced unconcern about the application of the Internal Security Act. On the other hand, even judges critical of security legislation frequently do no better than colleagues who favor the laws because they regard judicial intervention as undesirable meddling in politics.

For South African judges willing to risk a bolder stance, the cause of civil liberties could conceivably be bolstered in at least one area: the acceptability of evidence of witnesses held for long periods in solitary confinement. No law requires the courts to attach credibility to such evidence. If they had shown more skepticism about its reliability in the past, the mistreatment of detainees (resulting in some fifty deaths during the history of detention) might have occurred less frequently. However marginal their powers, this is an important area in which judges can still be effective.

IMPLICATIONS

For the present, it makes little sense to speak of civil rights in South Africa. "Right" implies something that can be enforced, while the reality in South Africa is that every civil right may be denied if the authorities so choose. Few safeguards of a substantive or procedural kind exist, and the citizen is effectively at the mercy of the state. "Civil rights" have become privileges exercisable at the discretion of the government.

The flickers of open opposition do not belie any of this. Blacks who speak out frequently suffer for it. *Effective* aboveground opposition is generally not permitted, although, as in the case of press criticism, some antigovernment political activities by whites are tolerated. It is this selective approach in the application of laws infringing on civil rights, says Anthony Mathews, that "creates the illusion of civil rights and that distinguishes South Africa from totalitarian states where there are no pretenses about repression of freedoms."

Now and then there are hints that changes for the better are on the way. A major address in 1979 by D. P. de Villiers, a leading lawyer who is a prominent Nationalist supporter, called for reform of internal security legislation. This was followed by the 1979 appointment of a commission to study the security laws with an eye to recommending changes. But as of early 1981 the government had yet to repeal or even loosen by amendment any law restricting civil rights. Indeed, the converse is true. After the official report on a 1978 Information Department scandal* suggested that excessive secrecy in government operations was partly responsible for the mess, the government pushed through several additional secrecy laws. Even while the commission was reviewing security legislation in 1980, the government was in the process of introducing a law that would bar unauthorized press reports on antiterrorist activities by the police, apparently including the names of persons detained under the Terrorism Act or similar laws. Moreover, during the 1980 school boycotts the government placed hundreds of people in detention. If anything, recent actions by the government indicate a hardening of attitudes on civil rights under the national security rubric.

The repression of civil rights in South Africa has far-reaching implications. It means that the framers of policy are increasingly out of touch with the grievances of the majority and with the consequences of failure to respond adequately to them. It means that freedom is denied not just to persons com-

---

*The scandal, one of the major political developments of the late 1970s in South Africa, involved irregularities in the now-disbanded Department of Information. Officials in the department, including the minister, Connie Mulder, and the secretary, Eschel Rhoodie, had secretly and illegally established a partisan English-language newspaper, the *Citizen*, using public funds without cabinet authorization. Besides this abuse of authority, it was alleged that several department officials had misappropriated public funds for their own use. These charges were never proved in court, however. The scandal precipitated the departure of John Vorster from public life. He resigned as prime minister in September 1978, became state president, and then resigned from that post in June 1979.

mitted to violence but to all who fundamentally oppose the apartheid policies of the government. The result of such indiscriminate repression is that moderate black leaders are either discredited and replaced by those with more extreme views or that the moderates themselves become more extreme. This, in turn, means that the chances for an accommodation based on middle-ground or moderate positions grow ever slimmer as the clampdown on civil rights tightens.

Chapter 5
The Workplace

South Africa runs on black labor. At the automobile plants in the Indian Ocean city of Port Elizabeth, blacks run the assembly lines. In the sweltering depths of the Witwatersrand gold mines, the drillers and shovelers working at the face are black. On the vast farms that stretch to the horizon in the Transvaal and the Orange Free State, blacks drive the tractors, tend the herds, mend the fences.

Some statistics: Of the total South African work force of 9.4 million, 80 percent are black. Of the blacks, 85 percent are African, 11 percent Coloured, and 3 percent Asian. In manufacturing 77 percent of the work force are black; 70 percent of this are African and most of the rest Coloured. In mining 90 percent of the work force are black, almost all African. Virtually all the workers in commercial agriculture are black, again mostly Africans except for a sizable number of Coloureds in the western Cape.

Incomes of black workers, particularly Africans, trail far behind those of whites, but blacks made gains during the past decade. The ratio of white wages to African wages in manufacturing dropped from 5.8 to 1 in 1970 to 4.3 to 1 in 1979. In mining it dropped from 19.8 to 1 to 6.6 to 1 over the same span. Because of the wages earned by Africans in the growing industrial economy, the per capita income of Africans in South Africa undoubtedly ranks near the top for black Africa, though precise comparative figures are lacking.

All the same, there is little reason for complacency about the economic well-being of blacks in South Africa. Despite the recent gains, the wage gap has widened in absolute terms over this period. Moreover, comments Stanley B. Greenberg of Yale, an authority on South African labor practices, "the pattern of income inequality in South Africa remains extraordinarily skewed by almost any international standard." Millions of Africans still scrabble for subsistence in the impoverished "homeland" areas, their lives relatively untouched by the advances of the industrial sector of the South African economy. By one estimate, more than a quarter of the African population is unemployed. Those who are employed are almost always found in the worst-paying and least-prestigious positions. In factory tool-and-die shops the skilled craftsmen are white, and in management and supervisory offices the only black face is likely to be that of an African bringing around the tea.

This pattern partly reflects the composition of the black population, with its high proportion of newcomers to an industrial, urban way of life. It must also be noted that parts of the pattern—low black wages and status, high black unemployment—still find echoes in the United States. But conditions in South Africa reflect to a considerable degree a special circumstance: a conscious, systematic effort over the years to control black labor, to channel it where it will benefit whites and to raise barriers against it where it is not needed or where it seems to compete with whites.

This system of labor apartheid is of particular concern to Americans because it is a system in which many major U.S. corporations have acquiesced in the past. The whole field of employment is of particular interest to all who seek change in South Africa because it appears to be one of the areas offering possibilities for peaceful accommodation of some black-white differences. Polls show South African whites less resistant to change in the economic sphere than in other fields, and the government has taken steps on the economic front that hint at change but whose full import is not yet clear. Turning to prospects for more fundamental changes, some analysts maintain—although others disagree—that economic advances for South African blacks could be a first step toward political and social gains.

THE STATE AND THE LABOR MARKET

Government control of the black labor market in South Africa has a history dating back to the introduction of slavery in the early years of the Cape settlement. By the middle of the nineteenth century the system whites used to control the labor they employed was developing into a legal apparatus that forced many of the most numerous inhabitants, the Africans, to work for white farmers and severely limited African freedom of movement in seeking new jobs. The creation of the mining industry in the late 1800s brought new refinements in controls, including tightened pass laws and the system of migrant labor, which shuttled African workers between the mines and the reserves as they were needed by the whites. In the view of the Chamber of Mines, says Greenberg, "Such a labor framework . . . best suited the cultural and financial needs of workers new to industry, the cost requirements of the mines, and the maintenance and security needs of a civilized, European community in South Africa." The commercialization of agriculture and the development of industry in this century led to still further state constraints on African labor. The resulting control apparatus, says Greenberg, "is now an integral part of South Africa's modern, developing economy."

The previously described pass laws and "Section 10" rules sharply restricting Africans' presence in urban areas are key elements in the control of labor. An "unqualified person" from a homeland or a white farming district must run a discouraging gauntlet in trying to carve out a new life in a city. The best a man in this group can hope for is employment as a contract worker, usually for one year, without his family, housed in an all-male hostel. The granting of independence to the Transkei, Bophuthatswana, and Venda has resulted in new travel documents but has not altered the form of contract labor in any important way. Opportunities for women to do contract work in urban areas are severely limited, with domestic service the most likely prospect.

Since the 1960s the government has made a concerted effort to hold down the size of the permanent African population in urban areas. The administrative regulations that limit employment contracts to one year also require that workers visit their homelands annually to reregister with tribal labor bureaus before beginning new one-year stints. Except for those born to or married to "qualified persons"—Africans already legally entitled to live in an urban area—this rule effectively blocks the granting of new urban residence rights by making it impossible to establish the requisite period of continuous residence or employment. Delays in the construction of new family accommodations for African urban workers and checks on the growth of squatter communities have further limited the numbers able to take up permanent urban residence. These and other restrictions have operated with particular force in the western Cape, which the government in 1966 declared a "Coloured preference area."

Rudimentary controls on the movement of Africans into the urban areas of South Africa have existed at least since the 1920s. Under the Native Urban Areas Act of 1923 and other legislation, white municipalities established African townships. They began registering African employment contracts and, with varying degrees of vigilance, rooting out "redundancy." But these efforts, even when coupled with a law barring Africans employed by white farmers from leaving their jobs to go to the city, failed to prevent the large-scale influx of Africans into the urban areas during and after World War II. When the National party came to power in 1948, it promised to erect a legal barrier between urban and rural areas and provide the administrative machinery necessary to enforce it.

The Native Laws Amendment Act of 1952 and subsequent legislation provided for the administration of the African labor market by labor bureaus: local bureaus in white urban areas, district bureaus in white rural areas, and tribal bureaus in homeland areas. Overseeing the local and district bureaus since the early 1970s—and ensuring central government control—has been a layer of administration boards covering large geographical areas.

To some extent, the labor bureaus operate as labor exchanges, with job seekers registering their availability and employers their openings. But the bureaus are also essential to influx control. Registration for work is compulsory. A local labor bureau may not recruit African workers from homeland areas unless local, "qualified" labor is unavailable. In no case may it place farm laborers in urban employment. African farm workers registered at district labor bureaus are not referred to urban employers. Africans in the homelands are supposed to register at tribal labor bureaus and wait to be recruited, although many circumvent this requirement. Those who go illegally to the cities generally find work in the "informal sector," as peddlers, small-scale merchants, backyard mechanics, or in other low-paying fields. If they can get a job legally, they must return to their homelands to have their contracts attested at tribal labor bureaus. If they cannot, they face the prospect of arrest or of being "endorsed out" of the white area.

In 1977, 2.8 million African workers were registered at urban labor bureaus, including nearly a million contract workers. Another 900,000 were registered with district labor bureaus in the white rural areas. These figures do not include mine workers. The mine-recruiting organizations constitute, in effect, a state-delegated labor bureau system. Nor do the figures include illegally employed Africans, unregistered job seekers, unregistered casual and full-time farm workers, or most job seekers in the homeland areas.

Even though Africans continue to slip through the net, state control of the African labor market is pervasive and sweeping. The influx controls and the labor bureaus restrict the mobility of African labor and limit African urbanization. They foster migrant, contract labor and often impose artificial ties to impoverished homelands. Efforts to resolve the fundamental inequities of South African life must inevitably include changes in the labor control system.

DISCRIMINATION IN EMPLOYMENT

Race very largely determines the job a person holds in industry, commerce, and government. Partly as a result, in 1977 fewer than 1 of every 100 unskilled workers in these sectors was white and fewer than 1 of every 200 company managers was African. Eighty-two percent of African workers held semiskilled or unskilled jobs in 1977; 9 percent held clerical positions, but only 5 percent skilled, 1 percent supervisory, and 3 percent professional positions. Even now in gold mining all rock breakers and laborers at the mine face are black and all those with blasting certificates, a prerequisite for the best-paid jobs, are white.

State action is directly responsible for some of the color barriers in em-   **83** ployment. One field where such state-imposed bars have long been the rule is mining. The Mines and Works Act of 1911, passed almost immediately after formation of the Union of South Africa, reserved blasting certificates and thirty-two mining occupations for whites. But a much broader range of legal racial discrimination in employment resulted from the "civilized labor policy" announced by the government in 1924:

> The Prime Minister desires it to be understood by all Departments of State that it has been decided as a matter of definite policy that, wherever practicable, civilized labour shall be substituted in all employment by the Government for that which may be classified as uncivilized. Civilized labour is to be considered as the labour rendered by persons whose standard of living conforms to the standard generally recognized as tolerable from the usual European standpoint. Uncivilized labour is to be regarded as the labour rendered by persons whose aim is restricted to the bare requirements of the necessities of life as understood among barbarous and undeveloped peoples.

Pursuing this policy, the government substituted white labor for Africans and Coloureds employed by the railroads and harbors. It also established tariff protection for domestic manufacturers giving special consideration to "civilized labor." When the National party took office in 1948, it reissued the 1924 declaration and affirmed the policy for the central and provincial administrations.

After 1948 specific, legal employment color bars, previously confined to mining, became more general in industry. Beginning in 1951 African construction workers could no longer be trained for work outside "the Bantu's own area." Legislation enacted in 1956 authorized the government to "reserve" occupations for specific racial groups or to fix racial employment ratios for particular industries or types of work. Using these powers, the minister of labor reserved for whites, for example, a number of occupations in the meat-packing, construction, and metal and engineering industries; sampling, surveying, and ventilating jobs in the mines; and truck driving for the city of Durban. Other government initiatives strengthening the racial division of labor include the Physical Planning Act of 1967 (now entitled the Environment Planning Act) and the Coloured labor preference policy promulgated in 1966, which placed ceilings on the employment of African workers on the Witwatersrand and in the western Cape.

Largely because of pressure from employers unable to fill positions reserved for whites, the government showed considerable flexibility in enforcing job-reservation rules in the private sector beginning in the late 1960s. Many exemptions were granted, and after 1975 no new job reservations were imposed. Thus, although state-mandated job color bars are still widespread in government and mining, employers in manufacturing and commerce now operate primarily outside such legal restrictions.

More prevalent than state-imposed racial obstacles are those negotiated by trade unions and employers. Under the umbrella of industrial councils set up under the Industrial Conciliation Act, unions and management have stipulated a range of contractual provisions barring Africans from major sectors of industry, including the more skilled jobs. In the mid-1950s, spurred by government prodding, the industrial council for the iron, steel, and engineering industry, covering a sizable proportion of industrial workers, reserved higher-grade positions for those eligible under law for trade union membership—which then included whites, Coloureds, and Asians but not Africans. Similar provisions are spread across the industrial landscape, creating color barriers in such fields as automobile repair and the building and electrical trades. Closed-shop arrangements, which, according to a 1979 government report, were contained in forty-nine industrial council agreements covering 346,000 employees, are even more restrictive. The long exclusion of Africans from "registered"—officially recognized—unions has combined with the closed-shop agreements to prevent the employment of Africans in most skilled occupations in industry.

Affecting fewer workers but nonetheless critical to the overall racial labor hierarchy are apprenticeship restrictions. Although the law does not formally provide for color discrimination in apprenticeship programs, the makeup of the screening committees—largely white, plus a few Coloureds and Asians—has effectively barred Africans from working as skilled tradesmen in white areas. Furthermore, it was government policy for a number of years not to enroll Africans as apprentices in white areas.

The education available to blacks in South Africa is inferior to that for whites (see chapter 6), and this disparity extends to training in industrial skills, creating yet another kind of racial barrier. Until the mid-1970s organized industrial training was restricted to whites, plus some Coloureds and Asians, and even now the barriers against African apprentices remain in place. Reflecting the lack of training, in 1976 only 207 Africans took examinations to qualify as artisans, as skilled craftsmen are known in South Africa; 10,000 whites took examinations in 1977.

Opportunities for Africans to learn trades and technical skills are expanding. A new advanced technical college for Africans was preparing to open in 1981, bringing the total to three. Despite this, an immense gap remains between training for blacks and whites. By one tally, 1,146 Africans were enrolled in technical high schools in 1977. This compared with more than 32,000 whites taking similar training in 1975. In 1977 technical colleges for Africans had 541 students, compared with 27,000 whites receiving advanced technical training in 1976.

THE INDUSTRIAL RELATIONS SYSTEM

For most of this century South Africa has had an industrial relations system that met the problem of dealing with the largest body of workers, the Africans, by simply leaving them out of the bargaining process. Unions representing whites, Coloureds, and Asians got together with management representatives under government auspices and struck deals that satisfied the parties around the table. By and large, the Africans were left to accept what those in authority gave them.

The basis of this system is the Industrial Conciliation Act, passed in its initial form in 1924 following a long period of tumultuous relations between white workers and mine management that culminated in the violent 1922 mine strike. The act allows registered trade unions and companies to form industrial councils empowered to set wages and working conditions for their industries.

From the outset, the act excluded African workers from its coverage by omitting them from its definition of "employee" and by limiting membership in registered unions to employees. As a result, African wage levels were left to market forces that inevitably were distorted by influx control measures, to industrial council agreements in which the Africans had no say, and to sporadic determinations by the Wage Board, a body that sets pay for some unorganized workers. African workers and their organizations had few legal rights in the workplace, and police and influx-control officers regularly made a mockery of state impartiality in labor-management relations. Moreover, the industrial council agreements reserving the best jobs for whites smothered African aspirations for advancement.

The Industrial Conciliation Act did not burden Coloured and Asian workers with the disabilities inflicted on Africans, but the extension of segregation under the Nationalists has weakened the Coloured and Asian roles in industrial relations. Before 1956 Coloured and Asian workers were eligible for membership and leadership posts in racially mixed registered trade unions. Amendments to the law passed that year declared that no new mixed unions could be formed and compelled existing mixed unions either to split into fully separate, segregated unions or to form segregated branches under an all-white executive.

Since the early 1950s the government has allowed African workers highly circumscribed organizational rights in industry. Under the Bantu Labor Relations Act, passed originally in 1953 and revised in the 1970s, these took two forms: liaison committees, comprising management and worker representatives in equal numbers, and works committees, made up entirely of worker representatives and more oriented toward bargaining. Management, however, has rushed to form liaison committees, thus minimizing the collective bargaining aspect of the legislation. By 1978 companies had established 2,626 liaison but only 302 works committees.

Over the years, however, most of the important collective actions by African workers have taken place outside any legal framework. These actions have extended to strikes (the Bantu Labor Relations Act permits "legal" strikes but under procedures so cumbersome that workers have generally ignored them). In the years preceding and after World War I, African mine workers struck many times for higher wages, better jobs, and better living conditions. After World War II 76,000 striking African miners closed twelve mines and slowed production at others. One demand was recognition of an African mine workers' union. More recently, in 1973 and 1974 as many as 75,000 African workers staged general strikes in the industrial areas around Durban. Sporadic strikes in other urban centers ensued.

With the possible exception of the Durban strikes, which achieved higher wages and limited movement toward industrial relations reform, these protests accomplished few tangible results. Furthermore, the government intervened under the Suppression of Communism Act to remove many labor leaders from further active involvement in industrial relations. Neither management nor the government was willing to recognize African trade unions as bargaining representatives, which was a frequent demand in the strikes.

Although African work stoppages trailed off after 1974—only 10,000 Africans struck in 1978—there was a marked resurgence in 1979 and 1980. Starting in 1979 the western Cape was hit by a wave of strikes involving stevedores, meat and cold-storage workers, construction workers, textile mill hands, fishermen, and engineering workers. In 1979 and 1980 the eastern Cape experienced strikes at Ford and Volkswagen auto plants, auto parts plants, tire factories, and steel and paper mills. Africans have also struck large textile mills in Natal and automobile assembly plants, bus lines, and dairies in the Transvaal.

What distinguished these strikes by Africans from most earlier walkouts were their wide focus and broad community support. While wage demands were often raised, workers also vented their anger at firings of African union and political organizers and pressed for recognition of African trade union representatives. Coloured workers sometimes joined with African workers in the protests, and the African and Coloured communities participated in the work stoppages. A strike in 1979–80 at Fattis and Monis, a western Cape food processor, led to a nationwide boycott of the company's pasta products, and the meat workers' strike touched off a boycott of red meat in the Cape and the Transvaal. At the center of the Ford dispute was the Port Elizabeth Black Civic Organization, a group formed in 1979 with the stated objective of obtaining a better deal for urban Africans.

Unregistered unions representing African and some Coloured workers have been involved in many of these stoppages. Indeed, they figure increasingly in the whole area of African industrial relations. As far back as the 1920s and

1930s organizing efforts were carried on among African workers. Some large unions emerged, but severe legal obstacles, employer hostility, and other problems led to their decline. World War II saw a resurgence of African organization and strikes. By 1945 an umbrella organization called the Council of Non-European Trade Unions claimed a membership of 158,000, including the big African Mine Workers' Union. But by 1950, with the suppression of the mine workers' group and other unions, total African membership fell to about 17,000 in African unions, plus another 3,700 members in mixed African and Coloured unions.

At the start of the 1970s, there were still only about ten African unions, with a total of 20,000 members, 17,000 of whom were in one organization, the National Union of Clothing Workers. The 1973–74 Durban strikes, however, ushered in a period of unprecedented ferment and organization. By 1979 there were more than thirty African trade unions in South Africa. Their membership approached 130,000. Some of the unions joined together into coordinating bodies, and efforts to create national alliances began.

The Federation of South African Trade Unions (FOSATU), established in 1979, has about 45,000 African and Coloured members, mainly in Natal but also in the Transvaal and the Cape. Another group of unions, predominantly African and with a total membership of about 30,000 located mainly in the Transvaal, have formed the Council of Unions of South Africa (CUSA). There are also two large general workers' unions with predominantly African memberships. Aside from such black groupings, the Trade Union Council of South Africa (TUCSA), which for some years has consisted of white, Coloured, and mixed unions and had included African unions until 1968, has reopened its ranks to Africans. As of 1979 seven African unions with a combined membership of more than 20,000 had joined TUCSA. (TUCSA is one of the two established trade union federations in South Africa. The other major federation, the South African Confederation of Labor, remains all white, drawing its membership from the public sector and the white industrial unions.)

PROPOSALS FOR CHANGE

The mounting discontent among African workers, coupled with growing white uneasiness over its effects in industry, led the government in the late 1970s to undertake two major explorations of possible changes in South Africa's system for controlling its African labor force. One study, carried out by the Riekert Commission, examined the controls on Africans' presence and movement in "white" South Africa. The other, the work of the Wiehahn Commission, looked into unionization rights and other aspects of the treatment of African workers in South African industry. Both efforts were well publicized and initially raised expectations of change. But the implementation of their proposals thus far has not produced significant changes.

Labor Control: The Riekert Commission

The Riekert Commission, an inquiry into "Legislation Affecting the Utilization of Manpower," was appointed in August 1977. The commission actually consisted of one man: Pieter Riekert, economic adviser to Prime Minister John Vorster. Its report was released early in 1979. Chief Gatsha Buthelezi, the Zulu leader, cited it as "one of the first signs of meaningful change in South Africa." The secretary of TUCSA anticipated that it would "contribute to an improved economic climate and better race relations." After the publication of both the Riekert and Wiehahn commissions' reports, the *Wall Street Journal* commented that "blacks, whites, liberals, and conservatives in this racially divided country agree their government is making efforts to modify racial laws that would improve the conditions for some blacks."

The Riekert Commission report's stated objectives encouraged such optimism. The report declared that "discriminatory measures should be avoided as far as possible by not drawing any distinction on the ground of race, colour, or sex in legislation or administrative rules." It also stressed the desirability of a free labor market, with the elimination of administrative rules limiting the geographic mobility of laborers.

Some analysts of the report, however, are skeptical about the commission's commitment to fundamental change. The skeptics contend that its opposition to racial discrimination operates only at the level of appearances. Throughout the report they find resort to substitute mechanisms that are superficially nonracial in character but nevertheless discriminatory in effect—the use, for example, of "independent Black states," the government-created homelands, as instruments of an "immigration" policy whose effect is to keep Africans out of white areas. The call for freer markets and greater mobility for labor is nullified by the pervasive emphasis on "control." The report is replete with assertions that "reforms" can be achieved without loss of control, particularly over the influx of Africans into urban areas. Where there are apparent attempts to relinquish control or to foster mobility, such as within or between urban areas, say the critics, they are achieved only by exercising greater control and by further restricting mobility in other parts of the labor market.

Influx control. The Riekert report reaffirms the necessity of influx control. "Owing to the potential extent and the nature of the migration of Blacks [Africans] from rural areas to urban areas, serious social and sociological welfare problems will arise in urban areas in South Africa for both the established populations in urban areas, White, Coloured, Asian, and Black, and the new entrants, if the migration process is left uncontrolled." Even if such controls do limit growth, the commission concludes that "control over the rate of urbanization is, in light of circumstances in South Africa, an absolutely essential social security measure." The government white paper accompanying the report accepted this conclusion and observed: "In this connection, therefore, the question to which both the Commission and the Government had to find an answer was not whether there should be influx control, but what the right mechanism for influx control would be in South Africa's circumstances."

In the view of the Riekert Commission, the "right mechanism" would admit Africans to urban areas according to the availability of housing and employment and the unavailability of local job seekers. The report proposed that the government tighten control over employment, providing steeply increased penalties on employers who hire illegal, unregistered workers, and maintain barriers against illegal squatting and lodging. If tight control were maintained over access to employment and housing, it reasoned, the government would no longer need to use its police powers to restrict African access to the cities. Specifically, the government might relax the rule that limits Africans not legally "qualified" to live in an urban area to seventy-two-hour stays in cities. Said the commission: "The seventy-two-hour prohibition can disappear from the statute book without the abandonment of any principles in connection with control over urbanisation or without any detriment to the effectiveness of control."

The government, however, proved reluctant to yield its traditional forms of control, even as it recognized "the human relations problems" attached to enforcement of the pass law in urban areas. Therefore, it accepted the recommendations that fines on employers be increased—in fact, they were quintupled—but declined to repeal the seventy-two-hour rule "for the time being." In early 1980 the minister of cooperation and development announced that the government would abandon the seventy-two-hour rule on an experimental basis in Pretoria and Bloemfontein, but just how much relaxation will take place is unclear. In any case, implementing legislation introduced a year after publication of the Riekert report did not contain any provision to relinquish the old labor control mechanisms.

Local labor mobility. At the same time that the Riekert Commission and the government were defending influx control, they were displaying willingness to allow more freedom of movement for those not subject to influx control—that is, city-dwelling Africans with permanent residence rights. For this part of the African population—not quite half of the urban African labor force and a quarter of the total African labor force—the commission report recommends voluntary use of labor bureau services to find better jobs; perhaps special bureaus catering to the needs of professional, clerical, and more skilled workers; and freer movement between cities, subject to the availability of work and housing. As part of the effort to protect the jobs and living standards of those with permanent residence rights, says the report, "labor bureaus should exercise strict control over the admission of contract workers." The government went along with the recommendation for relaxed controls on permanent African urban residents, and in 1980 it proposed legislation allowing them to move freely between cities provided housing and jobs are available.

Besides backing strict limits on contract workers, the Riekert Commission urged action on another front to limit the growth of a privileged group of urban insiders. It endorsed the continued development of an African commuter population consisting of persons who live in the homelands and go to work each day in industries in white areas. In 1970, according to the government, there were 250,000 such commuters, but by 1979 the number had grown to 725,000. If the Africans "live in their own country and travel on a daily basis to South Africa," the senior deputy minister for the Department of Cooperation and Development commented, "then the political problem will be solved."

Racial discrimination. There are numerous examples of the Riekert Commission's efforts to put an acceptable face on racial discrimination without doing away with the underlying reality. African vagrants, it suggested, should be prosecuted under a law dealing with drunkenness and vagrancy that applies to all racial groups rather than under another law aimed specifically at African idlers, as had been the practice. Requirements for proof of accommodation should be extended to all racial groups, although the ready availability of housing for whites and the restricted supply for Africans mean that Africans are the ones for whom the rule creates difficulties. On paper, the labor bureaus' employment functions for Africans should be placed under the Department of Manpower Utilization, which serves all races. Even though the actual operation of the bureaus would not change, said the commission, the arrangement should "dispose of criticism that the Black worker was being discriminated against."

The Riekert report also unquestioningly accepts a number of explicitly discriminatory policies that fall outside its charge. Thus, it does not reexamine the Coloured labor preference policy in the western Cape or the basic principles of the Group Areas Act. Nor does it review the all-important Section 10 provisions that establish rights of residence in urban areas and the basic legal distinction between permanent and contract workers. The commission and the government white paper nevertheless justify the continued application of such a distinction to Africans but not to other racial groups. The white paper comments:

> The Commission finds justification for this in the fact that the process of urbanisation is far less complete in the case of Blacks than in that of the other population groups, that it is therefore mainly Blacks who are streaming into the cities in large numbers, and that it is therefore in the interests of the established and new residents in the Black urban residential areas to apply some measure of control there. Influx control is not now needed to the same extent in the case of the other population groups in their residential areas, because urbanisation is almost complete in their respective cases. The Government finds this line of thinking convincing, and therefore accepts this recommendation too.

Trade Union Rights: The Wiehahn Commission

The Durban strikes and the subsequent growth of unregistered African unions reverberated on several fronts. The new unions posed challenges for the registered unions, which were organizing a declining portion of the labor force; for employers, who could no longer rely on the existing industrial councils to ensure harmony between labor and management; and for the state, which watched uneasily as an informal industrial system emerged outside the one it had sanctioned. The government's response was to establish a Commission of Inquiry into Labor Legislation in 1977. Appointed to the commission were academics, including Nic Wiehahn, a professor of labor law at the University of South Africa, who served as chairman, and representatives of business and registered unions. Its first report, issued in February 1979, called for major changes in industrial relations in South Africa.

Acknowledging the rapid growth of unregistered African unions, the commission argued that it was in the best interests of the government to incorporate them into the system. Otherwise, it said, "Black trade unions are subject neither to the protective and stabilising elements of the system nor to its essential discipline and control. . . . The interests of the members of the Black trade unions . . . would clearly be better served within a more structured and orderly situation." Moreover, bringing African unions into the system would permit official surveillance of their operations and the prohibition of political activity and would encourage "responsible behavior."

The commission therefore recommended that African workers, even migrants and commuters, be considered "employees" under the Industrial Conciliation Act and thus eligible for membership in registered unions, either all African or multiracial. At the same time, it favored retention of safeguards that have been used to limit trade union activity in the past, including broad legal definitions of sabotage and terrorism and controls on publications and gatherings. The commission also urged—over the objections of employer representatives—that closed-shop provisions and union veto rights over admission to industrial councils be left intact. These would allow all-white unions to limit the role of newly registered African or multiracial unions.

Despite the emphasis on "control" and the acceptance of continued discrimination, the commission's recommendations represent a broad departure from traditional practice. They open up opportunities for legitimate trade union activity by African workers and promise to introduce greater balance in relations between management and the African labor force.

The government's first response to the Wiehahn Commission recommendations was to reject two key recommendations and adopt a more restrictive approach. Then, in a pattern of actions resembling those it has taken in other sensitive areas, the government partially restored the rejected Wiehahn proposals by means of exemptions.

In one instance, the government initially narrowed the redefinition of "employee" to permanent residents, excluding migrant and commuter workers, and said that registered unions could not admit a "nonemployee" to membership. But this was promptly followed by a blanket exemption allowing unions to enroll migrant and commuter workers. Similarly, after initially refusing to go along with the commission's acceptance of multiracial unions, the government granted exemptions permitting a number of established registered unions to admit African members and allowed African unions affiliated with FOSATU to apply for registration on a multiracial basis. It further confused the issue of multiracial unions in early 1981, however, by deciding to register several FOSATU unions only on a segregated basis.

Though the government's overall intent is not yet clear, a three-pronged policy appears to be emerging. First, the government seeks to achieve control over unregistered African unions and thereby to institutionalize industrial relations for the entire labor force. Second, it seeks to confine African trade union activity within narrow limits, removed from politics and closely linked to the activities of old-line registered unions. Third, it aims to reassure white and Coloured workers that they will not be displaced and that their wages will not be undercut.

Trade union reactions. The executive body of the all-white Confederation of Labor initially voted by a slim margin to accept the Wiehahn recommendations, but the action was negated by subsequent denunciations of the report by the confederation and its member industrial unions. The report was seen as a repudiation of the white worker. "Never before in the history of the country," a confederation statement asserted, had white workers received such a "slap in the face." The secretary of the Mine Workers' Union called the government's response to the report "the greatest treachery against the white employees of South Africa since 1922." Such antigovernment tirades underscore the growing estrangement between the government and the organized white workers represented by the Confederation of Labor, a traditional ally of the Nationalist leadership.

TUCSA welcomed the Wiehahn recommendations. Its member unions responded by organizing "parallel" African unions closely associated with existing registered unions. The first new African organization granted registration was the African Transport Workers' Union, organized by a registered Coloured union. Other parallel unions were quickly established in the auto repair and the electrical and engineering industries. Parallel unions in garments, textiles, and leather predate the present organizing drive, although some of these have recently expanded their operations. With the government's seeming willingness to accept multiracial unions, some registered unions have applied for multiracial status, apparently with the intention of merging with their parallel African unions.

The parallel African unions have stressed their ability to work with management, a traditional TUCSA theme, and have been noticeably absent from the African work stoppages of recent years. Not surprisingly, they have come into conflict with the existing independent African unions. Some of these conflicts—in the liquor trade and in engineering, for example—have been jurisdictional. But more fundamental issues are also involved. FOSATU, the organization of independent African and Coloured trade unions, claims that the less-militant parallel unions undermine the African unions operating on their own. Moreover, it is alleged that the "parallels" often operate in league with management, which grants them cooperation denied other African unions.

Many African unions not linked to established registered unions have expressed grave doubts about registration and its consequences for the African trade union movement. Three large independent African unions active in the food industry and on the docks remain opposed to registration, arguing that it brings too many restrictions and that the industrial council machinery will not protect the interests of African and Coloured workers. These unions prefer instead the limited forms of union recognition they won through strikes against Fattis and Monis and the Cape Town Stevedores Association. FOSATU unions have also won limited recognition at a number of companies, including Ford, but they have doubted that refusing registration is a tenable course in light of current pressures and consequently have applied for registration. Some unions belonging to CUSA have also moved to register. Following the government's recent rejection of multiracial registration for several FOSATU members, however, some of the independent African unions that had been inclined to cooperate with the system were having second thoughts.

Employer reaction. Employers and business organizations reacted favorably to the Wiehahn recommendations. For some, such as the Associated Chambers of Commerce, the registration of African unions represented a long-term policy objective and "a very positive picture on the labor relations front." For others, including the Afrikaanse Handelsinstituut (Afrikaans Institute of Business), African trade unionism was a recent discovery but nonetheless welcomed as a stabilizing force: "As an instrument for negotiation [the trade union] is essential to peace in labour. We wish to see it as a new safety valve so that we do not land in the minefield without warning." The Federated Chamber of Industries commended the report "as welding together a coherent approach permitting a new integrity to South Africa's system of labour relations."

During the present transition period, employers have taken varying attitudes in the workplace. Some companies appear to have encouraged parallel unions in the hope that more cooperative unions, linked to the established registered unions, would gain a foothold and claim membership on the industrial council. A few firms have proved willing to deal with African unions without ties to established unions, and some have signed formal agreements with unregistered African unions. Which pattern becomes dominant in industry may strongly influence the course of African trade unionism and the role of African workers on the job and in society.

Discrimination: The Wiehahn Commission

Besides calling for trade union rights for Africans, the Wiehahn Commission proposed changes in the racial allocation of jobs. The commission urged an end to legal job reservation, and the government accepted the recommendation, announcing the gradual elimination of the five remaining categories of work restricted by law to whites (excluding mining). But government-decreed job reservation amounts to only a fraction of the de facto job reservations found in industry. Most stem from closed shops, various other negotiated arrangements, and custom. In regard to these, the commission report and the government white paper moved much more cautiously.

A majority of the Wiehahn commissioners found the closed shop "so firmly entrenched in South Africa that it cannot be abolished." A minority, including all black members and employer representatives, urged its abolition, declaring: "A prohibition on closed-shop agreements in a situation of union plurality is a self-evident necessity if extreme inter-union and union-employee tensions— with the danger of industrial unrest on racial lines—are to be avoided." The government sided with the minority in principle, but it left existing agreements intact and did not include a closed-shop prohibition in the new legislation.

While opposing statutory racial barriers in employment, the commission report is ambiguous on negotiated arrangements that secure positions for white workers. Indeed, at times it seems to encourage mutually-agreed-upon private party discrimination. The commission also refused to bar racial discrimination by employers:

> The Commission submits that subject to the obvious necessity for control of labour migration, it would be unwise to apply a policy in South Africa whereby employers would be deprived of the freedom to appoint persons of their own choice as employees: not only would such a policy constitute gross interference in the affairs of employers but it would also have other undesirable results such as the sub-optimal allocation of manpower and unemployment. If freedom of choice gives rise to practices deemed undesirable, the remedy must be sought in the education and development of the people.

The commission recognized the need for more African apprentices in industry in white areas and recommended that Africans, like all other groups, be trained under the country's basic apprenticeship law. Legislation subsequently drafted by the government could eventually have the effect of opening up the system to Africans by adding African union representatives to the committees that pass on apprenticeship applications. It remains to be seen, however, just how much impact the proposed changes would have in fields where conservative white unions hold sway, and significant gains in apprenticeships for Africans are unlikely to come quickly. Moreover, training facilities are still segregated.

So, while South Africa has made a start on removing some of the legal apparatus mandating racial discrimination in employment, it has yet to take the major steps required to eliminate discrimination in fact. Closed shops, negotiated agreements, employer bias, and apprenticeship barriers will continue to allow race to determine most job assignments.*

FOREIGN FIRMS AS EMPLOYERS IN SOUTH AFRICA

Foreign companies are deeply involved in the South African economy (for a full analysis of their role, see chapter 7), and their involvement extends to the labor market. Businesses based in Great Britain, the United States, West Germany, and France are the most important foreign employers, with Britain looming largest by a wide margin. Some 350 American companies do business directly in South Africa. They employ about 100,000 workers there, of whom as many as 70,000 are Africans. Taking the workers' families into account, Desaix Myers III, deputy director of the Investor Responsibility Research Center (IRRC), estimates that employment practices of U.S. firms may directly affect 300,000 to 350,000 Africans. The ripples go wider, however, because of the extensive publicity given the policies of the American companies.

In recent years foreign businesses operating in South Africa have come under organized pressure to adopt various codes of conduct to guide their employment practices. The first such code was devised in 1974 by a subcommittee of Britain's House of Commons. It was followed almost immediately by a European Economic Community (EEC) code. In 1977 came the Sullivan Principles, a code drawn up for U.S. firms by the Reverend Leon Sullivan, a black clergyman from Philadelphia, whose concern about American involvement in apartheid was sharpened by his membership on the board of General Motors, a major investor in South Africa. The foreign codes were followed in 1979 by standards adopted by the Urban Foundation, an organization financed by some of South Africa's largest firms.

From the American perspective, the Sullivan code is obviously of greatest interest. The code was adopted by a dozen companies when first announced in 1977, and by late 1980 the list of signatories had grown to 137 and included most of the major American firms operating in South Africa. As amplified in 1978 and 1979, the Sullivan Principles call for desegregation of "all eating, comfort, and work facilities"; equal and fair employment practices, including

---

*Two new governmental bodies relevant to labor relations were established as a result of the Wiehahn Commission report: the Industrial Court, which is charged with settling a variety of labor disputes, and the National Manpower Commission, an information-gathering and advisory agency on labor matters. Some analysts see both these bodies as potentially beneficial to black workers, offering a new forum for their grievances and improving understanding of their plight. What actual impact the Industrial Court and the National Manpower Commission will have in the workplace cannot be predicted at this time.

support for the "elimination of discrimination against the rights of Blacks to form or belong to government registered trade unions"; equal pay for comparable work and "equitable" wages "well above the appropriate local minimum economic living level"; the development of training programs; the advancement of blacks into management positions; and the improvement of the "quality of employees' lives outside the work environment," including "housing, transportation, schooling, recreation, and health facilities." (The full text of the Sullivan Principles is set forth in Appendix B.)

While the Sullivan code stresses desegregation, the EEC code emphasizes trade union rights. It begins with this injunction:

(A) Companies should ensure that all their employees irrespective of racial or other distinctions are allowed to choose freely and without any hindrance the type of organisation to represent them.

(B) Employers should regularly and unequivocally inform their employees that consultations and collective bargaining with organisations which are freely elected and representative of employees are part of company policy.

In addition, the EEC code calls for trade union access to plants and offices, display of trade union notices, and paid time off for employees to carry out union duties. Like the Sullivan code, it backs "equal pay for equal work," advises company support for housing, education, and pension programs, and, finally, urges company efforts to "abolish any practice of segregation."

The code of the Urban Foundation begins by emphasizing the role of free enterprise in improving the quality of life, noting that progress has already been made in a number of areas. The recommendations to the private sector emphasize good-faith efforts rather than measured accomplishments. It suggests that employers "strive constantly for the elimination of racial discrimination from all aspects of employment practice," particularly in selection and promotion of employees, wages, and fringe benefits, and advocates "recognition of the basic rights of workers of freedom of association." It urges cooperation with other organizations to promote job opportunities and "the progressive transition to a system wherein the rates of remuneration paid and any assistance given by the employers will be such as to render unnecessary any general differential subsidy based on race or colour."

The monitoring of these codes varies. Sullivan code signatories are asked to file semiannual reports on standard forms which are then summarized by Arthur D. Little and Company. There is no regular on-site inspection or involvement of black employees in the monitoring process. In the case of the EEC code, the British government has required regular reporting since 1974. While Sweden and Denmark have considered making the EEC code mandatory, the French and Italian governments have proved indifferent. Relatively few European business associations or company home offices have lent support to the code or brought pressure to bear on European subsidiaries in South Africa. A number of South African organizations—including trade union councils (CUSA, TUCSA, FOSATU), the Urban Foundation, and the Black People's Alliance—have volunteered to monitor company performance, but no reliable and consistent mechanism has yet been created.

Changes in foreign business practice over the past few years have unquestionably brought some improvements in the lives of black South Africans. Desegregation of facilities, particularly in U.S. firms, is the most obvious area of change. Most companies have made at least some attempt to introduce integrated facilities. Still, an IRRC survey suggests that these efforts are "by no means universal." Some companies have only partially integrated facilities, and others have not acted at all.

There have been increased efforts in two other areas, training and housing. Most companies have begun providing in-service training, and many have joined collective efforts, such as the training centers organized by foreign auto companies in the Port Elizabeth area and a commercial high school in Soweto financed by the American Chamber of Commerce. Numerous foreign companies have attempted to provide housing directly or, more often, indirectly through loans to their employees or to the government's administration boards, which, as part of their labor-control responsibility, administer African housing in the townships. At the start of 1981, however, these efforts, along with a related government program to assure urban Africans of long-term property rights, were stalled. (Housing problems are discussed in chapter 6.)

It is difficult to tell whether wages have advanced faster at foreign companies than in industry as a whole, although African wages have certainly increased at foreign firms since 1970 and at rates exceeding those of whites. Some U.S. businesses have been "inching their minimum wage level up toward the minimum effective level [150 percent of the poverty level] in the last three years," the IRRC reports, "but most companies continue to start workers below the poverty datum or household subsistence level." In 1978 virtually all signatories to the Sullivan code paid some wages that were below the minimum effective level for Johannesburg.

In the area of African trade union recognition, U.S. companies have proved only slightly more progressive than the average South African firm. The overwhelming majority of American businesses, like most South African companies, rely on liaison committees. Some, Ford among them, have reached informal agreements with African unions; a few, including Kellogg, have signed formal contracts; others, including General Motors, have allowed trade unions dues deductions and access to premises.

In all these areas—desegregation, wages, and trade union recognition—company performance is uneven. The IRRC reports:

98   To sum up, response to the codes is measurable and sometimes

impressive. A number of the signers have taken tangible and often dramatic steps toward improving opportunities for black workers. But the effort has not been universal among those affected by the codes or among those who have endorsed the [Sullivan] principles. The speed and interest with which companies are carrying out the code vary considerably.

Companies attempting to implement the codes face a number of constraints. For example, availability of housing is limited by government policy and provision of equal pay for equal work is restricted by the barriers that effectively close some of the higher job categories to blacks. Nevertheless, the Study Commission was repeatedly told by management of the U.S. companies that practical ways around many of these constraints could be found if determined and persistent efforts were made. The government, they said, was often willing to ignore violations of regulations; and blacks could be hired to do a "white" job labeled as something else and could be paid the going rate for the job.

In the highly charged atmosphere of South African labor relations, however, even genuine efforts at fair treatment do not guarantee smooth sailing. This is nowhere more apparent than at Ford. The firm made a concerted attempt to comply with the spirit of the Sullivan Principles, integrating facilities, equalizing pay within grades, promoting African workers, raising wages, and recognizing an African trade union. A study of company practice, sponsored by Ford but conducted by independent academic specialists, observes that "Ford is probably the best employer in the Uitenhage–Port Elizabeth industrial region." Still, the report notes that African employees are skeptical about the considerable attention devoted to desegregation of facilities, fearing it distracts "attention from the far more fundamental problems of economic and social justice in the company and the community." Management attempts to ensure equal and fair employment practices are seen as "being implemented with notable lack of enthusiasm." Despite efforts to increase wage rates, short weeks leave 80 percent to 95 percent of African employees below the household subsistence level. African workers also are skeptical of Ford's role in the larger society, whatever its commitment to fair employment practices in the plant. The report finds that "good relations between the company and the Administration Board, expressed in substantial loans or donations by the company to the Board, lend credence to the belief that the Ford management is part of an unholy alliance between white employers and the two most hated arms of the state (the Security Police and the Administration Boards)."

In 1979 Leon Sullivan stated: "It is intended that the activity associated with the Principles will be of massive proportions and will promote programs which can have a significant impact on improving the living conditions and quality of life for the non-white population, and will be a major contributing factor to the ending of apartheid." Although the Sullivan Principles and the other codes have changed employment practices, company reform has not been of "massive proportions." Nor has compliance with the codes threatened the basic structure of apartheid. The state role in the labor market, particularly state control over African labor, is virtually unaffected. Moreover, the changes proposed by the Riekert Commission place an increasing burden of enforcement on employers. This means that both foreign and South African companies will find it difficult to avoid being caught between the necessity of dealing with governmental authorities in day-to-day operations and management of employee-benefit programs and the growing resentment among their workers of the overall apartheid structure and all institutions that function, however reluctantly, within it.

Chapter 6
Housing, Education and Health

HOUSING

A view of Soweto:

> The visitor . . . is struck by the litter lying in the streets, the absence of proper pavements and gutters, the ruts and potholes in many of the roads (most of which are untarred), the monotony of the rows of tiny houses—the Soweto "matchboxes"—and the generally bleak appearance of the township. He is struck too by the ragged children playing in the streets: there are some large open spaces, where wrecks of old cars and the occasional dead animal can be seen, but few proper parks, lawns, or playgrounds. On windy days dust from the streets and fine sand from nearby mine-dumps envelop the township so closely that the chimneys and cooling-towers of the Orlando power station on the outskirts are almost hidden. . . . At night the smog [from cookstoves] once again covers everything. . . .

These are the words of John Kane-Berman, a South African journalist. While they accurately convey the dominant reality of Soweto, they do not present a complete picture. There are homes in Soweto that would not look out of place in the suburbs of New York or Chicago. And since all urban Africans—whatever their income—are required by law to live in townships, Soweto includes a broad social and economic mix. Living standards vary widely. However monotonous in appearance, Soweto's housing is better than that found in the hillside favelas in Rio de Janeiro or the slums that fringe Lagos. And many of Soweto's houses are more comfortable than the shanties found in rural areas throughout Africa—including South Africa. Soweto is especially jarring because it is right next door to Johannesburg, a great gleaming city where white

South Africans live in comfort. And because even those who have the money and the desire to move into the city are forbidden to do so by law.

The South African government has made recent promises to upgrade the quality of life in African townships. In 1980 sizable programs to provide more housing for blacks were begun. The government has also indicated that it will gradually make housing available on a long-term basis to all income groups, giving special priority to the needs of low-income families. The ratio of per capita expenditure on white and black housing, historically higher for whites, is changing.

These changes, however, are all taking place within the framework of racial separation. Housing policy in South Africa continues to maintain the racial and ethnic distances separating communities and to preserve the existing structure of inequality. In South Africa, perhaps more than anywhere in the world, where a person lives is determined by law. Africans, Coloureds, and Indians all feel the burden of these restrictions, but of all black South Africans, the Africans feel the burden of apartheid most heavily. For that reason, Africans are the focus of this section.

Legal Framework

The main statutes governing residential segregation in urban areas are the Native Urban Areas Act of 1923, now the Black Urban Areas Consolidation Act of 1945, the Bantu Laws Amendment Act as amended in 1963, and the Group Areas Act of 1950 (reenacted and consolidated in 1957).

The Native Urban Areas Act, by far the most important measure regulating the presence of Africans in urban areas, has been more and more strictly enforced since the Nationalists came into power in 1948. It established compulsory residence for urban Africans in separate areas known as "locations" on the outer edges of white areas and regulated the entry of Africans into cities. The Group Areas Act of 1950 and later amendments provided for separate white, Coloured, Asian, and African residential areas. To further discourage contact, the act provided for buffer strips between the areas.

History of Apartheid in Housing

Whites have historically regarded urban areas as their domain. Policies of segregation in towns were designed to ensure the preservation of towns as places of undisputed white hegemony. Because labor was needed, Africans were permitted in urban areas. Policies of influx control reflected the state's desire to correlate the number of African town dwellers with the needs of the South African labor market.

The principle of the impermanence of African laborers in cities was explicitly stated in 1922 by a government body known as the Stallard Commission: "It should be a recognized principle of government that Natives—men, women, and children—should be permitted within municipal areas in so far and for so long as their presence is demanded by the wants of the white population." In this view—which until recently has been the basis of government policy—the urban African was a "temporary sojourner" with no permanent rights in white areas, tolerated only to the extent that he or she was instrumental in advancing the nation's economic objectives, at least as seen by whites.

With the discovery of minerals, Africans had streamed into the diamond and gold mines to seek employment. Working primarily for short periods, they created makeshift settlements in and around white settlements. During the early twentieth century, outbreaks of disease focused attention on the slum conditions in these settlements and led to the provision of public housing for Africans as an emergency measure. In 1913 the Native Lands Act was passed, which prohibited Africans from acquiring land, except in the native reserves (at that time about 10 percent of the country), without special permission. The 1923 Native Urban Areas Act required local authorities to assume responsibility for providing accommodation, in villages or hostels, for the African population within their jurisdictions. This act further stipulated that the villages were to be segregated and provided for the limitation of the number of Africans in towns. The Bantu Trust and Land Act in 1936 prohibited Africans from buying land outside the reserves under any circumstances. Plots in townships were made available to Africans only on a leasehold basis, and Africans who owned real estate outside the townships generally had to dispose of it. In a few areas Africans with freehold titles were allowed to remain. Upon the death of the householder, however, the heirs were obliged to sell the property.

In the 1940s, in response to the demand for labor in war industries and also because of poverty in the reserves, massive numbers of Africans moved to the urban areas, particularly on the Witwatersrand.

Serious social problems were compounded by the vast influx of people. Large squatter camps made up of shanties constructed from cardboard boxes, packing crates, corrugated iron sheeting, and scrap metal sprang up around the fringes of Johannesburg. Although local authorities made modest attempts to alleviate the situation, by the end of the 1940s Soweto, originally a dormitory township for migrant mine workers, had become a sprawling slum.

During World War II the operation of pass laws was suspended in all the major towns, largely in response to the booming economy's demand for labor. Influx controls were tightened with the coming to power of the National party in 1948. Africans without jobs were forced to return to rural areas. Africans legally employed were compelled to move from locations where they had held freehold rights. In many cases the move meant additional expense and longer traveling time to work.

As "surplus" Africans were removed from urban areas, programs were **103** established to house the black labor force remaining behind. (See chapter 8 for discussion of resettlement of Africans.) Construction of government housing in African townships was actively pursued, and in 1949 a thirty-year leasehold scheme was introduced for Africans. In 1951, the government introduced the Bantu Building Workers Act, which provided for the training and employment of black builders to construct houses within their own areas. The Bantu Services Levy Act was passed in 1952, making it compulsory for employers to contribute monthly to finance certain services in African townships. In 1954, the government introduced a "site-and-services scheme," under which local authorities provided sites and essential services for families who wished to erect their own shelters. And in 1956 the mining industry, spurred by Sir Ernest Oppenheimer, the mining magnate, provided a loan of R6 million for the construction of housing. Between 1948 and 1966 more than half a million dwellings were constructed. The vast majority of these houses were occupied by Africans. Almost 50,000 houses were constructed in Soweto.

At the same time, the ideology of apartheid was being refined by the newly formed National government. Although separate living patterns had been long established in custom and in law prior to Nationalist rule, the government further strengthened segregation by enacting the Group Areas Act in 1950. Section 10, passed in 1952, extended the authority of the Native Urban Areas Act and entrenched the principle of the impermanence of urban Africans in "white" areas. And in 1954, in anticipation of the policy of "separate development," the government introduced a system of ethnic segregation within African townships. Zulu were to live in one area, Xhosa in another, and so on.

For the urban African the 1950s brought a curious mixture of expanding potential material well-being and contracting social rights. As the decade wound down, however, housing development subsided. During 1958 the government decided that no further loans would be granted for low-income housing. In 1959, with the advent of plans to create self-governing "homelands," government attention shifted to housing needs in the reserves.

From 1962 to 1974, 188,000 houses were built in black homelands as part of the policy of promoting settlement there, but African areas in other parts of South Africa were largely neglected. In 1968 the government proclaimed that the building of homes by Africans on thirty-year leasehold plots—permitted since 1949—was to be discontinued, and declared that people should instead be encouraged to build homes in the homelands. Thirty-year leases could no longer be transferred and improvements could be sold only to local authorities. During this period, the forced removals of Africans to homelands gathered momentum, reaching a peak in the mid-1970s.

Entitlements also narrowed at the municipal level. During that year the Johannesburg City Council decided that Soweto should be self-financing. This principle was gradually extended to cover all African townships. Townships under Black Affairs Administration Boards—all-white local governing bodies created by a 1971 enactment—were to receive no financial assistance from the state and black housing was not to be supported from the general revenues. The major sources of income were to come from rents and from liquor sales through board-owned liquor outlets in the townships. Moreover, some of the revenue generated by townships was to be spent in the homelands.

Since 1975 there have been a number of significant changes in the status of urban Africans. These developments, at least on the surface, seemed hopeful. In January 1975 an official directive restored home ownership on a thirty-year leasehold basis. Qualified blacks were allowed to buy houses from the administrative boards in their areas. The events of Soweto in 1976 led to a reappraisal of housing policy. In July 1977 the Community Council Act was passed, providing African communities with certain limited rights of self-government by transferring to community councils some of the powers of the administrative boards, in which many Africans had little faith.

In August 1977 the Riekert Commission was appointed to inquire into, report on, and make recommendations concerning the major laws relating directly or indirectly to any economic aspect of manpower use (except that administered by the Department of Labor). The legislation investigated included the Black Urban Areas Consolidation Act, the Black Affairs Administration Act, provincial ordinances, and municipal bylaws.

One of the major recommendations put forward by the commission was that the entry of Africans into urban areas should be determined solely by the availability of housing, jobs, and local labor. Recommendations relating specifically to housing, all of which were later accepted by the government, included the following:

Permitting purchase of houses in black townships by employers who wish to provide housing for their employees to reduce the financial burden carried by the state.

Permitting the private sector to develop housing schemes on a business basis for sale to black buyers within the terms of the leasehold system.

Leasing plots for ninety-nine years to Africans wishing to build their own homes.

Using income from the sale of houses in black residential areas only for the provision of housing in such areas.

Providing housing subsidies for African employees of the state on the same basis as for public servants from other population groups.

Providing government subsidies for African housing on the same basis as for other population groups.

Establishing homes for the African aged in the urban residential areas.

In April 1978 the government announced the introduction of a ninety-nine-year leasehold system. Home ownership under the ninety-nine-year leasehold system became available to Africans who qualify for urban rights under Section 10 of the Urban Areas Act. Leaseholders would be able to sell, let, and bequeath property in designated urban African areas as well as in rural townships. The scheme is described as "leasehold in name but freehold in practice." In December 1978 the government issued regulations that gave Africans for the first time the right of title required by building societies for mortgage loans.

In 1980 Pieter Koornhof, minister of cooperation and development, introduced bills he described as creating greater security of tenure and mobility for Africans legally residing in urban areas. They were withdrawn for parliamentary review after analysis indicated that the bills as written would have restricted rather than enlarged the rights of urban Africans.

Current Picture

A housing shortage of crisis proportions looms ahead in the 1980s. In 1978 official estimates of the housing needs—generally considerably lower than estimates by representatives of the communities concerned—were nearly 141,000 for Africans, 45,000 for Coloureds, and 20,000 for Asians. (There is no shortage for whites.) In 1980 the government estimated the total housing shortfall for blacks at 40,000 units. The Urban Foundation has estimated it at more than 500,000.

For the period 1972 to 1976 the cost to the Department of Community Development of erecting 40,862 housing units for Africans was R34.8 million, 5.7 percent of the total R611 million spent on 151,153 dwellings for all races during these years. For other racial groups, of the R611 million spent, 42 percent was for housing for whites, 40.9 percent for Coloureds, and 11.4 percent for Asians.

The government has estimated that 4 million more houses will be needed before the end of the century to eliminate the existing backlog and provide for the growing black urban population. George de V. Morrison, the deputy minister of cooperation and development, has said that the state alone will not be able to meet black housing needs and has called for greater participation by the private sector.

With the growing realization in the private sector of the close relationship between living environment and labor productivity, employers are becoming increasingly involved in providing housing. The Urban Foundation, formed by a group of socially conscious white businessmen shortly after the Soweto riots, has been particularly active in encouraging the mobilization of private capital to augment public funds for black housing. Some companies contribute directly or indirectly to employees' housing. To help their employees obtain a house under the ninety-nine-year leasehold, employers can make an outright grant, give a loan repayable through monthly deductions (not exceeding 25 percent) from the employee's earnings, build a house and donate it to an employee as a grant or advance, give an employee time off on full pay to build his own house, or arrange a guarantee or loan for an employee with a financial institution. The government now offers tax deductions as incentives to employers to help in housing.

Foreign participation in black housing ventures is also a new development. The Bank of America is currently studying a plan to finance the $500-million development of Alexandra, a township northeast of Johannesburg, although this is still in the planning stage. And in late 1980 the South African government obtained a loan of $250 million from a consortium of European banks and Citicorp in New York specifically earmarked for black community development.

Soweto

While all black townships are theoretically affected by the new government programs it is apparent that they are focused most directly on Soweto.

Louis Rive, Soweto's city planner and special coordinator of Soweto projects, has said that he is determined "to transform Soweto from a nondeveloped dormitory into an economically viable, self-run city." And Koornhof has pledged that the government will make every effort to eliminate Soweto's housing backlog. Massive building projects are planned to begin in 1981, marking a reversal of policy dating back to the early seventies.

Soweto with all of its ills enjoys a position of privilege relative to other African townships. It has more cultural and sports facilities than other African townships and South Africa's largest and most modern hospital for blacks. Soweto is also different from other townships because of the diverse ethnic composition of its African groups and the size of its population. The 1970 census lists Soweto's population at 600,000. Current official government estimates, however, place it at 1.2 million, making it South Africa's largest urban community. Unofficially, its population is estimated as high as 1.5 million, placing it third in size only to Lagos and Kinshasa among black African cities.

Despite the uniqueness afforded by its size and complexity, Soweto is in many ways representative of other townships. Like other African townships, it is to a large extent a bedroom community for a white city. Roads and services are poor, and poverty and crime are prevalent. Also, like other townships, Soweto is overcrowded. The housing shortage in Soweto is officially estimated at 25,000 units. The Urban Foundation has estimated that the shortage is closer to 32,000. Dr. Nthato Motlana of the Soweto Civic Association and the Committee of Ten has speculated that the shortage is twice that. A standard four-room house is usually occupied by an average of nine persons, although occupancies of twenty have been found. Overcrowding has been cited as a primary cause of the high levels of psychological and social stress that exist in Soweto, which has one of the highest crime rates in the world.

The effect of unrelieved monotony in Soweto and other African townships is created by the rows and rows of standard municipal houses. Until recently, individual choice of residence has been severely limited. All Africans, whatever their income, were allocated similar housing by the local board. The average house in Soweto is brick, built during the late fifties or sixties, forty-eight square meters (approximately 520 square feet), and divided into three or four rooms, including a kitchen. (According to the *South Africa Yearbook, 1978,* "Most Whites live in single-family, single-story dwellings ranging from 90 to 180 m² [approximately 1,000-2,000 square feet].") A sample survey of houses in Soweto in 1979 revealed that only 5.8 percent of the houses had inside baths, and only 12.8 percent had inside toilets. Twenty-one percent had running (cold) water inside the houses. Fewer than 20 percent of Soweto's houses have electricity. Most homes have coal or wood stoves, accounting for the pall of smoke that usually hangs over much of the township.

Future housing in Soweto, according to the government, will be of better quality. Design will no longer be restricted to the monotonous pattern of concrete matchbox dwellings one story high. And all future housing will have electricity and internal bathrooms and toilets. (The first phase of the R30-million project to install electricity in about 100,000 homes in Greater Soweto began in August 1980. The entire project, the minister of cooperation and development has promised, will be completed by the end of 1982.)

The sterility and monotony common to most African townships may also be alleviated by the ninety-nine-year leasehold scheme, which is intended to permit construction of a greater variety of housing sizes and styles. Community councils are expected to introduce differentiated charges for rent, site, and services based on family income, with the wealthier ninety-nine-year lease-holders paying more. The government's theory is that families in higher income brackets will welcome the opportunity to leave municipal housing to purchase better-appointed houses available under the ninety-nine-year leasehold scheme. It is also hoped that lower-income families will buy the homes they are renting and make improvements upon them. (Many observers doubt that this will actually happen, as ownership would mean higher monthly expenditures without appreciable benefits.)

The ninety-nine-year leasehold scheme has gotten off to a slow start. By the end of 1980, there were only five hundred applications registered nationally—four hundred in Soweto. This plan's difficulties have been variously attributed to complex legal and administrative procedures, lack of cooperation by bureaucrats, Africans' desire to own the land a house stands on, the shortage of building sites, and strict controls regulating residential use (for example, it is a criminal offense to sublet a dwelling without the written approval of the town superintendent). Costs of purchase and lack of financing also inhibit response. Furthermore, while the ninety-nine-year leasehold arrangement has been introduced ostensibly to provide a more secure form of tenure for Africans, this reform, like others, operates within the context of apartheid, often creating contradictions in policy and thus uncertainty and suspicion among Africans.

The status of dependents with regard to the ninety-nine-year leasehold is also problematical. In spite of an appeals court decision in 1980 that appeared to establish the right of dependents of Section 10-qualified men to remain legally in urban areas, some officials have interpreted the decision narrowly, contending that each case must be decided on its own merits. For the most part, a woman, even if qualified under Section 10, gainfully employed, and married to a qualified man, cannot qualify in her own right for a loan to purchase a home under the ninety-nine-year leasehold scheme. Women married by customary law have the legal status of minors and thus can take on no financial responsibility. A woman married by civil law fares no better. "If a loan is granted to a woman married under civil law and she loses her husband and remarries under tribal law, we get caught," said the managing director of the United Building Society. Measures to discourage women from settling in townships resulted from past official emphasis on the temporary status of urban Africans.

This view was also the basis of restrictions on industrial and commercial development in townships. Until the Soweto riots in 1976, commercial and industrial activity were effectively prohibited. Africans were forbidden to operate anything larger than corner-store businesses. Following the Riekert recommendations, free enterprise was extended to townships, and business activity has begun. The wholly black-owned Blackchain has already put up Soweto's first supermarket, and another is planned. The introduction of measures to stimulate business activity in African townships has not been without problems. The idea has been resisted by white businessmen in Johannesburg, who fear that a business district in Soweto will divert business from Johannesburg. On the other hand, prospective African entrepreneurs need to be assured that Soweto's residents, who work and traditionally shop in Johannesburg (where they make 82 percent of their purchases) will patronize African businesses in Soweto.

In most urban societies, municipalities derive the bulk of their revenue from property taxes, with commercial and industrial property generating the most significant portion. But because no freehold rights or significant commercial and industrial activity have existed in the townships, normal assessments could not be levied. Local community councils have had to rely almost exclusively on rents and liquor sales for revenue to finance the townships' infrastructures. Such revenues have been unpredictable and unreliable. Community councils, almost always operating with a deficit, are frequently at odds with residents over threatened rent increases.

In Soweto, for example, rent increases were finally instituted in the summer of 1980 after a long battle between Soweto's residents and local authorities. The Soweto council justified the increase on the ground that the cost of maintaining services exceeded revenues. Local officials argue that Sowetans contribute little more than 10 percent of their monthly incomes toward rent. But the issue is as much political as it is economic. Many residents say that the community council does not represent their interests and that in the past moneys collected in African townships have been diverted to homelands and to research groups studying the effects of apartheid, while services in townships declined.

Hostels

Whatever the difficulties of life for residents of Soweto, to migrant laborers the urban African is a privileged "insider." Prevented by legal restrictions from becoming full members of urban communities, migrant laborers exist in a kind of limbo, living without their families in single-sex barracks for the period of their labor contracts in South Africa, and returning to their respective homelands before contracts can be renewed. Hostel dwellers live outside the network of community relationships that usually encourage responsible behavior, and consequently suffer high incidences of crime, violence, alcoholism, and emotional disorders. Tensions between hostel dwellers and community residents often run high.

Before the mid-sixties local authorities generally provided accommodation for all "single" workers not housed on their employers' premises. Beginning in 1966 employers requesting permission for additional migrant laborers were required to provide housing. Municipalities and private employers, including labor-intensive industries such as mining and construction, traditionally put up hostels, compounds, or other forms of collective residences to house workers. Typical were dormitory-type sheds or warehouses, which contained fifty or more bunks in two tiers. Originally meant to be temporary, and thus built to minimal standards, many of these structures were later upgraded to meet municipal building regulations and categorized as permanent housing. The effects of the upgrading were often negligible, however.

Recent investigations of hostels have revealed many of them to be squalid and overcrowded. Earlier this year Cape Town's medical officer described accommodation provided for contract workers in Langa township, north of Cape Town, as "unfit for human habitation." Employers were instructed to upgrade the facility immediately to an acceptable minimal standard.

The *Financial Mail* reported the results of its own investigation of Cape area hostels in its January 18, 1980, issue:

> The housing can only be described as minimal. Large overcrowded draughty sheds, concrete floors with occasional meagre or patchy covering offer scant comfort during the Cape winter, though occasionally a coal heater is supplied. Only one dormitory was seen to have an interior ceiling and often the asbestos roofs leak.
> In summer, they are hot, stuffy, and smelly. Three bare bulbs—or three fluorescent lights—are the sole standard lighting provided, serving to illuminate two dingy rows of 20-25 metal double bunks. . . .

The bunks and foam mattresses are generally the only furniture supplied by employers, along with narrow wire lockers which serve as storage space for personal possessions.

There is no privacy. Only one employer has attempted to alleviate this by erecting brick partitions defining living spaces for four to six occupants. Some men have constructed makeshift partitions of plastic sheeting, cardboard, or wood—all considerable fire hazards.

In addition to the lack of privacy, the absence of interior ceilings often results in condensation and moisture dripping onto those sleeping on the upper bunks. In the sheds, life at the top is therefore even worse than at the bottom.

A corridor formed by the arrangement of the bunks down either side of the walls is the only recreational space. Some employers have supplied a table or two, usually steel with attached chairs. Kitchens are sometimes separate rooms, often not. One sink and tap for a dormitory's occupants is the norm, but not the rule—some employers provide neither.

One unit has no fully separated kitchen space, no sink, and no tap. One outside tap is shared by the occupants of two sheds.

Ablution and toilet facilities are sordid—one toilet and shower for every 20 persons is common. In the makeshift ablution facilities of one firm, only eight out of 20 showers are in working order. This does not even meet the requirements of the Slums Act, which specifies a minimum of one toilet for every 12 people. Sinks or basins in ablution blocks are a rarity—water generally falls to the floor and eventually evaporates. Laundry facilities are unheard of. . . .

Subsequent investigations have found conditions in many Cape hostels significantly improved. Living conditions in most hostels elsewhere in South Africa, however, are generally agreed to be poor. Approximately R275 million will be needed just to construct new units projected to be required by 1982.

Squatter Settlements

Hostel dwellers often abandon single-sex facilities to live illegally with their wives and children in squatter camps. Squatter settlements have proliferated despite legal restrictions. For many, squatting is a desperate response to the shortage of housing or to prohibitive living costs. For others, it is an attempt to escape the poverty of the homelands. Roughly one million Africans and Coloureds are estimated to be living in squatter settlements—usually collections of corrugated tin shanties without electricity, heat, sewage, or any amenities other than water spigots.

In 1978 one such squatter camp, Crossroads, outside Cape Town, defied government efforts to raze the area. The incident sparked international criticism of the South African government, and the camp, composed primarily of African men employed in Cape Town and their families, was given a reprieve.

In 1980 New Crossroads, two miles away from the original siting, was officially declared an African township. New homes have been built and services provided. This was made possible by efforts of the South African government, the Urban Foundation, and a $9-million loan from an American bank. Other problems have arisen, however. New Crossroads will not be able to accommodate all Crossroads' present residents, and rent payments may strain the resources of those chosen to stay there. In late 1980 the government indicated that it was preparing a plan for "a controlled amount" of squatting. "Without condoning the phenomenon, we shall have to live with a certain amount of it as part of the emancipation of the Third World." If this plan is implemented, it would signal a significant change in official attitudes.

EDUCATION

Like housing, education is a key issue for blacks. Inequalities in education cause deep frustration and discontent among South Africa's black youth. In 1980, four years after the Soweto riots, a new wave of student unrest swept across South Africa, catching up in its swell the anger and dissatisfactions of the larger black community and emerging as a major political issue.

In spite of government warnings, thousands of Coloured and African students at schools and universities joined in boycotts and demonstrations to protest inequalities in the country's racially segregated educational system. The student protest, centered mainly in the Cape province, did not reach 1976 proportions, but expressions of solidarity were almost universal, and sympathetic work strikes were larger than during the Soweto disturbances. By the end of the year more than seven hundred schools—primarily African schools in the eastern Cape—had been closed, an estimated fifty people killed, and many others injured.

The introduction of Afrikaans as a medium of instruction in African schools sparked the Soweto protests. The refusal of administrators to address Coloured students' demands at a western Cape school for improved conditions and greater representation in decisions affecting their welfare precipitated the 1980 boycotts. In both instances, student demands quickly transcended the original issues and became a strongly articulated expression of dissatisfaction with the South African system of education, which students say is designed to perpetuate blacks' inability to compete on an equal footing with whites.

The boycotting students' first demand was for the provision of free and compulsory education for every school-age African child up to and including high school. Second, they called for one national education department for all races and for equal expenditures on all racial groups. At present the school system of each black group is administered by a separate department. White education, for which government spending is significantly higher, is largely controlled by the provincial governments.

Other student demands included equality in teacher-pupil ratios, parity in salaries for white and black teachers, improved teacher training colleges for black teachers, and equal job opportunities for black graduates. Blacks also demanded the revision of textbooks, which they say reflect white, not black, history, culture, and achievements. Finally, blacks called for curriculum changes, charging that not enough attention is given in black schools to mathematics and science. Without these subjects, they say, blacks will remain in a position of inferiority, unable to make progress within the society or to improve their standards of living. The government counters that syllabi in all schools, regardless of race, are the same, and that members of the black community are involved in drawing up the syllabi for black schools.

African education is markedly inferior to white education. To a lesser extent, the education of Coloureds and Indians is also inferior. Physical facilities for blacks are poor compared with those for whites. Textbooks in black schools are not equal in quantity to those in white schools. A serious teacher shortage exists in black communities: In 1979 the teacher-pupil ratio for Africans was 1 to 48, and for Coloureds 1 to 30, compared with 1 to 20 for whites. The preparation of black teachers is generally poor. This is particularly true for African teachers, who average only eighth-grade educations. Black schools are chronically overcrowded, with double sessions or platoon systems (two teachers and two classes using one classroom simultaneously) to accommodate the overflow. And, according to official estimates, a shortage of 7,000 to 8,000 classrooms exists in black areas. (In the homelands, resources for education are even scarcer.)

Dropout rates in African schools are high. Between primary and secondary school there is a sharp rate of attrition. Out of the total number of African pupils who entered primary school in 1967, only 15 percent reached the final year of high school. And despite the fact that there are four and a half times as many Africans as whites in South Africa, by 1970 there were only 1,400 African university graduates in the total population, contrasted with 104,500 white university graduates.

But in the continuing debate on South African education, the figures most often cited as evidence of the gross injustice of apartheid are expenditures on white and black education. In terms of per capita expenditures, in 1978–79 the government of South Africa spent roughly $940 on each white child, $290 on each Coloured child, and $90 on each African child.

Measured by such indexes as its industrial capacity and the level of education of its whites, South Africa exhibits the characteristics of a developed nation, running second only to the United States in its proportion of (white) university students. In marked contrast, the proportion of Africans receiving higher education in South Africa is similar to that of a developing nation, such as Zambia.* Some educators and laymen have warned that South Africa must immediately address the needs of black education if current levels of economic

---

*South Africa has a smaller percentage of its African population at the university level than do Ghana, the Ivory Coast, Kenya, and Nigeria.

growth are to be maintained. There seems to be a growing recognition on all levels that the South African economy will need to rely increasingly on the skilled labor of Africans, who are expected to account for 70–75 percent of the work force in the year 2000. In its publication "Focus on Key Economic Issues," the Bureau for Economic Policy and Analysis at the University of Pretoria states: "A high rate of economic growth is necessary for both the creation of employment opportunities and the narrowing of the 'race gap.' To achieve this growth, a much larger number of non-whites and particularly Blacks will have to move into skilled occupations, simply because there are not and will not be enough whites available to achieve the potential rate of economic growth. The removal of policy barriers on the advancement of non-whites without the provision of appropriate training opportunities will not close the 'race gap' as is frequently argued. . . . Large numbers of workers—particularly Blacks—are poorly equipped for the labour market from an educational point of view."

Despite criticism from many quarters on its policies toward African education, perceived by some to be the most basic inequality of the system of apartheid, the South African government stresses that advances in black education are taking place. According to the Department of Education and Training, the ministry that controls African education, more than 20 percent of the total African population now attends primary and secondary school. Of black-ruled nations, only Kenya—and possibly Nigeria since its recent introduction of free and compulsory education—exceeds this percentage. The Coloured and Indian populations have even larger percentages of children attending schools.

While acknowledging that disparities between white and black education exist, the National party contends that there have been great strides in African education under National party rule—especially in recent years. Dr. Ferdie Hartzenberg, minister of the Department of Education and Training, pointed out in an interview in the *Rand Daily Mail* that only 36 percent of school-age African children (7–16) were at school in 1954, as compared with more than 75 percent in 1975. The 1970s saw a very rapid increase in the number of African students remaining in the higher classes of secondary school, a level at which they had traditionally not been well represented. During this period significantly increased numbers of African students also passed matriculation (a basic requirement for university admission) and earned senior certificates after twelve years' schooling by successfully completing an examination, although in absolute terms these numbers remained comparatively small.

As further evidence of the government's commitment to increased African enrollment, the minister indicated that compulsory education for African children was being phased in on a "selective" geographic basis. This process was to have begun in early 1981 in three black townships in the Transvaal.

The minister also referred to the rise in spending for black education as concrete evidence of the government's commitment. In 1952–53 expenditures for black education were R15,712,388; in 1980–81, R249 million, or an increase of more than R233 million. In the past two years alone, Hartzenberg maintained, the budget for African education outside the homelands has increased by 26 percent and 36 percent respectively. (Spending on education in homelands, which depend upon the central government for their revenues, is also on the increase. In 1979, expenditures for education totaled R120 million, as compared with R96 million in the previous year. The *Financial Mail* reported that in 1980 estimated allocations for most homelands increased by more than 30 percent. There are approximately 2 million primary and secondary students in homelands, and 1.5 million African students in white areas.)

According to Hartzenberg, expenditures will continue to increase. Increased expenditures, he said, will result in the building of additional facilities and the upgrading of existing facilities, the lowering of the teacher-pupil ratios, the introduction of parity in the salaries of teachers from different racial groups, and the improvement of teacher preparation. He projected that the current shortage in classroom accommodation for Africans might be eliminated by 1985 "if the present financial climate prevailed and progress was not retarded by disrupting activities."

As for Coloured education, which is controlled by the Department of Coloured Relations, expenditures are expected to approach R200 million in the new fiscal year, up from an annual average of R100 million over the past ten years. After meeting with Coloured teachers in response to Cape student protests, Prime Minister Botha announced that Coloured education would be given top priority and that R14 million would be spent to make up the shortage of textbooks for Coloured students. Official statements indicated that greater expenditures would also be made to alleviate the serious shortage of classrooms existing in Coloured communities.

Increased government spending on black education would certainly seem to be dramatic. But some educators and others argue that the figures, particularly those for African education, are misleading. The *Financial Mail* warned in its April 11, 1980, issue:

> The important point is not the percentage increase in educational spending—which is in any event from a low base—but whether the [amount] is sufficient in the first place to educate the existing African population to meet the employment needs of commerce and industry. Inflation and the number of African school children will absorb a large chunk of this year's increases. The number of African children is climbing by around 90,000 in the white areas each year, giving a 6% growth rate.

SYNCOM (Synergy Communications), a futures research organization, has projected that the number of school-age South African children will increase from the present 8 million to 15 million by the end of the century. In order for the government to fulfill its promise of compulsory education for Africans, said SYNCOM, more than 186,000 new classrooms will be needed, just under 10,000 per year for the next two decades, plus 226,000 additional teachers and 36,000 new schools—at a total cost of R4 billion ($5 billion). The state, SYNCOM added, will not be able to meet singlehandedly the rising costs of black education. For black education to remain viable, SYNCOM contends, costs will have to be borne to an increasingly greater extent by the private sector and the black community itself.

Concerning students' demands regarding black teachers, officials said that efforts were under way to narrow the gap in the salaries of black and white teachers. Moreover, they said, the government had introduced programs to generate more black teachers and to improve the level of education of present teachers. Three new teachers' training colleges for Africans are scheduled to open next year, and various upgrading programs are to be instituted to allow African teachers to improve their academic qualifications. Among these will be a system of grants awarded to teachers for every recognized course successfully completed at the University of South Africa, a nonresidential institution offering correspondence degrees.

Educational requirements for black teachers will gradually be raised to a twelfth-grade level. At present, the majority of African teachers have eighth-to-tenth-grade qualifications and one year's teacher training. Only a handful are university graduates: In 1979 only 2.3 percent and 4.2 percent of African and Coloured teachers, respectively, were university graduates, as compared with 19.4 percent of Indian and 32 percent of white teachers.

Of all the students' demands, the one for a single education department for all races most fundamentally challenges the philosophy of apartheid, and is therefore meeting strong official resistance. In making its case for the continued existence of the system of separate education departments, the government argues that disparities in the academic qualifications of black and white teachers preclude the creation of a unitary system, which demands a certain uniformity of qualifications for all teachers. Since the majority of South Africa's 90,000 black teachers are deficient in their academic qualifications, special attention must be paid them, the government contends. This special attention can be given only by maintaining separate departments, which puts the government in a better position "to effect the progress desired by budgeting specifically with a view to eliminating backlogs and to provide for special needs."

Critics see a certain irony in this argument, contending that the existing system itself is in part responsible for these disparities.

Resistance to a single department of education is also strong among the larger white population, since many fear that a unitary system would mean greater bureaucratic control from Pretoria and less provincial and community autonomy. Moreover, while blacks tend to view it as a move toward the equalization of standards, whites tend to perceive a unitary system as a move toward integration.

Although the system of differentiated education has a long history in

South Africa, the National government, upon coming to power, introduced more rigid measures of racial separation. The limits of black education were clearly defined by Henrik Verwoerd, assassinated as prime minister in 1966. In a 1954 Senate speech on "Bantu" education, Verwoerd stressed that education should prepare blacks for service within their own communities and should not encourage the development of unrealistic "unhealthy white-collar ideals," which would cause "widespread frustration among the so-called educated Natives."

Verwoerd believed that there was "no place for [the African] in the European community above certain forms of labour." While this philosophy has had a continuing effect on the condition of black education, economic imperatives appear to be gradually changing this perspective. A member of the current administration said that because black education was ignored in the past, industry has been left with a bottleneck in skilled labor that is a major brake on South Africa's economic growth. Owen Horwood, South Africa's minister of finance, has said that the entire country would benefit from giving priority to black education.

While the Verwoerdian philosophy of black education has essentially been abandoned by the current administration—which has formally pledged the equalization of standards in the education of blacks and whites—the present government remains ideologically committed to the principle of separate systems of education for each racial group. However, Prime Minister Botha has asked the Human Sciences Research Council to investigate the implications of a unitary system—as well as ways in which "equality in education for all population groups" can be attained. The research body was scheduled to deliver its report to the cabinet in June 1981.

History of Apartheid in Education

Until formation of the Union in 1910 the responsibility and cost for educating Africans was borne largely by missionaries. In 1850 the Cape government began making grants to missions from the "Aborigine Fund," the purpose of the grants being to train young Africans in industrial occupations as well as to produce evangelists and schoolmasters who would work among their own people. In 1865 mission schools in the Cape were drawn into the local educational system and local taxes collected from Africans were used for teachers' salaries. By 1910 roughly similar arrangements obtained in the other three provinces.

The education of white and Coloured children remained intertwined until around the turn of this century. In 1893 provision was made for separate schools for white and Coloured pupils in the public system, and in 1911, after creation of the Union, that legislation prohibited Coloured children from attending schools with white children. Between 1910 and 1948, when the National party came to power, the responsibility for controlling and financing African, Coloured, and Indian education was divided among the central government, the provincial administrations, the churches, and the community.

The National party's early legislative measures at both national and provincial levels were intended to promote separation between the various racial groups and between English-speaking and Afrikaans-speaking whites. In 1948 the government appointed the Eiselen Commission, whose task was to formulate "the principles and aims of education for Natives as an independent race, in which their past and present, their inherent racial qualities, their distinctive characteristics and aptitude and their needs under ever-changing social conditions are taken into consideration."

The immediate effect of the 1953 Bantu Education Act, which resulted from the Eiselen report, was to pass the control of education for African pupils from the provinces to a division of Bantu education within what was then the Department of Native Affairs. At the local level, church involvement was minimized in African education through the progressive elimination of subsidies to mission schools over a four-year period. Teacher training was transferred from the churches to the state. This process resulted in the loss of the most competent white teachers and the increase in teacher-pupil ratios from 1 to 40 to 1 to 50 (and in some places 1 to 60). The central government also later assumed control of Coloured and Indian education pursuant to the Coloured Persons' Education Act of 1963 and the Indian Education Act of 1965.

The passage of these three acts provided the legislative framework within which nearly total separation of the various racial groups was achieved in the ensuing years. This legislation also enabled the government to use education as a means of advancing the policy of separate development. A shift to mother-tongue instruction in place of an official language (English or Afrikaans) at the primary level of African schools was recommended by the Eiselen Commission. This shift reflected the government's view of South Africa as a number of separate "nations" which included whites, Coloureds, Zulu, Tswana, Xhosa, Venda, and so on. Africans living in "white" South Africa were considered "temporary sojourners" who would eventually return to a homeland. In keeping with this philosophy, the government organized primary schools on an ethnic basis to provide for specific ethnic groups, each of which had been assigned to physically separate residential areas within African townships.

In 1956 new syllabi for primary schools were introduced that provided for exclusively mother-tongue instruction at the lower primary grades and the gradual introduction of both official languages, English and Afrikaans. The government explained the required use of vernacular instruction as an attempt to maintain the viability of indigenous languages and to preserve cultural and linguistic diversity.

Africans, however, saw the policy as a divide-and-rule tactic and an effort to retard Africans' social and economic development in South Africa. At a conference held during 1956, a group of prominent Africans decried the policy of vernacular instruction, saying that it inhibited the transmission of modern scientific concepts and did not otherwise prepare African students for the wider world. For several years the policy of instruction in three languages could not be implemented properly because of a shortage of teachers adequately proficient in all the languages. The poor language preparation of teachers and the need to change languages during the course of a day proved frustrating to African students. When the requirement for Afrikaans as a medium of instruction was reinforced in 1976, students marched in protest in Soweto.

The Education and Training Act of 1979, largely an outcome of events in Soweto, introduced greater flexibility in the choice of language of instruction and lowered the grade in which teaching in either English or Afrikaans would begin. Mother-tongue instruction is now required only up to and including standard two (fourth grade). Thereafter, students are to be instructed in an official language chosen by their parents. (English is the popular choice.) The act also waived tuition fees for African children, and empowered the minister of education to build and maintain both state and community schools. In addition, it set requirements for the registration of private schools serving black children. As a result of students' demands in 1976 the word *Bantu* was eliminated from official nomenclature, the Education and Training Act replaced the Bantu Education Act, and the Department of Bantu Education became the Department of Education and Training.

The organization of African, Coloured, and Indian education is structured on a centralized, racially homogeneous basis, each black group having its own system of schools, teacher training facilities, technical facilities, technical colleges, and universities. High-level control is largely in the hands of white public servants, and a significant number of white teachers, lecturers, and professors are employed in the three black systems, primarily at the higher levels. White civil servants also hold key positions in homeland education systems. In addition to its role within white South Africa, the Department of Education and Training also acts as a central liaison, and the planning and coordinating authority for the homelands.

Higher Education

The pattern of separation that exists in lower education also exists at the university level. Until the passage of the Extension of University Education Act in 1959, universities had been free to determine who should be admitted to degree courses. The universities of Cape Town and the Witwatersrand had, in fact, been "open" universities. The passage of this inappropriately named act limited the black student's choice of university and gave the ministers in charge of education affairs of the three racial groups the right to regulate through issuance or denial of permits the entry of black students to those white universities that offered them places. The act also provided for the establishment of separate universities for African, Coloured, and Indian students, the examinations, degrees, and diplomas to be those of the University of South Africa, a nonresidential institution offering degrees through correspondence to students of all races.

At the same time, control of the University College of Fort Hare, a black institution established by missionaries in 1916, also passed to the Department of Bantu Education. Coloured and Indian students were phased out of the college and admission was limited principally to students of Xhosa origin. (Fort Hare is located in the Ciskei.) The other ethnic colleges established under the 1959 act are:

University of the Western Cape (for Coloureds)
University of Durban-Westville (for Indians)
University of the North (Turfloop) (for Sotho, Venda, and Tsonga)
University of Zululand (for Zulu and Swazi)

In 1969 these ethnic colleges became autonomous state universities and obtained full university status. Subsequent legislation dispensed with ethnic segregation in these universities and envisaged enrollment by all African people. Bophuthatswana and the Transkei also have universities. Legislation enacted in 1977 and 1978 made it possible for whites and Africans to register at the universities of the western Cape, which are primarily Coloured, and at Durban-Westville, which is primarily Indian, subject to the agreement of the ministers concerned. Black students can also seek special permission to pursue studies in a white university in disciplines not offered at black universities. In recent years, there has been a considerable increase in the number of blacks enrolled at white universities. Gerritt Viljoen, minister of national education, reported in February 1981 that 4,034 black students were registered at predominantly white universities in 1981, an increase of 20 percent since 1979. The greatest number of blacks are enrolled at the University of Cape Town, Rhodes University in Grahamstown, and the University of the Witwatersrand in Johannesburg, all English-speaking. At Cape Town, for instance, Viljoen estimated that blacks accounted for about 1,600 of the university's 11,000 students. Of this number, Africans formed a small minority. In 1979 there were 62 Africans at Cape Town, 356 Africans at Natal, and 145 at Witwatersrand. Tuition and living expenses at white universities, which may run between $2,000 and $2,500 a year, are beyond the means of most black students, and universities are able to assist only a limited number.

Despite increased black enrollment at both white and black universities, the disparity between white and black university enrollment has remained essentially unchanged. According to the Institute of International Education:

> Despite the fact that there are four and a half times as many Africans as whites in South Africa, in 1970 there were only 1,400 African university graduates, contrasted with 104,500 white university graduates. In 1979 university enrollment on a full-time, residential basis included 80,000 whites and only 7,000 Africans. Despite the

recent growth in university places for Africans, a white child still has 100 times more chance of becoming a university graduate than an African child.

Students at black universities tend to graduate in arts, education, and social science rather than in specialized fields such as architecture, medicine, dentistry, engineering, law, agriculture, and veterinary science. In the latter fields there were only 216 black graduates in 1976 as compared with 3,516 whites. White universities can admit only blacks who enter these specialized disciplines. The universities of the Witwatersrand, Cape Town, and Natal have support programs to assist students from disadvantaged academic backgrounds.

Medical Education

The first medical training for blacks dates back to the 1920s, when a missionary doctor trained black medical orderlies. Before the establishment of a medical school for blacks at the University of Natal in 1951, the University of the Witwatersrand, which is "white," admitted black medical students on a quota basis. From 1946 to 1956, when it was legal for African students to attend white universities without special ministerial permits and when Witwatersrand alone was graduating Africans as doctors, the average number of graduating black medical students was 6.2 per year. From 1957 to 1966, when the universities of Witwatersrand and Natal were both graduating Africans as doctors, the total average per year was 13.2. And from 1967 to 1975, when Natal alone was graduating Africans as doctors, the yearly average was 13.1. Over the period 1976–78, the University of Natal has averaged 31.3 African medical graduates a year.

In 1979 a new medical university for blacks, the Medical University of South Africa, was established in Bophuthatswana, and it is expected to increase the number of black doctors significantly. (For further discussion of medical education for blacks, see following section on health.)

Technical Education

Formal technical education or training is offered at different levels within the various school systems in technical high schools. It is also offered to people who are no longer of school age through technical institutes, technical colleges, and technikons, which are colleges for advanced technical training. As in the school systems, technical education is structured on a racial basis and is available primarily to whites.

Technikons offer advanced training in technical, commercial, and other **121** courses. Training in a technikon is intended to ensure direct entry to commerce or industry. In fields such as engineering, the purpose of the technikons is to offer an alternative to university training. Their best products are highly trained technologists who have greater expertise in specialized areas than the more academically and broadly trained university graduates. There are six technikons for whites, one for Indians, one for Coloureds, and two for Africans, one of which was established through private funding. It is possible for blacks to gain entry to white technikons, but admission procedures are cumbersome.

The Department of Education and Training is currently building another technikon for Africans, as well as two technical institutes and eighteen orientation centers in the urban areas. In the next four to six years it plans to build eighteen technical centers and twelve technical institutes. The technikon is scheduled for completion in 1990 at an estimated cost of R55 million. Once completed it will have an annual enrollment of 5,000 students.

The Riekert Commission, anticipating future demands for manpower, stressed the importance of technical training in its report. The government is also experiencing growing pressure from the private sector to open white technikons to people of all races and to exempt students from the provisions of the Group Areas Act in order to provide residential facilities for black students.

Direct private sector involvement in manpower development programs is increasing. The American Chamber of Commerce has built an ultramodern, private coeducational commercial high school for six hundred students in Soweto. The school, for which $5 million has been pledged by American companies in South Africa, is scheduled to open in 1981. Also, Anglo-American Corporation, South Africa's largest company, has so far committed $3.5 million toward a project whose aim is to produce a generation of management leaders. The project, which is highly selective, will train twelve black students a year for the next five years. It will involve one year of intense general preparation, four years of engineering or three years of commercial training at university levels, followed by employment as managers in Anglo-American.

Religious groups are also involved in the effort to upgrade the level of Africans' skills. Notable among adult education programs established by religious groups are Saint Antony's Education and Training Centre, located near Johannesburg, and the Saint Francis Adult Education Centre in Langa, near Cape Town. Saint Antony's Centre, which is close to the East Rand industrial areas, incorporates an industrial training unit funded by local industries and a variety of continuing education opportunities.

And at the primary and secondary levels, the church, which assumed responsibility for black education before the government took it over in the 1950s, has again played a decisive role. In 1977 the Roman Catholic church, recently outspoken in its criticism of racial separation, quietly opened the doors of its private schools to blacks, in defiance of the government's threats to decertify integrated schools. After threats to close the schools and to prosecute the parents of the children involved, the government finally decided to leave the matter for provincial authorities to resolve. Admissions in the Cape and Natal provinces proceeded rather smoothly. However, the provincial authority of the Transvaal, in which Pretoria and Johannesburg are located, took a more rigid line. Nevertheless, black students from Soweto are reportedly presently attending a variety of private schools in Johannesburg.

As of the 1979–80 school year it was estimated that about 6 or 7 percent of the 24,300 pupils registered in Catholic schools are black. However, only a small percentage of these are African. Anglican and Methodist church schools followed the lead of Catholic schools, and at the request of the West German government, German schools in South Africa opened their doors to pupils of all races. Some Africans have rejected the idea of sending their children to integrated schools, saying that integration has no relevancy for their communities. Reformist groups, however, have hailed these developments as important in creating a climate for change.

HEALTH

The South African government invites international bodies to examine its health care system and the manner in which health services are extended to all racial groups. It points with pride to Baragwanath Hospital in Soweto. With 2,500 beds and 12 well-equipped operating theaters, it is the largest and most technologically advanced hospital for blacks on the African continent.

Public health services are government subsidized. Theoretically, health care for the poor, mostly blacks, is free or at a nominal cost. "The aim of South Africa's health services," official literature states, "is to promote the health of all the peoples of South Africa, both generally and individually." In a preface to a review of the country's health services, Dr. J. de Beer, secretary of health, wrote: "A full curative and preventative service is available to all citizens, of whatever population group, wherever they may reside in the country."

Yet the health status of black South Africans is generally low. The infant mortality rate, usually regarded as an index of a population's health, is high. The mortality rate for black infants between one and four years old is ten times as high as that for white infants. And 50 percent of deaths among Africans and Coloureds are those of children under five years old. Life expectancy for Africans is fifty-eight years, for Coloureds fifty-six, and for whites seventy-two. Most hospitals for blacks are poorly equipped and overcrowded. Even the showcase hospital in Soweto does not meet the health needs of its populous community. Moreover, health care is deficient in rural areas and homelands, where the largest number of blacks reside and where the greatest need exists.

Finally, while racial bias is not explicitly written into health legislation, economic and political inequalities inevitably influence health care. Like all other spheres of life in South Africa, health care is affected by the law and **123** custom of apartheid, which determine decisions regarding the distribution of resources. As a result, there are serious discrepancies in the quality and quantity of services provided to blacks and to whites.

The major causes of death among black adults in South Africa include gastroenteritis, measles, and hypertensive diseases. Other significant causes are rheumatic fever, homicide, and accidents. Among black children, gastroenteritis, measles, and pneumonia are said to account for the majority of deaths. Africans in South Africa tend to have diseases common to developing countries, whereas whites in South Africa show a profile of disease typical of developed countries, with cancer and heart disease being the major causes of death. Coloureds, who occupy an intermediate position between whites and Africans culturally and in terms of income levels, exhibit the health traits of both developed and developing nations. Among Coloured infants there is a high incidence of enteric (intestinal) and diarrheal diseases, and among adults a high incidence of circulatory or cardiovascular diseases.

According to the South Africa Institute of Race Relations (SAIRR), infant mortality figures per 1,000 live births in South Africa are 12 whites, 64 urban blacks, and 240 rural blacks. For comparison, in Niger, infant mortality per 1,000 live births is 200, in Zaire 160, in the United Kingdom 16, in the United States 14, and in Sweden 9.

Malnutrition and infectious diseases, major causes of deaths among African infants, are referred to as "diseases of poverty." They result from poor education, overcrowded and inadequate housing, poor sanitation, and a generally harsh living environment. Mortality rates based on malnutrition, a disease that may arise because of inadequate diet or result from illness, are exceptionally high. Diarrheal diseases and intestinal parasites, both of which are related to poor sanitation and unsafe water supply, are major contributory causes of malnutrition because they interfere with food absorption. Also, malnutrition, which lowers resistance to disease, aids the spread of tuberculosis and other infectious diseases.

Malnutrition is particularly prevalent in the homelands. According to SAIRR, 52 percent of all two-to-three-year-olds in the Ciskei are malnourished, and one in ten urban and one in six rural children suffer from *kwashiorkor,* a condition of protein deficiency, and marasmus, a wasting disease that is also a result of inadequate nutrition. Recently, a severe drought in KwaZulu focused attention on malnutrition in the homelands, a problem doctors there say has always been severe.

The correlation between poverty and poor health figures prominently in the discussion of black health care. Studies indicate that improved economic conditions among blacks are generally accompanied by longer life expectancy and a shift in disease patterns. According to L. G. Wells, author of *Health, Healing and Society,* "When a large white group lived in poverty in South

Africa during the depression in the Thirties, their health was more like that of the present blacks than whites. Those blacks who have attained a high standard of living show a health pattern similar to the white group."

Michael Savage, assistant professor of sociology at the University of Cape Town, shares this point of view: "It is a well known fact that TB declines in a population when malnutrition and inadequate housing are overcome. Rheumatic fever declines when poverty and overcrowding are effectively attacked; typhus declines when sanitation and inadequate water supplies are improved."

Michael McGrath, senior lecturer in economics at the University of Natal, says that the low socioeconomic status of blacks in South Africa has two immediate effects: "The first is the lower level of health which results from poor diet and environment. . . . The second direct effect of low black incomes is on the levels of consumption and the amount of income available for the purchase of health services. In 1968 per capita consumption expenditure of urban whites was more than 6 times that of urban Africans."

Larger per capita incomes enable whites to spend greater amounts for health services in the private sector. In 1974 white expenditure represented approximately 94 percent of private expenditure on health care. On the other hand, the vast majority of blacks are dependent on government-subsidized public medicine.

Just as poverty is a determinant of health care in a society, so too is the availability of institutionalized health care systems. White hospitals are often underutilized, whereas African hospitals are generally overburdened, thereby causing services to be deficient. While no figures are available on the distribution of public sector expenditures for each racial group, the racial distribution of hospital services reveals a bias in favor of whites. In 1960 official sources indicated there were 100 whites per bed, compared with 186 blacks per bed. By 1975 the white ratio had fallen slightly, although the black ratio remained unchanged. Some question these statistics. In Soweto, for example, Baragwanath Hospital's 2,500 beds do not begin to serve the population adequately. Even considering the availability of beds for Sowetans at Johannesburg General Hospital and at smaller health care facilities in Soweto, the bed-to-population ratio, based on the official population estimate for Soweto of 1.2 million, would still be no lower than 1 to 400. (In the United States it is 1 to 50, in Britain 1 to 20.)

But even if bed-to-patient ratios were equal for both population groups, McGrath argues, blacks would still be at a disadvantage. "The [greater] needs of blacks as indicated by health standards and the smaller quantity of private services available [to blacks] require that this proportion should be even higher if racial equity is to be achieved. In addition, the services provided to blacks are of inferior quality in relation to those supplied to whites."

Emphasis upon curative rather than preventive health services has also had a disproportionately adverse effect on blacks because they, particularly

Africans, tend to have nutritional and infectious diseases, which are responsive to preventive measures. Government resources have traditionally been directed at curative services, which are aimed at diseases found predominantly among the white population. Says Wells: "Concentration on illnesses such as heart attacks and cancer may not have much negative effect on a population for whom these are major illnesses. When the major killers are infection and malnutrition, though, the results are tragic."

The South African government has indicated that it is now attempting to reverse this trend. Health Secretary de Beer said in mid-1980: "This year the Department of Health is spending 20 percent of its budget on prevention and health care promotion, whereas five years ago, it was well below 10 percent." According to J. V. Reid, professor of physiology at the University of Natal, only about 2 percent of the annual health care expenditures have been directed to preventive services in the past. "Such a distribution between the curative and preventive aspects [of health care] can be regarded as a severe misallocation of funds because the African population, which in 1977 was estimated at 69 percent of the total population, suffers primarily from preventable diseases."

In this sense, South Africa is not unlike many other Third World countries that have massive unmet health care needs but channel resources into a few expensive, essentially middle-class curative facilities instead of into many modest structures equitably distributed. In the South African context, the question may be whether it is better to build another hospital like the one in Soweto or to use the same amount of money to create an extensive network of clinics in both urban and rural areas.

The pattern of geographical distribution as it stands now is highly discriminatory against blacks. Hospitals in homeland areas, where approximately one-third of the African population resides, are few and far between. Bed-to-patient ratios exceed 1 to 1,000. While an urban bias in the location of services and doctors is a common pattern around the world, in the South African context it has a disproportionate impact upon Africans, who need legal authority to be in white urban areas where health care is better than in the homelands.

Despite the fact that the central government is responsible for health and health services for Africans in the homelands, the homeland health system is still based largely on a sprinkling of former mission hospitals, many of which run outlying clinics. Black patients must often travel long distances for medical attention. In some areas, clinic services may be available only once a week. The South African government has recognized the value of mission hospitals, and in some instances gives them financial support. In the case of self-governing homelands, all functions related to health care services have been or are in the process of being transferred. "Where responsibility for health matters has been handed over to the homeland authorities, the Republic has supplied about 70 percent of total annual expenditure on health and health services within these areas in recent years," said Reid.

Although statutes relating directly to health in no way differentiate between races, racial segregation in health care is indirectly accomplished through general apartheid legislation such as the Group Areas Act, the Workmen's Compensation Act, influx control regulations, and legislation that separates control of health services and puts them under the various homeland governments. "The general effect of the Group Areas Act is to limit interracial health care," said Reid. "Hospitals are either wholly segregated, or are segregated by wards. Black doctors may not normally see patients in a white hospital or ward, except with special permission, or treat their own patients in a hospital if it involves being in control of white nurses. Separate ambulances are normally provided for black and white, except under emergency circumstances. Black nurses may care for whites in hospitals only if no white nurses are available." White doctors are allowed to treat black patients.

Generally poor medical facilities for blacks are aggravated by the lack of sufficient medical staff. There is a severe shortage of black doctors. This holds true particularly for Africans. There is an even greater shortage of African, Coloured, and Indian dental personnel. Available evidence indicates that there are few if any African psychiatrists. At the paramedical level, training programs for African personnel are in their infancy. In contrast, nursing is well established among Africans. In 1977 there were 18,000 African and 4,000 Coloured (and 27,000 white) general or specialized nurses.

Legislation controlling the separation of medical and training facilities has had a strong influence upon the quality of black health care because it has affected the opportunities for medical education for blacks and the resulting shortage of black doctors. In 1973, there were only 69 African medical doctors in the entire country. Over the period 1968–78, an average of 85.4 percent of medical graduates in South Africa were white, 3.4 percent Coloured, 8.4 percent Asian, and 3 percent African.

According to a recent survey of South African health systems conducted by the Southern Africa Labour and Development Unit of the University of Cape Town, there is 1 doctor to every 600 whites and only 1 to every 40,000 blacks in rural areas. (In the West a doctor/population ratio of 1 to 800 is considered ideal.) This survey also found that the overwhelming majority of South African doctors—81 percent—live in urban areas. And out of 17,374 registered doctors, only 2.8 percent work in the homelands. "This maldistribution of doctors is a mirror of the maldistribution of resources in South African society," the study concluded.

In 1978 there were nearly 6,000 registered students in medical schools in South Africa. Of these, 5,061 were white, 494 were Asians, 306 were African, and 107 were Coloured. The recent opening of the Medical University of South Africa in Ga-Rankua, Bophuthatswana, has led to a modest increase in African enrollment. However, social and economic conditions and bottlenecks in the output of qualified students from African secondary schools will probably hold down the rate at which African doctors will be produced for some time to come.

Chapter 7
The Economy

South Africa's economy is inextricably bound up with the politics of apartheid. In few other countries do political considerations affect economic decisions in such a stark fashion. Indeed, for many years economic requirements have been subordinated to the overriding political imperative of racial separation, especially in the field of labor.

Foreign investment, both direct and indirect, has played a key role in the development of the South African economy, and remains an important factor in maintaining a high rate of economic growth. In particular, it provides advanced technology for South African industry. But foreign investment is heavily influenced both by current South African events and by international political pressures. Moreover, decisions made by South Africa affecting its major area of vulnerability, energy, are based as much on political factors as on economic ones. For example, the development of alternative energy sources, such as synthetic fuels, has been dictated primarily by the threat of an international oil embargo.

The importance of economic growth has become a political issue as well as an economic one. Many people in South Africa see it as the hope of the future and the source of liberalizing social and political developments. Others see economic growth as continuing to benefit whites almost exclusively while making little or no contribution to changes that would significantly benefit the other population groups.

MAJOR CHARACTERISTICS OF THE ECONOMY

South Africa's economy is one of the success stories of Africa. In 1978 South Africa accounted for approximately 20 percent of the continent's output of goods and services (larger than that of oil-rich Libya and second only to Nigeria, with three times South Africa's population), 86 percent of its steel production, more than 50 percent of its electric power production, 60 percent of all rail traffic, 43 percent of registered motor vehicles, 42 percent of telephones, and 40 percent of industrial production. South Africa has the continent's highest per capita income and life expectancy. The country is also the only major food exporter on the continent. Because of its controversial status in the international community, South Africa has consciously tried to develop a self-sufficient economy.

According to the World Bank's 1980 listing, however, South Africa is only a "middle-income developing country," a category that includes over forty-five nations, among them Argentina, Brazil, Israel, Nigeria, and Spain. As measured by most of the important economic indicators of development, South Africa still lags far behind the major industrialized countries.

The country's economy, like many other aspects of South Africa, is a study in contrasts and inequality. South Africa has modern cities like Johannesburg and Cape Town, but many areas outside the cities are characterized by the rural poverty of an underdeveloped country. The economy is, in fact, a dual economy, divided not only between an urban industrial sector and a rural subsistence sector but also, as the enormous differences between income levels and living standards show, between black and white.

Mining

Today's South African economy has its roots in the discovery and exploitation of diamonds and gold in the last third of the nineteenth century. And although the years that followed the initial mineral discoveries saw the economy diversify greatly, minerals are still the cornerstone of South Africa's economic progress. Its mining industry now extracts over forty different minerals in mines all over the country, but gold and diamonds remain synonymous with South Africa. It is the world's major producer of gem-quality diamonds and the third largest producer of industrial diamonds, after Zaire and the Soviet Union. South Africa also produces some 60 percent of the world's gold, and gold sales are by far the country's single most important source of foreign income. With the price of an ounce of gold averaging $613 for 1980, the value of gold exports in 1980 exceeded the value of all other exports combined, and South Africa experienced an impressive 8 percent growth rate for the year.

In 1979 the mining sector contributed 18 percent of the country's total production of goods and services, or gross domestic product (GDP), compared with a 10 percent contribution in 1972. With higher gold prices and increased mining output, that percentage was certain to increase. However, because mining is such a capital-intensive industry, it provided jobs for only a little more than 700,000 workers in 1980, less than 10 percent of the national work force.

The sector's most important contribution to the economy is its export earnings: In 1980, minerals accounted for 76 percent of South Africa's total foreign exchange earnings of $26 billion, up from 66 percent of $19 billion the previous year. Apart from gold, the major export earners are coal, diamonds, platinum, uranium, iron ore, and copper, as well as the strategically important ferroalloys, ferrochrome and ferromanganese.

Although gold output has declined in the past decade—a consequence of the increase in mining of lower-grade ores as existing mines exhaust their reserves—output of most other minerals has expanded. Since 1950, the volume of mineral production has increased more than 300 percent. The sector is currently involved in a $15-billion, five-year investment program, the bulk of which is devoted to coal and gold mine expansion. The result of this expansion should be a significant increase in gold and coal production.

Agriculture

Like other developing countries, South Africa has seen its agricultural sector decline as the mining and manufacturing sectors have grown. Still, nearly one-third of the labor force is in agriculture, although the sector contributed only about 7 percent of the GDP in 1979. By way of contrast, in 1911, one year after the establishment of the Union of South Africa, agriculture's share of goods and services was 22 percent and its share of employment was 64 percent.

The economic disparity between white and black South Africa is most visible in the agricultural sector. The commercial farming sector is dominated by whites, while the subsistence sector consists of African family and traditional communal holdings. Although each sector employs roughly the same number of people, the large white farms of the commercial sector cover nearly six times the land area of the subsistence sector, and the output per commercial worker is almost twenty times the output of a subsistence farmer.

Over the course of this century commercial farming has grown dramatically, transforming South Africa from a food importer in the 1920s into a significant food exporter. Major export commodities have been sugar, maize, wool, fruit, and tobacco. From 1927 through 1976 the value of agricultural exports grew at an annual rate of 6.7 percent, and in 1976 they accounted for 30 percent of South Africa's foreign exchange earnings, excluding those from the sale of gold.

The modernization of agriculture has slashed the manpower requirements of the commercial farming sector. Although the numbers employed on commercial farms increased in absolute terms up to 1971, the increase did not keep pace with the resident population growth in white rural areas. The movement of whites, Coloureds, and Asians away from white farms to the expanding industrial sector of the cities began as early as 1921. This trend was offset before 1960 by the large number of African workers who went to work on white farms. But in the next two decades, as commercial farming became more mechanized, the net movement of Africans was also away from the farms. In many instances, this involved the forced resettlement of African farm laborers to the "homelands."

Subsistence farming is almost entirely confined to the homelands. The productivity of the subsistence sector has remained at a very low level for the past thirty years, and the output per capita has actually fallen during this time. Because agricultural production in the African rural areas cannot support the resident population, many are forced to seek work in white areas as migrant workers. In addition, between 1915 and 1950 nearly one million Africans left the homelands to settle permanently in towns or on commercial farms.

However, notwithstanding these outflows of people, the population of the African rural areas tripled between 1936 and 1970. With subsistence farming output growing much more slowly than the number of people dependent on it, and with virtually no industry in the homelands, per capita income in the various rural areas has remained static and in some cases has fallen. At present the homelands contain more than one-third of South Africa's population, but produce less than 5 percent of the country's goods and services. Any increases in the living standards of rural Africans in the past twenty years have been due to the remittances sent back by migrant workers to their families in the homelands.

Manufacturing

Industrialization has been the dominant economic force of the twentieth century in South Africa. In 1911 industrial production accounted for only 4 percent of South Africa's GDP. By 1940 the manufacturing sector was contributing 12 percent of the country's goods and services. The Second World War, which cut off the economy from foreign sources of industrial goods and thereby opened up domestic markets for South African products, further stimulated industrial development. Industrialization has continued unabated to the present day. During the thirty years from 1950 to 1980, manufacturing output has grown at an annual rate of 7 percent, and today the sector accounts for 22 percent of South Africa's GDP. Urbanization has accompanied industrialization. In 1911 only 25 percent of the population lived in towns; now, including migrant workers, about half of South Africa's population lives in urban areas.

Unlike mining and agriculture, the manufacturing sector is a net importer of goods and services. In fact, in 1975 the ratio of imports to exports in manufacturing was greater than three to one, an indication of the large percentage of foreign-made industrial machinery and equipment imported for use in South Africa.

Government

The South African government has played an important role in the development of the modern economy. In the early days of mining, the state helped establish a system of worker recruitment to ensure a stable supply of cheap labor to that expanding industry. Today, the public sector controls 58 percent of South Africa's fixed capital stock and contributes 26 percent to the country's GDP. Many of the country's largest industrial entities are the government-owned and -run corporations known as parastatals: the Armaments Development and Production Corporation (ARMSCOR), the Electricity Supply Commission (ESCOM), the South African Iron and Steel Industrial Corporation (ISCOR), the Industrial Development Corporation (IDC), to name some of the major ones. The government is especially active in energy development and exploration, operating the South African Coal, Oil, and Gas Corporation (SASOL)* and the Southern Oil Exploration Corporation of South Africa (SOEKOR).

In the past few years the government's role in the economy has come under attack. All three of the recent economic commissions of inquiry (the Wiehahn and Riekert commissions in the field of labor, and the De Kock Commission on monetary policy) have emphasized the need to reduce the degree of state involvement in the economy. For example, the Wiehahn Commission stated:

> The commission accepted the premise that full involvement, participation and sharing in the system of free enterprise by all population groups with as little government intervention as possible would not only give all groups a stake in the system, but would also ensure a common loyalty to both the system and the country.

The Migrant Labor System

Seventy-two percent of South Africa's work force is African. The complex of apartheid laws limiting the residence and movement of Africans has led to the development of a migrant labor system in which many Africans working in urban areas cannot gain permanent residential rights there and are required to return periodically to their homeland areas. In 1970 almost 60 percent of African men employed in the modern urban sector were migrant laborers, and an additional 5 percent commuted daily to white urban areas from nearby homelands. In addition, 35 percent of the African women who worked in white metropolitan areas were migrants or commuters.

Some migrant workers come from neighboring countries, such as Bo-

---

*Officially, SASOL is no longer a parastatal. In October 1979, the government sold 70 percent of SASOL's stock to the general public in order to finance the building of a new synthetic fuel plant (SASOL III). However, SASOL's board is still controlled by government nominees, and for all practical purposes it remains a parastatal.

tswana, Lesotho, and Mozambique, nearly all recruited for work in the mining industry. Since 1970 there has been a substantial reduction in the number of foreign migrants working in South Africa, and by 1978 fewer than 200,000 were still employed in the mines.

Migrant workers earn less, on the average, than their settled African counterparts. And migrant workers who lose their jobs cannot legally remain within white urban areas, except for a short period of time allowed for a job search. By separating husbands from wives and parents from children, the migrant labor system has also placed tremendous strains on the African family.

Economic Aspects of Racial Inequality

White South Africans are wealthier, better educated, have better jobs, and live longer than any other group in South Africa. In descending order of economic well-being come Asians, Coloureds, urban African men, urban African women, and, at the bottom of the economic ladder, rural Africans, who are considerably poorer than anyone else.

There has always been a large gap between the average incomes of whites and blacks in South Africa, and the disparities have not markedly diminished during the course of this century. In 1924 Africans made up 68 percent of the total population and earned only 18 percent of the country's personal income; in 1970 they made up 70 percent of the population and received 19 percent of the income. During the same period the ratio of white to African per capita income rose from 13 to 1, to 15 to 1.

The greatest jump in African wages in modern times came during the first half of the 1970s. African wages grew an average of 6.6 percent per year while the increase in white wages averaged only 1 percent, bringing the African share of total income to almost 24 percent. Still, the gap between white and African income remains large. Jill Nattrass, an economist at the University of Natal, has estimated African per capita income for 1975 at between R200 and R250, compared to a white per capita income of R2,500.

FOREIGN ECONOMIC RELATIONS

Total foreign investment in South Africa at the beginning of 1979 was $26.3 billion, an amount equivalent to 20 percent of the value of South Africa's industrial plant. Of this, approximately 40 percent was direct investment—primarily foreign company ownership in South African subsidiaries or affiliates—and 60 percent was indirect investment—international bank loans and foreign ownership of stock in South African firms.

Five countries—Great Britain, the United States, West Germany, Switzerland, and France—hold 80 percent of the foreign investment in South Africa.

Britain has an estimated 40 percent, or more than $10 billion, the United States 20 percent, West Germany 10 percent, and Switzerland and France approximately 5 percent each. In all, two-thirds of foreign investment in South Africa is held by European countries, 20 percent by the United States, and 15 percent by the rest of the world. A decade earlier Britain had held 60 percent of total foreign investment, the rest of Europe 20 percent, and the United States 15 percent. In dollar amounts, British investment has declined slightly over the past ten years while that of the United States and West Germany has increased.

Foreign investment has been of fundamental importance to the South African economy. It has helped offset the balance of payments deficits that have accompanied every period of rapid growth. And, in recent years, economic growth has become the prime goal of South Africa's economic and political policy. According to the government's economic development program for 1978–87, "a strong and vital economy is one of South Africa's best weapons against the coordinated onslaught being launched against her from outside her borders on the political, economic, military, and psychological fronts."

The economic development program also calls for reduced reliance on foreign capital. This reflects concern that South Africa has been overly dependent on foreign investment in the past, making the economy vulnerable to the effects of domestic political and social unrest on outside investors. For example, the drop in foreign investment following the Sharpeville shootings in 1960 prolonged and deepened the recession of 1959–63, while the reaction of foreign investors to the Soweto riots of 1976 had a similar impact on the 1974–78 downturn.

Direct Investment

At the beginning of 1979 direct foreign investment was $11 billion, with $8 billion held by Europe and $2 billion held by the United States. Britain, which for historic reasons has had the closest economic ties with South Africa, may have as much as $6 billion directly invested in the country. The British figure is equivalent to 10 percent of its worldwide foreign direct investment, while the U.S. total represents approximately 1 percent of its worldwide investment. In the past decade foreign direct investment in South Africa has increased only negligibly in real terms. Fifty percent of this investment is in manufacturing, 25 percent in finance, 15 percent in trade, and less than 10 percent in mining. Many of the world's major automobile and oil companies are represented in the manufacturing sector. The bulk of the investment in finance is held by subsidiaries of British banks, notably Standard Chartered and Barclays Bank International.

U.S. direct investment in South Africa has increased an average of $100 million a year since the mid-1960s, when it stood at $500 million. In the 1970s most new U.S. investment came from the reinvested earnings of South African subsidiaries. Return on all U.S. investment averaged over 15 percent for 1970–74, declined to 9 percent in 1975, and then rose to 14 percent for the period 1976–78. Over 50 percent of U.S. direct investment is held by four companies: Ford, General Motors, Mobil, and Caltex Oil. Altogether, some 350 American companies have subsidiaries in South Africa and over 6,000 do business there.

International Credit

At the beginning of 1979 indirect foreign investment in South Africa was between $13 billion and $15 billion, 80 percent of which consisted of U.S. and European bank loans. The U.S. portion of international bank lending has declined in the last few years, from over $2 billion in 1976 to $1.3 billion at the end of 1979. U.S. banks have also become more reluctant to make long-term loans to South Africa—in 1976, 57 percent of U.S. loans had maturities of more than one year, but by 1980 only 41 percent were long-term. Although it is difficult to determine the precise reasons for this large drop in U.S. lending, the following factors appear to have played a part: (1) a post-Soweto reluctance to lend to a potentially economically and politically unstable South Africa; (2) a general cutting back by U.S. banks on their loan exposure in less-developed countries; (3) increasing domestic pressure on banks not to lend to South Africa; and (4) the reduced need for South Africa to seek international credit because of large balance of payments surpluses generated by higher gold prices.

Foreign government trade credit agencies and the International Monetary Fund also on occasion provide loans or loan guarantees to South Africa. However, U.S. government credit agencies—the Export-Import Bank and the Department of Agriculture Commodity Credit Corporation—have not done business with South Africa since 1978.

Portfolio investment, especially the foreign ownership of South African gold-mining stock, is also an important component of indirect investment. Americans alone hold 25 percent, or $2 billion, of South Africa's total gold-mining stock, and foreign ownership overall is approximately $3 billion.

Gold

Gold continues to be the basic stimulus of economic expansion, which in turn is the magnet for foreign capital. Foreign exchange earnings from gold typically have been equivalent to 30 to 50 percent of merchandise import costs and 25 to 40 percent of the annual domestic investment in industrial facilities. The roller-coaster ride taken by the South African economy in the 1970s is, to some extent, a result of the wide fluctuation in the price of gold. After the decoupling of the dollar from the gold standard in 1971, the price of gold quadrupled by 1974 and South Africa's gold earnings tripled. Led by gold's performance, in terms of both increased foreign exchange earnings and increased domestic investment in the upgrading, expansion, and creation of new gold mines and other mining facilities, South Africa experienced an investment boom capped by a 1974 growth rate of 8.3 percent. The bubble burst when gold dropped from a high of $198 an ounce in 1974 to a low of $103 an ounce in 1976. The decline in gold earnings contributed to South Africa's mid-seventies recession and lower growth rates of 2.9 percent for 1975, 1.3 percent for 1976, and zero in 1977.

In 1978, however, the price of gold once again began to rise, and the new increase in gold earnings offset increased oil and merchandise import costs. Gold earnings more than doubled, from $3 billion to $7 billion in 1979, and the growth rate increased to 2.5 percent in 1978 and 3.7 percent in 1979. In 1980 gold earnings were above $13 billion and the growth rate reached 8 percent.

For the three-year period 1978–80, the rising price of gold was a major force liberating South Africa from balance of payments constraints. Rebounding from substantial payments deficits during the mid-1970s, South Africa registered surpluses of $1.6 billion in 1978 and $3.7 billion in 1979. Nevertheless, South Africa remains concerned that a booming economy will result in an increased import bill that will outweigh gold's huge foreign exchange earnings. Indications are that this is already happening. Although South Africa had a substantial balance of payments surplus in 1980, its imports for the year rose 45 percent over 1979. That plus a stagnation in the level of South Africa's industrial mineral exports because of sluggish world demand, and aggravated by a drop in the price of gold (every decrease of $10 in the gold price reduces South Africa's annual foreign exchange earnings by approximately $220 million), caused the country once again to face a balance of payments deficit in 1981.

Forecasters at the University of Stellenbosch Bureau for Economic Research warned that the price of gold must average $570 during 1981 for a deficit to be avoided. Thus, even though South Africa has benefited tremendously from the large increases in the price of gold, the volatility of the gold price means that the country, despite its concern about overreliance on foreign capital, cannot completely ignore outside investment as a source of funds. This may at least partly explain why Owen Horwood, South Africa's finance minister, actively sought foreign capital during 1980 and 1981, and succeeded in negotiating at least one new Eurocurrency loan of $250 million in late 1980. An additional motivating factor in seeking new loans was South Africa's desire to demonstrate its creditworthiness in the international market.

Trade

South Africa is an "open" economy, that is, its trading activities are so extensive that imports plus exports make up more than 50 percent of its GDP. This means that it is particularly sensitive to global economic conditions. When the world economy booms, South Africa benefits from an improved export market; when the world economy moves into recession, South Africa's economic growth rate suffers. In either case, there is usually a lag of twelve to eighteen months before these global conditions are fully felt in South Africa. Moreover, since the recent trend has been for the price of gold to rise during a recession (and, conversely, fall in response to a healthier world economy or a stronger U.S. dollar), increased gold earnings may balance the drop in South Africa's other export earnings, and the South African economy may have become less susceptible to world economic downturns than it once was.

Five countries—the United States, Great Britain, West Germany, Switzerland, and Japan—account for two-thirds of South Africa's trade. South Africa's principal exports are gold, other minerals, and agricultural goods; its principal imports are oil, machinery, electrical equipment, and transportation equipment. The United States has replaced Great Britain as South Africa's number-one trading partner, having sold $1.5 billion of U.S. goods to South Africa in 1979 and imported $1.9 billion of South African products in the same year. Since 1974, U.S. trade with South Africa as a percentage of U.S. world trade has remained constant at 1 percent. U.S. trade with black Africa in 1979 was significantly greater than its trade with South Africa: $13.7 billion as compared with $3.4 billion. Even excluding the United States's large oil import bill from Nigeria, U.S. trade with black Africa still totaled over $5 billion. Similarly, European trade with black Africa, excluding oil imports from Nigeria, was more than double Europe's $11 billion total trade with South Africa for 1979.

In recent years South Africa has moved to diversify its world markets. Switzerland has become a major export market, principally for diamonds, Krugerrands, and gold bullion, and South Africa has increased its trade with Israel, South Korea, Taiwan, and a number of Latin American countries. Trade with the rest of Africa topped $1 billion for the first time in 1980. However, for political reasons, South Africa's dealings with other African countries remain unacknowledged or "secret," and thus South Africa provides no country-by-country breakdown of its African trade.

Technology

Direct investment has been crucial to the development of several key industries in South Africa: the automotive industry, the oil-refining and petrochemicals industries, the telecommunications and computer industries. Even if high gold prices make direct investment no longer indispensable for the foreign capital it brings, South Africa remains dependent on Western technology for the continued development of many of its most modern and strategic industries.

South Africa's dependence on foreign technology is most marked in the areas of sophisticated electrical equipment, scientific instrumentation, computers, and nuclear energy. The United States dominates the South African computer and scientific instrument markets, and has a substantial share of the petroleum and gas technology market. Of the approximately $1.5 billion of annual U.S. exports to South Africa, 50 to 60 percent are high-technology items, and South Africa spends at least $75 million annually on licensing fees and royalties for the right to use U.S. technological processes in South Africa.

South Africa is, however, a modest exporter of technology. There has been some interest in the United States in the proven but expensive South African coal-gasification technology, as well as in its deep-shaft mining technology. South Africa's other exports are older technologies in agriculture, mining, and manufacturing. They are of particular interest to the states of the southern African region.

ENERGY

South Africa is a major producer and consumer of energy, using eight times more energy per capita than any other country in Africa. This reflects the central role in South Africa's economy of the energy-intensive mining and metallurgical industries. Coal, which South Africa has in abundance, provides nearly 75 percent of the country's energy needs. After Poland, South Africa is the largest supplier of coal to Western Europe, and one of the world's major coal exporters in general, averaging 20 million tons a year and approximately $200 million in foreign exchange. Balancing the desire for foreign exchange against domestic demand and the maintenance of an assured energy supply, South Africa has decided to limit coal exports over the next thirty years to no more than 5 percent of the country's extractable reserves. The government has said it will allow coal exports to rise to 44 million tons a year by 1985, a figure that is supposed to be the export ceiling for the foreseeable future. However, there are already indications that the government may soon increase the ceiling to 60 million tons.

South Africa consumes nearly 20 percent of its energy in the form of electricity, over 85 percent of which is produced by coal-fired power stations. The remainder comes from hydroelectric power and oil-fired power plants. In 1976 South Africa began importing electricity generated by the large Cabora Bassa hydroelectric dam in Mozambique. Until sabotage, allegedly carried out by the Mozambique Resistance Movement, cut the power lines in December 1980, South Africa had been drawing almost 10 percent of its electrical supplies from Cabora Bassa. Since then power has been intermittently restored and cut off, and the South African Electricity Supply Commission has been making up the loss from its own reserve generating capacity. ESCOM has warned, however, that without reliable and continuous service from Cabora Bassa, South Africa could face an electricity shortage by the end of 1981.

Nuclear Power

South Africa is the world's third largest uranium producer, ranking behind the United States and Canada. Although nuclear power makes no present contribution to South Africa's domestic energy requirements, the rising cost of other fuels has made it potentially competitive with conventional power sources. Nuclear power plants cost considerably more to build than coal-fired facilities, but less to operate. This is especially true in the western Cape region, far from South Africa's coal mines, and thus South Africa's first nuclear power plants have been located at Koeberg, near Cape Town. In mid-1975, an official projection put South Africa's reliance on nuclear power at nearly 25 percent of total electrical generating capacity by the year 2000. However, soaring capital costs for nuclear plant construction and the political uncertainty surrounding imports of reactor technology and enriched fuels have already altered this projection.

At present, the United States is withholding all supplies of reactor fuel to South Africa because of South Africa's refusal to sign the Nuclear Non-Proliferation Treaty. South Africa has begun to develop its own capability to process uranium ore into reactor-grade fuel, but the present facility located at Valindaba, near Pretoria, is only a small-scale prototype. Thus, unless South Africa is able to secure access to a foreign source of reactor fuel, the Koeberg nuclear reactors may stand idle for at least the first year following completion in late 1982. If and when they do become operational, it is estimated they will come close to meeting the electricity requirements of the western Cape region. The contribution of nuclear power to South Africa's electricity supply, however, is now estimated at 5 percent by 1985 and only 11 percent by the year 2000.

Oil

South Africa has no known commercial oil or gas deposits. Oil consumption is currently estimated at just over 20 percent of South Africa's total energy usage.* Although this is a relatively low figure (in some major industrialized nations oil accounts for as much as 65 percent of all energy consumed), two of

---

*Oil has been classified by South Africa as a strategic material, and all energy-use data is considered confidential information. Therefore, the estimates made by experts consulted by the Commission are derived from figures that have appeared in the press, oil industry trade journals, and other publications.

South Africa's key sectors—transport and agriculture—are heavily dependent on oil products, thus making reliance on oil imports a major concern of the South African government.

South Africa's cars, buses, and trucks run on imported fuel, and the transport sector in general depends on petroleum products for almost 80 percent of its energy needs. Commercial agriculture requires oil for the operation of farm machinery and irrigation equipment, and uses petroleum-based fertilizers in much of its cultivation. The railroads, on the other hand, are not as dependent on liquid fuel as they once were, because of a recent program to electrify the nation's rail lines.

The industrial sector, the largest consumer of energy, is fairly well insulated against a sudden drop in the availability of oil. More than 90 percent of its energy comes from coal, and this figure can be expected to increase as a result of government measures designed to encourage a shift away from the use of oil.

Before the 1973 OPEC oil embargo against South Africa, which is still in effect, most of South Africa's oil was supplied by Iran and other Persian Gulf producers. From 1973 until 1979, almost 90 percent of South Africa's oil imports came from Iran. With the coming to power of the Ayatollah Khomeini, Iran's oil exports to South Africa were stopped.

Before 1979 it had been argued that the loss of Iranian crude oil would place South Africa in a desperate situation. This did not happen. South Africa was able to survive the loss of its principal supplier without substantial disruption. Prior to the Iranian revolution, South Africa's domestic oil consumption was approximately 250,000 barrels per day (bpd). Yet it is estimated that South Africa imported anywhere from 300,000 to 400,000 bpd of crude oil plus some 15,000 bpd of specialized refined products. Adding South Africa's domestic oil-from-coal production of 5,000 bpd, this amounted to a supply of 320,000 to 420,000 bpd. Even at the lower figure, South Africa had a surplus of 70,000 bpd to be allocated to strategic stockpiles, reexported to neighboring countries, sold as fuel to ships on the Cape sea route, or consumed in the refining and conversion process. In other words, South Africa had considerable flexibility to adjust its oil imports downward and to bargain with suppliers and exporters to arrange new sources of nonembargoed oil.

In addition, the South African government instituted a number of measures to counter the Iranian oil cutoff. It is estimated that fuel prices doubled within six months, with much of the increase taking the form of new taxes to support stockpiles and alternative liquid fuel development programs. Conservation measures were also adopted to help curb consumption. Nevertheless, South Africa's oil import bill, estimated at $2 billion in 1978, probably nearly doubled in 1979, in large part because South Africa was forced to buy its oil on the spot market at much higher prices.

Energy Self-Sufficiency

In the early 1960s, facing increasing political isolation, South Africa began taking measures to reduce the country's dependence on foreign oil and consequent vulnerability to a cutoff of supplies: (1) the establishment of a national oil stockpile; (2) the production of synthetic fuels; (3) oil exploration; (4) energy conservation; and (5) the regulation of multinational oil companies operating in South Africa.

Oil stockpile. South Africa began stockpiling petroleum products in the mid-1960s. Accurate information about the size and location of the present oil reserve is difficult to obtain. Claims have been made that it is as large as 400 to 450 million barrels of oil, but it appears more likely that the actual stockpile is about half that amount. Even so, at current levels of consumption, a 200-to-250-million-barrel reserve would supply South Africa's oil needs for two and a half years without further conservation measures. Strict conservation plus increased production of synthetic fuels could significantly extend the life of the stockpile.

South Africa has recently announced its intention to increase stockpile amounts. South African law also requires each of the major oil companies to maintain separate thirteen-week inventory reserves of oil, and a twelve-month supply of lubricants, catalysts, and other chemicals used in refinery operations.

Synthetic fuels. South Africa is a world leader in the development and application of oil-from-coal technology, running one of the world's few successful coal-gasification programs. The first plant, SASOL I, has been in operation since 1955, producing approximately 5,000 bpd of gasoline, or about 2 percent of domestic consumption. Although SASOL-produced gasoline was originally far more expensive than that refined from imported crude oil, in recent years it has become competitive in price. In fact, after years of operating at a loss, SASOL announced a profit for the first time in 1978.

In 1974 the South African government approved construction of a second SASOL plant more than three times the size of SASOL I, at a total estimated cost of over $3 billion. In addition, the government announced the construction of a third plant in 1979, planned as a duplicate of SASOL II, to be completed by 1983. SASOL III will cost another $4 billion.

Estimates of the SASOL plants' contribution to meeting South Africa's oil needs vary widely. One view holds that the coal-gasification plants will not even keep up with the growing oil needs of an expanding South African economy. This minimum estimate puts SASOL's 1982 contribution at 13 percent of domestic oil consumption, with the figure rising to at most 25 percent when SASOL III becomes operational. However, if one assumes that conservation and other measures will slow the growth of oil consumption, then SASOL I and II may be able to meet 20 percent or more of the country's oil requirements, and all three plants may be able to meet almost 40 percent of the country's oil needs. The South African government claims that the three SASOL plants will be capable of producing a total of 120,000 bpd of liquid fuel, or 48 percent of net domestic needs at 1978 consumption levels.

In addition to its SASOL programs, South Africa is also experimenting with the production of alternative fuel supplies such as methanol and ethanol. However, the large-scale development of these synthetic fuels is not now considered a priority item, and they are unlikely to make a significant contribution to South Africa's energy needs in the near future.

Oil exploration. For the past fifteen years the South African government has conducted an extensive search for oil within its borders. In 1965 it established the Southern Oil Exploration Corporation of South Africa to oversee the search for oil. SOEKOR is responsible for both leasing drilling concessions to foreign firms and developing its own drilling capability. The onshore search for oil has been unsuccessful. More than two hundred holes were sunk between 1965 and 1978 by SOEKOR and private companies. Traces of gas and oil in isolated pockets were the only result. In fact, prospects for land-based oil discoveries were so unpromising that onshore drilling was abandoned in 1978, despite political pressure to continue. There was some possibility, in late 1980, that onshore test drilling might soon resume, this time in northern Namibia.

In 1972, SOEKOR launched a major offshore search for oil. It has had to depend heavily on multinational oil companies and American drilling companies to provide the necessary technology for offshore exploration. In 1978 some offshore oil was found thirty miles off South Africa's coast near the town of Mossel Bay. Recently, another offshore find of natural gas was made, which South Africa claims is the best strike to date. It is not clear, however, how large the deposits are, or whether they are commercially exploitable. Up to the end of 1980, fifty holes had been sunk offshore and the combined cost of the onshore and offshore exploration since 1965 had exceeded $280 million. SOEKOR's new five-year budget provides it with $550 million for continued offshore drilling.

Energy conservation. It has been estimated that South Africa could reduce oil consumption by 10 to 15 percent with a program of voluntary conservation, and that a determined rationing program could cut consumption by 20 to 25 percent without crippling the economy. Cuts by industry, government, car owners, and overland transport would provide most of the reduction. Another possibility for saving imported crude oil would be to reduce or eliminate the sale of oil and gasoline to neighboring African states and to ships calling at South African ports. However, many of the products sold, especially the bunker oil for ships, are heavy distillates that South Africa does not need but that are necessarily produced by refineries along with the lighter-grade diesel fuels and gasolines used domestically. Moreover, the sale of bunker oil is important in maintaining South Africa's position in international shipping and its trade ties with the outside world.

Regulation of oil companies. Five foreign oil companies—British Petroleum, Mobil, Caltex, Shell, and Total—control more than 85 percent of petro-leum-refining operations in South Africa. The South African government has established a stringent set of regulations to ensure that these companies act in South Africa's national interest. Pursuant to the Petroleum Producers Act of 1977, the minister of economic affairs has the authority "to regulate the purchase, sale, or use of any petroleum product." In addition, oil refiners can be required to set aside oil for purchase by the government for its strategic oil stockpiles. The government also has the authority, under the National Supplies Procurement Act, to make priority purchases of oil products for the South African military. And, under the South African Official Secrets Act, foreign oil companies may not disclose information regarding the sale or distribution of oil within South Africa.

Universal Oil Embargo

It is frequently said that South Africa's principal point of vulnerability is its dependence on imported oil, and that oil sanctions may be the only effective pressure on South Africa available to the international community, short of total economic sanctions. A full oil cutoff, it is argued, would be relatively painful to South Africa but relatively painless for its major trading partners in the West. Measures would have to be taken, however, to ensure that those countries that rely on South Africa for most of their oil supplies—Botswana, Lesotho, and Zimbabwe especially— would continue to receive their necessary imports.

Would such an embargo, even if universally observed, achieve its first-stage objective of creating economic stagnation and hardship? In 1963, a report by the Carnegie Endowment for International Peace expressed doubt that an oil embargo would bring about desired changes in South Africa. The report assumed that with no deliveries and only a six-month inventory, the country's economy could function near its normal level for two years. At the time of the report, oil provided only 12 percent of South Africa's energy needs, a figure that has now almost doubled. Despite this increase, South Africa's ability to withstand an oil embargo has grown. It now has a two-year strategic stockpile and produces increasing amounts of oil from coal.

The available evidence indicates that South Africa's vulnerability to even an effective oil embargo is decreasing with time. The combination of stockpiles, rationing, conservation, and alternative fuels should be able to keep vital South African industries and essential security and administrative machinery functioning for years. An embargo implemented after the mid-1980s would probably have little chance of significantly damaging the country's economy. **143**

ECONOMIC GROWTH

South Africa's economy has grown dramatically over the course of this century. Between 1950 and 1979 South Africa maintained an overall growth rate, adjusted for inflation, of 4.4 percent annually. To a large extent, this steady growth rate was achieved by the use of cheap black labor. Modern sector employers have effectively kept labor costs down by replacing white workers with blacks in the unskilled and semiskilled job categories. This substitution process, combined with increases in labor productivity, has allowed wages for both groups to increase without cutting into profit margins.

For most developed countries, a growth record like South Africa's would be cause for rejoicing. Yet the South African economy needs a growth rate of more than 5 percent per year to create enough jobs to accommodate its growing population. African unemployment is now about 16 percent in urban areas and about 20 percent in the homelands. South African economist Charles Simkins has estimated that overall African unemployment may be as high as 26 percent, and has calculated that between 1960 and 1977 the number of unemployed Africans almost doubled from 1.2 million to 2.3 million.

Even the South African government's substantially lower figures are pessimistic. According to the official economic development program, with an annual growth rate of 3.6 percent (the actual average for 1970–77), African unemployment will increase in ten years from 13 percent to over 26 percent. With a growth rate of 4.5 percent, African unemployment will still rise, according to the government, to 18.7 percent. A growth rate of 5.3 percent will keep the unemployment *rate* constant, but even so the *absolute* numbers of unemployed will continue to rise with the rising population. Simkins estimates that a growth rate of 6.7 percent is needed to stabilize the number of unemployed. South Africa's economy grew by 8 percent in 1980, but that was in large measure a result of the unprecedented gold price rise, an occurrence that is not likely to be repeated every year.

The steady growth of unemployment over the past twenty years, during a time of fairly regular economic growth, is an ominous sign. Not only is it an indication of the large number of new workers (estimated at 230,000 a year) that South Africa must strive to employ each year, but it is a reflection of the inability of the homeland economies to provide additional productive employment. Unemployment is likely to grow larger except under the very best economic circumstances.

Ironically, at the same time South Africa faces a growing labor surplus, it also faces a serious shortage of skilled labor—a shortage that poses perhaps the greatest threat to continued economic growth. Professor Gideon Jacobs, director of the Graduate School of Business Administration at Witwatersrand University, has estimated that industry has been unable to fill more than 100,000 jobs because of the lack of skilled workers. In a recent survey by the Natal Chamber of Commerce, a third of all respondents said that the skilled labor shortage was "the major factor limiting increased output." Forecasts of a skilled labor shortfall of 750,000 workers by the end of 1990 have been made.

This shortage is a legacy of the apartheid system and its inadequate educational and job-training programs for blacks. Even without the legal and other institutional barriers to the employment of black South Africans in many of the more skilled and professional jobs, there are not nearly enough qualified and properly trained blacks to begin to alleviate the skilled labor shortage. Thus, South Africa faces a chronic dilemma. Economic growth is vital for the improved economic prospects and general upward job mobility of blacks, but rapid expansion may be hindered by a lack of blacks trained to fill key skilled jobs.

With the black population growing at 2.6 percent a year, compared to a white population increase of 1.4 percent, the ratio of black workers to white in the workplace will continue to increase as the modern sector expands. The consumer purchasing power of blacks will also grow, as will the reliance of South Africa's economy on that purchasing power. One estimate puts the 1980 disposable income of Africans at more than R9 billion, or nearly 40 percent of the consumer market. The retailers of Johannesburg's central business district already depend on black customers, almost all from Soweto, for more than 50 percent of their total sales.

This is not to say, though, that growth, even phenomenal growth, will necessarily remove the economic disparities between whites and blacks. The wage gains made by blacks during the past two years, for example, have already been eroded by the accelerating rate of inflation. South Africa's consumer price index (CPI) rose 16 percent during 1980, and the CPI for lower-income groups went up 20 percent during the same period, pushed by a 30 percent increase in the cost of basic foodstuffs. In the early part of the century there was a similar disparity between English and Afrikaner South Africans. And despite steady economic growth, it was only with the acquisition of political power in 1948 that the Afrikaners began their rise toward economic equality with the English-speaking population. This was accomplished through Afrikaner domination of the civil service and the parastatals and the deliberate favoring by an Afrikaner government of Afrikaner financial institutions.

One recent result of growth has been an increasing spread in economic well-being among Africans. In the past ten years urban Africans have been able to advance, albeit slowly, into some semiskilled, skilled, clerical, and even professional positions,* while rural Africans have lost ground economically. By the mid-seventies, the ratio of African urban to rural income was more than eight to one, a figure that approaches the overall white-African wage disparity.

To some extent there is a growing recognition within the government that

---

*In 1977, 90 percent of the African work force classified as being in technical and professional occupations were employed as teachers or nurses.

the ideology of separate development must be accommodated to economic realities. This is reflected in the acceptance of the need for a larger pool of skilled black labor permanently resident in urban areas, improved education for blacks to create these skills, and the abolition of statutory job reservation.

Economic growth has helped to break down some racial barriers in the urban industrial society. But whether growth alone will result in black political emancipation is a matter of controversy. Harry Oppenheimer, chairman of the Anglo-American Corporation of South Africa and a leading exponent of the "growth hypothesis," has repeatedly argued that the growth of a modern, free-enterprise economy will modify South Africa's social and political structure in fundamental ways and undermine apartheid. Others counter that black living standards have not risen appreciably in the first century of capitalist development in South Africa, and that the stark economic and political inequalities between whites and blacks have not been diminished by economic growth and may well be enhanced by it.

The prospect of economic-growth raises other questions. Some members of the Afrikaner establishment worry that Oppenheimer's thesis is correct. They are concerned that growth will not only undermine traditional racial barriers in the workplace, but will also weaken Afrikaner political control. On the other side, some blacks see growth within the context of separate development as a means by which the white establishment hopes to divide the black community: middle class against working class, and both against the rural poor.

Wherever the truth lies in this debate, the whole concept of economic growth has increasingly taken on political overtones. The central economic issue is now whether the economy can expand sufficiently to absorb a rapidly growing population, and whether blacks as well as whites will benefit from that growth.

Chapter 8
The Homelands

In the running controversy over apartheid, the "homelands" are often reduced to political abstractions—theoretical constructions viewed either as the basis for a new, equitable racial order in South Africa or as devices to assure continued white domination and exploitation of Africans. Often overlooked is the reality behind the rhetoric. Millions of Africans live in the homelands and millions more shuttle between the homelands and "white" South Africa. Homeland economies strain to rise above subsistence levels. Homeland governments take shaky command of local affairs, while their leaders grope for coherent policies toward South Africa and struggle with the separate-development design in which they find themselves caught.

Until the 1960s the homelands—or, as they were formerly known, the reserves—attracted little attention. Economically they were seen as irrelevant backwaters existing in the shadow of a dynamic, industrialized society. Politically they were regarded as peripheral areas observing the larger South African drama from the sidelines. Sophisticated urban Africans tended to look disdainfully on the homelands, with their traditional tribal social systems and retarded economic development. Most whites simply ignored them. But no longer can anyone concerned about South Africa's future disregard the homelands.

THE LAND AND THE PEOPLE

Except for the Transkei, the ten African "homelands" created by the government of South Africa bear little resemblance to the original African homelands. Rather, they are the relatively small areas of African occupation that remained after the military and political defeats of the various African communities and kingdoms in the eighteenth and nineteenth centuries and after adjustments based on two laws passed by the South African Parliament in the twentieth century. The first of these laws, the 1913 Native Land Act, assigned 10 percent of South Africa's total area for exclusive African occupation. At the same time, by prohibiting Africans outside the Cape from purchasing land outside the reserves, it ensured that the remaining 90 percent would eventually belong to non-Africans. The second law, the Native Trust and Land Act of 1936, authorized the addition of enough acreage to the reserves to increase the Africans' share of the country to about 14 percent. These acquisitions have yet to be fully implemented, and the homelands—including those designated as "independent"—now comprise 13 percent of the total land area of South Africa.

Only one homeland—tiny Qwaqwa, with a population of little more than 50,000—consists of a single, contiguous territory. Of the others, the Transkei, which approximates fairly closely the ancestral land of its present occupants, the Xhosa, most nearly approaches geopolitical coherence; it is made up of one large area plus two adjacent smaller territories. For the most part, the homelands consist of scattered and fragmented pieces of land varying greatly in size. According to a government map, the most fragmented homeland is the Zulu homeland, KwaZulu. In 1975 it was scattered among forty-eight major pieces of land and scores of smaller tracts. Bophuthatswana was next with nineteen major pieces of land, followed by the Ciskei with fifteen, Lebowa with fourteen, Gazankulu with four, the Transkei, Venda, KaNgwane, and Ndebele each with three, and then Qwaqwa with one.

Although the homelands are generally thought of as rural, they have a relatively dense population. Based on official figures, the density in the "white" or common areas of South Africa is about 30 persons a square mile, but in the homelands it is more than 120. The homeland density ranges from a high of more than 170 a square mile in KwaZulu to a low of about 60 in Bophuthatswana.

These figures refer to de facto populations—the persons actually living in the homelands. Given South Africa's policy of regarding all Africans as citizens of a homeland, no matter where they actually live, the official totals for homeland populations are far larger than the de facto figures. For South Africa as a whole, preliminary results of the 1980 census indicate an African population of 19.8 million.* This total, the official figures indicate, is divided into 9.5 million, or 48 percent, resident in the white areas and 10.3 million, or 52 percent, in the homelands. Africans counted in the white areas include both those living there permanently and migrant workers. Africans classed as homeland dwellers include sizable numbers who commute daily to work in the white areas.

---

*The figures used here are based on the preliminary 1980 census results for South Africa proper and the nonindependent homelands, plus 1980 estimates for the three independent homelands.

From the government's point of view, the 1980 figures represent an improvement. The 1970 census found 52.5 percent of Africans in white areas. But the 1980 census results give the government little cause for complacency. For one thing, the figures for Africans in white areas do not include those living there illegally. It is widely believed that a more complete count of Africans in both white areas and the homelands would show the African population about equally divided between the two sectors, perhaps approaching 11 million in each. That is not an impressive achievement for the government after two decades of promoting the homelands policy. Moreover, the number of Africans in the common areas has continued to increase. Only the *rate* of increase has been held down by separate development, with the African population of the common areas growing at an annual rate of 1.5 percent, compared with 5 percent in the homelands. The faster homeland growth reflects both expulsions from white areas and boundary changes made to bring concentrations of Africans within homeland borders.

THE HOMELAND ECONOMIES

South Africa has long had a dual economy: a relatively advanced industrial economy, employing both black and white labor, alongside a rural subsistence sector. Labor has flowed from the subsistence sector to the industrial sector.

Under this pattern, economic stagnation in the homelands was of minimal concern to whites, and under the most cynical, callous formulation of separate development, it still is. The overriding aim, according to this concept, should be to reduce the number of Africans in the common areas to a minimum regardless of the state of the homeland economies. This would be achieved by wider use of migrant and commuter labor, population resettlement, and boundary changes between homelands and common areas that would maximize the homeland populations. To some extent, the homelands would simply serve as dumping grounds for Africans not essential to the industrial sector of the economy.

That version of separate development has not, however, been the one promoted by the Nationalist leadership over the years. At its most ambitious level, as articulated by former prime minister Hendrik Verwoerd, the policy calls for genuine racial separation between white and African based on separate territories. If such a goal is to be more than idle fantasy, the economic growth rates of the homelands would have to be high enough to absorb not only the indigenous population increase but at least some of the Africans working in the common areas. Verwoerd was the last major political leader to espouse this ideal. (He believed—erroneously, as it turned out—that 1978 would be the year when the flow of blacks back to the homelands would begin.) Today only fringe groups cling to his vision. A more modest formulation of separate development seeks to develop the homeland economies to the point where they can absorb all or most of their new potential workers while leaving largely untouched those Africans already employed in white South Africa. This is the present goal of the National party.

Whatever the shadings and permutations of their policy goals over the years, South Africa's leaders have found it extremely difficult to modify the traditional relationship between the peripheral subsistence sector and the industrialized core. Indeed, the proportions of income generated in the homelands and in the common areas have barely changed since the mid-1950s. In fiscal 1954–55 the gross national product of the homelands constituted only 2.5 percent of South Africa's total GNP. As of 1973–74, more than a decade after the homelands policy had become a priority goal of policy makers, this percentage remained almost unchanged. Thus, in the two decades since 1954 the economic growth rate of the homelands had only just kept pace with the growth rate in the common areas. Although accurate statistics are not available for the 1975–80 period, the growth rates in the homelands possibly exceeded the growth rates in the common areas. At best, however, the gross national product of the homelands remained less than 5 percent of the South African total by 1980.

The homelands are poor. In 1975 per capita gross domestic product ranged from a low of R49 in KaNgwane to a high of R108 in Bophuthatswana, which has a sizable mining industry. The average was R73. In the common areas of South Africa the per capita GDP in 1975 was R1,546. If the homelands statistics accurately reflected the living standards of the populations, starvation and misery would be worse than is actually the case. The incomes of many homeland residents are supplemented, however, by the earnings of migrant workers, and this income makes the difference between starvation and survival for many. The R73 average per capita income from sources in the homelands in 1975 increased to about R300 when the earnings of migrants were included. Thus, only a quarter of the income earned by the homeland population was generated in the homelands. The rest came from the other parts of South Africa.

This dependence is increasing. In 1960, 55.4 percent of the homelands' gross national product was generated by workers employed outside the homeland boundaries. By 1970 this had risen to 69 percent, and by 1976 to 71.6 percent. It is scarcely an exaggeration to say that the homeland "economies" are really located in the common areas of South Africa. The contribution of migrant-labor earnings to the GNP of the homelands reflects the fundamental inability of the homeland economies to provide paid employment for more than a fraction of their working-age populations.

A dominant trend in recent decades has been accelerating growth in the number of homeland-based Africans employed in the common areas. In 1951, 503,000 male workers left the reserves on short-term labor contracts. By 1960 this number had increased to 651,000, and by 1970 it had spurted to almost a million. By 1980 the total was between 1.4 million and 2 million workers—a clear indication of the continuing inability of the homelands to support their growing populations.

A newer trend has been an expansion in the ranks of commuter workers, Africans who work in industry in the common areas but reside in their homelands. Between 1970 and 1979, the total increased from 250,000 to 725,000. This growth has been fostered by government policy emphasizing industries located near the homeland borders, mass transportation, and a redrawing of homeland borders to bring them closer to the industrial centers. For example, in Durban, as a result of boundary changes, black workers formerly resident in white areas now live within KwaZulu and commute daily to work.

Because of the growth of commuter labor, all of the homelands except the Transkei, which is not located near any major industrial centers, have more of their residents in industrial employment in the common areas than in jobs within their borders. Moreover, this situation seems certain to persist. Between 1973 and 1975 only 28.4 percent of the new African entrants to the job market in the homelands managed to obtain employment there. The Transkei was able to place only 15.2 percent of its new job seekers in paid employment. Only Venda and KaNgwane, two of the smaller homelands, were able to find employment for more than half of the new laborers. Seven homelands were able to employ fewer than 40 percent of the potential new workers. A significant proportion of the new job seekers who failed to find jobs in the commuter or migrant labor markets remained unemployed in the homelands or took illegal work in the common areas.

Excluding the elusive "illegals," about a third of the homeland labor force work in the common areas as migrants, another third work as commuter labor in the border areas, and the remaining third are either employed in the homelands or, more likely, jobless. Unemployment in the homelands has not been accurately measured, but reasonable estimates place it at 20 percent to 30 percent of the total homeland work force.

A number of circumstances help explain the sluggish economic pace of the homelands. Industry in South Africa developed initially around the ports of Cape Town, Port Elizabeth, and Durban and in the mineral-rich areas of the Witwatersrand, and growth has continued to concentrate there. Even today about three-quarters of the total South African income is generated in these four regions.

The homelands themselves are poor in resources. With the exception of Bophuthatswana, they lack readily exploitable minerals. The major mineral deposits are all located in the common areas of South Africa. Although a few homeland areas, such as parts of the Transkei, have considerable agricultural potential, much of the rest consists of low-rainfall areas with limited capacity for raising crops. In the Ciskei and KwaZulu the land is badly overgrazed and eroded and overpopulation hampers the development of large-scale commercial agriculture. The homelands cannot feed themselves and must import food from farms in the common areas.

Traditional tribal culture also inhibits economic development. Communal land tenure, which allocates to all members of the group a section of the land for cultivation, often characterizes tribal organization. This system does not recognize and reward efficient producers, and thus does not promote optimum use of scarce resources. Moreover, the close relationship between the economy and the social organization in tribal societies delays the acceptance of economic innovations because such changes disturb age-old patterns.

While the white economy serves as a major source of income for the homelands, the structural relationships between the white and black economies have contributed to the underdevelopment of the latter. The migration of African workers to the white areas has drained the homelands of the most productive segment of their populations. At the same time, the insecurity that plagues Africans in the white areas as a result of influx control and expulsions makes them unwilling to risk severing all ties with the homelands. This has hampered the development of efficient homeland agriculture by causing members of the homeland group who live in the common areas to hold on to land rights.

One consequence of the low level of economic activity in the homelands is almost total dependence on the balance of South Africa for funds to pay for government and public services. Even if expenditures of the South African Railways and Harbours Administration and the former Department of Posts and Telegraphs (now the Department of Posts and Telecommunications) are excluded, the contribution of the homelands to their public expenditures was only 14 percent in 1972–73, 11 percent in 1974–75, and about 12 percent for the 1975–80 period. If a pro rata share of national defense and other common services is taken into account, the homelands' contribution drops to 5 percent for the 1970s. Not only is there no overall trend toward self-sufficiency but also no individual homeland comes close to balancing its budget without South African central government assistance. The three independent homelands continue to receive substantial South African aid.

Despite continuing financial dependency on South Africa, an important change is occurring in the form of such aid. South Africa is reducing its direct expenditures in the homelands and increasing its subsidies to the homeland governments, which means that a growing proportion of public expenditure now comes under the control of the local authorities. Typically, South Africa's undesignated grants to the Ciskei government rose from 16 percent of the Ciskei budget in 1971–72 to 34 percent in 1979–80. Clearly, South Africa's purpose is to strengthen the homeland governments and increase their legitimacy in the eyes of their citizens and the rest of the world.

This approach appears doomed to failure. The economic foundations of the

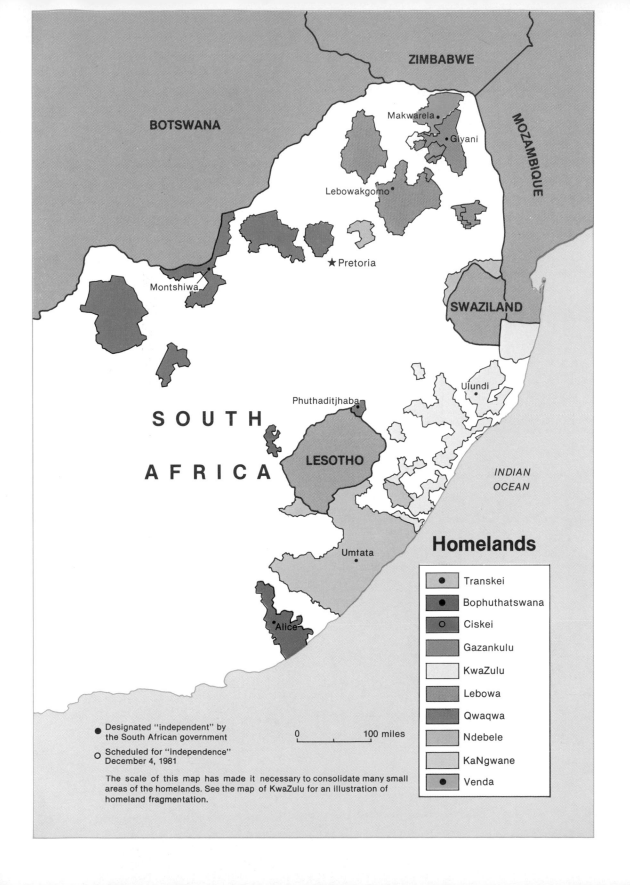

BOTSWANA

ZIMBABWE

MOZAMBIQUE

Makwarela •

• Giyani

Lebowakgomo •

★ Pretoria

Montshiwa

SWAZILAND

S O U T H

Phuthaditjhaba

Ulundi •

A F R I C A

LESOTHO

INDIAN
OCEAN

Umtata •

Homelands

Alice •

•	Transkei
•	Bophuthatswana
○	Ciskei
	Gazankulu
	KwaZulu
	Lebowa
	Qwaqwa
	Ndebele
	KaNgwane
•	Venda

• Designated "independent" by
the South African government

○ Scheduled for "independence"
December 4, 1981

0   100 miles

The scale of this map has made it necessary to consolidate many small
areas of the homelands. See the map of KwaZulu for an illustration of
homeland fragmentation.

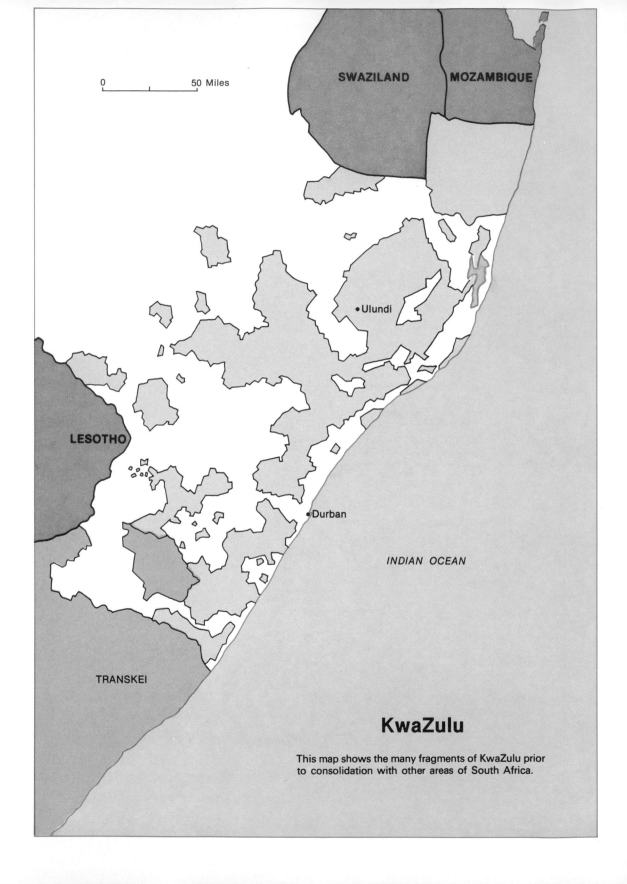

0   50 Miles

SWAZILAND   MOZAMBIQUE

•Ulundi

LESOTHO

•Durban

INDIAN OCEAN

TRANSKEI

KwaZulu

This map shows the many fragments of KwaZulu prior
to consolidation with other areas of South Africa.

policy of separate development are so weak that they undermine the whole concept. Given the experience of the past two decades, it is unrealistic to anticipate that the growth rate of the homelands will accelerate sufficiently to reduce the number of Africans living and working in the common areas. At best the homelands may be able to increase the proportion of new workers employed within their borders.

Whatever economic grounds may have existed for viewing separate development as a workable policy have thus evaporated. The most that can be said is that government policies have slowed the increase in the African population in the common areas. But this has been achieved not through the creation of more attractive opportunities in the homelands but by compulsory resettlement schemes, the acceptance of massive unemployment in the homelands, and an increase in migrant and commuter labor.

For both black and white the gap between illusion and reality, between promise and performance, has become too great to be ignored. The government, while continuing the policy of separate development, has begun to recognize the impossibility of creating ten viable homeland economies. Many urban and rural Africans will remain a permanent component of the population of the common areas. And homeland self-government, or even independence, will not end the economic ties between the territories and the peoples of the former unitary state of South Africa. The homelands will continue to lack a fundamental autonomy based on viable economies. Structurally they will remain part of the South African system, their economic fortunes linked inextricably to South Africa.

HOMELAND POLITICS

In the eyes of many, homeland politics are largely irrelevant—a sideshow featuring debates over relatively minor issues while the real struggle over the role of blacks in South Africa rages in the main arena. To some extent, that is true. Nevertheless, as South Africa presses ahead with separate development, the homelands governments increasingly affect the lives of Africans. Moreover, the governments and their leaders are themselves involved in the debate. Thus, no examination of South Africa today can omit the Nationalists' efforts to devolve political power to the homeland governments and the response of the African leaders.

South Africa has guided the constitutional development of the homelands at every step. The pattern has been to start with the existing traditional systems of chiefs and councillors and to graft onto them new administrative organs and partially elected assemblies. Table 8-1 summarizes the political status of the homelands as of 1980.

The process leading toward increased self-rule has three stages. Except

TABLE 8-1.

Homeland	Constitutional Status/Date	Political Leader	Ethnic Group
Transkei	Independent/1976	Chief George Matanzima*	Xhosa
Bophuthatswana	Independent/1977	Chief Lucas Mangope	Tswana
Venda	Independent/1979	Chief Patrick Mphephu	Venda
Ciskei	Self-governing/1972	Chief Lennox Sebe	Xhosa
Gazankulu	Self-governing/1972	Prof. Hudson Ntsanwisi	Shangaan/Tsonga
Lebowa	Self-governing/1972	Cedric Phatudi	North Sotho
Qwaqwa	Self-governing/1974	Chief Kenneth Mopeli	South Sotho
KwaZulu	Self-governing/1978	Chief Gatsha Buthelezi	Zulu
KaNgwane	Pre-self-governing/1975	—	Swazi
Ndebele	Pre-self-governing/1977	—	Ndebele

*George Matanzima recently succeeded his brother Kaiser as prime minister and political leader in the Transkei.

for the Transkei, which has a long history of self-government, the initial stage entails the creation of the first "national" political institutions. These consist of traditional chiefs and councillors transmuted into appointed territorial assemblies with sharply restricted powers and a small number of departments for basic government services. So far eight of the homelands have passed through this stage of development en route to self-government status, while two homelands are still classed as "pre-self-governing."

The second stage is self-government. The councillors become ministers and the administrative departments increase in number, size, and authority. A parliamentary system begins to take shape, with the cabinets nominally responsible to the partially elected and partially appointed legislative assemblies. During this stage South Africa retains direct control of security, economic policy, and foreign relations and can veto all decisions taken by the homeland governments. Nonetheless, the homeland governments do enjoy considerable de facto autonomy in local affairs.

The third and final stage of the constitutional process as envisioned by the South African government is independence. At the start of 1981 three of the homelands held this status, and the Ciskei had decided to accept independence in due course. Although several homeland leaders have expressed unalterable opposition to independence, it seems probable that some others will accept it eventually.

How real is such independence? Judging from the three homelands already in that category, it is genuine in terms of the abstract criteria for sovereignty accepted in international law: established boundaries, a settled population, and a government in effective control of its territory. But looked at pragmatically, it is a hollow proposition. A wide range of economic, technical, and defense agreements give South Africa powerful authority in the affairs of the independent homelands. And the homelands' overwhelming economic dependence on South Africa also drastically limits their autonomy.

The political institutions of the homelands are a compromise between Western concepts of representation and traditional African tribal government. All the homelands have unicameral legislatures in which appointed members—mostly chiefs or their representatives—play a central role. In 1980 the legislatures of the homelands were divided this way:

TABLE 8-2.

Homeland	Elected Members	Nominated Members	Total
Transkei	75	75	150
Bophuthatswana	48	52	100
Venda	42	42	84
Ciskei	22	29	51
Gazankulu	26	42	68
KaNgwane	0	36	36
KwaZulu	55	81	136
Lebowa	40	60	100
Qwaqwa	20	40	60
Ndebele	—	—	—

The representation of the chiefs has tended to decline after the achievement of self-government. For example, in 1963 the Transkei legislative assembly had sixty-four appointed members and only forty-five elected members. Similarly, Bophuthatswana had forty-eight appointed and twenty-four elected members in 1972, while in 1975 Venda had forty-two appointed and eighteen elected legislators. Nevertheless, all the homeland legislative bodies continue to be dominated by chiefs and headmen. Moreover, in several of the homelands, including KwaZulu, the constitution requires that the chief minister be a chief.

It is theoretically possible for an individual with only limited popular support to become chief minister because of strong backing from the traditional leaders. The only clear-cut example of this, however, was the elevation of Chief Patrick Mphephu to the chief ministership and then to the presidency of the independent homeland of Venda even though his rival attained a clear majority in elections. But Venda is the exception. Usually the chief ministers have been leaders who enjoyed both the support of the chiefs and a considerable popular following. Chief Lucas Mangope of Bophuthatswana, for example, had the backing of the tribal leaders when self-government was attained in 1972 but also won twelve of the sixteen contested assembly seats and all eight of the uncontested seats. Chief Gatsha Buthelezi is even more dominant in KwaZulu. He commands virtually unanimous support among both elected and appointed legislators.

Personalities and tribal roles carry more weight in homeland politics than parties and ideologies do. The most powerful leaders have been those who combined traditional rank with charismatic appeal or skill in bureaucratic politics. Chief Buthelezi has used his base as the leader of a traditional clan and a member of the Zulu royal family to build a strong political following in both KwaZulu and the common areas. While his opposition to separate development has undoubtedly contributed to his popularity, his support in KwaZulu is not primarily a reflection of this opposition. Chief Kaiser Matanzima of the Transkei has generally gone along with separate development, but he has nonetheless succeeded in using his position as chief of an important Xhosa clan—coupled with control of public resources and bestowal of patronage—to rally wide backing.

Although the rates of political participation in the homelands do not compare unfavorably with some other countries—including the United States—voting has tended to fall off after self-government has been achieved. In the Transkei, for example, 68.3 percent of the electorate voted in 1963 but only 43.5 percent did in 1976. Such declines reflect a de-emphasis on participation by both the South African and the homeland governments. South Africa has regarded the initial self-government elections as important evidence of the legitimacy of its race policy and consequently has worked hard to turn out the vote on these occasions. But once the governments are functioning, South Africa's concern about popular participation diminishes. Similarly, the homeland rulers, whose positions are based in large part on support from the traditional elites, lack the incentive to build mass political organizations or to encourage participation.

One exception to this trend is the policy of the KwaZulu leadership. In KwaZulu an effort has been made to increase participation through the creation of Inkatha, a mass political and cultural organization (see chapter 9). In the other homelands, by way of contrast, political parties have usually emerged from the membership of the legislative assemblies and have not sought broad support.

Incumbents tend to increase their electoral support and become entrenched. Again, events in the Transkei are illustrative. In the first Transkei elections, in 1963, Chief Kaiser Matanzima's Transkei National Independence party was overwhelmingly defeated in the voting for the elected members of the legislature by the anti-separate-development Democratic party, which won twenty-nine of the forty-five seats. But because of strong support from the chiefs in the assembly, Matanzima became chief minister. Since then he has steadily increased his popular support, capturing seventy-one of the seventy-five elected seats in the expanded assembly in 1976. The explanation is that Matanzima has used his position as head of the government to consolidate his support through the use of patronage and other official prerogatives. Such powers are formidable in the homelands, since government expenditures are the mainstay of the economy. Indeed, only one major homeland chief minister has been removed from power since 1963.

In assessing the legitimacy of separate development, perhaps the most telling aspect of homeland politics is the almost total lack of participation by urban Africans. They were to have been compensated for their lack of a political voice in South Africa proper by the homeland ballot. Although recent statistics are not available, fewer than 10 percent of the urban Africans eligible to vote in homeland elections are believed to exercise the right. A survey undertaken by the Quail Commission, an independent body charged with assessing the feasibility of independence for the Ciskei, confirmed that the overwhelming majority of urban Xhosa did not identify in any way with the politics of the homelands. On the contrary, they almost unanimously rejected homeland politics as a substitute for political rights in the areas where they lived and worked. In the most recent Bophuthatswana election, only 3 percent of the eligible Tswana living in the urban areas of South Africa voted.

None of this should be taken to mean that some of the current homeland leaders do not have substantial support. Many would probably retain office without the ability to dispense favors and to control the electoral process. On the other hand, political activity is now constrained by the pervasive influence of South Africa, making outcomes of open political contests in the homelands in which the African National Congress and other groups were free to participate difficult to predict. Moreover, even when chief ministers and their governments are chosen in relatively free elections, the resulting regimes are not models of democracy. The legislative assemblies hold brief sessions in which debate is largely perfunctory and important decisions are made by elite groups.

BLACK ATTITUDES TOWARD SEPARATE DEVELOPMENT

All important homeland leaders have rejected South African racism, but their attitudes toward separate development vary widely. Some, including the Transkei's Kaiser Matanzima and Bophuthatswana's Lucas Mangope, attack South Africa's treatment of blacks in the common areas and the inequitable distribution of land and resources, but they quarrel more with the implementation of separate development than with the basic policy. Others, such as KwaZulu's Gatsha Buthelezi and Gazankulu's Hudson Ntsanwisi, reject the entire philosophy of separation.

Even where the leaders, or, as in the Transkei, the opposition parties, vehemently oppose separate development, however, in day-to-day politics the issue has not loomed large. In part this is because the constraints that limit political discussion in South Africa proper also apply in the self-governing homelands (although not in the independent ones). The whole apparatus for curbing dissent—the Internal Security Act, detention, bannings—prevents many issues from even being raised in the self-governing homelands. It also eliminates the more radical African leaders. Moreover, the bans on such organizations as the African National Congress and the Pan-Africanist Congress also inhibit political activity in the homelands.

Debate has also been circumscribed by the absence of any opportunity for Africans to choose between a multiracial South Africa and separation. The only choice has been whether to participate in the separatist institutions created by South Africa or to shun them. Participation risks loss of standing with African nationalists. A boycott of these institutions runs the risk of handing power to Africans more susceptible to South African pressures and, ultimately, of political irrelevance or destruction.

Those who chose participation and emerged as homeland leaders have followed one of two courses. A number of leaders seek to use the separatist institutions to undermine white domination. They argue that they can use their legitimacy in white eyes and the resources it gives them to increase the political awareness and capabilities of Africans. Other homeland leaders, a minority, accept separation and use the new institutional framework to advance the cause of their own ethnic and regional unit—or, as more cynical observers suggest of some, to further their own interests.

Attitudes toward independence most clearly differentiate advocates of these two strategies. Those who have accepted independence have taken one or more of the following positions:

- The homeland was not the creation of South African policy but had existed as a state prior to apartheid (Transkei).
- Independence was necessary to prevent domination of a smaller African ethnic group by a larger one (Venda and Bophuthatswana).
- The choice was not between multiracialism and separation but between a racist status quo and the increased although flawed freedom resulting from independence.

Those who oppose independence say that independence:

- Legitimates white rule in the common areas.
- Fragments African political opposition and thereby strengthens white rule.
- Reinforces the rural-urban inequities in South African society and deprives the homeland populations of their birthright in a common South Africa.
- Postpones and makes peaceful change and genuine reform more difficult to achieve.

All public opinion surveys indicate that the African population would prefer a single multiracial democratic South Africa to any of the separatist alternatives. Urban Africans, who have put down roots in the common areas and have much at stake there, are most opposed to homeland independence. Homeland Africans, while more willing to accept a second-best separatist solution if other alternatives are closed off, also prefer a multiracial society.

Acceptance of independence by three homelands (and, scheduled for late 1981, a fourth, the Ciskei) in the face of such opposition reflects the proindependence arguments cited above, plus despair over the prospects for change in

South Africa. But there are other factors, too. The homelands have created a new African elite that benefits from the separatist structure. Traditional leaders now dominate the homelands. For them, independence increases both power and the opportunity for spoils. Perhaps the real surprise is not that several homelands have accepted independence on South Africa's terms but that so many have thus far refused it.

A final point is that ethnic nationalism continues to operate. Separate development has revived and heightened ethnic awareness, and some homeland groups are thinking in increasingly ethnic terms. Chief Mangope of Bophuthatswana, for example, has frequently expressed fear of Zulu domination, a theme echoed by leaders of several of the smaller ethnic groups.

As part of its effort to encourage separatist tendencies, South Africa is believed to have brought its weight to bear against multiracialism in homeland politics. It has been claimed that white officials played a role in Kaiser Matanzima's victory in the Transkei in 1963 by pressuring the chiefs to oppose the multiracial Democratic party of Victor Poto. Chief Buthelezi of KwaZulu has frequently alleged that South African officials have tried to undermine his advocacy of multiracialism by supporting his opponents. "Divide and rule," which critics of apartheid have long insisted was South Africa's strategy, would seem to be the guiding principle here.

ARBITRARY RULE AND CORRUPTION

The records of the homeland governments in administering local affairs vary, but on the whole they have not been encouraging. In particular, civil liberties have often fared poorly and official corruption has thrived.

In the nonindependent homelands the restrictions on civil liberties and personal freedom in part reflect continued enforcement of South African law and social practices, including segregation. But the homelands have also devised repressive policies of their own, including sweeping arbitrary powers of detention and banishment similar to South African practices. Even in Chief Buthelezi's KwaZulu, the style of politics is said to be increasingly authoritarian, and the chief is markedly impatient with criticism, whatever its source.

In many homelands the traditional elites have used their new offices to further enrich themselves. Chiefs' salaries, set by legislative assemblies dominated by the chiefs themselves, have climbed steadily. Outright stealing of government funds has been reported. As a result, the ruling establishments of the homelands are often islands of affluence amid oceans of poverty.

The clearest sense of official attitudes toward public office can be obtained in the independent homelands, where the leaders have the greatest latitude to determine their own course. In Bophuthatswana corruption appears less prevalent, and effort has been made to protect civil liberties. The credit goes largely to Chief Mangope. He has always believed that South Africa's racism reflected white fears of African "barbarism," and he has set out to allay these fears by trying to establish an exemplary multiracial democracy in Bophuthatswana. Shortly after independence, racially based South African laws, including the Mixed Marriages Act, were abolished. A bill of rights has been incorporated in the constitution—something unique for the region—and security legislation inherited from South Africa has been tempered. Although some civil libertarians would argue that excessive discretionary power remains in the hands of the executive, few would dispute that Mangope's reforms represent a considerable advance.

In the Transkei the record is more mixed. Its government is perhaps more personalized than in any other homeland. Kaiser Matanzima, the first prime minister, now serves as president. His brother George succeeded him as prime minister. Other members of his family have made careers in the armed forces and in government-related business activities. Corruption is said to be rampant, and only frequent infusions of South African aid prevent the government from going bankrupt. After some delay the most offensive racial laws were removed from the statute book, but civil liberties are not highly valued by the administration. Arbitrary arrests of prominent opposition leaders are commonplace, as are allegations of police brutality. Censorship remains stringent, and the government has issued some arbitrary and eccentric decisions, such as a ban on the Methodist church.

By far the worst record belongs to Venda, however, particularly in the field of civil liberties, which can only be described as nonexistent. Clinging to power despite the loss of two elections, President Patrick Mphephu is attempting to eliminate all opposition. Before independence he tried to ban the opposition party, and more recently he has ordered arrests of opposition members of Parliament.

The homelands are not beacons of liberty and government probity. About them, however, two things can be said. Whatever their shortcomings, the harshest aspects of South African racism are not felt there, and the potential of the Africans of South Africa for effective, fair, and honest self-government cannot be judged on the basis of a handful of corrupt, dictatorial homeland officials. Many of the most competent and public-spirited African leaders of integrity have disappeared from the political scene as a result of the repressive policies of the South African government.

SOUTH AFRICA'S RELATIONS WITH THE HOMELANDS

Now and then the homelands—in particular the independent ones—get their way in contests of will with South Africa. The Transkei has successfully pressed for increased financial aid from South Africa, and it persuaded Pretoria to cede Port St. Johns to it. Similarly, Bophuthatswana has received additional land, including the historically important town of Mafeking. The independent homelands have also dissuaded South Africa from major resettlements within their borders. Indeed, a South African threat to destroy Crossroads, a squatter community near Cape Town populated mainly by Xhosa, brought a public protest from the Transkei, and the South African government beat a partial retreat. Prime Minister Pieter W. Botha has indicated a far greater willingness than his predecessors to consult with homeland leaders, and should his proposed southern African "constellation of states" ever materialize, the independent homelands' position could be enhanced still further.

For now and for the foreseeable future, however, South Africa is firmly in command of its relations with the homelands. The fundamental inequalities in the division of wealth and resources between Africans and whites persist. All key elements of the homeland policy—white-formulated consolidation plans, homeland citizenship for all Africans, resettlement programs—remain essentially intact despite homeland opposition.

The fact is that the homelands lack the leverage to bring about significant changes in South African policy. They are weak and dependent, and South Africa, if it so chooses, can ignore their protests and demands. This was demonstrated in 1978 when the Transkei broke off diplomatic relations with South Africa to protest Pretoria's decision to turn over to Natal a piece of territory sought by the Transkei. Essentially, South Africa ignored the cutoff, leaving its consular officials on duty, continuing financial assistance, and maintaining the normal flow of labor from the Transkei to the common areas. When the Transkei resumed diplomatic relations in 1980, the difference in the conduct of affairs was imperceptible.

In 1955 a government-appointed panel of inquiry known as the Tomlinson Commission concluded that a successful homelands policy would require massive outlays of money for economic development and for territorial consolidation. The commission recommended the expenditure of £104,486,000 over the first decade alone to begin economic development. Consolidation would require additional sums.

The Tomlinson report posed a dilemma that South Africa has been trying to resolve ever since. On one hand, whites were attracted by the ideal of a separate-development policy based on the homelands. On the other hand, they were not at all eager to pay the cost of a fundamental restructuring of the nation.

Over the years the trend has been to increase government spending for the homelands, but the amounts have always fallen far short of what was needed to implement the policy fully. Ironically, one of the most tightfisted officials when it came to spending on the homelands was Hendrik Verwoerd, the prime mover in the development of the policy. He rejected consolidation as unrealistic, refused to permit private capital to flow into the homelands, and increased public expenditures for development programs only marginally. Under his leadership, first as minister of Bantu administration and development

161

and then as prime minister, government outlay for homeland development amounted to R7 million in fiscal 1957–58, R22.6 million in 1962–63, and R45 million in 1967–68, the last budget he had a hand in shaping. Under his successor, John Vorster, expenditures on the homelands soared from R95 million in 1970–71 to R1,108.7 million in 1977–78. Recently they have been rising at an average annual rate of slightly more than 10 percent.

The initial efforts to spur economic growth in the homelands focused on the Bantu Investment Corporation (later the Corporation for Economic Development). Established by the government in 1959, it was to channel public funds to new business enterprises in the homelands. But its resources were so small—it started with capital of only R1 million—that it was able to create only a relative handful of jobs and was clearly inadequate to get development off the ground. Thus, one of the first actions of Prime Minister Vorster when he succeeded Verwoerd was to open the homelands to white private capital. With the help of such funds, between 1971 and 1978 eight "growth centers" were created within the homelands and some 300 industries were launched.

In recent years, however, economic development within the homelands has clearly taken a back seat to the creation of border-area industries, whose African workers live in the homelands and commute daily to jobs in the white areas. The policy of promoting border industries actually dates back to 1960, when such industrial decentralization began on a voluntary basis. Progress was slow, and an element of coercion was introduced in 1968 with the passage of the Physical Planning Act, which limited the number of Africans employed in the established industrial areas. This speeded up the creation of border industries and contributed substantially to the growth in the number of commuter workers noted earlier.

How much the homelands benefit from the border industries is open to question, however. Some of the new border industries have sprung up at established industrial centers—such as Rosslyn, twelve miles from Pretoria, and Hammarsdale, thirty miles from Durban—that already provided substantial numbers of jobs for homeland Africans. Other homeland areas desperately in need of more jobs for their populations have been completely untouched by the border-industries scheme and lack any adjacent industrial complexes. The Transkei is in this category.

If the border industries become major economic factors, they could pose serious obstacles to internal homeland development. White industrialists are likely to favor them over homeland locations because on the white side of the border they run no risk of uncertain treatment under an independent African government. Of more immediate concern to the homelands is the seepage of resources to the white areas. The homelands derive only marginal economic benefit from the border areas because most of the income generated by them is spent in them. As a result, the contention of South African policy makers that economic growth in the white border areas would spill over into the homelands has proved wrong.

A glance at a map of the homelands shows that they make little sense as "nations." Even if all the bits and pieces were adequately endowed with resources their fragmentation would defy rational political and economic organization. Africans have long complained bitterly about the allocation of land, and the South African government does not dispute that a workable separate-development policy requires that the map be redrawn. White leaders have, in fact, been working at consolidation of the homeland territories for years. But, as in the case of economic development of the homelands, the will and the means to achieve the professed goal have generally been lacking.

Consolidation involves three separate undertakings: (1) the addition to the homelands of adjacent white-owned territory that was assigned to the African areas in the 1936 land act but was never turned over to them; (2) the eradication of "black spots"—thousands of parcels of land in white areas that were acquired by Africans before such holdings became illegal—by buying up the African-owned tracts and purchasing new land adjacent to the homelands on which to resettle the uprooted Africans; (3) the exchange of noncontiguous homeland territory for contiguous land. All these programs involve massive relocations of people—mainly Africans.

In early 1981 the territorial promises of the 1936 legislation still had not been fulfilled. Indeed, the government has been so fearful of antagonizing whites that the acquisition of white-owned land has actually slowed in recent decades. Between 1936 and 1949, 4,708,000 acres of land were purchased for addition to the reserves, and an additional 5,819,000 acres were purchased between 1949 and 1959. But between 1959 and 1971, only 2,116,000 acres were purchased, and through the rest of the 1970s acquisitions continued at a relatively slow pace. In recent years the slowdown has reflected not only the political obstacles but also rising land prices and a tendency to make cuts in expenditures on the homelands during economic slowdowns. A downturn that lasted from 1975 to 1978 resulted in a drop in land purchases for the homelands from R59 million in 1975 to R40.3 million in 1978. Since land prices continued to rise, the amount of land acquired declined even more sharply. At the end of 1980 almost 10 percent of the land allocated to Africans in 1936 remained to be purchased.

Recent consolidation has proceeded—haltingly—under an interim plan adopted by Parliament in 1975. Even if completely implemented, this strategy would still leave the homelands badly fragmented. The 112 major pieces of homeland territory existing in 1975, excluding the "black spots," would be reduced to 35. Only one major homeland, the Ciskei, would be fully consolidated. All the other large homelands would continue to consist of several separate areas. KwaZulu would have 10 and Bophuthatswana 6, while the Transkei would remain at 3. All told, more than 5.6 million acres—an area not much smaller than New Hampshire—would have to change hands, causing enormous human and economic dislocations. More than a million people—

mostly Africans living in scattered bits of homeland territory—are scheduled for relocation under the plan.

The 1975 proposals satisfied no one. Among the relatively progressive supporters of separate development they were rejected as selfish and inadequate. Conservative white economic interests grumbled about the costs. Africans protested both because only whites had participated in formulating the plan and because the allocation of land and resources remained unsatisfactory.

The widespread criticism, coupled with the budget squeeze stemming from the 1975–78 economic slowdown, led the government to adopt a go-slow policy on homeland consolidation, and only limited progress has been made since 1975. In 1979 Prime Minister Botha appointed an all-white commission made up of members of Parliament, academics, businessmen, and civil servants to take a fresh look at the entire consolidation issue. Botha also stated publicly that the government would not necessarily be bound by the 1936 legislation.

The commission report, a massive, multivolume effort, was delivered to the government in the latter part of 1980. As of early 1981 none of its conclusions had been disclosed, but leading members of the commission have outlined some of its guiding principles. These included maximizing the number of Africans in the homelands, ensuring that future population growth takes place in homeland territories adjacent to the common areas, minimizing the amount of white land that must be ceded to the homelands, and ensuring that most of the resources, ports, dams, roads, and railways remain in the common areas.

Although some efforts at consolidation are likely to continue, a number of Afrikaner leaders, including Prime Minister Botha, are cautiously seeking alternatives. They have recognized the enormous costs, both human and material, of even the limited consolidation schemes now constituting official policy. One low-cost plan that would salvage the separatist approach calls for consolidating the homelands by simply redrawing the boundaries and leaving the present populations intact. So far, however, this idea has been firmly rejected by the government because it would leave a number of whites under the jurisdiction of black governments. The other suggestions to date have been extremely vague, though they generally involve some sort of interracial administration of certain economic areas. The most publicized scheme of this type is the so-called Lombard Plan drawn up on behalf of white business interests in Natal.

Whatever alternatives may eventually emerge, it seems clear that new ideas must be developed to replace consolidation as it has been envisioned. For whites, even the modest goals set by existing laws appear increasingly burdensome. For Africans, even full implementation of the most ambitious consolidation plans considered so far would not suffice. Without sweeping redistribution of resources, they view consolidation as an ultimately irrelevant adjustment of boundaries. Thus, the Africans insist, in territorial consolidation, as in economic development, South Africa's commitment to the homelands

164

falls hopelessly short of anything that would make separate development a realistic policy.

AFRICAN RESETTLEMENT

One of the basic aims of the homelands policy has been to reduce the number of Africans living in the parts of South Africa claimed by whites. The goal has not been realized, but the government has continued to press efforts to hold down the permanent African population in the common areas. Programs to achieve this have included economic development of the homelands, expansion of border industries employing commuter labor, greater use of migrant labor, and forced resettlement of Africans from white South Africa to the homelands. Of these, resettlement has provoked by far the most controversy and criticism. The arbitrary expulsion of Africans from the common areas has caused as much human suffering, hardship, and despair as any other apartheid measure.

The efforts to consolidate and rationalize the homeland territories have been responsible for much resettlement. The eradication of "black spots" caused the uprooting and resettlement in the homelands of almost one-third million Africans between 1970 and 1979. As noted earlier, implementation of the interim consolidation proposals of 1975 would probably entail the relocation of more than one million Africans.

Government efforts to shift areas of dense African settlement near established homelands to the jurisdiction of the adjacent homelands have also led to resettlement on occasion. It is true that often the borders of the homeland have simply been redrawn so that the African population becomes officially resident in the homeland, but in other cases, such as in East London in the Cape, the African townships have been closed down and the local populations resettled in new dormitory towns located within the homelands. Although this policy has not produced the disruptions of the other types of resettlement, it has made getting to work more expensive and time-consuming and given rise to other hardships for those affected.

The modernization of agriculture, including increased mechanization and the use of herbicides, has also resulted in extensive resettlement by making many African farm workers "surplus." The labor tenant system, under which an African living on a white farm exchanged his labor for the right to cultivate a plot for himself, has been abolished, and the only Africans the government will allow legally in "white" farming areas in the future will be hired laborers, preferably migrants. From 1970 to 1979, more than 300,000 Africans were expelled from the white rural areas. Africans in these areas, unlike those legally resident in the white urban areas, cannot acquire the Section 10 rights that give some protection against arbitrary expulsion to the permanent urban African population.

Even Africans legally qualified to be in cities cannot escape the threat of **165** expulsion altogether. Despite the Section 10 rights, which are usually honored, all Africans live and work in urban areas strictly on sufferance. No African enjoys unrestricted and inviolable rights to urban residence. Section 10 privileges may be modified or revoked by administrative fiat, and unemployment or political activities displeasing to the government are usually sufficient grounds for expulsion. Moreover, a significant proportion of the urban African population lacks even the limited protection of Section 10. These "illegals"—male job seekers present in the white areas without permission and the families of migrant workers—have recently been settling in squatter communities, such as Crossroads near Cape Town. The government can demolish these illegal settlements and remove their residents to the homelands at any time. No figures are available for the number of such expulsions, but a clue can be found in the 279,957 prosecutions under the influx-control regulations in fiscal 1977–78. This represents a sharp drop from a decade earlier, when the number approached 700,000, but the threat of expulsion still hangs over every urban African.

In the two decades since 1960, resettlement under various separate-development policies has uprooted more than three million Africans. Many were forced to leave established communities where they had lived with at least modest comfort and convenience and begin life anew amid surroundings that are often ugly and barren. The new settlements are frequently far from urban centers and jobs. Housing has sometimes consisted of tents or corrugated metal shacks, while sanitation facilities and water supplies have been primitive or nonexistent. Some resettlement areas lack schools and clinics. The millions of relocated Africans are left impoverished and embittered. And yet the South African government is no closer to its original goal of reducing the African population in the common areas. On the contrary, the number of Africans in the common areas continues to increase.

The Nationalists have sought acceptance of the homelands policy by three constituencies: the international community, the Africans of South Africa, and the white voters, especially the Afrikaners. They have failed with the first two, and the whites have been forced to alter their concept of the policy drastically.

Foreign response has been unambiguous: Not one nation besides South Africa has recognized the independence of the three homelands so far granted that status. The view of most of the nations of the world is that the homelands are a transparent device for furthering apartheid—a scheme designed to frustrate rather than advance African aspirations. South Africa now seems to have resigned itself to this lack of acceptance and is making no serious effort to win international recognition of the homelands.

The attitudes of the Africans directly affected by the homelands policy are less uniform. Some homeland leaders argue that cooperation with the whites is justified on pragmatic grounds: The homelands offer a platform from which to oppose apartheid. Also, some homeland leaders have benefited personally from the development of the homelands. Nevertheless, almost all important African leaders reject the current version of separate development and have indicated a preference for a common citizenship and a united South Africa. As for rank-and-file Africans, the Quail Commission report made clear that most see independent homelands only as a last-resort escape from South Africa's racial policies. Like their leaders, they prefer a nonracial unitary democracy. This is particularly true of urban Africans, who are almost unanimous in demanding political and economic rights where they live and work.

Among Afrikaners, there is widespread acceptance that separate development is not destined to work out the way their leaders told them it would when the policy was being shaped. The homelands are not going to draw enough Africans from the common areas to reduce their numbers there. At the same time, there is still a consensus that the homelands can serve one of their original purposes: supplying labor for the core economy without diluting white political dominance. Homeland-based labor, the sophisticated whites are keenly aware, has economic as well as political advantages for them. Traditionally, of course, the low wages paid African workers widened the potential profit margins of their employers, but even as the differential between black and white pay shrinks, separate development transfers at least part of the social cost of maintaining an African work force to the homelands. When workers become unproductive due to age or ill health, South Africa can send them back to the homelands. Moreover, when the economy slows, South Africa can export many of the jobless to the homelands, where they are hidden from sight.

With the benefits to whites tangible, and with alternatives that would be equally beneficial to whites still far from clear, separate development remains the political orthodoxy of the South African government. The policy remains in effect and the government clings to its goal of ten independent African homelands. Whatever path South Africa ultimately takes, the homelands exist and will have to be taken into account in all future political calculations. Few believe, however, that the present homeland policy promises a permanent resolution of South Africa's racial crisis. At best the homelands may be viewed as a first step toward a more equitable political, territorial, economic, and social arrangement—some kind of federal or confederal system, for example. At worst, they can be seen as barriers to progress, too often giving rise to corruption and political elites that sometimes cooperate with whites to exploit their own people.

Chapter 9
Black Challenge

On the morning of June 16, 1976, 20,000 African students marched through the streets of Soweto on their way to a mass meeting in a stadium. They appeared, in the words of one observer, "good-humoured, high-spirited, and excited." As they approached the stadium they encountered a large contingent of South African police. There is confusion about the ensuing sequence of events. A South African judge who later investigated the clash concluded that the police opened fire on the demonstrators only after some youths threw stones at them. According to South African journalist John Kane-Berman, apparently no order to disperse was heard and no warning shots were fired. One of the first police bullets hit a thirteen-year-old and then several other youngsters were shot dead.

The Soweto shootings touched off a series of protests and disturbances around the country which involved Coloureds as well as Africans. Over a period of sixteen months, some 700 deaths were publicly recorded, with most of the victims shot by the police. At least 50 Coloureds were killed, most of them in Cape Town. A handful of whites also died, including two who were beaten to death in Soweto on June 16. Some estimates of the deaths run much higher than the recorded figure, in some cases exceeding 1,000 by the end of 1976. Estimates of the number of injured top 5,000.

Thomas G. Karis, an American scholar specializing in the politics of black South Africans, lists the "Soweto uprising" of 1976 as one of the "four watersheds in black politics during the past half century." The others are "the defeat of liberalism" in 1936 with the removal of Cape Africans from the common voters' roll; the adoption by the African National Congress (ANC) in 1949 of a program of "militant and sometimes illegal though nonviolent action—boycotts, strikes, and passive disobedience"; and the outlawing of both the ANC and the Pan-Africanist Congress (PAC) and their turn to violence after the shootings at Sharpeville in 1960.

But the bloody encounter between the students and the police in Soweto was "the most important turning point of all," says Karis. "A new generation of African and Coloured youth, conditioned by Black Consciousness, displayed a qualitatively new level of defiance and fearlessness, produced the first substantial exodus for armed guerrilla training, and contributed to the resurgence of the ANC. . . . What especially and repeatedly stunned observers . . . was . . . the readiness of youthful blacks to stand up to an aroused antagonist and to face death. This stance came increasingly to be accompanied by confident determination expressed in the clenched-fist black power salute and the cry 'Amandla!'—Zulu for 'power.' "

THE HERITAGE OF STRUGGLE

Blacks in South Africa—in particular, Africans—have been struggling against white domination for a long time. The roots of the 1976 Soweto protest run back a century, when Africans turned from armed resistance to white rule to peaceful petitions for equal treatment. Over the years black opposition has taken different forms and has waxed and waned in intensity, but there has been a steady trend toward more forceful challenge of the white minority.

One of the first broadly backed protests emerged from the South African Native Convention, a counterassembly held by Africans in 1909 when whites were meeting to write a constitution for the Union of South Africa; Africans objected to the draft's failure to provide "full and equal rights and privileges . . . without distinction of class, colour, or creed." Three years later, in 1912, a group of educated members of the small African middle class, including a number of professionals, formed the African National Congress. The ANC is still a leading champion of African rights.

From the start of the black opposition movement, impatience over the lack of progress has erupted periodically in boycotts, strikes, and other forms of defiance of white authority. The pass system has long been a prime target. In 1913 African women in the Orange Free State refused to carry passes and eventually got their way when their protest threatened to fill the jails. In 1919 several thousand Africans turned in their passes. The Africans drew some of their inspiration from Mahatma Gandhi, who lived in South Africa from 1893 to 1914 and used some of the same civil disobedience methods in campaigning for Indian rights in South Africa that he later used against British rule in India.

Potentially the most militant force was the mass of African workers in the cities. This potential has been tapped sporadically and with varying success since World War I. In the late 1920s white and black members of the Communist party led union organizing drives among African workers and initially met

169

with considerable success. After a decline, African trade union activity spurted in the late 1930s and in the 1940s, especially among the Africans moving into the growing industrial sector. During World War II punitive regulations did not deter these African workers from taking part in a wave of illegal strikes. After the war, in 1946, whites were shaken by the most threatening spectacle of African labor protest in South Africa's history, the strike of 76,000 mine workers, politically the least-advanced group of urban workers. Ignoring the law, they responded to the call of the African Mine Workers' Union, which was led by a longtime member of both the Communist party and the ANC, by refusing to enter the gold mines.

For the most part, however, African opposition from the 1880s through the 1940s relied mainly on tactics that were within the law. Africans had grounds for believing such methods would work. Mission schoolteachers had persuaded many that their place in a common South Africa would be based on merit, not race. Since 1853 a nonracial qualified franchise in Cape Colony had enabled African men to vote on the common roll, a right that existed until 1936. Another source of encouragement late in the nineteenth century was the thinking of black Americans—notably Booker T. Washington—who were optimistic about white goodwill. Many early ANC leaders opposed confrontation, mass action, and militant trade unionism, fearing they would alienate potential white sympathizers. The ANC's 1919 constitution stressed "resolutions, protests . . . constitutional and peaceful progaganda . . . deputations . . . enquiries." When the government established the advisory body known as the Natives' Representative Council in 1936, the ANC cooperated fully and some of its leaders became members.

If tactics were essentially moderate, so were goals. The ANC initially sought gradual reform through moral and political appeals. ANC leaders and other African representatives urged an end to discrimination and called for a nonracial, qualified franchise for all Africans rather than an immediate transition to one person, one vote and majority rule. In the first three decades of its existence, for example, the ANC advocated "the removal of the 'Colour Bar' in political, educational, and industrial fields" and, echoing Cecil Rhodes's formula, "equal rights for all civilised men." A widely representative All African Convention held in 1935, when the government was in the process of removing Cape Africans from the common voters' roll, accepted social and cultural separation but insisted that Africans and whites possessed a common citizenship and should participate in common political institutions. It accepted as "equitable" a qualified franchise that limited black voters to those who could pass a "civilisation test" based on "an education or property or wage qualification"—a policy almost identical to that adopted by the Progressive party more than two decades later. "Such measures," the convention said, "would adequately protect the interests of the White population in whose favour the dice are already heavily loaded in view of the extension of adult suffrage to White men and women." Literacy and economic qualifications for the white franchise had been removed by 1931.

Whether moderate or militant, however, the Africans' approaches were rebuffed by the government at every turn. The 1910 constitution of the Union of South Africa embraced the color bar, and the 1936 franchise revision further weakened the Africans politically. The land legislation of 1913 and 1936 strengthened separation by sharply delimiting where Africans could live or own property. Strikes were brutally repressed. It was the violent breaking of the 1946 mine workers' strike by Prime Minister Jan Smuts's government that led to the collapse of the Natives' Representative Council; so angry were the Africans serving on the council that they suspended its sittings, and government efforts to reactivate it were unavailing. Africans' hopes for integration into the political life of the country were dashed in 1948, when Daniel Malan and the National party came to power. The era of apartheid had begun.

By then the black opposition was taking a tougher stance, too. Most African leaders had stopped talking about a qualified franchise and were demanding one person, one vote. By the mid-1950s the ANC, along with Indian, Coloured, and white organizations working together in the Congress Alliance, had adopted the Freedom Charter. It said: "Every man and woman shall have the right to vote for and stand as a candidate for all bodies which make laws."

Within the ANC a younger generation of African nationalists had been rising to prominence. Stimulated by wartime idealism and by the militancy of the African trade unions and left-wing activists, they had founded the ANC Youth League in 1944. They were mainly teachers or students of medicine or law, comparable in their middle-class status to the people who had founded the ANC in 1912. But they were impatient with the organization's traditional, moderate tactics and dissatisfied with its failure to develop into a mass movement. Under their prodding, in 1949 the ANC adopted a program of militant African nationalism and mass action.

The chief result was the "Defiance Campaign" of 1952, a nationwide civil disobedience movement aimed at boldly challenging white supremacy. It was the largest effort at nonviolent resistance ever seen in South Africa and the first mass campaign pursued jointly by Africans and Indians. More than 8,000 Africans and their allies went to jail for defying apartheid laws. The ANC's membership soared from less than 20,000 to perhaps 100,000, and the number of adherents and sympathizers was undoubtedly much larger. Toward the end of 1952 the campaign began to spread from the "white" areas where it had started to the rural reserves. The movement never came close, however, to sparking the general strike it had hoped for, and after sporadic, unsanctioned violence late in the year and the prosecution of its leaders for promoting communism, the Defiance Campaign expired.

The trials in Johannesburg and Port Elizabeth, ending in suspended sentences, were part of a general tightening of the screws—the government's only response to the Defiance Campaign and subsequent protests in the 1950s. Surveillance, harassment, banning, and imprisonment became the lot of many black leaders and their white sympathizers. Repressive laws already on the books, including the sweeping Suppression of Communism Act, came into play. New laws further limiting meetings and demonstrations were enacted, and whipping was added as a penalty for committing any offense "by way of protest."

In 1956 the government brought treason charges against 156 blacks, mainly ANC leaders, and whites, contending that their efforts to achieve equal rights for all in South Africa "in their lifetime" would "necessarily involve the overthrow of the state by violence." The court eventually rejected the argument that the ANC's policy was one of violence, but elsewhere the government encountered few setbacks in its systematic efforts to still black dissent. Thus, 1956 saw the removal of the Coloureds from the common voting roll, accelerating their descent into political impotence. In 1959 came the Promotion of Bantu Self-Government Act, which completed the long deterioration of African political rights by eliminating African representation by whites in Parliament. Henceforth, Africans were expected to find political outlets in the rural "homelands."

In the face of the government assault, the ANC and its allies shelved mass civil disobedience as a tactic. Smaller-scale public protest meetings and demonstrations continued, however. Thousands of African women, especially in rural areas, staged spontaneous demonstrations against the extension of the pass system to them. There were also strikes and "stay-at-homes," consumer and bus boycotts, pamphleteering, and the symbolic lighting of lamps and bonfires. Even the old practice of deputations was used in 1956 when pro-ANC representatives of the Johannesburg advisory boards, elected by Africans in the townships, attempted to meet with Hendrik Verwoerd, then the minister dealing with African affairs. He refused to see them.

Late in the 1950s smoldering resentment over unpopular policies in rural areas burst into open revolt in the Sekhukhuneland and Zeerust areas of the northern Transvaal, and disorder and rioting flared in eastern Pondoland in the Transkei. The huts of Africans thought to be collaborators with the white regime were burned and some people were murdered. There were angry tribal meetings, burning of women's passes, refusals to pay taxes, and bloody clashes with the police. The involvement of ANC members appears to have been minimal, but the government declared the ANC "an unlawful organization" in certain areas.

Within the ANC the leaders debated the course the organization should follow. Radicals talked of building a disciplined, cell-based underground organization. But most leaders favored continued efforts to build a mass political organization, though they no longer held any illusions that its efforts could bring down the regime in the foreseeable future. ANC rhetoric increasingly contained passages that might be interpreted as a call to eventual violence, but for the moment, the leadership was anxious to avoid any action that might provoke all-out retaliation by the police. Indeed, throughout the decade non-violence remained the official policy of the ANC.

Then, in 1960, Sharpeville exploded and this attitude began to change. The next two decades saw the rise of a black generation more opposed to compromise and more willing to risk armed confrontation than its predecessors. The ANC abandoned nonviolence as a policy. The debate over whether it should operate underground or in the open was resolved by the government, which outlawed the organization completely under the newly enacted Unlawful Organizations Act. That law was only part of an expanded security apparatus created by the government in an attempt to eliminate radical black opposition. For a time the government succeeded in silencing that opposition, but its inability to eliminate it was demonstrated by such developments as the rise of Black Consciousness in the late 1960s, the Soweto uprising of 1976, and the bombing of SASOL oil-from-coal plants in 1980.

FROM SHARPEVILLE TO RIVONIA

Sharpeville is an African township in the industrial complex of Vereeniging, thirty-five miles south of Johannesburg. On March 21, 1960, a large crowd of Africans gathered around the local police station there to stage a demonstration. It was to be part of an antipass protest organized by the Pan-Africanist Congress, the first major campaign launched by its president, Robert Sobukwe, and other leaders since the founding of the PAC in April of the preceding year. Opposed to joint tactics with whites, the PAC leaders represented a deeply rooted "Africanist" strain within the ANC resembling the Black Consciousness that emerged a decade later. The plan called for "a sustained, disciplined, nonviolent campaign," and from all evidence the demonstrators in Sharpeville were complying with the nonviolence edict. Nevertheless, white police opened fire on them. The police continued to fire for ten to thirty seconds as the demonstrators fled. Sixty-seven Africans—including some women and children—were shot dead, the great majority hit in the back; 186 others were wounded.

The events of the following three weeks, mainly on the Witwatersrand and in Cape Town but also in Durban, Port Elizabeth, Bloemfontein, and elsewhere, had a cumulatively devastating impact on Africans and seemed almost cataclysmic to whites: mass gatherings; surrenders for arrest; pass burnings; a threatening but nonviolent march of 30,000 into downtown Cape Town; workers' stay-at-homes; baton charges by the police; diving aircraft; tear gas and shooting; indiscriminate assaults on workers at home by police using clubs and whips; a brief tactical suspension of the pass laws; countrywide arrests and detentions, including for the first time white Liberal party leaders; the declaration on March 30 of a state of emergency under legislation enacted following the 1952 Defiance Campaign; gun buying by whites; international condemnation, including a U.S. State Department rebuke (coupled with an expression of hope that Africans in the future would "be able to obtain redress for legitimate grievances by peaceful means"); U.S. support for the first United Nations Security Council resolution critical of South Africa; massive selling on the Johannesburg Stock Exchange; urgent pleas from the parliamentary opposition and from business for concessions to Africans; the banning of the ANC and the PAC on April 8. In Parliament the minister of justice asserted that the combined membership of the two organizations was "only about 70,000 . . . not at all representative of the Bantu . . . just a small coterie of terrorists" who want "our country." The Bantu "has not yet reached the standard of civilization of the white man," he commented.

The African leadership reeled. Recriminations flew about inadequate planning, lack of organization. The ANC criticized the PAC for sloppy preparation for its antipass campaign. But the ANC was no better prepared than the PAC for the government's crackdown or for clandestine operation. Although many Africans had at least glimpsed the potential power of civil disobedience and economic disruption, as well as the thinness of white South Africa's veneer of self-confidence, demoralization soon set in. The PAC became virtually leaderless overnight. Subjected to mass raids and arrests, it rapidly fell into a state of disarray from which it has still not recovered. Among the PAC leaders jailed was its president, Robert Sobukwe, who remained in detention or under ban until his death in 1978. Poqo (Xhosa for "alone"), a post-Sharpeville offshoot of the PAC that was ready to kill whites indiscriminately, was completely crushed.

After the lifting of the state of emergency late in the year, prominent Africans who were not under ban and who represented nearly all shadings of the political spectrum came together once more to try to forge a united front against white authority. Long-standing suspicions and differences soon undermined the temporary unity, but early the next year one more abortive attempt was made to organize a nonviolent protest. Planned mainly by ANC leaders, it was to culminate in a three-day stay-at-home timed to coincide with the inauguration of the Republic of South Africa on May 31, 1961.

The response was scattered and organizers called off the campaign on the second day in the face of the most formidable array of official intimidation and force ever mustered to quell African protest. The government followed up that action with legislation giving it emergency powers to deal with dissent without the necessity of proclaiming a national emergency, which could have a severe impact on the climate for foreign investment. The most significant new act was the "90-day detention law" of 1963, the first of South Africa's preventive detention laws.

Even as they struggled to regain their equilibrium after Sharpeville and laid plans for the peaceful protest of May 1961, African leaders and their allies had been reassessing their attitudes toward violence. Until this time, Nelson Mandela, by then the leading figure of the ANC, apparently retained the hope that nonviolent pressures might still persuade the whites to change their policies. But the suppression of the protest on the eve of the inauguration of the Republic led Mandela to conclude that the government was "relying exclusively on violence with which to answer our people and their demands." "Fifty years of nonviolence," he declared, had "brought the African people nothing but more and more repressive legislation." Now "only two choices" were left: "submit or fight." In June 1961 Mandela and other ANC leaders agreed the time had come to fight. Even then and until the 1970s, however, violence was to be limited to property such as power pylons and symbols of the state.

Although the ANC, operating underground, could still build black morale and inspire public demonstrations, there was no question of transforming a mass political movement into an instrument of sabotage and guerrilla warfare. Thus, late in 1961 members of the ANC and the Communist party, including whites and Indians, formed Umkonto We Sizwe ("spear of the nation" in Zulu) to serve as a small, close-knit organization to carry out sabotage. On December 16, 1961, the Afrikaners' sacred Day of the Covenant, commemorating the Zulu defeat at Blood River in 1838, Umkonto saboteurs began a new phase in the struggle against apartheid by exploding homemade bombs at symbolic targets in Johannesburg and Port Elizabeth. By mid-1963 Umkonto claimed more than seventy acts of sabotage. Then, on July 11, 1963, the security police captured Umkonto's leaders in Rivonia, a white suburb of Johannesburg. The decapitation of the major underground movement (another small group of saboteurs composed mainly of white former Liberal party members was soon eliminated, too) demonstrated the growing professionalism of the police. By the mid-1960s, the regime had not only uprooted most of the underground but had also demoralized and routed the entire radical opposition.

POST-RIVONIA SILENCE

Although frustration simmered beneath the surface throughout the rest of the 1960s, especially among black university students, the years immediately following Rivonia were characterized primarily by unprecedented silence. The government moved rapidly to solidify white support and to strengthen the economy and the security police. At the end of the Rivonia trial in June 1964, Mandela and other ANC leaders, including Walter Sisulu and Govan Mbeki, were sentenced to life imprisonment. They had admitted sabotage and preparation for guerrilla war but had denied that a decision had been made to begin guerrilla activity. (At the start of 1981 Mandela, Sisulu, and Mbeki were still serving their sentences in the prison on Robben Island near Cape Town.)

The responsibility for planning for armed struggle now fell to ANC leaders outside the country, whose functions originally were to have been only diplomatic and propagandistic. ANC and PAC leaders had already tried to organize a South African United Front abroad, along with Indian and South-West African representatives, but tensions and suspicions had led to the dissolution of the front by early 1962. After Rivonia, however, the various black groups united in calling for caution. They warned that African police spies and informers were increasing the danger of new police crackdowns and mass reprisals. Opponents of the regime were also coming up against the tough new laws aimed at curbing dissent: the Sabotage Act of 1962, the Terrorism Act of 1967, and the Prohibition of Political Inference Act of 1968, which outlawed multiracial political parties.

Uncertainty about the future gripped the liberation movement. Chief Albert Lutuli, banned president of the ANC (and a Nobel Peace Prize winner in 1961), worried about a "vacuum of leadership" after the Rivonia trial. Others renewed the old debate about using government-sponsored institutions as vehicles for pressure and for building African self-confidence. Prime Minister Hendrik Verwoerd sought to speed the development of such institutions as outlets for African political demands.

But the brooding political silence persisted. Writing at the end of the 1960s, Edgar Brookes, a longtime white supporter of black causes who had been elected to the Senate by Africans, said it was "nauseating to hear those who have reduced Africans to silence . . . boasting of that silence as a proof of happiness and contentment."

"BLACK CONSCIOUSNESS" AND WORKERS' DEMANDS

A highly politicized generation of African, Indian, and Coloured students arose in the late 1960s. Within a few years they had transformed the outlook of large segments of South Africa's black population. They spread a doctrine of "Black Consciousness," but they also made use of straightforward symbols of defiance, including the clenched-fist salute of black power.

The assertive new black student movement represented a breaking away from an alliance with liberal white students. Lacking political outlets of their own in the early and mid-1960s, African university students had sought a role in the English-speaking, antigovernment National Union of South African Students (NUSAS). But by 1967–68 they had come to view the NUSAS leadership as part of a paternalistic white liberalism that was inherently incapable of acting in the interests of the mass of people oppressed by white domination. Thus, in December 1968 African and Indian students formed the South African Students' Organization (SASO) as a federation of student representative councils at black universities. The first president was Steve Biko, a charismatic personality with a penetrating and analytical mind. His own political awakening had come three years after Sharpeville when, as a sixteen-year-old, he had been expelled from school after being interrogated about his older brother, who had been jailed as a suspected Poqo activist. Later he attended the University of Natal's "nonwhite" medical school, the only South African school where African, Indian, and Coloured students studied and lived together.

SASO was influenced in its thinking by intellectuals in black Africa and by black Americans. The organization defined "black" not as a color but as a term for all those suffering from racial oppression, thus encompassing Africans, Indians, and Coloureds. "Nonwhite" was discarded; in SASO's view it diminished blacks by defining them in terms of whites. In 1971 SASO described Black Consciousness as "an attitude of mind, a way of life" and called for "group cohesion and solidarity" so that blacks could wield the economic and political power they already possessed. Self-definition, self-reliance, black pride—these were the answers to what was seen as the immediate problem, a psychological one of overcoming black attitudes of inferiority and subservience. "Black man, you are on your own" was a key slogan.

Long-range political and economic policies were not spelled out and provocative identification with banned organizations was avoided, but SASO's thrust was clearly political. Marxists accused Black Consciousness of failing to understand the nature of capitalism and class struggle. But SASO rejected all approaches that might confuse or blunt popular anger, viewing racial polarization and confrontation with the white enemy as necessary stages in the struggle for full citizenship and majority rule.

Biko and his colleagues did not always see violence as inevitable, however. Though before he was killed in 1977 Biko apparently had come to expect white-initiated violence, at other times he indicated a belief that white rule might give way peacefully if the masses were organized to make demands and to withdraw their labor. A frequent SASO theme was the need for painstaking planning and organization in preference to the PAC's reliance on heroic leadership to trigger spontaneous mass action.

Liberal fears that Black Consciousness was antiwhite were understandable in light of SASO's "black" appeal and its repudiation of joint action with whites. Nevertheless, SASO never excluded whites from its vision of a future South Africa. In 1970 Biko wrote: "Once the various groups . . . have asserted themselves to the point that mutual respect has to be shown then you have the ingredients for a true and meaningful integration."

Between 1969 and 1972 SASO swept African, Coloured, and Indian colleges. It also established itself at black theological seminaries, where "black theology" had aroused intense interest. Through well-organized conferences and publicity, including the circulation of 4,000 copies of the *SASO Newsletter* by 1972, SASO raised black university students to "a level of political education and ideological diffusion never before achieved by any black political organization" in South Africa, according to Gail M. Gerhart, an American political scientist.

Reflecting the emphasis on step-by-step organization, the Black Consciousness movement spread to other sectors of the black community. An "adult" wing, the Black People's Convention (BPC), was formally launched in July

1972. One of its early decisions was to reject contact with homeland leaders and "to make known to black people that there shall be no cooperation with government institutions." SASO's influence also spread through the organization of local community projects, mainly in rural and semirural areas, to promote literacy and education, health and welfare. Such projects, along with others in black art, black theology, and publishing, were assisted by Black Community Programmes (BCP), an independent organization sponsored initially by the multiracial South African Council of Churches and the Christian Institute of Southern Africa, an ecumenical and multiracial body committed to fundamental change.

Also important was proselytizing in the high schools and even primary schools by new youth organizations. The South African Student Movement (SASM) was formed in Soweto, and similar bodies sprang up elsewhere in the country. Student activism was spurred in mid-1972 by the expulsion of a student leader, Abraham Tiro, and his sympathizers from the University of the North, an African university in the northern Transvaal. This led to black student boycotts and demonstrations throughout the country, resulting in additional expulsions and withdrawals from school.

Meanwhile, outside South Africa the ANC was responding to the new currents that had produced the Black Consciousness movement. In 1969, shortly before SASO's formal inauguration, the ANC adopted a heightened emphasis on African "national consciousness" in the liberation struggle. At a conference in Tanzania it singled out as the enemy a growing "all-white solidarity" and foresaw a "confrontation on the lines of color—at least in the early stages of the conflict." The first priority was "the maximum mobilization of the African people as a dispossessed and racially oppressed nation. . . . It involves a stimulation and a deepening of national confidence, national pride, and national assertiveness."

In warning of "all-white solidarity," the ANC excepted a small number of revolutionary whites. It also saw unity with both Coloureds and Indians as essential since they share "a common fate with their African brothers." While abandoning the Congress Alliance, which had often been criticized by Africans as dominated by other groups, the ANC made a point of welcoming Indians, Coloureds, and white revolutionaries to become "fully integrated [within the ANC] on the basis of individual equality." The National Executive Committee, however, was to be exclusively African for the time being.

The government cracked down on the Black Consciousness movement for the first time in March 1973, banning Biko and seven other leaders. Biko could no longer speak publicly and was restricted to King William's Town, in the eastern Cape. There he founded and directed a branch of Black Community Programmes until he was barred from such work two years later. The 1973 bans were followed by a series of restrictions culminating in the suppression of all Black Consciousness organizations in late 1977. But the government had begun its counterattack too late to forestall the spread of the new black attitudes.

One reason for the March 1973 bannings may have been a wave of strikes—some organized, some spontaneous—by Africans in and around Durban in January and February of that year. The government may have viewed them as evidence that the Black Consciousness leaders were dangerously influential. But whatever the spark that touched off the strikes, they were a harbinger of the new labor militancy described in chapter 5.

In the Durban strikes of early 1973, this militancy had few political overtones. At mass meetings at their working places, the largely unskilled workers often sang "Nkosi Sikelela I-Afrika" ("God Bless Africa"), the anthem of both the ANC and KwaZulu, but they made no overt political demands and focused instead on a generally successful effort to win wage increases. The strikes were inspired by leaders from the workers' ranks and were often spontaneous. As far as is known, the black political underground played little or no role. All the same, the strikes had nationwide political significance, for they demonstrated the potential power of black workers.

RISING ANGER: 1973–76

Squeezed by inflation and a strained economy, more than 200,000 black workers, mainly Africans, took part in strikes throughout South Africa from 1973 through mid-1976. Maintaining that the strikes affected far more people than did SASO and the BPC, Baruch Hirson, a South African Marxist, has asserted that they "helped create the atmosphere of revolt" that led to the Soweto uprising of 1976.

But there was much else to fuel the spirit of revolt. Black Consciousness leaders became more defiant, more uncompromising in their demands, and more militant in their language after 1973. Dozens of leaders were banned or detained; others left the country, in some cases seeking out the ANC or the PAC abroad. Despite the risks of open membership, the BPC claimed to have forty-one branches in late 1973. The government's countermeasures, including torture of detainees and crackdowns on strikers, and the murder of student leader Abraham Tiro in February 1974 by a package bomb, intensified black anger.

Two months after Tiro's death the black mood became one of exultation. The Portuguese government collapsed, foreshadowing the successful conclusions of the struggles for independence in Mozambique and Angola. On September 25, 1974, SASO and the BPC defied a government ban and held a "Viva Frelimo" rally in Durban to celebrate the victory of the Mozambican liberation movement. A similar rally took place at the University of the North. The police showed up in force at both and arrested many blacks. The great majority of those detained at these gatherings and on other occasions in the mid-1970s came from a new generation that had been in primary school when the ANC and the PAC were outlawed.

The most important consequence of the Viva Frelimo rallies was a nearly two-year trial of nine SASO and BPC leaders. With the evidence consisting primarily of Black Consciousness literature, including poetry and plays, the proceedings became, in effect, a public trial of Black Consciousness itself. The accused were charged with conspiring to use unconstitutional or violent means to bring about a revolutionary change and "to oppose and denigrate the Black homeland leaders . . . to support and eulogize persons who had been convicted of subversion . . . and to treat them as heroes and as the true leaders of the Blacks." Another issue cited in the court's judgment was a BPC resolution "calling upon foreign investors to disengage themselves from the White-controlled exploitative system."

The atmosphere of the Black Consciousness trial differed markedly from the decorum that had previously characterized such proceedings. The accused Africans regularly entered the courtroom singing freedom songs. They raised their fists in the black power salute and shouted, *"Amandla!"* (Power!). Returning the salute, black spectators in the courtroom cried in response, *"Ngawethu!"* (Is ours!). The press kept blacks throughout the country informed of this continuing demonstration of defiance.

The trial ended December 15, 1976, when the court held that neither SASO nor the BPC was a revolutionary group. But the accused were found guilty of organizing the pro-Frelimo rallies and of other activities—essentially speech—designed "to create among the Blacks a hostile power bloc oriented for action, more particularly political violence." Some were sentenced to five years in prison, others six.

Whatever credibility the homeland leaders had as allies in the struggle against apartheid was severely damaged in March 1974 when Chief Kaiser Matanzima announced his readiness to negotiate for Transkeian independence even though demands for more land had not been met. He thereby broke the united front for more land and against unilateral deals that homeland leaders had displayed in a summit meeting at Umtata in the Transkei late in 1973.

Against this background, black urban intellectuals generally regarded as moderates met in the "Black Renaissance Convention" near Pretoria in December 1974 and condemned separate development. Organized by black Catholic and Protestant leaders, the convention brought together some 320 African, Coloured, and Indian participants, including businesspeople, trade unionists, journalists, teachers, and other professionals from all parts of South Africa. No more than twenty SASO or BPC activists were present, according to the convention's official report, but the discussion nevertheless focused on Black Consciousness themes.

180   The convention reaffirmed long-standing black goals: "a totally united and

democratic South Africa . . . one man, one vote . . . an equitable distribution of wealth." It called upon "all the countries of the world to withdraw all cultural, educational, economic, manpower, and military support to the existing racist Government and all its racist institutions." It also emphasized the importance of organizing African trade unions and concluded, said the convention report, with "a massive vote of Black solidarity."

Among the more militant segments of South Africa's black population, the jubilation over the independence of Mozambique and Angola soon gave way to a new wave of frustration. Though troubled by dissension among exiled members, the ANC managed to circulate revolutionary literature within South Africa. It also established a recruiting network that sent young men through Swaziland and Mozambique for guerrilla training abroad.

"The serene prosperous face" shown by South Africa to the world and to casual visitors, said the Christian Institute at the end of April 1976, was a mask covering "the real faces; the intractable face of the White rulers and the Black face contorted with suffering and suppressed rage." At about the same time a British journalist contrasted the "bland confidence" of officials "in the geniality of the urban Blacks" with the sentiment expressed by a Soweto student: "I could take you down this street and you'll find they all talk about Black Power. . . . Even with all the arms the White man has, I fear the day when Africans take their revenge." On a visit to Soweto in early 1976 Alex Boraine, a Progressive Reform party member of Parliament, was troubled not so much by the expected anger of the younger blacks as by the "accumulated anger" of the "middle-of-the-road respectable people" who told him "they couldn't go on any longer apologizing to their sons."

In a letter written on May 8, 1976, Desmond Tutu, an African then serving as the Anglican dean of Johannesburg, warned Prime Minister John Vorster that the situation was "rapidly deteriorating." Reviewing the "blatant injustice and suffering" from such practices as forcing African men to leave their families to work as migrants, detention without trial, and police harassment, he professed "a growing nightmarish feeling that unless something drastic is done very soon then bloodshed and violence are going to happen in South Africa almost inevitably." Vorster dismissed the letter as "propaganda."

Officials were later to blame the Soweto uprising of June 16 and the months of unrest that followed on Communist agitators. But Judge Pieter Cillie, serving as a one-man investigatory commission, finally reported on March 1, 1980, that the outbreaks of violence were largely attributable to government policies and the insensitivity of officials. Racially discriminatory policies, he said, "did not only cause dissatisfaction, but among many, a great hate. This dissatisfaction and hate was one of the foremost creators of a spirit of unrest."

Students had particular grounds for dissatisfaction. They resented "Bantu education," which symbolized inferior status and prospects. And both the students and their parents had a long string of other complaints about education.

They included, according to one account, "the overcrowding, high wastage [dropout] rates in the middle schools, the racist content of school programmes, inadequate facilities, especially in scientific, technical, and vocational fields, low standards and poor examination results, the high costs to parents who have to pay fees, buy books, and even contribute directly to school buildings or maintenance, and so on."

Politically conscious students moved beyond educational issues to condemn "the system" in general, and some student placards on June 16 called for the release of political prisoners. But the immediate issue leading to the Soweto mass demonstration was the use of Afrikaans as a medium of instruction. In 1974 the government had decreed that by the next year all African schools must conform to its policy of equal use of Afrikaans and English in the classroom. The subjects to be taught in Afrikaans were mathematics, social studies, history, and geography. In itself instruction in two languages was a heavy burden for the students, who often spoke an African language at home, but they had also come to view the language policy and Afrikaans itself as symbols of white oppression.

Anger over the policy was not limited to Soweto. It had been the cause of scattered school strikes and boycotts in many parts of the country earlier in 1976, and teachers, parents, and community leaders had pleaded with Bantu-education officials to reconsider. The response had been negative. But it was in Soweto that the issue came to a head. When the complaints of Soweto residents about the use of Afrikaans were rebuffed, the students there decided to organize a demonstration.

The student leaders who organized the rally at Orlando stadium, which never took place, were experienced activists. They belonged to the South African Students' Movement, which had begun forming in Soweto high schools in 1971. SASM had spread rapidly to other schools in the Transvaal, Durban, and the eastern Cape, and by 1976 was functioning in the Orange Free State and in a Coloured high school in Cape Town. It promoted discussion, community work, and fund drives. In 1976, with the help of money from abroad, it was able to hire a full-time organizer. As a result of SASM initiatives, an action committee that included two delegates from each Soweto school was formed to plan the June 16 demonstration. It later became the Soweto Students' Representative Council.

SASM functioned openly and legally. Its activists reached out to representatives of the older political generation—for example, Winnie Mandela, wife of the imprisoned ANC leader, and a number of ANC militants who had been released from Robben Island. There is thus some evidence that SASM, unlike other Black Consciousness organizations, had links with the ANC. Such contacts undoubtedly contributed to its outlook, but the students learned primarily from their own experience, which, for many, included detention or imprisonment. According to Alan Brooks and Jeremy Brickhill, who have studied the

1976 uprising, the new generation was "reared in a climate even harsher than its forebears knew . . . a climate of terror, in which torture has become routine, indefinite detention normal, lengthy imprisonment unavoidable, and violent death an ever-present possibility . . . a climate of fear and suspicion fueled by the insidious threat of informers." Such backgrounds inevitably gave rise to discussions of violent strategies, but the student leaders nevertheless appear to have planned June 16 as a day of peaceful protest.

The government was not in a mood to respond in kind, however. James Kruger, the minister of justice, made his feelings clear on the occasion of the reenactment of the old Suppression of Communism Act under the new title of Internal Security Act. The government would use its full powers, said Kruger, not only against those it labeled "Communist" but also against "other people as well who, in an absolute spirit of un-South Africanism, are trying to smear, disparage and injure our country at every turn." He was thinking of "young Black Power members who, with the help of the Christian Institute of Beyers Naude [a distinguished Dutch Reformed church theologian and former member of the Broederbond who had been deprived of his status as a minister for accepting the directorship of the institute], . . . are creating a polarization" and of people who were "organizing these black people into trade unions . . . so that at a certain point they can use strikes to proceed to a revolution."

He spoke only a month before June 16.

THE SOWETO UPRISING OF JUNE 1976 TO THE CRACKDOWN OF OCTOBER 1977

The figures for those killed or wounded in the Soweto uprising, plus others for those imprisoned or flogged, only begin to convey the depth of the passions aroused on both sides by the clash between students and police. There are also hundreds of eyewitness accounts of youthful black fury and of indiscriminate police shooting and brutality. The combination of anger and fear stirred in the youths is suggested by the fact that two years afterward, according to the head of the security police, 4,000 of those who had fled were in guerrilla training camps outside the country, three-fourths of them with the ANC, and most of the rest with the PAC. Suggestive of the government's implacable and enduring hostility toward black militants was the death of Steve Biko while in the custody of the security police on September 12, 1977. Bernard Levin of the *Times* of London commented that Biko was the forty-fourth black South African to die since September 1963 while in police custody on security grounds and "in circumstances sufficiently suspicious to warrant investigation."

"Soweto" has come to mean not only the June 16 uprising but also a whole series of subsequent events: school boycotts and strikes; marches of tens of thousands; demonstrations extending into downtown Johannesburg; the burning or sabotage of symbols of white oppression, including government offices, beer halls, and liquor stores in African townships; clashes with police; police attacks on gatherings at funerals, where the slogan often heard was "Don't mourn—mobilize." Soweto reverberated in almost all parts of South Africa, crescendos of violence alternating with periods of uneasy calm until the end of 1977. Even after that, disturbances continued for several more months in Port Elizabeth. Among the major population centers, only Durban escaped large-scale violence, probably in part because of the influence of Chief Gatsha Buthelezi. KwaZulu remained generally quiet, but protests and arson spread to the University of Zululand as well as to the other homelands. In Bophuthatswana the legislative hall was burned down.

Power given to the police after Sharpeville made unnecessary the proclamation of a national emergency, but African and Coloured areas were ruled, in effect, by martial law. On the black side, there was no central leadership or overall strategy. The Soweto Students' Representative Council provided almost the only organized direction, and in time even this dynamic group was worn down by repeated raids on schools and homes and the detention of successive leaders. Yet the campaign against Bantu education intensified, and protest widened to encompass the entire system of white domination.

The African community did not present a united front. Divisive strains and tensions had always existed, and the uprising and the subsequent events tended to bridge these differences in some cases but exacerbate them in others. The young people themselves were a far from homogeneous group. More than half of Soweto's population was estimated to be under the age of twenty, but in 1976 only some 170,000 were registered at school. Youths who could not afford school or who had dropped out could not be expected to sympathize with protests about education. On the other hand, once demonstrations got out of hand, those among them who were jobless or who had become the petty gangsters known as *tsotsis* were not at all averse to violence against the police and other symbols of white authority.

Some straining of relations between students and parents, traditionally accorded special respect in African society, might also have seemed inevitable. Many in the older generation did not share their children's militancy. Yet one of the major consequences of Soweto was a narrowing of this generation gap. Parents responded to events with a mixture of shame for their own comparative docility, pride in the bravery and initiative of their sons and daughters, and rage at the devastating violence inflicted on them by the police.

The students' relations with older Africans in their roles as workers and breadwinners were another matter. Student leaders had few ties with workers and little appreciation of their overriding concern with bread-and-butter issues. Calls for political strikes like the three-day stay-at-homes of the 1950s met with only spotty cooperation in Soweto and elsewhere in August and September of 1976. A later effort at a five-day strike failed. The students met with outright hostility from migrant workers living in bachelor hostels. Resenting student demands that they participate in a stay-at-home in August 1976—and evidently encouraged and even assisted by the police—more than a thousand of these workers went on a rampage in Soweto lasting several days. Burning, looting, raping, and beating, they left at least ten Africans dead and more than a hundred injured, mostly teenagers.

In the broader black community, Soweto had an impact on the historic division between Africans and Coloureds. This division had been narrowing since the Nationalists came to power in 1948 and made it clear that all black groups were to bear the burden of apartheid. Coloureds had been active in the Congress Alliance of the 1950s, had been accepted as part of the black opposition by Steve Biko, and had forged links with Chief Buthelezi and other homeland leaders opposed to independence. But the most dramatic evidence of growing black unity was the participation of Coloured students in the protests that followed the Soweto uprising. The Coloured youths were particularly militant in Cape Town, marching through the downtown in September and November 1976 in a show of solidarity with African students.

Soweto brought to the fore the question of where the real leadership of the African community lay. During the period of turmoil several groups held center stage successively, with the general trend toward increasing militancy.

Shortly after June 16 government officials met for nine hours with the "Committee of Thirty," a group of prominent Africans representing, according to the press, "moderate and conservative black opinion." The committee was derided by younger leaders, and its initial program—a call for limited policy changes to alleviate certain chronic grievances—was predictably cautious. But even it could not ignore the long-standing black demand for fundamental change in political arrangements. "The focal point of all the issues they raised," said a reporter, "was political rights for Africans." Stressing deliberate rather than hasty change and avoiding talk of one person, one vote, the committee "asked for the powers of the Urban Bantu Councils to be expanded as a preliminary step toward African representation in the provincial councils and, ultimately, Parliament."

Seeking a more credible adult ally and a link to the black community at large, the Soweto students turned to the Black Parents' Association. The BPA was formed following the start of violence to meet the sudden need of many families for medical, financial, and legal assistance and for help in arranging funerals. Manas Buthelezi, a distinguished Lutheran theologian and an exponent of Black Consciousness, was elected chairman. The BPA represented "a vast number of influential black organizations," including the BPC, SASO, and SASM, said Buthelezi, and its contacts reached beyond Soweto. Rather than assuming a leadership role, the BPA functioned mainly as a conduit to transmit the students' grievances to the authorities. But its request for a meeting with the minister of Bantu education was refused, and in August 1976, acting under the Internal Security Act, the government detained a large number of black civic leaders and journalists, including the BPA committee. Manas Buthelezi himself, however, was said to have been detained by "mistake" and was quickly released. The other detainees were held till the end of the year.

The BPA was eventually eclipsed by the Soweto Local Authority Interim Committee, popularly known as the Committee of Ten. It was formed in June 1977 in the wake of the collapse of the Soweto Urban Bantu Council, whose members had resigned under pressure in face-to-face encounters with student leaders. The students had rejected such government-sponsored bodies as "collaborationist" and had mounted a successful campaign against a rent increase that the council had accepted.

The committee emerged from an extraordinary meeting of almost one hundred representatives of nearly all Soweto organizations, including Chief Buthelezi's Inkatha. Dr. Nthato Motlana, a physician who had been a member of the ANC and was prominent in the BPA, served as its chairman. One of its chief proposals was for an autonomous, self-governing Soweto, and the differences that remained even within the militants' own ranks were suggested by the divergent responses to the plan. Some radicals and Black Consciousness activists criticized it as indistinguishable from acceptance of the homelands. On the other hand, some of the older Black Consciousness leaders viewed it as a step toward a gradual, piece-by-piece takeover of South Africa.

As other groups waxed and waned, the underground ANC appears to have experienced a steady expansion of its influence after June 16, 1976. In his report on Soweto and its aftermath, Judge Cillie found that the ANC, the PAC, and the South African Communist party had all played an active role in encouraging the riots. Yet in reality the ANC seems to have been largely oblivious of the passions building in the Soweto schools over the Afrikaans language issue and to have been taken unaware by the explosion of June 16. That was almost certainly spontaneous, and both before and after, student leaders appear to have acted almost entirely on their own.

At the same time, as the disorders spread students did seek out ANC leaders for advice, for assistance in producing leaflets, and for help in escaping from the country. During this period the ANC became an increasingly prominent presence through the arrests and trials of its activists, the circulation of its clandestinely prepared literature, and its "Freedom Radio" broadcasts from outside the Republic. A few students joined its cells. Its underground recruiting network became more active, and the occasional capture of guerrillas revealed caches of weapons. On June 13, 1977, the "Goch Street incident" occurred, occasioning much premature commentary about the start of urban guerrilla war. It involved three former Soweto students who had taken military training outside South Africa after 1976. Apparently acting in panic, they killed two whites with Czech-made submachine guns near the police headquarters in downtown Johannesburg. This occurred on the eve of an elaborate trial of eleven men and one woman alleged to be key recruiters for the ANC's military wing. Some of these were convicted. It might seem that the successful prosecutions, coupled with the guerrillas' failures, would tarnish the appeal of the

ANC, but there was no sign of this. Even the failures signified that something was happening.

In the months following the June 1976 Soweto uprising, the school boycott spread to many other areas, both urban and rural, and broadened to include upper primary schools as well as high schools and junior highs. Again, government buildings, this time including schools, were burned. Some five hundred secondary school teachers resigned in protest against Bantu education. From the government's viewpoint, the situation seemed on the way to becoming uncontrollable, with no end in sight, and that judgment presumably weighed heavily in a decision to crack down on October 19, 1977. Although the authorities had relaxed the Afrikaans requirement soon after the troubles began and had taken other ameliorative steps and promised more, the concessions had gained it little. Its détente initiatives in Africa had virtually collapsed, and its image abroad had been further damaged. Western governments and businesses were reassessing South African stability. Fear and uncertainty gripped the white community. The outrage at home and abroad over Steve Biko's death in September 1977 had heightened the government's sense of being under assault from all sides.

Defending the crackdown—the most extensive since Sharpeville in 1960— the minister of justice assailed "a small group of anarchists" and organizations bent on subversion that hid behind a smokescreen of "sweet-sounding names and aims." Communists had taken advantage of the situation, he said, and the United States had contributed to unrest by indicating it wanted one man, one vote in South Africa.

On October 19 the government declared unlawful the Black Parents' Association, the Black People's Convention, Black Community Programmes, the South African Students' Organization, the South African Students' Movement, twelve other Black Conciousness organizations, and the Christian Institute, which had opposed apartheid for fourteen years despite continual harassment. The funds and property of these groups, including the BCP mobile clinic, were confiscated. The government also closed down the white-owned but black-edited *World,* which, with a circulation that topped 200,000 on weekends, was the largest publication aimed at a black audience. Forty-seven black leaders were detained. Besides the *World*'s editor, Percy Qoboza, the detainees included Dr. Motlana, chairman of the Committee of Ten. The government also banned seven prominent whites, including Beyers Naude of the Christian Institute and Donald Woods, editor of the East London *Daily Dispatch* and a friend of Biko.

"Most of the organizations outlawed and persons arrested . . . are noted for their moderation and their Western middle-class values and their public commitment to achieving change through peaceful means," Jim Hoagland reported to the *Washington Post.* One of the banned whites was the Reverend Theo Kotze, an Afrikaner who had been serving as director of the Christian

Institute in the western Cape. Nine months later Kotze fled South Africa for Britain. Only economic sanctions, he told the *Times* of London, could bring white South Africans "to their senses."

THE CONTEMPORARY PERIOD: 1977–80

In October 1980 Percy Qoboza, by then freed from detention and editing the Johannesburg *Post,* successor to the banned *World,* said that under the "relatively peaceful surface" of South Africa, "there is a volcano of anger and discontent. It is only a matter of time until the volcano will erupt." Early in the year the successful conclusion of the armed struggle against white rule in Zimbabwe stirred new speculation about a black "war of liberation" in South Africa.

Revolution is in the making in South Africa. But despite the talk of imminent upheaval, it must almost certainly be viewed as a process of undermining and eventually overcoming white power rather than as a single eruption or cataclysmic event. It is true that the rapidity with which nearly uncontrollable disorder can spread and threaten to immobilize the economy has been demonstrated on a number of occasions. But it is difficult to envision a revolutionary turnover in power in the absence of a largely unified, well-organized, and well-led opposition movement, and such a movement has yet to take shape.

Although in 1980 Bishop Tutu, by then secretary-general of the South African Council of Churches, envisaged Nelson Mandela as prime minister within five to ten years, leaders of the African National Congress are preparing for a longer effort. While committed to the necessity of "armed struggle" and "the seizure of power," they place greater emphasis on mass politicization and unarmed action. They are essentially in accord with the conception of revolution advanced by the lawyers for the prosecution in the treason trial of the 1950s, who saw it as the "consummation" of "a long and flexible process involving boycotts, strikes, civil disobedience, and stoppage of work." In contrast to the limited tactic of sabotage in the 1960s, ANC guerrillas are prepared to kill armed antagonists, but the ANC declares that it rejects terrorist killing. It is the first liberation movement to sign the protocol of the Geneva Conventions on the "humanitarian conduct of war," which extended the conventions to wars of national liberation.

This process has been developing, irregularly and with major setbacks, since the end of World War II, but by 1980 the pace had quickened. Whereas Sharpeville was followed by a lull in black activism, the post-Soweto years have been marked by the resurgence of the underground ANC and by growing radicalism, evident in renewed political activity and in waves of strikes and boycotts that have become endemic.

188

CONTINUED REPRESSION

Concerned about its international reputation, the government has attempted to use its arsenal of powers with restraint. It has intimidated the black political opposition with warnings, close surveillance, and limited restrictions. While avoiding the banning of more organizations, it has incapacitated them by banning or detaining any individuals who appeared threatening.

The government's reaction to a meeting of black activists at the end of April 1978 was typical. More than sixty blacks, including Bishop Tutu, met at a church center near Soweto to launch the Azanian People's Organization (AZAPO). This was essentially a reincarnation of the banned Black People's Convention. A few days after the meeting, before a constitution could be drafted and a planned public rally held, police detained the principal organizers under the Terrorism Act.

Bishop Tutu was not detained, but early in 1980 the government seized his passport (it was restored a year later and recently seized again) after he called for a boycott of South African coal while on a visit to Denmark. Prominent blacks who had been detained in the 1977 crackdown were similarly kept under tight rein after the government began to release them in March 1978. Some were banned and others were subjected to tailor-made restrictions designed to induce self-censorship. Shortly after Dr. Motlana made a fiery speech on the anniversary of Soweto in 1978, the minister of justice banned him for a month.

Presumably the authorities exercised caution in their treatment of persons as prominent as Motlana and Tutu, who were well known abroad. On the other hand, the government displayed its continued readiness to repress when it renewed its persecution of black journalists at the end of 1980 by banning Zwelakhe Sisulu, news editor of the *Sunday Post,* president of the Media Workers' Association of South Africa (described later), and son of imprisoned ANC leader Walter Sisulu.

Security officials also may strike almost at random, as they did in going after the instigators of a spreading school boycott in the Cape in May and June 1980. The police detained without charge four hundred or more persons, including older Coloureds and Indians with reputations for moderation. The detainees also included primary-school children.

Since the death of Steve Biko, there have been no deaths of political prisoners while in the custody of the security police. But accumulated evidence and testimony in trials have indicated a continuing pattern of beatings, electric shock, and other forms of torture of black detainees, including people in their early teens. Of special importance because of the effect on parents have been the indiscriminate attacks by the police on schoolchildren engaged in boycotts and demonstrations.

THE BLACK VIEW OF OFFICIAL POLICY

As Prime Minister Pieter W. Botha entered his third year in office in October 1980, virtually no black leader saw any sign of basic change in National party goals. Some had professed to find encouragement in the government's recognition that long-standing policies on the homelands and urban Africans were unrealistic, but even these black leaders shared the common belief that the government and its supporters were unshaken in their determination to confine change to the framework of white supremacy.

In its search for accommodation, the government has been unable to win the cooperation of popular black leaders, not only Africans but Coloureds and Indians as well. Among Coloureds, the ten-year-old Labor party, much criticized by young and radical blacks for its participation in the Coloured Persons' Representative Council, brought about the collapse of the council by late 1979. A move by the government to replace this largely elected body with an entirely appointed one has fared no better. Even Indians who have served on the half-elected South African Indian Council have become disillusioned, and some have resigned. Elections for a new, wholly elected council were postponed in 1979 and 1980.

The new President's Council, charged with advising the government on constitutional change, has been shunned by all significant black leaders. Its foes include not only the militants opposed to participation in all instrumentalities of separate development but also the leaders of the parties represented in the Coloured and Indian councils, who object to its exclusion of Africans. Chief Buthelezi's Zulu-based national movement, Inkatha, views the body as a step backward, and even the ordinarily nonpolitical Pretoria Chinese Association expelled a member who accepted a seat on the council.

The government's attempts to woo urban Africans with property-owning rights, greater freedom of movement, and more local autonomy also meet widespread black skepticism. Oliver Tambo, exiled head of the ANC, warned in January 1980 that the Nationalists intended "to buy some of us out by creating a black middle class." The Riekert Commission, said Bishop Tutu two months later, was "ruthless" about expelling unqualified Africans from urban areas and at the same time sought to create a "highly privileged black middle class who are surely going to be some of the best defenders of a status quo that provides them with such benefits and privileges." And Chief Buthelezi has described Pretoria's moves as an effort "to buy off black anger" and to separate urban from rural Africans.

BLACK LEADERSHIP

Who are the "real" black leaders in South Africa—the "true" or "genuine" representatives? Blacks who reject officially sponsored institutions frequently speak in these terms. So do white opinion makers whose sense of urgency about negotiation has grown since Robert Mugabe's election in Rhodesia in February 1980 shocked many white South Africans and demonstrated how badly they had overestimated popular support for the Bishop Abel Muzorewa.

"The lessons of Mugabe's resounding victory" were clear, said *Die Vaderland*, a leading Afrikaans newspaper, shortly after the vote. "The traditional leaders are not the men with the people behind them. The more radical, the greater the support. We must therefore talk to the true leaders." In the judgment of *Beeld,* seats at the negotiating table could not be reserved only for homeland leaders. On the contrary, room "would have to be made for the Motlanas and the Thozamile Bothas." Botha was head of the Port Elizabeth Black Civic Organization, an activist group that had been formed in October 1979 and reportedly attracted up to 10,000 people to its meetings. Restricted by a banning order, Botha escaped to Lesotho in May 1980 and joined the ANC.

Among the "traditional" leaders are the homeland officials. Whites have relied on their cooperation, but their standing among blacks has slipped badly, particularly in the case of the leaders who have gone along with homeland independence.

Comparable groups are to be found in the urban Community Councils, successors to the Urban Bantu Councils. They have some additional administrative duties but no real powers and little popular acceptance. Most members won office through elections in which relative handfuls of voters participated. All the same, the councils provide salaries, perquisites, and some personal power and influence to a small group of Africans. Perhaps the most publicized council member is David Thebehali, known as the "mayor" of Soweto. He was elected with ninety-seven votes in an election that turned out 4.4 percent of the voters in his district. Ebullient and self-assured, Thebehali dispenses favors much like an old-time American political boss. For this reason, and because of electrification and other improvements under way in Soweto, he predicts a great increase in support at the next election.

The government is reluctant to undercut those who collaborate with it by recognizing leaders outside its system. Nevertheless, Pieter Koornhof, the minister in charge of African affairs, has met privately with men like Motlana and in 1979 invited him, Bishop Tutu, Percy Qoboza, and the Reverend Sam Buti, the leading African in the Dutch Reformed church, then serving as president of the South African Council of Churches, to participate in an advisory committee on the future of urban Africans.

Motlana, Tutu, and Qoboza, who are sensitive to the attitudes of radical youth, refused to join what they regard as a powerless body headed by a government official. Buti joined the committee but soon quit in discouragement. In the end, most of the twenty-six Africans on the committee represented community councils or homelands and possessed almost no stature as popular leaders. Thus, even this rather modest government attempt to reach out to the "real" black leadership must be rated a failure.

Any discussion of black leadership must reckon with Nelson Mandela of the ANC. Imprisoned in 1962 and sentenced in 1964 to confinement for life on Robben Island, he has been a shadowy figure for the younger generation. But he has become a symbol of historic aspirations and of all leaders who have been silenced. Mandela is extolled even by blacks not committed, as he is, to armed struggle. In 1973 Chief Buthelezi declared that "real dialogue" required the participation of black "heroes": the exiled ANC leader Oliver Tambo, Robert Sobukwe of the PAC, and Mandela. "He represents all our genuine leaders, in prison and exile," said Bishop Tutu of Mandela in 1980, adding that "almost certainly" he would be the "first black prime minister." Some whites share these sentiments. A leading English-speaking editor has said privately that Mandela is South Africa's only hope.

Talk about a new national convention, which has recurred off and on for almost thirty years, often specifies as a prerequisite the participation of Mandela and others now in jail or in exile on the assumption that they would renounce violence. There does exist a sense that amnesty would be an important signal of fundamental change of direction by the government. On the other hand, such a change is itself a prerequisite for the renunciation of violence by revolutionaries.

On March 9, 1980, Percy Qoboza launched a petition campaign for Mandela's release in the *Sunday Post*. Qoboza is sympathetic to the Progressive Federal party—his stress has always been on nonviolent political activity—and his efforts are another indication of the breadth of Mandela's following. By early September 1980 more than 72,000 signatures and addresses had been collected on *Sunday Post* petition forms, but some supporters of the campaign complained that a better-organized, nationwide effort might have attracted a million signatures. In the meantime, *Race Relations News,* a publication of the nonpartisan and mainly white South African Institute of Race Relations, reprinted the petition form and endorsed the Free Mandela drive. The issue was banned, the official explanation being that "to plead for the release of Nelson Mandela is to propagate the aims of the ANC." In January 1981, the daily *Post* and *Sunday Post* were effectively banned.

Gatsha Buthelezi is also a force to be reckoned with. A descendant of Zulu royalty, he is a "traditional" leader who operates under separate development as chief minister of the KwaZulu homeland. But to a large extent he is in a class by himself. He has organized a political movement, Inkatha, whose membership exceeds that reached by the ANC when it functioned openly. Throughout the 1970s, he was one of the dominant black political figures in South Africa, regularly making headlines at home and also attracting attention on his frequent trips abroad, including many to the United States. By 1980, however, he had lost some of his support, especially among the youngsters who had marched in Soweto in 1976 and were now approaching maturity. Nevertheless, if only because of his role as the leader of the Zulus, the largest single ethnic bloc in South Africa, he remained an important figure.

Chief Buthelezi's expressed views are complex, have evolved with events, and appear from time to time to reflect the pressures of the difficult role he seeks to play. He won an early reputation as an African nationalist. He was a member of the ANC, and in 1950 he was expelled from Fort Hare College in the eastern Cape for taking part in an ANC Youth League boycott of a visit by the governor-general. At various times later in his life, he made statements supporting majority rule in an undivided South Africa. On March 14, 1976, for example, with new African governments in power in Mozambique and Angola, he declared in Soweto that "South Africa is one country" and the time had come to "move toward majority rule." In October 1977, shortly after the government crackdown on black activists, Buthelezi seemed to accept the necessity of violence to achieve change. "If so much violence is used to maintain the status quo," he said, "political realists will come to the conclusion that they should resort to violence to bring about change." Shortly thereafter the Johannesburg *Star* quoted him in apparent support of international sanctions against South Africa.

More often his statements run in the other direction, stressing accommodation and negotiation instead of confrontation and violence. He has been critical of much of the militancy of the late 1970s. A 1980 Inkatha publication asserted that uncoordinated strikes and boycotts had little prospect of winning "meaningful concessions." Buthelezi himself urged the ending of a 1980 school boycott in Natal, blaming it on a small group of outside agitators. He condemned, as mindless, damage done by demonstrators to schools in KwaZulu and also disorder at the University of Zululand. More often than not Buthelezi has denounced those who call for foreign firms to withdraw their investments from South Africa. Perhaps most important, he appears convinced that it is possible for blacks to strike a deal with the ruling whites and has engaged in lengthy discussions with whites of all political persuasions. In the course of these he has shown a willingness to consider new political arrangements other than majority rule in an undivided South Africa that he advocated in Soweto in 1976. He has, for example, displayed recurrent interest in a kind of federal or confederal arrangement that includes an autonomous area combining KwaZulu and Natal.

Chief Buthelezi has established himself as one of the most outspoken homeland leaders. For many years he blocked the creation of a Zulu Territorial Authority, the first step toward homeland status. When he acquiesced in the setting up of the KwaZulu homeland in 1970, he won election as chief minister and proceeded to use his official platform to assail apartheid. At the "summit" meeting of homeland leaders in Umtata, capital of the Transkei, in November 1973, he took the lead in a display of solidarity against the acceptance of formal independence—a solidarity shortly to be undermined, however, by Chief Kaiser Matanzima of the Transkei.

The importance of political organization in achieving change is a frequent Buthelezi theme. He has argued that carefully orchestrated grass-roots pressures—mainly workers' power and consumers' power—could bring radical change without violence by forcing the whites into a negotiating process that would culminate in a national convention. Inkatha demonstrates his faith in the power of organization. Founded in 1928 by King Dinizulu, his grandfather, as a Zulu cultural movement, Inkatha* was revived by Buthelezi in 1974–75 as the basis for a political mass movement open to all Africans, although the membership is still largely Zulu. By mid-1978 Inkatha—of which Buthelezi is president—was said to have 150,000 paid-up members; by mid-1980, more than 300,000.

While building a large black following, Buthelezi has also cultivated ties to whites. Some analysts suggest that he has calculated that as pressures mount for radical change, whites will turn to him as the most acceptable black leader. Both Nationalist and Progressive Federal party whites and Afrikaans- and English-speaking businessmen have been attracted by his promise of reform and stability within South Africa's capitalist system.

In January 1974, in a speech before the South African Institute of Race Relations, Buthelezi envisaged a federation—perhaps more accurately a confederation—comprising three types of states: those in which the interests of an "African ethnic group" were paramount, those in which white interests were paramount, and "multinational" states. By allowing each state to decide its own franchise and by giving limited powers to the federal Parliament, Buthelezi suggested, the controversial issue of control of a central Parliament "could at least be postponed for several generations." "The emphasis" of his proposal, he said, "is on constituent independent states that should be established in terms of the government's policy of separate development."

Despite this essentially moderate approach, Buthelezi's move to broaden Inkatha to include non-Zulus made Nationalist leaders initially uneasy. But by 1978 Inkatha representatives, including Buthelezi himself, had begun meeting with key Nationalists, and in time a continuing dialogue developed between the two groups. The Nationalist contingent included some of the most conservative members of Parliament. By the spring of 1980 four series of meetings had taken place, each lasting two or three days and growing in size to about thirty participants on each side. Some of the participating whites have noted that the Afrikaners and the Zulus are the two most powerful forces in South Africa and have suggested they should get together. Inkatha members have acknowledged that the meetings have aroused fears of an Inkatha-National party deal, but they have stressed the necessity of dealing with the holders of power. Believing that consensus on the need to share power must precede the holding of a national convention, Inkatha has looked upon the

*Inkatha's full name, Inkatha yeNkululeko yeSizwe, means "National Cultural Liberation Movement."

meetings as a way of bringing Nationalists to such a consensus. For their part, the Nationalists have continually raised the question of protecting "group rights." Inkatha has responded by saying that it recognizes that interest groups may consist mainly of members of one race.

Some Afrikaner Nationalists, but not Prime Minister Botha or his cabinet, have shown interest in giving Inkatha control of an area combining KwaZulu and Natal, whose white residents are largely English-speaking. The Nationalists' apparent aim is to advance separate development by pushing Inkatha toward acceptance of independence for the Zulu homeland. Inkatha has repeatedly refused independence for KwaZulu, insisting that South Africa is one country. But Buthelezi's plans for a federated South Africa that would include KwaZulu-Natal as one of its components conceivably could be reconciled with a modified version of the Nationalists' views, even though for now their stated goals remain homeland consolidation and independence. In 1980 Buthelezi and the KwaZulu legislative assembly appointed a commission to consider some form of provincial autonomy as a substitute for homeland independence. Many English-speaking white businessmen in Natal think along the same lines, as is evidenced by their sponsorship of the Lombard plan for a multiracial Natal (see chapter 8). Buthelezi, who would be the obvious choice for overall leader of the province if the plan were carried out, welcomed the proposal and said his own commission would consider it.

One of Buthelezi's strongest statements on the need "to negotiate with the Afrikaner and the Nationalist party" to avert violence came in a speech made on a trip to the United States in August 1979. "Persuasion backed by power from the people" could turn "opponents into allies," he said. Buthelezi dismissed "early cries for one man, one vote" as unrealistic. South Africa, he said, might have to "pass through phases" to "accommodate white fears, and other minority interests." Throughout the speech, Buthelezi expressed new confidence in peaceful change, an attitude apparently inspired by Botha and Koornhof. Those who took up arms were guilty of "barbarism," and "industrial sabotage" was out of the question "in the foreseeable future."

Nine months later ANC guerrillas carried out a dramatic act of industrial sabotage when they set fire to SASOL facilities. The bombing showed how different the approaches of Buthelezi and black radicals had grown.

The division had been in the making for many years. When Black Consciousness emerged as a force in South Africa, Buthelezi had moved cautiously to align himself with it. He accepted the Black Consciousness definition of "black" as embracing Africans, Coloureds, and Indians. Indeed, the South African Black Alliance, formed by Buthelezi in 1978 to promote black unity, still exists, though it has had little impact. It is an uneasy alliance of Inkatha, the Coloured Labor party, and the middle-class Indian Reform party, joined by leaders of the KaNgwane and Qwaqwa homelands.

As far back as the early 1970s, however, Buthelezi was beginning to part company with the more radical young black leaders. In 1972 Steve Biko described him as the "one man who has led the entire world to believe in the Bantustan [homeland] philosophy." By 1977 some black students were demonstrating against Buthelezi, and African newspapers were printing letters labeling him a "stooge" and a "sellout." The hostility of young radicals to Buthelezi took a violent turn when he appeared at the funeral of Robert Sobukwe, leader of the PAC, in the small town of Graaf-Reinet in the eastern Cape on March 11, 1978. Even though Sobukwe's brother had invited Buthelezi to speak at the funeral, some youths spat and jeered at Buthelezi and hurled stones, forcing him to leave.

The story of Buthelezi's relations with the ANC and the PAC is complex. Leaders of these organizations have often criticized Buthelezi, but at the same time they have respected his political skills and the size of his following. Sobukwe himself shared this ambivalence, telling a foreign journalist in 1975 that he admired Buthelezi personally but felt that he had inadvertently become identified with separate development. Similarly, the ANC, while critical of Buthelezi's continued support for foreign investment in South Africa and uneasy about his close ties to Nationalist leaders, generally refrained from attacking him throughout the 1970s. The ANC leaders distinguished between Buthelezi and homeland leaders who accepted independence, such as Matanzima. Unable to mobilize support openly within South Africa themselves, they saw Inkatha as a mass movement that might eventually mesh with the ANC.

Buthelezi reciprocated, speaking warmly of the ANC's "ideals." Inkatha adopted the ANC's anthem and its colors of green, gold, and black. The high point of Buthelezi's relations with the ANC occurred in the fall of 1979. Buthelezi and an Inkatha delegation met with Oliver Tambo and other ANC officials in London. Afterward Buthelezi said that Inkatha and the ANC were destined to form a "united front."

By June 1980 prospects for a "united front" were dim. The month began with the SASOL bombing, and then on June 29 the front page of the Johannesburg *Sunday Post* trumpeted: "ANC Slams Buthelezi." The ANC had many grievances against Buthelezi, but the immediate cause of the split was Buthelezi's condemnation of a rash of school boycotts by blacks that had spread to KwaZulu. Addressing a May 18 youth rally, he warned that "however much I may personally be committed to nonviolence," troublemakers might have "their skulls cracked." Later he told the Inkatha annual meeting that "we need to create well-disciplined and regimented *impis* [bands of warriors] in every Inkatha region" to keep order.

In the face of such assaults on the boycotts, the ANC felt it was no longer possible to smooth over its differences with Buthelezi. There was also a sense that events were leaving Buthelezi behind, a belief that may have been encouraged by the influx of Black Consciousness activists into the ANC. In the June 29 *Post* an ANC spokesman was quoted as saying of Buthelezi: "More and more, he has been identifying himself with the South African government. His action in calling on his *impis* to harass the children involved in the school boycott at KwaMashu and for them to attend school and the fact that he is not an enthusiastic supporter of the campaign to free Mandela show his attitude." (Although Buthelezi had backed the release of Mandela in 1973, he was averse to joining a "theatrical" petition campaign initiated by others.)

The ANC's break with Buthelezi may hamper Inkatha's efforts to further broaden its appeal beyond the Zulus. It may also weaken the loyalty of some of Buthelezi's present following. Nevertheless, he is likely to remain the leader of a large and powerful segment of the black population, as well as one of the black leaders most acceptable to whites. As such, he remains a major force in South Africa, on both the regional and national levels.

A widely publicized survey of black public opinion done for a West German study group in 1977 found that Gatsha Buthelezi was the political figure most admired by 43.8 percent of the Africans in Soweto, Durban, and Pretoria. ANC leaders came in second with 21.7 percent. Homeland leaders other than Buthelezi received 18.3 percent, Robert Sobukwe 7.4 percent, and Black Consciousness leaders only 5.6 percent. The survey found that 40.3 percent of Buthelezi's supporters among urban Africans were not Zulus. Among the survey's limitations were its exclusion of the Xhosa-speaking areas of the eastern Cape, an area long noted for its political awareness, and of the western Cape. Also, some current leaders, such as Dr. Nthato Motlana, became prominent after the study was conducted.

An early 1978 survey of educated urban dwellers yielded different results. The survey was limited to Soweto, an area "commonly considered to represent the political vanguard of Black South Africa," according to Lawrence Schlemmer, a South African social scientist who supervised the survey. To men sixteen years and older whose education was standard eight (mid-high school) and above, this question was posed: "Think of people like yourself in Soweto—people who live and work around you. Who would they see to be their real leaders?" The response to a list of possible answers was Soweto Committee of Ten, 54 percent; ANC people in jail or outside South Africa, 21 percent; former members of the banned Black People's Convention, 7 percent; former members of the banned (and short-lived) Black Parents' Association, 7 percent; and Buthelezi, 5 percent. Late in 1980 Soweto support for Motlana's Committee of Ten, Buthelezi's Inkatha, and Thebehali's Community Council was 69 percent, 9 percent, and 5 percent, respectively, according to a survey done for the Johannesburg *Star*.

BLACK POLITICAL ACTIVITY

Political activity unsanctioned by the government is risky. Except for Buthelezi, no black leader has been able to build an aboveground mass organization.

The police act quickly to crush any group involved in boycotts or demonstrations that appear threatening.

Even so, a great deal of black political activity takes place. Almost immediately after the government crackdown in October 1977, Africans who had not been banned sought to revive open political opposition. New groups sprang up in Soweto to take over from banned organizations and individuals. In 1979 there was a new surge in political organizing. In June the Congress of South African Students (COSAS), representing mainly African schools below the university level, was formed. In September the Committee of Ten formed the Soweto Civic Association. Later in the month AZAPO, which had been inactive after its formation the preceding year and the detention of its principal organizers, held its inaugural conference. The Port Elizabeth Black Civic Organization was formed in October. In November students from African and Indian universities formed the Azanian Students' Organization.

Organizations not overtly political in character serve political functions. The Writers' Association of South Africa moved into the vacuum created by the banning of the Union of Black Journalists in 1977. Later broadened to include all workers employed by newspapers, radio, and television and renamed the Media Workers' Association of South Africa, it has sought to strengthen blacks' editorial role. In December 1980 the Media Workers won recognition and demands for nondiscriminatory salaries in a two-month strike against white-owned publishing companies. The Methodist church, whose more than three million members are largely black, has called for one person, one vote. Also important in developing political consciousness and articulating demands are African business organizations; professional groups such as the Black Lawyers' Association, the nonracial Democratic Lawyers' Association, the South African Black Social Workers' Association, and large organizations of African and Coloured teachers; literary, cultural, and sporting groups; and black trade unions.

The political activities of such organizations are, of course, only the surface manifestations of deep and powerful currents of feeling. The intensity of these feelings is evident in the large crowds that often turn out on such occasions as the funeral of the occasional black guerrilla killed by security forces or the commemoration of an event like Sharpeville or the death of Steve Biko. It is also evident in the defiant demeanor of the young defendants in the continuing series of "security" trials. What would such intensity mean if it could be translated into unconstrained political activity? In 1976, shortly after Soweto, Sam Motsuenyane, president of the National African Federated Chambers of Commerce, offered an opinion. Asked by the *Financial Mail*, the country's leading business journal, for his estimate of support for the ANC and the PAC, he said he had "no evidence that they have widespread influence in the townships." But then he added: "If they had not been outlawed, they would have had massive support."

Predicting what will emerge from the welter of conflicting pressures in South Africa is risky. Nevertheless, there are some expectations that are all but truisms—for example, that the white regime will prove incapable of crushing all resistance permanently and that the black opposition will grow again after any crackdown. Six major trends in the black challenge to white authority that can be stated with almost equal assurance are set forth below.

1. *Acceptance of revolutionary violence.* There is a growing though reluctant acceptance—Chief Gatsha Buthelezi may be the most conspicuous exception—of the belief that fundamental change will come about only through revolutionary violence. Especially among young urban blacks, the watchword that has been gaining currency is "Which side of the gun are you on?" Africans began leaving South Africa for military training abroad about 1973. As noted earlier, during the two years after Soweto, according to security police sources, some 4,000 Africans left the Witwatersrand for such training. A small but steady exodus continues and now includes Coloureds.

These and other young people, believing that they have no stake in the system and facing dead-end or low-paid jobs or no jobs at all, chafe at inaction. Moreover, older blacks increasingly share their impatience, and many are resigning themselves to the inevitability of sabotage and guerrilla warfare as part of the overall pressure for change. Despite criticism from radicals, some continue to meet with the prime minister and otherwise to explore the possibilities of change through negotiation; in light of their long-standing opposition to violence, they can hardly close any doors. Yet those who take part in the exchanges with white leaders often emerge with their fears of a looming confrontation confirmed.

The fear of uncontrollable violence is probably as widespread among blacks as among whites, and disputes about alternative strategies continue. The appeal of Buthelezi's Inkatha lies partly in its vision of an organized force that one day will overwhelm white power without first plunging the country into a long period of disruption and violence. Another strategy being discussed is civil disobedience, even though ever since the government's harsh response to the Defiance Campaign of 1952, the conventional wisdom has held that civil disobedience cannot be conducted on a mass scale in South Africa. One influential advocate is Allan Boesak, a Coloured theologian at the University of the Western Cape. But civil disobedience appears likely to be of only marginal importance, reinforcing other more forceful pressures.

2. *Growing interest in radical ideology.* Since 1976 young blacks have become more interested in reading and discussing Marxism, socialism, and class analysis. Increasingly they use the rhetoric of radical ideology. Young adherents of Black Consciousness who are prisoners on Robben Island now refer to themselves as Marxists. In exile, some Black Consciousness activists

who have not joined the ANC claim a more radical position by virtue of new-found "scientific socialism." The ANC leadership, on the other hand, minimizes such ideological analysis and continues to stress its traditional themes of African nationalism and nonracial political power.

Although popular understanding of radical concepts is presumably low, in three major surveys urban blacks preferred to call themselves Communists, Marxists, or socialists rather than capitalists, according to a May 1979 report in the Johannesburg *Star*. Among the better educated, a serious effort appears to be under way to fuse Black Consciousness with class consciousness.

Radical ideology affects the attitudes of black South Africans in several ways—some positive, others disturbing to observers in the West. There is a tendency to see the liberation struggle either as one of both race and class or as one primarily of class. There is an inclination to take the longer view of the drive for equality and to discourage hasty or poorly planned action. Racial exclusiveness and antiwhite sentiment are muted. Interest is heightened in the role of Western capitalist states as underwriters and beneficiaries of the South African system. Barney Pityana, Steve Biko's close colleague who is now in exile, has given more attention to this role than did early Black Consciousness writings. Addressing a largely black audience at Howard University in the United States in 1979, he said, "Black Consciousness has a particular aversion for capitalism." He added, "The same Big Brother who oppresses in the States oppresses us in South Africa."

3. *Widening Coloured militancy.* Militancy is growing among all black South Africans: Africans, Coloureds, and Indians. "We have militant ten-year-olds and militant grandmothers supporting the same cause," said a Soweto educator after the 1977 crackdown. But it is among Coloureds, who once seemed willing to acquiesce in a role as second-class allies of the whites, that the rise in militancy has been most dramatic.

In August 1979 even the "collaborationist" leader of the conservative Freedom party within the Coloured Persons' Representative Council, W. J. Bergins, reversed himself and endorsed a single, nonracial Parliament. "When I look around me, all I can see are people in revolt. How can I still identify myself with the system that is propagating this?" The detention in 1980, almost at random, of Coloured leaders and academics with reputations as moderates increased alienation still further.

Coloured militancy was evidenced dramatically by the upheaval of mid-1980 in the Coloured townships in and near Cape Town, where Coloureds outnumber whites by more than three to two. Although Coloured students had joined African students in the streets of Cape Town in 1976, their actions in 1980 were unprecedented: They organized school boycotts, focused on broad political aims as well as educational concerns, and supported consumer boycotts linked to the demands of striking workers. Discipline was remarkable. There was far less violence and destruction than in Soweto in 1976, although in one three-day period in June at least thirty people died from police gunfire. In any event, the image of the Coloured community as politically apathetic and submissive was shattered.

As militancy has taken hold among rank-and-file Coloureds, the leadership of the Coloured Labor party, always the object of Black Consciousness attack because of its participation in the Coloured Persons' Representative Council, has been moving to the left. It has emphasized the futility of any constitutional proposals that exclude Africans and fall short of an eventual countrywide system based on one person, one vote. The Reverend Alan Hendrickse, the party's leader, has also stated that it will cooperate—in some as yet unspecified way—with the ANC. The Labor party has supported the withdrawal of foreign investment. Rumblings within the party suggest that it may break away from Buthelezi's South African Black Alliance.

In November 1980, seventy-five-year-old Ben Schoeman, who as a National party leader in the 1950s had supported the removal of the Coloureds from the common voters' roll, urged their restoration. "Circumstances have changed," he said. "I have said all along that we must make the Coloureds our allies, not our enemies. Today it is more imperative than ever." But it seems likely that the time when Coloureds could be expected to ally themselves with whites against Africans has passed.

4. *Growing black unity*. There is a narrowing of the gap between black students and their parents, black students and black workers, Coloureds and Africans, and Indians and Africans. The events of 1976 jolted the older African generation and strengthened its identification with the hopes and demands of the young. Equally noteworthy has been the disposition of many young African leaders to seek out and consult with political veterans. A similar process seems to have been under way among Coloureds and Indians in 1980.

Particularly devastating for many parents was the harsh response of the police to their children's participation in the school boycotts. Parents initially antagonistic to boycotts became sympathetic, and leaders among them became active in parents' committees. School principals and teachers also joined in protest.

Mindful of the clashes between students and hostel dwellers in Soweto in 1976, young black leaders increasingly reach out to workers. "We must not allow our action to become isolated in the schools," a Cape Town students' manifesto has warned. In a widely publicized action in 1980, Coloured and African students, assisted by a few white students, won wide community support in organizing a consumers' boycott of red meat in Cape Town and a fundraising campaign in support of eight hundred workers on strike for twelve weeks in the meat-packing industry. The boycott spread to other centers.

While unity appears to be the dominant trend, within black ranks important areas of real or potential disagreement remain. Some involve strategy—the duration of boycotts, for example. But others involve central issues, and one of the most important of these is the question of black tactics and aims regarding whites. Although Black Consciousness doctrines have held that during the struggle against apartheid racial polarization is necessary for unity against the white camp, the major black leaders and groups envisage a non-racial South Africa. Also, radical ideology stresses class over race. Yet there has long been a strong undercurrent of antiwhite feeling. Its virulence among young blacks could conceivably overwhelm the restraining influence of older leaders. Tsietsi Mashinini, one of the young Soweto activists who fled South Africa after the 1976 uprising, was asked on a New York television program if he hated whites. "I hate white people," he replied. "Everybody feels like taking a gun and wiping the whole white population off the face of the earth."

Other cracks in black unity could widen. The white regime's efforts to develop a contented African middle class in the urban areas could dilute the strength of the black opposition. Chief Buthelezi's split with the ANC may worsen. The independent homelands could align themselves even more closely with Pretoria's interests. Two of them, Bophuthatswana and Venda, are already involved in the military campaign against guerrilla infiltration.

5. *Growing political importance of black workers.* Many observers rate black trade unions as potentially the most powerful force for radical political change. Their reach is still very limited, however. Although membership in African unions has been growing, only about 2 percent of the African work force has been unionized so far. Moreover, the extension of black union power into the political arena must reckon with new government policies of tighter control of African and multiracial unions and with Pretoria's continuing practice of silencing individual leaders deemed threatening. Weak unions must take care not to jeopardize their existence by appearing to act in overtly political ways.

Nevertheless, significant changes are occurring in black labor. Black workers are moving into higher-skilled jobs. They are better educated, more militant, more politically aware. Their demands go beyond higher pay and deal with union rights and unfair dismissals. Workers are seeing strikes as weapons for achieving economic and social demands outside the workplace. As solidarity grows among workers and as they occupy more skilled positions, strikebreakers become scarcer. Workers are receiving support from their communities—the strike against the Ford Motor Company late in 1979 was encouraged by the Port Elizabeth Black Civic Organization—and from consumer boycotts linked to their demands. There is also a better understanding of how to take advantage of pressures abroad on foreign companies with interests in South Africa.

6. *Resurgence of the African National Congress.* As South Africa enters the 1980s, perhaps the most dramatic trend in black politics is the resurgence of the African National Congress. The ANC's renewed prominence was symbolized on the night of June 1, 1980, by the glow from burning SASOL oil-from-coal plants, which could be seen by people in Johannesburg some fifty-five miles

away. Infiltrators had cut through security fences and shot one guard in the course of a coordinated effort to sabotage three plants. Although damage amounting to nearly $8 million was done, there was no serious break in production. But the attack was the first sabotage of strategically crucial facilities. And the saboteurs escaped. South Africa has entered "a state of revolutionary war," the *Rand Daily Mail* proclaimed.

The newspaper was premature. The "war" was still at a very low level of intensity. That its escalation would be bloody was signaled by the regime's retaliatory raid on ANC houses in Maputo on January 29, 1981, reportedly killing at least eleven black South Africans. Government security officials have no doubt the level of conflict will rise.

After years of desultory amateurism, the ANC's military wing had begun demonstrating greater skill by the late 1970s. In a series of sporadic actions starting then, ANC guerrillas have attacked a handful of police stations and blown up rail lines. Black policemen, state witnesses, and informers have been killed, but the deaths have been few thus far and ANC policy continues to oppose the indiscriminate killing associated with terrorism. The Goch Street killing of two whites in Johannesburg in 1977 was an instance of panic, and the January 1980 death of two white hostages in a bank in the Pretoria suburb of Silverton resulted from an apparently impulsive and suicidal takeover of the bank by three ANC guerrillas who thought they were about to be apprehended. There have also been occasional clashes with the South African military and homeland forces in Bophuthatswana and Venda.

Goch Street and Silverton shocked whites. Their alarm was heightened by Soweto's according of hero status to the dead guerrillas, who during the bank siege had demanded the release of Nelson Mandela. More deeply disturbing, however, has been the long-term rise in guerrilla actions and the potential threat of industrial sabotage and destruction of oil pipelines, which would damage the climate for foreign business. There is also the danger of mass participation in simple forms of sabotage; already many defendants in security trials are untrained revolutionaries with no ANC connections.

As hundreds of security trials have indicated, infiltration has been stepped up, much of it through Mozambique. Zimbabwe is likely to be used as a route, and there appears to be frequent traffic between South Africa and Botswana. At present, however, the ANC has no military bases in adjacent countries. As many as 8,000 young blacks are believed to be in training outside South Africa, mainly in Angola but also in the Soviet Union, Tanzania, and elsewhere. East Germans do much of the instruction. Infiltrators need not be armed when they return home because large caches of weapons are available—as is evidenced by those periodically unearthed by the police. Thefts from the well-armed white population of South Africa are another source of weapons.

The ANC's strategy combines political and armed struggle. There are signs that future sabotage may be coordinated with political campaigns. In

October 1980, on the third anniversary of the 1977 crackdown, ANC guerrillas blew up rail lines and temporarily disrupted commuting between Soweto and Johannesburg. This coincided with demonstrations against higher rents and against a ceremony in which David Thebehali, head of the Soweto Community Council, was honoring Pieter Koornhof, the African affairs minister. There was also a concurrent disruption of bus service by stone-throwing youths seeking to enforce a stay-at-home by workers as part of the protests.

Much of the ANC's appeal lies in its historic reputation as the oldest African national movement. For the older generation it is comparable to a church that one is born into, the organization that has carried on while others have come and gone. It is, moreover, nondoctrinaire, with room for Marxists and non-Marxists, mildly socialist but not anticapitalist, open to whites even while envisaging a period of confrontation on color lines. Black Consciousness exiles and activists within South Africa have faced no ideological hurdles in turning to the ANC. The PAC's history of opposition to joint action with whites may make it seem more congenial to Black Consciousness, but internal disputes have left it largely ineffectual.

The new generation of exiles has found in the ANC a functioning organization with a well-established network of supporters and sources of money. Some 150 men and women work in its closely guarded offices in Lusaka, Zambia, some of them busy screening applications for membership. It also has offices in London, New York, Luanda, Maputo, and Cairo, among other places. The ANC stresses education of future leaders for South Africa. In 1980 about 100 members were studying in Cuba, 15 in Nigeria, and undisclosed numbers in both Eastern and Western countries, including the United States. The Soviet Union is the ANC's primary financial and military backer, but it also receives moral or financial support from Western European countries, the British Labour party, and the World Council of Churches.

Within South Africa the ANC remains a shadowy organization, but it is described by security authorities, in part perhaps to mobilize whites, as being everywhere. As the regime represses aboveground representatives of black causes, the vehicle for radical opposition is more and more likely to be the ANC. Indeed, one ally on which the ANC can rely in building its prestige both within South Africa and abroad is the South African government. The government's constant attacks on the ANC and its influence on South African blacks enhance its stature. The government also alleges that the ANC is a tool of the Soviet Union and that its masterminds are white, once again discounting the independence and capacity of the black opposition.

Shortly before the SASOL sabotage one ANC leader expressed his belief that "the countdown has begun." Most veteran leaders have cautiously avoided predicting when they might achieve success, but lately they have wondered if the timetable might be shorter than they had thought. "The long-heralded South African revolution remains a rebel's dream," two conservative American scholars, Lewis Gann and Peter Duignan, wrote in April 1980. In the same month Oliver Tambo acknowledged that "the liberation of South Africa . . . may sound like a remote dream at the moment." But, comparing himself to other liberation leaders whose struggles had also been dismissed as unrealistic, he said he was confident that "the day is not far off." The day may still be far off, but it is clear that blacks will persevere.

Chapter 10
White Rule

A revolutionary mood is spreading among the blacks of South Africa. Their numerical superiority suggests an inexorable move toward political change. But for now the whites are in charge, and the decisions made by the white political leadership—influenced, to be sure, by black demands and international pressure—control the pace and direction of change.

The majority of South African whites remain determined to resist any fundamental change in the political structure—certainly any change that would result in their living under a black-controlled government. Nevertheless, white attitudes are not static. The ruling Afrikaners argue openly about new political dispensations, in itself a radical departure from the past, when differences tended to be aired only within Afrikaner institutions and groups. Receptivity to new ideas is increasing and traditional ethnic loyalties and political allegiances are developing a measure of fluidity. There is widespread realization that the old answers will no longer do, and a fumbling for new solutions is underway. As yet none have been found, at least none that would satisfy the aspirations of the black majority, but there are signs of movement. And these give rise to hopes that the patterns of the past can eventually be broken.

THE PARTY SYSTEM

South Africa's white political structure is, at least in theory, a multiparty system. The ruling National party is challenged by three smaller parties: the official opposition, the Progressive Federal party (PFP), and two narrowly based groups, the centrist New Republic party (NRP), whose support lies largely in Natal, and the ultraconservative Herstigte Nasionale party (HNP), which has no seats in Parliament. Although elections frequently produce vigorous campaigns, the Nationalists clearly are the dominant party. As of early 1981, they enjoyed the support of about 55 percent of the white electorate and controlled about three-quarters of the seats in Parliament.

The National Party

Until very recently the National party was an exclusively ethnic movement representing Afrikaner interests. Founded in its present form in 1934, it elected its first English-speaking members of Parliament only in the 1960s. Even today only one member of the cabinet is of English-speaking descent and only a handful of the party's parliamentary caucus members are non-Afrikaners.

The Nationalists are the only mass party in South Africa. Although the number of activists is relatively small, more than 50 percent of the party's supporters are paid-up members. There is an elaborate structure for giving grass-roots members a voice in party affairs. Parliamentary constituencies are each divided into several branches controlled by card-carrying members, and these local organizations count heavily in the selection of candidates to run in parliamentary and provincial elections. The four provincial party organizations hold annual congresses at which party leaders explain policies. At the national level is the Federal Council, composed of representatives chosen by the provincial congresses and nominally the party's highest policy-making body. Despite the impressive multilayered party apparatus, however, the real power in the party—and in the country—lies in the hands of those who have risen through party ranks to the top government posts. This was never more conclusively demonstrated than in 1959, when Prime Minister Hendrik Verwoerd announced the "homelands" policy. Verwoerd had devised the new approach to dealing with the African population in consultation with a handful of his closest advisers, and only after the decision to implement the policy had been reached did he disclose the plan to the parliamentary caucus. Somewhat later the Federal Council and the provincial congresses ratified the homelands policy.

As such episodes suggest, the party's major function is less to formulate policy than to provide the pool of talent from which the leadership of South Africa is drawn. Most Nationalist members of Parliament emerge from the ranks of party activists or paid officials, and from Parliament, of course, come the prime minister and his cabinet. Thus, the political leadership of South Africa is derived from a highly circumscribed group. Besides their common bond of party activism, most Nationalist members of Parliament are middle-aged male Afrikaners who belong to one of the Afrikaans Calvinist churches. Their homogeneity contrasts sharply with the situation in some other nations, including the United States, where political leadership arises from various fields. Also, the limited size of the pool from which cabinet members have traditionally been picked means that talent has often been stretched thin.

Since broad backing within the party has generally been the key to executive power, most ambitious Nationalists adhere to centrist positions. In the 1980 cabinet only Pieter Koornhof, the minister responsible for African affairs, on the left, and Andries Treurnicht, minister of state administration and statistics and the party leader in the Transvaal, on the right, are clearly identified with either extreme. The powerful cabinet members, such as Prime Minister Botha himself and Chris Heunis, minister of internal affairs, are, by National party standards, centrists. So is Alwyn Schlebusch, chairman of the new President's Council, a post with cabinet rank.

Opposition Parties

If the National party's road to power lay in Afrikaner mobilization and unification, the English-speaking minority could hope to share political power only by creating an English-Afrikaner coalition. Before 1948 this strategy sometimes succeeded, resulting in control of the government by the center, but the trend was clearly toward Afrikaner nationalism. The 1948 victory of a coalition between the National party and the short-lived Afrikaner party entrenched ethnic political alignments.

Since 1948, two developments have worsened the prospects of the opposition parties. First, demographic trends have hurt them. A higher Afrikaner birth rate and increased Afrikaner urbanization, which has eroded liberal opposition parties' control of many urban constituencies, have changed the political arithmetic of the country. Increasingly, the English parties must win Afrikaner support simply to retain their relative position. Second, the National party has skillfully used its control of the government to further its electoral interests. The resources of the state have been used to build powerful blocs of support among farmers and government workers, including the large numbers employed by the railways and the post office. Constituency boundaries have been drawn—gerrymandered, to use the American term—so as to favor National party interests. Radio and television, controlled by the government, echo party positions and publicize Nationalist leaders.

Other circumstances also work against the English-speaking community. Most English-speakers are concentrated in a small number of the more populous urban constituencies, and they receive less representation in Parliament than their numbers warrant. Moreover, the Westminster system of winner-take-all, single-member parliamentary constituencies works against minority parties. English-speakers' parliamentary representation is further diminished by the fact that many do not vote. A significant proportion of South Africa's white non-Afrikaners are not South African citizens and are therefore not eligible to vote, while a sense of political powerlessness has left many other white non-Afrikaners apathetic.

The English-oriented parties' leadership, which itself has often been Afrikaans-speaking, has made no headway against these built-in obstacles. Policy has veered erratically from high principle to political pragmatism as successive leaders have attempted to win Afrikaner support while retaining their English base. For almost three decades the now-defunct United party engaged in this exercise, with the result that it shed support continually on both the left and the right. In 1953, for example, four liberal members of its parliamentary caucus resigned. In 1959 a major split led to the creation of the Progressive party. During the 1960s and 1970s several important leaders of the conservative wing of the party resigned; among them were Frank Waring and Marais Steyn, who subsequently became cabinet ministers in National party administrations.

In 1977 what was left of the United party officially became the New Republic party when it merged with the small Democratic party. As things worked out, the merger accelerated the decline of the center. The new party began life much smaller than the old United party because a great deal of its support, on both the left and the right, deserted. The conservatives eventually joined the National party and the liberals became part of a new, expanded Progressive Federal party. Today the New Republic party, with fewer than a dozen parliamentary supporters, is a declining force in white politics.

Of more significance is the official opposition, the PFP. The original Progressive party remained a minor party throughout the 1960s and was able to elect only one member—Helen Suzman—to Parliament during this period. During the 1970s, however, the party capitalized on the disintegration of the United party and experienced relatively rapid growth. In early 1981 the PFP held seventeen parliamentary seats. But its prospects for continued growth were not promising. The party remained dominated by English-speakers and drew most of its support from business and professional groups. It has yet to win a following among rank-and-file Afrikaners and the working class in general.

The PFP advocates a national convention representing all population groups to negotiate a new constitution. Its two stated nonnegotiable principles are (1) full citizenship for all South Africans with the right of participation in all levels of government; (2) constitutional and other safeguards against "group domination." Specific proposals that the PFP would present to the convention include a federal structure based on regional decentralization, a universal franchise, and a national assembly with a minority veto on some issues. Members of the party maintain that the fundamental choice is between negotiation and confrontation and that the PFP is the party of conciliation.

The PFP looms larger in South Africa than its small size might suggest. Although few blacks would identify publicly with it, many are influenced by its stands and look to it to articulate their grievances. It is at least conceivable that the PFP could play an eventual role as a bridge builder between the conflicting demands of African and Afrikaner nationalism. "The role of the PFP is to keep the voice of moderates alive in a polarizing situation and to keep a white-black dialogue going as far as possible," says the party's current leader, Frederik van Zyl Slabbert.

The opposition party at the opposite end of the political spectrum, the Herstigte (reconstituted) Nasionale party, was founded in 1969. The HNP, a fringe phenomenon within Afrikaner politics and society, represents an undiluted Afrikaner nationalism not markedly different from the original outlook of the National party. It won 13.8 percent of the vote in the 1981 elections and has nuisance value, creating an outlet for Afrikaner protest votes against the ruling National party. Nevertheless, the HNP's naked racism sounds anachronistic to most white South Africans, and they have never elected one of its candidates to Parliament. The party has also been hampered by a lack of funds and ineffective leadership.

PARLIAMENT

Parliament's most important function is to legitimate policy decisions made by the executive branch. Voting on substantive issues is almost always on strict party lines, and a victory for the ruling party is usually preordained.

Until 1980 South Africa had a bicameral legislature. The House of Assembly, the lower, politically dominant chamber, had 165 members elected directly by adult white voters. The Senate, whose members were chosen indirectly by party caucuses, was a smaller body and had minimal powers. It was usually filled with second-rank political figures who had been rewarded for loyal party service with a term in the Senate. In keeping with the 1980 constitutional revisions, the government abolished the Senate at the end of 1980, and during 1981 twelve additional members of the House of Assembly are to be chosen— four by the prime minister and eight by the elected members of Parliament on the basis of proportional party representation.

The power of the executive branch has increased as its parliamentary base has become more secure. The National party has experienced almost uninterrupted growth in its parliamentary contingent since 1948, moving from a bare working majority to overwhelming dominance. In the 1977 election, it won more than three-quarters of the seats. Especially since 1974 the once-powerful opposition had declined precipitously.

During parliamentary sessions the National party caucus, comprising all Nationalist members of the House of Assembly, meets every Wednesday, the day after the weekly cabinet meeting. At the caucus meetings ministers expound their legislative proposals. Although disagreements may have taken place in the cabinet, the ministers present a united front in the caucus. Ministers take into account the anticipated reactions of the caucus in formulating policy, and occasionally groups within the caucus may unite on a particular issue and deflect the cabinet from its chosen course. For the most part, however, caucus support for cabinet proposals is automatic. In South African government and politics the executive seldom faces a serious challenge.

THE PRIME MINISTER AND THE CABINET

South Africa has a tradition of strong prime ministers. This stems not only from the nature of the political system but also from the fact that since 1948 the leader of the government has also been the leader of a powerful ethnic movement. All Nationalist prime ministers have remained in office until death (Strijdom, Verwoerd) or voluntary retirement (Malan, Vorster).

Hendrik Verwoerd, a former university professor, dominated South African politics for almost a decade, from 1958 to 1966. Possessing a charismatic personality and brilliant intellect, he dazzled Parliament and overwhelmed his cabinet and caucus. In areas of his particular interest, such as foreign policy and race relations, he totally controlled policy, but he did not give adequate attention to a number of other important policy issues. While he established the official policy of homeland "independence," for example, his lack of interest in economics contributed to the neglect of the actual development of the African areas. This disinterest, coupled with inflexibility and an unwillingness to take advice that often marked Verwoerd's behavior, led him to reject all recommendations that white private capital be admitted to the homelands.

The Verwoerd legacy remains important today. His elaboration of the ideology of separate development is still accepted in many areas of life in South Africa. With the zeal of a true believer, he converted his party to the doctrine and drove the dissidents, such as the relatively liberal intellectuals in the South African Bureau of Racial Affairs (an Afrikaner think tank), out of the fold. Indeed, so successful was Verwoerd in building a core of followers committed to his views within the party and the public service that his present successor must reckon with it when he contemplates deviating from Verwoerd policies.

When Verwoerd was assassinated in 1966, John Vorster, then minister of justice, succeeded him as prime minister and party leader. His style contrasted sharply with Verwoerd's. Despite his strongman image, Vorster was cautious, conciliatory, more chairman of the board than decision maker. He tended to act only when a clear consensus existed and delegated considerable authority to his ministers and to departmental public servants. As a result, powerful figures within the cabinet built empires and there was a constant struggle for control of policy.

Although Vorster remained the dominant political figure in the country, under him the innovating role of the prime minister tended to be relatively limited. He carefully balanced conflicting interests and personalities in the

National party. To placate the conservatives he elevated Andries Treurnicht, then a prominent back-bencher, to subcabinet rank. To placate the reformers, he appointed Roelof F. Botha to the cabinet. Vorster made no effort to build an effective staff of his own, relying instead on a secretary and a single aide. In the view of close observers, he lacked the temperament, inclination, and means to strike off in new directions and to initiate radical change.

With the accession of the current prime minister, Pieter W. Botha, in 1978, the office changed its character. Operating in a manner different from either Verwoerd or Vorster, Botha showed himself to be a vigorous, activist prime minister.

He succeeded Vorster under inauspicious circumstances. The party was embroiled in a major scandal—the Information Department affair—involving misappropriation of public funds and having far-reaching political, ethical, and financial implications. In a way, Botha was an accidental prime minister, elevated to the highest office by the downfall of the heir apparent, Connie Mulder, who, as information minister, was held responsible for the scandal. Until it surfaced, Botha's support in the caucus had been limited mainly to his fellow representatives from the Cape Province. Most members of the Transvaal party were chary of his alleged liberalism. Even with his rival, Mulder, already discredited, he won only a narrow victory in the caucus vote for party leader, and thus prime minister.

Once in office, however, Botha quickly proved himself an adroit organization man. He immediately set about consolidating his position within the party and government. Using the great powers inherent in his office, he assembled a cabinet loyal to him personally. In two major cabinet reshuffles, he removed most of the ministers who did not support his policies. The minister of police was relegated to a politically unimportant ceremonial position. Several cabinet members without powerful political bases were retired. More powerful opponents were removed from the cabinet and appointed to the new President's Council. Treurnicht, the most influential conservative spokesman and thus a necessary member of the cabinet, was given an insignificant portfolio. At the same time, powerful allies were promoted or brought into the cabinet. Alwyn Schlebusch and Pieter Koornhof, for example, took on more significant roles, while General Magnus Malan, chief of the Defense Force, and Gerrit Viljoen, the reputed former head of the secret Afrikaner organization known as the Broederbond, joined the cabinet.

Prime Minister Botha also restructured the administration, institutionalizing and streamlining the machinery for making and carrying out policy. Permanent cabinet committees now oversee key policy areas, such as foreign affairs, race relations, economic matters, and state security. The most important panel is the State Security Council, which is headed by the prime minister and has representatives from the important ministries and the Defense Force. Moreover, for the first time the office of the prime minister has become a full-fledged department with sufficient budget and personnel to plan and coordinate overall government policy. The prime minister's hand has been strengthened further by an expanded advisory system that enables him to draw on the help of experts in a wide range of fields.

All these changes, coupled with effective use of patronage, have given Prime Minister Botha firm control over the executive branch. Although not as popular as his predecessors and like them obliged to take into account the views of the party at large and the voting public, he is nevertheless in a strong position to enforce his will in most important areas of policy.

THE PUBLIC SERVICE

South Africa has a large and powerful civil service. If the parastatals—corporations controlled and in large measure owned by the government—are included, more whites are employed by the public sector than by any other sector of the economy. Of the whites in government service, some 60 percent are Afrikaners, and at the highest levels the proportion is greater. The percentage of Afrikaners tends to be largest in the departments dealing with Africans, Coloureds, and Indians and in the Defense Force, and lower in the departments of finance, tourism, and foreign affairs.

The bureaucracy has expanded steadily since the creation of the Union in 1910, but it has grown especially rapidly since 1948 as the Nationalist government has penetrated ever more deeply into all areas of South African life. Its regulatory functions in the economy, including labor control, have increased year by year. So has its direct involvement in such fields as steel, mining, electric power, and synthetic fuel production. Government control of almost all aspects of the lives of blacks—jobs, education, residence—has required armies of administrators. Between 1950 and the late 1970s the number of government departments grew from thirty to forty-three, and there was even faster growth in the number of bureaus and sections.

Apartheid has compounded the waste and duplication inevitable in a mushrooming bureaucracy. The functional departments, such as education, health, and labor, in most cases are geared to serve the white community. Within the departments overseeing the African, Coloured, and Indian communities are sections dealing with the same functions. Health services, for example, are administered by the departments of health, African affairs, Coloured affairs, and Asian affairs. The old Department of Bantu Administration and Development was a veritable bureaucratic empire in itself, larger than half a dozen of the smaller functional departments combined and including an array of functional sections, such as health, labor, education, pensions, and sports.

When a bureaucracy becomes large and unwieldy, control from the top is weakened, and to some extent that happened during the period of decentralized administration under Prime Minister Vorster. Experienced top-level bureaucrats, such as Eschel Rhoodie in information and Brand Fourie in foreign affairs, amassed enormous independent power, and some officials operated in freewheeling fashion far beyond the normal confines of their positions. Some observers have even suggested that the bureaucracy became powerful enough to block policy changes of which it disapproved. The truth of the matter, however, seems to be that the bureaucracy can thwart government policy only when the political leadership is weak. When leaders fail to grapple forcefully with difficult issues, the bureaucracy is free to fill the political vacuum and chart its own course. In 1977, for example, the cabinet announced that urban Africans residing outside the western Cape would be able to obtain a ninety-nine-year lease on land for residences. M. C. Botha, the minister in charge of African affairs when the new policy was first proposed, supported it only reluctantly. His successor, Connie Mulder, who held both the information and African affairs portfolios, was already fully absorbed in the losing battle to salvage his career. Moreover, the reform was tentative, far short of the unrestricted freehold that Africans had sought. All these factors combined to allow civil servants to introduce the change in the most limited way possible. Even when ordered to step up the pace, they procrastinated in issuing the appropriate regulations and thereby delayed the program until 1980.

Prime Minister Botha has acted to keep the bureaucracy under tighter rein. Along with his reorganization of the policy-making machinery, he has reduced the number of government departments from forty-three to twenty-three and put them under the command of a small new cadre of high-level civil servants with clear-cut responsibilities. Many of the new posts have been filled by people sympathetic to Botha's policies, while a number of conservative officials have been moved aside. This appears to mean that if the Botha government is seriously committed to reform, the bureaucracy should not pose insuperable obstacles. If the status quo prevails, the most likely explanation is a failure of will at the top.

Another significant change in the bureaucracy under Botha is in the relative standing of certain sectors. Under Vorster, the conservative police and security apparatus achieved major influence. In the absence of an adequate staff of his own, the prime minister, a former minister of police, leaned heavily on the Bureau of State Security (BOSS), headed by a confidant, General Hendrik van den Bergh. BOSS influenced a wide range of domestic and foreign matters. After Van den Bergh resigned in 1978, a reorganization stripped the bureau of its operational functions and confined it to a relatively narrow intelligence-evaluation assignment. It is now called the National Intelligence Service.

Meanwhile, the military has gained ground under Prime Minister Botha. A former minister of defense, Botha has advanced the careers of many of his old military subordinates. Besides appointing General Malan minister of defense, he has staffed his new decision-making machinery heavily with military officers. What may make this significant is that the military, perhaps surprisingly, has lately shown signs of becoming one of South Africa's more flexible, adaptable institutions (see chapter 11).

Part I
South
Africa

PRESSURE GROUPS

Organized lobbying of the sort practiced in the United States is relatively rare in South Africa, but informal, highly personalized efforts to influence government policy go on all the time. Since power centers in the cabinet, most of the lobbying focuses there. Because South Africa's white community is small, and the dominant Afrikaner elite even smaller, the key participants usually know each other. Political and economic leaders may belong to the same church or be fellow members of the Broederbond, and not infrequently there are family ties. Afrikaner groups such as the Broederbond or the leaders of the Dutch Reformed church traditionally have had easy access to the inner circles of power. Black and English-speaking groups, on the other hand, have generally found it hard to obtain similar access.

Pressure groups' roles are not static, however. Although Afrikaner cultural and religious organizations retain great influence, they are not as powerful as they once were. The influence of the conservative white trade unions has also declined. When Afrikaner trade unions were confronting English-speaking capitalists twenty-five years ago over such issues as job security and protection from black competition, the support of the National party was automatic. But the rise of Afrikaner capitalism has blurred the old Afrikaner-English conflict in the marketplace, and increasingly the government sees white unionism as narrow and unrelated, if not antagonistic, to larger white interests. Similarly, white farmers carry less weight with the government as urbanization advances in South Africa. Meanwhile, other groups are gaining influence. Most important on the conservative side are the huge government bureaucracy and the parastatal organizations. Looming large among the forces more open to change is the fast-growing corporate sector, both English and Afrikaner.

A look at three major areas of pressure group activity—business, the churches, and the Broederbond—follows.

Business

When the National party came to power in 1948 business was largely controlled by non-Afrikaners—South Africans of English and Jewish extraction, and foreign citizens—who were almost universally hostile to a narrow ethnic party. Most Afrikaners were farmers, low-level civil servants, and blue-collar workers. Among National party leaders, ideological hostility to capitalism was widespread. In fact, one of the critical choices facing the new government in 1948 was whether to adopt a statist economic policy, including nationalization

215

of the gold mines, or to stick with capitalism. In the end the Nationalists straddled the issue. While they did not embark on a nationalization program, they poured resources into government-controlled business enterprises, including the South African Coal, Oil, and Gas Corporation (SASOL), the Iron and Steel Corporation (ISCOR), and the Industrial Development Corporation. At the same time, they encouraged the formation of private Afrikaner capital.

From Malan to Vorster, most members of the National party continued to view the English-controlled business sector as their natural enemy. Businessmen were regarded as unconcerned with the larger issues of white security and survival and as motivated solely by profit. Complaints by businessmen against influx control, job reservation, and other forms of racial discrimination were routinely ignored by the party.

For its part, English business, while in general opposed to Afrikaner nationalism, was largely inactive politically. Although a few prominent corporate leaders—notably, Harry Oppenheimer, chairman of the Anglo-American Corporation—participated in opposition politics, the business community as a whole was apolitical. Major business organizations such as the Associated Chambers of Commerce, the Federated Chamber of Industries, the Chamber of Mines, and the Steel and Engineering Industries Federation took strong public positions only during times of unrest. A continuous low-level dialogue did take place on issues such as influx control, industrial decentralization, migrant labor, and the pass laws, but it had little effect.

For two decades after 1948 the National party commanded the unquestioning loyalty of Afrikaner businessmen who were benefiting from its patronage. But while more influential than English-speakers, Afrikaner businessmen were, for the most part, political outsiders. Few became active party members or ran for Parliament, and few were appointed to important government commissions except in specialized areas such as monetary and fiscal policy. By the 1970s, however, some fairly basic differences were developing between Afrikaner business leaders and Afrikaner political leaders.

One reason was the growing doubts of businessmen about the government's heavy investments in state-owned industries. They had become aware that in times of recession the economy cannot support real expansion in both public and private sectors, and they had come to view the public sector as a rival for scarce capital, skilled labor, and markets. Another reason was that Afrikaner capital was expanding from its narrow agricultural base into a broad range of business activities: insurance, banking, mining, retailing. As it did so, and as Afrikaner business became big business, its leaders increasingly shared the interests and attitudes of the English business community. Contributing to their willingness to diverge from the Nationalists on occasion was the decline in the English-oriented opposition parties as credible electoral alternatives, which reduced the pressure for blind ethnic loyalty.

216   With growing frequency Afrikaner businessmen opposed some aspects of

old-style apartheid. While continuing to support the National party and the principle of white domination, they echoed—albeit in muted form—the long-standing English criticisms of the labor system and economic discrimination. They found, for example, that job reservation was as costly to them as it was to English interests.

The unrest in Soweto in 1976 imparted a new urgency to business activities in the political and social spheres. The most important innovation was the establishment by both Afrikaner and English business leaders of the Urban Foundation in 1976. The foundation, though ostensibly nonpolitical, has lobbied effectively for changes in such matters as residential rights and housing leases for Africans. It also played an important behind-the-scenes role in reversing the government's decision to remove the Crossroads squatter camp near Cape Town.

Under the leadership of Prime Minister Botha, the Afrikaner and English segments of government and business are moving closer together. Now that whites face an increasingly assertive black majority, conflict within the white community is viewed as an unaffordable luxury. The government recognizes that it needs the cooperation of business to develop the homeland economies, reduce unemployment, and provide an economic base for the security and survival of the state. The "constellation of states" concept and the attempt to maintain security through the creation of links of interdependence between South Africa and the West and parts of Africa are attempts to use economic forces for political ends. The corporate sector is of vital importance in establishing these links and ensuring that South Africa keeps its access to foreign technology, finance, and markets.

One indication of the new climate in business-government relations is Botha's appointment of a number of business leaders to executive and advisory posts in the government. Moreover, he has shown a much greater willingness than his predecessors to cooperate with businessmen. Harry Oppenheimer, the symbol of liberal South African business, has publicly praised some of Botha's actions. An Oppenheimer-controlled company, African Explosives and Chemical Industries, has made a major investment in the Bophuthatswana homeland, a significant departure from past policy.

A mutuality of interests is clearly developing between the government and business, including the Nationalists' old antagonists, the English-speaking corporate leaders. The government is showing increased sensitivity to business interests, from labor relations to relaxation of restrictions on the location of industry. Business, in turn, is supporting Botha's efforts to couple modest improvements in the lot of urban Africans with homeland development, hoping the prime minister's course will at least buy time for white South Africa.

217

The Churches

The traditional English-oriented churches—principally the Anglicans, the Methodists, and the Catholics—strongly oppose apartheid. Some of their church schools have been been desegregated. While these churches have helped raise black aspirations and have encouraged the development of a sophisticated black church elite, they have had no perceptible influence on government policy.

The Afrikaner churches, in contrast, are influential. Over 90 percent of all Afrikaans-speaking South African whites belong to one of the three Afrikaner churches—about 70 percent to the dominant Dutch Reformed church. Afrikaners take their religion seriously and most attend church services fairly regularly.

Historically, a close relationship has existed between the Dutch Reformed church and the National party. Political meetings usually begin with prayer, frequently led by a well-known cleric. Former prime minister Daniel Malan began his career as a Dutch Reformed pastor, as did several members of the present cabinet and Parliament, including Andries Treurnicht. John Vorster's brother was a senior Dutch Reformed official. Typically, a large number of cabinet members are active laymen, including Pieter Koornhof at present and Connie Mulder in the recent past.

Continuing a church-state partnership that dates back to the Boer republics, the government since 1948 has been sensitive to the Afrikaner churches' views on the regulation of individual morality. The churches helped create a "Christian" country where censorship protected the populace from "immoral" books, magazines, and movies and where Sunday was to be a day of contemplation and prayer. Even now movies and sports events are not permitted on Sunday in many parts of the country, and Sunday television runs heavily to religious programs. When apartheid became government policy, the Afrikaner churches sanctioned it, justifying separation of the races and black subordination in biblical terms. They also used their influence to build more support among voters for the National party, especially in rural areas.

The power of the Afrikaner churches reached its height during the first decade of Nationalist rule. Recently it has slipped a bit, the result, some say, of urbanization, increased education, and rising affluence. While the changes in Afrikaner society have not destroyed the traditional piety of the Afrikaners, they have weakened the ties between the individual and organized religion and have permitted the emergence of a wide range of different opinion leaders, interests, and values. Reflecting this changing climate, the government has introduced a lottery scheme to help raise funds for defense despite the strong opposition of the Afrikaner churches to legalized gambling. Also, censorship standards have eased modestly despite church opposition. Even within the Afrikaner churches there are some signs of change. The Dopper church, a small Dutch Reformed offshoot, has frequently opposed the government on important issues. The Dutch Reformed church, while remaining essentially conservative and loyal to the National party, contains outspoken ministers who criticize aspects of government policy. The tensions within Afrikaner religion are aggravated by worsening conflicts between the white "mother" Dutch Reformed church and the black "daughter" churches. These black Dutch Reformed bodies are impatient with the status quo and reject the conservative stance of the white churches.

The Afrikaner churches—in particular, the Dutch Reformed church—are still a potent force in South Africa. Using their ties to political leaders and working mainly behind the scenes, the churches remain a pillar of the status quo. But increasingly they stand aside from debate over the crucial issues of public policy. Inhibited by internal divisions, they have not taken strong stands on such matters as mixed marriages, interracial sex, and homeland consolidation. Their silence inevitably makes them a waning, though still far from inconsequential, force in national politics.

The Broederbond

The Broederbond (league of brothers) was established in 1918 to promote the interests of Afrikaners, then undeniably second-class members of South Africa's white society. It transformed itself into a secret organization in 1928. Membership, which today numbers about 12,000, has always been restricted to white, male Calvinist Afrikaners.

The Broederbond achieved great influence before 1948, championing the Afrikaner cause on several fronts. It focused academic attention on the plight of the poor Afrikaner, mobilized Afrikaner capital, and built a network of members able to open up new employment opportunities to Afrikaners. In the cultural field it supported Afrikaans literature. Afrikaner unity was a constant Broederbond theme.

With the rise of Afrikaners to political power in 1948, the Broederbond began to lose its central role. Once Afrikaners controlled the state, its resources were used to serve Afrikaner interests, supplanting many of the Broederbond's traditional functions. New sources of power and influence were also developing in Afrikaner business and industry. Moreover, by the 1960s and 1970s the internal divisions in the larger Afrikaner community were affecting the Broederbond. Many of the supporters of the Herstigte Nasionale party, including founder Albert Hertzog, an influential early member of the Broederbond, were expelled from the organization. In recent years the Broederbond's aura of power and mystery has suffered from periodic leaks of its confidential records, including membership lists, to English-language newspapers.

Although the opposition press has traditionally used the Broederbond as an issue on which to attack the so-called secret ethnic government, its real importance in the power structure of South Africa has probably always been exaggerated, and today it is clearly declining. Most influential Afrikaners, including key government officials, remain members, and the debates within the organization continue to generate new ideas that are guaranteed a full hearing by the cabinet. But the Broederbond increasingly plays a role subordinate to the National party and the government bureaucracy, and must compete with other pressure groups for influence.

THE NEWSPAPERS

Like many other institutions in South Africa, the press tends to split along ethnic lines. As a rule, the major Afrikaans newspapers support National party policy, while the English-language newspapers oppose it.

The English-language press, which is owned by English business interests, is dominated by two major chains. The Argus group, which includes the largest daily newspaper in the country, the Johannesburg *Star,* is regarded by many as more conservative than its rival, the South African Associated Newspapers, publisher of the *Rand Daily Mail.* But both chains advocate the elimination of racial discrimination and an increase in black political rights along the lines of the Progressive Federal party program. They are sometimes courageous; for example, they printed articles about the 1978 Information Department scandal in defiance of government pressure.

The English press is often viewed as the most important white opposition to the government, and the National party periodically threatens to restrict its freedom. The leading English newspapers on occasion have been branded unpatriotic by Nationalist leaders and their criticisms called threats to national security. Even though the Nationalists claim to ignore the English press, it has sometimes halted government action by exposing egregious examples of injustice under apartheid. Moreover, it is a major force in shaping the policies of the liberal opposition and to some extent acts as a kingmaker in PFP politics. It has a large and growing black readership, and many members of the black intelligentsia rely on it as a source of information about politics and current events.

The Afrikaans newspapers traditionally have been loyal instruments of the National party, with a mandate to rally its followers and do battle with its foes. Members of the party hierarchy, including cabinet ministers, have often served on the boards of newspapers, although that practice is now discouraged by the government. In the past, a few editors of Afrikaans newspapers regularly sat in on meetings of the parliamentary caucus.

The role of the Afrikaans press has changed markedly in the past decade, however. While there have always been independent-minded Afrikaner journalists, Afrikaner journalism in general is now moving away from party control. Afrikaans newspapers, even those that are nominally party organs, are developing into opinion leaders rather than propaganda vehicles. Most would define their new role as constructive opposition or loyal critic. Although they support the National party without reservation in elections, they no longer accept Nationalist policy unquestioningly but instead try to shape it in accordance with their editors' views. These views tend to be more pragmatic and moderate than government policy or Afrikaner public opinion. In various ways, such as adopting the use of *meneer* (mister) before a black man's name in their news columns, they are trying to modify their audience's racial views and to increase receptivity to limited changes in racial policies. Despite their overall support for separate development, they no longer hesitate to point out failures and problems. In August 1980, for example, the Afrikaans newspapers warned that a large increase in homeland populations shown in early census results, while superficially encouraging to separate-development proponents, was illusory. A decade earlier they might well have claimed a major breakthrough for the government.

The new look of the Afrikaans newspapers partly reflects intensified competition for readership and influence among today's better-educated, more affluent Afrikaners. The principal rivals are two chains, the Cape-based Nasionale Pers (*Die Burger* is its flagship) and the Transvaal-based Perskor (*Die Transvaler*). In the past the Cape chain tended to be more liberal than its Transvaal rival, but this corporate difference has blurred and individual papers now largely mirror the attitudes of their editors.

Although some prominent Nationalists have complained about attacks on them personally, the leadership as a whole appears to have decided that a more independent, progovernment press is a more credible ally than a toadying one. For their part, the editors of the Afrikaans newspapers now reason that the National party's unassailable electoral position eliminates the need for blind loyalty. Afrikanerdom is sufficiently well entrenched to countenance opposition from within the fold, they suggest.

If by chance an editor did move beyond acceptable bounds, it is likely the government would act to correct the situation. So, while the Afrikaans press has lately gained new credibility and influence, its freedom is still restricted by ethnic politics and its real impact on the political dialogue remains circumscribed.

THE WHITE ELECTORATE

Power is concentrated at the top in South Africa, but, at least for the whites, South Africa remains a relatively democratic country in which free elections are held. Thus, the National party remains in office at the pleasure of the white voters, and political leaders must reckon with white public opinion. For the Nationalists that means Afrikaner opinion, which is delineated most sharply when measured against the views of English-speakers.

Afrikaner-English Opinion

For several decades the Afrikaner and English communities have been moving closer together in their ways of life, but important differences remain. English-speakers still tend to be more urbanized, wealthier, better educated, and more widely traveled. Perhaps more significant, the cultural gap—different histories, languages, religions—persists. All this contributes to marked variations in the attitudes of the two groups on key public policy issues.

Table 10-1 underscores the greater willingness of English-speakers to see racial barriers partially lowered. It also points out that Afrikaners are most amenable to moves toward equality in economic areas and least amenable to changes in social and residential segregation. Another safe generalization is that Afrikaners are generally willing to accept extensive state intervention in day-to-day life to maintain traditional racial patterns, whereas English-speakers are more inclined to leave such matters to individual choice and market forces.

Wide variations in attitudes are also found when Afrikaners and English-speakers are asked about specific alternative political arrangements for the future. (See Table 10-2.) Once again, the English-speaking respondents were consistently more liberal than the Afrikaners. While 52 percent of the English

TABLE 10-1.

Afrikaner-English Views on Key Issues (1977)

	Percentage Accepting	
	Afrikaners	English-Speakers
Admission of blacks to the same jobs as whites	62	85
Equal salaries for whites and blacks	62	83
Blacks and whites together on sporting teams	61	92
Admission of blacks to white sporting facilities	40	81
Blacks and whites worshipping together in the same churches	32	88
Admission of blacks to all cinemas, theaters, etc.	28	66
Abolition of the Immorality Act	23	53
Permission to blacks to attend certain white schools	19	69
Use by blacks of white recreation areas	19	53
Permission to certain blacks to move into white residential areas	18	53

Source of information: Lawrence Schlemmer, "Change in South Africa: Opportunities and Restraints," in *The Apartheid Regime,* edited by Robert Price and Carl Rosberg (University of California Press, 1980), p. 254.

TABLE 10-2.

Political Arrangements Preferred for Different Black Groups According to Language Group of Respondents (1977) (In Percentages)

Political Arrangement	Coloureds		Indians		Africans	
	Afrikaans	English-Speaking	Afrikaans	English-Speaking	Afrikaans	English-Speaking
No representation whatsoever.	3	1	8	2	8	2
Representation by own people in a separate Parliament with sovereign powers in own territory.	19	7	16	7	45	16
Representation by own people in a separate Parliament with powers determined by the central white government.	28	9	27	8	15	7
Limited representation in the central white Parliament elected on separate voters' rolls.	20	12	19	12	6	6
Representation in a joint parliament for all population groups, the number of representatives and the powers of the joint Parliament determined by the white Parliament.	10	12	10	12	6	9
Representation of all races in the central Parliament on common voters' roll but with qualified franchise.	9	52	9	52	9	52
No choice.	11	7	11	7	11	8

Source of information: Schlemmer, "Change in South Africa," p. 259.

favored incorporation of all races into the present political system through a nonracial but qualified franchise, only 9 percent of the Afrikaners did. Conversely, 50 percent of the Afrikaners favored totally excluding Coloureds from the central political system and 68 percent would similarly exclude Africans. Only 17 percent of the English advocated such a policy toward Coloureds and only 25 percent felt so inclined toward Africans.

The English community views the racial situation as more serious and the need for remedial action as more urgent than do the Afrikaners. In 1977, when the Soweto uprising of the year before was still reverberating through South Africa, a survey found that only 17 percent of the English believed that the status quo could prevail five years or longer, compared with 34 percent of the Afrikaners. The English worried more about the impact of international pressures on South Africa. Also, the English were inclined to blame the racial unrest of the time on objective problems, while the Afrikaners attributed it largely to "agitators" and Communists.

Perhaps paradoxically, in light of the numerous divergencies of views, Afrikaners and English-speakers are in substantial agreement on the most fundamental issue: the danger to them of black control of government and political power. While Afrikaners and English differ in the degree to which they are prepared to compromise and to permit some black political participation, they are nearly unanimous that whites must retain a veto on important issues. This view is shared even by most of those willing to accept a central Parliament chosen by and open to all races; they clearly count on devices such as property or educational qualifications for voters to avoid black domination.

Two lines in the survey results shown in Table 10-3 are particularly important for any assessment of the obstacles to change in South Africa: 80 percent of Afrikaners and 50 percent of English-speakers believe that the order and security of society would be threatened by black rule. Only 3 percent of Afrikaners and 9 percent of the English believe that black control would not pose serious or permanent dangers for whites.

Policy Implications

While studies of white public opinion in South Africa show strong resistance to fundamental change, they also show that the government has a great capacity to shape white opinion, especially Afrikaner opinion. Henry Lever, an authority on South African public opinion, comments: "When the government takes a lead the opinions of the electorate fall into line with government policy. Whether the government gives permission for 'mixed' rugby or boxing, the desegregation of spectator facilities, or the narrowing of the wage gap, the approval of the electorate soon follows."

In general, the English-speakers are ahead of the government in willingness to desegregate South African society. On the other hand, a majority of

224

TABLE 10-3.

White Perceptions of the Consequences of Change (1977)

	Percentage Agreeing	
Type of Change	Afrikaners	English-Speakers
The order and security of our society would be threatened.	80	50
The jobs and work security of whites would be threatened.	37	29
The incomes and standard of living of whites would be lowered.	34	42
The way of life and culture of whites would have to change.	18	46
The language and culture of the Afrikaner would be undermined.	14	9
Whites would intermarry with blacks.	9	6
No serious or permanent dangers would exist for whites.	3	9

Source of information: Schlemmer, "Changes in South Africa," p. 267.

Afrikaners lag behind the more progressive elements of the government. In part, however, the views of Afrikaners reflect automatic support for long-standing party and government policies, and surveys indicate that the Nationalists would not lose significant backing if they moved toward less racist policies. Ethnic ties rather than policy details largely determine voting behavior. The results of relevant surveys are shown in Table 10-4.

Although these proposals represent fundamental changes in the government's most important policies, on proposals 1 and 3 more Afrikaners were prepared in 1977 to support the regime than to oppose it. Ironically, the proposal with the least support in 1977, proposal 2, was the only one of the three generally compatible with the existing policy of separate development. The less detailed 1980 results show a marked increase in the amenability of Afrikaners to political change. The power of ethnic bonds to maintain party unity despite policy changes is also confirmed by a 1977 survey that found that 89 percent of Afrikaners were "completely satisfied" or "fairly satisfied" with the National party. Moreover, 51 percent said they would not support another party even if they became dissatisfied with the Nationalists' performance.

The burden of all such studies appears to be that the Nationalist leadership is in a strong position to introduce at least some policy changes without being unduly concerned about electoral reverses. Providing that the party leadership

TABLE 10-4.

Afrikaner and English Attitudes Toward Proposals for Change (In Percentages)

1. If the present government should decide to grant full citizenship, social equality, and full franchise in our Parliament to Coloureds and Indians, would you:

	1977		1980	
	Afrikaners	English-Speakers	Afrikaners	English-Speakers
Support the policy	11 ⎫ 42	37 ⎫ 78	49*	82*
Accept the policy	31 ⎭	41 ⎭		
Oppose the policy	35	6		
Uncertain	23	16		

2. If the present government were to decide to considerably enlarge and make the Bantu homelands more viable by incorporating certain "white" areas (including industrial areas), would you:

	1977		1980	
	Afrikaners	English-Speakers	Afrikaners	English-Speakers
Support the policy	11 ⎫ 38	13 ⎫ 42	**	
Accept the policy	27 ⎭	29 ⎭		
Oppose the policy	39	30		
Uncertain	23	28		

3. If the present government decided to create a new legislative body where white, Coloured, and Indian leaders, homeland and urban Bantu leaders would have a say over national affairs without one group being dominated by another, would you:

	1977		1980	
	Afrikaners	English-Speakers	Afrikaners	English-Speakers
Support the policy	19 ⎫ 47	37 ⎫ 69	56*	78*
Accept the policy	28 ⎭	32 ⎭		
Oppose the policy	29	9		
Uncertain	24	22		

Source of information: 1977—Schlemmer, "Change in South Africa," p.261; 1980—Schlemmer, *Sunday Tribune.*
*The only figures available for 1980 are combined percentages for those who "support" and those who "accept" the policy.
**No comparable question.

remains united, the bulk of the Afrikaner voters would follow. Whatever losses do take place appear likely to be balanced by a growth in English support.

On the other hand, the government's freedom of maneuver is not unlimited. Without risking serious loss of support it could almost certainly push through reductions in statutory segregation in everyday life. But where fundamental white interests are involved, as they would be in a major redistribution of wealth and power, or where basic social patterns are threatened, as they would be by repeal of the Group Areas Act, the leadership would encounter formidable white opposition and would have a hard time carrying Afrikaner opinion along with it.

As it happens, however, the party leadership is unlikely to march so far in front of rank-and-file Afrikaners that a serious split would develop. A consensus as to the limits of reform continues to exist at all levels of Afrikanerdom. Most Afrikaners doubt that radical reform is either necessary or desirable. Most reject any genuine power-sharing arrangement in a common society, and most believe that the status quo, with some modification, will best serve white political, economic, and social interests. Underlying all these attitudes is their deep-seated belief in the racial superiority of whites and a fear of the consequences of black rule.

THE OUTLOOK UNDER BOTHA

Of all the steps taken by Prime Minister Botha to strengthen the executive, the most dramatic was his transformation of the cabinet into an instrument to advance his ideas. Past prime ministers have generally sought cabinets that represented the divergent views in the parliamentary caucus, but Botha has not given priority to balancing left and right. Instead, he has appointed a cabinet that represents predominantly the reform wing of the party. Its nature is shown by the breakdown of the caucus and the cabinet, in Table 10-5, in terms of members' views on a spectrum ranging from—to use the Afrikaans political labels current in South Africa—very *verlig* (enlightened) to very *verkramp* (narrow).

In the caucus more than half the members (seventy-five) were conservatively inclined, compared with only four of the eighteen members of the cabinet. Only one in ten in the caucus was very *verlig,* compared with almost a quarter of the cabinet. Indeed, as a result of a cabinet reshuffle that took place during the latter part of 1980, this position was reinforced; of the four conservatives in the cabinet in early 1980, two were replaced by more liberal figures. Also, at the time of the reshuffle the cabinet was expanded to twenty ministers, and the two new members fell into the *verligte* camp. Thus, as of early 1981 a predominantly conservative caucus coexisted with a cabinet comprising eighteen *verligtes* and only two *verkramptes.* Not surprisingly, given the power of

TABLE 10-5.

Caucus Opinion (early 1980)

	Transvaal	Cape	Orange Free State	Natal	Total
Very Verlig	8	4	0	1	13
Verlig-Centrist	12	25	4	4	45
Verkramp-Centrist	21	10	7	3	41
Very Verkramp	25	5	2	2	34
Total	66	44	13	10	133

Cabinet Opinion (early 1980)

	Transvaal	Cape	Orange Free State	Natal	Total
Very Verlig	3	1	0	0	4
Verlig-Centrist	4	4	1	1	10
Verkramp-Centrist	1	0	0	0	1
Very Verkramp	3	0	0	0	3
Total	11	5	1	1	18

Source of information: Christopher Hill and Steven Georgala, "Verligtes Appear to Be Gaining," Johannesburg *Star,* weekly airmail edition, July 26, 1980.

the executive, not one member of the caucus had publicly expressed concern about the situation.

If Botha stumbles badly, the caucus majority could turn to another leader, but at the start of 1981 the prime minister was in a powerful position to impose his views on the party. He was clearly dominant in both the cabinet and the caucus and had achieved effective control over the bureaucracy. His new prerogative to appoint additional members to Parliament should buttress his position further.

Just how Botha intends to use his power is not entirely clear, however. Some analysts say he is truly eager to eliminate some of the most noxious aspects of apartheid and is waiting for an opportune moment to act. Others insist he is a temporizer, concerned with modernizing apartheid enough to keep the lid on black dissent and mollify foreign critics. A closer look at *verligte* and *verkrampte* views within the National party may help place the prime minister more precisely in the political spectrum.

The *verligtes*—sometimes described as "pragmatic centrists"—have so far advocated only very limited changes. They argue that white security can best be safeguarded by a strategy of controlled change. Among other things, this entails the elimination of "unnecessary" discrimination, such as statutory so-cial segregation (mixed marriages, public facilities, sports), and the elimina-tion of barriers to economic efficiency, such as job reservation and other racially based constraints on industry. On the all-important question of new political arrangements, the *verligtes* are extremely vague—perhaps intentionally so. They advocate expanded rights for the Coloured and Asian minorities, perhaps along with sections of the urban Africans. For the African majority, they favor a decentralized scheme, with considerable control passed to subordinate eth-nically based organizations linked in a loose consultative framework. This framework would involve a confederal constellation of states, embracing the homelands and white South Africa, where institutionalized consultation, but not joint decision making, would take place. For the Coloureds and the Indians, the institutional structure has not yet crystallized in *verligte* thinking, but any acceptable mechanism for joint consideration of policy would have to provide for continued white control.

The ideological hard-liners, the *verkramptes,* insist that apartheid is a way of life, a system of laws, a moral vision. Yielding ground on any aspect of the policy, they argue, opens the prospect of fundamental change. Even small changes, according to this view, bring into question the overall legitimacy of apartheid, and once this happens the entire fabric begins to unravel. The aspirations of blacks inevitably increase as marginal reforms whet the desire for substantive changes. The whites, with the philosophical underpinnings of apartheid weakened, would not be able to withstand the escalating demands for concessions.

Verkrampte logic requires that statutory segregation and strict political separation on ethnic lines be perpetuated. Conservatives oppose reforms such as integrated sports and the removal of racial barriers in the workplace. They decline even to speculate on the possibility of limited power-sharing between whites and segments of the black population. "We are not prepared to let ourselves be talked out of our earthly paradise by so-called open dialogue or consultation," Andries Treurnicht told the Transvaal congress of the National party in 1980.

Despite the *verligte-verkrampte* rift, it cannot be stressed too strongly that the most basic differences involve means rather than ends. Both groups are in full agreement that Afrikaner power and leadership must continue to prevail, that white interests are paramount and must be safeguarded, and that the essential characteristics of contemporary South African society must be pre-served.

It should also be stressed that the vast majority of blacks regard these debates as irrelevant. As far as most are concerned, there are no genuine *verligte* members of the National party. The minimum demands of South Af-rica's blacks go far beyond the maximum *verligte* concessions.

However ambiguous remain the goals of Prime Minister Botha's admin-istration, he unquestionably belongs to the *verligte* wing of the National party.

229

While not committed to developing a nonracial society in South Africa, he is certainly far more committed to reform than was his predecessor, John Vorster. Moreover, he is more willing to confront opposition to his policies head on.

Even so, he has been forced to move more slowly than he may have desired. Perhaps the most important brake on more rapid change has been the desire of the party leadership, including Botha himself, to maintain party unity. Rapid reform and National party unity can be contradictory goals. Since the National party is the political arm of an ethnic movement, disunity within its ranks would shake to their roots all the groups and institutions that constitute organized Afrikanerdom. The bitterness and divisions that would result, virtually all Afrikaner leaders agree, must be avoided if South Africa's whites are to face up successfully to their enemies within and without.

Every prime minister since 1948 has placed a high premium on party unity and has tried to position himself near the center. The split by the Herstigte Nasionale party in the late 1960s was relatively insignificant; it was led by an elderly former cabinet minister, Albert Hertzog, who attracted only a small following of disgruntled members of Parliament. If any future split over policy could be contained within similar bounds, Botha would probably be prepared to accelerate the pace of reform. Some observers suggest that he probably would not be unhappy if Andries Treurnicht and his adherents left the party, but Treurnicht is aware of the danger of isolating himself and so far has sought to remain an opposition force within the party.

An early split in the National party—even a minor one—thus appears unlikely, though the possibility cannot be ruled out entirely. All factions have a vested interest in party unity, both for the preservation of Afrikanerdom and in furtherance of their own political interests. On the latter point, they see that the road to power lies not in challenging the party from outside but in capturing it from within. Prime Minister Botha turned sixty-five years old in 1981, and his rivals are already jockeying for power in anticipation of his retirement. One of the few developments that might suddenly alter the outlook would be a decision by Botha to act more boldly and attempt a major realignment of the political forces in South Africa. For example, if he advocated a full franchise for Coloureds, possibly through the President's Council, a party split would probably be inevitable. But there is little reason to expect such a change.

So far, Botha has moved with utmost caution in carrying out even such modest reforms as hotel and restaurant desegregation. The frequent practice of desegregating public facilities by granting special permits rather than by seeking blanket legislative approval is a manifestation of this caution, as is the heavy reliance on commission reports to justify policy changes in the other areas. Botha obviously believes that time is on his side. The *verligtes* are now firmly in control of the cabinet, the bureaucracy, and the military. The new Afrikaner power centers in the press and business are *verlig* in orientation. The influence of the bastions of *verkramptheid*—the cultural organizations, the

Dutch Reformed church—is in decline. All this suggests that support for reform is likely to grow with the passage of time.

Botha, in sum, appears to be a cautious reformer who is attempting to introduce a number of important but limited modifications of South Africa's racial order. He has given no indication that he grasps the depth of black discontent or the extent of the compromises required for a lasting accommodation. And yet, even if he did possess such an understanding, he would face immense obstacles in acting on it. White intransigence is still a powerful factor in South Africa.

VERLIGTE "REFORM" VERSUS GENUINE REFORM

In the next few years, the debate between *verkramptes* and *verligtes* may become largely a matter of historical interest. The differences between the two groups have probably always been overstated. More has united them than has divided them, and both *verkramptes* and *verligtes* remain committed to Afrikaner political hegemony. Now, with the *verligte* faction firmly in command of the government, the *verkramptes* appear to be a declining force, perhaps able to retard change but unable to take control of the party leadership.

Even as the old debate fades, however, the National party may be entering a new phase in which the real clash will be between the *verligtes* and those who might be called the genuine reformers. It is true that there have always been Afrikaners who refused to accept white supremacy as the natural order of things; writer André Brink and church leader Beyers Naude are two living examples. But rebels such as these have opposed the status quo from outside the National party and have thus been sharply limited in influence. In contrast, the small new group of genuine reformers represents the first effort to make a case for fundamental change as Afrikaners and from within the Afrikaner community.

In some respects their attitudes resemble those of the opposition Progressive Federal party. While they have not set forth a detailed program, several common themes run through their thinking. They advocate a new political order in which Afrikaner power is not entrenched but in which legitimate minority interests are protected. Whereas the National party has always stressed ethnic differences, the genuine reformers insist it is essential to minimize such differences. In the same vein, they say that the concept of Afrikaner identity should be demystified and suggest that the present regime's stress on preserving Afrikaner power at all costs in the long run threatens the very survival of Afrikanerdom. At the same time, they acknowledge South Africa's multiethnic nature and agree that this should be taken into account through such devices as consensus decision making or majority rule with minority safeguards. "Consociational" government, a rather hazy concept that involves separate ethnic political institutions capped by a joint democratic body to deal with matters of common concern, is also mentioned frequently by the genuine reformers. In further recognition of ethnic realities, they find acceptable some decentralization of power on a territorial basis, although they view the present homelands policy as completely inequitable.

The genuine reformers are a tiny segment of the Afrikaner community. They are most numerous in the academic world. To a lesser extent, they are found in the churches, the press, and the military. Not one member of the cabinet and only a handful of parliamentary caucus members have publicly advocated what could be classed as genuine reform as opposed to limited *verligte* reform. But the significance of the genuine reformers is greater than their number would suggest. Their ranks include some leading Afrikaner intellectuals, and, perhaps more important, their ideas have stirred considerable interest among Afrikaner students. If the 1960s and 1970s were dominated by the conflicts between the centrist *verligtes* and the hard-line *verkramptes*, the 1980s may hold at least the promise of a dialogue between the center and the advocates of genuine reform.

Chapter 11
Fortress South Africa

$\mathbf{M}$ilitary power reinforces the political power of the whites of South Africa. Their armed might relative to the black military strength they are likely to confront in the foreseeable future is so formidable that it is difficult to envision the government being overthrown by force. The seemingly contradictory lessons of the past decade from other countries usually do not hold up under close examination: Vietnam's jungle was more hospitable to guerrillas than South Africa's barren mountains and plains. The Shah's regime in Iran turned out to be a hollow shell, a far cry from the almost fanatical support that the Nationalist government commands among most Afrikaners. In Zimbabwe the blacks' numerical edge over the whites was more than twenty to one in a total population of two million, compared with five to one in South Africa in a total population of more than 26 million.

None of this means that a violent revolution will not someday topple the white rulers of South Africa, but it does suggest that such an event is unlikely without a drastic change in circumstances. Nor do the scant prospects for violent revolution mean that force will not be a factor in bringing change to South Africa. While the blacks are unlikely to be able to defeat the whites militarily, neither can the whites defeat the blacks, and an unending campaign of low-level violence, a ceaseless war of attrition on white resistance, could be one of the many pressures for change. But in any realistic assessment of current military strength, white dominance appears beyond question.

THE BUILDUP

White concern about security began to intensify after the antiapartheid passive resistance Defiance Campaign of the early 1950s demonstrated the extent of **233** black anger. It was heightened by the sabotage campaign that followed the shootings of unarmed black demonstrators in Sharpeville in 1960. Mounting international isolation also contributed to white fears. The whites' sense of standing alone was fed by the progressive European disengagement from most of black Africa, the United Nations' 1963 voluntary embargo on arms for South Africa, and the mandatory UN arms embargo of 1977.

White South Africa's rising concern about security led to major expansion of military strength throughout the 1960s and 1970s. Previously the country had relied mainly on the protective British umbrella provided by its Commonwealth membership and had maintained minimal peacetime forces of its own. Pretoria began to develop its own defense doctrines and priorities, to become more self-sufficient in weapons production, and to maintain growing numbers of whites, as well as some blacks, in the standing forces of the Republic. By the late 1970s, South Africa had acquired a substantial capacity to withstand embargoes on military equipment, created a very strong armed force, strengthened its repressive racial apparatus, and evolved new training and operational doctrines tailored to its perceived local needs. At the same time, the South African Defense Force (SADF) and other institutions involved in security had achieved an enhanced role in shaping national policy.

Before 1960 the SADF accounted for less than 1 percent of South Africa's gross national product (GNP) and less than 7 percent of the government budget. Then, between 1960 and 1965, defense expenditures soared. By the 1964–65 fiscal year they were running at a rate of between 2 percent and 3 percent of the GNP and accounting for 21 percent of the budget.* The SADF's small Permanent Force (professional regulars serving as a cadre for command, training, and maintenance) rose 65 percent. Citizen Force conscripts and reservists, who supplement the Permanent Force, increased nearly sixfold, and commando reserves, assigned primarily to defense of their home areas, increased 18 percent.

The rate of increase in the defense effort leveled off in the mid-1960s, and spending dipped to a low point of 12 percent of the budget in 1972. But another major spurt in South Africa's military buildup occurred from 1974 to 1977. By the 1977–78 fiscal year the defense appropriation was nearly five times its 1972 level (though less than three times if adjusted for inflation), and it edged close to 20 percent of the budget and 5.1 percent of the GNP. Over the same period the target level for standing forces rose by 18 percent, to 65,000 men on active duty. Measures taken to strengthen the forces included extending the national service requirement for white males from twelve to twenty-four months, recruiting more white women, improving military pay and benefits, and making a serious effort for the first time since World War II to enlist Africans, Coloureds, and Indians in the SADF.

---

234   *The defense spending figures in this section do not include outlays for the police, who perform major national security functions.

Local procurement of military equipment through South Africa's Armaments Development and Production Corporation (ARMSCOR) grew thirtyfold, to an annual rate of nearly Rl billion between 1968 and 1978. Increasingly, weapons were acquired according to their suitability for local African conditions, and today local designs or local adaptations of foreign designs are commonplace in the army, air force, and police inventories. Imported guns, combat vehicles, and other military items are of interest to Pretoria only if there is clear assurance of a secure supply pipeline and some potential for local manufacture.

In defense doctrine, the fundamental change has been a reorientation toward the "landward threat" and away from preoccupation with the old role as a partner of the West in the protection of the ocean lanes around the Cape. With most of its strategic ties to the West severed, the Nationalist government has turned its attention to such missions as riot control (largely a police function), close air support of mobile ground forces, counterinsurgency operations, coastal patrol and interdiction, and commando strike techniques. The termination of Western naval cooperation has meant a steady downgrading of antisubmarine-warfare capability and a conscious choice in favor of local naval defense. Procurement reflects these changes. Top priority goes to modernizing light and mobile ground forces with self-contained artillery and flexible air support. The aim is complete self-sufficiency in items consumed in sustained, low-level operations.

It can be argued that by the 1979–80 fiscal year the South African defense effort had once again leveled off. Defense spending for the year stood at R1.9 billion, up from R1.7 billion in 1977–78, but over the same span defense had declined a bit as a percentage of GNP (to 4.5 percent) and of the state budget (to 16.6 percent). All the same, South Africa appears to have arrived at a fairly secure military position. The security forces are believed to be better suited to the potential threats facing the government than in the past. Morale is said to be high. A substantial defense buildup has been carried out.

The full implications of the military's expanded policy role, in part a reflection of Prime Minister Botha's background as minister of defense, remain to be seen. But it does seem safe to assume that if Botha presses his reformist views against the opposition of conservatives in his party, the influence of the security forces leadership will be brought to bear on his behalf. In recent years SADF leadership has spearheaded articulation of the concept of a "total strategy" for South Africa, to meet the twin perils of "Marxist onslaught" from outside and domestic turmoil within. One key element of the strategy as defined by both Botha and the military is that it must include all population groups, not whites alone. The top officers are said to see their role as one of buying time for domestic political evolution, which will make the Republic more "defensible," less vulnerable to internal disorders, and better able to attract the support of the majority. This is what Defense Minister General

Magnus Malan is thought to mean when he says that the strategy for South Africa must be 90 percent political.

THE INTERNAL BALANCE

There is little evidence on which to question the short-term survivability of white power in South Africa. Analogies drawn from Iran, Nicaragua, or elsewhere ignore the realities of power in South Africa and the severe obstacles facing prospective revolutionaries. Although "revolutionary" is often used to describe the South African situation, "prerevolutionary" would probably be more accurate, and perhaps even that term stretches the facts. Threatening or potentially threatening organizations are ruthlessly controlled or repressed. The political system is backed by a substantial reservoir of trained and well-armed whites, including security forces that could exceed 400,000 if fully mobilized.

To be sure, some ingredients of a potential revolution are present: a heightened level of political awareness and unity among young urban blacks, an uprecedented degree of determination and even optimism about the potential for black power, and the pervasive allegiance to Black Consciousness. It appears likely that the gap between reality and aspirations is growing, expanding the level of frustration in the black community.

Both the government and its armed opponents recognize that the towns, cities, and key industrial installations are the primary targets and the points of potential vulnerability for political action and physical attack. The short-term threat includes mass protests, urban turmoil, strikes and boycotts, sabotage, and sporadic guerrilla or terrorist violence. The aim of such challenges, insofar as they are purposefully organized and led, is not a frontal and physical challenge to the system. They seek rather to wear down white resistance to change, discredit the government in Western eyes, instill political awareness and discipline among blacks, raise notch by notch the price of maintaining the status quo, and focus attention on specific grievances and demands.

It is too early to predict whether actual physical violence on a mass scale will ultimately prove more effective than other avenues for challenging minority control or even whether it will prove necessary. But in terms of organization, tactics, and resources, the revolution is still at an embryonic stage, and for the time being the military outcome of violent challenges to the white regime remains predictable. Physical represssion on a scale not yet seen is both possible and likely. White opinion would overwhelmingly support the maintenance of order, whatever the misgivings of some whites about official policies.

Currently urban blacks lack the means to raise a sustained physical challenge to the authorities. The government has the ability to cut off black townships from food, water, electricity, and telephone sources as well as transportation and jobs. Spontaneous violence in such circumstances can mobilize domestic and international opinion but probably cannot serve as an effective military tactic. Even under the most extreme assumptions about underground effectiveness in organization and the smuggling of arms and explosives, the current possibilities appear to fall short of enabling insurgents to carry out sustained mass violence in the urban areas.

In the countryside the maximum threat at present is the infiltration of small numbers of men who slip across the border from neighboring states and make their way to the major centers. There is no evidence to date of guerrilla success in establishing rural-based cells. Political and geographical factors hinder insurgent activity in the rural areas. Popular support is more likely to come from politically conscious and educated urban dwellers than from rural residents. Also, little of South Africa's rural landscape or borderlands lend themselves to guerrilla tactics.

It is true that homeland governments may find it difficult to enforce tight security in their scattered territorial fragments, assuming they would wish to do so. Similarly, there is a limit on the ability (and perhaps willingness) of neighboring Botswana, Lesotho, and Swaziland, which have small security establishments, to protect the Republic. Their attitude in the future is likely to reflect their own internal security needs and the posture adopted by South Africa's crucial neighbors, Zimbabwe and Mozambique. Even so, the constraints on a strategy of large-scale rural insurgency are severe. Perhaps the most important is that South Africa can use its military and economic power to hurt its neighbors that support or turn a blind eye toward more than a token guerrilla presence.

In the post-Soweto period public discussion about the internal threat of armed attack has become progressively less complacent. In fact, government and security force leaders have gone out of their way to spell out the reality of the problem in speeches, press interviews, and meetings with industrial and agricultural groups. The purpose presumably is to build public support for new security measures. In 1977–78 there were reports of nineteen "notable" incidents involving small-scale attacks or terrorist actions; they were concentrated in the Transvaal and northern Natal. Another pattern to emerge clearly in the post-Soweto period consists of direct attacks on police stations and individual acts of violence against off-duty black policemen.

While the quality of guerrilla training to date generally is not rated high, South African commentators agree it is improving, as the coordinated attack on SASOL in June 1980 demonstrated. Reflecting a new level of concern, the government, in recent years, has taken a number of new countermeasures. These include expanded civil defense preparations at over seven hundred centers throughout the country; government-supported small arms training for rural whites and subsidies for new radio networks and other security improvements on farms; security fences and new airstrips in some border areas and upgraded patrols on borders and road networks in outlying areas; and more rigorous counterinsurgency training—sometimes on a multiracial basis—for rural and urban-based commandos. By devising programs to make farming more attractive for whites, the government is also attempting to deal with the security problem created by unoccupied farmland in "white areas" near sensitive borders.

Despite such efforts, points of potential vulnerability are evident to even the casual visitor to South Africa. Airport security on domestic flights is lax by Western standards. Influx control in big cities like Durban and Johannesburg provides little real protection for white residential and shopping areas. Thousands of blacks live, squat, or hide in gardens, alleys, and warehouses every night. South Africa's sprawling and sophisticated infrastructure and economy could be hit by sabotage at many points, assuming a well-organized campaign were started.

That, however, remains a big assumption. The key point about South Africa's internal situation is the enormous contrast between actual and potential vulnerability. For the time being, bridging that gap appears beyond the reach of the government's opponents. The organization primarily responsible for domestic security is the relatively small South African Police force (SAP), a semimilitary, multipurpose force under the control of the central government in Pretoria. (Traffic police functions are locally organized, while the railway and harbor authority maintains its own force.) SAP's responsibilities include the full range of crime prevention duties as well as riot control, political intelligence work, disaster assistance, and counterinsurgency duty in border and rural areas. Its paramilitary units have been widely used in Namibia and Rhodesia as well as on the Republic's northern borders.

The SAP, rather than the SADF, bears the responsibility of maintaining internal security. The SAP is also the security force in which the greatest effort has been made to recruit and promote Africans, Coloureds, and Indians, who account for nearly 50 percent of its active-duty authorized strength of some 35,000 men. The SAP is the largest African security force in the country, and its programs for training cadres (officers and noncoms) are considered more advanced than other government services, including the SADF. Given its central role, it is surprising that the SAP is so small relative to the size of the country; the police-to-population ratio in South Africa is considerably lower than in most Western countries. Moreover, the SAP's financial and manpower needs appear to have been given lower priority in recent years than those of the SADF. Although authorized members grew by over 1,000 in the years following the 1976 Soweto riots, the SAP remains 4,000 men under its active-duty target strength of 35,000. Turnover among whites is reported relatively high, in part because of benefits less attractive than in other government services, including the military, with which SAP recruiters must compete.

The impression is widespread in South Africa that whites with limited education and few employment alternatives form the bulk of the new recruits. This perturbs the white leadership, since the SAP is highly exposed to public scrutiny as it confronts the hard realities of influx control, township law enforcement, strikes, and riots. The remedies being applied are in part financial, but the authorities are also having to come to grips with the fact that uniformed police service is one of the least attractive aspects of white South African life—and one that will not be adequately performed if left to dispirited and underqualified whites. This suggests a continued and perhaps expanded reliance on blacks and a larger effort to upgrade pay and benefits.

The shortcomings of the police do not suggest a major security weakness at this stage, however. The SAP's numbers are complemented by the part-time reserve police force (16,000 active and 7,000 nonactive) for evening, weekend, and holiday duty, plus a police reserve of 15,000 available for annual and emergency call-up. Efforts are under way to modernize tactics. Observers were struck by the SAP's greater reliance on nonlethal methods of crowd control during the June 1980 Coloured school boycott disturbances, though there is still much cause for complaint. Eventually, of course, the SAP's ability to cope will depend on what structure of laws, policies, and regulations it is asked to enforce.

THE REGIONAL MILITARY BALANCE

The Republic of South Africa is stronger militarily than any current African opponent or coalition. Its regional preponderance in armed strength and conventional military potential can be illustrated in several ways. In 1977, the last year for which comparative data are available, South Africa accounted for about one-third of all African military spending, excluding only Egypt. Until the late 1970s, when arms imports elsewhere in Africa started to soar and South Africa's began to fall due to the mandatory embargo, the Republic regularly accounted for some 50 percent of all sub-Saharan African arms imports. Another significant index of military effort—military spending per capita—shows that South Africa spends four to five times as much as any of its African neighbors; in all of Africa only Libya spends more per person on defense. In local manufacture of equipment South Africa ranks with such states as Brazil, Argentina, India, Israel, and Taiwan as a significant arms producer. Although its standing forces remain modest in size, even by African standards, they are probably the best trained and led on the continent, with the possible exception of Zimbabwe's battle-hardened regulars. They are backed by the trained, mobilizable strength of an additional 340,000 reserves and supported by the continent's strongest economy—the leading producer of electricity, steel, and motor vehicles. Other assets with military value include developed financial, communications, and transport systems and a pool of managerial and technological expertise.

The disparity between the Republic and its potential opponents is indicated by other factors as well. Table 11-1 provides a crude quantitative sketch

239

TABLE 11-1.

Indicators of the Southern African Military Balance (1979)

Country	Total Armed Forces	Combat Aircraft	Helicopters	Naval Combatants[1]	Tanks	Other Armored Vehicles	Def. Budget Million $
Angola	40,000	31	51	13	285	350	98
Botswana	2,260**	—	—	—	—	—	—
Lesotho	1,000	—	—	—	—	—	—
Malawi	5,000	—	2	—	—	10	13*
Mozambique	24,000	35	4	8	240	—	117
Swaziland	2,000	—	—	—	—	—	2*
Tanzania	50,000	20	6	33	40	—	140
Zaire	55,500**	31	20	33	38	135	164
Zambia	14,300	37	35	—	30	28	310
Subregional	194,060	154	118	87	633	523	844
Nigeria	173,000	21	30	12	50	118	1,750
Subregional & Nigeria	367,060	175	148	99	683	641	2,594
South Africa	63,250 (404,500 including reserves)	416***	170	23	270	3,610	2,228

Source: The Military Balance 1979–80 (London: ILSS)
[1]All armed naval units counted equally; only Nigeria and South Africa have armed units beyond patrol craft.
*Data for 1977 from *World Military Expenditures and Arms Transfers, 1968–77* (ACDA).
**Includes paramilitary forces.
***Does not include armed helicopters, transport and utility aircraft.

of the force relationships between South Africa and its neighbors plus Nigeria. The South African and Nigerian navies are the only ones possessing units heavier than patrol craft and neither has much capacity to inflict damage on the other in its own waters. The South African Air Force is the only one listed in the table with sufficient trained pilots, logistical support, and numbers necessary to be considered an operational combat force. Comparative strength in tanks gives an indication of South Africa's massive advantages in ground strike forces and if its inventory of more than 3,500 armored fighting vehicles (armored personnel carriers, scout cars, and armored cars) is included, the picture becomes clearer. South Africa's ability to keep complex armored vehicles operating under difficult combat conditions gives it a further edge.

Troop and equipment totals mean little without an analysis of other, less quantifiable variables. The capacity to deploy, maneuver, and resupply units in combat is perhaps the most decisive factor. South Africa has the military capacity to strike hundreds of miles beyond its borders. None of the African states listed in the table has the current capacity to deploy more than a token force to a potential combat zone on South Africa's periphery without substantial outside logistical and other support. There are both political and logistical advantages accruing from South Africa's unitary command structure and internal lines of supply when contrasted with a possible wartime coalition of African states. Not only are the African Frontline States (Angola, Botswana, Mozambique, Tanzania, Zambia, and Zimbabwe) militarily weak and preoccupied with their own internal security, they are also autonomous political units with their own specific interests. A common military stance would not be simple to maintain.

Thus, as South Africa contemplates its neighbors, it perceives an extensive vacuum of conventional military power—a vacuum that African states are not in a position to fill themselves for some time to come. South Africa does not face a significant conventional threat from African states. But this analysis must be pursued further on several points.

The southern African military balance cannot be assessed without considering the Soviet–Cuban–East German role. If there is any element of balance in the current situation, it is provided by the physical presence of Communist troops, advisers, and arms in support of Angola and Mozambique and the South-West African People's Organization (SWAPO), the Namibian movement. It is not so much their *military* presence in the region that constrains South Africa to a degree; the Cuban troops supporting the government of Angola are fully occupied in the effort to destroy the National Union for the Total Independence of Angola (UNITA) insurgency and are in no position to undertake fresh adventures. Rather, it is the *political* presence of a militarily engaged superpower in the region that South Africa must take into account. Although there is no immediate reason to anticipate a dramatic increase in Soviet–Cuban–East German involvement, the possibility cannot be ruled out. There is little question over the longer term that if South Africa were to overplay its military hand outside its borders, this escalation could be matched in scale and technology by the external Communist powers. The real question, therefore, is what level of South African military activity outside South Africa's borders the Soviet Union would be prepared to tolerate; of equal importance, what price would the USSR be willing to pay in East-West relations to maintain its stake in southern Africa?

The external threat facing South Africa is a guerrilla campaign, not a conventional one. So far, this has consisted of sporadic, low-level efforts to penetrate the Republic's own northern borders and the more substantial cross-border activity of SWAPO in Namibia. Given the conventional might of South Africa, exiled nationalist groups have no military alternative but to explore vulnerabilities, engage in sabotage and hit-and-run actions, and try to wear down South Africa's will to fight. For the time being, there is little prospect of that happening along the Republic's own borders to any great extent, but the counterinsurgency struggle in Namibia has demonstrated how a relatively small number of guerrillas can tie up substantial military forces. An estimated 20,000 to 25,000 South African troops were stretched out along Namibia's long northern border in 1980, even though less than 20 percent of SWAPO's 7,000 to 8,000 armed fighters were believed to be in the field at any one time.

A related consideration affecting the assessment of the military balance in southern Africa is the apparent reluctance of planners in Moscow and Havana to engage South Africa's forces directly. They are aware that they would bear the primary combat burden if the region's wars were to expand. The 1975–76 Angolan conflict demonstrated the extent of South Africa's diplomatic and political isolation more than its potential military weakness. South Africa did experience some difficulties in coordination and control over long lines, and its forces would have had an easier time with more helicopters, heavier artillery, and better antitank weapons. But by some accounts the small (1,500-to-2,000-man) South African expeditionary force in Angola acquitted itself well militarily, taking a fraction of the casualties of the Cubans and penetrating far into north-central Angola before the political decision was made to withdraw. It appears unlikely, according to Chester Crocker, an expert on the South African military, that South Africa is deterred by the prospect of tangling with a Cuban-African force—even one on the scale of 20,000 to 30,000 men—provided the stakes are deemed important enough.

A conflict could escalate well beyond this level. South African planners believe that Soviet enthusiasm for large-scale adventurism in southern Africa will decline as Moscow becomes aware of the difficulties of maintaining and operating major units over long distances in Africa. But at some level, South African air and maritime defenses could be neutralized by Soviet and/or East European (though probably not Cuban) combat forces. Major Communist ground and air forces could seek to harass lengthening South African supply lines and bog down the nation's forces in a costly war of attrition. South Africa does have technological limits, as its defense planners are quick to concede.

242

Moreover, a war that consumed quantities of key items like helicopters and produced substantial white casualties would not last long—assuming it occured beyond South Africa's borders. On the other hand, Soviet planners are aware that encounters of this sort could provoke a strong Western reaction, a fact that points up the importance placed on southern Africa by all parties in relation to other interests. (See discussion in chapter 15.)

A final consideration in evaluating the regional balance is its shifting geographic limits. Angola, Namibia, and, until recently, Zimbabwe (Rhodesia) have been the main fields of conflict; South Africa has played an important role in all three places. For the South African government, the situation of greatest risk may be one in which overextension results in a no-win war of attrition over a large area. South Africa's current level of military exposure is possible only because it is predominant militarily. When and if this situation changes, South Africa may be expected, according to Crocker, to reduce its defense perimeter and try to capitalize on the inherent advantages of defending familiar home ground using short, interior lines of communication. In the long run, then, a policy of strategic disengagement from neighboring territories may add strength to South Africa's ability to defend itself militarily.

MANPOWER AND MULTIRACIALISM IN THE SECURITY FORCES

Like most industrialized countries outside the Communist world, South Africa relies on relatively small standing military forces backed by a much larger pool of reserves subject to quick mobilization. The professional component is small. More than 70 percent of SADF active-duty strength consists of conscripts, and the percentage is more than 80 percent for the army.

If, like Israel, South Africa can expect to face low levels of threat interrupted by occasional major military actions, the system will work. On the other hand, if it becomes necessary to field substantial forces for months or even years at a time, it probably will not. The central role of whites in both the SADF and the economy means that prolonged mobilization could have important consequences for morale and for the economy. The Rhodesian experience may be relevant; in the view of many observers, the prolonged call-ups caused by the Rhodesian war lay behind much white emigration.

But while this suggests a potential Achilles' heel, South Africa does not have severe manpower problems today. Only in the late 1970s did it begin to impose on itself the kinds of military manpower burdens that are readily borne in other societies. For decades the white population has enjoyed a low level of defense burden, in terms of both economic costs and military service requirements. As late as 1977, the total SADF professional component consisted of no more than 16,000 to 17,000 men, while draft-age young men faced only a twelve-month commitment to active duty as national servicemen. However, it had already become apparent that this level of active-duty manpower was too

243

low for the role assigned to the SADF. The demands of the Namibian war had grown, and the burden was falling on Citizen Force reservists, who began to face call-ups for as long as ninety days. By 1977 SADF planners were finding themselves severely shorthanded for full-time regulars and conscripts; these accounted for only 17 percent of total SADF strength instead of the targeted 30 percent. As a result, Citizen Force and commando units (basically active reservists who had completed national service) were making up the missing 13 percent through periodic call-ups that drained these men from the civilian economy. The time had come when South Africa would have to make more men and more money available for defense, and over the past two years the government has taken a number of steps toward that end. For example, it doubled the national service commitment to twenty-four months of active duty. But it appears unlikely that South Africa will willingly move toward creating a largely professional standing army. South Africans, and especially Afrikaners, have a long, if romanticized, memory of relying on the citizenry at large for defense. There is a strong tradition summed up in the phrase " 'n boer en sy roer" (a farmer and his rifle), and modern-day SADF planners continue to believe in the merits of national service for citizenship training.

As part of the military buildup, the SADF has advocated a truly multiracial defense force. Describing the SADF as a "people's army" because of its primary reliance on draftees and reservists, former SADF chief of staff General Magnus Malan remarked in 1977: "I want to emphasize that the door of this people's army is open to people of all colors." He noted that blacks made up 20 percent of the South African force then in Namibia. Malan's comments may have come as something of a jolt to ideological hard-liners who have long fought to prevent or limit the arming of blacks. But the calls for increased recruitment of blacks have intensified in recent years, and opponents know they are fighting a rear-guard action against both military and political realities. It is no secret in South Africa that the civilian economy and the white manpower needs of the SADF are inevitably competitive; for now, the two-year national service commitment presents no major economic problem, but reserve call-ups are a different matter. The white manpower pool of 750,000 men between the ages of eighteen and thirty-five is basic to both the economy and the military, a point that has led one observer to term manpower "the greatest constraint" on defense policy.

The recruitment and training of Africans, Coloureds, and Indians has a long history in South Africa. The SAP has been a multiracial force since before World War I, and by the 1970s the percentage of blacks had risen to between 40 and 50 percent. Multiracial counterinsurgency units of the SAP have seen duty in Namibia, Rhodesia, and South Africa's northern border areas since the early 1970s.

Among military units, the Cape Corps—formerly known as the Cape Coloured Corps—is prominent, with a history stretching back to the seventeenth century. During World War I, several Cape Corps infantry battalions served in Europe and the Middle East, along with Coloured service units; some 45,000 Coloureds served in auxiliary roles with the Union Defense Force in World War II. Disbanded in the immediate postwar years, the unit was reconstituted as a noncombatant Cape Auxiliary Service Corps (cooks, drivers, medical orderlies) in the 1950s. This status continued until 1963, when the government reactivated the unit as the South African Coloured Corps, with its own training center and headquarters outside Cape Town; the training of Coloureds in a wide range of noncombat specialties, especially in the navy, dates from that time. By 1970, the decision to promote Coloureds to officer rank had been made.

In 1973 the government reversed its insistence on primarily noncombat roles for Coloureds and began to explore ways of expanding their assignments. An officer-training course was started. The Cape Corps itself was reorganized in that year to include volunteer national service combat units and to train Coloureds who wanted careers in the Permanent Force. The first Coloured infantry company saw duty in Namibia in 1974, and there have been similar units there ever since. Today over 3,000 Coloureds are serving in all branches of the military, and as of 1979, thirty Coloured officers had been commissioned or were due for commissioning. There have been parallel developments in the recruitment and training of Indians for the SADF, with emphasis on the navy.

SADF and government leaders have been more circumspect about recruiting Africans, though here also there is a long tradition of military service. During World War II, as many as 122,000 Africans served in a variety of noncombatant military roles in the Native Military Corps, constituting 37 percent of the Union Defense Force at one point. But the matter has always been highly controversial in white domestic politics, and African units were disbanded after the war. The government has switched only recently from minimizing its modest experiments with African military manpower to stressing the potential benefits for the SADF. So far efforts have focused not on the formation of large black units within the SADF itself but rather on the development of ethnically distinct units for service in Namibia and the homelands. The creation of "mini-armies" for the homelands began in 1974 for the Transkei; by the time of its independence in 1976 the Transkei force numbered about 250 men. Bophuthatswana and Venda have followed suit. In Namibia the recruiting of small ethnic battalions began with the Ovambos and Kavangos in 1974–75; ultimately ten such units were formed, at least on paper, and most of them have served with the SADF in northern Namibia, their total number probably not exceeding 1,200 men. In 1977, with the changing diplomatic-political environment, the SADF shifted its approach in Namibia. Recruitment into separate ethnic battalions was terminated, and a multiethnic territorial unit known as the Forty-one Battalion was organized as the nucleus of a future Namibian army.

The South African government backed cautiously into recruitment of Africans for combat roles in the SADF itself, starting in 1973. By 1975 formal approval was given for the recruitment of Africans into the Permanent Force, although on a very small scale. The basic organization is the Twenty-one Battalion, which is essentially a training unit, headquartered at Lenz, near Johannesburg. Twenty-one Battalion now comprises roughly five hundred men, some of whom form part of its one combat infantry company, while the remainder serve in administrative, training, and support roles as Permanent Force career men. Two full infantry companies have been trained, but only one is kept in readiness for operational use; it is deployed in Namibia. Twenty-one Battalion also serves as the SADF's main training center for homeland military units, for the Forty-one Battalion, and for a new type of formation called the regional company, which is aimed at providing small black units based in the nonindependent homelands. As of 1979, Zulu, Shangaan, Venda, and Swazi regional companies had been formed. It is possible that men drawn from this source will be posted to serve in a newly formed Fifty-two Battalion, a unit serving on the northern Transvaal border. Finally, a start has been made at forming African combat auxiliaries within the rural commandos, whose primary mission is counterinsurgency; urban commandos are also moving in this direction.

The proportion of blacks varies markedly from one branch of the security forces to another. Indians and Coloureds make up 20 percent of the navy's Permanent Force; this is not insignificant because nearly three-quarters of the navy consists of career regulars. Coloureds and Africans account for nearly one-third of the army's Permanent Force; however, the army's active-duty component is 80 percent draftees. The air force remains virtually all white. The SAP is nearly 50 percent black, but its reserves are primarily white. Excluding the SAP, it would appear that blacks make up perhaps 15 percent of the Permanent Force, 20 percent of the forces engaged in Namibia, 5 percent of the active-duty SADF, and an insignificant portion of the total SADF structure, including reserves. An indication of the direction of events can be seen from a Ministry of Defense announcement that Coloured and Indian manpower had risen 40 percent between 1977 and 1978, but this rate of increase is unlikely in the future. African recruitment is proceeding more slowly.

There are several obstacles to a rapid, large-scale buildup of black military manpower. It is unclear how far the trend can go if it is actively opposed by African, Coloured, and Indian leaders. A number have publicly attacked black recruitment. For example, Chief Gatsha Buthelezi, of KwaZulu, has posed questions about what these new black soldiers would be defending and whether blacks can be expected to defend a country under whose laws they may no longer be citizens. On one occasion, he wondered aloud if South Africa's biannual defense white papers were meant for whites only. On the other hand, the SADF has little difficulty attracting more black recruits than it can handle. The only evidence of resistance has come from highly politicized centers such as Soweto, where potential recruits have faced strong pressures against enlistment. Coloured and Indian leaders appear more ambivalent about the question.

The SAP's role as an agency of domestic repression undoubtedly deters many blacks from joining. Interviews with members of some black military units show concern that the SADF's mission as an external defense force be kept distinct from that of the police. Such interviews also evidence concern that black soldiers enjoy equal treatment with whites, and it would appear that the South African government is indeed moving toward "separate but equal" benefits and facilities. Among other things, it is closing the pay gap, with Africans in the Twenty-one Battalion reportedly at 70 percent of white pay scales and Coloureds in the Cape Corps at 88 percent as of 1979. The small Coloured officer element has pushed with apparent success to obtain full equality of rank and status in the SADF. As yet there are no African officers, except in the independent homeland units. Clearly, the morale and loyalty of black troops to the government will depend, in part, not only on decent treatment but on equitable treatment as well.

White attitudes also pose obstacles to black recruitment. At present a small number of top SADF officials plus a larger group of mid-career people are wholly in favor of a continued but carefully managed buildup. A majority of senior officers and lower ranks in the Permanent Force are more skeptical, however, and they will find it difficult to summon the racial sensitivity necessary to make a truly multiracial institution work. The attitudes of the national servicemen will reflect the full range of white South African opinion.

The net effect of these attitudes will probably lead to expanded recruitment among blacks but with certain constraints. Officer training is likely to be approached with considerable caution, especially for Africans, and there will be preference for officer recruitment from the ranks rather than from universities. This, in turn, will limit the pool of highly qualified applicants who could be genuinely competitive within a multiracial officer corps. There will also be greater emphasis, proportionately and perhaps even absolutely, on Coloureds and Indians than on Africans. The SADF establishment is likely to continue its recent hard sell on the subject of African, Coloured, and Indian participation in defense, at least as long as the current leadership in South Africa remains in power. Prime Minister Botha made his support for the policy clear at the September 1979 Transvaal National Party Congress: "I know I can get these people to stand with me against the hell of terrorism. . . . Must I keep insulting them while they are fighting alongside me? . . . We are not alone in our survival struggle. It is not a fight between black and white, for we have black and brown Christians with us."

All the same, whites will continue for some time to bear the primary defense manpower burden. The drain on white manpower could grow, although current demands are not extreme. Some 1.2 percent of men between eighteen and forty-five years of age are now serving in the armed forces; for whites alone, the figure is about 7 percent. When contrasted with such countries as

Turkey, Cuba, Vietnam, Taiwan, North and South Korea, several Arab countries, Israel, Bulgaria, and the USSR, this is not an overwhelmingly large percentage. But it is sufficient to give SADF planners a growing incentive to make greater use of black manpower in the coming period. By the mid-1980s, the SADF could be a far more multiracial institution than it is today.

That would be a development of political as well as military significance. At this point, the political implications are speculative. Some contend that black military recruitment is yet another means for the government to buy off a segment of the black population. Others say that the country's top military leadership is genuinely eager—if only for pragmatic reasons—to initiate a widespread lowering of racial barriers and that the close working relationships essential in the military will soften the racial attitudes of the rank and file. Still others suggest that the creation of a large, well-trained and well-armed black element could turn out to be a step in upsetting the power structure of South Africa.

ARMS SELF-SUFFICIENCY AND EMBARGOES

Until the voluntary UN arms embargo of 1963, Britain, the United States, and other sources openly sold military hardware to South Africa. From 1963 to November 1977, when the mandatory UN arms embargo was approved, France and Italy assumed the leading roles as arms sources; there was little secrecy about these transactions since neither country professed to adhere to the voluntary embargo. Jordan, Israel, India, and others also sold defense equipment to South Africa. The United States and Britain continued to provide spare parts for earlier sales, as well as dual-use equipment and components. Great Britain made an additional small-scale transfer of helicopters in the early 1970s under an agreement for naval cooperation with South Africa that was not terminated till 1975. More important than some of the shipments of equipment were several hundred licensing and coproduction agreements signed with various Western countries—especially France and Italy—helping South Africa toward self-sufficiency in arms production. In short, until the 1977 embargo South Africa had little difficulty acquiring, in one way or another, the imported hardware and technology to become a major regional power.

Even before 1977, however, South Africa's push for greater self-sufficiency in arms was well under way. The mandatory cutoff only accelerated the development and diversification of South African arms production. By 1980 South Africa had achieved a high degree of self-sufficiency in the manufacture of armored cars and personnel carriers; mortars and medium field guns; light observation and liaison aircraft and ground-attack fighter planes; hulls and some equipment for patrol boats; some missile types; heavy armored steel; basic infantry weapons and communications gear; night-vision sights, sensors, and some navigational instruments; mine-clearing devices; most ammunition types, bombs, fuses, and propellants; and chemical weapons, tear gas, and napalm. It is a long list, and it has grown steadily longer as more components, technology, and manufacturing processes have been mastered.

All the same, self-sufficiency is a continuing challenge. There is the possibility that observance of the 1977 embargo will become progressively more universal, covering not only end items such as tanks but also critical components and highly specialized raw materials needed in arms manufacture. A situation could also develop requiring South Africa to "spend" its limited inventory of arms before it can replace them from domestic production.

How effective is the 1977 embargo?

If the purpose of the embargo was to defuse African diplomatic pressure (and some domestic pressure in the West) for more extensive mandatory sanctions on trade or investment, the embargo has worked—at least through early 1981. If its purpose was to dissociate the West visibly from South Africa's policies, it has at least partially achieved this objective. If the goal was to throw South Africa back on its own resources and sharpen its awareness of its international isolation, it has met with some success. But if the goal was to weaken South Africa militarily or to coerce it to revise its policies, the results are mixed.

Even a mandatory embargo tends to operate at the lowest standard of observance of any of its adherents. Although the United States appears to have made good-faith efforts to close loopholes and to restrict sales of items with both military and civilian uses—"gray-area" transactions—it was not a significant arms source when the measure was adopted in 1977. The European record is less clear. There are few reported sales of major, visible end-items since 1977, but it is likely, according to Crocker, that trade continues in some items of clearly military application: marine diesel engines and communications gear from Germany, British-designed jet engines and avionics, Israeli missile components and electronic technology, French and Italian components and spares for aircraft and armored vehicles under pre-1977 licenses and co-production agreements.

The embargo unquestionably has further dried up the supply of major military end-items available to South Africa from the principal exporting nations. In today's climate, it would be surprising to find reports of transactions in such items that were approved by the government of the country in which they were produced. However, a secondary market continues in various forms. Military-related components are clearly still available to South Africa from some sources. If a proposed deal for a component becomes sensitive, it is often possible to disaggregate the component or technology in such a way as to "bury" it in trade data as a nonmilitary transaction. South Africa is still able to purchase used or reconditioned end-items from a government or through the private arms market. Although such deals are intended to be covered by the embargo, they are less traceable because the seller is not the original producer and intermediaries can be used to camouflage the transaction. South Africa's 1978 purchase of one hundred Centurion tanks from India would fall into this category.

It is safe to assume that the secondary market in end-items is considerably more extensive than public reports would suggest; the trade has been driven underground but is unlikely to stop. The saying often heard in Pretoria, "You cannot read an embargo document through a gold coin," continues to apply to South Africa's arms dealings. Indeed, South Africa most likely has offers of far more military equipment than it needs. The majority are no doubt turned down. South Africa's forces are not desperate for basic combat items, and ARMSCOR has little reason to rush about the globe in search of end-items from the arms market when the net result would be an assortment of noncompatible hardware. The purchase of 100 Indian Centurion tanks was logical because the SADF already possessed 150 of the same tank.

The most significant reason for South Africa's cautious approach to the postembargo arms market, however, is its determination to avoid vulnerability to cutoffs. Officials are aware that some Western governments are devoting greater effort to monitoring embargo observance. Activities by the UN anti-apartheid committee's staff and by various nongovernmental groups in the United States and Europe all point toward a progressively tighter embargo. As a result, South Africa can be expected to cover its tracks more carefully to avoid exposure. In practice, this has already produced new procurement guidelines that, combined with straightforward military considerations, add up to a new policy on arms imports. As far as possible, ARMSCOR will avoid buying end-items off the shelf. Preferring technologies that have a long life span and the potential for local manufacture, ARMSCOR conducts exhaustive testing of arms and components to determine their durability and the feasibility of local assembly and locally designed improvements. Because of the highly competitive nature of the arms sales business—especially after the loss of the Iranian market—ARMSCOR is able to bargain for deals that include the provision of manufacturing technology and data as well as finished products.

Another factor limiting arms imports is the SADF's reading of the southern African military environment. It was the specific defense requirements of South Africa, for example, that accounted for ARMSCOR's decision to develop a new type of infantry fighting vehicle. Now in production, the Ratel is a long-range (nine-hundred-mile) armored personnel carrier that operates on wheels at high speeds. It is considered relatively easy to maintain in rugged conditions without nearby logistic support, and it offers range and mobility for quick reaction throughout the region. With current production around three hundred vehicles annually, South Africa could soon have several thousand Ratels and might even begin exploring export opportunities.

Measuring embargo effectiveness also involves the question of licenses and coproduction agreements. The 1977 UN embargo called upon states "to review . . . all existing contractual arrangements with, and licenses granted to, South Africa relating to the manufacture and maintenance of arms, ammunition of all types and military equipment and vehicles, with a view to terminating them." No reliable figure is available on the number of such preembargo contracts, but some estimate them to total several hundred, perhaps more. Moreover, there is no reason to believe that many of these contracts have been unilaterally severed by the supplying state. The reason is simple: South Africa has considerable leverage on existing contracts and licenses. To force a halt in production of an item, the external party would need to possess control of indispensable imported components or know-how not available elsewhere. Once technical data and engineering designs have passed into South African hands, the government has the option to start up local assembly provided it can duplicate or substitute components. A unilateral breach of contract by the supplying firm would have the effect, in some cases, not of stopping production but of stopping the flow of income from South Africa to the firm. It is possible that some "contracts" have been terminated or have expired after production of a specific number of units, while profitable subsidiary licenses or subcontracts continue on components. There is evidence of continued local assembly since the embargo of a number of French and Italian aircraft and helicopter models and Israeli patrol boats. In other cases, South Africa has made design modifications and continues production under a new name with nearly 100 percent local content. An armored car of French origin, for example, is now manufactured in South Africa under the name Eland.

Thus, licenses and coproduction agreements continue to limit embargo effectiveness. Although the embargo may constrain some firms and governments from entering into new agreements, it would be unrealistic to expect them to inflict damage on themselves through unilateral measures to sever existing agreements. Over the longer term, other areas of embargo evasion could become more important to South Africa. These include the direct hiring by ARMSCOR of foreign experts in various weapons fields and the passing of designs and engineering technology through the local subsidiaries or associates of foreign firms. In Crocker's view, common sense suggests that both these practices are occurring and will continue to occur, though no concrete evidence has come to light. Assuming U.S. adherence to the spirit and letter of the embargo, the competitive commercial interests and differing political perspectives of European, East Asian, and Israeli firms and governments make it likely that some technology and components will continue to flow to South Africa.

THE NUCLEAR QUESTION*

Reports of planned or actual nuclear weapons tests in August 1977 and again in September 1979 have spurred growing speculation among some Western observers that South Africa has embarked on a nuclear weapons program.

---

*See examination of South Africa's nuclear power program in chapter 7.

South African official sources firmly deny the existence of such an undertaking. However, South African statements include an element of ambiguity designed to demonstrate that the government has options and will keep them open. Affirmations of commitment to strictly peaceful uses of nuclear energy have been followed by hedges.

In the case of the 1977 reports of what appeared to be a nuclear weapons test site in the Kalahari Desert, no alternative explanation has been offered by the South African government for the structures revealed by Soviet and U.S. satellite photography. The reports of a possible September 1979 nuclear test over the Indian Ocean have occasioned South African reactions ranging from amusement and astonishment to denials. These uncertainties about alleged nuclear activities in 1977 and 1979 have only fueled conjecture. Some U.S. experts have reportedly concluded that the 1979 event was a neutron bomb test, perhaps conducted jointly with Israel. But as of early 1981 there was no unanimity of opinion among American intelligence and scientific experts.

Perhaps the most important rationale for a South African nuclear weapons capability would be the straightforward diplomatic and status incentives. Membership in the small group of nuclear powers is seen as enhancing status in world politics, and the urgency with which nuclear powers are currently seeking to curb proliferation may reinforce status incentives for weapons development. South Africa's political isolation may make it peculiarly susceptible to such attractions. Moreover, the government may be motivated to some extent by an implicit desire to impress Africans, both at home and across its borders, with white technological prowess. Certainly, it has nothing to lose if one spinoff of its nuclear program is to reinforce the view among Africans that South Africa cannot be tackled militarily at this stage.

South Africa may also see diplomatic benefits from nuclear capability in its relations with the Western powers. The strong Western reaction to the purported test plans of 1977 probably confirmed the impression that a weapons capability would offer leverage: If South Africa is doing (or might do) something that the Western powers dislike, perhaps they will see the wisdom of offering something in exchange for its termination. The South Africans may expect that more attention will be paid to them if they possess nuclear weapons. The so-far-unsuccessful U.S. efforts to get South Africa to sign the Nuclear Non-Proliferation Treaty as a condition of supplying nuclear fuel are one form of such attention. The South Africans are aware that their nuclear potential is an issue of both concern and potential embarrassment for the West, and they are likely to continue to exploit whatever leverage this situation offers.

There are nevertheless definite limits to the use of such leverage. South Africa is not yet so self-sufficient that it can readily ignore all foreign links in the nuclear field. Foreign fuel supplies for the Koeberg nuclear plants will be sorely missed. Also, South Africa's nuclear leverage is presumably greater when there is ambiguity about its intentions. Overt testing and weapons deployment would be seen not only as provocative but would also make it virtually impossible for Washington to continue discussions about nuclear co-operation and would probably lead to further technological isolation or embargoes. South Africa can threaten to cut itself off from the West and become totally self-sufficient in the necessary technologies. But if South Africa were to resort to these tactics, it would lose the inherent bargaining advantages of flexibility and ambiguity. Hence, it would be surprising if overt weapons testing and assembly were to proceed at this stage, especially since the overall domestic and external security environment would not seem to require it. The reaction of African and Western states to allegations of South African testing would appear to have already conferred on the Republic many, if not most, of the diplomatic benefits of nuclear weapons capability.

SOUTH AFRICANS TALKING

A Clerk

He is thirty now, born in Soweto, of parents born in the Transkei. He is not a registered Transkei citizen and vows that he never will be. His parents technically are Transkei citizens but they, too, are now permanent residents of Soweto. "They would probably go back to Transkei without a murmur if they were told to go," he says. "They don't know anything about these things. They just agree with everything the government says. They don't understand."

He lives in a four-room house in Soweto with no electricity and with cold water supplied from an outside tap. The rent is 28 rand a month. He drives a 1976 model car, which costs him 107 rand in monthly payments out of his salary of 200 rand. He doesn't have a driver's license, and if he did he wouldn't carry it on his person, just as he refuses on principle to carry his dompas (passbook).

Although he has never been charged with any offense, he calculates he has spent about two and a half years in and out of detention. He has been in solitary confinement and says he has been beaten during interrogation. "They wanted to know what I've been doing since the day I was born. They beat me. A lot. I don't forget that so easy."

I am a clerk in a factory that supplies hardware to builders but I am registered as just a laborer. I can't get any better than that because they don't want me to work. I was expelled from school in Natal in 1975, so since then the government don't want me to get work. They are trying to force me to go back to Transkei.

When I was at school—it was a boarding school—we were confined to the school premises every day, and we decided we needed some recreation facilities, needed to improve our social life. I had a friend who was an advocate and he agreed to put a case before the court: a civil case appealing for our rights as students. We had an argument with the principal and the school inspectors, and I was expelled. Then I came to Soweto to try to get my matric [qualifying exam for university admission]. I sat my matric, but to this day I have never been able to find out my results. Once you are labeled as a troublemaker, that's it!

I work for an Afrikaner in a factory that supplies hardware. It is a job that a white man can do, and there is a white man supervising me. There's a big gap between his salary and mine. He's getting about seven hundred rand a month, I'm getting two hundred.

We are allowed to be members of a union, but I'm not interested in joining the one we've got. It's called the Furniture and Allied Black Workers Union. We are told we must be a member of this union without being told what are the conditions of membership, what are the policies, and why was it formed. I feel that as long as it is not formed by the people concerned it will never be a real association of workers. The secretary of the union is a Coloured man, and in the factory in South Africa there is discrimination between the blacks and the Coloureds. I don't think that man, being a Coloured, has any concern about the interests of the black workers. We don't get the same salary as the Coloureds. They get more than the black people even if they are doing the same job. The Coloured people don't experience what we experience daily.

I would like to do something else, something better, if I could, but I don't think I will ever get a chance, because I only got that job through a friend of a friend who just pushed me in there, and I know that I must work there my whole life. I can't get a job anywhere else. About three or four times when I try for a job the security police phone to say, "That man is no good." They want me where I am so they can keep an eye on me.

My wife is a teacher in Transkei. I get home to see her only on holidays, maybe once or twice a year. I am still trying to get permission for her to stay here with me. But even if she gets a Transkei passport to travel here she has no right to live in Johannesburg because she is a citizen of the homelands. So I will never be able to have her living here, permanently, with me. They are trying to force me out, to go to Transkei. But I'm not prepared to do this. There are jobs there, maybe, but there's no money there. At one time if there had been a job in Transkei worth taking I would have taken it. But not now that it's a so-called independent state. I wouldn't take a job there now on principle. I feel very bitter that most of the people who were born in Transkei can't get jobs in the cities of South Africa. They can't benefit from what little rights workers do have in the cities; they can only work here under a contract. They can work for thirty years in a factory here and they are still on a contract. They get no pension, and when they eventually leave, they leave with nothing.

You see in the factory there is no future for a black man, none at all. There have been people working there for thirty years, one man for forty-six years, but they are still getting low salaries and no benefits. With a black man there is no promotion.

The only time I get to talk to the white people where I work is when they tell me to do something, nothing else. They never ask me about my life. I never get a chance to talk with white people outside of the job. I might be interested to talk to them but they are not interested to talk to me—the black man is there just to work, that's all. Sometimes I am dearly interested to talk to a white man to ask about his life and things and what he has been doing at the weekends. But at the end of the day he goes one way and I go another.

I send some of my money to Transkei, but after paying for my car there isn't much left over. I cannot save. I need the money to eat, pay the rent, buy clothes. There's nothing left over.

I have thought about trying to buy a house in Soweto but not with the restrictions and the laws that we have to go through. I don't want to know about a ninety-nine-year lease. I want to be able to buy a house without those conditions attached. If I were offered a normal lease system I would buy a house, if I had enough money. But even then there's nothing to look forward to.

I feel that I will live in Soweto, like this, for the rest of my life, without any change. I feel safe among the people of Soweto. I feel sorry rather than afraid for the criminals of the township. They are dissatisfied with their lives, with the government, but have no direction to follow. I make my own protest—I refuse to carry the passbook—but as an individual my attitude has no effect on the government. Unless we can do it as a nation, only then can we have any impact. We will do it as a nation. It is only a matter of time before we get organized to that action. We talk about it together every day. Here in the township, at work. We talk in our own language, and the white people do not understand what we are saying.

I have a car but I don't have a driver's license. I'm not a criminal, I haven't stolen anything. I don't feel like carrying a pass either, so long as the white man doesn't have to carry a passbook. I tell the police that when they stop me. So they take me to the police station. Sometimes they release me, sometimes they take me to court. Then I tell them I won't pay the fine, I'd rather go to jail than pay their fine. So I go to jail for thirty-one days. Then I've been held in security detention. I've been in plenty of police stations and prisons. I was never charged with anything. But I still refuse to carry my passbook. I know the security police here very well by now. They watch me and I watch them. I don't really know what the police are after. I am not a member of any of the local political organizations. I don't mix with them. Sometimes I just start arguing with someone in a shop and the next thing they've called the uniformed police and from there they call the security police. That's how it goes. I'm the sort of guy who doesn't like to be pushed around.

An Investment Banker

The house is built on a ridge overlooking Johannesburg's zoo and its neat, green public parks. It is pleasantly furnished with lots of Cape yellowwood, pine, imbuia, and blackwood. Copper and brass pots and utensils from settler days hang on the walls. Two Mercedes cars, a sports model and a sedan, are in the garage. Between the ornamental goldfish pond in the courtyard and the all-weather tennis court, a drilling rig rises like a giant steel-girdered mantis.

"I'm drilling for water," the investment banker, who owns all this, says. He is a tall, burly, and handsome Afrikaner, thirty years old. He speaks in the cultured tones of a man educated at Stellenbosch University, the alma mater of Afrikanerdom, and later at American business schools. A Great Dane bounds up to him, followed by a spaniel and a blue-eyed weimaraner pup, a rare breed of German hunting dog. A servant in a crisply starched white uniform with a crimson sash around his waist lays out a tea tray on the terrace.

"I was up at dawn this morning," he says. "I had to take the girl friend of one of my house servants to the hospital. She'd been assaulted by some black tsotsis [thugs]. That black hospital on a Sunday morning is something else. A horror show." He pauses. "A battlefield."

As he talks, his fiancée pours tea. She is an elegant-looking blonde, an English South African. The wedding will be a high-society affair.

I look at friends of mine, they come from farming communities, they go to Stellenbosch and Pretoria University, and they go to the city. The Afrikaner is changing, and as he becomes urbanized some of his values and traditions are also changing. There's a difference between us and the prior generation in our politics and in the way we behave with other people in society. And it is often disturbing to the older generation.

As a young man I never got to know blacks at all. I was from the Cape, and the Cape Coloured is really only a slightly browner Afrikaner, almost completely Western in his culture. Then I went to the States. In my last year there I met a black chap from Soweto, a Zulu, who had been working for Coca-Cola and studying hair care and cosmetics in his spare time. He asked me if I'd go into a partnership with him in South Africa. He wanted to open a hair salon here. I said, sure, so we opened a hair salon in the Carlton Center, in downtown Johannesburg. It's a fifty-fifty partnership, in both of our names. We have nothing signed. We balance the books at the end of the month on a pure trust basis. And we're doing extremely well.

My partner and I invested $45,000, and we had a turnover of about $300,000 in the first year. The chap drives a Mercedes. It was no giveaway; he earned it. And now he can afford to live in a better area. His wife is a black American with an MBA degree. He doesn't want her to live in Soweto, so he lives in a Coloured area. But we're already looking at houses in some of the better white areas. He can't live in a bad white area because people there would kick him out, but he could move into an upper-class white area. In fact, I'd like him to go into a Progressive Federal party [predominantly English-speaking opposition party] constituency. Let's see how honest they are, let's see how far their progressive ideas go.

Now we're going to open a hair salon in Soweto also. There are legal restrictions to blacks opening up shop in a white area and vice versa. But we just break them. We just break the law because I believe when a law is immoral, unethical, and unjust, you must go ahead and break it. And I believe it's unjust that until recently a black businessman wasn't allowed to open up shop in Johannesburg. Now blacks are doing just that, and the Group Areas Act is being changed. But even if they hadn't changed the act, we would still have gone along and done what we did. Let them put us in jail if they want to.

If I could find properly trained blacks I would employ them immediately. The only thing that stops this country's economic growth is the lack of skilled personnel. We should be training people ourselves, and the whole education system, black and white, should be completely revamped. As the economy grows, we simply will not have enough whites or Coloured or Indians to fill the slots, so Africans will have to be advanced more rapidly. Free enterprise can be used as a tool for advancement and integration. First people work together, then they start eating together. That's one thing a businessman can do. Another is to make sure that the people he employs are well treated, treated like human beings. These changes can't be far off. It's got to happen. I believe we will have change in the next two to three years. It won't be five years. We don't have that kind of time. I mean, who are we kidding?

But I'm not too sure that the white democratic society we have here is going to give up or share power that easily. For us to do a great reform act is very, very difficult, looking at the realities of Africa. Personally, I see that we are going to have majority rule. The question is, How do we bridge the gap between majority rule and the stage we're in now—our white democracy, which I would call a meritocracy? I believe we're going to have an interim phase—a one-party state of some kind.

But the only way anybody's going to be able to change our society is as P. W. Botha is now going to try it: with a referendum. The only way around the right wing of the Nationalist party will be to go straight to the nation. Of course, that doesn't include Coloureds or Indians or Africans. I'm talking about a straight white referendum. But P. W. Botha's got the public-opinion formers behind him, and I think in a referendum he could swing it.

The Nationalists have always believed that the end justifies the means—and whatever happens in between is just bad luck. But I think we've seen a change in philosophy since P. W. Botha became prime minister. It's a change that foreigners and the English-speaking press might not be able to pick up on. You've got to be awfully close to the Afrikaner soul to understand what's happening now. Let's face it, a guy like P. W. Botha, or Education Minister Gerrit Viljoen, they know what the score is. They know exactly what's what. Viljoen is a former head of the Broederbond. I think that helps him understand the power struggle. When he says something should change, an awful lot of powerful people are going to listen. And P. W. Botha has already made some important changes. Look at the army—it's totally integrated now.

The blacks have exactly the same complaints today as the Afrikaners had under the British. We don't seem to remember our own history, and we go even further by creating martyrs. I knew Steve Biko and other Black Consciousness leaders back in the early seventies. Biko was like our Jopie Fourie, the Cape rebel who was executed by the British in 1914. It's as simple as that. I don't know who was in charge, but it is frightening to think they never realized how important Steve Biko was. He was a powerful, powerful man.

But there has been a change in mentality. Deaths in police cells have dropped dramatically. Someone at the top must have said, "We've had enough. Now let's work together to solve things." Because most of the Afrikaners could not take it, the treatment of Steve Biko. When it finally got into the press, the Afrikaners were ashamed. Afrikaners never really understood or realized what was happening until Biko's case was brought to light. But now I think there are going to be changes, so many and so fast that we'll surprise the world. I know this has been said in the past. John Vorster said, "Give me six months"—and nothing happened. But now we have no choice.

A Sculptor

His grandparents were Scots and Danes, and he grew up in a English-speaking community in Cape Town. A big man with broad shoulders and thick builder's hands, he sits on the patio of his house, surrounded by experimental sculpture. His wife's ceramics are scattered among his own works—twisted variations of the human figure, cast in metal or carved from South African hardwoods. Talking about an elaborate marble wall fountain he did recently for a South African spa resort, he says derisively, "Most clients here can hardly be bothered to look at your work. They just want to show that they're cultured and civilized— like Europeans. They're trying to say, 'I'm just as civilized as you are.' "

Why do I live here? I live here because I can operate here better than anywhere else. There's a boom here. In Europe it's nearly impossible now to make a living as an artist. I've had several one-man shows in a gallery in Barcelona, and now and then I sell the odd piece. But it would be very difficult for an unknown artist like me to get by in Europe. Here, in South Africa, you can make a good living in art, particularly if you take on the kind of big architectural commissions that I do—sculptures to go in places like airports and universities around the country. The people here are still interested. They still have enough money to be able to put some very good works of art into their buildings. There's an enormous output of art here in comparison to the population, and first-class British artists show here regularly. After all, this is where the money is. From that perspective, South Africa is a paradise today.

Still, I have to admit that I am happier overseas. We live in Spain for a while each year. And both of my daughters are abroad, one of them married to an Englishman. I feel happier that they're out of it. I think this is a very bad place for impressionable people to be brought up. As it was, several times just before they left it was bloody dodgey. They would come in at four o'clock in the morning after an evening with a black man. They were spending time in one of the townships and smoking pot with all sorts of rum blacks. It was a bad scene. And I think politics had a lot to do with it. Obviously the kids did these things to show their defiance. They figured, "To hell, if I want to go with a black, why shouldn't I go with him?" It was obviously politically inspired radicalism at heart.

I only come back here because this is where the business is. I have no feelings of attachment or patriotism or whatever. Quite honestly, I can't wait to shake the dust of this bloody country off my feet. Maybe it's because of my English background. These bastards have screwed me so hard that I couldn't give a stuff really.

I have no Afrikaner friends—except perhaps the one who's now left South Africa and gone to live in England. I first began to understand the psychology of the Afrikaner when I was studying at Stellenbosch. It was at the beginning of World War Two and the Afrikaners in my class were all very enthusiastic about Ossewabrandwag [a nationalist Afrikaner organization with pro-German sympathies] and other such mobs that were probably the precursors of the Broederbond. And boy, did those bastards give us English-speaking students a hard time. Even the teachers went along. There were six of us and forty-eight Afrikaners, and they really went out of their way to be as hard as they could on us. When one of us did something wrong, we'd be sent out by the teacher to cut a stick to be punished with. You'd cut it and strip it yourself and then he'd beat you with it. Like digging your own bloody grave. Afrikaners are a nasty bloody race. Absolutely humorless. They should never have been let loose here.

Not that any of this stops me doing business with them, rather an awful lot of business. It's the easiest thing in the world. You can always fool yourself: You say this is art and art is above politics. That's easy to say. But of course you know it's not like that at all. We're not such bloody great Michaelangelos that we fly above it. We're hack workers, really, working to order.

I just can't take Afrikaners seriously when they come across with all that mouthing about good-bye to apartheid and all that balls. And yet the funny thing is that if the Afrikaner were allowed to ease up, he'd find himself getting on with the black man like a house on fire. There's no doubt about it. I mean, the Afrikaner has an absolute identity of interest with the black man. That's the reason they're so hard on blacks—because fundamentally they are the same person: simplistic, very fond of their positions, tribalistic, preoccupied with the whole issue of the group's identity. Why the hell the Afrikaner chooses to fight the black, I can't imagine.

Of course, as soon as you get a hard-core black, what the Afrikaner would call a "cheeky kaffir," then there's trouble. Then you have a racial incident. But that's unusual. I'm struck over and over again with the extraordinary patience and real politeness of the blacks. Take for example the library right here in town. The reading room in the reference library is just one sea of black faces. And there hasn't been any sort of racial incident or friction there. Or take a petrol pump hand; you'd expect him to be a real hard case. But in fact he goes out of his way to be nice to you. I could just fall down and weep in that situation. I mean, how can these people go on day after day taking the stuff that is handed out to them?

I had hoped in my early days to possibly do something to change things—mainly by writing. I used to be a journalist. And then when I was working in the government tourist organization, I used the office typing pool and duplicating machines to put together a news sheet about the massacre at Sharpeville and things like that. I used to send it overseas. Of course, when the boss discovered this, I was dismissed.

I've also been brooding many years now on a book I want to write about South Africa. I've figured out how this place has to be assessed. It has to be done humorously—as a joke, a satire. Because it's so bloody ludicrous. Every single thing you come across is a joke. The book I've been planning—it's called *Milk Tart in Momma Street*—is about a Boer who comes back to South Africa after a fancy education in Europe and tries to readapt to society here. But although he is really a Boer at heart, he still can't get used to it again. He finds the tension growing and growing, until one evening he goes to a place like Soweto and gets caught up with a black woman and becomes her valet. He arranges her bridge appointments and lays out her clothes and so on. And he finds great satisfaction in this—the ideal of service. He thinks, "Why haven't I done this years ago?" It's a difficult thing to write. I rewrite it every few months. But each time it's so unsatisfactory I have to start it again.

In another scene in the book, a marvelous scene, a guy who has had a tremendous party wakes up hung over the next morning and goes out into the street. He sees all these blacks, thousands of blacks, passing him on the sidewalk, and he lurches into the Office of Racial Affairs or some such to report it. He says to the *oubass* [old boss] there, who's smoking his meerschaum [a Dutch pipe] and wearing a cap, "*Oupa* [old man], there are a helluva lot of black people in this town, eh?" The old man says, "Black people? What do you mean black people? I don't see any black people." And meanwhile they're passing by all the time. The guy with the hangover says, "But there, can't you see them? Have I got such a hangover? Can't you see them?" "No, my boy, I don't see any blacks here, no, no, no." "But look," the guy says desperately, "look at them," and he goes out into the street and tries to grab one of the passing blacks. "Watch out," one of them cries, "he's trying to catch us." And pffft, suddenly they're all gone. The street is deserted. And the old boss puffs on his pipe and says, "See, where are your black people now? As I told you, there are no blacks here."

Yes, I once hoped to change things by writing, but I've never tried to take action—like Alan Paton starting up a political party or going into the center of town to shout slogans or distribute leaflets. No, I've never been an activist. In some way, I suppose I'm really cynical about it. I mean humanity is a bit of a bastard all the way 'round, isn't it? Nasty bloody race. Anyway, I don't envisage spending my last years here. If I could I would rather not. Although God knows, it's got a lot to be said for it. I mean, the climate here is like paradise. You can live here like a king.

A Business Family

The mother is an Indian South African, a descendant of a warrior family from the region that is now Afghanistan. She was once a schoolteacher in Durban. Like her husband and their children, she has light olive skin—so light that she is often taken for Portuguese or Spanish or Italian.

When I first spoke to the ballet teacher on the telephone, she was afraid to tell me that her class was completely white. So one Thursday afternoon I took my child to her studio and told her how enthusiastic my daughter was about ballet. She told me she had eight children in her class. "Well," I said, "then one more won't make any difference." She was dillydallying, but I knew just what the problem was. And I had taken my child with me because I felt that if the teacher looked at my child, she might change her mind. I said, "I wouldn't mind my child doing ballet with white children. And if the white children wouldn't mind doing ballet with her, and their parents don't mind, then would you mind?" She said she would telephone me. I waited a week and she hadn't phoned, so I phoned her. I told her, "My child is anxious. It's either yes or no." So she took my child. But she said I must keep quiet about it, as really she shouldn't have more than nine pupils. I knew what she meant and I kept quiet about it, because in this country you don't cut off your nose to spite your face. And now my child does ballet with them. They've accepted her. They treat her very well. She has never once come home to say that they treat her differently. And she's a pretty good ballet dancer.

Her husband is a businessman whose grandfather arrived in South Africa before the Boer War, lured to the new country by stories about the gold that had been discovered in the Transvaal. He settled in Shakaskraal, north of Durban, and opened a trading store, where he sold clothing, textiles, and foodstuffs to the black laborers on neighboring farms. When he died, his sons sold the store and bought into a manufacturing concern that makes ropes and twines for farms, shipping, and industrial use. Now the family owns the business.

The husband is a small, neat man. He went to primary school in Shakaskraal and completed his matriculation in Stanger, on the north coast of Natal, about fifty miles from Durban, where the family business is centered. He has been able to buy property there in an area designated as an Indian residential area.

Maybe I'm different because I'm in business, in manufacturing, and when it comes to business, it's the color of your money that makes the difference. If somebody can do business with you or if they can make money from you, I don't think they are prepared to look at the color of your face. I work pretty hard. I'm making a good living. I'm very strongly for private enterprise. But I feel that I could certainly do better if the legal barriers separating the races were taken down. I feel that my business is inhibited by these barriers. If there was a good opportunity in Cape Town, I'd like to open up a shop there, or a factory. But in the present setup that's very difficult for me as an Indian, because the law has set aside certain areas where we can live and where we can trade, where we can open up factories and businesses. There is even a law that says that Indian people cannot be in the Orange Free State for more than twenty-four hours without special permission. You are allowed twenty-four hours for your passage through. I've been through, and I've never stayed longer than that.

My children are not yet conscious of the apartheid setup. We travel quite a lot—to the Far East and Europe and London. Here in South Africa we often eat at international hotels, and every year we spend a few weeks at the Holiday Inn on the Hlalalume River near Kruger National Park. There the kids swim in the pool and eat with their friends. They do anything they like. I don't think it has struck them yet that there are certain places where they can't go. Their lives have been, to some extent, sheltered by me—not intentionally, though, because I want them to know the problems they will have to face. But one thing we have already taught them is not to hate anybody, not to hate the white man. They can hate the political system as much as the blacks hate it. And when they grow up they must be prepared to fight it. They must be prepared to change it. But they must never hate another person. I'd like them to treat everybody as a human being, whether he is white or black or pink or any color. Color must never be a criterion.

My wife and I, we don't look at color. Color doesn't matter to us. We have African friends and white friends. We don't feel that as Indians we must stick with the Indians or that we mustn't associate with other people.

But most Indians here are not very active members in the community. They keep very much to themselves. In some conservative families it is still important to know where you come from in India. They feel they still belong to India. And religion is still very important. We are Moslems—and a Moslem wants to marry another Moslem. And let's face it, it's also very much political. It's the apartheid setup which tends to divide everybody. The Indian in his residential area, the white man in his area, and the African in his. So most of the Indian community is very insular. But not because they enjoy it. They don't. The Indian may seem introverted. But he is naturally friendly, and he wants to get out of his shell and meet people and mix with the rest of society.

We have made two trips to India and we liked it very much. It was a great experience. But as far as going back to live there, that is never in our thoughts. We don't see ourselves as Indians. Maybe in the food we eat and the paintings in the house—in this way we may be very much Indian. But these things are just part of our background. Even when we are in India, they feel we are foreigners. And I don't blame them, because our thinking is not as Indians. We are South Africans. Besides, it would be very difficult for us to go and live in India. I have a very strong business background, and I think I would survive in any part of the world. But I must be honest about this. To go and get a job in India or to start a business there—it's not impossible, but it would be very difficult. We would not be better off in India. And we don't feel that we belong to India.

The rebels in Afghanistan, my wife's people, are still holding out against the Russians. But there aren't many rebels in South Africa now. The Indians do make some noises, but the Indian is very much a pacifist. He doesn't like to fight. He would rather use his intelligence—which they are doing. It brings us back to Gandhi and his philosophy. But Gandhi wasn't in South Africa for a very long period, and the memory of him isn't very strong here. In any case, today the rebels haven't got a chance. They're all either in jail or banned or something. I'm afraid to express my real feelings even to my best friend, because he might be an informer. That is the situation right now.

Still, South Africa is a vital country. It's moving; things are happening. I think we Indians are changing, taking more interest in the rest of the community. The Indians in Stanger have a local-affairs committee. We have proposed for years that Stanger should be a multiracial town. We've always lived in harmony with the population here, white and black. And we don't want this to be an exclusively Indian town. We want it to be a multiracial town. We are fighting for that, and I think we are getting somewhere. It's a matter of time. It might come about. The government has made certain statements about giving local people more say in their own affairs, at the grass-roots level, and I see a little bit of light on the horizon. I'm very hopeful about the changes that are talked about every day.

But then, I don't think my African friends feel the same way. At this point in time they are not optimistic. And if it came to the choice whether to align myself with the whites or the blacks, I would go with the blacks. Sure, my wife and I can go into any hotel in town and order a meal, and there are no questions asked. We have been mistaken for Portuguese lots of times. But that doesn't really give me any comfort. It doesn't mean anything. What would our black friends say if they saw us going into a hotel where they can't go with us? How would they feel about that? Yes, if it came to a crunch, I would go with the blacks. Looking at history, I feel that is where the future lies—maybe not my future but the future of my children. Africans cannot be dominated or suppressed forever. When you look north—at Zimbabwe and Zambia—the black man is taking over. And I think the black man in South Africa has changed his ideas, and his thinking is now that the Indian is not his enemy. Because we are all part of the society here, and it is our country—just as much as it is his.

A Builder

He is an Afrikaner of Dutch and French descent. In the late 1920s his family, unable to maintain the farm, moved to the city. Later, during World War II, his father joined the South African forces to fight with the Allies.

He left school as a boy with a standard-seven [ninth-grade] education. He became a storeman and a mechanic before serving his apprenticeship as a boilermaker. He did some boxing in his younger days and, for a time, rode with a local motorcycle gang. He was a drill-and-field instructor in the army, and one of his passions is still the subject and sporting use of firearms. He and his wife go to shooting practice at a nearby rifle range once a week.

Today he is an independent small builder, one of many who live in and around Johannesburg. He built the house in which he lives with his wife and two daughters.

Yes, I served my time as a boilermaker, and I could go back into that business any time, but it's a dirty trade, with long hours, not much overtime, and you ruin your eyes with the welder. I found there was more money trying it on my own. I've always had the ambition to work for myself, to buy and build for myself. I've got a house that I've built from a *pondokkie* [hut] and I've bought land where I'm going to build. But I'll always stay in the Transvaal, where I was born and bred.

Recently, there was a slump in the building trade. A lot of the whites left and the blacks took over. You have more blacks in the trade now than at any time before. Bricklayers, carpenters, plasterers, they can do that by law now. For the six years I've been in business I've employed blacks. It's really hard to find a good guy. You run into many chancers, but if you hit upon a good guy you try and keep him by offering a good wage, finding him living quarters if you can, and getting him registered, because in this country you've got to register them. Guys that come from the homelands can't get a permanent sort of residence outside the homelands. You've got to have proof of where they stay, otherwise you can't register them.

I work with these guys on a friendly basis, not like

a boss over them. And if there's any problem with the job I pull them aside and discuss it with them. If I can't communicate with the guy, and he doesn't want to listen to me, it's just too bad—he goes. Now and then you've got to put your foot down, you've got to show them that you're the boss. Otherwise if you give them a hand, they'll take a foot, they'll take your whole body. I think the majority of the blacks do respect that you are white, and there are others, higher-class blacks, who respect you not because you're white but because you're on par with them. I mean, I treat a black who's done a standard six, standard seven, on a par. If he's come into the trade as a bricklayer, and I can afford to pay him, I would pay him the exact same wage as a white man. Because I treat every guy as he comes, no matter what color he is.

I employ nine boys: three Rhodesians who speak English, the Tswanas speak Afrikaans, the Zulu boys I speak Zulu to—not fluently but enough to communicate— and we've got one who comes from Vendaland who can only speak Venda. He's a hang of a good worker, a bricklayer; there's no end to his work, he's like a machine. We communicate with him through the other boys.

My day begins at seven-thirty and finishes at about quarter to five, and we all work a forty-five-hour week as a mutual agreement. We always end a bit early on a Friday. Once a month I buy beers and we have a drink together, socialize, talk about the job, see if there are any problems. At Christmastime we have a party at the house, I buy meat, give them a hang of a good bonus, plus leave pay. I've bought a couple of drinks every year since we've been going. And this year on the Easter weekend I'm going to take the whole lot down to the coast. They've never seen the sea. The whole nine—I'm going to pile them into the truck and drive them myself. The wife and kids are going with us and we're taking the servant, so there will be ten blacks.

You know, I've been accused of being too close to the blacks by my *boets* [mates]. I had a partner once, an English guy, you would call him an abuser because he's the type of guy who comes out here and treats the blacks like you've never seen, like dirt, and just abuses them, uses them for his own convenience. We never really got on, and we split company after a while. I believe today he's started up several businesses which have fallen through. He's since tried to get boys from me, but they don't want to go because they know what he's like. And he thought I was too soft, too easy on the boys. He used to come around when I wasn't there and tell my wife I was too soft on them, that I didn't treat my coons properly. He thought that I wasn't capable of dealing with them because I had only a standard-seven education. I didn't have the proper authority, that was his attitude. But I believe you don't have to express that type of authority on your guys. I mean, we work together. They're all more or less my age, and if you work with a guy and you treat him the way you would treat anyone else, he's going to respect you. If you look after him he's going to look after you. You don't have to step on him all the time and shout at him.

I treat everybody as they come. I could make a friend of anybody who's willing to be friends with me. And I think that a lot of South Africans are like me; if we were certain of what our destiny was going to be and if we were certain that the government was going to give us our true destiny, that we would be recognized and not stepped on by the rest of the world, we'd go for that. But who can be certain what's going to happen to them? No one can be certain. I mean, if I was sure that my family would be safe and I could live the life I'm living now, then I could live in a black country, under a black government. I'm a lover of my country; my father fought for my country, and I'm willing to give for my country. I don't want to see anybody being put down because of any policy.

On April 29 I'm voting for the Nats [Nationalists]. I feel it's every South African's duty to vote. If you don't vote you're not a true South African. I'm voting Nat because I'm not sure what the PFP [Progressive Federal party] policies are. I know they're going to help the blacks, which I'd like to do myself, but I'm not sure where the PFP policies would lead us. You know, it's not like the States, where it's either the Republicans or the Democrats. We've had a government here that's been governing since the forties.

The Nats have got something, all right. This is the government with the policies. You know, they're doing good in some way. We've got a place in the sun, the white people. Okay, so we've got a black majority in this country, but we didn't start off the homelands policy—the British did with Swaziland, Lesotho, and Bechuanaland [Botswana today]. So it wasn't us that started it. The British saw what the problem was and how to sort it out. Now, I believe this government's doing good as far as the homelands are concerned. You don't want to be put in an Angolan situation with three different parties, tribal parties, battling for power. There's civil war there. You can't have one black man rule. And it's the same in this country, you can't have one black man rule this country. So I believe the homelands policy is good. I don't believe the government is giving the blacks enough land, the whites are hogging the land, but I believe they may be on the right path. They may be.

But we live with this feeling of insecurity. I had a shaky upbringing; both my parents died, and my brother and I had to do a lot of things ourselves. I saw a lot of violence as a small boy, black violence, amongst blacks. One uncle of mine lived on a platinum mine, outside of Pretoria, where I once stayed when I was small. One day, I saw a faction fight, Zulu warriors against Tswanas. The violence I saw that day was unbelievable: blood everywhere and eyes torn out like you've never seen before. From that day I've felt that I must have some sort of protection. Because I feel that in Africa today, no matter where you live, you've got to have some sort of security against the blacks. I have guns and I know how to use them. I have a shotgun I use for shooting birds and clay pigeons, and I've got a .44 magnum I use for target shooting. I've never carried them in the street. Some guys get out of hand carrying guns, and you wonder whether they're really capable of protecting themselves. I believe there are also blacks who do carry guns, in the homelands police force and that sort of thing. But if there were no homelands and the majority of blacks in this country were carrying weapons, I would feel very insecure indeed.

When I went to Soweto to see the big fight [the World Boxing Association flyweight title fight between the Soweto title holder, Peter "Terror" Mathebula, and the Argentine challenger, Santos Laciar], that was the first time I'd ever been actually inside there. There were a lot of blacks there with hatred in their hearts. I felt that. We sang their national anthem, "Nkosi Sikelela I-Afrika" ["God Bless Africa"], the Argentinian national anthem, and the South African anthem, "Die Stem" ["The Call"]. And there was just continual singing of their anthem, and black power salutes. You know, I went there to support one of their guys. But then one South African fighter, Harold Volbrecht, an Afrikaner like me, came out and fought an Argentinian. They were both white, but the blacks booed Volbrecht. And they booed every decision that was for the South African.

There was more bad than good atmosphere at that place. I saw two white women with black guys. I don't know how they got there or obtained permits or whether they visit there regularly, but it makes you think. Now, it's up to you how you want to live your life. You know, if there could be peace in the land I would be happy. I'll never interfere, but I can't say the same thing would go for my daughters. And I don't think it would go with any white man in this country. Not because of racialism, not because I want to interfere with my kids' happiness or their choice. But because of the kids of my kids—the sort of life they might lead. I'd never go against my daughters, and when they come of age there's nothing I can do. But I would disapprove of it; I think every white guy would.

I've never been overseas, but my heart's always been in America. I feel Reagan is going to be the right man, because he can see the strategic advantage of South Africa's minerals and the sea route. I don't think he's going to stand with us as far as our racial policies, but he's going to be with us and protect us. I see him as a protector. I love my country, and I think this is the guy.

But I also feel that before the eighties are out there'll be a complete change in this country. Whether or not the blacks feel that too I'm not sure. The black guy is hard to understand. His views are totally different from ours. He'll agree with you one time and he'll be totally against you the next. Most of the blacks I've met say this is their country. But when you get down to facts, there were only the Bushmen in South Africa when the whites landed at the Cape. The blacks were in Rhodesia. Basically, we came here more or less at the same time. We both belong to South Africa. There is no one black man who can say that this is his country more so than a white. We belong here as much as they do. And I'm prepared to defend that right. And if ever anything happens where the blacks will suffer in this country, I'll suffer with them. If there's a Communist onslaught on our country and the blacks are going to be oppressed, I'll fight with them. My father fought for this country, for the free world, and I would do the same.

A Doctor

The acrid tear gas seeped into her yellow Mercedes, sting-ing her nose and eyes and making it difficult to breathe. At the entrance to Elsiesriver township the police had set up a roadblock. "You can't go in there," they told her. "They're stoning cars. Better turn back." She refused. "My surgery is in there," she said. "I'm needed in there." A few moments later, she found herself stuck in traffic, sur-rounded by a gang of children who were throwing stones at passing vehicles. She stopped her car and got out. "What the devil are you doing?" she shouted. "Don't you know who I am? Don't you know that if you get hurt or you get shot, I'm the one who's going to help you? I live right over there. Now let me through." For a moment, the angry youths stood frozen with their arms raised, the stones still in their hands. Then somebody waved her on. When she looked back, they were stoning the cars behind her. By the end of the day, she had patched up quite a few of their cuts and bruises and had tended one young girl suffering from shotgun wounds.

Elsiesriver is a Coloured township on the barren Cape Flats northeast of Cape Town, an area that Coloured people often call their "homeland." There are no class distinctions in the township. Workers and laboratory assistants live side by side; lawyers' bungalows are scattered among der-elict shanties made of cardboard and corrugated iron. Her trim house and surgery unit stand across the street from a block of high-rise tenements.

When the South African government first introduced official race groupings in 1950, she was classified as Indian. She appealed to the supreme court and was reclassified Ma-lay—a subdivision of the Coloured group. Some years later the government again ruled that she was of Indian descent, and again she appealed. Her current identity card lists her as Malay, like her husband, who is also a doctor. She is a vigorous woman who chain smokes and speaks perfect Eng-lish. She has also learned to speak the rough, slangy Afri-kaans that is used in the street in Elsiesriver.

I want to live here because this is where I work. If you are going to be a family doctor, you have to live among the people you serve. You can't isolate yourself from them. I can take a *skollie* [a young ruffian] off the street and I can talk to him in his own language, and he will listen to me because I live here. If I lived in Constantia [a plush white suburb] or Fairways [a middle-class Coloured area] and simply came and worked here, then I would break that sort of communication.

And I think it has become a matter of pride to the people here to know that their doctor is living amongst them. There used to be a bus terminus right in front of our house. And people started queuing up there from about five o'clock in the morning to catch the bus into the city to work. But we didn't hear a single peep from them. If someone put on a wireless they would be told, in Afrikaans, "Hey, stop that music. The doctor's asleep." The people here developed a protective instinct toward us. Throughout the riots of 1976, throughout the flare-ups that occurred last year, we were in the middle of it, and no one harmed us. Even when the bitterness and the frustration was at its explosive peak, no one touched us.

But the frustration isn't just here, it's all over South Africa. And it's not just with the schooling and the education standards. It's a frustration that goes right across the board. It's a question of knowing that when you've done your work, you've got to go back to those tenements. And even if you're in a job and you have some ability, you know that you're not going to rise further than a certain level. Or if you do go beyond that, you won't be paid what you should be paid. You know that your education is inferior. You know that when you go outside to get a bus, even in the pouring rain, you first have to check that there is no sign that says the bus is for whites only. Basically it boils down to that little piece of paper—your passbook or identity card—no matter what your standards or your education. That is what you are fighting. You get the sense that you are in a quagmire: You are trying all the time to get out and yet you know that the moment you get to the edge your heels are still stuck. And if you don't possess too much intelligence, you don't understand it, and you just turn to violence—senseless violence.

I don't think there can be any black South Africans— if they have any intelligence—who can really say that they have not been involved in anything political. And that doesn't necessarily mean joining a specific political party, because there isn't a single party standing at the moment that you could say is going to achieve something. That's why a lot of people are turning away from political parties: for the simple reason that they can see absolutely nothing that a party can achieve in South Africa now.

If I had to belong to one organization, I would belong to the African National Congress. The wife and children of Nelson Mandela [jailed leader of the African National Congress] stay with us whenever they come down to Cape Town, whenever she can visit him on Robben Island. She is allowed to come down once a month, but financially, of course, this is impossible, and she generally comes down every second or third month. Then she's allowed to visit him for half an hour each day for two days. At Christmas she was lucky: She was allowed Christmas Day and Boxing Day and the weekend that followed—four days. So I still have my ear to the tune of what's going on among black political leaders. And I can tell you they are not antiwhite, despite the specter of fear that's been raised up. Neither are they Marxist. They started off that way, as Zimbabwe's president, Mugabe, did. But basically they are pragmatists. And I can tell you this: If there is anybody who can really save South Africa, that person is Mandela.

My children are now five and six years old, and I have made up my mind that things cannot go on as they are. The eighties are going to be a crucial part in South African history: 1985 is going to see a change. Don't ask me why I have settled on that date. The main fact we have to take into consideration is that the black population is in complete ferment, and they are not going to take very much more of what has already been handed out to them. The youth of today are no longer patient. And they are willing to die in the struggle. So this ferment is not going to be stopped, or even contained. And it's not going to stretch on for years, to the year 2000, for example—the date the government is talking about as the time for the evolutionary changes to occur.

Now, the changes can still occur peacefully if Botha can make up his mind. If Botha became a dictator tomorrow, if he's firm enough, he could still lead South Africa out of the mess that it's in. The question is, Will the present government be subtle enough to bend where it should? Is it prepared to give more than it has given? Because all it has given so far has been promises. And if the government doesn't make some real changes soon, then there's going to be one unholy mess—and people are going to die for nothing. And I can assure you that I'll be here and I'll be one of them who's going to fight. And if I die in the process I only hope it will be better for my children.

It's a bleak prospect, but it's among the imponderables one has to look at. We don't want cosmetic changes. I don't want to know that I can go into any hotel or restaurant. That doesn't interest me. Because I can go home and have a proper, decent meal—and a lot cheaper too. But I want to know that vital changes have occurred. I want to know that when my children start school, as they have just now, their education is on a par with that being given at Bishops or Herschel [white private schools in Cape Town]. I want to know they will be taught South African history from an impartial point of view, and I want to know that when they grow up they will not be like us and sit and do nothing.

I'm inclined to be more positive than negative because I tend to say there is good in everybody, which there basically is. Nobody can be so bad that he can't change. The question I am most frequently asked when I go overseas is "Why on earth do you want to go back to that goddamn awful country?" And I say that "goddamn awful country" spawned me, and there are a lot of people back there who cannot leave. Besides, there's no greener grass anywhere in this world. There are problems all over—in England, in Australia, in America, in Canada, and in Africa. So where do you go? No, I can't think of leaving here. I may be one of the dying breed, but I still believe there is a little bit of patriotism left, not for South Africa as it is at present but for the South Africa I envisage.

An Executive

It is early morning and the smoke of wood and coal fires hangs heavy over a township outside Springs, about twenty miles from Johannesburg. He kisses his wife good-bye— she works too, but will leave later—and gets into a shining

*new car. It churns up the dust on the dirt road leading out
of the township. As he joins the traffic on the highway into
the city, he takes out a pocket tape recorder and dictates
a memo for his secretary, Diana. Diana is white. He is
black.*

*"My car," he says, laughing, "is my company's dues
to apartheid." According to South African law, he must
live in the East Rand, where he was born and raised; he
could not live in Soweto even if he wanted to. So the company must provide him with a car to travel from his home
near Springs to his office in Johannesburg. He says he
usually keeps a car for about eighteen months and then the
company replaces it with a new one.*

*A small, bespectacled man with a straggly beard, he
wears a dapper pin-striped suit and a ruby ring, and
checks the time on an expensive digital watch that he
bought, he explains, on a recent business trip abroad.*

When you come from a poor family, there's a lot of
pressure on you to get out and get to work. My father,
who was a policeman, died just after I wrote my final
matric, and it was only through my own tenacity that I
managed to keep on with my education. After my matric
I began a BA in social work at Turfloop [University of the
North at Turfloop, an all-black university in the northern
Transvaal], but I never completed it because midway I got
cheesed off with social work. That's the kind of blunder
you make in Bantu education, because for blacks there's
no vocational guidance. You just feel your way through,
you just choose a course without really thinking what you
want to do. Anyway, I changed my mind. I wanted to do
a degree in fine arts but none of the black universities
had that faculty. I applied to do one at Wits [University
of Witwatersrand] but was turned down because in order
for a black to be admitted to a white university you have
to have a junior degree in the first place and then you
have to get special permission from the minister of education. So I ended up with a BA in general education
without being specifically trained for any particular
profession.

In the township where I was born, we lived in a two-
room shack. After the authorities declared the township
abandoned [to make way for new white housing], we were

transferred to a new Springs township. My father owned two houses there, but he never owned the land. Today certain areas in the township have been declared ninety-nine-year-lease sites. In fact, my lawyer just telephoned me about this: The problem is that I want to build a house on a site outside of the ninety-nine-year-lease area. So before we start building, we need a reply from the minister. My new house will cost me thirty thousand rand. That's a hell of a long way from the original two-room shack in the old township. I don't know how we lived there, how we did it. It was ridiculous. Sometimes I go for a look at that shack. It's still standing.

I'm now a brand manager cum marketing consultant, concerned mainly with the nonwhite market. White people say to me, "Look where you are." And I say, "Yes, but there aren't many of us." And the blacks who do break into corporate management rarely get the big decision-making jobs. I'm an exception. I got a break from an English-speaking South African who felt it his duty that I should get a break. I was lucky, and I worked hard. Of course, I was pretty cocky. I talked my way behind this desk. But I know a lot of black people who are smarter than me, and they never got the breaks.

At an American company where I worked before, I was the first black marketing trainee in South Africa. And I remember the divisions within the company when I first started to work there. Some people, mainly Afrikaners and Nationalists, were saying, "We wish he fails, we hope he confirms our stereotypes, the way we think of blacks as lazy and irresponsible." All of that nonsense. And then there was a small group of Americans and English-speaking people who said, "We hope he makes it, just to show that given the chance black people can make it."

In this business there's a good deal of social mixing to be done, so I get plenty of invitations from my colleagues—an invitation to a *braaivleis* [barbecue] or from someone who's opened up a new pub. There aren't too many laws that make it difficult for me to mix socially with whites in a private capacity. In a white area the only problem comes when a neighbor phones the police to object to your host entertaining a black man. I'm not really affected by the curfew laws. Sometimes I work late at my office, and sometimes when I've had too much to drink I sleep over at my friends' places. But if I want to invite my friends out to my place, then there's a lot of red tape, and they've got to be out of the township by half past four in the afternoon.

Still, you can't really avoid the kind of harassment that reminds you of the color of your skin. The other week we had a Christmas party at a fancy downtown hotel, and I was dancing with a white woman. And in the middle of the dance there was somebody tapping me on the shoulder and saying, "We're sorry, but we aren't allowed to let you dance like this."

It's so crazy, so ridiculous, sometimes very laughable. But sometimes it makes you bitter. There are days when I feel very, very bitter about being a black in South Africa, and I suppose it shows in my dealings on that particular day. If I'm stopped by a policeman and he's very rude, then, when I get to the office, I'm hating all white men. Or sometimes you see people being treated very, very badly. And if at that moment someone said to me, "Why don't you cross the border and fight with the guerrillas," then I'd go and do it, really I would.

By definition I'm South Sotho and my homeland is Qwaqwa. But I don't think of myself as South Sotho really. It's not important to me. I'm a cosmopolitan person. I come from a rich, intertribal background. My ancestors didn't come from Qwaqwa, they came from Lesotho. In any case, Qwaqwa hasn't opted for independence yet. But the whole thing is ridiculous. Can you imagine the reaction of a white South African if there were a black government here that suddenly said, "You have no political rights in South Africa because you come from France, or Germany, or Holland. Even if you are fourth generation, if you want to vote you must go back to Europe. If you want a passport, you must get a European passport." You see, it's not his country anymore. He doesn't identify with these people. I've never even been to Qwaqwa. I'm third generation and that's that.

It's laughable, yes. Guys like myself may be able to afford to laugh at it. But I see more and more younger people who aren't laughing at it any longer. That's what's frightening about the future. There are two camps that whites have to negotiate with. One is the moderate black camp. "Okay," the whites say, "we can negotiate with those people right now and save ourselves a lot of problems in the future." But the generation that comes after that will not be concerned with any kind of negotiation. It will go for a takeover, the sort of thing that happened in Zimbabwe. You can only stall for so long, then you lose the initiative. From a long-term point of view, it's a very myopic solution—and a dangerous one.

And the worst thing is that the moderate guys in the first camp are being lured into the militant camp. The militants will tell you, "Forget about negotiation. Every time you go to Pretoria and talk to the minister, it's very nice, you have coffee and all that. But you come back empty-handed. We throw a couple of stones, overturn some vehicles, and things happen, man. So why don't you come into our camp?"

You see, change normally takes a long time. And the only area where I see even a little bit of change is in the mind, in people's attitudes. But unfortunately those kinds of marginal changes are very few and far apart, only happening among people in certain classes. I don't think the attitudes of the man in the street are changing. If anything, his attitudes are hardening, because he feels threatened, in a class sense, by blacks. An upper-class guy doesn't worry about having a black family living next door. He knows that his chances of having a black neighbor are very rare because he lives in an area that's too expensive for most blacks.

Change is like love in this country, it's in the eye of the beholder. No black person will tell you that there's been any real change in this country. The educational system hasn't changed. The opportunities within companies haven't changed. And the changes that are being talked about, however dramatic they may be, those changes are not initiated by the black people themselves. How could they be, when black people aren't represented in Parliament?

Businessmen boast about what they are doing for their black workers: integrating toilets and eating facilities. But who said blacks wanted integrated toilets or integrated eating facilities? These changes were defined by whites for black people—and that's not the sort of change we want. I don't particularly want my daughter to go to a white school. I want her teacher to be paid the same as a white teacher, and I want black education to be as comprehensive and efficient as white education. Just because I'm sitting here at this desk doesn't mean much change, because I'm only a tiny fraction of the total black population. And if only that tiny fraction can go to a white restaurant, then what change are we talking about?

Africans line up for bus from Soweto to Johannesburg

NON-WHITES ONLY
SLEGS NIE·BLANKES

Bus for blacks, Johannesburg

African workers, Chrysler automobile plant in
Johannesburg

Afrikaner surface worker, Western Deep Levels gold mine, near
Johannesburg

Prime Minister P. W. Botha

Dr. Fredrik van Zyl Slabbert, leader of the Progressive Federal party

Harry Oppenheimer (left) and Anton Rupert, two of South Africa's leading industrialists

Dr. Andries Treurnicht, minister of state administration and statistics

M. Gatsha Buthelezi,
chief minister of KwaZulu,
addressing rally, Soweto

Nelson Mandela,
imprisoned leader of
the African National Congress

(WIDE WORLD PHOTOS)

(INTERNATIONAL DEFENCE AND AID FUND)

(ALON REININGER/CONTACT)

Bishop Desmond Tutu, general
secretary of the South African
Council of Churches,
at Sunday Mass, Johannesburg

(INTERNATIONAL DEFENCE AND AID FUND)

Dr. Nthato Motlana, chairman,
Soweto Committee of Ten

*New housing provided by Ford Motor Company,
Port Elizabeth*

Garbage collectors, Johannesburg

Part II
THE WIDER STAGE

Chapter 12
South Africa in Africa

Pᵣesident Julius Nyerere of Tanzania once said that if he needed shoes and South Africa was the only place he could buy them, he would go barefoot. But if he needed food and South Africa was the only source of supply, he would buy food from South Africa.

Nyerere's comment points up the hard choices South Africa poses for many black African nations. On the one hand, they deplore apartheid and are eager to oppose it at every turn. That attitude is reflected in official African policy, as expressed through the Organization of African Unity (OAU): to "isolate South Africa both politically and economically." One manifestation of this policy is a long-standing OAU trade boycott.

On the other hand, they cannot escape the overriding reality: South Africa is the dominant economic force in southern Africa. That reality frustrates observance of the trade boycott and appears to rule out for now participation by many African states in other forms of economic sanctions against South Africa. In 1980 more black African states traded with South Africa than ever before, and in record volume. Neighboring black states depend heavily on South Africa for food and, in some cases, oil imports. Many of these states also earn much of their export income from shipments to South Africa. And economic links between South Africa and its neighbors are not limited to trade: Some of the key transportation routes of adjacent states go through South Africa, and often their only access to world markets is through South African ports. Electricity flows from South Africa into the power grids of neighboring states. In addition, several states in the region send migrant workers to South Africa, and South African capital finances development projects in a number of countries.

South Africa is seeking to expand its economic relations with the other states of the region. They, on the other hand, are seeking through greater mutual cooperation to reduce the imbalance in their economic relations with South Africa. Thus far it has been a difficult goal. Robert Mugabe, prime minister of Zimbabwe, stated the dilemma of southern African leaders in a New York television interview in 1980. "We know that apartheid is abominable," said Mugabe. "It is repugnant to the whole international community. But we must accept that South Africa is a geographical reality and as such we must have some minimum relationship with it." Mr. Mugabe said that Zimbabwe could not ignore the "economic reality that our country has been linked with South Africa over years . . . in trade and commerce."

TRADE

According to the Department of Customs and Excise in Pretoria, South Africa's exports to African countries in 1980 exceeded $1 billion, up more than 50 percent over the previous year. Imports from African countries rose to a record $345 million for the January–November period in 1980.

Although no breakdown of the trade between South Africa and individual African countries is available, evidence indicates that most of South Africa's trade is with states in the southern African region. For the neighboring states—Botswana, Lesotho, Swaziland, Zambia, Zimbabwe, Malawi, and Mozambique—the economic cost of enforcing the trade embargo would be prohibitive, and they do not observe it. Of the nine nations in the area, Tanzania and Angola appear to have the least volume of trade and commerce with South Africa.

What the dramatic increase in trade indicates, said a government official in Pretoria, is that "African countries struggling with massive economic and food problems are pushing aside political antagonisms and boycotts to trade in the best and the cheapest market—South Africa." African nations would not agree that they are pushing aside concerns about South Africa's racial policies, but they would agree that trade with South Africa is a necessity under present circumstances.

Food is the item that black Africa needs most. Maize (corn), wheat, processed foods, and meat accounted for the largest share of items purchased from South Africa by African states in 1980. For reasons ranging from fast-growing populations to a lack of capital or expertise, from adverse natural conditions to continuing rural-to-urban migration, most African nations do not yet produce enough food to feed their populations. South Africa, on the other hand, is a major food exporter. Moreover, its climatic conditions are ideal for growing maize, the staple food of neighboring African states.

Aside from food, South Africa is also the source of a large share of manufactured goods in the southern African region. The area relies upon South Africa for machinery, spare parts, and petroleum products. In 1976, 73 percent of machinery and equipment, 55 percent of chemicals, 89 percent of plastics

288

and rubber products, and 73 percent of transport machinery imported by neighboring black states came from South Africa.

TRANSPORT LINKS

Historically determined north-south transport routes are a major contributing factor to southern Africa's dependence on South Africa. When Cecil Rhodes was prime minister of the Cape Colony (from 1890 to 1895), he accelerated the construction of the railroad network that currently links the black states with South Africa. The network was originally designed to join the administrative centers of colonial powers, situated for the most part on the coasts, to the production areas in the hinterlands.

The railway line running through Botswana, for example, was intended to link the Cape Colony with Southern Rhodesia (now Zimbabwe). The line was later extended farther north to serve newly discovered copper mines of Northern Rhodesia (now Zambia) and into the mineral-rich Shaba province of the Belgian Congo (now Zaire). Still later, lines were added through Portuguese territory to link Angola with Shaba and to link Rhodesia with Mozambique. The main access remained the north-south link, and all exports were routed through South African ports.

During the Rhodesian civil war, Botswana took over the Rhodesian railway in Botswana. The line, which connects Botswana to Zimbabwe to the north and South Africa to the south, is used primarily to carry Botswana's imports and exports through South Africa. The independence of Zimbabwe will permit the restoration of normal transport patterns through that country and make it possible for Botswana to reduce the volume of transport through South Africa. Botswana has placed high priority on paving the "Botzam" road north to the Zambian border, now largely completed with help from the United States. Seeking to develop its transport potential further, Botswana has also established a national airline.

Surrounded by South Africa, Lesotho is also heavily dependent on South Africa's transport and port systems. Lesotho is building an international airport (scheduled for completion in 1983) and has recently established a direct air link to Maputo in Mozambique. Transit through Johannesburg will then no longer be necessary.

Swaziland has road and rail links with Mozambique and road links with South Africa. A rail link to Durban is under construction. Mozambique is less dependent on South Africa for transport, since it has several good harbors. However, Mozambique earns revenue from the export of South African goods through Mozambican harbors, and South African technicians are working on the economically crucial task of improving the efficiency of Mozambique's port of Maputo. In February 1979 South Africa signed a seven-year agreement with Mozambique to increase its exports through Maputo to 30,000 to 35,000 tons per day by 1981. (In late 1980, 70 percent of goods flowing through Maputo's port were South African.) Also, South African mining concerns will finance the upgrading of the rail line from Maputo to Komatipoort, on South Africa's eastern border.

Although Zimbabwe is exploring alternative export routes through Mozambican ports, it remains heavily dependent on South Africa to ship its goods to world markets. Zimbabwe and Mozambique have agreed to cooperate in improving the rail line between the ports of Maputo and Beira, in Mozambique, and Zimbabwe. The line was severely damaged during the war in Zimbabwe when Mozambique served as a base for Zimbabwean guerrilla forces. Until the railway is restored and improved, however, Mugabe is apparently reconciled to shipping his country's exports through the South African ports of Durban and East London, which surpass the Mozambique ports in capacity and efficiency.

The war in Zimbabwe increased Zambian and Mozambican dependence on South African imports and transports. Rhodesian forces bombed transportation routes in both countries, causing extensive damage. The closing of the Zambia-Rhodesia border from 1973 until 1978 and the Mozambique-Rhodesia border from 1976 until 1979, in compliance with UN sanctions, also had serious economic consequences for both countries.

A railway from Lusaka, Zambia's capital, to the Tanzanian port of Dar es Salaam was completed in 1975 so that Zambians would not have to use the rail links to South African ports. But the Tazara Railway, as it is now called, has proved inefficient and the port at Dar es Salaam is heavily congested. As of late 1980, only 40 percent of Zambian goods were shipped via the Tazara; South Africa handled the rest.

OIL AND ELECTRICITY

South Africa sells refined oil regularly to the BLS states (Botswana, Lesotho, and Swaziland), to Zimbabwe and Namibia, and on a limited basis to other states in the region. Discussion of an oil embargo as a sanction against South Africa raises the question of its impact on South Africa's neighbors. If South Africa's oil supply were cut off or greatly reduced, the BLS states would be particularly affected.

Alternative sources of varying degrees of reliability are available in some states. There is a refinery in Maputo, Mozambique, which gives Swaziland a choice in its source of imports; and efforts are under way to restore an oil pipeline between Zimbabwe and Mozambique. Zambia's Ndeni refinery and pipeline to Dar es Salaam already free that country from oil dependence on South Africa. Ndeni might also be able to service Botswana in an emergency.

Mozambique, Lesotho, Swaziland, and Zimbabwe receive electricity from the South African Electricity Supply Commission (ESCOM). In addition, Botswana and Namibia have asked to be linked to the South African power grid to cope with their peak electricity demands. South Africa itself buys electricity generated by Mozambique's Cabora Bassa hydroelectric power dam to supplement locally produced supplies. In late 1980 Mozambican dissidents sabotaged the power lines to South Africa, depriving ESCOM of almost 10 percent of power supplies normally available to it, for which it pays nearly $200,000 a day. Because ESCOM has a reserve capacity of 17 percent, service was not disrupted.

South Africa had regarded the Cabora Bassa project as the first step toward establishing a power network for all of southern Africa. Problems of security raised by the sabotage, however, may have dampened enthusiasm for this prospect.

FORMAL AGREEMENTS AND AID

The BLS states are formally linked to South Africa through the Southern Africa Customs Union (SACU) and, in the case of Lesotho and Swaziland, through membership in the Rand Monetary Area (RMA). Namibia, still under South African control, is also a member.

SACU, which establishes a common tariff area, provides the BLS states with more than 50 percent of their revenues through customs, sales, and excise taxes. In 1979–80, for example, Lesotho received almost $90 million in revenues from the agreement.

The de facto monetary union of South Africa and the BLS states was formalized with the creation of the Rand Monetary Area in 1974. In August 1976, Botswana withdrew from the RMA and issued its own currency, the pula, which was tied to the U.S. dollar. Swaziland's lilangeni and the new maluti in Lesotho remain tied to the rand, which remains legal tender in these two states.

South Africa has trade agreements with Zimbabwe, agreements with Mozambique and Malawi on labor supply, and tariff agreements for the use of Mozambican ports and rail systems.

MIGRANT LABOR

Foreign migrant workers from most of the states in the region except Zambia are employed in South Africa, most of them in the mines. While the number of foreign mine workers in South Africa has been substantially reduced in recent years, they still make up more than 40 percent of the total mining work force. Mining in South Africa is a major source of employment for neighboring states.

The exodus of adult males from neighboring countries causes social dislocation and, some believe, makes economic development in these countries

291

more difficult in the long term by removing significant numbers of men in their most productive years. On the other hand, remittances by migrant workers provide badly needed income for the individuals involved as well as critical foreign exchange for the neighboring countries. Earnings from the mines are a major support to Lesotho's and Botswana's economies.

INVESTMENTS

South Africa has investments in every nation in the region except Angola and Tanzania. The Anglo-American Corporation is the largest South African investor in the region. A company with approximately $10 billion in assets, it does about 6 percent of its business in the countries of the region other than South Africa and Namibia.

AID

In 1980 South Africa spent nearly $200 million on development aid and technical assistance in the region. South Africa cooperates with African countries in soil conservation, medical and health services, famine relief, and veterinary science.

THE AFRICAN QUEST FOR ECONOMIC INDEPENDENCE

Although the task has proven difficult, the nations of southern Africa are working to lessen their economic dependence on South Africa. In November 1980 Angola, Botswana, Lesotho, Malawi, Mozambique, Swaziland, Tanzania, Zambia, and Zimbabwe—informally called "the Nine"—attended the Southern African Development Coordination Conference (SADCC) in Maputo, Mozambique. (Zaire, which depends on South African ports to ship 50 percent of its copper, a principal export, participated as an observer.) Formally established in April 1980, the group aims to improve transport and communication links between their countries, expand cooperation in trade and industry, and coordinate aid programs for the region.

Political and economic cooperation among majority-ruled nations in Africa is not new. What is new is an independent Zimbabwe, with a highly developed industrial sector and infrastructure that make it a key factor for regional development. It is, in addition, the only nation in the region other than South Africa that is broadly self-sufficient in food. Mozambique, whose ports offer access to world markets, is also considered pivotal to the Nine's hopes of establishing a countervailing bloc to offset South Africa's regional economic dominance.

The cost of linking the Nine with road and rail lines is estimated to be $2 billion over the next ten years. Most of this will have to come in the form of international aid. At the meetings held in April and November 1980, the group gathered $650 million in such pledges.

In addition to measures to establish transport and communication links between their countries, the leaders of the Nine have also proposed:

(a) a Southern African Development Fund;

(b) a study of existing systems and customs instruments looking toward increasing trade among the Nine through bilaterally negotiated annual trade targets and product lists;

(c) the establishment in Botswana of a Southern Africa regional branch of the International Center for Research on Agriculture in the Semi-Arid Tropics (ICRASAT) to promote regional food security and environmental protection;

(d) a coordinated approach to the control of hoof and mouth disease through expansion of the existing vaccine-producing center in Botswana; and

(e) sharing training and research facilities and promoting the exchange of information to advance concerted policies in the fields of mining, industry, energy, and agriculture.

In order to monitor the results of these efforts and reach agreement on future plans, SADCC will meet annually.

CONSTELLATION OF STATES

As black nations in the region try to reduce their dependence on South Africa, South Africa, on the other hand, seeks to formalize its economic ties with nations in the region through its proposal for a "constellation of states." As envisioned, the constellation would include South Africa, the homelands, and the neighboring states. In July 1980 the South African government formally began to promote the concept, which would involve "voluntary cooperation in matters of common concern" to white South Africa, independent and nonindependent homelands, and black states in the region. Committees have been established to examine proposals for a multilateral development bank in southern Africa, industrial decentralization, and financial arrangements between the South African government and other participants.

Prime Minister Botha has suggested that private enterprise play a large role in economic development of the homelands and of southern Africa as a whole. To bring this about, restrictions on investment by white businesses in the homelands would be removed and an economic council for South Africa and neighboring states would be established. In addition, an Institute for Intermediate Technology would be established to use South Africa's technological capabilities for such regional objectives as increasing food production. Food production would be an important aspect of the arrangement, the South

African government maintains, and a common market would be established for the subcontinent.

Some elements of a "constellation" are already in place. The Southern Africa Customs Union is one example. Critics say, however, that South Africa's behavior in SACU demonstrates that South African interests would dominate an economic union with less powerful states.

Critics also characterize the constellation idea as a device to achieve international recognition of the homelands and say that it would tend to institutionalize and protect the central position of South Africa in the regional economy. The effect of this arrangement, they say, would increase South Africa's economic and political leverage in the area and decrease external pressures for reform.

Others argue that initiatives such as the constellation would force internal reforms. They see more private investment in neighboring states as a way to reduce economic and political imbalance in the region. They urge that the constellation concept be more fully examined, arguing that refusal to cooperate with South Africa in developing the area would be counterproductive. Still others point out that the concept is presently too vaguely articulated to be definitively evaluated.

No other country has yet supported the constellation initiative. In fact, the economic plan of the Nine is commonly referred to as the "counterconstellation," though the group has stressed that its activities are not specifically directed against South Africa. "It is misleading to present what we are doing . . . as confrontation between this part of black Africa [and] white rule in South Africa," said a government official from Zimbabwe. "The fact is that under the present circumstances which we have inherited, we are vulnerable, and it is simply poor economic sense to be so dependent on any single country. Of course, the fact that that country happens to be South Africa is a political spur to us to push ahead as far and as fast as we can."

SOUTH AFRICA REACHES OUT

With regard to African states to the north of the Nine, South Africa seeks to broaden and intensify trade relations. In addition to direct economic benefit, South Africa hopes that more substantial trade will lead to better political relations.

As early as the mid-1950s, National party leaders occasionally spoke of developing economic relations and extending technical aid as part of a policy of "peaceful coexistence" with black African states. Prime Minister Verwoerd, shortly before his death in 1966, met with Chief Leabua Jonathan, prime minister of Lesotho. South Africa's reaching outward has been variously called "dialogue," "détente," "good neighbor policy," and "outward policy." These

294

policies have extended not only to the southern African region, but also to West Africa.

In the late 1960s and early 1970s, some West African states took conciliatory initiatives toward South Africa. Kofi Busia, then prime minister of Ghana, said that he thought it was wrong not to communicate with South Africa, although he later reaffirmed his country's endorsement of OAU policy. In 1970 President Houphouët-Boigny of the Ivory Coast called for dialogue, stating that change in South Africa might be induced through a lessening of hostility and direct contact. Malawi, Madagascar, Gabon, and Dahomey (now Benin) announced their support for the initiative. During 1970–71 visits were exchanged between official representatives from South Africa and Madagascar, Mauritius, and the Central African Republic. But both Madagascar and Mauritius soon pulled back, and a successor government in Madagascar rejected the former president's policy of dialogue with South Africa. Vorster paid a state visit to Malawi in 1970, and President Hastings K. Banda of Malawi made an official visit to South Africa in 1971, the first African head of state ever to do so. During this period South Africa claimed to have established relations with a dozen African countries.

For the most part, however, African nations remained aloof. Except for Malawi, no African nation has established diplomatic relations with South Africa. South Africa had hoped that a clear divorce could be made between economic and political issues; however, its internal racial policies remained an insuperable obstacle to diplomatic rapprochement on the African continent. Senegal's former president Leopold Senghor was quoted as having said in 1971: "I am not against dialogue, but I believe in dialogue at the right time. South Africa must take the first step. She must prove that she has had dialogue with her own people."

The OAU officially opposed dialogue with South Africa in 1971, effectively silencing the movement.* In the mid-1970s, however, contact resumed. In 1974 Vorster met with Houphouët-Boigny in the Ivory Coast, and in 1975 with then-president William R. Tolbert in Liberia. All publicly acknowledged discussions between South Africa and the other countries of Africa north of the Nine abruptly ended with South Africa's foray into Angola in 1975, which unified Africa in a call for South Africa's isolation.

ISOLATING SOUTH AFRICA

African states have called for South Africa's isolation since their entry into the United Nations during the late 1950s and early 1960s. In 1960 a conference of African states in Addis Ababa initiated a trade boycott against South Africa.

---

*The declaration was supported by twenty-eight states. Six states—Gabon, the Ivory Coast, Lesotho, Madagascar, Malawi, and Mauritius—voted against the declaration, while Dahomey, Niger, Togo, Swaziland, and Upper Volta abstained.

This boycott was continued by the OAU upon its formation in 1963. Liberia and Ethiopia, former members of the League of Nations, took the case of South-West Africa (now Namibia) to the International Court of Justice in 1960 in behalf of African states. But these and other measures had little concrete impact upon South Africa, whose confidence in its ability to counter external threats grew with increasing military and economic strength. Still, the concentrated opposition of African states, including their political and moral pressure on the West, has played a significant part in increasing South Africa's diplomatic and ideological isolation.

The policy of isolation was reiterated by the Lusaka Manifesto of April 1969, drafted by Presidents Julius Nyerere of Tanzania and Kenneth Kaunda of Zambia, adopted at a meeting of east and central African states. The manifesto states:

> South Africa should be excluded from the United Nations Agencies, and even from the United Nations itself. It should be ostracized by the world community. It should be isolated from world trade patterns and left to be self-sufficient if it can. The South African government cannot be allowed both to reject the very concept of mankind's unity, and to benefit by the strength given through friendly international relations. And certainly Africa cannot acquiesce in the maintenance of the present policies against people of African descent.

The manifesto is striking for its tone of moderation. "We would prefer to negotiate rather than destroy, to talk rather than kill," it states, making this negotiation conditional on South Africa's commitment to human equality and dignity. The document condemns "reverse racialism" and asserts that African hostility is directed at "systems of minority control" rather than at the whites themselves. White South Africans are acknowledged to be Africans. "We believe that all the peoples who have made their home in the countries of Southern Africa are Africans, regardless of the colour of their skins. . . ." There is an implicit understanding in this document that change would be gradual and originate from within the country. If gradual and peaceful efforts fail, however, African nations would support other measures, the document indicates. Officially called the Manifesto of Southern African States, the document was later approved by the OAU.

THE ORGANIZATION OF AFRICAN UNITY (OAU)

Since its formation in 1963, the OAU has provided the institutional framework for activity against South Africa by black African states. Newly independent African states, divided from South Africa on the issues of apartheid, South-West Africa, and Rhodesia, intensified pressure on South Africa at the United Nations and in other international bodies.

Guided largely by OAU policy, African states, whatever their political and ideological differences, have tended to vote as a bloc in the United Nations on the issue of South Africa. They have spearheaded efforts resulting in South Africa's withdrawal from the British Commonwealth and its exclusion from the Economic Commission for Africa (ECA), the United Nations Educational, Scientific and Cultural Organization (UNESCO), and other technical and scientific bodies. African states also precipitated South Africa's suspension from the World Health Organization (WHO) in 1964. (South Africa is currently a member of WHO but is denied full participation.) African-led efforts to expel South Africa from the United Nations were frustrated by the Security Council vetoes of the United States, France, and Great Britain in 1974, although the African countries were influential in the 1974 and 1981 decisions by the General Assembly to reject the credentials of the South African delegation.

Since the establishment of the OAU, resolutions calling for commercial, diplomatic, and political sanctions against South Africa have been introduced regularly at the United Nations by the African states. In 1970 the OAU began a campaign for an effective arms embargo against South Africa. This embargo was adopted by the United Nations as a recommended action in 1975 and as mandatory policy by the Security Council in 1977. In the mid-1970s, the OAU sought to establish in a number of resolutions a connection between Israeli and South African governments. African states hoped to enlist Arab and other oil producing and exporting countries' support in their campaign against South Africa, just as the Arab states, during the October 1973 war, had persuaded them to cut their ties with Israel and support the Arab League. In 1973 OPEC imposed an oil embargo against South Africa. In subsequent years the OAU set up committees whose purpose is to find ways of making the oil embargo more effective.

In 1976, the OAU condemned France for its sale of nuclear reactors to South Africa and passed a resolution that effectively interrupted South Africa's participation in international sports events, including the Olympics.

African states have regularly introduced resolutions at the United Nations calling upon all governments—especially those of the United States, the United Kingdom, the Federal Republic of Germany, France, Japan, and other industrialized countries—to adopt legislative, administrative, and other measures to stop new investment in South Africa and progressively withdraw existing investments. While these particular efforts have had only minimal effect, Western nations have come under increasing pressure to be responsive to black African initiatives on South Africa because of the number of votes of the African and Third World blocs in the United Nations and growing Western economic interests in black Africa.

In its campaign against South Africa, African countries have given moral and material support to nationalist liberation movements. The OAU established the African Liberation Committee (ALC), which in 1970 recognized the

African National Congress (ANC) and the Pan-Africanist Congress (PAC) as legitimate liberation movements in South Africa.

The strategy of isolation favored by African countries brings into focus not only the question of U.S. economic interests in South Africa but also U.S. relations with African countries. South Africa is one of the issues on which the United States and African states have differed most frequently in the United Nations.

Only Nigeria, the second largest supplier of crude oil to the United States, currently has the ability to begin to make its economic relations with the United States conditional on policy changes toward South Africa. With 90 million people and oil revenues that brought in $25 billion in 1980, Nigeri is black Africa's most populous and wealthiest nation. It is Africa's largest oil exporter, and the sixth largest worldwide.

Nigeria's leadership among African nations and its position of influence in world affairs have grown with its economic power. OPEC and Commonwealth memberships have further enhanced its leverage in both the OAU and the United Nations. As one of South Africa's strongest critics, Nigeria has repeatedly used the forums available to it to focus attention on South Africa. In its various roles at the United Nations, including its capacity as head of the UN's Anti-Apartheid Committee, which it has held since that body's inception in 1963, Nigeria has actively prosecuted its case for sanctions against South Africa and for withdrawal of investment by Western multinationals. Along with the five Western members of the Security Council and the Frontline States, Nigeria has also been involved in the negotiations for free elections in Namibia. Further, Nigeria has provided moral and material support to anti-apartheid movements. It is reported to be the largest contributor to the OAU's Liberation Committee's fund.

South Africa has a long history as one of Nigeria's main foreign policy interests, predating Nigerian independence in 1960. At the very first Commonwealth Conference attended by Nigeria, Abubakar Tafawa Balewa, then prime minister, called for the withdrawal of South Africa from the Commonwealth. Nigeria's opposition to South Africa further hardened when South Africa lent support to the cause of Biafran secession during the Nigerian civil war in 1966.

Although South Africa has been a constant focus of Nigerian foreign policy, Nigeria's level of commitment has varied. In the years between 1960 and 1970 Nigeria's pursuit of an independent foreign policy was inhibited by civil war and economic dependence on Great Britain.

Commitment has also been influenced by changes in administrations. Lieutenant General Yakubu Gowon, beset by a civil war, tended to maintain a low profile in foreign affairs during his 1966–75 administration. His successors, General Murtala Muhammed and Lieutenant General Olusegun Obasanjo, followed a more militant and Africanist foreign policy. During Obasanjo's administration, Nigeria provided direct financial aid to the Popular Movement for the Liberation of Angola (MPLA) and adopted an open-door policy for African exiles from areas in which liberation struggles were being waged.

According to R. A. Akindele, research professor at the Nigerian Institute of International Affairs, Nigeria's general approach is not to allow any multinational company "to prosper through its involvement in our nation's economy only to strengthen apartheid South Africa." Specific information about enforcement of this policy is difficult to obtain, although there is some evidence that its application has varied from case to case. For example, Nigeria gave as its reason for nationalizing the Nigerian operations of Barclays Bank the bank's extensive involvement in South Africa; however, Standard Chartered Bank, also a British bank and the second largest bank in South Africa, has not been nationalized. Nigeria may be particularly vigilant in scrutinizing the conduct of oil companies. In 1979 British Petroleum's Nigerian interests were nationalized after it was discovered that it had been involved in supplying oil, possibly Nigerian, to South Africa.

Both Britain and the United States have large economic stakes in Nigeria. In 1980 Nigeria was expected to surpass South Africa as Britain's largest customer in Africa. Nigeria's trade with Britain is thought to have contributed to Britain's decision to support all-party elections in Rhodesia/Zimbabwe. Nigeria supplies 16 percent of total U.S. oil imports. Because it purchases little from the United States, the U.S. trade deficit with Nigeria was expected to exceed $13 billion in 1980.

Nigeria has indicated that it is willing to use its leverage to achieve its objectives in South Africa. In October 1980, President Shehu Shagari, on his first official visit to the United States, warned that Nigeria would "use any means" at its disposal, "including oil," to persuade the United States to use its "powerful economic position to discourage and eventually destroy apartheid in South Africa." President Shagari told the UN General Assembly that his country would "assist, encourage and support armed insurrection in South Africa" and called for a mandatory oil embargo. Before making a state visit to the White House, the Nigerian president said that it would be a "disaster" for the United States to veto a sanctions resolution against South Africa at the United Nations.

President Shagari expressed frustration over delays in UN-supported elections in Namibia and urged that the United States exert pressure to bring South Africa to the bargaining table. One of the Nigerian president's senior advisers, Chuba Okadigbo, said that Nigeria expected South Africa to yield control of Namibia within one year. After that, he said, Nigeria would set what it considers a reasonable timetable for majority rule in South Africa.

Weighing against Nigeria's desire to exert pressure on the West is its need for economic stability. Nigeria has embarked on an ambitious development program of educational, agricultural, and transportation projects that would be jeopardized by disrupting trade relations with the United States. The United States purchases almost half of Nigeria's oil, and income from oil accounts for 90 percent of Nigeria's revenue. Nigeria's wealth is unevenly distributed, and the standard of living for most Nigerians is low. Children under fifteen make up nearly 50 percent of Nigeria's population. Steady economic growth is needed to satisfy rising expectations.

Some Nigerians say that their government's preoccupation with South Africa does not accurately reflect the interests of most Nigerians. A few, as we learned in Lagos, are skeptical about the potential effectiveness of sanctions. In any event, it is virtually certain that Nigeria will play a major role in articulating the broader African viewpoint in discussions of these and other possible policies toward South Africa.

Chapter 13
South Africa's Relations with Western Europe, Japan, Israel, and Latin America

The United Kingdom, West Germany, and France subscribe to a European Economic Community (EEC) statement that condemns "apartheid without reservation." The statement, made before the United Nations General Assembly in December 1979, describes apartheid as "an evil system which violates the fundamental rights of the majority of the citizens of South Africa." The nine EEC countries, it continues, "are convinced that the apartheid system must end and they continue to urge the South African government to bring about rapid and fundamental change in South Africa. Change is inevitable. The nine earnestly hope that the South African government will respond to the wishes of the majority of its citizens and of the international community as a whole by ending apartheid before opportunities for peaceful change have passed."

EEC trade with South Africa—primarily that of the United Kingdom, West Germany, and France—is three times greater than that of the United States. Historically, Great Britain has been South Africa's largest trading partner. In recent years, however, both the United States and West Germany have surpassed Great Britain in total trade with South Africa.

European investment in South Africa is five times as great as that of the United States. Direct and indirect British investments represent nearly 55 percent of total foreign investment in South Africa; German investment makes up about 10 percent, and French investment nearly 5 percent.

Japan's official policy toward apartheid is more severe than those of the EEC countries. As Japan's representative to the United Nations told the General Assembly in 1980, "[T]he government of Japan has upheld its policy of not permitting direct investment, such as the establishment of local corporations in South Africa by Japanese nationals or corporate bodies under its jurisdiction. . . . Further, the government of Japan . . . has called upon Japanese foreign exchange banks and their branches abroad to refrain from extending any loans to South Africa and has strictly enforced this policy." Nevertheless, Japan has been South Africa's fourth largest trading partner since 1975, and Japanese banks, while restricted, are still allowed, according to a UN report, to make "trade-related" loans.

THE UNITED KINGDOM

In 1979, Lord Carrington, secretary of state for foreign and Commonwealth affairs in the Thatcher government, told the United Nations, "We share the international community's distaste of apartheid. It is neither just nor workable. But will threats and isolation bring about the changes we all wish to see? We in the British government doubt it. We believe that the better course is to accept that the Republic's plural society gives rise to unprecedented problems and to offer our help to the leaders of all races to work together to find just solutions. In this way we can all contribute towards peaceful change in South Africa. Otherwise the future promises only violence and misery for all the people of South Africa, whatever their race."

Former Labour prime minister James Callaghan, who described his party's philosophy to the Commission as "more persistent in its agitation against apartheid" than that of the Conservative party, said that he was still "not a sanctions man." Opposition to apartheid is not a major public issue, according to political leaders of both parties, and sanctions against South Africa would be unpopular because they would create unemployment in the United Kingdom. The London-based United Kingdom-South Africa Trade Association has estimated that a cutoff of South African trade would result in a loss of 70,000 jobs in the United Kingdom. However, a recent report in the *New Statesman,* a British publication, estimated that only between 13,000 and 14,000 British jobs were directly dependent on sales to South Africa.

While there is a trend of continuing decline in Britain's imports from South Africa, other areas of its involvement in the South African economy remain generally stable. About 10 percent of all British overseas direct investment is in South Africa; direct and indirect British investments constitute a majority of South Africa's foreign investment. And British banks continue to be important to the South African economy. Through their international links they have played a key role in South Africa's industrial development. As of 1978 Standard Charter and Barclays Bank International controlled 60 percent of all South African banking deposits.

British companies account for almost half of the 2,000 foreign companies in South Africa and are prominent among the top 100 South African industrial companies. British Petroleum (controlled by the British government) and Shell (jointly owned by Dutch and British interests) together supply about 40 percent of South Africa's petroleum. British companies also provide South Africa with up-to-date technology in the fields of computers, industrial processing, pharmaceuticals, and mineral development.

Antiapartheid groups have mounted numerous campaigns against Britain's economic links with South Africa. The Antiapartheid Movement, based in London, has sixty-two branches and about 3,000 members throughout Great Britain, drawing support from churches, universities, and unions. Despite predictions of job losses, unions have called for economic sanctions against South Africa, and have also given direct assistance to independent black unions within South Africa. The London-based International Defence and Aid Fund focuses attention on the plight of political prisoners in South Africa. The British Council of Churches and the Roman Catholic church have taken activist roles in opposing apartheid, and recently an interdenominational group called Christian Care for Southern Africa was formed.

The United Kingdom's interest in South Africa is in part based on strong historical and cultural connections. Some 1.8 million people living in South Africa are of British descent. Available figures show that up to 50 percent of white immigrants to South Africa come from the United Kingdom. English-speaking whites still make up a greater percentage of professionals and high-level managers than do Afrikaners, and South Africa receives more attention from the news media in Great Britain than in any other country.

On the other hand, Britain also has strong links with other African countries, particularly with former British colonies. Black-led states spend more than $3 billion a year on British goods, and British investment in these countries is now estimated to be greater than that in South Africa. Among Britain's African trade partners, Nigeria stands out as particularly important.

British business and political leaders are concerned about not antagonizing their important trade partners in black Africa, and are not, under current circumstances, willing to reduce trade substantially with South Africa or to withdraw British investments. Avoiding this choice is a key objective of British policy.

WEST GERMANY AND FRANCE

In the Commission's meetings with political and business leaders in West Germany and France, several themes consistently emerged. The director of a German bank with substantial investments in South Africa expressed surprise at the idea that racial policies of a foreign government should affect financial decisions. "Whereas we might feel as human beings that we should take a stand," he said, voicing the sentiment of those with whom the Commission spoke in both countries, "as bankers we have no political sympathies at all."

The Commission was repeatedly told that business and politics are mutually exclusive. Business executives pointed out that their companies are providing South Africa with "essential services" that are nonpolitical in nature and available to all governments, whatever their ideology. If and when the government of South Africa changes—and they expect it will eventually—then these same services will be available to the new regime.

Under current circumstances, France and West Germany do not expect their trade with South Africa to impede business relations with other African countries. Although Germany purchased more South African goods in 1979 than any country except the United States, Germany's oil imports from Nigeria and Libya in the same year surpassed in value its imports from South Africa. France relies on South Africa for certain strategic minerals, but its major African trade is with the francophone nations, primarily Algeria, the Ivory Coast, and Cameroon; and with Nigeria and Morocco. French and German officials expressed concern over the situation in Namibia (see chapter 16), which they see as an issue that may generate increasing African pressure for economic sanctions against South Africa. Like the British, they would not like to face the dilemma that a UN Security Council vote on sanctions over Namibia would pose.

West Germany

West German trade and investment with South Africa represent nearly 1 percent of its gross national product, compared to three-tenths of 1 percent for the United States. Germany imports 60 percent of its chromium, 50 percent of its manganese and platinum, and 90 percent of its asbestos from South Africa. Two-way trade between Germany and South Africa in 1979 was over $3 billion. German banks made a total of $2.4 billion in loans to South Africa from 1972 to 1978.

The thirty-three largest German companies operating in South Africa have approximately 22,000 employees. Germany's direct investment of $336 million makes it the third largest investor in South Africa. Investment is concentrated in Volkswagen, Daimler-Benz, Metal-Gesselschaft, Hoechst, AEG Telefunken, and Siemens. Lurgi, an engineering group, provided the design and special equipment used at the three South African Coal, Oil, and Gas Corporation (SASOL) plants. The process used in SASOL was adapted from a German technique, and German companies are heavily involved in the transfer of technology and expertise to South Africa. Of the 140,000 German nationals in South Africa, 15,000 to 20,000 are employed by German companies. German immigration, which had been heavy in the past, has recently begun to taper off.

Southern Africa
and the World

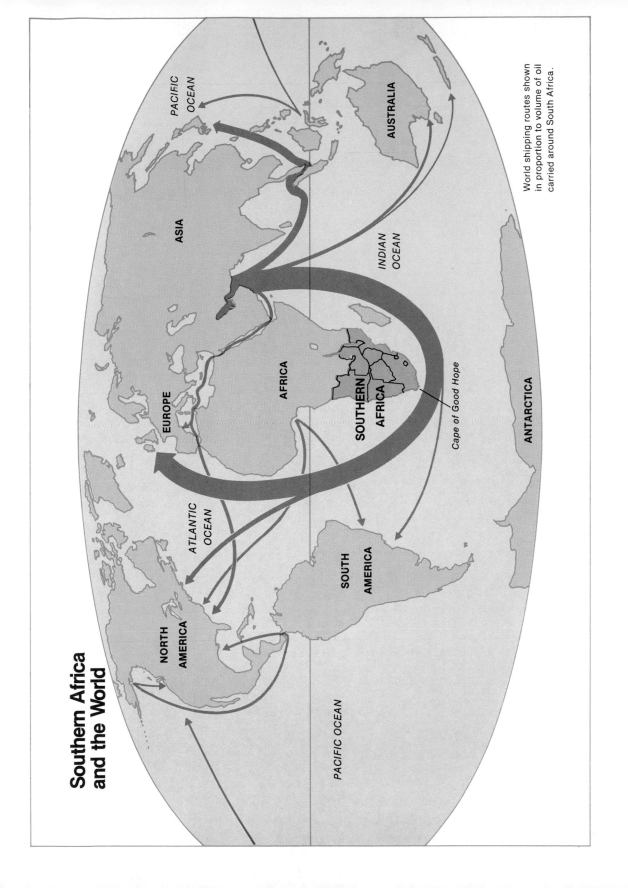

World shipping routes shown
in proportion to volume of oil
carried around South Africa.

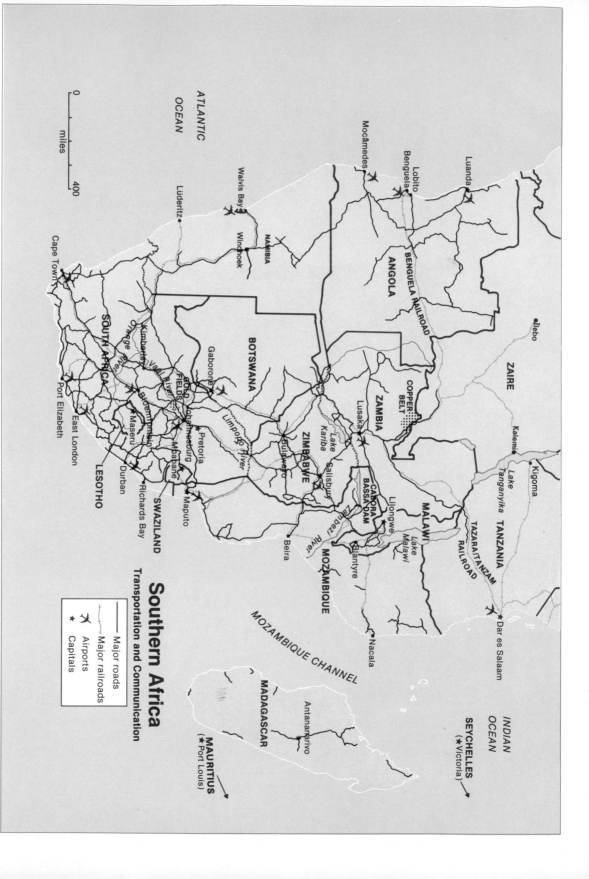

Southern Africa

Transportation and Communication

Major roads
Major railroads
✈ Airports
★ Capitals

As a precondition to the issuance of loan guarantees to companies doing business in South Africa, the German government now requires a declaration of support for the EEC Code of Conduct for Companies with Interests in South Africa. Delegations from German trade unions have visited South Africa to check on compliance. However, according to a 1980 study by Intecontecs Ltd., an international consulting firm, many German companies "have pursued a relatively independent policy in South Africa" regarding enforcement of the code, with some arguing that it limits their ability to compete with those companies not required to conform.

The German government does not support economic sanctions, trade boycotts, or prohibitions on investments. Chancellor Helmut Schmidt has said that it is not his government's policy "to destroy the economic structures of South Africa, plunge the country into economic chaos, and hurt the very section of the population most badly whom we would like to help the most: the black majority, which would have to suffer most from the resultant unemployment." A key official in the German Foreign Ministry told a delegation from the Study Commission that Germany has only limited political means to bring pressure to bear on South Africa. "Whatever we did alone," he said, "would weigh little."

France

In France the Commission was told by officials and others that the French government does not regard policy toward South Africa as an issue of high priority. French policy has developed as trade with South Africa has increased in the past few years, although it is not yet clearly defined.

From 1973 to 1978 French trade with South Africa increased 154 percent. In 1979 two-way trade between South Africa and France was $1.5 billion, and France was South Africa's fifth largest supplier of goods. The UN Center Against Apartheid estimates that in the period from 1972 to 1978 loans to South Africa by French banks totaled nearly $2 billion. There are, however, few French companies with significant operations in South Africa. French companies in South Africa have only about a thousand employees, and "French companies and the French government are decidedly lukewarm about the EEC Code of Conduct," according to Intecontecs Ltd.

Although the French government did not comply with the United Nations' 1963 voluntary embargo on arms sales, in 1977 it voted in the Security Council for the mandatory embargo.

At present, France's most controversial business activity in South Africa is the construction of nuclear power plants. Framatome, a privately owned engineering consortium, has built two power stations at Koeberg, South Africa, which are scheduled to begin operation in 1982 and 1983 if enriched fuel supplies are obtained. The French government, after granting its approval to export a nuclear plant, explained that "the interruption of any civilian nuclear cooperation with South Africa whatsoever would inevitably incur autonomous, unchecked development of nuclear activities . . . in all fields."

France relies heavily on South African minerals. Forty percent of French coal imports come from South Africa, and supplies from alternative sources would be more costly. France, which buys some uranium from Nigeria and could get more from Chad and Gabon, nevertheless imports more than 50 percent of this mineral from South Africa. France also relies upon South Africa for manganese, iron ore, chromium, and platinum. (See chapter 14 for discussion of strategic minerals.)

JAPAN

In 1973 the Organization of African Unity (OAU) published a message to Japan expressing the hope that Japanese business enterprises would sever their economic relations with South Africa. "It would be incomprehensible if [the Japanese people chose] to exchange the immense economic opportunity of the rest of Africa for the small South African market," the message read. Japan responded by promulgating investment and foreign exchange restrictions on those wishing to do business in South Africa.

Nevertheless, trade between Japan and South Africa has expanded significantly in recent years and was expected to set a record in 1980 for increases within any single year. In 1978 South African exports to Japan were more than $1 billion (up 85 percent in three years) and imports from Japan were $950 million (up 33 percent in three years). During the first six months of 1980, trade between the two countries increased by 45 percent.

Japan imports nearly 40 percent of its chromium, 43 percent of its manganese, 88 percent of its vanadium, and 41 percent of its platinum from South Africa. Its nuclear power industry relies heavily on supplies of uranium from South Africa. During the first half of the 1980s, an estimated 25 percent of Japan's coal will come from South Africa. Japan also imports food, primarily maize and sugar, from South Africa. Japanese companies have provided plant equipment for the construction and expansion of major South African enterprises.

Despite the Japanese government's restrictions on loans to South Africa, from 1972 to 1978 Japanese banks made loans totaling $503 million to that country—since 1973 by channeling these loans through overseas affiliates—according to information from the UN Center Against Apartheid. In the early 1970s a sizable portion of these loans went toward industrial development projects in South Africa, and were tied to long-term purchase contracts for South African mineral resources.

More than seventy Japanese firms operate in South Africa, primarily major automobile and electronics manufacturers. Because of their government's ban on direct investment in South Africa, Japanese companies operate through licensing arrangements with unaffiliated South African companies, enabling the local company to assemble and sell Japanese products in South Africa. Japanese companies also often provide technological know-how and management expertise.

In the 1960s the South African government tried to encourage trade with Japan by categorizing the Japanese as "honorary whites." However, members of the small Japanese community in South Africa continue to experience some racial discrimination.

ISRAEL

Recent debates about apartheid in the UN General Assembly have singled out Israel for special attention and have thereby stimulated considerable controversy in the world community and special interest in the United States regarding Israeli–South African relations. UN resolutions linking Israel and South Africa are at least in part an outgrowth of international political developments that followed the October 1973 war in the Middle East. When the Organization of Petroleum Exporting Countries (OPEC), as part of its opposition to Western support of Israel, instituted its oil embargo against the West, it sought support from other international groups. An informal working alliance developed in the United Nations between anti-Israeli Arabs and the anti-apartheid forces of black Africa. The result was a two-pronged attack against Israel and South Africa, condemning both by UN resolutions and seeking to establish that the two countries have unusually close relations.

In 1948 the newly victorious Afrikaner government of South Africa was quick to recognize the new state of Israel. In subsequent years, however, Israel joined in UN resolutions condemning apartheid and voted for sanctions against South Africa. Throughout the 1960s Israel pursued an active policy of friendship with black Africa, and offered technical and economic aid. Israel even offered financial assistance to the OAU's fund for liberation movements.

After the emergence of the alliance between black Africa and the Arab world in 1973, however, many African nations broke off relations with Israel. In late 1975 the UN General Assembly, in two separate resolutions, asserted that "[Z]ionism is a form of racism and racial discrimination" and condemned "the strengthening of relations and collaboration between the racist regime of South Africa and Israel in the political, military, economic, and other fields." In the General Assembly Africans pursued resolutions condemning apartheid that also contained language condemning Israel. In December 1980 Israel's permanent representative to the United Nations complained to the General Assembly that "the needless insertion of unending diatribes against my country has severely undermined the very purpose of the annual debate on apartheid." He reiterated what he said was Israel's position on apartheid: "unequivocal rejection of racism and racial discrimination in any form."

While there is antiapartheid sentiment among members of the Jewish communities in both South Africa and Israel, many Israelis express the need to cooperate with countries that are supportive of Israel's existence and willing to be friendly. South Africa views the situation as an opportunity to extend its own network of relationships.

At the beginning of 1981 it was difficult to define precisely the relationship between Israel and South Africa. Diplomatically there had been changes. During the early 1970s South Africa upgraded the level of its representation in Israel, replacing a residential representative with an ambassador. Israel had increased its official presence in South Africa, and in 1976 both countries signed an agreement on trade, technological, and economic cooperation. Tourism between the two countries has increased. In 1978 El Al Airlines and South African Airways carried 32,000 passengers between Israel and South Africa— 25,000 South Africans and 7,000 Israelis. Trade also increased. Estimates for 1978 placed Israeli exports to South Africa at $87 million. Imports from South Africa were $38 million. There is, however, considerable dispute about the nature of trade and technological cooperation. There have been reports that Israel has supplied South Africa with military hardware in violation of the arms embargo and with nuclear expertise. Israeli officials deny these reports. Israel sells potash, animal feeds, canned goods, textiles, and electronics to South Africa. South Africa supplies Israel with paper, timber, coal, chemicals, and machinery and—through London markets—with diamonds for Israel's cutting and finishing industry. Because the diamonds are purchased in London they are often not reflected in the figures for trade between South Africa and Israel. However, according to the *Financial Mail*, between 1970 and 1978 Israel increased annual imports of rough diamonds from $154 million to more than $1 billion.

LATIN AMERICA

Latin America's trade with South Africa is small but growing steadily. In 1977 and again in 1978 South African exports to Latin America increased by 41 percent over the previous year. The total was over $300 million in 1978, with most going to Brazil. In 1980 South Africa signed an agreement to supply Brazil with $117.5 million of phosphoric acid. Also, Brazil is likely to purchase South African coal.

South Africa is interested in forming a South Atlantic Treaty Organization to protect the South Atlantic. For both security and economic reasons, South Africa would like to expand its relations with Brazil and Argentina, which have relatively well-developed navies and long-range aircraft. In addition, all three countries are staunchly anti-Communist. Argentina and Brazil, however, appear reluctant to make a formal military alliance with a country regarded as a "pariah" state by the world community. Also, Brazil is seeking an increasingly active role throughout west Africa and with Portuguese-speaking African countries. Trade between Angola and Brazil, for example, has grown from $4 million in 1975 to $500 million in 1980, and Brazil is not eager to strain these relationships.

Chapter 14
Strategic Minerals

South Africa has rich and varied mineral resources. Occupying less than 1 percent of the earth's land surface, it is the world's fourth largest supplier of nonfuel minerals. It has the world's largest known deposits of chromium, manganese, platinum, vanadium, and gold, all minerals which are important to the West because of their strategic, industrial, or economic uses. In addition, South Africa has major reserves of many other valuable minerals, including asbestos, coal, copper, diamonds, iron, nickel, phosphates, silver, uranium, and zinc.

South Africa has exploited its mineral wealth with great success. Its mining industry is extensive, efficient, and sophisticated. World mining experts consider South African technology in deep underground mining to be without equal. According to available reports, the safety and health record of South African mine workers is among the best anywhere. The country's well-developed transportation system allows for the reliable shipment of extracted minerals to the region's ports. In 1980 minerals accounted for 76 percent of South Africa's $26-billion foreign exchange earnings, with gold alone accounting for more than 50 percent of this total.

FOUR KEY MINERALS

Chromium, manganese, and vanadium are indispensable in the production of steel. Platinum-group metals serve as catalytic agents in refining petroleum and in reducing automobile emissions. These four minerals—imported from South Africa—are essential to Western industry and defense. Table 14-1 shows the degree of U.S. reliance on South African imports for these minerals. While disruption in the supply of South African gold would have significant impact

TABLE 14-1.

U.S. Dependence on South African Supplies of Four Key Minerals

Mineral/ Alloy	Total Imports as % of U.S. Consumption (1978–79 av.)	Imports from South Africa	
		% of U.S. Imports (1978–79)	% of U.S. Consumption (1978–79)
Chromium:			
Ore	100	46	46
Ferroalloys	55	72	40
Manganese:			
Ore	98	15	15
Ferroalloys	71	58*	42*
Vanadium:			
Pentoxide	30	72	22
Ferroalloys	net exporter	—	—
Platinum- Group Metals	90	67**	60**

Source: U.S. Bureau of Mines, *Minerals Yearbook, 1978–79.*
*Includes an estimated amount for ferromanganese imports from France and other countries of ore originating in South Africa.
**Includes an estimated amount for imports from Great Britain of platinum-group metals originating in South Africa.

on world gold prices and affect international monetary stability, supplies of gold are not as crucial to the West from a strategic or industrial standpoint. U.S. production, government stockpiles, and the holdings of other developed countries would be sufficient to meet the industrial needs of the Western world for some time.

Chromium. Chromium is extracted from the ground as chromite ore and is used principally in its iron-alloy form, ferrochrome. Ferrochrome, when combined with nickel, produces stainless steel. Because of its high strength and its ability to withstand heat and corrosion, stainless steel is critical in the manufacture of jet engines, petrochemical and power plant equipment, and other products subjected to high pressure, extreme temperatures, and corrosion. Other heat-resistant, high-strength superalloys in the defense, aviation, petrochemical, and power-generation industries are formed from chromium. The mineral is also used in tanning leather and in manufacturing textile dyes, heat-resistant bricks, and metal coatings.

South Africa is the largest producer of chromite ore, mining a third of the world's supply and 44 percent of the chromium mined in non-Communist countries. It has more than 66 percent of the world's reserves. The 1979 world production and reserve figures for chromium, as well as for manganese, vanadium, and the platinum-group metals, are listed in Table 14-2. South Africa is the United States' principal source of chromium both as ore and as ferrochrome, and the absolute amount and relative percentage of South African imports have increased steadily in the past few years.

While the United States has some chromium ore deposits, none are sufficiently concentrated and accessible to be extracted profitably under current

TABLE 14-2.

1979 World Mine Production and Reserves of Four Key Minerals

Mineral	United States (%)	South Africa (%)	Soviet Union (%)*	Other (%)
Chromium:				
Production	—	33.0	24.5	Turkey (7.1), Zimbabwe (6.2), Philippines (5.7), Other (23.6)
Reserves	—	66.4	2.9	Zimbabwe (29.3), Other (1.6)
Manganese:				
Production	—	20.9	45.8	Gabon (8.3), India (7.5), Australia (5.8), Brazil (5.0), Other (6.7)
Reserves	—	37.2	50.7	Australia (5.6), Gabon (2.8), Brazil (1.6), Other (2.1)
Vanadium:				
Production	17.6	42.3	27.9	Chile (2.1), Other (10.2)
Reserves	0.7	49.4	45.9	Australia (1.1), Other (2.9)
Platinum-Group Metals:				
Production	0.1	47.5	47.5	Canada (3.7), Other (1.0)
Reserves	0.1	73.2	25.1	Canada (1.1), Other (0.5)

Source: U.S. Bureau of Mines, *Mineral Commodity Summaries 1980.*
*The Soviet Union production and reserve percentages for chromium and manganese include production and reserve figures for all the Soviet Bloc countries.

conditions. Therefore, the United States imports 100 percent of its ore. Also, there has been a rapid increase in ferrochrome smelting capacity at mine sites. This has given South Africa the ability to undersell U.S. and European processors. Two and one-half tons of chromite ore are required to produce one ton of ferrochrome, resulting in a 30 percent cost advantage for on-site smelters, the difference coming from the transport costs that foreign smelters must pay for the shipment of huge quantities of ore. As a result, the United States now also imports 55 percent of its ferrochrome.

In 1978–79, the United States imported 46 percent of its chromite ore from South Africa, up from the 35 percent average of 1974–77. To some extent, the increase in use of South African chromium is the result of the 1977 cutoff of Rhodesian chromium imports, which previously had been permitted into the United States under the Byrd Amendment. But, despite the recent resumption of shipments from Zimbabwe, South African exports continue at their increased level. In the first six months of 1980, the United States imported 76 percent of its ferrochrome from South Africa. Europe and Japan rely on imports for more than 95 percent of their chromium—both as ore and as ferrochrome—and most of it also comes from South Africa.

The West's ferrochrome production has dropped markedly in the past five years, with many of its furnaces now lying idle. Industry sources predict that by 1985 the vast majority of these furnaces will have been either scrapped or converted to other uses. To the extent that some smelting capacity will still exist in the United States and Europe, it will be the result of government actions specifically intended to preserve the West's strategic ability to convert ore to ferrochrome. In the United States, for example, some import relief was given to domestic producers in 1978 by the imposition of a "trigger price" mechanism on foreign ferrochrome. (Any producer importing ferrochrome to the United States at less than the so-called trigger price must pay a duty penalty.)

South Africa's booming ferrochrome industry is the result of a conscious decision by the South African government to encourage the on-site smelting of mineral ore into a finished product. Economically, the production of ferrochrome is seen as an important growth industry.

Since 1975, South Africa has provided various economic incentives for the development of its minerals-processing industry, including subsidies, tax concessions, low-cost loans, and rebates. The West's demand for ferrochrome is not expected to drop. Politically, South Africa can only be helped by increased reliance on imported ferrochrome. This reliance makes it more difficult for the West and Japan to diversify their sources of supply to other, less-developed producing countries which do not have on-site smelting operations. Thus, as the industrial countries' capacity to refine chromite ore diminishes, the strategic importance of South Africa's minerals trade increases.

In the event of a short-term (up to five-year) cutoff of supplies from South Africa, the United States would have to depend heavily on its stockpiles. The

313

present 2.3-year supply of chromite ore and 1.5-year supply of ferrochrome, coupled with privately held inventories, should enable the United States to continue to produce essential chromium products, provided that adequate provisions are made for converting presently stockpiled ore. America's other major sources of ore have traditionally been the Philippines, the Soviet Union, Turkey, and Zimbabwe. Foreign sources of ferrochrome have included Japan, West Germany, Yugoslavia, and Zimbabwe.

Some immediate relief from a shortage might come from recently renewed Zimbabwe chromium exports. However, Zimbabwe would not be able to fill the void entirely. Zimbabwe currently produces 16 to 20 percent of the world's supplies, up from 6 percent in 1979, when the United Nations embargo against Rhodesia was still in effect. Because of the geological formation of its reserves, production could be stepped up to 26 to 28 percent of world supplies at most. Moreover, a large percentage of Zimbabwe's exports travel overland on South African railroads and then exit through South African ports. Any disruption of South Africa's transportation system or closing of its ports that stopped South Africa's own mineral exports would affect those of Zimbabwe as well. The Mozambican port of Beira cannot handle Zimbabwe's current chromium shipments, much less an increased supply. The Mozambican port of Maputo, which has a large capacity, could not handle more than 50 percent of Zimbabwe's total production at stepped-up levels, assuming the completion of a reliable Zimbabwe-Maputo rail link.

The United States could respond to a chromium shortage by increasing the recycling of stainless steel scrap, which now supplies 15 to 20 percent of U.S. demand. In addition, much of the chromium used in the decorative stainless steel industry could be replaced by other materials, although such a substitution would require substantial lead times for effective implementation and, by raising costs and reducing quality, would place the U.S. stainless steel industry in a noncompetitive position with the rest of the world.

In response to a medium-term (five-to-ten-year) and long-term (more than ten-year) interruption, alternate supply sources would have to be developed. New technologies using substitute materials would be needed, and increased secondary recovery efforts would be necessary. It is estimated that a threefold increase in the world price of chromium—which could easily occur if there were a total cutoff of South African chromium—would make many of the world's subeconomic resources, including small U.S. chromium deposits (about 8 million tons in Montana and Oregon), profitable to extract. Reserve figures historically have increased as mineral prices have risen and technological advances have made it possible to exploit previously unworkable deposits. For example, world consumption of chromite ore during 1950–74 exceeded the total world listed chromite reserves for 1950, because during that period reserve figures increased sevenfold. More recent increases in reserve estimates have been just as dramatic. In 1977 the U.S. Bureau of Mines' chromite reserve figure for South Africa was 1.2 billion tons. The 1979 figure more than doubled to 2.5 billion tons.

According to experts, a threefold price increase for chromium would be manageable if supply was adequate. It would result in only a 13 to 15 percent rise in the cost of stainless steel. However, the development of new reserves under such circumstances would be a risky venture. Even if environmental issues are resolved quickly, start-up time for a new mine is five to ten years. If, in the interim, South African supplies once again began to reach the world market, the price of chromium would quickly return to its former level, wiping out the new ventures.

Manganese. Over 90 percent of all manganese produced is used in the manufacture of steel, with no known satisfactory substitute. In addition to manganese's desulfurizing and deoxidizing properties, it is an essential hardening and strengthening agent. Manganese is also used in the manufacture of dry-cell batteries and in the production of various chemicals. South Africa has more than 50 percent of the world's reserves and is the free world's largest producer. The United States and the other industrial countries are virtually 100 percent dependent on imports for their supply of manganese ore.

The two largest suppliers of manganese ore to the United States are Gabon and Brazil, followed by South Africa and Australia. Although South Africa provided on the average only 9 percent of U.S. imports during 1974–77, in 1979 the United States imported 20 percent of its manganese ore from South Africa. Europe and Japan relied upon South Africa for 40 percent of their needs.

As with ferrochrome, U.S. production of ferromanganese has been declining, unable to compete effectively with the lower-cost alloy refining done at the mine sites. The United States' capacity to produce ferromanganese is not as threatened as its capacity to produce ferrochrome, however. The principal form in which manganese is used by the steel industry is standard high-carbon ferromanganese, which can be produced in the same blast furnaces used to make pig iron. The remainder, about 30 percent, is in the form of silicomanganese and medium-carbon ferromanganese. These alloys require special electric-arc furnaces for smelting, and it is these furnaces, similar to the ones used to make ferrochrome, that face extinction.

In 1979, South Africa directly supplied 44 percent of U.S. ferromanganese imports, compared with 30 percent during 1974–77. Moreover, France and other industrialized countries also supply the United States with considerable ferromanganese, much of which is processed from South African ore. So, the actual portion of U.S. imports originating in South Africa now approaches 60 percent.

U.S. stockpiles of manganese ore are substantial (almost three years) but those of the ferroalloys provide little more than half a year's supply. Because world reserves of manganese are more widely distributed than are those of chromium, U.S. imports of ore are more evenly balanced among several countries. Ferromanganese is another matter, however.

In the event of a short-term cutoff of manganese from South Africa, the United States would have to rely on its stockpiles, private inventories, and other sources of ore to lessen the impact. Since manganese is indispensable in the production of steel, substitution is not a realistic alternative. The major concern is adequate supply rather than price, because manganese makes up only 1 to 2 percent of the cost of steel.

A medium-term shortage may be the most difficult to deal with, especially if countries like Brazil and India are unable to increase export production to meet new Western demand. This is a distinct possibility, because as these countries develop, more of their own natural resources are needed to meet growing domestic needs. Brazil, for example, is projecting a steady decrease in its manganese ore exports throughout the 1980s in response to the growth of its own steel industry. Increased exports to the West from the Soviet Union are also unlikely. Although the Soviet Union has been a major exporter, at present its production just about meets the needs of Soviet Bloc countries. The country most likely to be able to pick up the slack in the medium term is Australia, whose mining operations and deposits are particularly suited to rapid expansion and large-scale production.

A potential future source of manganese is the rich metal-bearing nodules on the ocean floor, which also contain cobalt, nickel, and copper. However, given the technical problems of mining 20,000 feet beneath the sea and the absence of international agreements governing such operations, successful deep seabed mining is estimated to be at least a decade away and can be considered at best a long-term solution.

Vanadium. Vanadium is used principally as an alloying element in the manufacture of lightweight, high-strength steels for jet engines, airframes, other transportation equipment, and the large piping needed for oil and gas pipelines. South Africa is the world's largest producer of vanadium.

The United States is potentially self-sufficient in vanadium. It annually produces more vanadium than it uses. Because a good portion is exported to Europe, the United States actually imports approximately 30 percent of its domestic requirements, with 72 percent of these imports (or 22 percent of domestic consumption) coming from South Africa. Domestic smelting capacity remains high, enabling the United States to be a net exporter of ferrovanadium. Even though there is only a one-month government stockpile of vanadium and no stockpile of ferrovanadium, the United States can adjust to a cutoff of South African vanadium more easily than to cutoffs of chromium, manganese, or platinum-group metals.

In the short term, the United States could reduce its exports. Some substitution would also be possible—columbium, manganese, titanium, and tungsten can be used almost interchangeably with vanadium in the manufacture of certain steel alloys. Vanadium and ferrovanadium are primarily by-products of the mining of other ores (most notably uranium) or secondary recovery from steel-making slag. In the medium and long terms, vanadium recovery from uranium mining and the processing of slag can be increased in both the United States and other uranium- and steel-producing countries.

Even though the United States has reliable domestic sources of vanadium, it is not entirely immune to the effects of a stoppage of South African exports. A total South African cutoff would leave worldwide production almost 25 million pounds short of demand, a shortage which could not be made up immediately by substitution or by increased production in the United States and elsewhere. The Soviet Union accounts for 31 percent of world production. Vanadium is also produced in Australia, Chile, Finland, India, Norway, and Venezuela. Nevertheless, Europe continues to rely heavily on South African imports. In the event of a stoppage, the price would rise. The United States would be under considerable pressure to increase exports and share its supply, just when U.S. domestic needs would require a reduction in exports and conservation of resources.

Platinum-group metals. The United States imports about 90 percent of its consumption of the platinum-group metals. South Africa supplies the United States directly with 57 percent of its platinum imports. In addition, the United States' platinum imports from Great Britain, approximately 10 percent of the total imported, actually originate in South Africa. Platinum and the other platinum-group metals (palladium, rhodium, ruthenium, iridium, and osmium), which are found and mined together, serve as catalytic agents, facilitating important chemical processes without being altered or consumed themselves. Platinum-metal catalysts are used in auto emission-control systems, petroleum refining, and the production of nitrogenous fertilizers. The corrosion-resistant properties of platinum also make it popular for use in medical and dental supplies, electronic equipment, glassware, and ceramics.

The United States consumes about 30 percent of the world's platinum production, almost all of it (98 percent) for industrial purposes. The largest single use (about 35 percent of domestic consumption) is in the catalytic converters of automobiles. By contrast, Japan imports 30 percent of the world's platinum production for jewelry use alone.

South Africa and the Soviet Union are the world's major producers, each with 47.5 percent of world production. The only other major supplier is Canada, which produces approximately 4 percent of world demand as a by-product of nickel mining.

Although U.S. reliance on South African platinum is high, the possibility for secondary recovery—in the event of a cutoff of supply—is good. This is because about 70 percent of U.S. platinum use is for catalytic purposes. About 10 percent of the platinum consumed in the United States already comes from the recycling of platinum catalysts and the recovery of platinum-group metals from scrap.

U.S. stockpiles provide only a four-month supply of platinum itself, the **317** most important and widely used of the platinum-group metals. Some substitution by the other platinum-group metals, of which U.S. stockpiles contain more than a one-year supply, is possible for many of platinum's catalytic functions. Substitution for platinum by nonplatinum metals is also possible for some of its noncatalytic applications, such as in electronic equipment, and worldwide demand is somewhat elastic because of the large, nonessential use of platinum in jewelry. For example, Japanese imports of platinum fell markedly in 1980 in response to the large price increases for the metal. For these reasons, the United States and the West could cope in the short and medium terms with a stoppage of South African exports.

In the long term, the practical development of new technologies, presently in the experimental stage, to replace the use of platinum catalysts for petroleum refining and auto emissions control would drastically reduce U.S. demand. If nonplatinum catalytic processes were not devised, then a continued denial of South African platinum would increase U.S. reliance on platinum exports from the Soviet Union.

VULNERABILITY TO STOPPAGES

An interruption in the supply of minerals from South Africa potentially could occur for any one of several reasons: (1) the United States, unilaterally or in concert with other nations, might voluntarily deny itself access to South Africa's mineral wealth by imposing economic sanctions, including a trade embargo, against South Africa; (2) the present South African government, in response to what it viewed as intolerable pressure from the United States and other nations, might retaliate by halting or reducing exports of some or all of its minerals; (3) internal upheaval in South Africa could hinder mining or transport operations, and for a time severely reduce or even halt entirely South Africa's mineral exports; (4) a new, unfriendly government in South Africa might manipulate, suspend, or discontinue the sale of some or all minerals to the United States and/or other Western countries.*

Since the 1950s the United States has stockpiled strategic materials, such as chromium, manganese, vanadium, and the platinum-group metals, as a precaution against the interruption of supplies. Table 14-3 shows the current U.S. stockpile objectives, and the size of both government and private inventories. Despite increased U.S. dependence on foreign processing operations, a major stockpile trend is the reduction in stockpile goals for processed ferroalloys and a corresponding increase in the target levels for unfinished ore. For example, the ferrochrome stockpile is projected to be cut to an eight-month

*The enumeration of these scenarios is not intended to suggest that any one of them is likely to occur or that each of them has the same probability of occurring. Those questions and the question of the likely duration of any stoppages are discussed in chapter 18.

TABLE 14-3.

U.S. Government Stockpiles and Private Inventories

Mineral/Alloy	Av. U.S. Consumption 1978–79	1980 Stockpile Objectives		Current U.S. Stockpiles		Private Inventories*	
		Amount (short tons)	U.S. Consumption	Amount (short tons)	U.S. Consumption	Amount (short tons)	U.S. Consumption
Chromium:							
Ore	1,100,000	3,200,000	2.9 yr.***	2,500,000	2.3 yr.***	910,000	10 mo.***
Ferroalloys**	510,000	350,000	8 mo.	780,000	1.5 yr.	57,000	1 mo.
Manganese:							
Ore	1,290,000	2,700,000	2.1 yr.***	3,600,000	2.8 yr.***	900,000	8 mo.***
Ferroalloys**	1,050,000	440,000	5 mo.	650,000	7 mo.	260,000	3 mo.
Vanadium:							
Pentoxide	6,600	7,700	1.2 yr.	541	1 mo.	110	<1 mo.
Ferroalloys**	5,800	1,000	2 mo.	0	0 mo.	840	2 mo.
Platinum (troy ounces):							
Platinum	1,300,000	1,310,000	1.0 yr.	450,000	4 mo.	310,000	3 mo.
Other five platinum-group metals	1,200,000	3,100,000	2.6 yr.	1,275,000	1.1 yr.	460,000	4 mo.

Sources: U.S. Bureau of Mines, *Minerals Yearbook, 1978–79*; Federal Emergency Management Agency, March 1980 Stockpile Report to the Congress.
*Inventories in private industry are constantly changing. Figures are for inventories held at the end of 1979.
**U.S. ferroalloy consumption is a combination of imported ferroalloys and ore (or pentoxide) which has been converted domestically into ferroalloys.
***These consumption figures assume the continued existence of adequate U.S. smelting capacity to convert unprocessed ore into usable alloy form. U.S. smelting capacity for ferrochrome and certain forms of ferromanganese is declining steadily.

supply, while the chromite ore stockpile is scheduled to increase to nearly a three-year supply.

The stockpile program in the United States is administered by the Federal Emergency Management Agency. According to the Strategic and Critical Materials Stockpiling Act, its purpose is "to sustain the United States for a period of not less than three years in the event of a national emergency." Where a reliable domestic supply of a strategic material is assured, only a minimal stockpile is maintained. This accounts for the small size of the current inventories of and stockpile goals for vanadium and ferrovanadium. U.S. production of both remains high.

A determination of a surplus or deficit for a given material does not mean that the inventory can immediately be brought into harmony with the stockpile goals. Care must be taken in the acquisition and disposal of materials to avoid disrupting domestic and international commodity markets with sudden large purchases or sales. Sales and purchases of materials are spread out over several years. Congressional approval is required before any stockpiled materials can be sold, and congressional approval of appropriations requests must also be obtained before any funds can be expended on stockpile purchases. In 1980, for example, although President Carter proposed an authorization of $237 million for the acquisition of strategic and critical materials, Congress imposed a spending limit of $50 million. Thus, adjustments to the stockpile are likely to take considerable time to achieve.

Private inventories are also held by domestic producers and consumers. Private supplies of ferrovanadium exceed government stockpiles. Although private supplies provide a useful buffer for their holders in the event of a disruption in imports from South Africa or elsewhere, they do not have the same strategic value as national stockpiles. In general, they are much smaller than government stockpiles, and their levels fluctuate as market conditions change.

United States stockpiles greatly exceed in absolute quantity and projected periods of coverage the stockpiles of all the European countries combined. Great Britain has no stockpiles. Germany recently abandoned a plan to require private industry to maintain one-year inventories of strategic minerals. France maintains a general government stockpile of only two months' duration, although it has made a special effort in the past year to stockpile chromium, of which it reportedly now has slightly over a one-year supply.

Stoppages in the flow of South African minerals will be harder on the other developed countries than on the United States. The European countries are just as reliant on South Africa for their supplies of chromium, manganese, and platinum (and more so for vanadium) as is the United States, but the absence of significant stockpiles makes them more vulnerable to short-term stoppages. Japan is even more dependent on foreign mineral resources than either Europe or the United States, but its long-established policy of long-term, multiple-source contracts with many different countries makes it somewhat less vul-

320

nerable than the European countries to a South African cutoff. However, neither Japanese nor European mineral resources are as great or as diverse as those found in the United States. Thus they rely on South Africa for a wider range of minerals. The European Community and Japan import more than 40 percent of their uranium from South Africa and Namibia and large quantities of coal from South Africa. Given the problems of oil supply and price, supplies of these alternate energy substances are particularly vital.

The heightened vulnerability of Western Europe and Japan has serious implications for U.S. policy. A worldwide stoppage of South African minerals leading to competition for reduced supplies and a struggle to afford increased prices would create tensions among the allies. To maintain a unified policy, the United States would have to consider sharing its stockpiles to alleviate strategic and economic dislocations. Under these circumstances, U.S. stockpiles could be depleted much sooner than expected. Even if other countries began stockpiling efforts today, it would be several years before they could adequately protect themselves against even short-term interruptions.

When there is a cutoff in supply from the major producer of a key mineral, the impact can be dramatic. For example, in May 1978, Zaire, which supplies more than 56 percent of the world's cobalt, began to ration sales to its customers in response to increases in demand which it was unable to handle. At the same time, a civil war in the Shaba Province halted cobalt mining and refining activity for nearly a month. The result was a tripling of cobalt prices by the end of the year and near depletion of Western inventories. South Africa produces several significant minerals which affect a wide range of industries. This compounds the problems of conservation and substitution should a cutoff occur. For example, one of the substitutes for vanadium in making high-strength steel alloys is manganese. Manganese would also be in short supply if South Africa's mineral exports were stopped. Moreover, increased demand for substitute minerals, even those not supplied by South Africa, would cause market dislocations. Since South African minerals are used in so many different industrial sectors, economic disruption caused by an across-the-board stoppage would be difficult to cope with. The inflationary effects of individual cutoffs would multiply. U.S., European, and Japanese reliance on a wide range of South African minerals thus makes them more vulnerable than a mineral-by-mineral analysis would indicate.

However, it appears unlikely that South Africa will use its mineral resources as a weapon against the West, except possibly in response to extreme provocation. The South African government stated in a 1979 report: "Continued access to South African sources of supply under prevailing free enterprise conditions in a stable political and economic environment is indeed the dividing line between orderly and disorderly minerals marketing, free access, cartelisation, and/or reliance on Communist-controlled sources of supply. Indeed with South Africa in the Western World's gold, platinum, chrome, manganese, vanadium supply line these mineral commodities need not be considered strategic or critical . . . without South Africa, they no doubt are."

South African government policy is designed to maintain South Africa's position as the number one supplier of minerals to the West. South Africa continually stresses the stability of the country as compared to other mineral-producing nations. Government officials cite the liberal mining, tax, and ownership laws which allow for profitable foreign investment and South Africa's unblemished record in fulfilling contracts and supplying minerals at reasonable cost. The South African economy and balance of payments are heavily dependent on continuing and increasing sales of mineral exports to industrialized countries, especially the United States. Over $19 billion annually of foreign exchange earnings from mineral sales cannot be ignored.

Should South Africa feel itself forced to respond to actions taken by the United States or the international community, a selective denial of a few strategic minerals would probably be the tactic used. In 1977 South African sales of the platinum-group metals and chromium, manganese, and vanadium ores totaled approximately $580 million, about half from sales of the platinum-group metals. (Export figures for refined ferroalloys are not disclosed.) In 1978 export earnings for chromium and manganese ore totaled $240 million. South Africa could stop sales of chromium, manganese, and vanadium without suffering major direct economic consequences. It would run the risk, however, of further alienating traditional trading partners and stimulating a harsher international response.

Chapter 15
The Communist States and Southern Africa

South Africa regularly plays on the fears of the West about Communist involvement in southern Africa. "The main object of the onslaught on the Republic of South Africa, under the guidance of the planners in the Kremlin," Prime Minister Pieter W. Botha told Parliament in 1980, "is to overthrow this state and to create chaos in its stead, so that the Kremlin can establish its hegemony here." Such rhetoric often strikes a responsive chord abroad. However distasteful South Africa's racial policies may be, some in the West insist, the Communist threat in southern Africa is of greater moment and the West must therefore maintain ties with South Africa. Proponents of this view regard South Africa as a vital bulwark against Communist expansion.

Another segment of opinion in the West holds that any policy linking the West to South Africa for the sake of checking communism will, in the long run, have precisely the opposite effect. According to this view, by retaining ties to the white regime of South Africa the West risks the loss of influence in the black-ruled states in the region and ultimately the accession to power of an unfriendly black government in South Africa. One American international relations specialist argues: "Support for South Africa, and visible ties with South Africa, is the one thing that will surely turn African opinion against the West and open opportunities for the Soviet Union and its allies to be the champion of African nationalism and the foe of white minority rule."

The Communist presence in southern Africa raises economic and strategic issues. Its potential implications for future Western access to the natural resources of the region, particularly its mineral riches, are a source of concern.* So are its implications for the continued free flow of shipping on the Cape sea lanes, the route traveled by much of the West's oil. How best to protect these Western interests over the long term is a major consideration for U.S. policy.

As background for the debate over the West's response to communism in southern Africa, this chapter examines the activities in the region of four Communist nations: the Soviet Union, Cuba, East Germany, and China. It considers the extent and nature of their involvement, their motives, their priorities, and their potential for expanded roles.

THE USSR

The Soviet Union is the dominant Communist factor in southern Africa. Since the demise of Portugal's African empire in the mid-1970s first convinced Soviet leaders that significant new opportunities were opening up in the area, the USSR has sought recognition as the prime supporter of local "antiimperialist" and antiracialist forces.

Its efforts have taken many forms. The USSR championed strong United Nations sanctions against Rhodesia until a settlement involving the guerrilla insurgents of the Patriotic Front was achieved, and for years it has urged the UN General Assembly to reject the credentials of the representatives of the current South African government and deny them South Africa's seat in the organization. It has moved to solidify relations with the professedly Marxist-Leninist states of Angola and Mozambique, signing treaties of friendship and cooperation with both. It has established itself as the chief patron of the South-West African People's Organization (SWAPO), the group conducting guerrilla warfare in Namibia, and has reinforced its long-standing ties with the African National Congress (ANC). It has even forged diplomatic ties with Botswana and Lesotho, two of the more conservative states in the region.

The most substantial Soviet undertakings have been in the military sphere. Not only did the USSR combine forces with Cuba to help the Popular Movement for the Liberation of Angola (MPLA) assume power in Angola, but in 1980 1,300 Soviet and East European military advisers and a large contingent of Cuban troops remained in the country to deal with opposition guerrilla forces continuing to operate there. It also established itself as the main arms supplier for Mozambique in the mid-1970s and for Zambia in early 1980. It is clear as well that the USSR has become the major source of weapons for the "national liberation" movements in the area. Until the March 1980 elections in Zimbabwe, the primary recipients among these movements were Joshua

---

*South Africa's minerals are described in chapter 14. The resources of southern Africa as a whole include oil, platinum, chrome, vanadium, gold, manganese, fluorspar, diamonds, nickel, uranium, zinc, phosphate, asbestos, antimony, lead, iron ore, coal, titanium, copper, quartz, alabaster, and silicate.

Nkomo's wing of the Patriotic Front, known as the Zimbabwe African People's Union (ZAPU), and SWAPO in Namibia, but with the settlement in Zimbabwe Soviet assistance to ZAPU has apparently ceased. While the African National Congress of South Africa may get some arms from the USSR, this flow has been modest so far apparently because the ANC has not managed to launch a full-fledged guerrilla struggle on South African soil.

To date, the fruits of these labors have proved decidedly mixed from Moscow's standpoint. Although both Angola and Mozambique continue to be militarily dependent on the Soviet Union, in recent years each has sought to expand its contacts with the West, especially in the economic sphere. Moreover, each has urged SWAPO to cooperate with the Western powers, working under UN auspices, in trying to bring about a negotiated solution to the conflict in Namibia. Zambia turned to the USSR for arms only with reluctance, and Lusaka subsequently reaffirmed its commitment to nonalignment by not supporting Moscow's version of the Soviet intervention in Afghanistan when the United Nations voted on the issue in January 1980. As the Soviets well know, President Kenneth Kaunda of Zambia has long harbored deep suspicions of Soviet intentions in the region. Aside from increased contacts, the new ties with Botswana and Lesotho have netted the USSR little. Certainly the two countries have not changed their basically conservative orientations.

Undoubtedly the most severe setback that the USSR has encountered has been in Zimbabwe. Because Moscow had backed ZAPU against the rival Zimbabwe African National Union (ZANU) before the formation of the Patriotic Front and had maintained rather distant relations with Robert Mugabe even after the front came into being, the USSR found itself at least temporarily shut out of Zimbabwe in the wake of Mugabe's election victory in 1980. It was not until 1981 that Mugabe's government agreed to open formal relations with Moscow.

A variety of motives have been advanced for the Soviet Union's involvement in southern Africa:

- It hopes to stake out a role for itself in the ultimate denouement of the racial conflict in the region, thereby reinforcing its claims to status as a global power.
- It seeks to promote the emergence of Soviet-leaning radical black governments in the area. It has already achieved a measure of success in Angola and Mozambique and hopes for eventual successes in Namibia and South Africa.
- It seeks to win local acceptance of a Soviet political, economic, and military presence. Among its economic interests is access to the area's minerals. Although the USSR itself possesses enough reserves of the minerals southern Africa has to offer to make it essentially self-sufficient, it faces additional demands on its supplies from other Communist nations, particularly those in Eastern Europe. Besides the supplying of arms and advisers, its military links

325

have included arrangements permitting Soviet warships to call at local ports and Soviet reconnaissance planes to use local airfields.

● It would like to see a weakening of the Western position in the region, not only politically but also economically and strategically. The USSR, some analysts assert, has an interest in impeding Western access to the minerals in the area and in disrupting Western use of the sea lanes around the Cape. Commenting on Africa as a whole, a Soviet analyst said in 1980: "Despite all efforts undertaken by the United States, the main tendency consists in the gradual weakening of the positions of the leading Western powers on the continent. With the material and moral-political support of the socialist community, the African people are inflicting one defeat after another on imperialism."

● It hopes to curtail Chinese influence in the area. Moscow has long seen China as a threat to the USSR's efforts to establish itself as the patron of national liberation and revolutionary movements throughout the Third World and especially in Africa. One example was China's backing of the National Front for the Liberation of Angola (FNLA) against the Soviet-supported MPLA in the Angolan civil war of the mid-1970s.

In pursuing its goals in southern Africa, the Soviet Union boasts important assets. It has several avenues by which it can exert political influence. There are two Communist parties in the area—the South African Communist party and the Lesotho Communist party—and both are pro-Soviet. The South African party is by far the more significant. Though in itself a weak and largely exile organization, it maintains close ties with the ANC of South Africa. Indeed, several of its members hold major posts in the ANC. Even though Soviet officials regard the ruling parties of Angola and Mozambique as "revolutionary-democratic" organizations rather than true Marxist-Leninist bodies, the Communist party of the Soviet Union has forged party-to-party links with them and has furnished ideological and organizational training for their cadres. The so-called nonaligned movement offers the USSR additional potential for shaping events in southern Africa because of the close Soviet relationship with Cuba and Havana's contention that the USSR is the "natural ally" of the nonaligned. This source of influence has dwindled markedly, however, as a result of the Soviet invasion of Afghanistan and the subsequent negative response of much of the Third World. Still another source of political leverage in southern Africa is the Soviet Union's status as a permanent member of the UN Security Council. Not only does this give Moscow a say in defining any threats to international security in the area but it also allows the Soviet Union to veto any UN attempt to deal with such threats.

The Soviet Union has so far played a rather minor economic role in southern Africa. The region received only $22 million in Soviet economic aid between 1970 and 1978, and trade was also relatively insignificant. But that Moscow could, if it chose, operate on a much larger scale is suggested by the fact that over the 1970–78 period the Soviet Union extended a total of $10.5 billion in economic assistance to Third World countries. The extent of Moscow's economic relations with southern Africa thus appears to turn less on its capabilities than on its priorities in committing its resources around the globe and on the attitude of the African nations themselves toward such aid.

The Soviet military potential in the region is also substantial. The USSR has long had the capacity to supply arms and military advisers to southern Africa to help sustain prolonged guerrilla struggles. It also has a growing capacity to project its own power and that of its allies into southern Africa. Since 1969 there has been a permanent Soviet naval presence in the Indian Ocean, and a Soviet West African patrol has operated in the eastern Atlantic since 1970. Both of these naval forces could move to the waters off southern Africa on fairly short notice. The USSR has improved its aircraft and sealift capabilities to the point where its own troops or those of its allies could be dispatched in strength to the area. Moscow has in recent years created several new airborne divisions, bringing the total to eight. In addition, it has some special-duty brigades, plus about 12,000 naval infantry—the equivalent of marines. Should the Soviet Union decide to commit all its various airborne and naval infantry units to an operation in southern Africa, the forces would total about 150,000 men.

A large-scale operation of this sort must be considered highly unlikely, however, for a number of circumstances work to restrain Moscow's activities in southern Africa. For one thing, the Soviet Union has interests in many parts of the world, and southern Africa does not appear to be high on its list of priorities. Europe, where the USSR and its allies confront the West directly, is obviously the principal focus of Soviet attention. East Asia has followed close behind Europe at least since the 1960s, when China's acquisition of nuclear weapons convinced Soviet leaders that a security threat existed on their eastern borders. Third place on the list has gone to the southern rimlands of the USSR—the countries lying in an arc to the south of the Soviet Union, from south Asia to north Africa.

Beyond these, it is hard to pin down precise rankings, but within Africa it is clear that the Horn of Africa enjoys a higher priority than southern Africa. By the early 1970s, the USSR had acquired access to various facilities of military utility in Somalia, including the port at Berbera, and soon thereafter it concluded a treaty of friendship and cooperation with Mogadishu—the first such document it had signed with any African country. When its efforts to cultivate ties as well with the revolutionary military government in Ethiopia resulted in the loss of its position in Somalia, Moscow moved to bolster its relations with Ethiopia by conducting a massive air and sea infusion of weapons, Cuban combat troops, and Soviet military advisers to help repel the invading Somali forces that sought to wrest the Ogaden area from Addis Ababa's control. This effort led to an investment of nearly $2 billion in arms alone. The USSR has evinced keen awareness of the Horn's strategic importance. This derives not only from its location at one end of the route between the Mediterranean Sea and the Indian Ocean but also from its proximity to the outlet of the Persian Gulf, from which flows much of the West's oil.

Soviet leaders are also restrained, many experts believe, by their desire to avoid escalating the racial conflicts and guerrilla wars of the area into a nuclear confrontation with the United States. While they have argued that détente does not prohibit them from assisting national liberation movements in the Third World, they have kept a close eye on the reactions of the United States as they stepped up their intervention in African countries such as Angola and Ethiopia. Only when it had become clear that the United States was not going to respond militarily to these interventions did they fully commit the USSR. Moreover, the Soviets are obviously aware that, should it choose to do so, the United States possesses an impressive capacity to project its conventional forces to remote theaters. American airlift and sealift capabilities far exceed those of the Soviets. The U.S. Marine Corps is fifteen times as large as the Soviet naval infantry and can sustain operations for a month without resupply, compared with a week for the Soviet forces. U.S. carrier-based aircraft greatly surpass the USSR's sea-based aircraft in range and firepower.

Moscow's disposition to act boldly in southern Africa may be further inhibited by a reluctance to fan the distrust that its invasion of Afghanistan generated among Third World countries. Although the USSR's growing proclivity for intervening in conflicts in Africa had produced misgivings on the part of some of these nations, the trend in the Third World prior to the Soviet incursion into Afghanistan was toward acceptance of the argument that the socialist states were the "natural allies" of the nonaligned nations. But Afghanistan drastically altered the situation. Not only did most of the Third World support the UN General Assembly resolution in January 1980 condemning the Soviet invasion—the only African states that backed the USSR were Angola, Mozambique, and Ethiopia—but a large number of countries also echoed the contention of Nigeria's UN ambassador that "in the end" the nonaligned countries had to conclude that "there are no natural allies." Without retreating from their established path in Afghanistan, Soviet leaders have evinced a strong desire to mitigate this damage to their standing in the Third World.

Perhaps the most plausible large-scale Soviet involvement in southern Africa would be intervention on behalf of black nationalists attempting to topple the white regime in Pretoria or, more immediately, on behalf of SWAPO in Namibia if a peaceful settlement is not forthcoming there. In both cases a powerful inhibiting factor would be the formidable South African military establishment described in chapter 11. Against a South African force that could approach half a million, including reservists, the Soviet Union would be able to deploy the 150,000 airborne and naval infantry troops it could dispatch quickly to southern Africa, plus perhaps at most 50,000 Cuban troops, and a much smaller contingent of East German troops. Thus, the Soviets would face enormous odds unless buttressed by army line units.

Providing logistical backup for such a military expedition would be a monumental task at the distances involved, even if the USSR gained access to transit facilities in nearby states. Moreover, the West, and especially the United States, could compound the difficulty by attempting to interdict both the sea and air supply routes. In this manner, the West might well succeed in thwarting the enterprise without becoming directly involved in the ground warfare.

All things considered, the Soviet Union's ability to launch an all-out assault on South Africa seems highly circumscribed for the present. Its real capacities lie more in aerial and naval harassment of South African forces. Yet even such ventures would probably require safe sanctuaries in neighboring states, and they would entail a substantial risk of escalation of the conflict by South Africa. Obviously, if the USSR chose to reorder its priorities, it could bring greater resources to bear in southern Africa, but such a possibility appears remote. Soviet analysts do not seem to envision rapid change in South Africa. On the contrary, their view seems to be that while a black government will ultimately emerge in South Africa, the struggle will be a protracted one.

One of the possible motives suggested for Moscow's involvement in southern Africa was to disrupt Western shipping around the Cape. It is conceivable that the Soviets could eventually attempt such interdiction even without installing a friendly government in South Africa, relying instead on air and naval harassment by forces based elsewhere. But whether such a move by the Soviets is a realistic prospect under any circumstances is a matter of wide disagreement.

The importance to the West of the Cape route is beyond question. Some 2,300 ships travel it each month. They deliver 57 percent of Western Europe's imported oil and 20 percent of U.S. imported oil. Some 70 percent of the strategic raw materials used by NATO is also transported via the Cape route.

Many strategists look at these figures and see potential danger for the United States and the rest of the West. Air Vice-Marshal Stewart Menaul of Britain writes: "Southern Africa is the key to the security of NATO's lines of communications . . . and South Africa in particular has the facilities . . . to provide the surveillance necessary for the security of European interests." Richard E. Bissell, of the Foreign Policy Research Institute in Philadelphia, describes the Cape route as a "choke point." General George S. Brown, former chairman of the U.S. Joint Chiefs of Staff, has written that "the threat to the Atlantic area is primarily from the Soviet Union maritime forces. Increasing Soviet naval capability to operate along the littoral of Africa has put increasing pressure on our ability to protect important South Atlantic trade routes which provide materials essential to the United States and Western Europe."

For many, South Africa becomes strategically important simply because it sits aside the Cape shipping lanes. The need to protect the Cape route is taken as a given and the South African government is seen as essential to this endeavor. If this argument is carried to its extreme, it can easily be maintained that the Cape route is so vital that the United States and its allies should have formal military ties with South Africa. Events have moved in the opposite direction, of course, and the West's military ties with South Africa have now largely been severed.

The West's disengagement from defense links with South Africa was motivated by political and moral considerations—a reluctance to be seen as an ally of the white minority government. But leaving such considerations aside, a number of analysts find the military case for the threat to the Cape route far from compelling. Comments one: "It is hard to think of the Cape route as a 'choke point' once you consider the logistical requirements of somehow blockading the sea between the Cape and Antarctica. . . . The logistical requirements that the Soviet Union would face to position its ships for such a blockade, let alone the likely political and military consequences that would quickly ensue, make the whole proposition dubious at best." In a 1977 book entitled *How Long Will South Africa Survive?* R. W. Johnson of Oxford University argued that "the whole idea of Russian submarines starving the West into submission by a strategy of protracted interdiction or blockage was . . . absurdly nineteenth century in its conception. The very first ship sinking, after all, would constitute a major act of war and the nuclear bombers and missiles would be in the air only a few minutes later."

More matter-of-factly, political scientist Robert Price asks two questions: (1) If the Soviet Union wished to interdict Western oil shipments, why would it do so at the Cape? (2) If the Soviet Union was prepared for a war with the West, why would it want its navy in South African waters?

Answering the first question, Price suggests that if the Soviet Union wanted to halt the flow of oil to the West, it could do so far more efficiently by bombing the oilfields or blockading the Strait of Hormuz. Because of their proximity to the Soviet Union, either of these operations could be carried out much more effectively than any operation off the Cape. As for the war that would almost certainly ensue from any such provocative Soviet behavior, Price notes that the Soviet Union would need its navy in the North Atlantic and the Mediterranean where it could assist in responding to the nuclear threat posed by U.S. submarine-launched ballistic missiles. Any ships based as far away as South African waters could easily be destroyed by U.S. air power.

CUBA

Cuba's recent activities in Africa are consistent with the foreign policy objectives it has pursued almost from the time Fidel Castro gained power in 1959. Even before forging its close relationship with the Soviet Union, Cuba sought to export its revolution by supporting like-minded governments and national liberation movements abroad.

In the 1960s efforts focused on Latin America. But even then Cuba was busy in Africa. Havana provided arms to the Algerian National Liberation Front, the nationalist movements in the Portuguese colonies, and the guerrillas fighting Moïse Tshombe in Congo-Leopoldville. Friendly governments in Congo-Brazzaville, Guinea, and Algeria received Cuban military assistance, and in 1963 Cuba committed regular combat troops abroad for the first time— to Algeria to assist the new government there in its border war with Morocco.

By the 1970s Cuba's foreign involvements were concentrated in Africa. Early in the decade there were military advisory missions and economic assistance to friendly governments, coupled with continued aid to the nationalist movements in the Portuguese colonies. Cuban policy in Africa attracted little notice in the United States until the eruption of the Angolan civil war in 1975, when Cuba escalated its decade-long assistance to the MPLA. When South African troops launched a major offensive in support of the rival Angolan movement—the FNLA and the National Union for the Total Independence of Angola (UNITA)—Cuba dispatched some 36,000 regular combat troops to defend the MPLA. Cuba and the MPLA triumphed, and Angola became an independent nation with an MPLA government.

Zimbabwe has been another Cuban concern in southern Africa. Cuba had long given diplomatic support to the nationalist guerrillas trying to oust the regime of Ian Smith, and after the Angolan civil war this backing was supplemented by military advisers and arms. Cuba followed the lead of the Soviet Union in channeling most of its aid to Joshua Nkomo's faction of the Patriotic Front, though Cuba often seemed to feel a closer ideological kinship with Robert Mugabe.

The close cooperation between Moscow and Havana in Africa was demonstrated decisively in Angola. By itself Cuba could not have undertaken a military enterprise of the scale it carried out there. Soviet logistical support was essential. The Soviet Union supplied arms and at several points in the war provided transportation for Cuban forces.

Yet it is not accurate to say that Cuba acted as a Soviet puppet in Angola. The deployment of troops was certainly unprecedented in size for Cuba, but it was nevertheless a logical extension of Cuba's long-standing policy of aiding the MPLA. Moreover, Soviet involvement in the Angolan civil war proceeded much more cautiously than did Cuba's. The USSR seemed hesitant to commit itself fully in a region that was not high on its list of geopolitical priorities. In mid-1975 the Soviets rejected an MPLA request for military advisers that the Cubans later filled. Twice, in December 1975 and January 1976, Moscow suspended its transport of Cuban troops to Angola because of diplomatic protests from the United States, even though the Cubans were urgently needed to check South Africa's rapid advance on the Angolan capital of Luanda. This pattern of events suggests that Cuba, not the Soviet Union, took the initiative for the socialist camp in Angola.

The Cuban-Soviet relationship in Angola, like the joint involvement that developed later in Ethiopia, has been a partnership. Either partner would find it hard to make a major military commitment in Africa without the cooperation of the other. Cuban troops could not be deployed or maintained abroad without Soviet logistical support, and the Soviet Union could not send its own troops to Africa without risking charges of Soviet imperialism of the sort that followed the invasion of Afghanistan.

Cuba's current policy objectives in Africa appear to differ little from those of a decade ago. Havana is committed to supporting friendly governments, with troops if necessary, and to aiding the national liberation movements in southern Africa.

Cuba is pledged to defend the MPLA government in Angola. Nearly 18,000 Cuban combat troops and 9,000 civilian advisers were serving in Angola in 1980. The MPLA government faced two principal security threats: South Africa, whose troops were stationed on Angola's border with Namibia, and Jonas Savimbi's UNITA, whose guerrillas continued to operate in the south-central region. These security problems appeared certain to persist until Namibia achieved independence, and so in early 1981 there was almost no prospect of major Cuban troop withdrawals from Angola until a resolution of the Namibian issue.

With Cuban support, Angola had provided arms, training, and safe haven for SWAPO guerrillas. South Africa had used this support as justification for both ground and air attacks on southern Angola, and there was always the danger that such assaults could trigger a wider war, possibly bringing Cuban and South African troops into direct combat, as in 1975.

In the struggle over the political future of South Africa itself, Cuba has supported the ANC and will probably provide it with the same sort of aid supplied to the anti-Portuguese nationalists and to Zimbabwe's Patriotic Front. But there is little likelihood that Cuba would send its own troops to South Africa. The South African military strength that would give pause to Soviet planners contemplating intervention in South Africa could also be expected to limit Cuban enthusiasm for involvement there. Moreover, Cuban intervention in South Africa would run counter to two decades of past policy that has restricted Cuban troop deployment to situations in which a friendly government requests aid to repel a truly external attack—risks of a different order from plunging into a revolutionary maelstrom in South Africa.

A variety of international and domestic considerations limit Cuba's freedom to maneuver in Africa. Internationally, Cuba must pay heed to two constituencies: the Soviet Union and the nonaligned Third World nations.

332   The Cuban-Soviet relationship is close. The Soviet Union provides all

Cuba's military equipment, along with several billion dollars' worth of economic assistance each year. Although in the past the two nations have sometimes differed sharply on policies in Latin America and Africa, lately they have been in agreement on most global issues. For Cuba to undertake military initiatives on the scale of Angola or Ethiopia, such agreement is essential. Cuba lacks the logistical capability to deploy or supply large numbers of troops abroad, and the need for active Soviet participation in major troop deployments obviously limits Cuba's ability to launch big operations on its own. The Soviet Union has a veto power over such ventures.

Cuba's concern with its standing in the Third World has been evident in its successful pursuit of a leadership role in the nonaligned movement. Its Third World prestige was clearly bolstered by its stand against South Africa in Angola. International reaction to Cuban intervention in Ethiopia was less positive. Although African states generally supported Ethiopia's efforts to defend its borders against Somali attempts at territorial annexation, the regime of Haile-Mariam Mengistu was not highly respected abroad. Soviet support of Ethiopia, much more extensive than that given Angola, was widely regarded as having been geopolitically motivated. Cuba's willingness to join in the Soviet effort to preserve Mengistu appeared considerably less principled than its commitment in Angola.

Since Cuba's greatest benefit from its policy in Africa has been the growth of its Third World prestige and influence, the Cubans are unlikely to pursue any policy that would significantly reduce those payoffs. This means that a prerequisite of any future Cuban military initiative abroad would probably be legitimacy in the eyes of the Third World peoples in the region involved. Such legitimacy may be harder to come by, however, as a result of the invasion of Afghanistan by Cuba's partner, the USSR. Caught between the Soviet Union and angry nonaligned nations, Cuba reacted by voting against the UN General Assembly resolutions condemning the invasion but refusing to endorse the Soviet action explicitly. Despite this attempt to finesse the issue, many nonaligned states remained uneasy about the intentions of both the Soviet Union and Cuba, and Cuba seemed likely to have more difficulty winning regional acceptance for military ventures abroad in the future. Nevertheless, it should be noted that South Africa is so universally despised in the Third World that any Cuban involvement against the South Africans would probably still command wide support among the nonaligned.

The chief domestic constraint on Cuban involvement abroad on the scale of Angola and Ethiopia is the heavy cost. Although the Soviet Union provides Cuba's military equipment free, Cuba bears most of the other costs of both its civilian and military aid programs. Since nearly half the 40,000 Cuban military personnel deployed abroad in 1980 were reservists, they represented a serious drain on the domestic labor force. The skilled technical personnel required by Cuba's foreign economic aid program also are badly needed at home.

These economic costs have political ramifications. Faced with economic austerity on the domestic front, the political leadership has inevitably been drawn into debates about how large a foreign aid effort Cuba can afford. Among the general populace, there is already some evidence of complaints that Cuba ought not to channel so much of its limited resources abroad. Neither the leadership debate nor the rank-and-file grumbling constitutes a serious political problem as yet, but their very existence should act as a brake on additional large-scale commitments in Africa or elsewhere.

EAST GERMANY

After the USSR and Cuba, East Germany plays the most significant Communist role in southern Africa. It works in alliance with the Soviet Union, and it echoes Moscow's themes of opposition to imperialism and support for national liberation.

East Germany has sought to cultivate close relationships with blacks in the region. It has forged strong links with Angola and Mozambique. In 1979 the head of the East German government, Erich Honecker, visited the two countries, and East Germany has signed treaties of friendship and cooperation with both. East German personnel are even believed to have trained the personal guards of President Samora Machel of Mozambique. East Germany has similarly endeavored to strengthen its ties with Zambia. Honecker called at Lusaka on his 1979 swing through southern Africa. East Germany has also developed close relations with liberation movements: the ZAPU wing of the Patriotic Front prior to the 1980 election in Zimbabwe, SWAPO in Namibia, and the ANC in South Africa.

Partly as a result of economic problems at home, East Germany's economic aid to Third World countries has been limited. Precise figures for such aid to southern Africa are lacking, but the total is believed to be small. East Germany appears to have confined its technical help largely to developing security and intelligence services and mass education programs. Trade, which is largely with Angola and Mozambique, is minimal.

In the military field, however, East Germany's activities are substantial. It makes and exports sizable quantities of arms. It began to supply the Front for the Liberation of Mozambique (FRELIMO) in 1969, before FRELIMO gained power, and it subsequently assisted the MPLA in Angola, ZAPU in Zimbabwe, SWAPO in Namibia, and exiled ANC guerrillas in similar fashion. Indeed, in the final stages of the Zimbabwean guerrilla struggle, East Germany appears to have assumed prime responsibility for supplying arms and ammunition to the ZAPU forces. Although East Germany has no independent capability to transport its own forces into the area, it does have the skilled manpower to supply technical military aid and training, and East German military advisers have in fact played prominent roles in both Angola and Mozambique. East Germans have also helped train ANC guerrillas. Should the occasion ever arise, East Germany could obviously contribute some combat forces to a combined military venture in the area with the USSR and Cuba. But such a contingent would probably not be large, considering the relatively small size of the East German army and its internal security role at home.

Like the Soviet Union, East Germany has encountered disappointments in southern Africa. The moves by Angola and Mozambique to expand dealings with the West could not have pleased it. Despite Honecker's visit to Zambia, relations with Lusaka remain fairly distant. East Germany's intimate association with the USSR has drawbacks from Kenneth Kaunda's standpoint. Because of East Germany's past identification with the ZAPU forces of Joshua Nkomo, it has met with distrust on the part of the Mugabe government in Zimbabwe, and not until 1981 did the East Germans establish diplomatic representation in Salisbury.

East Germany has no pretensions to global-power rank, but its activities in Africa nevertheless have something to do with status. It seeks constantly to reinforce its nationhood—its recognition as a nation standing clearly apart from West Germany. Solidifying and entrenching the division between the two Germanies is seen as strengthening East Germany's domestic stability and internal security. Involvement outside Europe—in southern Africa, for example—has been one means employed by East Germany to build a stronger identity of its own.

Southern Africa's raw materials also draw East Germany to the region. It has an interest in guaranteeing access to the minerals and other raw materials of the area as a hedge against eventual reduction of supplies from the USSR and other Communist trading partners. East Germany is poor in natural resources, so it must purchase a large share of its raw materials and food from abroad. A foothold in southern Africa represents a possible alternate source for some commodities.

A final likely motive for East German involvement in southern Africa is to demonstrate its ability to serve Soviet objectives in that area as a means of enhancing its influence on Soviet policy elsewhere, especially in Europe. The East German government, still hampered by its inability to achieve legitimacy in the eyes of large segments of the population it rules, must depend heavily on the USSR in order to remain in power. This dependence has often resulted in Moscow's riding roughshod over East German concerns. During the USSR's push for détente in the early 1970s, for example, Moscow forced East Germany to be more forthcoming than it wished to be on matters such as Berlin, and it even brought about the replacement of Walter Ulbricht as first secretary of East Germany's governing party. The only way East Germany can at least partially offset its dependence is to show Soviet leaders that retaining its goodwill has positive aspects, and southern Africa offers an opportunity to make this case.

As with the Soviet Union, there are built-in limits to East Germany's role in southern Africa. East Germany, like the Soviet Union, has higher priorities. Its fundamental concerns continue to lie in Europe, where the bulk of its trading relationships are centered and where it leads a sometimes uneasy existence as the Warsaw Pact member most geographically exposed to the West.

CHINA

China is the major Communist opponent of the USSR in southern Africa. Since the collapse of Portugal's African empire in the mid-1970s, China has acted on a number of fronts in an effort to bolster its position in the region.

In Angola the Chinese initially backed the creation of a coalition government with the expectation that the two Angolan factions with which China maintained links, Holden Roberto's FNLA and Jonas Savimbi's UNITA, would dominate such a coalition and thus restrict the influence of the Soviet-supported MPLA. Since the MPLA came to power in Luanda with the assistance of the USSR and Cuba, Peking has endorsed UNITA's call for the withdrawal of non-African forces from the country and for representation of UNITA in the government.

Elsewhere in the area, the Chinese have relied largely on exploiting long-standing ties to further their ends. For example, China had rendered assistance to both FRELIMO in Mozambique and the ZANU wing of the Patriotic Front in Zimbabwe during their guerrilla struggles, and has sought to capitalize on these historical links to ensure friendly relations with the governments that the two now control. During the early 1970s China had furnished Zambia with the capital and technical know-how for the construction of the Tan-Zam railroad between Zambia and the port of Dar es Salaam in Tanzania—the largest Third World aid project in which the Chinese have participated to date. When Zambia had trouble keeping the line running in the late 1970s, Peking came to the rescue by sending its specialists back to help. Chinese contacts with SWAPO of Namibia and with the Pan-Africanist Congress (PAC) of South Africa had begun well before the Portuguese revolution of 1974, and Peking has tried to expand these relationships as much as possible. To the extent that China has undertaken new overtures, these have focused on Lesotho and Botswana. In recent years Peking has opened diplomatic relations with both states.

At the start of 1981, the payoffs from these efforts were unimpressive. Soviet, Cuban, and East German military personnel remained in Angola, and UNITA's fight against the MPLA government continued. Although Mozambique had by no means severed its links with China, it had turned to the USSR for arms. Moreover, its ruling party had established direct relations with the

Soviet Communist party. Zambia had reluctantly looked to the Soviet Union for weapons, deeming other sources inadequate. SWAPO had become heavily dependent on sanctuaries in Angola and on Soviet arms to sustain its operations in Namibia, and was displaying an increasingly distant attitude toward China. The PAC had fallen into disarray and tended to be isolated from developments within South Africa. The one genuine triumph that the Chinese had achieved was in Zimbabwe. In contrast to its coolness toward the USSR, Robert Mugabe's new government had quickly entered into warm relations with China.

"The South African racist regime," Peking has declared, "is not only an insensate stone pressing upon the South African and Namibian peoples but also a catastrophe jeopardizing peace and stability in Africa." Furthermore, it has argued that since "the signal victory" of anticolonialist forces in Zimbabwe, "the days of colonialism and racism are numbered," and it has pledged that "the Chinese people will . . . firmly support the just cause for the total liberation of southern Africa."

Thus does China constantly express its alarm over the racial conflict in southern Africa. Such statements reflect a fundamental motive for China's activities in the region: a determination to establish its credentials as a power—though perhaps not a superpower—with global concerns. China appears to have at least three other reasons for its ventures in southern Africa.

One is an interest in aligning itself firmly with the anticolonial and antiracialist forces in the region to reinforce its identification with the Third World. Since 1974 Peking has analyzed global affairs in terms of three worlds—(1) the superpowers, (2) other industrialized states, and (3) developing countries—and it has associated China with the last of these. Although events in the late 1970s, and especially the Soviet invasion of Afghanistan, have compelled Chinese leaders to take stock of the purely military realities confronting them, Peking continues to maintain that "the rise of the Third World has brought about a radical change in the balance of power of the world's forces in favor of the people," and it insists that Third World countries can "preserve the stability and peace of the world" if they "join hands with all the justice-upholding countries and people in a resolute struggle to expose and thwart" the "aggressive design and war plan" of hegemonism, "the root cause of global unrest." From this perspective, mobilization of the Third World under the aegis of Peking affords China at least some protection against Soviet attack. To accomplish such a mobilization, however, China needs to demonstrate common purposes with other Third World countries.

China also hopes to block the expansion of Soviet influence. As Peking well knows, Soviet involvement in southern Africa has expanded greatly since the mid-1970s, and that trend has weakened China's position in the region. Chinese leaders' eagerness to undercut the Soviets was evident in Chinese comments after the elections in Zimbabwe in March 1980. Peking noted that the "ambitious superpower" that "has always coveted Zimbabwe and all of southern Africa" and "tried to meddle in the affairs of Zimbabwe" was "unhappy about the London agreement and the new Zimbabwean government which will soon be formed." It then cautioned that "once there is good opportunity," because of difficulties Zimbabwe might encounter, the superpower would not hesitate to "fish in troubled waters," and it warned that "this is a matter against which the Zimbabwean people should heighten their vigilance."

A final motive for Chinese involvement in southern Africa is to ensure access to at least some of the area's raw materials. China is largely but not entirely self-sufficient in minerals, and southern Africa offers a good source of supply for certain items in which China is deficient, such as copper and chromium. Peking is clearly aware of the mineral wealth of the region, for it has repeatedly accused Moscow of having designs on these riches. Moreover, China already has a long-term contract with Zambia for copper.

China's various interests do not always mesh smoothly. For example, to soften the hostility that Luanda now exhibits toward China, Peking would probably have to accept as legitimate the presence in Angola of the Soviets, Cubans, and East Germans.

There are also conflicts between China's interests in southern Africa and its larger global interests. In particular, Peking desires to avoid actions unsettling to relations with the United States and Western Europe, which Chinese leaders have worked assiduously to cultivate in both the political and economic fields in recent years. Indeed, China's ambitious new modernization plans will require major imports of technology from the industrialized Western nations and perhaps long-term credits as well. Chinese commentaries on Zimbabwe since Mugabe's election victory have confirmed that Peking is acutely conscious of a relationship between its expanded involvements with the United States and Western Europe and its behavior in southern Africa. These have stressed Mugabe's desire for reconciliation between whites and blacks, his willingness to coexist with South Africa, and his wish to develop links with the West.

However, as in the case of the other Communist states engaged in southern Africa, China's global priorities also restrain its actions. Asia obviously occupies the top place on China's list of geopolitical concerns, and southern Africa now appears to occupy a place below the Middle East on China's priority list.

China possesses distinctly limited capabilities for operating in southern Africa. In the political sphere, its seat on the UN Security Council lends some weight to its views. Another political asset, more difficult to explicate but nonetheless significant, is the predominant Third World view of China as a nation with which the Third World has much in common. Aside from these sources of influence, however, Peking has little political leverage. It has no ties with the two Communist parties in southern Africa, which are both pro-Soviet, nor has it entered into party-to-party relations with the avowedly Marxist-Leninist ruling groups in Mozambique or Angola.

China's options in the miliary sphere are exceedingly circumscribed. Although the Chinese have three airborne divisions and some aircraft to transport them abroad, the planes could not reach southern Africa without access to refueling facilities. Similarly, there are 38,000 marines in the Chinese armed forces, but the Chinese navy lacks the vessels to carry out an effective sealift. Moreover, even if China managed to get a few troops to the area, it could not supply them. China does have an arms industry and thus can supply at least some weapons to states and liberation movements. It can also provide military advisers. But involvement of even this sort is severely restricted by the demands of China's own security and the need to modernize its military forces. As a result, Peking has offered little military help in southern Africa. Total military aid in the region from 1973 to 1977 amounted to about $10 million at most.

Perhaps surprisingly, it is in the economic realm that China enjoys the greatest capabilities for exerting influence in southern Africa. The Chinese economy still falls into the underdeveloped category, but since the late 1950s its gross national product has averaged an estimated annual growth of more than 5 percent. Furthermore, even though per capita GNP in China still has not reached $400, the sheer size of the economy permits Chinese leaders to contemplate actions that the rulers of countries with smaller economies could not consider. Estimates of China's GNP in 1978 put it at $444 billion, the fifth largest in the world.

Moreover, it is possible to heighten the impact of available resources by committing them in a concentrated area, and Peking has shown a tendency to follow this course. Of the $3.7 billion in economic aid it extended to developing countries in 1970–78, for example, almost $2 billion went to states in Africa. The African allocation included $349 million in credits to southern Africa—an amount that is far from insignificant, even though so far Peking appears to have gained little in return.

Chapter 16
The United States and South Africa

For most Americans, including those who shape foreign policy, South Africa has never been a central concern. Even though a variety of groups have labored to focus attention on apartheid, their efforts have failed to persuade the public of the urgency of the issue. Most Americans strongly disapprove of apartheid when it is brought to their attention, but in a poll taken in December 1978, when the Carter administration was pressing for solutions in Zimbabwe and Namibia, only 4 percent of Americans picked *any* African issue when asked to name "the two or three biggest foreign policy problems facing the United States today."

Things can change, however. Not long ago most Americans were not particularly interested in Iran or Afghanistan. And South Africa, whatever its standing at any moment in the hierarchy of public concerns, will at minimum keep demanding attention until it moves toward fundamental change. That is assured by the moral issues it embodies and the forces for change they create. Foes of apartheid insist this moral dimension should be a consideration for the policies of countries around the globe. For the United States it is an inescapable consideration. Our history and the racial composition of our population make South Africa a special concern.

The links between the domestic politics of the United States and relations with South Africa are unmistakable. It was not by chance that friction between the United States and South Africa developed only as the United States began, in the years after World War II, to rectify its most glaring domestic inequity. Nor was it by chance that the pressure exerted on the South African regime by Washington has correlated with the commitment of particular administrations to advancing the civil rights of America's own black population. Thus, even though South Africa is still not a major focus of U.S. foreign policy, it is linked to domestic American politics. For good or ill, domestic political considerations will continue to influence U.S. policy toward South Africa.

THE HISTORY OF U.S. POLICY

Before World War II, when the United States at last accepted the necessity of playing a leading role in world affairs, its policies toward South Africa—like its policies toward most of the world outside the Americas—were the product of four traditional concerns: commerce, humanitarianism, anticolonialism, and political noninvolvement. At various times one or another of these concerns would take precedence. Of the four, the refusal to make a major political commitment on any African issue was fundamental. America's refusal to undertake formal responsibility in Africa (with the exception of Liberia) stemmed in large part from its commitment to the Monroe Doctrine: The United States had feared that participation in the scramble for Africa, in the words of one scholar, "would contradict the Monroe Doctrine's dogma of no American interference in [European spheres of influence] and so invite European meddling in Latin America." Political abstention in Africa thus helped to protect American commercial primacy in the New World and to assure friendly access to European capital for U.S. development.

The Open Door free-trade policy advanced by the United States at the start of the twentieth century provided the diplomatic principle for extending American commercial and financial connections with Africa, and American exports of goods, capital, and technical expertise helped build what was to become South Africa. Ford automobiles and Otis elevators reached South Africa in the first decade of the century, and the quantity of American exports rivaled German shipments for second position behind those of Great Britain. Colonel Edward McMurdo, an American investor, provided the initial financing for the Delagoa railway from Lourenço Marques, Mozambique (now Maputo), to the Transvaal, and American capital helped establish the Anglo-American Corporation (though it soon lost all but a fraction of its American backing). Even before these developments, American miners fresh from the California gold fields helped open the South African gold and diamond mines. Cecil Rhodes's mining empire in particular depended heavily on senior American engineers.

The Anglo-Boer war divided Americans in South Africa, American opinion at home, and American diplomats. A succession of American consuls in Pretoria defended the "freedom struggle" of the Boer republics against British imperialism, and that cause also received strong support in the United States, particularly from German and Irish communities, urban politicians, and not a few liberal journalists and intellectuals. A West Point colonel commanded a pro-Boer unit made up mostly of anti-British Irishmen. On the other hand, while the United States remained formally neutral, the weight of American policy and commerce clearly came to favor the British. American businessmen supplied the British war effort, and the secretary of state swung his department behind the British cause. The logic of this policy decision was complex. Britain, of all colonial powers, had been most amenable to the Open Door principle of free trade. Unlike the agrarian Boers, moreover, the British were committed to industrial development of South Africa, and, according to one historian, American officials assumed that this "would not only attract a large white population but also expose the African to a capitalistic moneyed system and eventually create a huge bloc of black consumers" presumably eager for American products. American missionaries—both black and white—also favored the British cause, judging it more sympathetic to the Christian uplifting of the black population, while many Americans believed that support for the British was tantamount to supporting democracy and enlightened progress.

Most of these hopes were dashed: Britain imposed restrictions on American trade and investment; the huge black consumer market never developed; and evangelization by Americans, particularly black Americans, did not take place on a significant scale. Rather than looking on the United States as a source of democratic ideals, South Africa increasingly looked to American racial segregation as legitimation for its own efforts and saw in American racial troubles a lesson that any weakening of racial barriers threatened their own version of "civilization."

In the years between the first and second world wars, South Africa received little official American attention. At the Paris peace conference, the United States initially supported handing German South-West Africa over "for incorporation in the self-governing Dominion of South Africa." The American expert on such matters argued that "the mandatory principle is inadvisable and really inapplicable in this case. In other areas, we are concerned mainly with derelict peoples, here essentially with land." On broader issues, only such strongly motivated persons as W.E.B. DuBois persisted in denouncing the South African racial order. "Responsible" and thoughtful white Americans were distressed by South Africa's "race problem" but few saw it as an issue for the United States to rectify. Rather, they tended to seize every hopeful straw as evidence that the progressive march of historical and economic development would in time provide a solution. As one such commentator, Raymond Leslie Buell, wrote in 1928:

> The obstacles to a solution of the race problem in South Africa are formidable almost to the point of despair. While the leaders realize the necessity of a new policy, the great masses of Europeans . . . find it difficult to shake off century-old beliefs and to support legislation involving the sacrifice of their immediate interests. Nevertheless there are many signs of a growing appreciation of the problem. . . . The present Prime Minister has shown an intelligence and courage which none of his predecessors has demonstrated. The mere fact that

the leader of the Nationalist party has dared to support measures giving natives a form of representation . . . shows how long a distance South African opinion has travelled during the last few years.

In the past the so-called "liberals" in both Europe and America . . . have been unduly harsh in their judgment of the South African people. They forget that Europeans came to this country with the same innocence as the Pilgrim Fathers came to America. . . .

They also forget that the white man settled in some parts of South Africa earlier than the ancestors of the present black inhabitants. . . . As the Natal Native Affairs Commission said, "Noted for their fecundity and virility, they [the natives] will not die out or succumb to ordinary adversity, and, as we can neither assimilate nor destroy them, political forethought and common sense alike call for a settlement of the question on a broad, enlightened, and permanent basis."

The principles sanctioned by the Hertzog Government are an important contribution to this settlement.

More than fifty years later similar hopes are expressed by many Americans looking for a solution in South Africa.

During World War II South Africa was a valued, if distant, partner in the fight against fascism. South African troops fought in the north African campaign and alongside Americans in Italy, and the United States signed a lend-lease agreement with South Africa. The section of the State Department planning U.S. policy toward colonial areas for the postwar world (known derisively as the "Hottentots and Crusaders" in distinction to the "hard-boiled realists" of the navy and war departments) thought well enough of South Africa to contemplate at one point opposing Portuguese colonialism by splitting Mozambique between southern Rhodesia and South Africa.

At the end of the war, Prime Minister Jan Smuts's prestige was augmented through his close cooperation with the United States in establishing the United Nations. Nevertheless, the United States found it advisable not to encourage Smuts's "Pan-African idea," which would have brought together much of central and eastern Africa under South African leadership. According to some historians, concern that such a move might close the door to American commerce and investment in other African countries seems to have been at least as strong a factor in U.S. opposition as any humanitarian disapproval of South Africa.

Aside from Smuts, South Africa was essentially unknown to and ignored by Americans, including top policy makers. Within the Department of State, South Africa was considered administratively part of Europe, and the European bureau had weightier matters to worry about as the Third Reich came to an end and the cold war began. Smuts's defeat by Daniel Malan in 1948 briefly raised eyebrows but caused no significant consternation in Washington and certainly not in the business community. The Malan government volunteered its support in the fight against worldwide communism. The United States gratefully accepted its contribution of an air crew for the Berlin airlift and a fighter squadron for the war in Korea but ignored Malan's efforts to have South Africa included as the North Atlantic Treaty Organization's southern flank or to establish a south Atlantic equivalent of NATO. In the immediate postwar years, economic relations with South Africa picked up but no more so than they did with most other parts of the Western world. During Harry Truman's presidency, South Africa was to all intents and purposes just another friendly country so far as America's bilateral relations with it were concerned.

It was in the multilateral context of the United Nations that South Africa first became a problem for the United States. Problems arose there because the United States had to take into account relations with third parties more exercised over South African practices than the American government was. Also, in the United Nations issues of international law involving South Africa were posed, calling into question the new structures of international order for which American troops and diplomats had labored so mightily. The United States, motivated in large part by sensitivity to potential foreign condemnation of its own racial policies, sought to focus the argument on the legal issues of "domestic jurisdiction" and the "rule of law" among nations. India had repeatedly sought UN support for the protection of Asians in South Africa. Since the status of these Asians was the subject of a treaty between India and South Africa—and hence already an international matter—and since the United States cared about its bilateral relations with India, Washington supported mildly worded resolutions counseling roundtable talks, negotiation, and mediation. South-West Africa was seen essentially as a "rule of law" issue in which South Africa's refusal to submit to the supervision of the Trusteeship Committee was interpreted as challenging a particular part of the UN structure whose establishment has been an important subsidiary concern of wartime interallied diplomacy. In 1947 John Foster Dulles, a member of America's UN delegation, strongly criticized South Africa's refusal to comply with a resolution calling for a trusteeship plan for South-West Africa. Two years later the United States supported a UN resolution referring the matter to the International Court of Justice and subsequent resolutions regretting South Africa's persistence in flouting the United Nations and the World Court's opinions.

In December 1952 apartheid itself became the target for the first time with the introduction in the United Nations of an Asian-Arab resolution. After strenuous debate within the American delegation between those arguing that this was exclusively a matter of domestic jurisdiction and those, including Eleanor Roosevelt, who felt it more important to support India and its cosponsors on a clear moral issue, the matter was finally resolved by the secretary of state, Dean Acheson. Acheson was a strong proponent of the view that the United States "should not intervene for what are called moral reasons in the internal affairs of another country. Moral reasons for interfering are merely a cover for self-indulgent hypocrisy." In the end, the United States abstained on the resolution (Britain and France opposed it), thereby setting what was to be the dominant pattern of American diplomatic activity with regard to apartheid for the next decade.

The pattern set by the 1952 UN vote continued through most of the Eisenhower years. The United States "regretted" certain internal developments in South Africa but felt obliged to abstain from interfering in matters within the domestic jurisdiction of a state, particularly one that regularly declared itself a staunch ally in the fight against communism. Although the United States and its allies continued to turn a deaf ear to South Africa's reiterated interest in joining or formally complementing NATO, military cooperation proceeded routinely. Under the 1955 Simonstown naval cooperation agreement between Britain and South Africa, the United States, as Britain's ally, acquired guaranteed access to South African naval and air facilities in time of war, whether or not South Africa was a belligerent. American warships regularly called at South African ports, and in 1959 U.S. ships joined British, French, Portuguese, and South African units in joint antisubmarine warfare exercises off the South African coast.

In 1954 South Africa, as an important supplier of uranium, was invited to join the United States, Britain, and other European states in forming the International Atomic Energy Board. Through membership South Africa acquired extensive technical information in the nuclear field. In implementation of President Dwight Eisenhower's 1954 "Atoms for Peace" program, which called for cooperation in the civil uses of nuclear energy between the United States and other nations, the United States and South Africa signed a twenty-year agreement in 1957 providing for cooperation in nuclear energy research and eventually in the development of nuclear power. As outgrowths of this agreement, some ninety-four South African nuclear scientists were trained at installations such as Oak Ridge and Argonne National laboratories, and Allis-Chalmers constructed South Africa's first research reactor, which went into operation in 1965. There is no indication that the 1957 agreement raised any unusual questions in Wasington.

Other sensitive relationships, such as regular contacts between the Central Intelligence Agency and South African security officials and the occasional visits back and forth of senior defense officials, continued as matters of routine. In 1953 the Commerce Department issued a report on investment opportunities in South Africa balancing that country's many attractions for American capital with references to "internal racial and social tensions" and the observation that "there is reason to believe that wide and adverse publicity accorded race relations and political discord in the Union has discouraged many potential investors." South Africa's protest that this was an "unfriendly act" upset neither the Department of Commerce, which continued similar cautions in subsequent editions of the report, nor American investors, who increased their South African holdings from $212 million in 1953 to $350 million in 1960.

Major changes were at work, however, both at home and abroad, and these inevitably had consequences for America's policies toward South Africa. Most important, during the second half of the 1950s Africa was slowly changing from a mere geographic label to an idea with political content. Ghana's independence in the spring of 1957 began a movement that by the end of Eisenhower's presidency made African states the largest geographical voting bloc in the United Nations. The 1956 Suez crisis led the United States to reassert its independence from its principal European allies, Britain and France, in matters involving former colonial areas. At home in the United States, the Supreme Court's *Brown* v. *Board of Education* decision in May 1954 declared that "separate" could not be "equal" and set American racial policy irreversibly on a path opposite to that taken by Pretoria.

Within the Department of State, in 1956 South Africa was administratively transferred from "Europe" to the African subdivision of the Bureau of Near Eastern, South Asian, and African Affairs. In mid-1958 the African section achieved administrative independence with the creation of the Bureau of African Affairs under an assistant secretary, Joseph Satterthwaite. Although it was the smallest and least prestigious of the geographical bureaus, the African bureau was now in a position to begin to think through African problems in regional terms and to speak directly on behalf of its conception of American interests in Africa to the most senior levels of decision making. And in the State Department, at least, South Africa was henceforth part of Africa.

The effects of these changes, if not dramatic, were soon apparent. On October 30, 1958, the United States abandoned its policy of abstention on UN resolutions critical of apartheid and with it acceptance of the supremacy of the "domestic jurisdiction" argument. Washington negotiated a weak enough resolution to permit it to vote with the majority in expressing "regret and concern" over South Africa's racial policies. Speaking with "humility" occasioned by the United States' own racial difficulties, the American representative nevertheless declared that South Africa's case was unique because discrimination was "sanctified by statute." Prior to May 1954, the United States could hardly have attributed such uniqueness to South Africa. There is little doubt that a desire to establish friendly relations with the independent nations of Africa and to block Soviet propaganda appeals to Africa played a major role in this decision to free American policy from total subservience to the "domestic jurisdiction" principle. "The African people look to the United States for assistance in achieving social, economic, and political progress," Assistant Secretary Satterthwaite explained subsequently. "They look to us for moral leadership and for a sympathetic understanding of their aspirations. . . . They expect us to apply our historic ideals to our foreign policy."

The Sharpeville shootings on March 21, 1960, shook Washington as had no previous South African event, and repercussions were quickly felt throughout the business community. The State Department, without consulting either its embassy in Pretoria or the White House, issued a statement on March 22 expressing its hope that "the African people of South Africa will be able to obtain redress for their legitimate grievances" and its regret for "the tragic loss of life resulting from the measures taken against the demonstrators." Over repeated South African protests the United States called a meeting of the UN Security Council and on April 1 joined a unanimous vote (Britain and France abstaining) for a resolution that expressed the view that continuation of the South African situation "might endanger international peace and security" and "deplored the policies and actions of the South African government." American business, reacting to what looked like dangerous instability, joined in a general flight of foreign capital that caused South Africa's foreign-exchange reserves to drop some $64 million in the first seven weeks following Sharpeville.

Despite these strong reactions, evident also in press commentary, the bloody events of March 1960 did not have the lasting consequences that many foresaw—either within South Africa or for U.S.-South African relations. Within a few months the South African government had throttled down the disturbances to the point where the world's newspapers ignored them. Whatever speeches and press releases critical of South Africa emanated from the State Department, they had little effect on day-to-day bilateral relations. On September 13, 1960, the National Aeronautics and Space Administration announced agreement with South Africa for the establishment of three tracking stations. (The informal understanding that only whites would be assigned to these stations was not announced.) In November General Motors said it was expanding its investment, and American and other foreign funds began flowing once again. With the help of substantial dollar loans from U.S. banks and multilateral lending institutions, South Africa soon resumed its dramatic economic growth.

What had changed in U.S. policy was the outward political symbolism of relations. American rhetoric hardened. UN votes and governmental statements put some distance between the United States and South Africa—and also between the United States and Britain and France over South African issues. Sharpeville was the catalyst that brought forth the verbal expressions of distance and dismay, but changes in America's own racial policies and in America's and South Africa's international environments provided essential ingredients for the reaction. This reaction was limited to words however. The United States voted to "regret" and "deplore" and "condemn" South African policies; it refused to "intervene" in such domestic affairs. A gap between rhetoric and action was opened wide, and it was to be maintained by the administrations that succeeded Eisenhower's. In the absence of firm governmental action, many American businessmen ignored the rhetoric and made their judgments on pure business criteria.

President John Kennedy gave Africa a prominent place in his New Frontier. Unlike any previous American president, Kennedy had Africa in his political background: His 1957 Senate speech denouncing French colonialism in Algeria was perhaps the first speech to bring him to international attention. He made what he viewed as the Eisenhower administration's fusty attitudes toward Africa an issue in his campaign against Richard Nixon. Africa, according to Arthur M. Schlesinger, Jr., appealed to Kennedy as a place where "no traditional doctrines guided . . . policy" and where he might make a difference without having to overcome the entrenched resistance of bureaucrats and bureaucratic precedent. Kennedy was convinced that winning Africa to America's side in the cold war required new policies clearly distinct from those of the old colonial powers. As for South Africa, the issue of apartheid apparently meant more to Kennedy and to his young advisers—many of whom had strongly supported civil rights campaigns in the United States—than it had meant to men of Eisenhower and Dulles's generation and backgrounds. Kennedy's African commitment was symbolized by his choice, in the very first appointment announced after his election, of G. Mennen Williams, a leading member of the Democratic party's liberal wing, as assistant secretary of state for African affairs.

South Africa was not pleased when on his first trip to Africa Williams used the phrase "Africa for the Africans"; Pretoria denied him a visa. In the United Nations Adlai Stevenson continued the policy of voting condemnation of apartheid and of South African administration of South-West Africa while opposing proposals for sanctions put forth with increasing vigor by the General Assembly's new African members. Kennedy was personally convinced that sanctions had no possibility of being implemented and was repelled by "unrealistic" and "grandiose" resolutions calling for them. More quietly, the State Department sent Pretoria an *aide-mémoire* in September 1961 stating that the United States would be unable "to cooperate with South Africa in ways which would lend support to apartheid." Kennedy also declined to respond favorably to a request from Prime Minister Hendrik Verwoerd for an invitation to visit Washington. On July 4, 1963, the American embassy for the first time invited black South Africans to a reception. South African government officials stayed home.

While the Kennedy administration accelerated the change in tone of American policy toward South Africa, South Africa itself was never the major focus of American policy, not even of American African policy. When it came to matters of strategic military importance, cooperation with South Africa proceeded. Naval ships continued to call, and in June 1962 agreement was announced for the establishment of an American military space-tracking station in South Africa, in exchange for which the United States agreed to sell South Africa arms "for use against Communist aggression." Similar expedient distinctions applied in the case of Portugal. The United States sold Portugal arms "for NATO use only" and protected Portugal from African-sponsored UN resolutions essentially because the U.S. military—and the president—felt that continued use of military base facilities in the Portuguese Azores was vital. In perfect illustration of the Kennedy administration's hierarchy of concerns, the first serious action taken by the United States against South Africa grew out of an attempt, as Schlesinger records it, to "do something in African eyes to make up for restraint in the case of Portugal." The decision was for the United States to announce a unilateral refusal to sell South Africa additional arms after January 1, 1964, and to vote in favor of a nonbinding UN resolution calling on all states to do likewise.

Under Lyndon Johnson, Africa faded from presidential attention. Yet the outlines of policy toward South Africa were maintained and in some respects strengthened, despite the growing preoccupation with Vietnam. Although Johnson made a brief trip to west Africa in 1961, while vice-president, he had none of his predecessor's personal involvement in Africa. Three factors conditioned the Johnson administration's response to southern African issues. First, Johnson's commitment to advancing the position of blacks in American society made South Africa an exemplary and easy target. As Johnson said in a May 1966 speech to the African diplomatic corps on the third anniversary of the founding of the Organization of African Unity, "The foreign policy of the United States is rooted in its life at home." In a sense, condemning apartheid was an adjunct to building the Great Society. Second, Williams and his deputy, J. Wayne Fredricks, continued to lead the African bureau for several years after Johnson took over, and they left behind them a well-established and increasingly confident bureau. Finally, the administration's preoccupation with the Vietnam war, while it made impossible any major initiative requiring presidential commitment, permitted the bureaucracy most concerned with South Africa to continue its policies when they involved no significant cost to the United States.

South-West Africa dominated much of American policy toward South Africa. It was clear that the suit brought by Ethiopia and Liberia in 1960 before the International Court of Justice with the aim of compelling South Africa to relinquish its control of the mandate over the region would be decided in 1966. In preparation for this, the United States in 1964 voted for a Security Council resolution establishing a committee of experts to study the practicability of sanctions against South Africa. Three days before the decision was to be handed down, the United States announced to South Africa its intention to see that the decision was enforced. The African bureau's firmness was backed strongly by the State Department's legal branch, and several American lawyers prominent in Democratic party affairs were involved in the case. (Both Phillip Jessup, one of the World Court judges, and Ernest Gross, who pleaded the case of Ethiopia and Liberia, had held prominent State Department positions during the Truman administration.) On July 18, 1966, the Court's eight-to-seven ruling confounded expectations by dismissing the case on technical grounds. The following fall, however, UN Ambassador Arthur Goldberg took a leading role in drafting a General Assembly resolution condemning South Africa for its continuing control over South-West Africa and asking the Security Council to take "effective measures" to bring about self-determination in the territory. The resolution contained enough loopholes to avoid the need for decisive action, and the following year the United States, along with Britain and France, refused to join the United Nations' Council for Namibia, which seemed stacked in favor of those pressing for more radical action.

In its bilateral relations with South Africa, the United States continued the Kennedy policy of "neither encouraging nor discouraging" American investment—which continued to grow. It tightened its observance of the voluntary arms embargo by refusing the sale of "gray area" material that could have both civilian and military applications, and annoyed the French by blocking the sale of Mystère 20 jets—small executive-type transports—equipped with American engines. In 1967, however, the nuclear energy agreement was renewed, and routine military and CIA contacts continued, although quietly. Perhaps most annoying to the South Africans (and revelatory of the pressures at work on the U.S. government) was the *FDR* affair. In February 1967 the carrier U.S.S. *Franklin Delano Roosevelt* was returning from nine months' duty off Vietnam and planned on refueling and giving the crew much-needed shore leave at Cape Town. The State Department was unhappy about the visit but recognized the force of the navy's contention that refueling at sea would cost some $200,000 and deny the crew leave. Word of the dilemma was leaked to the American Negro Leadership Conference on Africa, which was meeting in Washington at the time. The issue rapidly boiled up, involving thirty-eight members of Congress, the attorney general, and the president. A compromise was finally worked out whereby shore leave would be limited to "integrated activity only." The *FDR*'s captain found this order impractical, took on fuel, and refused the crew permission to go ashore. The South African government and press were incensed, but since then U.S. naval ships have called in South African ports only in emergencies.

The Nixon administration began with a conscious effort to change both the style and the substance of American relations with South Africa. The effort was embodied in a document known as National Security Study Memorandum 39. The preparation of NSSM 39 was not a sign that southern Africa had moved to stage center in U.S. policy concerns. Quite the contrary: NSSM 39 was one of eighty-five such reviews of American policy throughout the world ordered by Henry Kissinger, the president's national security adviser, during 1969. Kissinger's vision was focused on managing the central relationship between the United States and the Soviet Union. Southern Africa concerned him primarily as a region in which American policy seemed to drift unproductively under the influence of what he considered a client-oriented State Department bureaucracy. It was an area where U.S. policy should be "tidied up" and made more "realistic" so that top decision makers could concentrate on important things without distraction.

350
The policy review occasioned by NSSM 39 revealed the contradictions

inherent in prevailing American policy and the limitations on America's ability to resolve the contradictions and achieve its primary goals by employing politically acceptable means. As the review stated:

> The aim of present policy is to try to balance our economic, scientific, and strategic interests in the white states with the political interests of dissociating the U.S. from the white minority regimes and their repressive racial policies. Decisions have been made ad hoc, on a judgment of benefits and political costs at a given moment. But the strength of this policy—its flexibility—is also its weakness. Policy is not precisely recorded. And because there have been significant differences of view within the government . . . certain decisions have been held in suspense. . . . [U.S.] objectives are to a degree contradictory—pursuit of one may make difficult the successful pursuit of one or more of the others. Moreover, views as to the relative priority among these objectives vary widely. . . . But the range of feasible policy options is limited.

Nor did the review hold out much hope for change: "There is no evidence that the white regimes of Southern Africa will make constructive changes in their race policies in response to external pressure. . . . For the foreseeable future South Africa will be able to maintain internal stability and effectively counter insurgent activity." In South-West Africa there was "no solution in sight." In Rhodesia, "despite the effects of sanctions, the white regime can hold out indefinitely with South African help."

NSSM 39 also pronounced a realistic assessment of the rationale behind U.S. efforts on issues at the United Nations:

> The main U.S. political interest in Southern African issues at the U.N. is to keep these issues manageable. On the one hand, we seek to maintain a credible stance on racial questions in the eyes of the Black African nations, while on the other we attempt to discourage the adoption of unrealistic measures which would damage other U.S. interests in the area and the U.N. has also sought, through its itself . . . The U.S. has also sought, through its posture on Southern African issues, to enhance the prospects for support by the 42 African states on other U.N. issues, for example, on the Chinese representation question.

Of the five policy options offered, Kissinger is said to have recommended that Option Two be chosen as the basis for American policy. Option Two proceeded from the following premise:

> The whites are here to stay and the only way that constructive change can come about is through them. There is no hope for the blacks to gain the political rights they seek through violence. . . . We can, through selective relaxation of our stance toward the white regimes, encourage some modification of their current racial and colonial policies. . . . Our tangible interests form a basis for our

351

contacts in the region, and these can be maintained at an acceptable political cost.

Option Two appealed to President Nixon and his advisers. In subordinating "political" (i.e., black African and human rights) concerns to "tangible" (i.e., economic and strategic) interests, the administration tilted away from outside liberal constituencies and State Department primacy within the government toward an outside business constituency and Defense Department and Commerce Department primacy. Furthermore, just as interest in civil rights and support from black leaders had contributed to Kennedy's and Johnson's rhetorical opposition to South Africa, so Nixon's "Southern strategy" of courting racial conservatives made rapprochement with South Africa attractive. This political interest was symbolized in Nixon's appointment of John Hurd, a conservative businessman who had managed Nixon's campaign in Texas, as his ambassador to Pretoria.

Those in the State Department and elsewhere who were most concerned with protecting U.S. relations with black Africa and who strongly opposed supporting a racist society could take partial comfort from Option Two's stated goal of "constructive change" in South Africa and its recommendation for increased economic aid to black states in the region. The assistant secretary of state for African affairs, David Newsom, noted the potential benefits of a new policy of "communication" with the white regimes and told Congress that black Africa gave first priority to issues of economic development.

Although no public announcement of the new direction of policy was made, subsequent events make clear that such a shift took place. In the military field, gray-area sales involving light planes, helicopters, troop transports, and communications equipment were approved; the objection to France's sale of Mystère 20s was dropped. The head of the South African Defense Force, Admiral Hugo Biermann, was welcomed at the Pentagon, and Connie Mulder, then minister of the interior and information, was received by Vice-President Gerald Ford. In the economic realm, restrictions on long-term Export-Import Bank financing were relaxed, and the Commerce Department shifted informally from "neither encouraging nor discouraging" American investment to encouraging American firms to adopt progressive policies toward their employees when they did invest in South Africa. In the United Nations condemnation of apartheid and South African intransigence over Namibia was replaced by abstention, and abstention on resolutions requiring action was replaced by opposition. The administration chose a southern African issue (an Afro-Asian resolution calling for the withdrawal of consulates in Salisbury and extending Rhodesian sanctions to the principal sanctions breakers, South Africa and Portugal) as the one on which the United States would cast its first veto in the Security Council. The White House refused to back the State Department in lobbying against the Byrd amendment permitting importation of Rhodesian chrome. The Azores agreement was renewed on terms that were unusually generous to Portugal, and sales of military equipment to that country were substantially increased. The CIA dropped most of its contacts with Angolan and Mozambican liberation movements.

The policy of "communication" with South Africa may have gone further than its sponsors intended when Ambassador Hurd was the only major diplomat to attend the segregated state opening of the Nico Malan theater in Cape Town and when he accepted a South African cabinet minister's invitation to hunt small game on Robben Island—with political prisoners serving as beaters. The State Department did rebuke Hurd for these lapses and, furthermore, in 1973 assigned his embassy its first black foreign service officer. However, the appointment signaled no change in the embassy's policy of avoiding communication with black opposition figures.

The single most important American policy initiative during the Nixon administration, from South Africa's point of view, was taken for reasons having nothing to do with southern Africa. This was the decision, forced ultimately by the deficit financing of the Vietnam war, to allow the price of gold to float above $35 an ounce. For South Africa, source of three-quarters of the world's gold production, a $10 change in the price of gold represents some $220 million in foreign exchange earnings. From $35 in 1969, gold reached just under $200 an ounce by the time Nixon left office, giving South Africa substantial insulation against international recession and economic pressure.

The underpinnings of Option Two were shaken by the Portuguese coup of 1974 (some of southern Africa's whites were clearly not there "to stay"), and the policy approach collapsed under the pressure of African events during the brief administration of President Gerald Ford. The Lisbon coup, product in large part of the Portuguese army's frustrations in Africa, attracted Kissinger's attention to African affairs. Now secretary of state, Kissinger "saw Angola as part of the U.S.-Soviet relationship, and not as an African problem," said a former State Department official. Over the objections of the African bureau and two assistant secretaries, Kissinger approved a program of covert intervention that, together with the actions of the Soviet Union and Cuba, led to the escalation of the conflict. As part of the process of escalation, South Africa intervened with a small but initially effective military force in support of Jonas Savimbi's National Union for the Total Independence of Angola (UNITA) and Holden Roberto's National Front for the Liberation of Angola (FNLA), which were also supported by Zambia and Zaire, respectively. It seems unlikely that Kissinger specifically encouraged the South African intervention, but it is clear that he did not discourage it. South Africa's political leaders, taking heart from the general course of the Nixon-Ford policy, seized upon the opportunity to demonstrate their country's importance as an American ally.

If South African intervention did not in fact promote massive Cuban intervention, it effectively legitimated it in the eyes of black Africa and most of the world. Nigeria, which had initially supported UNITA and the FNLA, changed course overnight and brought Zambia along in its wake. The U.S.

Congress, acting more out of concern about congressional privilege, CIA dirty tricks, and new Vietnam-style involvements than out of concern about the African dimension of the war, brought the CIA's intervention to a halt. South Africa withdrew its troops in February 1976. The Popular Movement for the Liberation of Angola, now dependent on 30,000 Cuban troops, organized the government of independent Angola.

At this point, Kissinger realized that a new approach to southern African policy was necessary. In April 1976 he undertook what was planned as a major African tour. Its centerpiece was a speech in Lusaka, Zambia, in which the secretary of state pointedly threatened the Ian Smith regime in Salisbury with "our unrelenting opposition until a negotiated settlement is achieved." With regard to South Africa, Kissinger's words were carefully shaded:

> Our policy toward South Africa is based upon the premise that within a reasonable time we shall see a clear evolution toward equality of opportunity and basic human rights for all South Africans. . . . In the immediate future the Republic of South Africa can show its dedication to Africa—and its potential contribution to Africa— by using its influence in Salisbury to promote a rapid negotiated settlement for majority rule in Rhodesia. This, we are sure, would be viewed positively by the community of nations, as well as by the rest of Africa.

The speech signaled the South African government that the United States would give it time to enact a mild program of economic and social reform (political rights were not mentioned) in exchange for cooperation on Rhodesia. President Kenneth Kaunda of Zambia was cautiously impressed. The leaders of Mozambique, Nigeria, and Ghana, apparently less impressed, refused to receive the secretary of state.

South African Prime Minister John Vorster translated the remarks correctly and agreed to meet Kissinger in Bavaria at the end of June. Vorster had every incentive to do so. He, too, thought Smith had made serious mistakes and would have preferred a moderate African government to a white one that was a perpetual invitation to outside intervention in the region. Moreover, U.S. gold sales had driven down the price of South Africa's most precious commodity to $126 an ounce, with indications that Treasury Secretary William Simon intended to let it sink to $80, and South Africa was searching for international credit to finance arms and petroleum purchases. Above all, a public meeting with Kissinger promised to confer unprecedented recognition on Vorster and his government (the last prime minister to have a personal meeting with such a high-level American official had been Jan Smuts). The explosion of Soweto on June 16 added urgency to Vorster's mission and gave Kissinger another stick to apply to South Africa, all the more welcome in that it need not be brandished publicly. (The secretary of state left it to the acting **354** United States representative to the United Nations to comment on the "tragic events.") Following the meeting South Africa began to slowly put the squeeze on the Smith government.

Kissinger and Vorster met again in Zurich on September 4, and on September 17 Kissinger traveled to Pretoria. After two days of meeting with Vorster, and with South African blacks at the American embassy, Kissinger met with Ian Smith. Kissinger brought strong pressure to bear on the Rhodesian, and his message was reinforced separately by Vorster. U.S.-South African cooperation seemed to work. On September 24 Smith read out over Rhodesian television his agreement to negotiate a transition to majority rule.

The Geneva negotiations that began at the end of October dragged on past Christmas and finally collapsed. Kissinger has attributed their failure to Jimmy Carter's defeat of President Ford in the November election, which undercut the secretary's effectiveness. Other observers suggest that the talks failed in large part because the United States did not succeed in establishing an effective relationship with the principal Zimbabwean guerrilla leaders or with Presidents Julius Nyerere of Tanzania and Samora Machel of Mozambique. Smith was ultimately dependent on the goodwill or at least the blind eye of the West and of the United States in particular. Robert Mugabe and Joshua Nkomo had other sources of support for their guerrilla forces and were hardly likely to recoil in horror at the prospect of Cubans besieging Salisbury or to be seduced by promises of Western aid for buying out white farmers and paying pensions to white civil servants. Something more and different was needed.

POLICIES UNDER CARTER

When President Carter took office in 1977, his administration, like those of John Kennedy in 1961 and Richard Nixon in 1969, encouraged a broad reassessment of international and domestic trends affecting foreign policy. These trends included:

1. The overall decline of American political and economic power relative to that of Western European nations, the petroleum-exporting nations, and on many issues the Third World as a whole, which meant there were few major issues on which the United States could go it alone.

2. The spread of American business overseas and the significant increase in American dependence on foreign supplies and markets, particularly those in the Third World.

3. The Soviet Union's acquisition of the ability to project military power sufficient to play a determining role in Third World conflicts where it was not opposed by substantial modern forces and its demonstrated willingness, under some circumstances, to project such power.

4. The collapse of the cold-war consensus in the United States that had united liberals and conservatives in a reflexive anticommunism.

5. The increasing connection of domestic and foreign policy issues and attitudes, with the result that domestic ideological positions increasingly influenced attitudes toward foreign affairs and domestic concerns were increasingly projected onto the international scene.

6. The increased role of Congress in making and executing foreign policy, with some sixty-seven congressional committees, many staffed by foreign policy specialists, attempting to play a role in foreign policy.

7. The rise to middle and, in a few cases, senior leadership positions in the private and especially the public sector of significant numbers of black Americans, together with an increasing awareness of black voting strength.

Recognition of these trends underlay the Carter administration's initial approaches to foreign policy generally and was strongly reflected in President Carter's first major foreign policy statement, the speech at Notre Dame University on May 22, 1977. The effect was also felt in the development of policy toward southern Africa.

Jimmy Carter came to the presidency concerned that the United States should do something to right the racial injustices in southern Africa. As he himself stressed in an interview, this concern was anchored in his personal regret that he had been slow to support the struggle for black civil rights in his own country. For the president, and for some of his closest advisers, notably Secretary of State Cyrus Vance and UN Ambassador Andrew Young, commitment to "doing something about southern Africa" had deep personal meaning and reflected attitudes formed long before they assumed their new offices. All three likewise shared the view expressed in Carter's Notre Dame speech that concentration on East-West antagonism should be subordinated to a new emphasis on North-South cooperation.

To the State Department, and to a lesser degree other branches of government dealing with foreign affairs, Carter brought with him a new generation of assistant secretaries and bureau directors, most of whom were critical of the preceding administration's conduct of foreign affairs. They were particularly disturbed by what they saw as its disregard of human rights issues and its concentration on East-West relations. For them, too, southern Africa was a major focus of interest and a chance to promote their general foreign policy vision. Their interest gave the State Department's Bureau of African Affairs a prominent role and unaccustomed backing both in the State Department and in the White House. The new assistant secretary for African affairs, Richard Moose, found himself confronted with the pleasant task of leading the bureaucracy in the direction it already wanted to go.

The African bureau saw black African nationalism as the driving historical force on the continent, as opposed to Soviet or other Communist imperialism or subversion. It assumed that in the long run black nationalism was a force whose development was largely consonant with American interests in Africa and that mature nationalism was the best—and for the United States the least expensive—defense against Soviet penetration. Black nationalism, furthermore, was judged to be a force whose eventual triumph in white-ruled southern Africa could only be delayed—at great cost—and not permanently thwarted. Working with nationalist forces, channeling their efforts productively, rather than confronting them or shoring up a losing minority, was seen as the only sensible policy for America to follow. It was also seen as the policy most likely to make it possible for whites to continue to live in southern Africa. The bureau was aware that the United States had increasingly important interests in black Africa, especially in Nigeria, which in 1973 had surpassed South Africa in total trade with the United States and in the rate of new American investment. Apart from U.S. reliance on South Africa's strategic minerals, American investment in and trade with South Africa, while significant (about 1 percent of both total U.S. foreign investment and total U.S. trade), are not indispensable. In this respect, the United States differs markedly from Great Britain, which depends heavily on a continued high level of business with South Africa. From Washington's viewpoint, appearing to coddle the white regimes of southern Africa could permanently jeopardize more important relations.

The South African government was aware that it was in for trouble from the new administration even before it took office. In a somber message delivered on New Year's Day 1977, Prime Minister Vorster concluded:

> It is my firm conclusion that if a communist onslaught should be made on South Africa . . . then South Africa will have to face it alone, and certain countries who profess to be anti-communist will even refuse to sell arms to South Africa to beat off the attack.

At first only scattered hints of a policy shift came through. In his Senate confirmation testimony, Andrew Young suggested that the United States might support a Swedish proposal for limited economic sanctions against South Africa and that "a rather hard-line policy might be necessary to make South Africa move internally." Sympathetic House and Senate subcommittees on Africa were promised an "urgent and comprehensive review" of the "whole question of U.S. policy toward southern Africa" by another administration official. In April, in an offhand reply to a journalist's question, Young indicated that he agreed with the characterization of South Africa's government as "illegitimate." Although the State Department issued a formal retraction, a National party newspaper concluded, "There is no doubt that relations between South Africa and the United States of America have reached an all-time low."

A month later Vice-President Walter Mondale met with Prime Minister Vorster in Vienna for "a day and a half of very frank and candid discussions." In contrast to the Kissinger approach, which was to concentrate initially on the problems of Rhodesia and Namibia, the new policy sought to focus directly on South Africa as well. As Mondale told the press:

Put most simply, the policy which the President wished me to convey **357** [to Vorster] was that there was need for progress on all three issues: majority rule for Rhodesia and Namibia and a progressive transformation of South African society to the same end.

Mondale registered "basic and fundamental disagreement" with Vorster's contention that separate development was not inherently discriminatory and insisted that South Africa must take steps toward "full political participation by all the citizens of South Africa—equal participation in the election of its national government and its political affairs." Although he did not initially use the words "one person, one vote," when a journalist used them and asked if Mondale was talking about something different, he replied, "No, no. It's the same thing. Every citizen should have the right to vote and every vote should be equally weighted." Mondale held out no hope that the United States would recognize any homeland's independence and with regard to Namibia firmly rejected any solution based on the ethnic representation foreseen in Vorster's Turnhalle initiative, which critics saw as a device to perpetuate white dominance.* The following day Young visited Pretoria and Johannesburg and further irritated the South African government by receiving a warm welcome in Soweto and by espousing the American civil rights movement's economic boycott tactics as the sort of nonviolent action that South African blacks might want to adopt.

Relations hit rock bottom in the second half of 1977. On August 6 the Soviet Union informed the United States, and in succeeding days France, Britain, and West Germany, that Soviet intelligence had spotted installations for detonating an atomic explosion in the Kalahari desert. The United States quickly redirected satellite cameras and verified the information. It then coordinated with its allies a strong joint warning to South Africa not to proceed. South Africa issued a series of categoric denials that any explosion was contemplated and coupled them with a public display of indignation about the way the United States had treated South Africa. Nevertheless, President Carter was able to announce at his August 23 press conference that South Africa had assured the United States that "no nuclear explosive test will be taken . . . now or in the future." What seems particularly to have impressed, and distressed, the South African government was the clear demonstration that the United States and its allies were willing to collaborate with the Soviet Union against South Africa. The following month Prime Minister Vorster announced that parliamentary elections would be held in November, almost a year ahead of time. One of the reasons given was that he wanted a strong mandate to deal with "outside interference" in South Africa's internal affairs.

South Africa promptly provided new ammunition for its foreign critics with the death of Steve Biko on September 12 and the October 19 crackdown

---

*The initiative emerged from a conference of Namibian internal factions organized by South Africa in Windhoek. It was held in the Turnhalle, a former German gymansium, and ran from September 1975 to March 1977.

on dissident black leadership. South African officials were nonplussed when
Donald F. McHenry, deputy American ambassador to the United Nations,
broke off participation in negotiations in Pretoria over Namibia to attend
Biko's funeral. In Washington Assistant Secretary of State for African Affairs
Moose gave strong support to a "resolution of concern" over the October 19
bannings and arrests sponsored by the Congressional Black Caucus, and the
House subsequently passed the resolution overwhelmingly. Of more consequence, the United States joined the United Nations in voting mandatory
sanctions against arms transfers to South Africa. Vorster's National party
directed its electoral campaign against Jimmy Carter and won by the largest
margins ever in the November elections.

There is no doubt that the style of American policy changed with the
Carter administration and that the South African government reacted angrily
to the change. Aside from style, substantive changes in policy were less clear,
but in relations between nations style cannot be neatly divorced from substance. The United States for years had condemned apartheid in the United
Nations. It took a change in style to register the message that the U.S. government actually meant it and that relations were bound to "deteriorate"
further if South Africa made no domestic changes. Similarly, it took both
Mondale's words and American cooperation with the Soviet Union over the
nuclear test site to begin to convince Pretoria that it was seen as a liability
and not as an ally against communism and that South Africans, as Mondale
put it, should "not rely on any illusions that the United States will, in the end,
intervene to save South Africa."

The style of official American representation in Pretoria changed as well
and inevitably brought a change in what was communicated to Washington as
well as to Pretoria. Carter's ambassadors, William Bowdler and William Edmondson, were both career diplomats. They themselves reached out to meet
black South Africans, and young embassy officers, black and white, were instructed to seek the widest possible contacts. The embassy regularly sent observers to political trials, and Bowdler was the only ambassador to attend the
funerals of both Steve Biko and Robert Sobukwe. The naval attaché, representing the service that had traditionally been closest to its South African
counterpart, was withdrawn, and the other attachés were instructed to concentrate on collecting information. After the October 19 crackdown, both Bowdler and the commercial attaché were recalled to Washington for "consultations."

At the same time, American communications under Carter were not always clear or systematic. Statements following Mondale's at Vienna asked for
"significant progress" toward the "elimination of discrimination" and "full
political participation" but failed to define the terms further. The reasons for
this reticence were understandable. Greater precision would have opened up
the United States to even stronger charges of interfering in South Africa's

domestic affairs. Equally understandable, however, was South Africans' frustration with what they construed as open-ended demands that no actions short of ceding all political power to blacks could satisfy.

To this must be added considerable confusion in the signals emanating from Washington. For all the administration's stern words, Carter at one point referred to South Africa as a "stabilizing force" and Mondale spoke of South Africans as "good friends." Some of Young's more provocative sallies were subsequently repudiated by the State Department, and National Security Adviser Zbigniew Brzezinski's statements about the Communist menace, confused the South Africans. South African frustration was typified in the cartoon in a Johannesburg Afrikaans newspaper that showed Carter gesturing to a lineup of his aides and saying: "This is what my liberal policy towards South Africa looks like: Walter has one, Hodding another, the Pentagon has one, Vance has one, and Andy has quite a few!"

A final source of confusion—and one present under all administrations—is that the United States always speaks in many voices besides those of the government. Among the most important of the unofficial voices, at least to South Africans, are those of the American business community. Vorster went almost directly from his meeting with Mondale in Vienna to address the Young Presidents' Organization, an international but largely American business group, which gave the South African prime minister a standing ovation. A month after the October 19 arrests the U.S. Chamber of Commerce opened a branch in Johannesburg. The South Africa Broadcasting Company took particular note of the opening speech of the head of the chamber's international division, in which he asserted that "Washington could not ignore the stake of American business in, or its long historical association with, the Republic" and declared that "commerce could disagree with the wishes of politicians and trade with whomsoever it chose."

Visiting American politicians can also add to the confusion of voices. Some do so inadvertently, as when Representative James Wright of Texas visited SASOL and, meaning to praise the technological prowess demonstrated there, found himself quoted in the local press as saying that "South Africa has provided the leadership and inspiration which we in America will follow." Others are less misunderstood. Barry Goldwater told a South African audience that he was "ashamed" of U.S. policy on South Africa and Rhodesia. If South Africans claim confusion over American policy, some of the reason is inherent in the way the United States regularly conducts its public business.

In the military field, besides the largely symbolic withdrawal of the naval attaché in Cape Town, the Carter administration moved by executive order to end the gray-area sales permitted during the Nixon and Ford administrations. It also sought to investigate more vigorously the transfers of American-made equipment to Rhodesia via South Africa. U.S. representatives at the United Nations helped shape the Security Council's mandatory arms embargo voted on November 4, 1977, and the executive order from the Department of Commerce on February 16, 1978, implementing the embargo was in some respects more restrictive than the Security Council's provisions. Still, as critics have charged, the embargo has never been totally effective, and on occasion some American corporations and their overseas affiliates have been among those evading restrictions. Most notable was the illicit export by the Space Research Corporation in 1977 and 1978 of substantial supplies of advanced-design 155-millimeter artillery shells whose range outmatched the Soviet-made artillery that had earlier harassed the South African troops in Angola. American officials have said privately that enforcement resources are so limited and jurisdiction is so divided among government departments that it is impossible to make embargoes airtight. By mid-1980 the State Department had taken steps internally to strengthen enforcement, and the Space Research Corporation's president had been convicted and his organization sent into bankruptcy.

Relations involving nuclear energy posed a particularly difficult set of problems for the Carter administration. A sense of the dilemma and the consequent policy decisions can be derived from Brzezinski's reply to a Black Caucus suggestion that the United States end all forms of nuclear cooperation with South Africa:

> The question of the U.S.-South African nuclear relationship is an extremely difficult one. It is our judgment that a complete break now would put South Africa on an irrevocable "do-it-alone" path, which would compound the already serious problem of nuclear proliferation. The U.S. Government has for the past two years withheld export licenses for shipment of highly enriched uranium to South Africa, and to date we have not approved shipments of low enriched uranium for use in the power plants now under construction, even though both varieties of fuel are subject to full international safeguards. We will not permit shipments of any nuclear material or technology until we have clear assurances from the South African Government that it will adhere to the NPT [nonproliferation treaty] and submit its nuclear facilities to effective safeguards.

The United States was caught in a clear dilemma: To advance its African policies and to put pressure on South Africa, it should cease all cooperation; to restrain the spread of nuclear weapons, it should increase cooperation. Different parts of the American government gave different priority to these two goals, and policy tended to straddle the issues. South Africa meanwhile did nothing to relieve the dilemma. It had stated that it had no intentions of developing nuclear weapons but had not signed the nonproliferation treaty. While no one doubts its ability to develop and deploy simple nuclear weapons, experts disagree as to whether or not it actually conducted an atomic test in September 1979. As the administration of President Ronald Reagan took office in 1981, the issue remained undecided, and so did the extent of American nuclear cooperation with South Africa.

Although the tone and urgency of the Carter administration's policy toward South Africa in economic matters differed from that of its predecessors, in substance policy was essentially an extension of that followed by previous administrations. From the beginning, administration officials gave strong support to the Sullivan Principles and in public and private statements urged American businesses in South Africa to adopt them as their own and to accept effective monitoring and reporting procedures. In the fullest public statement of U.S. economic policy, Assistant Secretary Moose observed that the Sullivan initiative "springs from the private corporate world and that it brings together American companies voluntarily to pursue a common objective," and thus may be expected to survive a change in administrations. Moose and other administration officials quietly encouraged private stockholder pressures on corporations and, in contrast to preceding administrations, neither discouraged nor disparaged private actions to reduce investments in South Africa. They, in short, hewed somewhat more closely than their predecessors to an evenhanded interpretation of "neither encouraging nor discouraging investment."

Although under Carter there were occasional hints that harsher action might have to be contemplated, with great consistency the administration emphasized the positive side of economic relations and enlightened capitalism as a positive force for change within South African society. Andrew Young, drawing on what he saw as the positive effects on black civil rights of industrialization in Atlanta and the rest of the American South, endorsed the "Oppenheimer thesis," the argument advanced by Harry Oppenheimer of Anglo-American Corporation, among others, that economic gains for South African blacks will ultimately produce social and political progress as well. Young and other Carter administration representatives also endorsed the efforts of the South African Urban Foundation to extend a Sullivan-like code to South African-controlled firms, and in a speech to the Johannesburg Chamber of Commerce in August 1978, Ambassador William Edmondson encouraged the South African business leaders to "express their concerns about political policies that they see as incompatible with a stable future and with South Africa's image in the rest of the world."

The avoidance of the punitive use of economic relationships was most apparent in 1978 when, following the support for a mandatory arms embargo against South Africa, the United States joined Britain and France in vetoing a motion to impose general economic sanctions. As Zbigniew Brzezinski told the Black Caucus members, "We are opposed to the use of mandatory trade embargoes as a political instrument except in the most exceptional cases. It is important, moreover, that we retain flexibility for the future, should developments in South Africa warrant further U.S. or international response."

SEEKING A SOLUTION IN NAMIBIA

The Carter administration began efforts to find solutions to the Rhodesian and Namibian issues immediately on assuming office. It did not have the time to carefully stage its initiatives. By January 1977 John Vorster's government was proceeding in Namibia to implement what would amount to an internal settlement based on ethnically divided representation that would give effective control to whites and black minority groups dependent on whites. It would put at a severe disadvantage the Ovambo, who constitute about half the population and provide the principal ethnic base for the South-West African People's Organization (SWAPO) insurgent movement.

Such a settlement would fly directly in the face of Security Council Resolution 385, adopted unanimously a year earlier, which called for "free elections under the supervision and control of the United Nations . . . for the whole of Namibia as one political entity." The black African states, thoroughly frustrated that their long efforts to make South Africa respect the United Nations' writ in Namibia had come to naught, let it be known that they were preparing in the Security Council to push for mandatory sanctions on the basis of South Africa's clear defiance of Resolution 385. Although the Western nations could have vetoed such a motion once again, it would have been particularly embarrassing for the United States, whose new permanent representative would, by the luck of rotation, have been in the chair. Furthermore, a veto would have undone any attempt to generate the goodwill among the African states necessary for the success of the Rhodesian negotiations.

The American response, following intensive discussions with Western and African states, was to organize an initiative of the five Western members of the Security Council—the United States, Britain, France, West Germany, and Canada—to try to find a solution in full accordance with Resolution 385. In large part because of the personal diplomacy of Andrew Young, the African states gave a tacit—if still suspicious—go-ahead to the Western Contact Group.

Hewing closely to the wording of Resolution 385, the Contact Group concentrated on procedures for setting up elections under UN supervision and insisted that it favored no particular Namibian faction. By April 1977 the Contact Group, led by Ambassador McHenry of the United States, had completed consultations in New York and held extended consultations in Pretoria. These succeeded at least to the extent of getting the South African government to quietly shelve its plan for an interim government. A year later the Contact Group was able to present to both sides a plan for implementing Resolution 385 that received their "provisional acceptance" and whose key element was adopted by the Security Council on July 27, 1978. (The importance of the Security Council vote lay in the fact that this was the Soviet Union's chance to block the Western initiative by a veto. When the time came, the Soviet representative yielded to the pressures of the Frontline States and abstained.)

But when UN Secretary General Kurt Waldheim sought to proceed on the basis of the new plan, the South African government balked. It revived as an objection the 1973 General Assembly resolution, voted through by the African states, declaring SWAPO to be the "sole authentic representative of the people of Namibia" and providing modest support for SWAPO's representation in New York. South Africa took the resolution as a sign that the United Nations was bent on imposing a SWAPO government and that no negotiations satisfactory to Pretoria were possible within the UN framework. Pretoria assumed this stance even though the Western Contact Group made clear that its effort was under the aegis not of the General Assembly but of the Security Council, which had not given SWAPO any particular status, and that it was thus starting from a neutral stance.

The history of the Namibia negotiations is inordinately complicated and will not be detailed here. Donald McHenry, who succeeded Andrew Young as the U.S. ambassador to the United Nations, has said of the process:

> It could not have been undertaken without modern communications. Five nations have operated as one negotiating team. . . . Each step has required careful coordination among our missions in New York, our capitals, our embassies in the Frontline states and Nigeria, and our embassies in South Africa.

The African states, Angola in particular, played crucial roles in working out arrangements on the ground and in helping SWAPO get itself organized for the difficult negotiations. All the Western governments involved deployed very substantial diplomatic resources, including considerable amounts of their foreign ministers' time.

As of early 1981, the Namibian initiative had not succeeded. In 1980, both South Africa and SWAPO appeared to be pursuing two-track strategies, negotiating but drawing out the negotiations while they attempted to maneuver in search of more favorable outcomes. For South Africa the second track meant punitive raids almost at will into Angola and across the Caprivi Strip into Zambia, together with establishing new political structures inside Namibia that could be used for an internal settlement. SWAPO's second track was primarily diplomatic—appeals to the African states to stick by it and, preferably, help it obtain de facto the status voted as "sole authentic representative." This was not as weak a position as it may seem, since no solution premised on bypassing SWAPO completely has a chance of receiving either international recognition or widespread acceptance within Namibia.

As 1981 began, SWAPO reiterated its acceptance of the arrangements worked out by the Contact Group and the UN Secretariat. In January, however, face-to-face negotiations in Geneva involving South Africa, the internal Namibian parties, and SWAPO broke off with no progress. The purpose of the talks was to draw up a timetable for a cease-fire as a preliminary to elections held under UN supervision. Sam Nujoma, the head of SWAPO, quickly announced that he was ready to sign a cease-fire agreement. South Africa refused, asserting that such action would be "premature." So in the early months of 1981 South Africa was playing for time on the Namibian issue.

SOUTH AFRICANS TALKING

A Lawyer

In 1980, one of several groups sent to the operational zone in northern Namibia as guests of the government consisted of professional women from various parts of South Africa. Among them was a lawyer of British descent, born and raised in Namibia.

Our trip was fascinating and I learned a great deal about what's going on there, but I'm afraid I'm a bit out of touch with the situation as a whole. When I lived there, I was involved politically. One of my father's friends was Chief Clemens Kapuuo, the head of a coalition of moderate whites and blacks [known as the Democratic Turnhalle Alliance]. When I left Namibia, he felt I was running from the cause. But I explained that I had to leave for professional reasons; I felt isolated there, but I still believed strongly in what he was trying to accomplish. Unfortunately, two teenagers and my practice don't leave much time for work on other things I consider important—the Institute of Race Relations, for one.

At the moment, I've taken on some work through the Lawyers for Human Rights. We have several cases dealing with Indians and Coloureds who were occupying so-called white residential areas. They've been called to court under the Group Areas Act. That sort of policy on the part of the government is difficult to defend; but it's law, it's on the statute books, so my clients have to appear in court.

I think apartheid has worked. There isn't really a national black feeling here; it's been systematically eroded. Perhaps the government's plan for their confederation of states will work, given enough time. It may work on an economic basis. And I'm afraid I haven't seen the rest of Africa working particularly well on that score. But I don't know whether blacks are still in an accommodating mood. Young people are very impatient. They haven't got time. That's why, in the long run, I am less optimistic.

There's so little communication between blacks and whites. You pride yourself on being a liberal but then you can count on one hand how many blacks you communicate with. I know a lot of blacks, but what do I do about it? I studied with blacks in Namibia and I lived with them. My father's closest friends were black leaders, often guests in our house. But here there's virtually no contact, and we go and break off what few contacts we do have. We isolate these people, and I think it's absolutely crazy.

I find not having blacks in the President's Council unacceptable. You can't have a workable constitutional solution with three-quarters of the population not being represented. That's crazy. As long as you've got these huge urban complexes like Soweto, with a middle-class elite, an educated elite—and some of the people I've met there are superb even though I don't have much social contact with them—it's absurd to exclude these people from any kind of constitutional solution.

Furthermore, I felt absolute horror at the banning of the two black newspapers [The *Post* and the *Sunday Post*]. The government is mad! It is crazy, so much so that for the first time the Afrikaans press has come out vociferously against it. You don't get rid of the opposition by stifling it. It's still there. I would have thought it far safer to hear these people, to listen to what they have to say.

So I vote for the Progressive Federal party, though I've never really been a card-carrying member of any party. I would classify myself as a liberal, although in South Africa today even the blacks don't like white liberals. I think one has to be very pragmatic with the changing situation. Recently I've been feeling more and more that while I know that there are thousands of things absolutely wrong with the laws of this country and the situation in this country, there are also a lot of things wrong with just going overboard the other way. You become schizoid in South Africa. There's an element of overkill on both sides. But I'm afraid things are never going to be such that you can get out of that overkill situation. I think that time is against us; I think the mood is against us.

I have two daughters. The army hasn't called up girls yet but if they were sons and they had to go to Namibia, I wouldn't be very happy about it. First of all, I know there's a lot of soul-searching going on in South Africa, among mothers in particular: why their sons are fighting virtually on foreign soil, why they are dying there. And I think a lot more are dying or being hurt than we're being told about. The other thing is, I think you've got to make up your mind what you are fighting for. While I'm totally against guerrilla activities and terrorism and sabotage, I don't know if these people have any alternative. Although that doesn't mean to say you've got to sit back and take it, you've got to do something about it.

The government is trying very hard to mount a big civil action campaign to educate the people. It has built an enormous number of schools and sent up a tremendous amount of equipment to Namibia. Its financial commitment up there must be colossal. When I was up there last September, I found the whole thing very exciting. You can't help being impressed by what they are doing; the standards of the thing are exceptionally high and there's a huge commitment to the people up there. The bulk of South Africans who have gone up are young Afrikaner fellows who are teaching these people agriculture, teaching the children in school—they're committed! I know of somebody's son who is a music teacher, and the army sent up his piano to Ovamboland so that he could teach them music. Vast amounts of money are being spent to educate them. But I have to ask myself why they aren't spending that kind of money in South Africa, in Soweto.

I see that for the government it's a vastly complex problem. We all tend to be overly simplistic. There have been changes, and they are trying to follow a course of sorts. I think there would be a tremendous groundswell of support if Botha really moved. I think he could survive—probably—without the right wing. I feel sorry for the Nationalist Afrikaner, I honestly do. I think he's in a terrible dilemma, and the fact that I'm in the middle of it, between the two rival nationalisms, as an English-speaking white, is tough. But I really feel for him. I can see he's got an identity crisis, and he wants to preserve his culture and his power. He's got an enormous mass against him, and if he can bring out the different identities and different cultures and thereby not have a single mass against him, perhaps the whole thing will work. Perhaps he can save himself that way.

Could somebody else do a better job than the Nationalist government? I don't know. I don't know if the Progs would do any better. I heartily endorse their call for an all-race convention to try to work out this country's future. But I don't know whether there's any time left for them. I don't think that there will ever be another white government of South Africa that is not Nationalist.

A Civil Servant

Following the National party victory in 1948, the Nationalists moved to Afrikanerize the civil service and turned it into the largest employer in South Africa. Today more than 60 percent of the country's civil servants are Afrikaners.

He is a senior official on one of the Black Administration Boards that oversee black affairs in "white" South Africa. Descended from the first Dutch who arrived at the Cape in 1652, he is married and has four grown children. He and his wife are active members of the Dutch Reformed church and of various Afrikaans and church societies. He is also a member of the Broederbond, the influential Afrikaner secret society.

As a small boy, I grew up among the Tswanas on a farm in the western Transvaal, which now forms part of the Bophuthatswana state. We played traditional games, such as clay stick and knucklebones, and made clay oxen. And we hunted and roasted birds together. I could speak the language fluently and still use it today, though I am less fluent.

President Mangope was then a teacher not far from

my father's farm. He often visited us and had coffee on the *stoep* [veranda]. My grandfather and Mangope's grandfather also visited each other decades ago in Mangope's village. There they spoke as equals to each other. I can show you many letters between Chief Lennox Sebe of Ciskei and myself. So you see, these people trust me. They believe in me and speak the same language.

I fully understand the black man, his thinking and his aspirations. I am convinced that we have a beautiful future, on the condition that the majority of blacks and whites keep cool heads. And I have no problems in working every day with blacks. It's a challenge for me. With my black leaders in the community, there are no differences or problems. From the beginning, we have worked together amicably. For practical reasons I do not meet them socially at home. You see, I'm out almost every night; weekends I keep for my family, and I don't entertain much.

We deal with a number of black community councils representing black towns. Our task is to act as a link between the various councils and the administration. We believe in consultation not domination. We attend their meetings, but only at their request, of course. They have little experience in the running of council administration. They must still be taken by the hand. It is true that we also administer the influx control and pass laws, but with great fairness and care. An uncontrolled influx will cause chaos in housing and employment. After all, it is in the interests of the blacks themselves. We protect those working in the white areas from being swamped by others from the outside.

The urban Bantu Administration Boards will eventually change to Development Boards, meaning that these boards will be better able to assist with the developing and funding of black towns. I must admit that legally these community councils still have not got the same full powers as those of the white municipalities, but we do not believe in dictating to them. We discuss everything with them first, although we have the power to make decisions on our own. For instance, matters such as housing allocation are dealt with in conjunction with the black councils, so they have got a measure of control over them. I think that is the reason why our area had comparatively little trouble from school boycotts in 1976. There was only about a week of unrest. After we discussed the issue with the community leaders, it came to an end.

I believe in Dr. [Hendrik] Verwoerd's policy of strong development of the homelands, but I think there should be a change in emphasis. I have always advocated joint economic growth points between black and white areas, stretching from Rustenburg in the western Transvaal to the Tugela valley in Natal. On the northern side of this line would be the political areas of the blacks, but they would be working in a joint development area and earning money for their own countries.

Eighty percent of the income tax of Bophuthatswana comes from the districts north of Pretoria and those bordering on Pretoria, and the other twenty percent comes from that state. The money earned by blacks from Bophuthatswana working in and outside Pretoria enables them to bring money back into their homeland. Money creates money. I disagreed with Dr. Verwoerd not allowing private initiative to assist in homeland development. For example, he prevented Dr. Rupert from establishing his tobacco factory in Umtata [the capital of the Transkei]. It was then built in the Paarl in the western Cape province. All those Xhosas are now working in the Paarl. They could all have lived and worked in Umtata, which would have helped in the development of the Transkei. I am still trying to encourage this development, but the private businessman is not very interested. This is why I encourage the idea of a growth axis with economic growth points where the black man can come across the border from his area and the white man can come from his side and both will work together.

What I have been spelling out is in full accordance with government policy and is one of the twelve points of the prime minister's plan. There is no deviation from government policy.

In areas for which we are responsible, we have never forced ethnicity down somebody's throat. In our area, though, most of the community councils have been established along ethnic lines. There are no geographic voting areas, but each ethnic group votes for his own representatives. Political efforts from outside to infiltrate my black urban areas have failed because of this *volksbande* [strong ethnic ties] among the blacks themselves—they resist such pressure.

I think the Verwoerd policy over the last twenty years has been further developed, not diluted. Of course, I agree that if the whites could not maintain their physical majority in a given white area the idea of separate development could not be morally justified. But the black majority is not a real problem because, in fact, you do have a number of separate nations, each with a specific ethnic population, and these must be developed further for the good of all.

I can assure you that among those community councils composed of ethnically related members, one finds a truly beautiful restfulness in the town as a whole. An ethnic representative grows into a cultural "father." Others come to him with their problems. And inside the community councils, where elected leaders of the various nations work together, there are no fights or clashes between the various nations. There is no dilution of government policy with regard to the question of national ties. The only exception might be Soweto, and even there the ties are much stronger than one might believe. And anyway, I think it would be a mistake to say that if one loses ties with his tribe he no longer has national ties. This would cause much widespread confusion.

These ties are undeniably strong among blacks of all classes. I recently had a long discussion with an educated black, a Ph.D. in philosophy. I asked him whether he wanted to live in a white residential area. The man, currently earning a very good salary, said, "No, sir. It would mean that I had turned my back on my people. My people would no longer accept me. I can perhaps discuss political or educational matters on an equal basis with whites and feel at home, but I think my children must first prove themselves before they move into the white camp. Such a move would be unfair to them." You see, this man fears the rejection of his own people and, more important, he wants to bring them up in their own black cocoon before they're forced to confront broader national influences.

In my position, I meet many whites who are dissatisfied with the government's rapid moving away from discrimination. Resistance is building up; I am concerned. It should be remembered that Dr. Koornhof did not specifically say that he wanted to abolish the discrimination affecting the urban blacks. Rather, he emphasized the positive development of that which the blacks had in their towns. He called it "a better way of life," but with blacks still remaining separate, linked to their homelands.

And personally, I do not feel that all facilities should be open to all races. I truly believe that for the white man there should also be a place of withdrawal where he can be on his own. I can honestly say that in my daily contact with blacks I have come to realize that they do not want whites with them. They too want a place where they can withdraw to. I am talking of the large mass and not of a few individuals. These few can be accommodated in specially reserved places. Blacks today are financially well off and can afford the prices of top restaurants. But whites should have the right to reserve certain areas for themselves where they can be at home with their friends.

I find no fault with the Twelve Point Plan of the prime minister. That is the basis for the future, although it should be given much more contents and detail. If there was not such a basis, I might have been unhappy. In other words, it is important to spell out where the policy of separate nationhoods is going because, of course, no Zulu or Xhosa or Afrikaner or Englishman would submit to rule by any other single nation. The future government as I see it is a system whereby the prime ministers from the various states consult at the top. That means that the white state or white government will be in a minority but with a guaranteed retention of all present rights—in other words, a totally solid future.

But a majority government in one geographical country on a one man, one vote basis could only come after my lifetime. I think there are too many blacks who are illiterate and who are isolated in their own black states. These people are uninformed and too easily influenced by leftist Communist ideologies. This will lead to the same situation as that now found in Rhodesia and South-West Africa. But should there be an historical freak and we end up with a majority rule as did Rhodesia, I would be forced to live with it. Where else could I go? My life and the lives of my descendants are irrevocably linked to South Africa.

I ask myself, in view of recent oil sanction moves, what the Western nations hope to achieve if there is a total boycott. Because whites will not be the only ones hurt. I then have to ask myself to what extent the West is still important for me as a white. I think we must accept the West as an historical fact. After all, we are its descendants. But that is merely historical. And while we still have trade links with the West, I believe we have reached a stage in the world market where we can compete with other countries. We have good trade relations with Japan, for instance; Japan is not part of the West. If only we can realize that we are a strategic point on the world map for the anti-Communist camp, I think we can then regard ourselves as an important part of the West.

I am optimistic about the future. I have had many discussions with leaders of black states and have many friends among them. We all believe that the big danger will be the ultras to the left and right. If they can be handled there will be a beautiful future, provided a large number of heads remain cool among blacks and whites. Then there should be no problems.

A Homeland Teacher

The Ciskei, scattered in many pieces in the eastern Cape, was set aside by the South African government for members of its Xhosa-speaking population. It is the home of the University of Fort Hare, whose graduates include Zimbabwe's president, Robert Mugabe, and Chief Gatsha Buthelezi. There, too, marked by a stone bearing the slogan: One Azania, One Nation, lies the grave of Stephen Biko.

A woman from the Ciskei has missed her bus and stands with a heavy parcel, hoping for a lift to Port Elizabeth. An assistant teacher at a lower primary school that serves a rural community, she lives at the school during the week, returning home to her mother on weekends. She can't afford to travel home each evening, she explains to a white woman who has offered her a ride.

My father was a laborer for many years; he died in 1969. We didn't ask for a pension, so we didn't get one. My mother has no pension, so I must give her money and pay for her rent. And I pay for the family food and support my daughter since my husband left us.

It is difficult teaching here. There are so many poor children. They are clever, but they are hungry, and a child can't learn if the stomach is empty. I ask the children who have money to pay two cents and then we buy bread, which we share. There are some families where the parents have gone away and left the children alone in the house. Some of the fathers have gone to work on farms, and the mothers look for work in East London, but they don't come back and they don't send money. There is one family of five—very clever children—where there are no parents. We teachers gave ten rand each to help them, and the principal said she would pay for the eldest one to go to boarding school. The vice-principal buys shoes for the two other children.

My pay is 256 rand a month, but 42 rand is taken off in deductions. My pension is a Ciskei government pension, but if I die, my mother and child will get nothing. If I live until I stop working, I will get the money; but they will get nothing if I die first. We all know this because we know of many families who have asked and asked for the pension money, but it never comes. We have complained through the Teachers' Association, but nothing happens. Last year we were suppose to get an increase in October, but it never came. Even this year it never came. Now they have revised the scales again and we are getting that increase, but we never got those others—only the principals and vice-principals did.

The thing is all the money you have to pay. They are now collecting two rand from every female and three rand from every male for the new Ciskei stadium. You have to pay. If you refuse you lose your job. Even the people who aren't working have to pay. I have to give my mother two rand so that she can pay. I told her to tell them that she is sick and not working and has no pension, but she says she must pay because she wants a pension. She also says they will take the house away if she does not pay.

When Chief Minister Sebe goes away we have to pay one rand for his journey, and when he comes back we have to pay fifty cents for his reception at Zwelitsha. Even pensioners have to pay because otherwise they take the pensions away. My mother has joined a cell of Chief Sebe's party. I asked her why she did that and she says it is because she wants a pension and won't be able to get it otherwise.

The Ciskei voted for independence [in December 1980] but Chief Sebe must not go for independence. We blacks cannot do things properly. It's better to be under the whites because you know where you are. We blacks are lazy. Take a look at this land. If whites owned it, it would be ploughed and things would be growing. No, it's not because there is no water—all this irrigation makes no difference. I know black people who have bought the farms where whites used to be. There is irrigation there, but they don't use the land. They are friends of the government, and they only bought the land because they wanted to live in a beautiful farmhouse. They work somewhere else. I think, though, that equality is a good thing. We should share everything in this country. That would be better than independence because blacks can't manage a country like whites can. Everywhere I have heard of, blacks don't do things properly, like in Swaziland.

["What about Zimbabwe?" she is asked.]

Zimbabwe?

["Rhodesia. What about Mugabe?"]

Oh, Rhodesia. The man is just beginning and you can't tell. You see, I am a peasant, and I will always be a peasant because I am not related to any of the big men who are the government. You can never stop being a peasant if you are in a black country. I know many people who have been teaching for many years—fifteen years and more—who are still assistant teachers like me. We are peasants and we can never be anything else. With a white government you get a better chance, because you get promotions if you work hard and not because of your relations.

Even the police now don't keep the law in the Ciskei like they should. Law is supposed to be there so we can live quietly and not be afraid. We had a burglar in our house. He locked himself in our outdoor toilet. I asked him nicely to come out, so he ran into the house with an ax and said he would chop us all up—my mother and the neighbors who were in the house. I ran to the police, but they told me I was drunk and should not come complaining about my boyfriend. They finally came and got the burglar, but he came back the next day to pick up his *dompas* [passbook], which he had left in the toilet. He laughed at us and told us not to think we could do anything, because he was a friend of the policemen.

When there's anything I have to go to the police for, I go to the white police in town because it is much better. They will listen to a person.

A Union Leader

*His father, a black South African, was a migrant laborer,
killed in an explosion in a dynamite factory the day after
the boy was born. The father was not insured, and the
family received no industrial compensation. As soon as the
boy was old enough, he left the Transkei to find a job.*

When I went to Johannesburg, I was not yet circumcised. I was still a boy. I had worked in Umtata selling
used mealie [maize] sacks to miners, who used them to
make jackets. And I had worked underground in the
Transvaal mines, driving a hauling engine. I lasted about
six weeks, until I ran away and came to Egoli [the golden
city, Johannesburg] to look for a better job. The first thing
I did here was to register at the Labor Bureau. My reference book number was 426515266. I worked as a newsboy and then as a clerk in the Johannesburg City Council.
Then I made an application to the Central News Agency,
where they needed boss-boys to check and count the newspapers that the vendors took out. My number was three—
I was BB3—and in my time off I learned how to drive at
the Eazy Driving School. It was then that I went home to
Transkei for my tribal circumcision. It was only then that
I became a man.

When I came back I started to look for a better job.
The National Cold Storage Company took me on part-time as a driver. All the full-time drivers were whites,
and we were allowed to do the job only if a white driver
was not available. During that period I studied my matric
at Union College by correspondence. I wanted to earn
more money, so I applied for a city council bus-driving
job. The council had decided that black drivers could drive
black buses, but we were not paid the same rate as the
white drivers. We were paid twelve rand a week. I understood there was a union, but we were not allowed to join
it. So we went on without a union. Still, we were trying
to investigate how a union works when I became involved
in SACTU—the South African Congress of Trade Unions.

I resigned from the city council and started to work
as a long-distance truck driver. It was then that I became
aware what people were being paid for driving these long

distances, sleeping out in the *veld* and driving for a week and arriving back in Johannesburg with sore backs and aching kidneys. We were getting twenty-five rand to drive from Johannesburg to Cape Town—a thousand miles. There were no allowances for staying on the road, there was nowhere to stay—we slept underneath our trucks.

Today I am heading this Black Municipality Workers Union with the experience I got from those earlier days. It all started in 1979, when we were approached by the city council to join their union, called the Union of Johannesburg Municipal Workers. It was a black union, but the organizers were white. We said, "No, we cannot join a union organized by our employer. You can help us, but you cannot form a union for us or tell us that we must join a certain union which has an executive already." When we said we were going to form our own union, they tried to tell us not to. They told us we could only organize transport workers. They said they would not provide a free hall where we could have a meeting, as they did for the union they were backing. So we collected money out of our own pockets to pay for the hall—even people who were not yet members contributed.

Of course, we are still struggling. Our organizers are not officially allowed to enter the Johannesburg compounds where our members live. But the men who work at the compound gates are sympathetic to us and they do not bar us from entering. We think we have about 12,500 members. But we're not sure because they don't all carry our cards. Some of them cannot carry cards because they might lose their jobs. They are being victimized every week—and not just for racial reasons. There are people in the city council who are sympathetic to us, people in the opposition. I communicate with some officials on a personal basis, but they don't want it to be known. They, too, are afraid of losing their jobs.

In July 1980 some 10,000 black municipal workers went on strike for a minimum wage of sixty rand a week and recognition of the new union, which claimed to have the support of 80 percent of the workers. City engineering and electrical workers, gas, transport, and maintenance workers, traffic policemen, parks services, messengers, sewage workers, garbage collectors, and cleaning services were affected. It took the council a week to break the strike.

During the strike, our lawyer told us we had no case because the people who were striking worked in essential services and, according to the law, essential services are beyond a strike. So I tried to negotiate with the city council. I wanted to be allowed to address the strikers so we could arrange to go back to work. But first the workers needed some assurances from the city council. The council's reply was that we could not negotiate with them because we were illegal and not registered. Now, the council had been talking with the other union, which was also not properly registered and had only forty paid-up members. We asked for the same status: We would talk with the city council if they recognized our members as their employees and recognized themselves as our employers. Their answer: No way. Again I sought legal advice, and was told to tell the men to go back to work. Meanwhile, I heard that some of the strikers had been fired and that the city council was organizing buses to take them back to their homelands.

I went to the high court to get an injunction against the city council to prevent them from busing the strikers home. And right there in the courthouse three gentlemen came up to me and said, "Let's go." My advocate asked them what they were doing. They said they were arresting me. He asked under what law. They said, "Section 15." He wanted to know section 15 of what act. They said, "Under the usual act." Even the judge came out and wanted to intervene. They said, "No, we have already arrested him." [He was charged and later acquitted.]

What our union needs is recognition. Not recognition by the government, but recognition between employers and employees. Why not by the government? Because most of the members of our union are not citizens of South Africa. The South African government says they belong to the governments of the homelands and, according to the law, we should register our union with ten different homeland governments: the Ndebele government, the Transkei government, the Ciskei government, and so on. But before we register our union, we want to know which government recognizes these people.

Right now, no one would employ me. They wouldn't employ a person who asks as much as I'm asking. They forget the duties that us drivers are responsible for. They think to pay a man for this responsibility is to throw the money away. Even a humble sweeper has a responsibility to keep a place clean, to prevent disease. Workers handle chemicals, poisons. They need protection, not only insurance but also decent wages. My aim is to get a man a good wage for his work before he dies—as well as a pension for his family after he dies.

People talk about black and white consciousness. But it's not black consciousness, it's hatred. It's not white consciousness, it's hatred. Someone has said, "To hell with the other person." What we need are ways and means of living together. We must recognize ourselves as humans because of our two feet, two hands, one head, and we must recognize that we are equal.

These are petty things we are doing in South Africa when we say blacks must live here and whites must live there, blacks must live one way and whites another. Do you know we do not even drink the same water? I know because I worked in the water services. They have water for whites and water for blacks. If the government wanted to, it could kill us with the water it gives us.

What if America said the South African government must change? What if the United States threatened to use force? I'm afraid it would be like rushing at a child who is sitting next to an open window. The child might get a shock and fall out. The person must gently tell the child to move away from the window. You see, South Africa has reached a point of hatred of which we are very afraid.

A Student

She is a young woman of Zulu background, still wearing her light-brown school uniform and still talking of favorite memories from her student days: the basketball games played in the dust of the schoolyard and singing in the choir. In 1976 she was one of the children who defied their parents' wishes and went out to join the protests against the use of Afrikaans as the medium of instruction in schools. She was fifteen when the Orlando march began in June of 1976, when the first shots were fired and the first schoolchild fell.

We were at a good school, a good high school. We liked

our teachers and we studied hard. But when the word went out, we knew we had to join the rest. We were not sure of what the ideals were, except that we were joining in a demonstration against discrimination. I used to say to my mother and father, "Do you know what discrimination means? Do you know what it does to people? It kills them very slowly." They would tell me to hush, and look at me as though I was saying something that was very bad, very evil. "You are getting a good education," they would say. "Why do you want to destroy what we have done for you?" I could not give them an answer.

My parents were worried and afraid. They didn't want me to go with the crowds, because they said they didn't want me to die. They tried to stop me, but each time I slipped out. I would climb the fence at the back of our house.

The schools were closed in 1976 after the June riots. They opened in 1977 but closed again after more riots. I was involved in the crowds at that time. I got the tear gas many times. Even now my chest bothers me from it. Some of my friends were hurt and some died. One of my girlfriends was killed. There is a boy who lives next door to us now who was blinded. He stays at home, and there is no one to teach him.

Altogether I missed about a year of school. The schools were opened again in 1978, but it was a struggle to get in and we waited for weeks to get registered. We were taught in English and Zulu, and I took Afrikaans as a separate subject. I was never taught in Afrikaans. They tried to get us to study in Afrikaans before the riots but after the riots they stopped trying.

I was sad that I did not qualify for the university. I only got a senior school-leaving certificate. I was tested in six subjects but failed biology and English. To be able to apply for the university, I'd have to write these subjects again. But I can't because I don't have the money. Even if I had my matric, I couldn't get into the university without a scholarship. It would cost two thousand or three thousand rand—too much. I have applied for training in nursing at a hospital, near Krugersdorp. I would like to get a job as a nurse because I can't study at school anymore.

Only two people in my family went to school, and since I've left there is only one. The others are not working. They can't get jobs. We are Zulus from the Orange Free State. My father was an electrician, but now he is sick and not working. One of my brothers is in jail. We don't know why he is there. All they will tell us is that he was not taken by the security police. We haven't been able to find out anything.

We pay for the rent with what my mother earns. The rent now for our house is twenty-one rand a month and it will soon go up to twenty-six and then thirty-five rand a month. My mother is working but only at temporary jobs, earning four rand a day. She does washing, ironing, cleaning houses. Then she has to take the train. That is sixty cents a day. When you take that off how much is left? Sometimes she has to borrow from other people to make it through the month, and when she gets the money she repays them. We do not know where we will get the money if they put up our rent to thirty-five rand. If we don't get the money the house will be locked against us and we will be put outside. Then we will have to sleep outside. They are doing it with other people.

Sometimes I go into Johannesburg to see the big city. I look around and I think that things there are for the people who earn more or who are high. And if you come to Soweto you can see that this is low and not very well developed. They say it is being developed and that is why they are increasing the rent, and yet I cannot see it. We have no electricity in our house. We have cold water from a tap outside the house. When we studied at school we stayed at the school at night because it had electricity. Otherwise we studied by candlelight at home. I enjoyed school. I like it. But now it's all finished. I can't go anymore. I am sad about that.

A Sunday in Soweto

St. Paul's Anglican Church is not large. It has a tower but it is really a long shed that holds a congregation of about 350 people. There is a wooden crucifix above the altar and a life-sized Virgin and Child, in painted plaster, in the corner. The altar rail is made of wood and on the altar itself there is a bowl of freshly cut flowers. The black priest wears olive-green vestments that match the altar cloth. His acolytes wear red cassocks beneath crisp white surplices. There is an organ, but it is not played. Kneeling pads, squares of carpet, really, are handed out randomly as the congregation—all black except some foreign visitors—file into the church.

The service is simple, multilingual, and moving. Windows and doors remain open, and small children come in at different times and sit along the chancel rail, facing the congregation. In the two-and-one-half-hour service there are eleven hymns, the number and page being called out in English, Tswana, and Zulu. The church throbs with song, deep resonant voices, and wonderful harmony. At times the congregation sways and claps hands. From the moment they enter the visitors are made welcome. Seats and hymnals are shared and participation is warmly encouraged.

The children, many of whom sing without hymnals, are immaculately dressed. Among them are two albinos, one looking very sad. Most of them, like the adults, are formally attired, although one has on a sweatshirt with the legend: Behind This Shirt Is. . . . Throughout the service a diminutive acolyte swings a smoking censer.

The sermon, in Tswana, is based on the first chapter of John, the meaning of Passover. There is a message for the white government: "We have our leaders, great leaders, among us. In spite of their rivalry and jealousy, they will show how all God's children should live—not by the color of their skin but as human beings." At one stage there is applause.

The climax of the service comes with the entire congregation singing "Nkosi Sikelela I-Afrika" ["God Bless Africa"], the national anthem of several black African states and a hymn closely associated with the banned African National Congress.

After the collection and a special offering for the unemployed, the congregation dissolves into a milling crowd around the foreign visitors, one of whom turns out to be the U.S. assistant secretary of state for Africa. There is much shaking of hands, touching, smiles, and laughter. "Peace be with you," they say. "Welcome. Peace be with you." There is a sense of resolve, well-being, joy, even exultation.

The churchgoers spill out into the sunlight. The smell

of incense drifts after them. Only then is it clear that a generation is missing from the congregation. There are no young people attending service at St. Paul's Anglican Church in Soweto this summer Sunday morning.

Afrikaner at his home, Stellenbosch

Indian spice dealer, Johannesburg

Soweto youths pose in front of "Azania" sign on wall of
community hall

Antiriot policeman, Johannesburg

Bowlers in Cape Town suburbs

*Statue of a nineteenth-century
voortrekker, Church Square,
Pretoria*

*Voortrekker monument outside
Pretoria*

African migrant workers, Vaal Reef gold mine,
near Johannesburg

Kitchen, Soweto home

Antiriot police with demonstrator,
Johannesburg

Beach for whites, East London

Grocery store, Soweto

Guarding the Parliament Building, Pretoria

Umtata, capital of the Transkei

Part III
POLICY

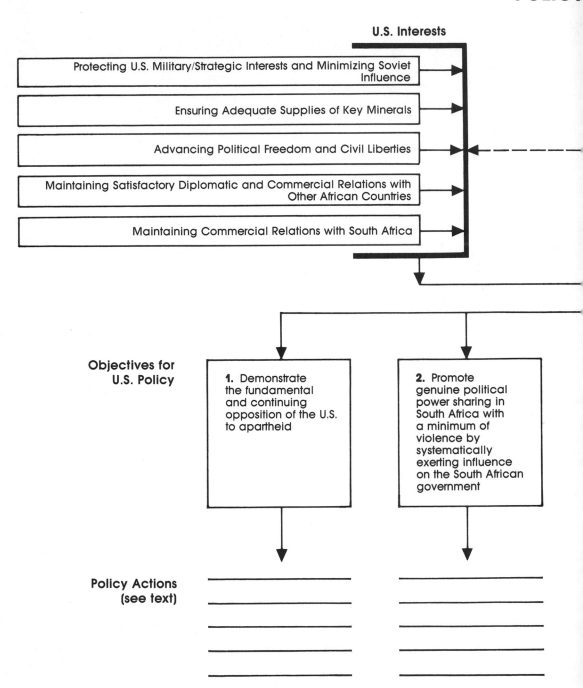

U.S. Interests

Protecting U.S. Military/Strategic Interests and Minimizing Soviet Influence

Ensuring Adequate Supplies of Key Minerals

Advancing Political Freedom and Civil Liberties

Maintaining Satisfactory Diplomatic and Commercial Relations with Other African Countries

Maintaining Commercial Relations with South Africa

Objectives for U.S. Policy

1. Demonstrate the fundamental and continuing opposition of the U.S. to apartheid

2. Promote genuine political power sharing in South Africa with a minimum of violence by systematically exerting influence on the South African government

Policy Actions (see text)

FRAMEWORK

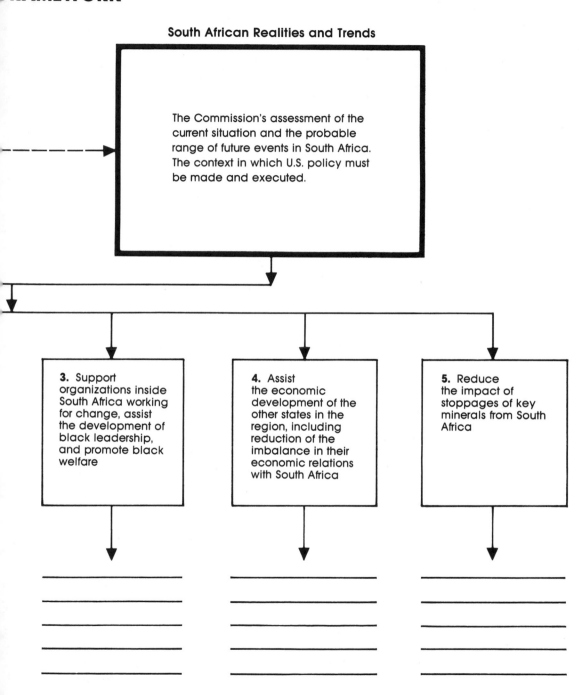

South African Realities and Trends

The Commission's assessment of the current situation and the probable range of future events in South Africa. The context in which U.S. policy must be made and executed.

3. Support organizations inside South Africa working for change, assist the development of black leadership, and promote black welfare

4. Assist the economic development of the other states in the region, including reduction of the imbalance in their economic relations with South Africa

5. Reduce the impact of stoppages of key minerals from South Africa

Chapter 17
U.S. Interests

Although South Africa seems remote to many Americans, what happens in that country inevitably affects the United States. Past U.S. governments have accepted this, analyzed American national interests in South Africa, and tried to advance them. U.S. policy has sought to protect strategic interests, including the Cape sea route and access to important minerals, minimize Soviet influence, promote multiracial and democratic governments in southern Africa, maintain good relations with other African states, and protect U.S. trade and investment. Political instability and armed conflict in the region have been acknowledged as the greatest direct threats to our interests, and U.S. policy has aimed at minimizing those dangers.

Although there is general agreement about the legitimacy of American interests, there is some disagreement over their relative importance and even more about the most effective ways to protect and advance them. These issues have already been touched on briefly in the introduction to this report. We analyze them here in greater detail and in the next two chapters examine their South African and international contexts and the manner in which U.S. interests can best be protected. The interests are not addressed in any deliberate order. All are important and in our judgment together establish a compelling case for a comprehensive and integrated U.S. policy toward South Africa.

Unimpeded use of the Cape sea route, along which much of the West's oil passes, is of great strategic importance to the United States as well as to other Western countries. So is curbing Communist influence in the southern African region. The problem is how best to advance these interests. One group of analysts sees the Cape route as a potential "choke point." They suggest that the Soviet Union could pose a serious threat to the route if it controlled, or had friendly access to, South Africa. A close relationship with the South African government, it is argued, is therefore indispensable to counter the Soviet threat, especially since South Africa has modern ports with sophisticated repair and refueling facilities.

Other analysts argue that if the Soviet Union wished to stop the flow of oil to the West it would do so by "choking it off" closer to home—by blockading the Straits of Hormuz, for example—rather than in remote southern African waters. Moreover, such a provocative action would trigger a major war in which the Soviet Union would be unlikely to deploy major naval forces off South Africa at the expense of more vital positions elsewhere. Blockading the route at the Cape would be difficult, the argument continues. Ships usually take advantage of calmer seas and a shorter passage by traveling close to the Cape, but, if necessary, they could make a much wider sweep through the long stretch of navigable water between the Cape and Antarctica. Therefore, the argument concludes, neither the small South African navy nor its surveillance and logistical facilities are important factors in keeping the Cape route open to the West.

The information we have gathered supports the latter view. In our judgment, the active collaboration of the South African government, whatever its ideological leanings, is *not* an important factor in protecting the Cape sea route. A greater source of danger to U.S. interests is the growth of Soviet influence promoted by political instability and armed conflict in the region. U.S. access to minerals, freedom to trade, and political influence could all be adversely affected by the transformation of South Africa into a close ally or satellite of the Soviet Union.

Political instability and armed conflict in the region open the door to Soviet involvement and penalize the United States. This is especially true because the Soviet Union can plausibly characterize its military backing for black South African liberation movements as support for the cause of racial justice. Direct requests from insurgents for arms would be met by the United States' customary reluctance to support armed attack against an established government with which it has diplomatic relations. The Soviet Union, however, operates under no such constraints. The most effective way for the United States to counter Soviet influence is by encouraging a negotiated resolution to South Africa's problems. The United States has a distinct initial advantage over the Soviet Union in pursuing this track because of its higher political standing with all parties and its greater economic resources.

Maintaining adequate supplies of key minerals exported by South Africa is another U.S. strategic interest. The South African government describes nearly all of its mineral exports as strategically vital to the West. We have concluded that in fact only four groups—chromium and ferrochrome, manganese and ferromanganese, platinum, and vanadium—are critically important. Even for these minerals, uses fall into different categories of importance. Some are vital to military preparedness, others are economically but not strategically significant, and some are merely convenient. The consequences of stoppages would depend on a number of variables: the specific minerals, the

391

length of time involved, the extent of the cutoff, and the steps taken previously by the United States to prepare for this eventuality.

A central question is what the impact on supplies would be if widespread conflict broke out in southern Africa or if a government hostile to the West took power in South Africa. Our judgment (explained more fully in chapter 18) is that stoppages in exports of these minerals, should they occur, are likely to be partial, intermittent, and short term (less than five years) in duration. Medium-term (five-to-ten-year) and long-term (more than ten-year) interruptions appear unlikely.

Another interest grows out of our history, values, and institutions, which place Americans in basic sympathy with people seeking political freedom and civil liberties throughout the world. We struggle to apply these ideals at home, and they are part of the example we seek to provide the rest of the world. Influencing other nations to adopt them, as former secretary of state Cyrus Vance has said, "improves our relations and strengthens our own security, not on the temporary basis of accommodation to a repressive regime but on an enduring basis of shared commitment to democratic values."

The promotion of political freedom is not a new element in American foreign policy. Woodrow Wilson's commitment to self-determination, Franklin Roosevelt's pressures on the Allies to decolonize after World War II, and U.S. participation in framing the United Nations Charter and Declaration of Human Rights are instances in which the United States has formally committed itself to the advancement of political freedom and civil liberties beyond its shores. In 1958, the Eisenhower administration voted for the first of a long series of UN resolutions critical of apartheid. Beginning in 1974, Congress has enacted a substantial body of legislation injecting human rights considerations into economic aid, trade, and military assistance programs. An amendment to the Foreign Assistance Act in 1976, for example, directs that no economic aid be provided "to the government of any country which engages in a consistent pattern of gross violations of internationally recognized human rights, including torture or cruel, inhuman, or degrading treatment or punishment, prolonged detention without charges, or other flagrant denial of the right to life, liberty, and the security of person, unless such assistance will directly benefit the needy people in such country."

Human rights strictures have been applied at various times to the Soviet Union, Uganda, Ethiopia, Brazil, Argentina, Uruguay, Chile, Nicaragua, Guatemala, El Salvador, Cuba, Vietnam, and Cambodia. They have been and are being applied to South Africa, most notably in the form of an embargo on shipments of arms and other goods for the South African police and military. Although the list of target countries is fairly long, it by no means includes all the nations whose commitment to political freedom and civil liberties is dubious: South Korea and the Philippines are missing, for example. Nor have such pressures always been consistently applied. The absence of evenhandedness stirs criticism, and this leads to another fundamental question about the justification for American efforts to promote change in South Africa. In a world where arbitrary rule, political assassinations and kidnappings, the jailing of dissidents, and torture are commonplace, why single out South Africa's apartheid for special attention?

A preliminary response is that in the real world neat "ideological symmetry"—to borrow a phrase used in this context by *New York Times* columnist Anthony Lewis—is seldom possible. A report on the role of human rights in American foreign policy issued in 1979 by the United Nations Association of the United States agrees that selectivity in human rights policy is unavoidable. "The United States should be as consistent and evenhanded as possible in its responses to human rights violations by other governments," said the report, but "complete consistency is neither possible nor always desirable." Inevitably, the emphasis placed on human rights varies from place to place and from time to time. Sometimes we may deplore a situation but lack the leverage to press for change. At other times competing interests, such as military security or the need for an essential commodity, may inhibit our actions. But our inability to deal with every evil on the globe does not mean that we should not act where we have the latitude to do so and where there is a chance that we can make a difference. We are convinced that South Africa qualifies on both counts.

Beyond this, a strong case can be made that South Africa does in fact warrant special attention. Its violations of human rights fall into a category of their own. As Henry Kissinger, then secretary of state, put it in a speech at Lusaka, Zambia, in 1976: "The world community's concern with South Africa is not merely that racial discrimination exists there. What is unique is the extent to which racial discrimination has been institutionalized, enshrined in law, and made all pervasive." The controlling minority group understands and itself enjoys political freedom and many civil liberties. Finally, South Africa clings to its system of institutionalized discrimination even while continuing to profess membership in the community of Westernized "free world" nations. These factors make South Africa a special case for the international community and especially for the United States.

South Africa's racial policies also stir special concern because they could eventually lead to a race war that could have serious ramifications in the United States. Frustration is building among blacks within South Africa. Many have left the country to join the armed liberation movements. If open conflict should break out between white and black in South Africa—and in particular if the Communists should choose to help wage a "war of liberation" against the white regime—the United States would face difficult questions in deciding how to react. Many Americans—black and white—would have intense feelings about events there, and strong, conflicting pressures to support one side or the other would emerge. The resulting debate could quickly develop divisive racial overtones, damaging to race relations in the United States. That possibility gives the United States direct interest in a negotiated resolution of the political struggle in South Africa.

393

Another major interest, linked to events in South Africa, is U.S. relations with other African countries. The United States has $4.5 billion in direct investments in these states and annual trade of $13.7 billion. Nigeria is particularly significant as the United States' second largest foreign oil supplier and a leading African opponent of apartheid. The diplomatic, political, and, in some cases, military cooperation of these countries is also important to the United States. U.S. policy toward South Africa and the actions and statements taken to implement it are closely watched by other African governments. Leaders of black African countries who view the racial doctrines of South Africa as a denial of their own human dignity have called for concerted action against apartheid and are supporting the South African liberation movements with money, training, and arms. Any intensification of the conflict in southern Africa is bound to put pressure on U.S. relations with these nations.

Finally, there is the U.S. interest in maintaining commercial relations with South Africa itself, where there is direct American investment valued at $2 billion and trade with the United States totaling $3.4 billion a year. Pursuit of this interest raises the possibility of conflict with the pursuit of good relations with other African states. Increased violence in South Africa may pose a direct threat to this interest as well as lead to greater pressure by the African states for the West to reduce or cut its economic ties with South Africa.

Chapter 18
South African Realities and Trends
The Commission's Findings

Foreign policy cannot be made in a vacuum and, to a large extent, the course of events in South Africa will determine the choices open to U.S. policymakers. The Commission makes no claim to predict the future of South Africa. Instead, using the information we have gathered, we analyze the current situation and then lay out two broad scenarios suggesting the range of events that U.S. policy makers are likely to have to deal with. A number of key findings are presented at the end of the chapter.

SOUTH AFRICAN REALITIES

There has been little noticeable change in the basic structure of apartheid. But there have been a number of developments reflecting contradictory trends within Afrikaner society, particularly in the National party. The nature of Afrikaner society has been changing for some time and the divisions between *verligte* (enlightened or reformist) and *verkrampte* (narrow or reactionary) wings of the ruling National party have been deepening.

The prime minister, Pieter W. Botha, has strengthened his office, remodeled the constitution, and tightened his hold on the bureaucracy, thus consolidating control over the machinery of government. Although the National party and its parliamentary caucus seem to be fairly evenly balanced between *verligtes* and *verkramptes,* Botha's cabinet is almost exclusively drawn from the reformist wing of the party.

Much attention has been focused on Botha's introduction of the President's Council, a multiracial consultative body consisting of whites, Coloureds, and Asians but excluding Africans. Key developments have also taken place in black education, labor, and housing policies. The budget for African education was increased by 26 percent and 37 percent respectively in the fiscal years 1979 and 1980, and many new schools, as well as additional classrooms in existing schools, are being built. The government has announced plans to phase in compulsory primary education for Africans in selected areas—it is already compulsory at the primary level for Coloureds—and to introduce parity in the salaries of teachers from different racial groups.

Glaring disparities nonetheless remain between white and black education. The government is still spending ten times as much on each white child as it does on every African child, and the teacher-pupil ratio in white schools averages 1 to 20 compared with 1 to 48 in African schools. The government has begun to provide free textbooks to black schools but claims that the program has been slowed by the loss of the books by pupils. (All textbooks in white schools are free.) Government spending on education in the "homelands" increased by 30 percent in 1980—education in the "independent" homelands is the responsibility of the individual governments—but there is no provision for the needs of the many schoolchildren in squatter camps and resettlement areas around the country.

The government has increased expenditures for black housing. It has borrowed $250 million from American and European banks to finance new housing, hospitals, and schools for blacks—the first foreign loan of its kind designed specifically for black needs in South Africa. But there is still a huge and growing shortage of housing. Also, Africans are confused and skeptical about the government's new program of leasing township houses to them for ninety-nine years, which does not meet their basic demand for the same freehold rights as whites.

The government put forward legislation removing restrictions on blacks relocating from one township to another, provided those relocating had jobs and living accommodations, but withdrew it after a detailed critique by the Urban Foundation. The proposals would have made it more difficult for "illegal" residents to remain in the townships and for job seekers from rural areas to enter them.

In the labor field, the government has adopted the Wiehahn Commission recommendations to recognize black labor unions and to abolish statutory job reservation. The implications of this move for the future of black labor are unclear. Some black unions are at present reluctant to avail themselves of the new right to register and become legally recognized because they fear government control of their activities. On the other hand, there is the argument that if black unions are admitted to industrial councils and if legally sanctioned procedures for resolution of industrial disputes are made workable—including the right to strike—black labor leaders, as major players in a government-established tructure, may gain some protection against harassment and arrest.

Another government commission has proposed that township community councils be given more powers of self-government. Black entrepreneurs, hitherto severely restricted, would be allowed greater freedom to establish and run commercial enterprises in the townships. But they would continue to be excluded from "white" commercial areas, an exclusion that remains a major grievance within the black business community.

Homeland policy, the keystone of apartheid, remains unchanged. The government continues to press homelands to become independent, although it has publicly acknowledged that they can never be economically viable independent units. Proposals for further geographical consolidation of individual homelands by granting the fragmented entities more land are a sensitive subject with the white electorate. But Mafeking, formerly a white town, has been made the capital of independent Bophuthatswana and the South African prime minister has not excluded the possibility of additional land for some or all of the homelands in the future.

While the government is clinging to the basic homeland blueprint, it appears to be searching for new models of economic and political development through its "Constellation of States" proposal. In the meantime, it continues to resettle large numbers of "surplus" Africans in impoverished homelands and to deny South African citizenship to those with ethnic links, however remote, to the independent homelands.

The basic cohesion of the National party has not yet been disturbed by the direction of the prime minister's policies. Conservative dissent, led by Andries Treurnicht, the Transvaal leader, has been fierce at times but has been kept within the confines of the party, the caucus, and the cabinet. In addition, a small group of reformers who believe in authentic political power sharing has emerged for the first time within the Afrikaner community. It is a new ingredient in the political flux. Threats of a major party split along *verligte-verkrampte* lines have not materialized, but the possibility cannot be ruled out.

The ethnic unity of Afrikanerdom nonetheless remains a compelling preoccupation of every Afrikaner leader and in the past almost invariably dominated Afrikaner public concern. While Botha might not be averse to losing a small number of the most *verkrampte* members of his party, he gives no evidence at present of willingness to sacrifice party unity in the cause of reform. Perceiving that some form of change is inevitable, National party leaders are searching for alternatives that do not undermine their power nor the essential unity of the Afrikaner people. Ethnicity remains a powerful force in white politics.

Many *verligte* academics, however, believe that Botha should have moved more positively by this time and are worried about the continuing strength of the *verkramptes* in the party. They feel, for instance, that Africans should have been included in the President's Council. A new constitutional provision that permits a number of members of Parliament to be appointed has resulted in

397

the addition of more *verkramptes* to Parliament than expected. A suggestion by *verligtes* of some form of common citizenship for all South Africans, including those in the homelands, has been rejected by the National party.

The debate over apartheid is not confined to the National party but is reflected with varying degrees of passion in other important Afrikaner institutions, including the universities, the churches, the Broederbond, and cultural organizations. Growing urbanization, education, and wealth have helped to transform Afrikaner society in the last three decades, producing changes in the relative importance of different segments of that society. The Dutch Reformed church, though still powerful and conservative, has probably never been as divided as at present and is thus not as influential as in the past.

The growth of the Afrikaner business sector is important because it tends to share the more enlightened views and international outlook of the English-speaking business community. Further, the corporate sector's influence, although still limited, is growing as the economy expands and the government draws the business community into its "total strategy" for "defense" of the country. Part of that strategy involves the South African military, whose leadership is thought to share the *verligte* tendencies of the government. As long as the National party maintains its cohesion and huge parliamentary majority, the role of the English-speaking minority in South African politics would appear limited. However, the small liberal Progressive Federal party, the official opposition, could be significant as a stimulus to public debate and understanding.

Other factors thought by some to facilitate change are at work in South African society. One is economic growth. A school of thought led by Harry Oppenheimer, chairman of the Anglo-American Corporation, holds that economic growth leads to political change. It argues that as an economy becomes more sophisticated and dependent on advanced technology, the greater the need for an educated, well-paid, stable, and satisfied work force. The business community therefore becomes more averse to political disruption and is guided by "rational" rather than "ethnic" or "racial" considerations and thus exerts effective pressure for political reform.

Other analysts reject this argument. They note that after almost thirty years of South African economic growth, blacks still have no effective political power, and over the same period have been subjected to increasingly repressive measures. Critics of the "growth" hypothesis also point out that timing is important. Economic reform may come too late to make a significant impact on the political situation.

Yet others, agreeing that economic growth does not automatically bring political reform, observe that it does produce benefits for the black population useful in themselves and also creates more favorable conditions for political change. The hypothesis is that better-educated, healthier, and more prosperous black South Africans will become more concerned and active about their political rights. They will also tend to develop, along with their white compatriots, a greater stake in finding a political solution with a minimum of destruction and violence.

Whether or not economic growth helps to produce political change, there is some evidence of reformist trends in the private sector. A number of private schools, including some that are church-affiliated, have begun to integrate classrooms despite official policy prohibiting integration in primary and secondary schools. The Urban Foundation, which was created after the Soweto upheavals as a vehicle for corporate efforts to improve the quality of life in the townships, is expanding its operations, although it is too soon to assess its real impact. Implementation by a number of foreign companies of the Sullivan Principles and the European Economic Community's corporate code in the workplace has brought benefits to some blacks, and many South African companies have taken similar measures based on the Urban Foundation's own code of conduct.

Blacks in general have reacted to these developments with extreme skepticism. Both the details and the ultimate intentions of the government's policies are often unclear, and there is a tendency among many black leaders to reject the concept of staged progress because they are not now being offered anything they consider significant. Most blacks, as the Quail Commission discovered, prefer a nonracial unitary democracy, but, given the existing restraints, their immediate objectives tend to be social and economic reform rather than political change. They appear ready to accept a phased dismantling of apartheid if offered by the government. However, the overwhelming majority of blacks require that a genuine and equitable sharing of political power be part of the program. Many are willing to defer achievement of this goal but virtually none will give it up.

There is increased politicization among blacks, attested to by the growth of organized labor, the impact of Black Consciousness organizations and banned nationalist movements, and the expansion of cultural-political organizations like Inkatha. Many younger blacks are becoming more radical, and some are leaving the country to join the exiled liberation movements, particularly the African National Congress. There are signs of increasing solidarity among Coloureds, Indians, and Africans. The principal Coloured and Indian political parties have refused to participate in the new President's Council unless Africans are represented. There also is a tendency among Coloured and Asian youth to identify with the African population.

The growing stake of blacks in South Africa's expanding economy and the increasing reliance of that economy on black purchasing power are also important. So is the rapid growth of the black population compared to the white. In 1980 blacks outnumbered whites by five to one. By most forecasts, in the year 2000 it will be seven to one, and by 2020, nine to one. The economy is currently experiencing new growth fueled by higher gold prices, renewed foreign investment, and the expanded development of South Africa's minerals for export, all of which is accompanied by relative stability. Higher wages, better working conditions, unionization, and greater upward mobility for black labor are all serving to increase the black stake in the economy and their potential leverage over it.

The situation in South Africa, then, continues to reflect a number of fluctuating and contradictory forces. On the one hand, there is continued government repression of black dissent. On the other, public debate at different levels and involving all races is taking place. Numerous commissions have been established to hear grievances and to discuss issues affecting the various racial groups. One such body, the Buthelezi Commission on the future of KwaZulu and Natal, is the result of black initiative.

Despite restrictive laws and a degree of self-censorship, the white South African press remains relatively free to report and comment on some important questions. The critical stance of certain English newspapers helps to publicize black demands and views. But the government is far more repressive with the black press, shutting down newspapers and banning leading black journalists, regardless of foreign and domestic criticism.

SCENARIOS

Where might all this lead South Africa? In the conflicting developments just outlined there is no clear answer. There is change. Some of it is reformist, although its significance is debatable. And some of it is repressive, undermining the credibility of the government's reforms.

The state of flux in South Africa suggests alternative scenarios for the future. These are presented to establish the probable range of events in South Africa, along with their regional and international implications, as a backdrop for policy formulation. The scenarios are not meant to be self-contained predictions. No more credence is attached to one than to the other. They inevitably overlap, and the actual course of events may include elements of both scenarios or, conceivably, some not in either.

The first scenario describes a process of change that avoids sustained, large-scale violence. The second scenario posits retrenchment and intransigence by the government, leading to major violence and civil war.

Until Namibia has gained its independence through negotiation or by other means, that problem may attract more international attention than South Africa. For the purpose of the scenarios put forth here, however, we assume the Namibian issue will have been resolved.

Scenario One

> The first scenario has reformist trends prevailing over regressive ones. It recognizes an inevitable increase in black opposition to the government whose strategy would be perceived to be the moderni-

zation of apartheid rather than its removal. Sabotage inside South Africa and guerrilla activity along the borders by the African National Congress and other nationalist movements would escalate over time. Civil disobedience in the form of boycotts, stay-aways, demonstrations, and strikes would continue to be a feature of South African life. The government would meet such developments with overwhelming force. Assuming its reformist intentions were genuine and sustained, the government would also be expected to select its targets carefully to avoid sweeping away black leaders and organizations needed to implement its economic and social policies and maintain a functioning economy.

The government would be unlikely to change its homeland policy dramatically, no doubt continuing to seek ways to make the homelands more viable and encouraging those not already independent to accept independence. In the urban areas residential segregation would almost certainly be maintained but the resettlement of surplus Africans, Coloureds, and Indians might not be pressed, and the current policy of sometimes accepting squatters as permanent residents would continue. In theory urban Africans would remain citizens of the homelands, but in practice the government might turn a blind eye to those who refused to accept homeland citizenship. The government would spend substantial sums to improve black education, housing, and job skills, and the private sector would continue to assist this process. The South African economy, bolstered by high gold prices, reasonable internal stability, development of the nation's valuable mineral resources, and diminishing dependence on imported oil, would be able to support these actions. The government's policies would be shaped to attract the support of industrialists at home and investors overseas and would include a "deconcentration of industry" to create greater economic development outside the major cities.

Outside South Africa, the government's reforms would be viewed with suspicion by the African states, which would, at least diplomatically, continue to isolate South Africa. The Frontline States would find themselves pressed by the ANC and other South African nationalist movements to take part in the guerrilla campaign. Those organizations could also be expected to step up their recruiting and their requests for arms and training from the Soviet Union and other Communist countries. The South African government would probably use its economic and military strength to dissuade its neighbors from cooperating with the guerrilla movements. The extent of involvement by the Communist countries would vary with the level of tension in the region and their relations with the Frontline States. As long as the South African government showed it could effectively contain the guerrilla threat, however, the likelihood of a greatly increased Soviet or Cuban presence in the region would appear limited. African pressure would probably focus on South Africa's Western trading partners in the United Nations. Those countries would have to assess their interests in South Africa and elsewhere on the continent. An argument would be made that since reform had begun in South Africa, sanctions should not be imposed until the government had more time to follow through with its policies.

At various stages in the scenario the South African government would presumably try to co-opt moderate black leadership without conceding meaningful political rights. Inducements might include offers of more financial aid for the homelands, separate concessions for Coloureds and Indians, government jobs for urban leaders, and greater authority for government-created institutions like the township councils. While some leaders, including homeland rulers, might cooperate with the government, the expectation would be that many black leaders would resist the temptation, sensing that the growing power of blacks, especially in the economic sector, could be better used if blacks remained united. Co-option would in any case slow the course of events. Dramatic activities by black nationalist organizations—guerrilla attacks and sabotage, for example—could result in the temporary eclipse of black leadership that rejected cooperation with the government yet refused to espouse violence. But as the government's ability to suppress rising violence became clear and as social and economic reforms began to have an impact on the lives of millions of Africans, support could gradually shift from those who back violence to more moderate leaders.

International pressure on South Africa to make fundamental political changes would undoubtedly continue, perhaps forcing the question of mandatory sanctions to the UN Security Council. But given the strength of the South African government and the relative stability of the country and its region, international pressure might well level off as the political atmosphere inside South Africa changed and representative black leaders began to talk to the government about new political and constitutional arrangements.

Internal reform and external stability would have produced some improvement in the racial climate in South Africa. The edge on some of the whites' deepest fears about political change would have been dulled, and blacks, with some of their important social and economic grievances redressed, would be less frustrated about those issues and would be pressing harder for political reform. Each side would remain aware of the other's nonnegotiable premise. For whites this would be the unacceptability of a winner-take-all form of majority rule in a unitary state, and for blacks it would be the unacceptability of continued denial of genuine power sharing. On the surface those nonnegotiable premises might seem to be as difficult to reconcile as ever, but underneath a search for new political solutions would be intensifying, assisted not only by greater racial harmony in some sectors of society but also by a shift in the balance of power between the races.

A number of factors would have contributed to the shift. The government's social and economic reforms would lose potency as devices to delay political change as they became effective and blacks turned their attention to explicitly political goals. Growing black economic power would be making itself felt. Black internal leadership would be gaining in experience and sophistication as the black population became more politically active. Certain institutions, such as universities and professional organizations, that had acquired influence during the reformist phase might also contribute to behind-the-scenes pressure for political change. And, although the government would have contained the black guerrilla and sabotage campaigns, the threat of continued and possibly escalating violence would remain.

Under these circumstances, the whites would begin to realize it was in their interest to negotiate some form of power sharing to ease black pressures, rather than to try to keep those pressures bottled up and thereby increase the likelihood of an eventual explosion. White fears of sharing power would begin to be offset by their fears of what would happen if they did *not* do so. It would be unlikely that whites would take the initiative. Rather, blacks would begin to acquire power through an uneven, incremental process accompanied by economic and social dislocations and doubtless some violence. The pattern would probably be one of increasingly forceful black demands, cautious and limited white concessions, increased black capabilities, more black demands, more white concessions, and so on, until a new, more just and more viable political order emerged. Eventually, whites would see it in their interest to concede some of their power, and blacks would regard it in their interest to not demand all of it.

Willingness to accept certain general political criteria would tacitly run through the search for a new political system. These would include some decentralization of power, a combination of universal and qualified franchises so that blacks would not overwhelm whites with their greater numbers, a federal structure that would give much local autonomy yet maintain central control over foreign policy and key economic matters, and the opportunity for everyone to retain South African citizenship. The process would probably be

403

diverse, piecemeal, and hesitant. For example, one formula might work in the province of Natal, where English-speaking whites, Zulus, and Indians might reach agreement on universal suffrage, whereas a racially based solution might serve the Coloured population in the Cape, with all of South Africa's Coloureds exercising their political rights at the national level through that subunit. The concept of city-states might hold some appeal for places like Soweto, while the independent homelands could possibly be reintegrated into South Africa as part of a newly created federal structure. Constitutional devices would have to be created to ensure that one racial group did not dominate the others. Universal suffrage within the units of a federation might be acceptable, but representation of those units in the central authority would not necessarily be in direct proportion to population. Finally, the process, though sporadic, would be continuing and would not end after the first important reform.

External pressures would be expected as negotiations proceeded but would abate if substantial political gains for South Africa's blacks resulted. Eventually, with a multiracial government installed, external recognition of the changes that had occurred would follow. The new government would be friendly toward the West and would continue to export key minerals to the West. Although it might establish relations with the Soviet Union as a matter of diplomatic form, it would adopt a cautious attitude toward all Communist states and deny them military facilities.

Scenario Two

The second scenario is essentially the reverse of the first. The conservative wing of the National party would successfully block *verligte* reformist policies. The *verkrampte* view that alterations in the fabric of apartheid make political change inevitable—the underlying thesis of the first scenario—would block the government's reforms.

Verligte leadership would then face a choice.

It could break with the *verkramptes,* splitting the National party and Afrikaner ethnic unity. If the split were deep enough, the leadership would look to support from the English-speaking electorate to stay in power and continue its reforms.

Or it could change its policies, seeking to maintain party and Afrikaner unity. If so, the government would return to more orthodox apartheid policies with a few cosmetic modifications. Influx control and resettlement of surplus urban blacks would be more rigorously enforced. The trend toward treating squatters as permanent residents might be reversed, totally eliminating Indian and Coloured "black spots" in white areas. Black labor unions might continue to be recognized, but the government would try harder to drive a wedge between those affiliated with white unions and those trying to maintain their independence. The government might well use its extensive powers to destroy independent black union leadership. The townships would be given limited autonomy but kept firmly under white administrative control. There would be some economic and social reforms benefiting urban blacks, Coloureds, and Indians, but the government would clearly have other priorities.

The black response would be as before—guerrilla activity, growing politicization—but more bitter and determined. Government repression, by the same token, would probably be more harsh and sweeping. The government would be less concerned about preserving certain black organizations and leadership, and would be reconciled to the negative impact of its policies on South African business and on foreign investors. The economy, underpinned by sales of gold and other minerals and a growing self-sufficiency in fuel, would probably remain strong. Despite the absence of major reforms, blacks would be playing a larger role in the economy, both as an expanding middle class and as consumers through the increase of buying power. The government would use its power of patronage to try to co-opt black moderates, including homeland leaders who rejected independence, and might have some success as the black community became more divided over the most effective ways of achieving their goals.

External pressures would escalate as it became evident that no significant changes were taking place in South Africa. The black liberation movements would acquire greater legitimacy as the only credible forces left to confront the South African government and would exert pressure on the Frontline States to assist them. Those states, in turn, might be drawn more deeply into guerrilla campaigns, albeit at considerable risk and cost to themselves. At the United Nations, African states would ask the Security Council to impose economic sanctions on South Africa, probably with emphasis on communications and oil embargoes. Bilateral pressures would come from African countries like Nigeria that supply the West with oil or minerals. There might also be threats to boycott multinational corporations that do business with South Africa.

The Soviet Union, Cuba, and other Communist countries would see an opportunity to increase military support of the liberation movements without risking direct confrontation with the West. Western nations would be increasingly restrained by the South African government's reactionary policies and by the popular support enjoyed by the government's black opponents inside and outside the country. The Soviet Union would probably proceed with caution as long as South Africa maintained its military superiority in the region. The South African government might gain time through successful co-option of some internal black leadership, but, unchecked by any sustained program of reform, the polarization of the races within the country would continue. Coloureds and Indians would align themselves more positively with Africans and the influence of older blacks on the younger generation would weaken as violence and disruption grew.

The expansion of the guerrilla campaign would lead to more South African reprisal raids across the borders of the Frontline States and the use of economic pressures. Racial strife in southern Africa, vividly reported, would stimulate a strident and polarizing debate in the United States over what role it should play. This debate would exacerbate racial tensions across the country. African pressures on the West for sanctions against South Africa and economic disengagement would increase, forcing Western powers to make clear choices. As fighting on the borders of South Africa expanded, Cuba might be asked for help by one or more of the Frontline States. Within South Africa, violence would begin to seriously disrupt the economy and would raise anxieties among whites about their capacity to defend themselves. Labor unrest, boycotts, demonstrations, and other forms of civil unrest would play an important part in weakening the government. White emigration would increase as individuals' security and livelihoods were undermined. Co-opted black leaders, especially those in the more remote homelands, would become increasingly irrelevant. Slowly and over a long period the country would descend into civil war involving massive destruction of life and property, making the South African issue a critical U.S. and international concern. In the end, the South African government's belief in victory would collapse, leading to de facto partition or a Zimbabwe type of power-sharing arrangement.

During the struggle, the West would experience difficulties in obtaining regular supplies of minerals from South Africa. Cutoffs of long duration would be unlikely, however. The government would want to maximize its exports as a source of foreign exchange. But the United Nations, with Western support, would probably impose some form of mandatory economic sanctions, creating a new and highly unpredictable situation.

It seems likely that a new South African government, whatever its ideological or political orientation, would export minerals to the West, its natural market. It, too, would need the foreign exchange.

A new government might well demand higher prices, though, and might try to manipulate the supply of chromium, a mineral critical to the West and not a major foreign exchange earner for South Africa. The attitude of the new government toward the West in general would depend largely on the behavior of the Western powers during the civil war. Since the African National Congress would probably have had a major part in the struggle, a close relationship with the Soviet Union, East Germany, and Cuba would be expected. Nonetheless, if the record of other African revolutionary movements that have won long, bitter racial wars is any guide, South Africa's new government would probably not compromise its hard-won sovereignty by granting the Soviet Union military base rights. It might, however, grant requests for less important facilities.

FINDINGS

The two scenarios unavoidably portray events as more mechanically linked than, in reality, is likely to be the case. But we believe they are helpful to our effort to formulate U.S. policies that, first, are tailored to the probable range of developments in South Africa and, second, attempt to influence those developments in ways consistent with U.S. national interests.

Some analysts believe that reinforcement of the status quo in South Africa, with minor modifications, is the most probable outcome. We do not share that judgment. Whatever the government of South Africa does to perpetuate the status quo, in the long term black forces inside the country will alter it. This judgment is central to our analysis.

Division and fluctuation in white politics and strong black pressures for basic change are not new in South Africa and, despite their intensification, the country has not yet reached a climactic "turning point" in its affairs. We are convinced that final battle lines have not yet been drawn and that sufficient ferment exists in both white and black communities to suggest that fundamental political change could eventually come without sustained, large-scale violence. But such an outcome is far from certain. Opportunities for dialogue and accommodation may not be taken and irreversible confrontation could result. It is this uncertainty, however, that offers opportunity and challenge to U.S. policy makers.

Any analysis of South Africa must begin with a fundamental reality: Both blacks and whites hold certain positions to be nonnegotiable. For blacks, an acceptable solution must give them a share in genuine political power. For whites, that solution cannot be based on a winner-take-all form of majority rule. This is the core of the problem. Short of an outcome involving sustained and large-scale violence, any solution to the South African problem must incorporate those two positions. Whether such a solution can be achieved with a minimum of violence is an open question.

A new, more just political order will not come in South Africa without a shift in power from whites to blacks. We do not favor or advocate a particular political configuration for South Africa. South Africans will make their own choices. If South Africans of all races do ultimately freely choose a strong unitary state, or a looser federal structure, or a confederation of separate sovereign states, or partition, the choice should be respected by the United States and the rest of the international community.

There are, unfortunately, no painless alternatives in South Africa. The choice is not even between a slow process of "peaceful change" and a quick process of "violent change." Instead, the situation is one in which a slow, uneven, sporadically violent pattern of events including bargaining, compromises, and agreements could preempt the other alternative, an equally slow but much more violent descent into civil war. Both paths, of course, could lead to genuine political power sharing.

We prefer the first because it holds the promise of less bloodshed and suffering and a greater likelihood of a government responsive to the rights and needs of all groups. It would also minimize the chances of Soviet involvement and superpower confrontation, pose less of a threat to the flow of strategic minerals and other commerce, place less strain on our relations with other African countries, and reduce the inflammatory impact of South Africa's problems on race relations in the United States.

Economic and social reforms will not necessarily lead to political change. They might, but they might not. They may, however, help produce conditions more conducive to political change with a minimum of violence and bring intrinsic benefits to the black population. In any event, consistent, long-term pressure is indispensable for fundamental political change.

By power sharing we mean arrangements that will give all South Africans some form of effective participation in the political system. The exact form of those arrangements will be less important than the fact that all groups have come to agreement on the issue. For the present, whites controlling South Africa talk about the need to share power in minor ways but have not yet begun to address this issue in a way satisfactory to blacks. Nor do whites consider blacks presently capable of exercising power. On the other side, blacks do not yet possess sufficient leverage to compel the whites to share power.

Finally, we attach no timetable to these events, nor do we predict when reform or revolution may come. Over the decades South Africa has confounded students of its affairs, and we see no merit in joining the legions of discredited soothsayers. Outsiders tend to focus on the conspicuous manifestations of South Africa's unique racial system, yet, as in most countries, there are different layers of meaning in its political dialogue and policies. Politicians, government

408

officials, and persons outside government often speak to several audiences in different idioms, and what they say does not always match what they do. The result is frequent and sometimes pervasive ambiguity.

We do need to be as clearheaded as possible, however, about present realities and the probable range of future developments in South Africa if we would understand better what U.S. policies toward that country should be.

Chapter 19
Policy Objectives and Actions

What objectives should be pursued to protect and advance U.S. interests in the context summarized in the preceding chapter? The Commission recommends a policy based on five distinct but related objectives:

1. To make clear the fundamental and continuing opposition of the U.S. government and people to the system of apartheid, with particular emphasis on the exclusion of blacks from an effective share in political power.

2. To promote genuine political power sharing in South Africa with a minimum of violence by systematically exerting influence on the South African government.

3. To support organizations inside South Africa working for change, assist the development of black leadership, and promote black welfare.

4. To assist the economic development of the other states in southern Africa, including reduction of the imbalance in their economic relations with South Africa.

5. To reduce the impact of stoppages of imports of key minerals from South Africa.

These objectives constitute a framework for policy that is presented as a guide for private American organizations as well as for government. In shaping policy, we are aware that U.S. influence in South Africa is limited, that the implementation of policy is less than a precise science and its results never entirely predictable. Nevertheless, we believe these objectives, pursued simultaneously, constitute a workable framework for a policy toward South Africa. Each objective is intended to serve one or more U.S. interests but none is itself a sufficient basis for policy, and the pursuit of one without the others would be damaging to U.S. interests.

Specific actions follow each objective. Many of the actions serve more than one objective but are listed where they are considered to be most effective.

With the exception of the actions for Objective 2, they are intended to be put into effect as soon as possible and remain in place until a genuine sharing of political power, acceptable to all races, is implemented in South Africa. For Objective 2—promoting power sharing by influencing the South African government—we recommend a flexible approach. The actions described there are illustrative, possible pressures and inducements that the U.S. government could use in response to changing developments in South Africa.

The actions as a whole, while reflecting the limits of U.S. influence, cover a wide range of activity. Our main concern has been to construct a realistic framework for policy that serves the full range of U.S. interests. In practice, the specific actions taken will depend to a great extent on developments in South Africa. As time passes, some actions may lose their value while others assume greater relevance. But the basic structure of U.S. policy, as embodied in the objectives, should remain unchanged until a satisfactory political outcome is reached in South Africa.

OBJECTIVE 1

To make clear the fundamental and continuing opposition of the U.S. government and people to the system of apartheid, with particular emphasis on the exclusion of blacks from an effective share in political power.

Pursuit of this objective serves U.S. interests in South Africa. It does so by transmitting on a continuing basis to black and white South Africans and to all others concerned the message that U.S. opposition to apartheid is profound, and that the actions taken in pursuit of this objective will be withdrawn only when South Africa's blacks have obtained an effective share in political power. Until that time, the United States will continue to support the exclusion of South Africa from full membership in the Western community of nations, an exclusion about which white South Africans, including Afrikaners, appear to care a great deal.

If this point is made clearly and continuously, misunderstanding of U.S. motives in recognizing and encouraging partial progress in South Africa (see Objective 2) and in remaining engaged with that country in other ways (see Objective 3) should be minimized.

The United States also demonstrates that it does not accept the view that South Africa, under its white minority government, is a bulwark against communism. Rather, the opposite: the United States sees apartheid as a target and an opportunity for the growth of Communist influence in the region.

U.S. disapproval of apartheid is a source of hope to black South Africans and others opposing that system. That disapproval—and that hope—constitute a form of moral pressure on the South African government. As long as black

411

and white South Africans retain the capacity to compromise, that pressure is likely to increase the chances that the apartheid system will be dismantled through a process involving less rather than more violence.

The United States thus makes a contribution to reducing the potential for violence during what will inevitably be a difficult transitional period in South African politics and, at the same time, accumulates political capital with a more representative South African government. Both factors help to minimize Soviet influence in the area and to maintain Western access to South Africa's key minerals.

Looking further ahead, a future South African government that had been denied any form of American moral support during the period leading to its formation is likely to become more dependent upon the Soviet Union and other Communist allies. However, an American posture that condemned apartheid and gave hope and encouragement to legitimate black concerns in South Africa could be expected to assist in establishing good relations between the new government and the United States.

As to minerals, it is our judgment that in the long run any government coming to power in South Africa will be obliged for economic reasons to sell to the West. However, a government that had enjoyed a degree of moral support from the United States during its formative stages would be less likely to interfere with or manipulate the flow of mineral exports to the West for political or other advantages.

The U.S. interest in maintaining good trade and diplomatic relations with the other countries of Africa and the rest of the world is also served by a clear policy of opposition to apartheid. For the people of many nations, apartheid is an affront to their fundamental dignity as human beings. A belief, even if mistaken, that the United States is willing to ignore apartheid in its dealings with South Africa is a growing impediment to good relations. And, among African countries able to exercise economic leverage against the United States, notably Nigeria, the United States' second largest foreign oil supplier, it is a potential cause of economic reprisals.

Finally, pursuit of this objective responds to a deeply felt need shared by many Americans, black and white, to follow a course of action that expresses their moral opposition to apartheid. In U.S. domestic politics, unambiguous opposition to apartheid is a prerequisite for taking other steps to promote constructive change in South Africa. Without it, there can be no viable consensus in the United States to support the next three policy objectives.

Actions for Objective 1

1. U.S. Government
   - (a) Broaden Arms Embargo to Cover Foreign Subsidiaries of U.S. Companies.
   - (b) Broaden Nuclear Embargo.

    (c)   Increase Number of Blacks—Americans and South Africans—in U.S. Embassy and Consulates.

    (d)   Continue Policy of Statements and Actions Expressing U.S. Opposition to Apartheid.

    (e)   Expand Contacts with Black South African Leaders.

    (f)   Withhold Recognition of Homelands.

    (g)   Support Humanitarian Aid Programs for Black South Africans.

2. U.S. Corporations
    (h)   No Expansion and No New Entry.

    (i)   Social Development Expenditure Standard.

    (j)   Sullivan Principles.

3. U.S. Shareholders: Some Guidelines

1. U.S. Government
    (a)   Broaden Arms Embargo to Cover Foreign Subsidiaries of U.S. Companies.

The United States announced an arms embargo against South Africa in 1963 and, shortly afterwards, supported a United Nations Security Council resolution calling on all member states to institute a voluntary embargo on "the sale and shipment of arms, ammunition of all types, and military vehicles to South Africa." In 1964, the United States issued its own guidelines for implementing this embargo by prohibiting new sales of (1) military equipment of significant use to military, paramilitary, or police forces in training or combat and (2) equipment and material for the production and maintenance of arms and ammunition.

The 1964 guidelines also contained a provision covering "gray-area" goods, dual-use items such as civilian aircraft, computers, and other electronic and communications equipment that find application in both military and civilian situations. While allowing such U.S. goods to be exported to South African civilian users, the guidelines give the relevant government department the discretionary power to review and, if necessary, prohibit such sales.

In 1968 the embargo provisions were amended to forbid the use of U.S. components by foreign companies in the manufacture of arms, ammunition, and weapons-related items destined for South Africa. But under President Richard Nixon, after a policy review in 1970, a new directive effectively reversed the Johnson administration presumption that dual-use equipment would not be sold unless there were strong assurances that it would not be put to military uses. Under the new policy, a sale was approved unless there were strong arguments against it.

Following the 1977 UN Security Council resolution establishing a mandatory arms embargo, the Carter administration in 1978 promulgated new regulations which once more broadened the embargo to prohibit all exports destined for use by the South African military or police. These restrictions go beyond what is required by the UN ban.

Responsibility for implementing the embargo is divided among the Department of Defense, which handles arms transfers by the government, the Department of State, which controls commercial arms sales, and the Department of Commerce, which controls commercial sales of some military-related equipment and enforces the ban on all other sales to the South African military and police.

The arms embargo covers all arms and weapons-related technology, including any tangible (blueprint, model, and so on) or intangible (technical expertise) data. All export, release, or reexport of such technology is prohibited, as are (1) visual inspections of equipment originating in the United States and of facilities in the United States or abroad, (2) oral exchanges of information in the United States or abroad, and (3) the applications to situations abroad of personal knowledge or technical experience acquired in the United States. This ban also extends to any direct or indirect product of the embargoed data and is intended to cut off all avenues of transfer between the United States and South Africa.

The U.S. regulations for implementation of the arms embargo, however, do not prohibit sales to South Africa of goods originating in countries other than the United States. Thus, subsidiaries of U.S. companies incorporated abroad, whether in South Africa itself or in other foreign countries, may sell foreign-made commodities to the South African military or police, and may even sell foreign-made arms to South Africa, if not forbidden by the laws of the countries in which they are incorporated or operate. At the same time a U.S. company is prohibited from selling a component part to a foreign company if that component is to become part of an embargoed product to be sold to South Africa.

We are aware of the sensitivity of governments, including our own, to attempts by other nations to regulate the conduct of corporations established under their laws and operating within their boundaries, and of the conflicting legal obligations that frequently arise from such efforts. However, in situations involving important interests, we have given our domestic laws extraterritorial reach—in the antitrust area, for example. In our judgment, the significance of the interests involved in the effective implementation of the arms embargo warrants extending the reach of U.S. law to cover the actions of foreign subsidiaries of U.S.-based companies. The severity of potentially conflicting legal obligations should be mitigated, moreover, by the fact that all UN member states are bound by law to observe the mandatory arms embargo against South Africa. The scope of the ban imposed by the United States on companies operating within its jurisdiction extends beyond the minimum required by the embargo and beyond the policies established by some other countries to implement it. But the existence of the mandatory UN embargo guarantees that U.S. law and the policy of the countries in which the affected U.S. subsidiary is incorporated or operating are not in basic conflict.

(b)   Broaden Nuclear Embargo.

In 1957, the United States, in furtherance of the "Atoms for Peace" program, signed an agreement with South Africa for cooperation in the development of peaceful uses for atomic energy. U.S. companies under government license provided South Africa with information, technology, and fissionable materials for the construction and operation of South Africa's nuclear reactors. However, the export of fissionable materials to South Africa was halted in 1976 by a Nuclear Regulatory Commission proceeding brought by the congressional Black Caucus.

In 1978, Congress passed the Nuclear Non-Proliferation Act. The Carter administration took the position that any agreement by the United States to supply nuclear fuel to South Africa was contingent upon South Africa signing the Nuclear Non-Proliferation Treaty and accepting the safeguards laid down by the International Atomic Energy Agency. South Africa has refused to sign the treaty, and therefore the United States continues to deny fissionable materials to South Africa. For similar reasons, neither the Nuclear Regulatory Commission nor the Commerce Department has approved the sale of any nuclear-related equipment to South Africa since 1977.

South Africa has begun to feel the impact of the U.S. cutoff of nuclear fuel. The Safari-1 nuclear reactor, South Africa's first research reactor, operates only occasionally. The two Koeburg reactors, not yet ready for operation, were originally intended to run on enriched uranium provided by the United States. If this fuel is not forthcoming, and the few other potential suppliers do not fill the gap, the Koeburg reactors will remain idle and South Africa will lose an important source of energy. But the present policy leaves open the possibility that if South Africa signs the Non-Proliferation Treaty and agrees to monitoring and the other safeguards required by the treaty, the United States would consider resuming sales of nuclear materials, technology, and services to South Africa.

To provide a comprehensive basis for the embargo of nuclear technology, we recommend a broad ban equivalent to that in effect in the arms embargo. All nuclear collaboration with South Africa should be ended by broadening the nuclear fissionable materials embargo to include the transfer of nuclear-related technology and equipment, and by imposing a prohibition against the provision of nuclear expertise to South Africa by American companies. Although it can be argued that there is an advantage to leaving the question open in terms of bargaining with South Africa for its adherence to the Nuclear Non-Proliferation Treaty, we believe that this speculative benefit is outweighed by the consideration described above.

(c) Increase Number of Blacks—Americans and South Africans—in U.S. Embassy and Consulates.

The State Department assigned the first black foreign service officer to the U.S. Embassy in South Africa in 1973. At present, the State Department's official policy is to encourage black Americans to work in the South African mission, but not to assign anyone unwilling to go. Understandably, family and other considerations often discourage black foreign service officers from accepting positions in South Africa. Of the sixty-seven American foreign service officers working in the U.S. Embassy and consulates in early 1981, two were black: the deputy chief of mission in the embassy and a public affairs officer in the Johannesburg consulate.

We recommend that the State Department embark on a high-priority program of recruiting more black foreign service officers to serve in South Africa, as indeed it should in all other areas. Assignments to South Africa should, however, remain on a voluntary basis. There should also be more black officers in the upper levels of the embassy; the selection of a black ambassador would have a particularly strong symbolic effect.

In early 1981, approximately 110 South Africans worked for the U.S. Embassy and consular offices in South Africa. Of these, roughly 50 percent were black. While whites hold the majority of responsible jobs available to South Africans, about 25 percent of the senior positions are filled by blacks.

In view of its stated policy objectives, the United States has a special responsibility to demonstrate through its local embassy work force that equal employment opportunity can be a reality in South Africa. This responsibility has been recognized recently through the institution of affirmative action and job training programs in the embassy and consulates, and of a number of employee benefit programs of the kind suggested in the Sullivan Principles. This is a good beginning and we urge that these initiatives be vigorously pursued.

(d) Continue Policy of Statements and Actions Expressing U.S. Opposition to Apartheid.

The United States has in the past taken a number of steps to express its disapproval of the South African government's racial policies, including sending U.S. officials to the funerals of black South African leaders and having its embassy staff attend political trials. It has made it clear to the South African government, publicly and privately, that movement toward genuine political power sharing is a prerequisite for improved relations between the two countries. The United States has also warned the South African government that it should not expect American military assistance in the event of major internal violence or external aggression. Such actions and statements, which express and publicize the United States' position, should continue.

(e)   Expand Contacts with Black South African Leaders.

Whatever the future holds for South Africa, black leadership will play an increasingly important role. The U.S. government presently maintains informal contact with black South Africans, including church, labor, and business leaders and representatives of the exiled African National Congress and Pan-Africanist Congress. These contacts demonstrate that the U.S. government regards them as important and increase the government's knowledge of South African affairs. But it is also important that dealings with the black leadership not be construed as support for one group or another, or as recognition of claims to be the sole representatives of the South African people. With that caveat, we recommend that these contacts be maintained and, if possible, expanded.

(f)   Withhold Recognition of Homelands.

The South African government continues to pressure the homeland governments to accept "independence." We believe this de facto partitioning of the country must be opposed and that the homelands should remain an integral part of South Africa until all South Africans have full political and citizenship rights and are thus in a position to make a free choice. Until this happens, we recommend that the United States continue to withhold recognition of the homelands as sovereign states. The homelands that have not accepted independence should be treated like any other part of South Africa. Government and private assistance, for example, should be subject to the same restrictions and exceptions as those proposed for the rest of the country. We recommend that homelands that have accepted independence should receive only humanitarian aid in emergencies and that U.S. governmental or private agencies, whether business or nonprofit, not now operating or doing business in them should stay out. We are aware of the depth of human need in the independent homelands but believe that to do otherwise would give unacceptable recognition to the homelands policy. It should also be noted that since human needs in the rest of South Africa greatly exceed available resources, choices have to be made in any event. (See further details in the discussion of actions to support Objective 3.)

417

(g) Support Humanitarian Aid Programs for Black South Africans.

The UN General Assembly established the UN Trust Fund for South Africa in 1965 to provide legal, educational, and relief assistance for South African political prisoners and refugees and their families. The Trust Fund relies on voluntary contributions, primarily from UN member states but also from private organizations and individuals. In 1979, the United States resumed annual contributions to the UN Trust Fund after failing to contribute for a decade. Since 1978 the U.S. government has also contributed $1 million annually to the UN Educational and Training Program for Southern Africa, and in 1980 it gave $25,000 to the UN-affiliated International Defense and Aid Fund for Southern Africa.

The United States is not in the forefront of this effort. The Scandinavian countries routinely contribute more in absolute terms to the UN humanitarian organizations, and a number of other countries make considerably higher per capita contributions. We recommend that the United States increase its contributions to these organizations and to others providing legal, medical, educational, and other assistance to black South Africans.

2. U.S. Corporations

The thrust of our policy recommendations, insofar as they relate directly to South Africa, is twofold. We recommend action by the U.S. government to make clear its opposition to South Africa's racial policies. We also propose that the United States remain actively engaged in South Africa as a means of exerting the maximum possible constructive influence. Some tension will always exist between these two strategies, but it can be minimized.

The presence of U.S. corporations in South Africa raises this conflict in sharpest form. Is it possible for American companies to remain in that country and simultaneously reflect the United States' opposition to apartheid, improve the lives of black South Africans, and attempt to influence the South African government on important issues? And, if that is not possible, should not U.S. corporations be urged to withdraw from South Africa?

We believe that economic withdrawal—disinvestment—is not the answer. U.S. corporations can remain and perform their functions in ways fully consistent with the objectives of U.S. policy—but not while doing business as usual. A clear commitment by American companies is necessary, a commitment in deeds as well as words that aligns corporate economic interests with movement toward a more just society. To achieve this, we make three recommendations.

First, U.S. corporations and financial institutions operating in South Africa should commit themselves to a policy of nonexpansion and those businesses not already there should not enter the country. Second, a generous proportion of corporate resources—determined in accordance with a specific "social development expenditure standard"—should be set aside to improve the lives of black South Africans. Third, U.S. companies that have not yet subscribed to the Sullivan Principles should do so, and compliance should be effectively monitored.

Each of these measures could be made mandatory through enactment into law. In fact, a bill that would require U.S. companies in South Africa to comply with the Sullivan Principles has been introduced in Congress. Its supporters argue that it would ensure wider compliance and send a stronger signal to the South African government and all concerned. It would also answer the criticism of corporate managers that the U.S. government has, by default, left them to make foreign policy.

Those who oppose making the Sullivan Principles mandatory argue that it would subject corporate management to conflicting U.S. and South African legal obligations. Enactment into law and the imposition of penalties for violation would create requirements of precision in monitoring and standards of proof in enforcement that would be difficult to meet.

The difficulty of formulating a clear definition of "expansion" would also create problems of monitoring and proof if the ban on new investment were made mandatory. Enacting the social development expenditure standard into law would not be feasible because of the problems of finding a formula or even a small number of formulas that could be applied equitably to all the different U.S. companies operating in South Africa.

Each would raise the troublesome question of whether U.S. companies in other foreign countries should be subject to the same requirements, and, if not, how such determinations should be made and monitored. Finally, it is argued that enactment of the required legislation would be a long, drawn-out process, and many corporations might use its pendency as an excuse for inaction.

Although there is merit on both sides, we find the arguments against trying to make these measures mandatory more convincing under present circumstances.

We therefore suggest that for the time being the measures be implemented on a voluntary basis (including the development and implementation of a better monitoring system for the Sullivan Principles) and that the U.S. government strongly endorse them as an important part of overall U.S. policy. They should remain in effect until a new system based on a genuine sharing of political power is put into effect in South Africa.

High-level management of American corporations operating in South Africa should consider meeting periodically in the United States to discuss these measures and, where appropriate, formulate common strategies for their implementation. Informal assurance that these meetings and policies would not violate the antitrust laws should be sought from the Department of Justice.

These proposals are also put forward as a guide for church, university, and other groups in the United States that have taken a close interest in corporate behavior in South Africa. Before discussing each proposal in detail, however, we should explain why we have rejected the use of major economic sanctions against South Africa under current circumstances.

The Sanctions Controversy. There has been a long and divisive debate in the United States over economic sanctions against South Africa, a debate that is likely to continue until a satisfactory solution to South Africa's political problems is found. It takes place in churches, on university campuses, in labor unions and corporate boardrooms, in Congress and the executive branch, in civil rights organizations, in the media, and even on Madison Avenue.

The debate is complicated by the multifaceted nature of the sanctions "weapons," and by the fact that some people who support the use of minor sanctions balk at major ones. In the minor category, various groups have chosen to boycott the handling or sale of South African goods, as when the longshoremen's union refuses to unload South African cargoes or television stations reject Krugerrand advertising.

The U.S. government and American corporations active in South Africa have imposed their own forms of sanctions from time to time. The government has curtailed trade by banning arms sales, limiting Export-Import Bank facilities, and restricting the transfer of computer technology to the South African government and the sales of dual-use items to the military and police. Some U.S. corporations have cut back on new investment, reduced their South African holdings, stopped lending to South Africa, or, in the case of those not already in South Africa, refrained for political reasons from entering what is otherwise perceived as a promising market. But more drastic actions, such as trade embargoes and disinvestment, have so far been rejected by the U.S. government and the private sector.

Further complication arises when an attempt is made to evaluate the effect of sanctions already applied to South Africa. The arms embargo, although reasonably well observed, has resulted in South Africa developing a thriving indigenous arms industry. An oil embargo imposed by the Arab members of OPEC, at the request of the Organization of African Unity, in place for almost a decade, has not seriously curtailed South Africa's access to oil but has spurred the development of oil production from the country's abundant coal reserves. Despite the OAU ban on all commercial dealings with South Africa, some African states have become more economically dependent upon the Republic.

Although advocating disinvestment is a serious criminal offense in South Africa, black South Africans readily make their views clear on the issue. A thorough examination of black opinion by the U.S. Embassy in South Africa in 1977 concluded: "Our impression is that blacks who reflect on foreign investment as an issue are now roughly divided between those favoring disinvestment and those who would like to see it remain in instances where it contributes to black aspirations directly and in the near term." Our own contacts with black South Africans confirmed this division.

420   The United States' economic stake in South Africa is relatively small.

Direct investment amounts to about $2 billion (compared with $6 billion for the United Kingdom), about 17 percent of total foreign investment in South Africa, and 1 percent of the United States' world total. The 350 American corporations there employ approximately 70,000 black South Africans, 2 percent of the total black labor force. The United States' trade with South Africa, though important, is a fraction of American world commerce. The only critical area is the purchase of several key South African minerals—chromium, manganese, platinum, and vanadium—which are important to a wide range of U.S. industries.

Yet this modest profile does not properly reflect the symbolic importance that the U.S. presence has for South Africans. America's leadership of the West, its economic strength and influence, and its belief in democracy and racial equality mean that the U.S. commercial relationship with South Africa has a significance out of proportion to actual economic size. That significance is heightened by the activities of special interest groups in the United States and by African states calling on the U.S. government and American corporations to use their economic leverage to exert pressure on the South African government to change its policies.

The arguments for and against are familiar to many people but are worth reviewing to explain why under present circumstances we reject the two major forms of economic sanctions—a trade embargo and disinvestment—and why we think U.S. corporations should stay in South Africa but limit their expansion. The arguments turn on a number of factors that include the economic and political impact of sanctions on South Africa, the cost to those imposing them, their effects on South Africa's vulnerable neighbors, the capacity of the Republic to retaliate, and the likelihood of their being adopted multilaterally. Of the two major kinds of sanctions, a trade embargo is regarded as the more powerful. A discussion of disinvestment follows later.

Trade Embargo. Supporters of a trade embargo against South Africa argue that it would have serious economic consequences if it were effectively imposed. South Africa is heavily dependent upon a relatively limited number of foreign suppliers for high technology and capital goods such as heavy machinery. The impact on growth, employment, and productivity would be dramatic.

Opponents of sanctions concede that South Africa's dependence on imports constitutes its greatest vulnerability. But they point out that the country could meet some of its needs through import substitution, and that increased oil-from-coal production, conservation, and rationing would make the economic impact of an oil cutoff minimal for a period measured in years rather than months. South Africa would not be short of foreign exchange because its exports—principally gold and unprocessed minerals—could be marketed with relative ease. Demand for these commodities would presumably remain strong and their origin, the Rhodesian experience shows, would not be difficult to disguise. The country would also have no trouble feeding itself. The embargo would undoubtedly make South Africa more self-sufficient in a number of industries, although at higher cost.

The debate then focuses on the likely political and psychological effects of the embargo. Proponents of sanctions argue that economic hardship would produce political change, either through the whites introducing change to cause the embargo to be lifted, or, if they became more intransigent, through the collapse of the economy and the creation of a revolutionary situation. Blacks, they agree, would probably suffer more than whites, but blacks are suffering under apartheid anyway, while whites are secure and prosperous. For blacks, the hardship would be a short-term sacrifice for a long-term gain.

Opponents of sanctions disagree. The political effects of sanctions have historically not been determined so much by economics as by cultural, social, and ethnic factors. The Afrikaners, in particular, are conditioned to turn inward and resist outside pressures. A trade embargo would make the white community more united, more resourceful, more determined to preserve its identity and its power. Sanctions would also probably strengthen the reactionary elements in South Africa and weaken the reformers, as well as dry up resources that could have been used to implement reforms. Whites who found the hardship brought by sanctions unacceptable would probably leave the country, but the majority would stay and accept a reduced standard of living as the inevitable price of survival. The government would ensure that the white community was adequately cushioned against severe economic effects of sanctions. The black population would have to bear the brunt of the assault.

A trade embargo, even if an exception were made for purchases of key minerals from South Africa, would not be cost free. The United States would probably be the least affected of South Africa's principal trading partners, although the South African government could retaliate by withholding some of its key minerals. Even if mineral supplies were not affected, the cost to Great Britain would be considerable—causing a major loss of export earnings and jobs. West Germany, France, and Japan would also be hurt, although less seriously than Great Britain.

South Africa's neighbors, particularly Botswana, Lesotho, and Swaziland but also landlocked Zimbabwe and Zambia, would be vulnerable both to the side effects of the embargo—the South African government would be unlikely to permit the shipment to its neighbors of oil and other important products that were in short supply at home—and to deliberate South African retaliation. There would also be a strong temptation for South Africa to use its neighbors' vulnerability as a bargaining counter to weaken or even end the embargo.

The question of implementation provides the opponents of trade sanctions with their strongest case. At present, there is no sign that Britain, West Germany, France, and Japan would agree to a multilateral embargo against South Africa over its apartheid policies. The British government has made it clear that the political and economic costs are far too severe. Without their cooperation, as even the supporters of boycott concede, the unilateral American embargo would have little more than a symbolic effect that would quickly dissipate as South Africa filled the gap by increasing its trade with the other industrial nations.

A multilateral trade embargo mandated by the UN Security Council remains a possibility. But the doubts that surround sanctions as an effective instrument of coercion in international affairs and the difficulties of applying them to South Africa as a means to force the government to share political power with blacks make it unlikely that they will be used for this purpose under current circumstances. For example, a call for sanctions over Namibia was vetoed by the United States, Great Britain, and France in the Security Council in April 1981. Nevertheless, deadlock over Namibia, if sufficiently protracted, and the possibility of a serious deterioration of conditions in South Africa keep the option alive.

The problems of imposing a multilateral trade embargo against South Africa have caused someadvocates of strong economic pressures to propose a selective attack on the country's most critical dependency: oil. They argue that an effective oil boycott, like an effective trade embargo, would have a substantial impact on South Africa if continued for an extended period. But the same questions arise. Is it feasible? And, even if it were, would it lead to the desired goal, political change?

An oil embargo, its supporters contend, is easier to implement than comprehensive trade sanctions because oil is a single product and can be monitored from its points of origin outside South Africa. Oil is delivered by sea, making shipments susceptible to identification and confiscation. Deterrent action by naval forces can be taken as tankers are on their way to South Africa or on their way back. About 20 percent of South Africa's energy needs are met by oil, the bulk of which is still imported. Until the country's second and third coal-to-oil plants come into operation in 1982–83, only a marginal percentage of its oil requirements will be covered by domestic production.

Critics of the oil embargo point out that South Africa has already successfully circumvented two serious attempts to cut off its oil, the OPEC boycott in 1973 and the Iranian embargo imposed in 1979. (Before 1979 Iran supplied 90 percent of South Africa's oil imports and ignored the OPEC ban.) Oil also tends to lose its national identity and accountability in a free-trading world market. Opponents of the boycott stress that as long as South Africa has sufficient foreign exchange to pay top prices and is not subjected to a costly naval blockade, oil is likely to get through. Meanwhile, South Africa is increasing its stockpiles and developing its own alternative energy resources. By 1983, SASOL plants should provide between 30 and 40 percent of domestic oil needs. Finally, Western countries that are themselves potential hostages to an oil embargo can be expected to be extremely cautious about using it as a weapon against any other country.

Disinvestment. The arguments over disinvestment are similar to those used in the trade sanctions debate, but there are some differences. Advocates of disinvestment say that continued economic engagement damages U.S. interests in several ways. It shows a lack of concern about apartheid that is at cross-purposes with the United States' public condemnation of the system. The United States is ready to take a rhetorical stand, supporters of disinvestment stress, but is not prepared to pay a price by denying itself direct access to the profitable South African market.

The presence of the U.S. corporations, it is argued, provides valuable moral, economic, and political support for the South African government. American corporations pay taxes to the government, and foreign loans help finance South Africa's purchases abroad, including arms and oil, and sustain the country's growth. The presence of foreign capital is seen as insurance for South Africa, protecting it against international economic sanctions.

Although U.S. investment may be a relatively small proportion of total foreign capital in South Africa, it is concentrated in a number of key industries: oil (constituting about 44 percent of the petroleum industry), automobiles and trucks (33 percent), and computers (approximately 70 percent). All these industries, advocates of disinvestment argue, are critically important to the South African government's capacity to maintain control and develop its economic and military strength. And, in the broader context of Africa, more than a third of American investment in the continent is concentrated in South Africa alone.

Those favoring disinvestment also contend that the flow of foreign capital has not improved conditions for blacks in South Africa. The gap between white and black wages was not significantly altered during the years in which economic growth was fueled by foreign investment. Moreover, few blacks have been accepted in managerial positions in commerce and industry. In some cases increased American investment has made industry more capital intensive and actually reduced the number of black employees. And, during the period of great economic growth, black political rights have, if anything, been reduced by the growth of discriminatory and repressive legislation and the implementation of the homelands policy.

U.S. investment is not apolitical, the argument continues. The automobile industry sells vehicles to the South African military and police; the oil companies supply them with fuel; American computer firms in South Africa provide the government and its agencies with the means to administer the apartheid system more effectively; and the government can, whenever it wants, direct foreign companies' production to meet its own needs. Even foreign loans serve a political function, regardless of their actual purpose. The South African government is borrowing aggressively abroad, despite record foreign-exchange earnings from gold, to maintain a high profile in Western credit markets and to test its creditworthiness after a period of economic depression and investor fears of political instability.

Finally, it is argued, black South Africans support disinvestment, and their wishes should be respected. Organizations such as the liberation movements, banned in South Africa but believed to be well supported among the black population, the Black Consciousness movement, and prominent leaders of the South African Council of Churches favor disinvestment. Although they are not free to say so directly, it is possible to infer from their public statements that Bishop Desmond Tutu, Dr. Nthato Motlana, and Bishop Manas Buthelezi are all opposed, in varying degrees, to continued foreign investment in the country.

Opponents of disinvestment argue from three different standpoints. First, some oppose it on purely pragmatic grounds: It just won't work. To have any chance of being effective, disinvestment would have to be supported by the other major foreign investors in South Africa, especially Britain, and there is no possibility that they will join a multilateral withdrawal at present. If the United States were to pull out on its own, the vacuum would be filled by foreign and South African firms eager to expand their market shares. The influence exercised by American companies would be lost and their replacements might be less favorably inclined toward the black labor force and less likely to press the government for constructive change.

The South African government has legal authority to restrict the repatriation of equity capital and to block overseas repayments of loans by foreign subsidiaries, authority which has never formally been applied but which exerts a constraining effect on foreign companies. Although this makes disinvestment more difficult, it appears that over a period of time much, if not all, American capital could be withdrawn on an individual, voluntary basis. Assets could be sold to other foreign companies and payment made outside South Africa. Since profits are allowed to be repatriated, some capital could be recovered by permitting plant and equipment to run down over a period of time. Disinvestment mandated by U.S. law, however, could provoke a much harsher response by the South African government—freezing of foreign assets, for instance—which would change this picture.

Others argue that, as with trade sanctions, even if multilateral disinvestment were practicable, there is no demonstrable causal connection between the economic pressure it would create and political change in South Africa, nor between disinvestment and improvements in black living conditions.

A third group rejects disinvestment on the grounds that foreign capital is beneficial to South African blacks and that disinvestment would harm them more than the better-protected whites. There is, it is emphasized, a considerable trickle-down effect from foreign investment that benefits at least those members of the black labor force who work in the modern sectors of the economy. Economic growth and prosperity, it is argued, will open up new and more skilled jobs for blacks, produce better wages, and narrow the black-white income gap. Economic growth will generate strong forces that over time will modify, if not completely change, the apartheid system. The redress of some of

425

the blacks' major grievances—job reservation, influx control, and deplorable living conditions in the townships—could be made substantially easier by economic growth. Also, U.S. firms, by good labor practices and affirmative-action policies, can set an example for others to follow.

Having considered both sides of the argument, we conclude that there is not much of a choice. If there were a serious possibility of South Africa's principal European trading partners voluntarily joining an American withdrawal, disinvestment—and perhaps other large-scale economic sanctions—might become a credible instrument of policy. But it is clear to us that the Europeans would not follow an American lead under current circumstances. Britain, we were told bluntly, simply cannot afford disinvestment. Government and business leaders of other European countries, although not as economically constrained, also told us unequivocally that disinvestment was out of the question. Instead, companies from Europe and elsewhere would probably move to fill the gap left by a voluntary U.S. withdrawal.

Many of the other arguments against disinvestment are also persuasive. There is no evidence that, even if there were a concerted move by foreign corporations to pull out of South Africa, such an action would produce the kind of changes black South Africans want and the United States supports. And, as we saw in South Africa, the presence of foreign companies does bring tangible benefits to a segment of the black population.

Finally, we gained the impression there that many blacks who favor disinvestment as a means of creating the economic and political climate they consider necessary for meaningful change do so because they do not believe U.S. corporations are sufficiently committed to change. If these blacks could be convinced of a serious corporate commitment, many more, it appears to us, would favor the conditional presence of U.S. companies.

For one or more of these reasons all of us, after much thought and discussion, recommend against disinvestment under current circumstances.

At the same time, major sanctions must be kept in the U.S. policy arsenal. The situation in southern Africa may change. If widespread violence, massive repression, or civil war engulfed South Africa, the international community and individual nations would feel a strong need to respond. Trade embargoes and disinvestment remain legitimate instruments of policy for such circumstances. Comprehensive, multilateral, and mandatory sanctions would inflict substantial economic damage on South Africa, even though it is not clear that the desired political change would result.

Thus, we do not rule out their use. The United States and other countries may be compelled to react to what is considered an intolerable situation. With all other actions exhausted, sanctions could be the only available means of expressing international outrage.

Although opposed to disinvestment, we believe that U.S. corporations in South Africa should align themselves more closely and more visibly with the objectives of U.S. policy. Hence our three proposals: no expansion and no new entry; the "social development expenditure standard"; and broader adherence to the Sullivan Principles. These are all things we think U.S. corporations can reasonably be expected to do if they wish to continue operating in South Africa. We propose that the policy of nonexpansion be adopted by all U.S. companies already in South Africa. In addition, American corporations not currently operating in the country should not enter.

A moratorium on new investment would align U.S. companies more clearly and strongly with the declared aims of U.S. policy. It would create an economic incentive—removal of the ban—for American businesses to work for a more just society in South Africa. Yet black South Africans would continue to benefit from their presence because, although the corporations would grow more slowly, they would still provide employment, training, and social benefits for their employees and dependents.

Equally important, the South African government would no longer be able to interpret and publicize new American investment and increased lending—newsworthy items in South Africa—as signaling the United States' underlying acceptance of the status quo. Although there may be no difference in the potential benefit that blacks derive from old and new investment, the negative symbolism of new investment is greater and, in our judgment, outweighs its benefits.

We recognize the difficulty of establishing a uniform and comprehensive definition of "expansion" for the diverse group of American companies in South Africa. Limiting new investment—and the level of lending in the case of banks and other financial institutions—to amounts necessary for maintaining a company's market share might serve as one rule of thumb, although the term "market" is also open to many different interpretations. We are not recommending disinvestment through the "back door." Corporations should be able to make capital outlays to keep pace with product refinements and market growth.

We are, however, against expansion that clearly steps outside these boundaries. Diversification of South African operations into new lines of business would be a breach of the nonexpansion commitment. Examples of such diversification would be an oil company deciding to turn to coal or uranium mining, a corporation that makes only automobiles building a new plant to make trucks, or a drug manufacturer branching into cosmetics. Banks and other financial institutions, whose business in South Africa consists of a portfolio of expiring loans, must be able to make new loans. But they should restrict their overall level of lending in South Africa to conform with the principle of nonexpansion.

427

We recommend that each company set its own explicit nonexpansion guidelines and report annually to its shareholders on their implementation. Several major companies, active in South Africa, already factor into expansion decisions the degree of progress that the South African government is making toward reform. For example, the chairman of the board of General Motors has declared that "until South Africa demonstrates convincing improvement in the extension of human rights, General Motors will not expand its operations there."

Other companies have made similar statements. Eastman Kodak stated that until "significant progress" in reaching a solution "that is fair to all the people of South Africa" has been made, Kodak's "best interests would not be served by considering expansion of productive facilities." Burroughs's policy is that it will not inject new investment capital into South Africa "under present social conditions." And Gulf and Western has stated that although it has had a number of opportunities to invest in business ventures in South Africa, it has declined to do so "for a number of reasons, not the least of which are the policies of the South African government."

There may, of course, be occasions when a project planned by a company is of such value to black South Africans that it would be counterproductive to the basic aims of U.S. policy to forego it.* Control Data, a company that operates in South Africa but has declared a moratorium on new investment, recently cited the case of a computer-based educational system for blacks that it had decided to develop and treat as an exception to its nonexpansion policy.

Although we propose that the nonexpansion policy be adopted on a voluntary basis, in our judgment pressures for a mandatory ban are likely to grow if voluntary action is not taken. The Swedish and Norwegian governments have passed legislation banning new investment and loans, but the laws contain loopholes and affect only a small group of business interests since neither country has a significant economic stake in South Africa. Japan bars direct investment in South Africa yet does a large amount of business there through licensing agreements and other indirect forms of involvement.

A moratorium on expansion may have a greater chance of acceptance than disinvestment by some European countries because it is prospective only and thus less immediately costly to them. Over a period of time, if adopted by other foreign investors in South Africa, such a freeze would have a significant economic impact on that country. In addition to its direct effects, it would inhibit the transfer of Western technology, thus slowing the growth of the more advanced sectors of the South African economy.

*See a more detailed discussion of possible exceptions under the list of actions for Objective 3.

(i)   Social Development Expenditure Standard.

The special circumstances of South Africa require, we believe, a higher-than-usual level of corporate social and community development expenditures for black South Africans. The purpose of the standard we propose is to provide an objective and verifiable means of ensuring that U.S. corporations discharge these responsibilities. The standard, to some extent an elaboration of the sixth principle of the Sullivan code, would remain in effect until blacks had achieved an effective share of political power. It would thus create a further economic inducement for corporations to use their influence with the South African government to encourage change.

Ideally, all corporations would observe exactly the same standard, one based on the same indicator—for example, profit, sales, number of employees, or any combination thereof. But the significance of the indicators varies so widely from company to company that efforts to develop a uniform standard for corporate philanthropy within the United States have so far been unsuccessful. In our judgment the next best approach is to build on the individual standards for corporate giving within the United States, which have been developed over the years and are in many cases a matter of public record.

One possibility is that each corporation set aside at least twice as much annually from its net pretax profits, in proportion to the size of its South African operations, as it does for corporate philanthropy in the United States. For example, if three corporations had policies in the United States of giving X percent of net pretax profit, Y percent of sales, and Z dollars per employee respectively to philanthropic enterprises, they would devote at least $2X$ percent of net pretax profit derived from the South African operation, at least $2Y$ percent of sales made in or to South Africa, and at least $2Z$ dollars per employee respectively in South Africa to such expenditures. Expenditures would be for the benefit of the company's black employees and their dependents or of other black South Africans. The purposes and programs for which expenditures are made should be determined by the corporation in full consultation with unions or, in their absence, with other employee organizations, as well as potential beneficiaries, and black community leaders.

The standard should apply to corporations that are not currently making a profit from their South African operations as well as to those that are. Some companies, although operating at a loss, appear to be staying in South Africa in the hope of being well positioned for larger markets in the future. Others may be in various stages of projects with long capital outlay and start-up periods. They choose to remain in South Africa in pursuit of their basic profit objective, and it is thus appropriate that they should share the same responsibilities as other businesses.

The standard would create a quantifiable target for each corporation's social development responsibilities, ensure high-level-management attention,   **429** and permit the companies operating in South Africa to show that they are playing a constructive role there.

(j)   Sullivan Principles.*

Many foreign companies in South Africa have stated that they cannot adopt progressive practices because such practices are contrary to South African law. Yet the adoption of the Sullivan Principles—several of which conflict with South African legislation—was done openly by the subscribing corporations with the knowledge of the South African government. We were told repeatedly by representatives of major U.S. corporations in South Africa that it is possible to introduce fair employment practices despite proscriptive legislation. Nevertheless, more than half of the American companies there have still not subscribed to the Sullivan Principles.

The Sullivan Principles have often been criticized for providing U.S. companies with a relatively low-cost rationale for staying in South Africa. The code is not designed to change the basic structure of apartheid. But, as we saw firsthand, it has produced real benefits for black employees of some U.S. corporations and their dependents. It has made the managers of U.S. corporations—both American and South African—more aware of the need to introduce reforms and has stimulated acceptance of the concept of corporate social responsibility in South Africa among non-U.S. firms. The code, however, should not be regarded as a static development. Companies that have already subscribed should be prepared to extend the scope of their reforms.

We recommend that businesses adopt the principles as an important step in making a clear commitment to reform in the workplace in South Africa. We also urge that a more effective monitoring system be established, although we are aware of the difficulties of doing this. The present system is based exclusively on reporting by management on a standard form, and has no provision for on-site inspection of company facilities or any other independent means of checking corporate performance. Black employees and their unions should be involved. The Council of Unions of South Africa, a federation of black trade unions formed in September 1980, has already declared itself prepared to participate in monitoring implementation of the various codes of conduct.

3. U.S. Shareholders: Some Guidelines

In recent years, Americans have been paying increasing attention to the social, environmental, and political behavior of the corporations they invest in, as well as exercising their traditional function of monitoring the company's economic progress. Shareholders have brought their concerns to the attention of management through personal advocacy and shareholder resolutions at

*The full text of the Sullivan Principles is set forth in Appendix B.

annual meetings. When corporations have failed to respond satisfactorily, some have chosen to sell (divest) their stock.

The divestment debate has been particularly heated over South Africa. Stock in U.S. corporations operating in South Africa is held by individuals, universities, churches, foundations, public and private pension funds, bank trust departments, and mutual funds, and all these different kinds of shareholders have been drawn into the discussion.

Those favoring divestment assert that a series of well-publicized sales by prominent shareholders can have a shock effect on management, motivating it to rethink its policies. Divestment also satisfies the impulse to express a moral position and, it is argued, enables the divestor to disengage honorably from the issue.

On the other hand, opponents of divestment point out that when a shareholder sells its stock it gives up its voice in shaping company policies. The shares sold will be bought by others, presumably less concerned about the company's practices in South Africa, and the number of shares likely to be voted for reforms will decline. In addition to these general considerations, share-holding institutions must reconcile their commitment to social responsibility with their primary responsibility of protecting and increasing the value of the funds they manage. Sales of stock for noneconomic reasons can sometimes be costly.

Claiming no greater wisdom than others who have thought hard about this issue, we offer the following guidelines.

We suggest that shareholders of U.S. corporations in South Africa try first to persuade the businesses to adopt and implement the no-expansion and no-new-entry proposal, the social development expenditure standard, and the Sullivan Principles. Only if a corporation remains unresponsive should the shareholders consider selling their stock. The decision to hold or sell under these circumstances should be made on a case-by-case basis, taking into account which course of action will have the greatest practical effect on the conduct of the company, as well as the other responsibilities of the shareholder. If a decision is made to sell, the shareholder should consider retaining a nominal number of shares to retain a voice at stockholders' meetings with which to continue trying to influence the company's policies.

It is worth noting that the success of efforts to promote corporate social responsibility are sometimes due more to the nature of the effort than the size of share holdings. A well-planned and sustained campaign by a small group or even an individual, based on nominal share holdings but involving an informed, continuing, and responsive dialogue with management, can produce results. The recent campaign urging corporations to increase the percentage of their annual profits devoted to philanthropy in the United States is a case in point.

Finally, shareholders who sell their shares in protest against corporate

431

policies in South Africa should feel free to reinvest if the problems that caused them to sell are resolved.

OBJECTIVE 2

To promote genuine political power sharing in South Africa with a minimum of violence by systematically exerting influence on the South African government.

Effective pressure for change requires not only a clearly communicated overall posture toward apartheid, but also continuing government-to-government contact to maximize the weight and credibility of the United States' views on particular events in South Africa. Blacks in South Africa often say that change must come from within, a perception we share. A realistic analysis of the situation in South Africa does not hold out much hope for major changes in the political system in the immediate future, regardless of the methods—violent or nonviolent—used to pursue them. Most likely, such changes will come in a series of uneven, erratic increments, increments hopefully neither too small nor too slow.

The South African government, like others, takes repressive measures or keeps them in force principally because it believes them important to its survival. To give them up, the government must be convinced that they are not required for survival or that a greater threat is created by failing to remove them. The United States does not have the leverage to alter the terms of this calculation radically. But it can affect the outcome when the calculation is already close, in cases where a modest incentive or disincentive might shift the balance.

To make most efficient use of the leverage that it does have, the United States should focus its attention on the nuances of change as they occur. The available range of pressures and inducements should then be used to try to steer the South Africans toward policies that favor constructive change.

Underlying this objective is the judgment that there is still time for a process of change that could lead to a new political system in which all races share political power. The process could begin with limited reforms, including some of those currently under discussion. Each significant move forward may make possible further changes that were previously unthinkable. Of course, there is no guarantee that this will happen, and there is a risk that the process could backfire, producing an explosive situation in which black demands for further change, fueled by the government's reforms, outpace white capacity to adjust to them. But accepting the risks of change, in our view, is the only morally acceptable course and, in any event, is far less dangerous in the long term than trying to reinforce the status quo.

432   The hardest part of the journey for whites will be to move to the point

where they are ready to deal with the central issue of sharing power with blacks. The various stages of that journey will provide the most important targets for U.S. influence. We recognize, however, that the implementation of policy is never as precise and unambiguous as this or any other formulation suggests. There is a risk that black and white South Africans as well as others, including our own citizens, may misread U.S. approval of limited progress as complacency concerning the slow pace of change overall. This danger makes it imperative that the first and second objectives be pursued with equal vigor and consistency.

Actions for Objective 2

1. The Approach

The United States, like most governments, pursues a wide range of interests by means of pressures and inducements aimed at influencing the actions of other governments. The U.S. government has also taken steps in the past to cause the American private sector to promote the same objectives. Within the range contemplated in this report, these actions are recognized and permitted by international law.

There are a number of recent precedents. The United States severed diplomatic relations with Idi Amin's Uganda and, later, Congress imposed comprehensive economic sanctions against his government because of his policy of wholesale politically motivated murder. The U.S. government has used a number of devices to pressure the Soviet Union on the issue of Jewish emigration, notably restrictions on grain sales and the export of technology. In these cases, the focus of the United States' attention was the *internal* affairs of the country concerned, the way in which the government of that country was treating its citizens.

Application of this approach to South Africa requires careful monitoring of events in that country. When the South African government shows signs of taking a serious initiative, it will be important for the U.S. government to signal its response during the decision-making process—before positions have hardened—rather than after the decision has been made. In some situations that will be impossible, and the United States will then have to act after the fact, almost certainly with less effect.

If a genuine debate began within the South African government about the possibility of opening all universities to blacks, coupled with significant movement toward closing the gap between expenditures for black and white primary and secondary education, the U.S. government might communicate to the South African government that such steps would be recognized as positive and that an appropriate response would be made. This could be communicated by a public or private statement of support and approval or by a reduction in pressure in some area of U.S.-South African relations.

If the U.S. government saw the South African government taking steps that indicated a move toward genuine dialogue with black leaders, such as revoking banning orders or releasing political prisoners, it could convey its approval and support by increasing diplomatic and other contacts and by lowering some of the commercial barriers between the two countries. The more substantial the progress in South Africa, the greater the positive response.

Conversely, pressures would be used to attempt to discourage negative actions by the South African government. Thus, if it looked as though the government were seriously thinking of backtracking on its policy of permitting the development of black labor unions, the U.S. government could indicate that new pressures would be applied—the tightening of export controls on oil exploration services and technology, for example. Comprehensive economic sanctions would be at the extreme end of this scale, although we are not convinced that they are an effective means of producing political change in South Africa. If the South African government were to turn away from the path of progressive change and adopt a policy of massive violence against blacks, the United States could be forced by international and domestic pressure to use economic sanctions, either alone or, more likely, on a multilateral basis through the United Nations.

We are not suggesting that the U.S. government can or should respond to each initiative by the South Africans. Doing so would quickly exhaust the U.S. repertory of responses, and would be impossible to defend against the charge of trying to influence the internal conduct of another country at an inappropriate level of detail.

The impact of all U.S. responses will be enhanced to the degree that other countries support them. The United States should try to persuade its Western European allies and South Africa's other major trading partners to cooperate with this policy.

Given the limits of American influence and the need to follow South Africa's internal dynamics, why should the South African government take notice of what the United States will or will not do? Despite official disclaimers, the South African people and government do in fact care deeply about ending South Africa's present international isolation in general, and about South Africa being accepted as a member of the Western family of nations in particular. That finding underlies the strategy recommended here.

2. Illustrative Pressures and Inducements

Many of the pressures normally used by the United States to pursue its foreign policy are already in use in the case of South Africa. We have recommended others for the purpose of achieving the first objective. Those actions should remain in effect until a political solution, satisfactory to all races, is reached in South Africa. There are, however, still other measures that the U.S. government could apply. Inducements—frequently, but not always, the reverse of the pressures—are also discussed. We are not proposing these pressures and inducements as specific recommendations for action. Rather, they are described to illustrate the range of responses that could be made to positive and negative actions by the South African government (a list of which is found in Appendix C).

(a) Current Measures.

First, it is worth noting the military, diplomatic, and economic measures already in force. Traditionally, the United States and South Africa had maintained close contact in naval matters. South Africa's attraction for the U.S. Navy was its location in the South Atlantic and its excellent port facilities, especially the Simonstown naval base which can handle major ship repairs. The U.S. Navy called regularly at South African ports until February 1967, when the discriminatory treatment of black American sailors at Cape Town resulted in a ban on future visits. Since then U.S. naval vessels have stopped at South African ports only in emergencies.

In 1975, the United States closed down its NASA/Defense Department space tracking facilities near Johannesburg and two years later withdrew its naval attaché. The United States currently has two military attachés in South Africa, and the South African government has one in its embassy in Washington. The American attachés' principal function is to keep the United States informed about South Africa's military capabilities. The United States and South Africa do not officially exchange intelligence, and the South African government has no official relationship with the North Atlantic Treaty Organization, although it has sought continually to establish one. From time to time the U.S. government has recalled officials from its embassy to Washington to show displeasure at actions taken by the South African government.

Since the early 1960s, the United States has neither encouraged nor discouraged U.S. investment in and trade with South Africa. A 1965 National Policy Paper description of U.S. policy is still accurate today:

> Consistent with our balance of payment goals the U.S. aim in the field of foreign trade with respect to South Africa should be to keep commercial channels open and to maintain U.S. trade in non-strategic commodities in this market. However, in view of overriding political considerations, interested government agencies should continue to refrain from undertaking trade promotional projects involving substantial and readily identifiable government participation and sponsorship.

Thus, while the U.S. government provides information to U.S. exporters and investors on economic conditions and opportunities within South Africa, it does not arrange or participate in promotional projects or send trade missions to South Africa, as it does to many other countries.

The U.S. government has the authority to control trade with South Africa **435** through the Export Administration Act of 1969, which authorizes the use of export controls for three purposes: (1) to protect national security, (2) to advance U.S. foreign policy, and (3) to protect the economy against shortages and inflationary price increases caused by excessive foreign demand. Restrictions on exports to South Africa rest on the foreign policy authority of the act.

The power to implement export controls was delegated by President Jimmy Carter in 1977 to the Department of Commerce, which uses a system of export license requirements to carry out its mandate. A comprehensive Commodity Control List (CCL) covers virtually all items that are exported commercially with the exception of items (for example, military goods) subject to export control by other agencies. No commodity on the CCL may be exported unless it is authorized by a license issued by the Commerce Department's Office of Export Administration. Different licenses are required depending on the nature of the commodity and its destination. Three main types of license have been established:

1. General license—represents the least amount of export control; does not require an actual application to the Commerce Department but is effective automatically for any items covered by the license and shipped to authorized destinations.

2. Special license—issued in cases of repeated shipments; avoids the need for multiple licenses for related transactions.

3. Validated license—most stringent licensing control; requires approval by the Commerce Department before a particular export transaction may take place.

The Commerce Department implements the embargo on U.S. exports to the South African military and police through the use of validated licenses. This has been done by (1) requiring such a license for these exports and (2) prohibiting its issuance.

(b) Additional Measures.

There are additional pressures that could be considered if the South African government were to move toward or to adopt more repressive policies. They fall into several categories.

From time to time the United States has made public statements condemning specific acts by the South African government. In addition, the ambassador and other mission staff members have been recalled, high-level U.S. officials have gone to the funerals of black South African leaders, and embassy staff have regularly attended political trials as observers. However, in contrast to the public statements the United States has made on behalf of political prisoners elsewhere, it has been less vocal about such individuals in South Africa. The United States could show its strong disapproval of South African actions by all these means. It could also reduce the levels of its diplomatic representation in South Africa and South Africa's representation in the United States.

One of the more flexible foreign policy tools is the system of licensing authorized by the Export Administration Act. By shifting individual commodities or classes of commodities from one license category to another, the Department of Commerce can exercise control over the flow of various goods, services, and technology to South Africa. The U.S. government could use this power to control exports in a flexible manner to demonstrate approval or disapproval of actions taken by the South African government.

A specific application of this authority is worth special mention. South Africa depends heavily on American technology for oil exploration. It has been searching for oil for many years through its own state-owned Southern Oil Exploration Corporation (SOEKOR), which hires American drilling companies to do much of the work. American expertise dominates this aspect of the oil industry. Restrictions on the transfer of U.S. exploration and drilling technology to South Africa would have a direct impact on that country's ability to search for oil, the only major energy resource it lacks.

The U.S. government should also be ready under appropriate circumstances to respond to requests for defensive weapons from other states in southern Africa. Care must be taken not to precipitate or intensify direct military confrontations. Nevertheless, the supplying of defensive weapons may serve as an important counter to South African moves. If guerrilla activity based in the Frontline States escalates, South Africa will almost certainly carry out reprisal raids, forcing the Frontline States to turn to the industrialized, arms-producing countries for weapons, as Zambia and Mozambique did during the war in Rhodesia. U.S. willingness to consider arms transfers to meet legitimate defensive needs will also help to minimize the growth of Soviet influence in the region by reducing the need for the Frontline States to appeal to the Communist countries for arms.

The U.S. government's response to requests for arms assistance should not be governed by the level of violence in the region alone, but by the overall configuration of events we wish to influence. There may be merit in supplying certain Frontline States with arms even if there is no serious military threat present at the time. Similarly, a high level of violence in the region should not place the United States under an automatic obligation to provide arms. The appropriate levels and terms of arms transfers will also vary. In certain circumstances small shipments, symbolizing U.S. support, may serve U.S. policy goals most effectively. Much would depend on the scale of the conflict in the region, and how far the South African crisis had gone.

If the situation seriously deteriorated as the result of repressive policies by the South African government, the international community, including the United States, could find itself looking for more forceful ways of expressing its opposition. One possibility would be communications sanctions against South Africa.

The U.S. government has the authority to cut off all direct communication links with South Africa, including flights by U.S. airlines to that country, South African Airways' landing rights in the United States, and postal, telephone, telegraph, and other telecommunications services. If this were done unilaterally, the effect would be to establish an upsetting precedent but not to seriously damage South Africa economically. A multilateral cutoff would be far more severe in its effects. South Africa's most valuable exports travel by air. But even the unilateral embargo is, in our view, an important pressure and should remain an option. The United States should also be prepared to offer inducements to the South African government in response to positive initiatives.

In the diplomatic field, the United States could make official statements of approval, increase diplomatic representation, expand political, parliamentary, and cultural contacts between the two countries, and press for the approval of South Africa's credentials so that it can again participate in UN General Assembly proceedings and be readmitted to other international organizations. This might not be a popular move with some of the African states, but under appropriate circumstances it would be a good way of showing the international community that the United States believed South Africa should no longer be consigned to a "pariah" status. Expression of official U.S. approval for actions taken by the South African government could be done privately or publicly, depending on the extent and nature of the changes and the sensitivities of the South African government.

Expansion of both countries' diplomatic representation would make it clear that relations had improved. The U.S. government could reinstate the post of naval attaché in its embassy in South Africa. The United States could once again permit the exchange of visits by high-level military personnel. In the important area of commerce, the U.S. government could relax restrictions on exports of goods, services, and technology to South Africa, using its powers under the Export Administration Act.

Finally, there is one category of action that does not fall within the framework of government-to-government pressures and inducements. That is the potential influence that individual American sports figures and entertainers—and the organizations that sponsor their events—have with the South African government. Although some decentralization has taken place with regard to athletic competitions, racial policies on sport and entertainment in South Africa are still largely controlled by the central government. Actions by American sports organizations and athletes to influence their South African counterparts are recommended under Objective 3, but the same tactics can be used to exert pressure on the South African government. Reversals of boycotts can provide inducements, if, for example, the government moves positively to end discrimination in an area of sports or entertainment.

To support organizations inside South Africa working for change, assist the development of black leadership, and promote black welfare.

The purpose of this objective is to strengthen the internal forces for change. Both the U.S. government and private institutions can play useful roles.

The lack of a policy framework has made it difficult for private organizations to focus their energies and resources on South Africa in a fully constructive way. Efforts to assist in the development of educational and other institutions serving blacks in South Africa, for example, are sometimes criticized as condoning or collaborating with apartheid. The structure recommended here seeks to relate the actions of private institutions to U.S. national interests and to the policies of the U.S. government, and thus to provide the private sector with a mandate for constructive action.

The U.S. government and private American organizations may be accused of favoring one or another group among those opposing apartheid by providing financial and other assistance to organizations in South Africa. But we believe that risk can be minimized if support is channeled through such groups as civic and labor organizations and the churches. In any case, the risk is outweighed by the potential benefits of such assistance. Support would be given to organizations working for change through nonviolent methods.

Training and other forms of assistance to develop the skills, education, and experience of black South African leaders in every walk of life will serve all U.S. interests. Aid for black leaders will benefit the individuals themselves and may indirectly contribute to the process of change. The more experienced and skilled black leaders are, the more adept they will be at devising and implementing effective strategies for change.

U.S. governmental and private assistance will help improve the abilities of black leaders to function at all levels of government, business, education, and the labor movement. That experience will be valuable whether blacks reach those levels through evolutionary or revolutionary change.

For the black population as a whole, improvements in education, health, housing, and nutrition are important in themselves. Better-educated, better-fed, better-housed, and healthier individuals can also be a more potent force for constructive change in South Africa. They will be better able to take advantage of opportunities opened to them by progress on the political front.

U.S. assistance to black South Africans will also increase their understanding of our values and help us to understand theirs. This base of common experience and personal contact, especially at the leadership level, will strengthen relations and help protect U.S. interests when those individuals reach positions of power in South Africa. The experience and working rela-

439

tionships of private organizations in South Africa will also help in the task of monitoring and assessing changes in that country.

It is important that the rural black population is not overlooked in actions taken to pursue this objective.

Actions for Objective 3

1. Support Public Interest Organizations Working for Change.

2. Encourage Antiapartheid Activities by Private Groups in South Africa through U.S. Counterparts.

3. Support the Research Efforts of South African Organizations and Individuals Working for Change.

4. Support Programs Providing Educational Aid for South African Blacks.

5. Aid African and Multiracial Unions.

6. U.S. Corporations:

    (a) Support Black Economic and Social Development through Investments and Loans.

    (b) Adopt and Implement Social Development Expenditure Standard and Sullivan Principles.

7. Continue Leadership Exchange Programs.

8. Continue Monitoring of South African Government Repression by Private U.S. Organizations.

1. Support Public Interest Organizations Working For Change.

In August 1980, a South African appeals court ruled that the wives and children of African men residing legally in urban areas were entitled to live with them without obtaining special lodgers' permits. Previous practice had separated many of these men from their families. This case, one of the most important in recent years, was brought by lawyers from the Legal Resources Center, a public interest law firm. The center, supported by several South African corporations and at least three U.S. foundations, supervises the work of four clinics in South Africa offering free legal services to poor blacks.

Other public interest organizations in South Africa engaged in projects and research efforts that promote nonviolent social, political, and economic development for all segments of South Africa's population include the South African Institute of Race Relations, the South African Labor and Development Research Unit, the Urban Foundation, the Center for Intergroup Studies, and the Center for Applied Social Sciences. We recommend that U.S. private institutions support organizations of this kind in South Africa.

440

2. **Encourage Antiapartheid Activities by Private Groups in South Africa through U.S. Counterparts.**

The expressed opinions of professional peers and social associates often have greater impact than any amount of repetition of the same point of view by others. We encourage private U.S. organizations and professional associations, such as national civic organizations, women's groups, and medical and legal societies, to make use of their influence with their South African members or counterparts.

An organizational stand of general opposition to apartheid, coupled with an examination of the impact of apartheid in the area with which the particular organization or association is concerned and involving, if possible, the participation of South African members or counterparts, would effectively complement the policy actions available to the U.S. government. For example, South Africa's current racial policy on sports leaves a great deal of discretion to private associations and teams. Pressure by U.S. teams and sports associations on their South African competitors and counterparts who continue to discriminate on racial grounds is certainly appropriate.

Where a South African group is already engaged in antiapartheid activities, it is important for the American branch or related organization to show its support and solidarity. The ways in which this can be done will vary from organization to organization and can best be determined by each in the context of its particular activity and relationship to its counterpart.

3. **Support the Research Efforts of South African Organizations and Individuals Working for Change.**

To enhance their ability to negotiate with the government and mobilize their constituents, black organizations have begun to develop research and analysis capacities. For example, the Inkatha Institute, the new research arm of Chief Gatsha Buthelezi's cultural movement, is charged with "providing a resource and information service to Inkatha in the definition and analysis of national problems and in the formulation of a black response to critical issues of current debate." It is expected to pay particular attention to problems affecting black labor, including formulation of strategies for eliminating influx control and the migrant labor system.

Outreach programs based in universities and other South African institutions have begun to provide research and technical assistance to a variety of black organizations, including self-help groups. We recommend that private U.S. institutions support these and other worthwhile efforts. Assistance, however, should be given with due regard to the risk of placing the receiving organization or individual in political jeopardy.

441

4. Support Programs Providing Educational Aid for South African Blacks.

A number of programs are in existence, both in the United States and in South Africa, to increase the educational opportunities available to black South Africans. The U.S. International Communications Agency annually brings two hundred blacks from South Africa to the United States to receive professional career development training in such diverse fields as business management, social work, journalism, and so forth. In addition, a sizable Fulbright student program brings black South African graduate students to the United States to complete Master's degree programs before returning to South Africa. The U.S. government also supports programs that help refugee students from South Africa attend universities in other African countries and in the United States.

In 1980 a new program—the South African Education Program, funded by U.S. corporations, foundations, and universities under the auspices of the Institute of International Education—was established to provide U.S. college and graduate scholarships for qualified South African blacks to continue their studies in the United States. In its first year thirty students, chosen by black leaders and community groups in South Africa, were placed in American universities.

Within South Africa, correspondence programs for black students have been functioning for many years. The largest, run by the University of South Africa, enrolls as many students at post-high-school levels as attend the government-run black universities. In Soweto, Project Pace, sponsored by the American Chamber of Commerce in South Africa, is nearing completion. The project includes construction of Soweto's first vocational high school—Pace Commercial College—which will train six hundred students. There is also the South Africa Committee for Higher Education, established in 1958 to advance and supplement black education, and the Council for Black Education and Research.

We suggest support for these programs and also urge the consideration of programs specifically designed to provide educational opportunities for black South African women, who face even more hurdles in their pursuit of higher education than black men.

In addition, we recommend private U.S. assistance to South African educational institutions that have shown a commitment to providing educational opportunity regardless of race, color, sex, or national origin. Some universities, for example, have begun to develop outreach programs and adult education programs in the black community, academic support programs for disadvantaged students, and teacher training programs designed to improve the teaching standards of the black school system. The South African government has substantial resources and must bear the ultimate responsibility for improving black education. Nevertheless, these specialized initiatives deserve support and could produce significant results.

5. Aid African and Multiracial Unions.

International trade unions follow developments in South Africa closely, sometimes sending representatives to provide industrial-relations training and to assist in wage disputes. International unions have also contributed to the strike funds of South African unions, although on occasion such overt foreign support has led the South African government to cut off funds from outside sources. In the United States, the African-American Labor Center, an organization with close ties to the AFL-CIO, has a special work/study program that brings a group of five to ten black South African trade unionists to the United States each year for a ten-week training period. The center is also establishing a special unit to coordinate all U.S. labor activities in connection with trade union development in South Africa and is creating a special labor fund to finance trade union activities.

The existing training programs for black South African trade unionists should be expanded, and more U.S. government financial support should be given through U.S. unions and other private organizations to African and multiracial unions when this can be done without jeopardizing their status within South Africa.

6. U.S. Corporations.
    (a) Support Black Economic and Social Development through Investments and Loans.

We recommend the adoption by U.S. corporations of a policy of nonexpansion in South Africa as one of the actions to implement Objective 1. In so doing, however, we noted that exceptions to the ban should be made for investments or loans for projects of unusual and direct benefit to South African blacks.

Decisions on exceptions should be made on a case-by-case basis but should include consideration of the following factors: (1) the effect of the specific project in assisting the development of black leadership and promoting black welfare, (2) the views of South African blacks directly affected and of South African black leaders about the project, (3) the extent of black South African participation in planning the project, (4) the practical availability of South African resources for the same purposes, (5) the compliance of the new project, if it will be an employer, with nondiscriminatory employment practices and, if it is to be part of a U.S. corporate operation, with the social development expenditure standard, and (6) the symbolic and psychological effect of the project on South African blacks, the South African government, and other concerned parties and governments. The creation of job opportunities for blacks should not by itself justify an exception to the ban. Projects that might qualify under these criteria could include development of new housing, educational, and health facilities for blacks and loans to black-owned industry.

443

(b)   Adopt and Implement the Social Development Expenditure Standard and the Sullivan Principles.

Described in detail earlier, these are also important actions in support of Objective 3.

7.   Continue Leadership Exchange Programs.

The U.S. International Communication Agency operates an International Visitor Program that brings twenty-five white and twenty-five black prominent South Africans to the United States each year for one-month visits. A private organization, the United States-South African Leader Exchange Program, has conducted leader exchange, science education, and faculty exchange programs between the two countries for more than twenty years. We favor such programs and recommend their continuation.

8.   Continue Monitoring of South African Government Repression by Private U.S. Organizations.

A number of private organizations in the United States and elsewhere monitor actions taken by the South African government to suppress internal opposition to apartheid. In many cases South African government actions are directed against organizations and individuals committed to change through peaceful methods.

American monitoring organizations convey the message of U.S. concern, focus public attention on particular cases, and help mobilize U.S. governmental efforts on behalf of victims of political repression. Some organizations provide financial assistance to South African attorneys defending individuals accused of political offenses. We endorse these efforts and, recognizing that they are properly dependent on private funding, recommend that such organizations be generously supported.

OBJECTIVE 4

To assist the economic development of the other states in southern Africa, including reduction of the imbalance in their economic relations with South Africa.

The other states in the region are Angola, Botswana, Lesotho, Malawi, Mozambique, Swaziland, Tanzania, Zambia, and Zimbabwe. They are some-times referred to as the Southern African Development Coordination Confer-ence (SADCC) or, more briefly, the "Nine." Pursuit of Objective 4 serves the U.S. interests in a variety of ways. Greater economic strength of the other states in southern Africa would reduce, although certainly not eliminate, South Africa's ability to exert pressure on them for political purposes. (South Africa's small immediate neighbors—Botswana, Lesotho, and Swaziland—would always remain highly vulnerable to such pressure.) In dealing with the South African government, all nine states in the region would have a greater degree of political maneuverability, and, by extension, so would the Organization of African Unity and the United Nations, particularly if multilateral coercive action, such as economic sanctions, become a live issue.

Some analysts have suggested that the Nine cut their economic links with South Africa. But these countries possess little economic leverage over South Africa, apart from that derived from control of the port of Maputo and hydroelectric power from the Cabora Bassa dam, both of which are beneficial but not vital to the South African economy. Costly efforts to do without South Africa's goods and services would have minimal political impact. These realities, though unpalatable, are recognized by leaders of the Nine. An approach that denied them would be counterproductive, for it might, by adding to the existing economic strains in those countries, threaten their political stability.

Instead, we call for a policy aimed at reducing the imbalance between these countries and South Africa. Aid is needed to develop alternative transport routes and facilities to those that pass through South Africa or are dependent upon South African personnel. Those routes make the Nine particularly vulnerable since South Africa can choke off their exports and imports at will. Alternatives could be developed that avoid South Africa and would remain economically viable even if relations were eventually normalized. Development aid should also be channeled into agriculture and technical training, which, together with improved road, rail, and harbor infrastructures, have been flagged as major priorities by the Nine themselves.

Assisting the economic development of these countries may also have an important symbolic effect. Zimbabwe, with its racially mixed population, its recent change from white to multiracial rule, and its political and economic prominence in the region, is of particular relevance. White South African fears of sharing power with blacks would be strongly reinforced if Prime Minister Robert Mugabe's carefully balanced policies on race and private ownership were discredited by economic failure, produced at least in part by a lack of Western aid and investment.

A major U.S. effort to help the economic development of the Frontline States and to reduce the imbalance in their economic relations with South Africa would be seen as evidence of our seriousness of purpose in aligning ourselves with the forces working for change in South Africa. U.S. relations with the Nine should improve. A closer relationship between the United States and the countries of southern Africa is important because the latter play a key role in formulating African strategy on South Africa, both in the Organization of African Unity and in the African caucus at the United Nations.

Our global and regional interests will also be protected by assisting the development of stable governments in the region open to constructive relations with the United States. With such governments in control there is less likely to be political turmoil in the area and less chance of calls for military or other assistance from the Soviet Union, Cuba, or other Communist powers. They would be more likely to look to their friends in the West if they need help to defend themselves.

Aid will facilitate the flow of key minerals to the United States, particularly ferrochrome produced in Zimbabwe and exported through Mozambique. In the long term, infrastructural development—transport and electric power— may lead to the discovery and exploitation of important mineral deposits in these countries, possibly providing alternative sources for some of the minerals the United States imports from South Africa. Sound economic development and its effect on political stability may also reduce the possibility of disruptions in mineral exports to the United States.

Actions for Objective 4

1. Provide Assistance on a Regional Basis.
2. Provide Bilateral and Regional Aid to:
    (a) Assist Agricultural Development.
    (b) Assist Development of Transport, Communications, and Energy Infrastructures.
    (c) Assist Vocational and Management Training.
3. Increase Aid to Zimbabwe.
4. Encourage Trade and Industrial Investment in the Region.

1. Provide Assistance on a Regional Basis.
Historically, U.S. assistance to the countries of southern Africa has been on a bilateral basis, with U.S. aid being targeted to individual countries to fill individual needs and support development projects. In 1977, Congress asked the Agency for International Development (AID) to conduct a "comprehensive analysis of the development needs of the southern Africa region." That analysis concluded that southern Africa's varied distribution of resources and natural geographic interdependencies require regional cooperation to improve economic development. Accordingly, in its 1981 budget proposal AID called for aid to southern Africa on a regional basis in addition to the traditional bilateral approach. Specifically, AID has requested $39 million in general aid to southern Africa to address regional transport problems, provide assistance for regional training, and assist the development of regional agriculture projects and small-scale enterprises.

This approach by AID coincided with the recent formation of the Southern Africa Development Coordination Conference, grouping the nine southern African countries of Angola, Botswana, Lesotho, Malawi, Mozambique, Swazi-land, Tanzania, Zambia, and Zimbabwe. While it is too early to tell whether the SADCC will be an effective organizational umbrella for regional develop-ment, it is important as a political symbol and as a potential mechanism for long-term regional cooperation and coordination. An organization has been established, specific countries have accepted responsibility for exploring poten-tial areas of cooperation in different sectors, and efforts have begun to coor-dinate external assistance with regional objectives.

The possibility of successful regional development has been markedly en-hanced by the independence of Zimbabwe. All of the countries of the region suffered economic hardship from the observance of UN sanctions against Rho-desia and from the effects of the fighting in that country and across its borders. Since the end of the war and the independence of Zimbabwe, much of the regional transport system has been reopened. This will help to reduce the reliance of the Nine on South Africa's railways, roads, and ports.

At a meeting of SADCC in November 1980 in Maputo, the organization sought foreign aid in support of an ambitious $1.9-billion regional development program. Western nations, international organizations, development funds, and banks responded by pledging $650 million. Although much of this consists of renewals of earlier pledges of bilateral loans and aid, the uses to which the money will be put are now to be determined by SADCC. Its stated priorities are (1) the establishment and improvement of the region's communications and transportation infrastructure, (2) increased agricultural production through rural development, livestock disease control, and improved technology, and (3) manpower training.

We endorse both this regional approach to foreign assistance in southern Africa and the priorities for development of the region set by AID and SADCC.

The recommendation that follows provides more detail.

2. Provide Bilateral and Regional Aid to:
(a) Assist Agricultural Development.

The most important of South Africa's exports to the region is food. The Nine annually import hundreds of thousands of tons of maize and other grains, as well as beef, eggs, and other foodstuffs. In 1980 the United States provided $46.4 million in direct food shipments to southern Africa. If properly developed, the region could be not only self-sufficient but also a major exporter of food to the rest of Africa. In addition to continuing to send food to the region, AID has proposed providing more than $65 million in bilateral and regional support for agricultural development. The projects range from the construction of food storage facilities at important transport points in the region to agricultural research and water development in Malawi and resource conservation projects in Botswana. We recommend support of this approach.

447

(b)   Assist Development of Transport, Communications, and Energy Infrastructures.

Of the nine SADCC countries, six are landlocked: Botswana, Lesotho, Malawi, Swaziland, Zambia, and Zimbabwe. Many rely heavily on South Africa's transportation networks to trade with the outside world. A reliable transport, communications, and energy (electricity) infrastructure is needed to move goods between the ports of Mozambique, Tanzania, and Angola to the hinterlands of these countries and the six landlocked SADCC countries. In recognition of this need, the SADCC countries have established the Southern African Transport and Communications Commission, which is charged with coordinating the use of existing systems and the financing and construction of additional facilities in the region. Its first projects are the development and enlargement of the Beira and Maputo ports of Mozambique and the improvement of the Mozambique-Zimbabwe railway links.

Major AID projects scheduled to begin in 1981 include the upgrading of existing road links between railheads in Malawi and Mozambique and major supply routes within Zambia. Numerous smaller projects for the development of rural feeder roads are also planned. We endorse the priorities of the Southern African Transport and Communications Commission, noting that in addition there is a pressing need for the development of reliable communications networks among the countries and an energy infrastructure that can assure the reliable provision of electricity to the Nine.

(c)   Assist Vocational and Management Training.

For long-term economic development, southern Africa badly needs mid-management personnel, vocationally trained workers, skilled technicians, and farmers schooled in modern agricultural methods. SADCC has noted the necessity for manpower training, and AID has targeted $24 million in fiscal 1981 for institutional development, manpower training, and educational programs in its regional and bilateral aid to southern Africa. Included are programs for direct training of individuals in the United States. We urge support of these programs.

3.   Increase Aid to Zimbabwe.

Because Zimbabwe occupies a place of special importance, both politically and economically, in southern Africa, the U.S.-Zimbabwe bilateral aid program should be given very high priority. In the first year of Zimbabwe's independence, the United States provided approximately $50 million in grants and $50 million in loans. We strongly recommend a major increase in the level of U.S. aid to Zimbabwe.

4. **Encourage Trade and Industrial Investment in the Region.**

The Nine need more investment and trade to develop their economies and reduce their dependence on South Africa. In Zimbabwe, the ability to attract foreign investment is likely to be vital to the success of the government's moderate multiracial approach. We recommend that the U.S. government take steps to encourage trade and industrial investment in the region. U.S. government insurance and financing programs, such as those of the Overseas Private Investment Corporation (OPIC) and the Export-Import Bank, should be made available to companies seeking to operate there. Negotiations for a U.S.-Zimbabwe agreement authorizing OPIC insurance and financing for investors in Zimbabwe should be completed as rapidly as possible. The U.S. Trade and Development Program (TDP) finances project planning services at the request of a host country for development projects that either TDP or the host country has found to be feasible, and then locates U.S. firms that may be interested in investing in or providing services for the project. At present it spends about $100,000 annually on projects involving southern Africa. Consideration should be given to expanding this program.

Trade missions should be organized and conducted by the U.S. government. Initiatives taken by countries such as Zimbabwe and Mozambique to welcome new trade and investment from the West should be explored and encouraged by the U.S. government. In the long run, these actions could prove more valuable than all the direct aid the United States is able to give to the region.

OBJECTIVE 5

To reduce the impact of stoppages of imports of key minerals from South Africa.

Pursuit of this objective is intended to minimize the effect on the United States of cutoffs in the supply of the key minerals imported from South Africa. Interruptions in the supply of South African chrome and manganese ores, and their iron alloys, ferrochrome and ferromanganese, would have the most serious impact. Adjustments could be made more easily to shortages of platinum and vanadium. For all these minerals, medium- (five-to-ten-year) and long-term (over ten-year) stoppages would pose substantially greater problems than short-term (less than five-year) stoppages.

We are not suggesting that the United States can or should attempt to end its use of South African minerals. The volume of South Africa's mineral sales to the West makes this impractical. However, actions can be taken to prepare the United States to cope with possible stoppages and to reduce the extent of U.S. reliance on South African imports. This objective calls for such actions to be identified and carried out.

449

The factors that could disrupt the supply of South African minerals to the United States and the likely consequences of such disruptions have been examined elsewhere in the Commission's report (see chapters 14 and 18). Our judgment is that stoppages, if they should occur, are likely to be partial, intermittent, and short term. We consider a medium-term stoppage to be unlikely and a long-term cutoff extremely unlikely.

Pursuit of Objectives 1 through 4, it should be noted, will reduce the chances of political developments causing such stoppages. Avoidance of widespread violence in South Africa, movement toward a genuine sharing of political power, assistance for black South Africans, and increased economic well-being in southern Africa will make stoppages or anti-Western manipulation of South African mineral exports less likely. Objective 4—U.S. aid for the economic development of the Nine with emphasis on their transport and communications networks—will also help to reduce U.S. dependence on South African chromium and ferrochrome by increasing the ability of Zimbabwe to produce and export these minerals.

Actions for Objective 5

1. Increase Stockpiles of Ferrochrome, Ferromanganese, Platinum, and Vanadium.
2. Develop a National Minerals Policy and Contingency Plans.
3. Diversify Sources of Supply.
4. Develop Transport Sectors of the Nine.
5. Encourage Allies to Take Parallel Measures.

1. Increase Stockpiles of Ferrochrome, Ferromanganese, Platinum, and Vanadium.

The U.S. government maintains a strategic-materials stockpile of more than 90 minerals, metals, and industrial materials. The stated purpose of the stockpile is to ensure an uninterrupted supply of strategic materials to meet the country's vital military, industrial, and civilian needs during times of war or when, for other reasons, foreign sources of supply are cut off. The Strategic and Critical Materials Stock Piling Act of 1979 requires a national stockpile able to "sustain the United States for a period of not less than three years in the event of a national emergency," a limit based on the theory that nuclear weapons make a general war lasting more than three years unlikely.

Four minerals imported from South Africa are strategically important: chromium, manganese, vanadium, and the platinum-group metals. A detailed discussion of these four minerals and U.S. stockpiles of them can be found in chapter 14.

The general stockpile goal of sufficient strategic materials to cope with interruptions of up to three years is sensible. This does not mean that full three-year supplies must be maintained for every strategic material, but rather that the combination of government stockpiles, domestic production, and reasonable conservation efforts should be able to meet U.S. needs for three years. For chromium and manganese, we recommend that full three-year inventories be kept. The platinum metals stockpile can be somewhat smaller (on the order of an eighteen-month-to-two-year supply) because of the feasibility of recycling platinum-group metals, which are used primarily as catalysts. A one-year stockpile of vanadium should be adequate because of the large domestic production capacity of the United States.

In addition, the emphasis should be shifted from stockpiling unconverted chromium and manganese ore, which cannot be used by industry until processed into ferroalloys or pure metal, to stockpiling ferroalloys of these minerals. The development in South Africa, and to some extent elsewhere, of smelting facilities at or near mine sites has made conversion in the United States of chromite ore into ferrochrome and to a lesser extent manganese ore into ferromanganese so economically uncompetitive that smelting capacity for these purposes is expected to all but disappear over the next several years. This makes the stockpiling of adequate supplies of ferrochrome and the grades of ferromanganese processed in electric furnaces imperative. The stockpiling of ferrovanadium is not as crucial, because the United States, as a major world producer of vanadium, will retain the ability to convert vanadium ore into ferrovanadium and other alloys. Even so, the production of any ferroalloy requires time and the expenditure of large amounts of energy. By stockpiling more ferroalloy and less ore of any mineral, the government would also be stockpiling labor, time, and electrical power—valuable resources likely to be in short supply during national emergencies requiring stockpile usage.

Inventories of chromium and manganese ferroalloys in early 1981 were markedly below what is necessary to survive a three-year supply interruption—the ferrochrome stockpile contained an eighteen-month supply; the ferromanganese stockpile only a seven-month supply. U.S. 1980 stockpile goals call for reduction from even these levels to just an eight-month supply of ferrochrome and a five-month supply of ferromanganese. These goals should be raised to the three-year level, and the large existing stockpiles of chromium and manganese ore should be converted almost entirely into ferroalloys while U.S. electric furnace capacity still exists. The processing of the stockpiled ore has the additional advantage of permitting a faster buildup of ferroalloy inventories than could be accomplished by purchases of the ferroalloys, which would have to be made over substantial periods of time to avoid disrupting world markets.

We are not recommending that all the ore be converted. There is a loss of flexibility when only end-products are stockpiled. Small quantities of ore should be retained which can be processed, when needed, into other, less widely

451

used alloys or other products that are in short supply at the time of need. In general, however, there is no logic in stockpiling large amounts of unconverted ore that the United States will not have the capacity to refine. At early 1981 prices the cost of increasing the stockpiles as recommended is in the $1.5 billion to $2.5 billion range. Spread out over a three-to-four-year period, this would amount to less than one half of one percent of the annual national defense budget.

Finally, a necessary part of any stockpile program is the development of criteria and administrative mechanisms for allocating available supplies in time of emergency. These would have to be adjusted and fine-tuned constantly during an actual rationing period, but it is important to have a basic program and administrative structure worked out in advance. We recommend that the government develop up-to-date plans for the key South African minerals.

2. Develop a National Minerals Policy and Contingency Plans.

In 1980 Congress passed the National Materials and Minerals Policy, Research, and Development Act. Based on the determination that "the United States lacks a coherent national materials policy and a coordinated program to assure the availability of materials critical for national economic well-being, national defense, and industrial production," the act directs the executive branch to develop a national materials policy, dealing not only with stockpiling but with such measures as conservation and recycling of strategic materials. The act also provides for a "continuing long-range analysis of materials used to meet national security, economic, industrial, and social needs; the adequacy and stability of supplies; and the industrial and economic implications of supply shortages or disruptions."

Insofar as it is intended to deal with stoppages of mineral supplies from South Africa, a national minerals policy should include contingency planning for:

Substitution of materials: For many of the strategic and nonstrategic uses of chromium, manganese, platinum, and vanadium, substitute materials are available, although they often cost more and perform worse. Where substitutes can be used without unacceptably undermining performance (for example, substituting magnesite bricks for chromite bricks in refractories) and without creating severe economic problems because of either the higher price of the substitute material or the costs of retooling, plans should be prepared for possible changeovers to available substitutes.

Conservation efforts: Not all uses of these four minerals are critical or indispensable. For example, the decorative uses of chromium could be cut back without affecting the strategic capacity of the United States. Plans should be drawn for conserving these minerals.

Recycling: Recycling already provides approximately 15 percent of America's stainless steel and approximately 10 percent of its platinum. The potential for greater recycling of platinum is especially great because the metal is neither physically dispersed nor chemically altered by its principal use as a catalyst in automobile emission-control devices and in chemical processes. In the case of an extended stoppage, recycling efforts will certainly have to be expanded, and plans should be made now.

3. Diversify Sources of Supply.

The past few years have seen substantial increases in U.S. imports of strategic South African minerals, especially ferrochrome and ferromanganese. To counter this trend of increasing U.S. reliance on South African minerals, we recommend a concerted effort on the part of the United States and private U.S. mining companies to develop alternative sources of supply of chromium, manganese, and platinum. Diversification is not required for vanadium, because domestic production is adequate. Diversification means developing domestic reserves when and where economically feasible as well as cultivating other foreign sources. Although the latter practice will not reduce U.S. import dependence per se, it will reduce the impact of a supply interruption from South Africa or any other single country.

We recognize the economic and political factors that have led to the concentration of U.S. mineral imports from South Africa: the abundance of proven resources; a government that facilitates foreign investment; low, steady prices and reliable supply; a modern infrastructure; and, at least in the past, relative political stability. The difficulties of doing business with more politically volatile, less-developed countries have made many mining corporations wary of undertaking major long-term projects in such countries.

Government incentives may be necessary to encourage new exploration and mineral development within the United States and in other countries. Although it is beyond the scope of our expertise to make specific recommendations on this subject, we urge the government as part of the development of a national minerals policy to consider the question of whether tax or other incentives are needed to encourage the development of more diversified sources of key minerals, including resources within the United States that are not commercially viable at present prices.

4. Develop Transport Sectors of the Nine.

Of the four key South African minerals, the United States is most vulnerable to a cutoff of South African chromium ore and ferrochrome. The principal alternative source of this mineral and its alloy is Zimbabwe.

Zimbabwe has the potential to produce up to 28 percent of the world demand for chromium and the on-site smelting capability to produce high-grade ferrochrome. But the limited capacity and operating difficulties of the rail, road, and port systems of Zimbabwe and Mozambique (the country through which landlocked Zimbabwe's exports would most efficiently exit to the West) mean that most of Zimbabwe's chromium production must be exported through South Africa. Because of the poorly developed transportation infrastructure of the other states in the region, exploitation of future finds of key minerals in the Nine may also be dependent on access to South Africa's rails, roads, and ports.

In the event of a stoppage of South African mineral exports, South African transport facilities may also be unavailable, either by government decision or as a result of armed conflict. To help assure that Zimbabwean chromium exports and other mineral commodities from the region continue to flow to the West, we recommend that U.S. aid be specifically targeted to the Nine for the upgrading of existing transportation networks and the development of new systems, and we endorse the priority given this matter by AID in its 1981 budget proposals.

5. Encourage Allies to Take Parallel Measures.

With the possible exception of Japan, which for decades has made an effort to diversify its sources of supply, the current capacity of the other OECD countries to cope with stoppages in imports from South Africa is greatly inferior to that of the United States. They have no significant stockpiles. Their vulnerability will lead them in times of emergency to put pressure on the United States to share its stockpiles at the same time that harsher competition for supplies on the world market will force the United States to rely on them more heavily. The political freedom of European governments to exert constructive influence on South Africa along the lines recommended in this report may also be reduced by their extensive dependence on South African minerals. For these reasons, we suggest that the U.S. government encourage its European allies and Japan to take actions similar to those we recommend for the United States and, in particular, to create their own strategic stockpiles.

Conclusion

In discussions of U.S. policy toward South Africa it is frequently said that the region is not of vital importance to the United States compared to Western Europe, Japan, or Latin America. While this is true, all the ingredients of a major crisis are present there. The dangers of political instability, large-scale racial conflict, and the growth of Communist influence are real. The initiative now lies with the South African government. It has the power to minimize these dangers by adopting policies that produce constructive change and movement toward a genuine sharing of political power. Or it can reject that course and try to reinforce the status quo.

To deplore, condemn, and ridicule Afrikaner stubbornness and blindness will not change these attitudes. Indeed, it may strengthen them. Only when Afrikaners see change as a workable alternative to a more frightening fate may they become pragmatic and flexible about sharing power. In seeking to encourage this understanding, U.S. policy must take into account Afrikaner reluctance to surrender any of their political power for fear of losing all of it.

There are, as we have suggested, no easy solutions in South Africa. Change will be a piecemeal and uneven process. U.S. policymakers will find tension, frustration, and moral uncertainty as they deal with specific day-to-day issues while simultaneously keeping ultimate goals in focus.

Most Americans want change in South Africa. Foreign policy, unfortunately, has a price tag, and South Africa is no exception. Stockpiling of key minerals, diversification of sources of supply, assisting black South Africans, providing economic aid for South Africa's neighbors, and a policy of nonexpansion for U.S. companies in South Africa will cost money. It is our firm conviction, however, that if we do nothing or adopt the wrong policies, the eventual costs will be much higher.

We conclude with three general recommendations for the U.S. government. **455**

First, the effect of the policies proposed will be greater if South Africa's trading partners, which are also close to the United States, adopt a similar approach. They should be urged to do so. These countries include Britain, West Germany, France, Italy, Japan, Taiwan, and Israel. Second, we urge the government to issue a white paper defining American interests in the southern African region and outlining the overall structure of policy toward South Africa. Its purpose would be to develop broad understanding and support for U.S. policy among Americans and to make clear to South Africa our fundamental interests and objectives. Finally, we recommend that a high-level interdepartmental committee to oversee policy toward South Africa be established. This will help ensure that the issue is given continuous and coordinated attention.

The United States can constructively assist the process of change in South Africa. There is time, but, as we have stressed, not much time.

Appendix A
Organizations and Individuals Contacted

The Study Commission solicited the views of American organizations and individuals, representatives from state and local governments, and special groups affiliated with Congress on U.S. policy toward South Africa. Individuals and representatives of organizations who addressed the Commission in person are indicated by an asterisk; those who submitted written statements are indicated by two asterisks. Where applicable, the name of the representative responding for the organization appears in parentheses after its name. Federal officials involved in the formulation or administration of U.S. policy toward South Africa who addressed the Commission are also listed below.

PRIVATE U.S. ORGANIZATIONS AND INDIVIDUALS

  *The African-American Institute (Donald Easum, President)
   African Heritage Studies Association
   African Studies Association
   Africa Resource Center
**Professor Henry S. Albinsky, Pennsylvania State University
  *American African Affairs Association (J. A. Parker, Co-Chair)
   American Baptist Church of the United States in America
  *American Committee on Africa (George Houser, Executive Director)
**The American Coordinating Committee for Equality in Sport and Society
     (Richard E. Lapchick, National Chairperson)
   American Enterprise Institute
**American Federation of Labor—Congress of Industrial Organizations

457

American Federation of State, County, and Municipal Employees
American Friends Service Committee
The American Jewish Committee
American Lutheran Church
Americans Concerned About Africa
American Security Council
*Amnesty International (Susan Riveles, South Africa/Namibia
    Coordinator)
*Association of Concerned African Scholars (James Turner, Co-Chair)
*Bank of America (Irv Gubman, Corporate Secretary)
**Professor Albert Blaustein, Rutgers Law School
The Business Round Table
Robert Cabelly, National Journal
The Center for International Security
Coalition for a New Foreign and Military Policy
Coalition for Southern African Freedom
**Coca Cola Company (William Pruett, Vice-President, Corporate Affairs)
**Envirotech International (Paul R. Gibson, President)
Episcopal Churchmen for South Africa
**Ethics and Public Policy Center (Professor Ernest W. Lefever, President)
Federation of Protestant Welfare Agencies, Inc.
*Ford Motor Company (William Broderick, Director of Research and
    Analysis, International Governmental Affairs)
**Freedom House
*General Motors Corporation (Robert Price, Director of International Social
    Action)
**John C. Harrington, President, California Alternative Investment Task
    Force
*Harvard University (Derek Bok, President)
*The Heritage Foundation (Jeffrey Gayner, Director, Foreign Policy
    Studies)
*Peter Duignan, Senior Fellow, the Hoover Institution
Howard University
Howard University Student Association
*Interfaith Center on Corporate Responsibility (Timothy Smith, Executive
    Director)
International Association of Machinists and Aerospace Workers
**International Defense and Aid Fund for Southern Africa
International Freedom Mobilization
International Longshoremen's and Warehousemen's Union
International Longshoremen's Association
Institute for Foreign Policy Analysis
*Lawyer's Committee for Civil Rights Under Law (Millard Arnold,
    Director, Southern Africa Project)

Liberation Support Movement
Professor Richard Logan, University of California, Los Angeles
Madison Wisconsin Area Committee on Southern Africa
Michigan State University
**Mobil Oil Company (E. S. Checket, Executive Vice-President,
      International Division)
Professor Edwin S. Munger, California Institute of Technology
 *National Association for the Advancement of Colored People (Michael
      Meyers, Assistant Director)
National Association of Black Social Workers
**National Council of Churches of Christ U.S.A. (William Howard,
      President)
National Council of Negro Women, Inc.
National Urban Coalition
**National Urban League (Vernon Jordan, Executive Director)
 *New Jersey Coalition of Black Student Organizations (Adimu Changa,
      Coordinator)
Newmont Mining Corporation
Northeast Coalition for the Liberation of Southern Africa
Operation-People United to Save Humanity
Dr. Earl R. Parker, Department of Science and Mineral Engineering,
      University of California, Berkeley
 *Phelps Stokes Fund (Franklin H. Williams, President)
People for Southern African Freedom
Professor Morris Rothenberg, Advanced International Studies Institute
San Antonio Committee Against Mercenary Recruitment and U.S.
      Intervention in Foreign Countries
**South Africa Catalyst Project
South African Military Refugee Aid Fund
Southern Africa Liberation Committee, Michigan State University
Southern Africa Media Center
Southern Africa Support Project
Southern Center for International Studies
Southern Christian Leadership Conference
 *Reverend Leon Sullivan, International Council for Equality of
      Opportunity Principles (Daniel W. Parnell, Executive Director)
 *Students for Economic Democracy (Dallas Burtraw, Spokesperson,
      Northern California Office)
**Professor Lewis A. Tambs, Arizona State University
**Professor Frank N. Trager, Director, National Security Program, New
      York University
 *Transafrica (Randall Robinson, Executive Director)
**United Automobile Aerospace and Agricultural Implement Workers of
      America (Leo A. Suslow, Director for International Affairs)

The United Church Board for World Ministries
United Methodist Church
**University of California (David Saxon, President)
*U.S. Catholic Conference (Reverend Rollins Lambert, Adviser for
African Affairs)
U.S. Chamber of Commerce
*Washington Office on Africa (Edgar Lockwood, Director)

STATE AND LOCAL GOVERNMENT OFFICIALS AND SPECIAL GROUPS AFFILIATED WITH CONGRESS

*Perry Bullard, State Representative, Michigan
**Ernest Chambers, State Senator, Nebraska
*Congressional Ad Hoc Monitoring Group on South Africa (Senator Paul
Tsongas, Co-Chair)
*Congressional Black Caucus (Francis Kornegay, Staff Assistant to
Congressman Charles Diggs)
City of Davis, California
**Herman Farrell, State Assemblyman, New York
*Governor's Office of Planning and Research, California (Barry Steiner,
General Counsel)
Albert Vann, Assemblyman 56 A.D., Brooklyn, New York

FEDERAL GOVERNMENT OFFICIALS

Pauline Baker, Staff, Senate Foreign Relations Committee
C. Fred Bergsten, Assistant Secretary for International Affairs, Department
of the Treasury
Charles Bray, Deputy Director, International Communication Agency
Goler T. Butcher, Assistant Administrator, International Development and
Cooperation Agency for Africa, Department of State
Johnnie Carson, Staff Director, Subcommittee on Africa of the Committee on
Foreign Affairs, House of Representatives
Nancy Ely, Assistant Legal Adviser for African Affairs, Department of State
Frank Galino, Labor Officer, U.S. Embassy, Pretoria
Franklin D. Kramer, Principal Deputy Assistant Secretary for International
Security Affairs, Department of Defense
460 Anthony Lake, Director, Policy Planning Staff, Department of State

Stanley J. Marcuss, Acting Assistant Secretary for Industry and Trade Administration, Department of Commerce

Richard Moose, Assistant Secretary for African Affairs, Department of State

Charles Runyon III, Assistant Legal Adviser for Human Rights, Department of State

James Woods, Director, Africa Region, International Security Affairs, Department of Defense

Appendix B
Sullivan Principles for U.S. Firms Operating in South Africa

The Sullivan Principles, first drawn up by the Reverend Leon Sullivan in March 1977, have been amplified twice—in July 1978 and in May 1979. The text of the principles as amplified in May 1979 follows.

PRINCIPLE I.

Nonsegregation of the races in all eating, comfort, and work facilities.

Each signator of the Statement of Principles will proceed immediately to:
- Eliminate all vestiges of racial discrimination.
- Remove all race designation signs.
- Desegregate all eating, comfort, and work facilities.

PRINCIPLE II.

Equal and fair employment practices for all employees.

Each signator of the Statement of Principles will proceed immediately to:
- Implement equal and fair terms and conditions of employment.
- Provide nondiscriminatory eligibility for benefit plans.
- Establish an appropriate comprehensive procedure for handling and resolving individual employee complaints.
- Support the elimination of all industrial racial discriminatory laws which

impede the implementation of equal and fair terms and conditions of employment, such as abolition of job reservations, job fragmentation, and apprenticeship restrictions for blacks and other nonwhites.
- Support the elimination of discrimination against the rights of blacks to form or belong to government-registered unions, and acknowledge generally the right of black workers to form their own union or be represented by trade unions where unions already exist.

PRINCIPLE III.

Equal pay for all employees doing equal or comparable work for the same period of time.

Each signator of the Statement of Principles will proceed immediately to:
- Design and implement a wage and salary administration plan which is applied equally to all employees regardless of race who are performing equal or comparable work.
- Ensure an equitable system of job classifications, including a review of the distinction between hourly and salaried classifications.
- Determine whether upgrading of personnel and/or jobs in the lower echelons is needed, and if so, implement programs to accomplish this objective expeditiously.
- Assign equitable wage and salary ranges, the minimum of these to be well above the appropriate local minimum economic living level.

PRINCIPLE IV.

Initiation of and development of training programs that will prepare, in substantial numbers, blacks and other nonwhites for supervisory, administrative, clerical, and technical jobs.

Each signator of the Statement of Principles will proceed immediately to:
- Determine employee training needs and capabilities, and identify employees with potential for further advancement.
- Take advantage of existing outside training resources and activities, such as exchange programs, technical colleges, vocational schools, continuation classes, supervisory courses, and similar institutions or programs.
- Support the development of outside training facilities, individually or collectively, including technical centers, professional training exposure, correspondence and extension courses, as appropriate, for extensive training outreach.
- Initiate and expand inside training programs and facilities.

PRINCIPLE V.

Increasing the number of blacks and other nonwhites in management and supervisory positions.

Each signator of the Statement of Principles will proceed immediately to:
- Identify, actively recruit, train, and develop a significant number of blacks and other nonwhites to ensure that as quickly as possible there will be appropriate representation of blacks and other nonwhites in the management group of each company.
- Establish management development programs for blacks and other nonwhites, as appropriate, and improve existing programs and facilities for developing management skills of blacks and other nonwhites.
- Identify and channel high management potential blacks and other nonwhite employees into management development programs.

PRINCIPLE VI.

Improving the quality of employees' lives outside the work environment in such areas as housing, transportation, schooling, recreation, and health facilities.

Each signator of the Statement of Principles will proceed immediately to:
- Evaluate existing and/or develop programs, as appropriate, to address the specific needs of black and other nonwhite employees in the areas of housing, health care, transportation, and recreation.
- Evaluate methods for utilizing existing, expanded, or newly established in-house medical facilities or other medical programs to improve medical care for all nonwhites and their dependents.
- Participate in the development of programs that address the educational needs of employees, their dependants, and the local community. Both individual and collective programs should be considered, including such activities as literary education, business training, direct assistance to local schools, contributions, and scholarships.
- With all the foregoing in mind, it is the objective of the companies to involve and assist in the education and training of large and telling numbers of blacks and other nonwhites as quickly as possible. The ultimate impact of this effort is intended to be of massive proportion, reaching millions.

Appendix C
South African Government Actions

The following is an illustrative list of the kinds of actions by the South African government, both positive and negative, that the U.S. government might link to appropriate inducements and pressures.

I. POLITICAL RIGHTS

Positive Actions

1. Explicit rejection of separate development as the solution to the challenges posed by a multiracial society.

2. Acceptance of the principle of bona fide negotiation with genuine leaders of each population group as the only basis for resolving the question of political rights.

3. Commitment to a goal of genuine power sharing and extension of meaningful political rights to all groups, while providing protection for the basic rights of all segments of the population.

4. Creating a forum for genuine negotiations on power sharing. This could take one of many forms, including:
   (a) A formal national convention with representative leaders from all major segments of the population.
   (b) A broadened intergovernmental conference with provisions for urban

465

African representation (e.g., Soweto urban council, African local government).

(c) A wide range of formal and informal consultations.

5. Conducting such negotiations in apparent good faith.

6. Release of significant numbers of political detainees, including key black leaders.

7. Revocation of banning orders.

8. A program of amnesty for exiles not accused of serious crimes of violence.

9. As an integral part of the negotiation process and a demonstration of the good faith of the South African government, a "guaranty of security" for political leaders not carrying out or advocating violent activity aimed at overthrow of the South African government.

10. Nonimplementation of homeland legislation and resettlement programs.

11. Reversal of the policy that denies South African nationality to Africans and forces homeland nationality upon them.

12. Repeal of internal security laws that restrict both whites and blacks from achieving an open political dialogue:
(a) Pretrial and preventive-detention laws.
(b) Censorship laws (Publication Act, Official Secrets Act, Defense Act of 1957, Prisons Act).
(c) Laws that restrict the freedom of association (Internal Security Act, Unlawful Organizations Act, Affected Organizations Act).
(d) Laws that restrict the freedom of assembly (Riotous Assemblies Act, Internal Security Act, Black Consolidation Act).

13. Repeal of legislation (Political Interference Act) that prohibits multiracial political parties and other forms of interracial political cooperation.

14. Implementation of decentralized measures including:
(a) Extension of urban African administrative organs with genuine authority and resources.
(b) Communal institutions (Coloured and Asian) with genuine governmental powers.
(c) Multiracial consultative bodies with an effective voice in policy determination.

15. Introduction of legislation to broaden the base of the electorate for parliamentary elections (e.g., nondiscriminatory voting qualifications).

16. Adoption of a governmental system acceptable to black South Africans with constitutional protection of the basic rights of all groups (e.g., federation; confederation; consociation; one person, one vote in a unitary state).

Negative Actions

17. Statements of continued commitment to separate development.

18. Unusually racist and provocative political rhetoric.

19. Accelerated implementation of homeland policy, including:
    (a) Increase in population resettlement schemes.
    (b) Additional pressures (e.g., financial) on homeland leaders to accept independence.
    (c) Formulation/implementation of consolidation schemes carried out on a unilaterial basis with an unequitable allocation of land and resources.
    (d) Erosion of rights of urban Africans, including citizenship rights.
    (e) Accelerated homeland independence through changes in statutory process for granting independence.

20. Further isolation of African political groups from other societal groups.

21. Decrease in Coloured/Asian political rights:
    (a) Further limitations on authority of Coloured/Asian local governmental bodies.
    (b) Abolition of partly elected assemblies coupled with increase in direct white administration.

22. Increased repression, including:
    (a) The banning of African political and cultural organizations such as Inkatha, Soweto Committee of Ten, and AZAPO, and their leaders.
    (b) Increased restrictions on the holding of public gatherings and free speech.
    (c) Further restraints on freedom of the press.

23. Massive repression and violence against black South Africans, including mass killings of black South Africans.

II. THE APARTHEID SYSTEM

This section refers to the apartheid system narrowly defined to include only group areas, influx control, residential segregation, and so-called petty apartheid.

Positive Actions toward Ending Apartheid

24. Consistently liberalized administration of the Group Areas Act:
    (a) Ending or greatly reducing prosecution of violators.
    (b)

Reducing the effective penalties for violating the law.
(c) Increasing the scope and availability of exemptions.

25. Changes in areas of property ownership and residential restrictions:
    (a) Limited removal of statutory barriers, e.g., establishment of "free zones" to which no residential restrictions based upon race apply.
    (b) Large-scale and rapid implementation of ninety-nine-year lease program with ancillary programs (e.g., low-cost mortgage funding) which would permit Africans to make practical use of the legal opportunities.
    (c) Removal of all restrictions on Africans, Coloureds, and Asians purchasing land: (i) in the common areas, (ii) anywhere.
    (d) Repeal of Group Areas Act.

26. Changes in the area of social segregation and separation in access to facilities and amenities, including:
    (a) Refusal to administer racist legislation.
    (b) Substantial administrative desegregation of facilities by the widespread granting of exemptions.
    (c) Legislation removing categories of facilities/amenities from coverage of current restrictions.
    (d) Repeal of all "petty apartheid" laws and regulations, including laws under which municipalities might enact local ordinances requiring segregation.
    (e) Antisegregation legislation (e.g., fair-housing laws, public accommodations and amenities).

27. Ending of segregation in:
    (a) Higher education.
    (b) Secondary education.
    (c) Primary education.

28. Ending prohibition on mixed marriages and sexual relations:
    (a) Decriminalization of interracial sex.
    (b) Removal of prohibition on mixed marriages.

Negative Actions

29. Increase in effective enforcement of existing discriminatory legislation, especially in areas of relative relaxation (sports, culture, education).

30. Decrease in willingness to grant exemptions from racial legislation restricting residence, access to public accommodations, attendance at "white" institutions of higher education, etc.

31. Failure to implement announced changes within reasonable periods of time.

III. HEALTH, EDUCATION, OTHER PUBLIC SERVICES

Positive Actions

32. Clear rejection of race as a valid criterion in allocation of resources; commitment to goal of equal allocation of public goods and services:
    (a) Formulating timetables for greater equalization in expenditure on health, education, housing, and related services.
    (b) Taking action to reflect these new priorities in the national budget.

33. Commitment to and creation of mechanism for greater intergroup participation in policy (especially the development of school curricula).

34. Reorganization of racially based departments along functional lines (e.g., new Department of Education would include old, separate departments of white, Coloured, Asian, and Bantu education).

35. Equalization of salaries and pensions of teachers of all races.

36. Implementation to the same academic levels of compulsory and free education for all races.

37. Increased provision of lighting, sanitation, and electrification to black areas.

38. Building substantially more family housing for Africans in urban areas.

Negative Actions

39. Justifications of existing inequalities.

40. Statements in support of continued preferential treatment for whites.

41. Failure to follow through on commitments to significantly reduce the gap between white and black services and facilities within reasonable periods of time.

42. Increase in white control of educational policy and administration affecting blacks.

IV. LABOR AND EMPLOYMENT

Positive Actions

43. Acceptance of principle that race should not be a factor in the structure and functioning of the industrial relations system.

44. Acceptance of effective equality of opportunity in employment.

45. Rapid implementation of progressive recommendations of Wiehahn Commission, especially:
   (a) Desegregation of workplace.
   (b) Elimination of job reservation.
   (c) Expeditious registration of African trade unions and admission into industrial councils.

46. Development by Manpower Commission of a Code of Fair Labour Practices prohibiting discrimination in employment, promotion, and training, and prohibiting segregation in the workplace.

47. Effective enforcement of said code by the Industrial Court.

48. Rapid implementation of Riekert reforms, especially:
   (a) Abolition of the seventy-two-hour rule restricting African presence in urban areas.
   (b) Decriminalization of pass-laws offenses.

49. Changes extending beyond Riekert and Wiehahn, especially:
   (a) Influx control:
      (i) Use of nonracial criteria for influx control, such as housing availability, skill requirements, job availability, etc. The use of such criteria would be justified provided sufficient resources were allocated to promote housing, education, etc.
      (ii) Abolition of migrant labor category for non-mine workers, i.e., non-mine workers would have to be accepted on a permanent basis.
      (iii) Elimination of all forced separation of workers' families.
      (iv) Complete abolition of influx control system.
   (b) Greater freedom for trade unions to determine their organization, membership, and strategy:
      (i) Ability to form multiracial unions.
      (ii) Ability to engage in political activity (i.e., lobbying).
      (iii) Cessation of arrests of leaders of registered and unregistered trade unions for offenses under the security laws that do not involve violence.
   (c) Greater employment opportunities in the public sector:
      (i) Active program of training and promotion of blacks within all branches of civil service and parastatals.
      (ii) Appointment of black judges in courts of general jurisdiction.
   (d) Adoption of a legislative program of affirmative action for the private sector.
   (e) Elimination of all restrictions on black business, including:
      (i) Restrictions on place of business.
      (ii) Restrictions on type of business (e.g., factory in Soweto) and size of business (e.g., number of employees).
      (iii) Restrictions on building and employment without a permit.

Negative Actions

50. Reaffirmation of race as the criterion for labor control and employment opportunity.

51. Repudiation of Wiehahn and Riekert reforms.

52. Maintenance or increase in gap between white and black wages.

53. Harassment and/or tightened controls over both registered and unregistered African trade unions, including restrictions on ability of trade unions to receive funding from outside sources.

54. Continued and heightened restrictions on black businesses.

55. Diminished employment opportunities for blacks in both public and private sectors.

Glossary

African	Under South African law, the word is a racial classification that encompasses the majority of the population of South Africa. It refers to any person "who is, or is generally accepted as, a member of any aboriginal race or tribe of Africa."
Afrikaans	A language developed in South Africa from seventeenth-century Dutch. It is one of the two official languages (the other being English) of the Republic of South Africa. Afrikaans is spoken as a first language by Afrikaners and a majority of the Coloured population.
Afrikaner	A South African white descended from the early Dutch, German, or Huguenot settlers who immigrated to South Africa beginning in the seventeenth century.
apartheid	Apartness; a racially based policy of segregation and political and economic discrimination against blacks in South Africa. The philosophy of apartheid was first enunciated officially by the National party of Prime Minister Daniel Malan in 1948.
BLS states	Botswana, Lesotho, and Swaziland.
baasskap	Bossdom; supremacy; a term frequently used to describe white domination under apartheid.
banning	An action taken by the minister of justice under the authority of the Internal Security Act to restrict an individual's freedom of movement, association, and expression. In some cases, banning can amount to house arrest. Organizations and publications can also be banned.

Bantu	In South Africa the term, which has pejorative connotations, means any African person. It has been dropped from official government parlance.
blacks	As used in this report, a collective noun to include Africans, Coloureds, Indians, and other Asians.
black spots	Areas of land in "white" areas "illegally" inhabited by blacks; may be expropriated by the South African government.
Boer	A white South African of Dutch, German, or Huguenot descent, especially a rural descendant of the early Dutch settlers. As *boer* it is a generic word meaning farmer. Sometimes a synonym for Afrikaner.
Broederbond	Brotherhood; league of brothers; an exclusive, male-only secret organization established in 1918 to promote the interests of Afrikaners.
Cape route or Cape sea route	The sea route around the Cape of Good Hope, which is heavily used to transport oil from the Middle East to Western ports.
Coloured	A racial classification denoting South Africans of mixed race, mainly African-Euorpean descent. A Coloured person is sometimes defined as one who is not a white or an African, a definition that can include Indians and Asians.
common areas	"White" South Africa; all of South Africa excluding the homeland areas.
community councils	Local government bodies of elected black officials with limited powers over black urban communities.
direct investment	Investment of capital in the physical assets of an enterprise or a controlling interest in the business entity owning such assets.
disinvestment	As used in this report, the withdrawal of capital from investment in South Africa.
divestiture	As used in this report, the sale of stock in a corporation that has direct investments in South Africa.

473

Dutch Reformed church	Established by early Dutch settlers who brought their native Calvinism to South Africa. Today more than 90 percent of its membership are Afrikaners. The church includes three white "sister" churches: the Nederduitse Gereformeerde Kerk (NGK), the Nederduitsch Hervormde Kerk (NHK), and the Gereformeerde Kerk (GK). Until recently the church also included three black "daughter" churches: the Nederduitse Gereformeerde Kerk in Afrika (NGKA) for Africans, the Nederduitse Gereformeerde Sendingkerk (NG Sending) for Coloureds, and the Reformed Church in Africa (RCA) for Indians. The black churches have all split from the Dutch Reformed church.
English-speaker	A South African white of British descent for whom English is spoken as a first language.
ferroalloy	Any alloy containing iron.
francophone Africa	French-speaking African nations.
Frontline States	Angola, Botswana, Mozambique, Tanzania, Zambia, and Zimbabwe.
grand apartheid	Government policy designed to create separate, independent states (homelands) for the various African ethnic groups in South Africa.
gray-area goods	Dual-use products such as aircraft, computers, and other electronic and communications equipment that have both military and civilian applications.
Group Areas Act	Legislation that governs ownership and occupation in specified geographic areas according to race.
homelands	Areas designated by the South African government as homes for the various African ethnic groups. The ten homelands are: Bophuthatswana, the Ciskei, Gazankulu, KaNgwane, KwaZulu, Lebowa, Ndebele, Qwaqwa, the Transkei, and Venda.
indirect investment	As used in this report, loans to corporations or other entities for use in South Africa; ownership of a non-controlling stock interest in a business entity operating in South Africa.
influx control	Regulation of the movement of Africans into urban areas.
job reservation	The reservation by law of many skilled jobs for whites.

laager	An encampment protected by a circle of covered wagons.
the Nine	The nine nations that make up the Southern African Development Coordination Conference: Angola, Botswana, Lesotho, Malawi, Mozambique, Swaziland, Tanzania, Zambia, and Zimbabwe.
ninety-nine-year leasehold	A form of land tenure available to "qualified" Africans in certain townships that carries the right to occupy or build houses on designated plots that are leased from the government for a period of ninety-nine years.
parastatals	Corporations controlled and in large measure owned by the South African government.
passbook (*dompas*)	Identity document required to be carried by every African over the age of sixteen.
pass laws	Legislation restricting the movement of Africans by requiring them to carry passbooks.
petty apartheid	Term used to describe the laws and regulations that enforce racial segregation. Petty apartheid includes segregation in public facilities, transportation, sports, hotels, and restaurants.
rand	Unit of South African currency equivalent to U.S. $1.25 on March 31, 1981.
reserves	Former name for the homelands.
Robben Island	Maximum-security prison for political prisoners near Cape Town.
Section 10 rights	A key section of the Black Urban Areas Consolidation Act which regulates the residence and mobility of Africans in urban areas. Section 10 defines the qualifications required for Africans to remain permanently in "white" areas.
total strategy	Prime Minister P. W. Botha's call for military preparedness, economic growth, and political reform to counter South Africa's adversaries.
townships	Designated residential areas for Africans in South Africa, generally located near white cities. The largest township is the *south*west *to*wnship, or Soweto, located near Johannesburg.
trek	Arduous journey; migration.

trekboers	Seminomadic Afrikaner farmers who traveled to the interior of South Africa by ox wagons, often in organized groups, during the eighteenth and nineteenth centuries.
uitlanders	Immigrants; foreigners. Term used by Afrikaners to describe the British subjects who came to work in the Witwatersrand gold fields in the latter part of the nineteenth century.
veld	Open grassland with scattered shrubs and trees.
verkramp, verkrampte	"Narrow-minded" or reactionary.
verlig, verligte	"Enlightened" or reformist.
volk	Nation; people; rank-and-file Afrikaners.
voortrekkers	Literally "forward trekkers"; pioneers; refers to the Afrikaners who left the Cape Colony and took part in the Great Trek of 1834–37.
Western Contact Group	Five Western members of the United Nations Security Council—Canada, France, Great Britain, United States, West Germany—that have worked to bring about a settlement in Namibia.

Abbreviations

AID	Agency for International Development
ALC	African Liberation Committee
ANC	African National Congress
ARMSCOR	Armaments Development and Production Corporation
AZAPO	Azanian People's Organization
BCP	Black Community Programmes
BLS	Botswana, Lesotho, Swaziland
BPA	Black Parents' Association
BPC	Black People's Convention
CCL	commodity control list
CPI	consumer price index
CUSA	Council of Unions of South Africa
ECA	Economic Commission for Africa
EEC	European Economic Community
ESCOM	Electricity Supply Commission
FNLA	National Front for the Liberation of Angola
FOSATU	Federation of South African Trade Unions
FRELIMO	Front for the Liberation of Mozambique
GDP	gross domestic product

GNP	gross national product
HNP	Herstigte Nasionale party
IRRC	Investor Responsibility Research Center
ISCOR	South African Iron and Steel Industrial Corporation
MPLA	Popular Movement for the Liberation of Angola
NSSM 39	National Security Study Memorandum 39
OAU	Organization of African Unity
OECD	Organization for Economic Cooperation and Development
OPEC	Organization of Petroleum Exporting Countries
PAC	Pan-Africanist Congress
PFP	Progressive Federal party
RMA	Rand Monetary Area
SACU	Southern African Customs Union
SADCC	Southern African Development Coordination Conference
SADF	South African Defense Force
SAP	South African Police
SASM	South African Students' Movement
SASO	South African Students' Organization
SASOL	South African Coal, Oil, and Gas Corporation
SOEKOR	Southern Oil Exploration Corporation
SWAPO	South-West African People's Organization
TUCSA	Trade Union Council of South Africa
UNITA	National Union for the Total Independence of Angola
ZANU	Zimbabwe African National Union
ZAPU	Zimbabwe African People's Union

Selected Bibliography

Listed below are some of the published and unpublished sources of written information used by the Commission, its staff, and consultants. Each appears under only one of several broad topic headings, although many are pertinent to several.

The Commission made regular use of a number of newspapers published in the United States and South Africa. Newspapers from the United States included the *New York Times, Washington Post, Christian Science Monitor,* and *Wall Street Journal.* South African newspapers included the *Post* (Transvaal), *Sunday Post, Star, Sunday Times, Rand Daily Mail,* and *Voice.* Others published in the United States, South Africa, and Europe, were also consulted. The *Financial Times,* published in London, was especially useful. The Commission received English translations of editorials from Afrikaans-language newpapers and retained an Afrikaans-speaking consultant who kept it informed of important issues covered in the Afrikaans press.

The Commission regularly consulted specialized journals and periodicals published in the United States and elsewhere. The publications and materials of a number of organizations concerned with southern Africa were also used. Lists of each of these source materials appear below.

The Chatham House Southern Africa project of the Royal Institute of International Affairs, London, generously permitted the Commission to use its unpublished working papers. They were especially important for the Commission's understanding of Western Europe's involvement in South Africa.

JOURNALS AND OTHER PERIODICALS

Africa News
Africa Report
Africa: The International Business, Economic and Political Magazine

Africa Today

African Affairs

African Index

African Studies Review

Financial Mail

Foreign Affairs

Frontline

International Security

Journal of Modern African Studies

Journal of Southern African Affairs

SASH

SECHABA

Social Dynamics

South Africa/Namibia Update

South African Labour Bulletin

Southern Africa

The Economist

The World Today

To the Point

ORGANIZATIONAL PUBLICATIONS

Annual surveys and occasional publications of South African Institute of Race Relations

Company reports of the Investor Responsibility Research Center (IRRC)

Occasional papers of the South African Institute of International Affairs, University of Witwatersrand

South African Yearbook (Annual)

Who's Who in South Africa (1980)

Working papers of the South African Labour and Development Research Unit (SALDRU), University of Cape Town

BOOKS, ARTICLES, AND UNPUBLISHED PAPERS

I. History and Overview

Davenport, T. R. H. *South Africa: A Modern History*. London and Toronto: University of Toronto Press, 1978.

De Kiewiet, C. W. *A History of South Africa: Social and Economic*. Oxford: Clarendon Press, 1941.

Elphick, Richard, and Giliomee, Hermann, eds. *The Shaping of South African Society 1652-1980*. London: Longman, Inc., 1979.

Fredrickson, George M. *White Supremacy: A Comparative Study in American and South African History*. New York: Oxford University Press, 1980.

*Marquard, Leo. *The Peoples and Policies of South Africa*. London: Oxford University Press, 1969

Muller, C. F. J., ed. *Five Hundred Years: A History of South Africa*. Pretoria and Cape Town: Academica, 1969.

Pakenham, Thomas. *The Boer War*. New York: Random House, 1979.

Thompson, Leonard, and Wilson, Monica, eds. *The Oxford History of South Africa*. New York: Oxford University Press, 1969, 1971. 2 volumes.

Thompson, Leonard, ed. *African Societies in Southern Africa*. London: Heinemann, 1979.

II. Apartheid/Separate Development

Adam, Heribert. *Modernizing Racial Domination*. Berkeley: University of California Press, 1971.

Adams, John; Butler, Jeffrey; and Rotberg, Robert. *The Black Homelands of South Africa: The Political and Economic Development of Bophuthatswana and KwaZulu*. Berkeley: University of California Press, 1977.

Brotz, Howard. *The Politics of South Africa: Democracy and Racial Diversity*. London and New York: Oxford University Press, 1977.

Butler, Jeffrey, and Thompson, Leonard, eds. *Change in Contemporary South Africa*. Berkeley: University of California Press, 1975.

*Carter, Gwendolen. *The Politics of Inequality: South Africa Since 1948*. New York: Praeger, 1958.

---

*Denotes those books that are particularly important for an introduction to South Africa.

Carter, Gwendolen, and O'Meara, Patrick, eds. *Southern Africa: The Continuing Crisis*. Bloomington: Indiana University Press, 1979.

Ciskei Commission Report. Pretoria: Conference Associates Ltd., 1980.

Desmond, Cosmas. *The Discarded People: An Account of Resettlement in South Africa*. Harmondsworth, Middlesex: Penguin Books, 1971.

*de St. Jorre, John. *A House Divided: South Africa's Uncertain Future*. New York: Carnegie Endowment for International Peace, 1977.

Dugard, John. *Human Rights and the South African Legal Order*. Princeton: Princeton University Press, 1978.

Duignan, Peter, and Gann, L. H. *South Africa: War, Revolution or Peace?* Stanford: Hoover Institution Press, Stanford University, 1978.

Halberstam, David. "The Fire to Come in South Africa." *The Atlantic Monthly* (May 1980).

Horrell, Muriel. *Laws Affecting Race Relations in South Africa 1948-1976*. Johannesburg: South African Institute of Race Relations, 1978.

Jenkins, Simon. "South Africa, the Great Evasion: A Survey." *The Economist* (June 21, 1980).

Lapchick, Richard. *The Politics of Race and International Sport: The Case of South Africa*. Westport, Connecticut: Greenwood Press, 1975.

Lapchick, Richard, and Urdang, Stephanie. "The Effects of Apartheid on the Employment of Women in South Africa and a History of the Role of Women in the Trade Unions." New York: Background Paper, World Conference of the United Nations Decade for Women: Equality, Development and Peace (June 11, 1980).

Mare, Gerry. *African Population Relocation in South Africa*. Johannesburg: South African Institute of Race Relations, 1980.

Mathews, Anthony S. *Law, Order and Liberty in South Africa*. Berkeley: University of California Press, 1972.

*Price, Robert, and Rosberg, Carl, eds. *The Apartheid Regime: Political Power and Racial Domination*. Berkeley: Institute of International Studies, University of California, 1980.

Rhoodie, Nic, ed. *South African Dialogue*. Johannesburg: McGraw-Hill, 1972.

Rogers, Barbara. *Divide and Rule: South Africa's Bantustans*. London: International Defence and Aid Fund, 1976.

Stultz, Newell, M. *Transkei's Half Loaf: Race Separatism in South Africa*. New Haven: Yale University Press, 1979.

The South African Homelands. Foreign Policy Document No. 1. London: Research Department, Foreign and Commonwealth Office, Great Britain, June 1978.

Wilkins, Roger. "The Heart of Whiteness: A Journey to South Africa," Part I, *Village Voice* (January 14, 1980); Part II, "Thrills and Chills in South Africa" (January 21, 1980); Part III, "South Africa's Empty Promises" (January 28, 1980).

Woods, Donald. "South Africa's Face to the World." *Foreign Affairs* (April 1978).

III. Labor/Economy

Bailey, Martin, and Rivers, Bernard. *Oil Sanctions Against South Africa*. New York: UN Centre Against Apartheid, 1978.

Barber, James, and Spicer, Michael. "Sanctions Against South Africa: Options for the West." *International Affairs* (July 1979).

Clarke, Duncan, and Simkins, Charles. *Structural Unemployment in South Africa*. Pietermaritzburg: University of Natal Press, 1978.

Desmond, Cosmas, and Simkins, Charles, eds. *South African Unemployment: A Black Picture*. Pietermaritzburg: Development Studies Research Group and Agency for Industrial Mission, 1978.

Feit, Edward. *Workers Without Weapons*. Hamden, Connecticut: Archon Books, 1975.

Godson, Roy. *Black Labor as a Swing Factor in South Africa's Evolution*. Washington, D.C.: International Labor Program, Georgetown University, Spring 1979.

Horrell, Muriel. *South African Trade Unionism*. Johannesburg: South African Institute of Race Relations, 1961.

———. *South Africa's Workers*. Johannesburg: South African Institute of Race Relations, 1969.

Houghton, D. Hobart. *The South African Economy*. Cape Town: Oxford University Press, 1964.

The Importance of South African Non-Fuel Mineral Supplies to the United States and Its Allies. Braamfontein: South Africa Minerals Bureau, 1978.

Imports of Minerals from South Africa by the United States and OECD Countries. Prepared for the Committee on Foreign Relations, U.S. Senate. Washington, D.C.: Congressional Research Service, September 1980.

Imrie, Ruth M. *A Wealth of People: The Story of Trade Union Council of South Africa.* Johannesburg: Trade Union Council of South Africa, 1979.

Johnson, Willard. "Why American Firms Must Quit South Africa." *First World* (March-April 1977).

Kahn, E. J. "Annals of International Trade: A Very Emotive Subject." *New Yorker* (May 14, 1979).

Leftwich, Adrian, ed. *South Africa: Economic Growth and Political Change.* London: Allison and Busby, 1974.

Lombard, Jan. *Freedom, Welfare and Order: Thoughts on the Political Co-operation in the Economy of Southern Africa.* Pretoria: Benbo, 1978.

Luckhardt, Ken, and Wall, Brenda. *Organize or Starve: The History of SACTU.* London: Lawrence and Wishant, 1980.

Magubane, Bernard. *The Political Economy of Race and Class in South Africa.* New York: Monthly Review Press, 1979.

Mineral Commodity Summaries, Mineral Industry and Mineral Commodity Profile. Washington, D.C.: U.S. Bureau of Mines, 1980.

Minerals Yearbook, 1978-1979. Washington, D.C.: U.S. Bureau of Mines, 1980.

"Multinationals [in South Africa] a Survey." *Financial Mail* (June 27, 1980).

Nickel, Herman. "The Case for Doing Business in South Africa." *Fortune* (June 19, 1978).

Oppenheimer, Harry. "Why the World Should Continue to Invest in South Africa." Address to the International Monetary Conference, Mexico City, May 22, 1978.

Raiford, William N., et al. "International Credit and South Africa." Washington, D.C.: Congressional Research Service, 1978.

———. "South African Mineral Resources—Importance to the United States and the OECD Countries." Washington, D.C.: Congressional Research Service, 1978.

South Africa: An Appraisal of the Sovereign Risk Criteria. Johannesburg: The Nedbank Economic Unit, 1977.

Spandau, Arnt. *Economic Boycott Against South Africa: Normative and Factual Issues.* Kenwyn: Juta and Company, 1979.

Stockpile Report to the Congress. Washington, D.C.: Federal Energy Management Agency, March 1980.

Prepared for the Committee on Interior and Insular Affairs, U.S. House of Representatives. Washington, D.C.: Subcommittee on Mines and Mining, July 1980.

"Top Companies [in South Africa]." *Financial Mail* (April 25, 1980).

van Rensburg, William. "Mineral Supplies from South Africa—Their Place in World Resources." London: The Economic Intelligence Unit, 1978.

Walker, Ivan, and Weinbren, Ben. *2000 Casualties: A History of Trade Unions and the Labour Movement in the Union of South Africa.* Johannesburg: South African Trade Union Council, 1961.

Webster, Eddie, ed. *Essays in Southern African Labour History.* Johannesburg: Ravan Press, 1978.

Wicker, Tom. "Should American Business Pull Out of South Africa?" *New York Times Magazine* (June 3, 1979).

Wilson, Francis. *Labour in the South African Gold Mines.* Cambridge: The University Press, 1972.

————et al., eds. *Farm Labour in South Africa.* Cape Town: David Phillip, 1977.

IV. White Politics

Adam, Heribert, and Giliomee, Hermann. *Ethnic Power Mobilized: Can South Africa Change?* New Haven: Yale University Press, 1979.

Botha, P. W. "Address at the Carlton Centre." Johannesburg: November 22, 1979.

Johnson, Richard W. *How Long Will South Africa Survive?* New York: Oxford University Press, 1977.

Moodie, Dunbar. *The Rise of Afrikanerdom: Power, Apartheid and the Afrikaner Civil Religion.* Berkeley: University of California Press, 1975.

Munger, Edwin S., ed. *The Afrikaners.* Cape Town: Tafelberg Publishers, 1979.

Starcke, Anna. *Survival: Taped Interviews with South Africa's Power Elite.* Cape Town: Tafelberg Publishers, 1978.

Thompson, Leonard, and Butler, Jeffrey, eds. *Change in Contemporary South Africa.* Berkeley: University of California Press, 1975.

V. Black Politics

Berman, John Kane. *Soweto: Black Revolt, White Reaction.* Johannesburg: Ravan Press, 1978.

Biko, Steve. *I Write What I Like.* San Francisco: Harper and Row, 1978.

Brooks, Alan, and Brickhill, Jeremy. *Whirlwind Before the Storm: The Origins and Development of the Uprising in Soweto and the Rest of South Africa from June to December 1976.* London: International Defence and Aid Fund, 1980.

Buthelezi, Gatsha. *Power Is Ours.* New York: Books in Focus, Inc., 1979.

Gerhart, Gail. *Black Power in South Africa: The Evolution of an Ideology.* Berkeley: University of California Press, 1978.

Hirson, Baruch. *Year of Fire, Year of Ash: The Soweto Revolt: Roots of a Revolution?* London: Zed Press, 1979.

Johns, Sheridan. "Obstacles of Guerrilla Warfare—A South African Case Study." *Journal of Modern African Studies* (1973).

Karis, Thomas, and Carter, Gwendolen, eds. *From Protest to Challenge: A Documentary History of African Politics in South Africa 1882-1965.* Stanford: Hoover Institution Press 1972-1977. Vols. I-IV.

Mandela, Nelson. *No Easy Walk to Freedom.* New York: Basic Books, 1965.

van der Merwe, Hendrik, W., et al. *African Perspectives on South Africa: A Collection of Speeches, Articles and Documents.* Cape Town: David Phillip, 1978.

VI. Education/Health/Housing

Dewar, David, and Ellis, George. *Low Income Housing Policy in South Africa.* Cape Province: Citadel Press, 1979.

Hellmann, Ellen, and Lever, Henry, eds. *Conflict and Progress.* Johannesburg: Macmillan and Company, 1979.

Troup, Freda. *Forbidden Pastures: Education Under Apartheid.* London: International Defence and Aid Fund, 1976.

Westcott, Gill, and Wilson, Francis, eds. *Economics of Health in South Africa,* Vol. I. Johannesburg: Ravan Press, 1979.

VII. South Africa and the International Community

A. United States

Arkhurst, Fredrick S., ed. *U.S. Policy Toward Africa*. New York: Praeger, 1975.

Baker, James; O'Flaherty, Daniel; and de St. Jorre, John. "Full Report/Public Opinion Poll on American Attitudes toward South Africa." New York: Carnegie Endowment for International Peace, 1979.

————. "The American Consensus on South Africa." *Worldview* (October 1979).

Baker, Pauline. "South Africa's Strategic Vulnerabilities: The Citadel Assumption Reconsidered." *The African Studies Review* (September 1977).

Barron, Deborah, and Immerwahr, John. "The Public Views South Africa: Pathways Through a Gathering Storm." *Public Opinion* (January-February 1979).

Bissell, Richard, and Crocker, Chester, eds. *South Africa into the 1980s*. Boulder: Westview Press, 1979.

Bowman, Larry. "South Africa's Southern Strategy and Its Implications for the United States." *International Affairs* (January 1971).

Committee on Foreign Affairs, House of Representatives. *U.S. Policy Toward South Africa*. Washington, D.C.: U.S. Government Printing Office, 1980.

Committee on Foreign Relations, United States Senate. *U.S. Corporate Interests in South Africa*. Washington, D.C.: U.S. Government Printing Office, 1978.

Crocker, Chester. "South Africa: Strategy for Change." *Foreign Affairs* (Winter 1980/1981).

El-Khawas, Mohamed A., and Cohen, Barry, eds. *National Security Study Memorandum 39: The Kissinger Study of Southern Africa*. Westport, Connecticut: Lawrence Hill and Company, 1976.

Ferguson, Clyde, and Cotter, William. "South Africa: What Is to Be Done?" *Foreign Affairs* (January 1978).

Foltz, William. *Elite Opinion on United States Policy Toward Africa*. New York: Council on Foreign Relations, 1979.

————. "United States Policy Toward Southern Africa: Economic and Strategic Constraints." *Political Science Quarterly* (Spring 1977).

Jackson, Henry. "A Policy with No Plan." *Black Enterprise* (April 1979).

Kitchen, Helen A., ed. *Options for U.S. Policy Toward Africa*. Washington, D.C.: American Enterprise Institute for Public Policy Research, 1979.

Lake, Anthony. "Caution and Concern: The Making of American Policy Toward South Africa 1946-1971." Ph.D. dissertation, Princeton University, 1974.

Lemarchand, Rene, ed. *American Policy in Southern Africa: The Stakes and the Stance*. Washington, D.C.: University Press of America, 1978.

Munger, Edwin S. *Notes on the Formation of South African Foreign Policy*. Pasadena: Castle Press, 1965.

Myers, Desaix. *Labor Practices of U.S. Corporations in South Africa*. New York: Praeger, 1977.

—— et al. *U.S. Business in South Africa: The Economic, Political and Moral Issues*. Bloomington: Indiana University Press, 1980.

Nielsen, Waldemar A. *The Great Powers and Africa*. New York: Praeger, 1969.

Nyerere, Julius. "America and Southern Africa." *Foreign Affairs* (July 1977).

Ottaway, David. "Africa: U.S. Policy Eclipse." *Foreign Affairs* (January 1980). Annual Review.

Rogers, Barbara. *White Wealth and Black Poverty: American Investments in Southern Africa*. Westport, Connecticut: Greenwood Press, 1976.

Seidman, Ann and Neva. *South Africa and U.S. Multinational Corporations*. Westport, Connecticut: Lawrence Hill and Company, 1977.

Seiler, John. "The Formulation of U.S. Policy Toward Southern Africa 1957-1976: The Failure of Good Intentions." Ph.D. dissertation, University of Connecticut, 1976.

"South Africa Under Botha." *Foreign Policy* (Spring 1980). Three articles: Rotberg, Robert I., "How Deep the Change"; Myers, Desaix, and Liff, David, "The Press of Business"; Robinson, Randall, "Investments in Tokenism."

Western Massachusetts Association of Concerned African Scholars, eds. *U.S. Military Involvement in Southern Africa*. Massachusetts: South End Press, 1978.

Whitaker, Jennifer, ed. *Africa and the United States: Vital Interests*. New York: New York University Press, 1978.

B. The West and South Africa (excluding the United States)

Barber, James. *South Africa's Foreign Policy 1945-1970*. London: Oxford University Press, 1973.

Decter, Moshe. "Arms Traffic with South Africa: Who Is Guilty?" New York: American Jewish Congress, 1976.

Geldenhuys, D. J. "South Africa and the West." *In South Africa: Public Policy Perspective,* edited by Robert Schrire. Cape Town: Juta and Company, 1980.

"On the Dawn of Shalom: Israel," *Financial Mail* (September 14, 1979).

Stevens, Richard, and Elmessiri, Abdelwahab. *Israel and South Africa: The Progression of a Relationship.* New York: New World Press, 1976.

United Nations Centre Against Apartheid. *Relations Between Israel and South Africa.* New York: Report of the United Nations Special Committee Against Apartheid, 1977.

C. South Africa and Sub-Saharan Africa

Akinyemi, A. B., and Vogt, Margaret. "Nigeria and Southern Africa: The Policy Options." Conference paper, Conflict and Change in Southern Africa: Scandinavian and Canadian Perspectives and Policy Options. Ottawa: Carleton University, 1978.

Barratt, John. "Southern Africa: A South African View." *Foreign Affairs* (October 1976).

Breytenbach, W. J. "South Africa's Involvement in Africa." Occasional paper No. 42. Pretoria: Africa Institute of South Africa, 1978.

Burgess, Julian. *Interdependence in Southern Africa: Trade and Transport Links in South, Central and East Africa.* Special Report No. 32. London: Economist Intelligence Unit, 1976.

The Frontline States: The Burden of the Liberation Struggle. London: Commonwealth Secretariat, 1978.

Gordon, Robert J. *Mines, Masters and Migrants: Life in a Namibian Mine Compound.* Johannesburg: Ravan Press, 1977.

Leistner, G. M. E. "Economic Interdependence in Southern Africa." *Africa Institute of South Africa Bulletin* (October 1978).

D. South Africa and the Communist World

Albright, David, ed. *Communism in Africa.* Bloomington: Indiana University Press, 1980.

Dominguez, Jorge. "Political and Military Consequences of Cuban Policies in Africa." *Cuban Studies* (July 1980).

Legum, Colin. "The Soviet Union, China, and the West in Southern Africa." *Foreign Affairs* (July 1976).

LeoGrande, William. *Cuba's Policy in Africa 1959-1980*. Policy Papers in International Affairs No. 13. Berkeley: Institute of International Studies, University of California, 1980.

Rothenburg, Morris. *The U.S.S.R. and Africa: New Dimensions of Soviet Global Power*. Washington, D.C.: Advanced International Studies Institute, 1980.

Biographies of the Study Commission and Selected Staff

Commission

Robert Crocker Good   President, Denison University, since 1976. Received Ph.D. international relations, Yale University, 1956. Assistant professor international relations, Social Science Fund, University of Denver, 1953-58; research associate, Washington Center for Foreign Policy Research, 1958-61; director, Carnegie Endowment Seminars in Diplomacy, Washington, 1960-61; director, President-Elect Kennedy's Task Force on Africa, 1960; director, Office of Research and Analysis, Africa Bureau, Intelligence and Research, Department of State, 1961; U.S. ambassador to Zambia, 1965-69; dean, Graduate School of International Studies, University of Denver, 1970-76; consultant and/or member of board, Center Global Perspectives, 1974-, Global Perspectives in Education, 1975-, Patterson School of International Diplomacy and Commerce, University of Kentucky, 1975-77; external board of governors, National University, Lesotho, Roma, 1977-. President, Neighbors, Inc. (Washington, D.C.), 1961-65. Kent fellow, 1951; recipient, Superior Honor Award, Department of State, 1964. Member, American Political Science Association, International African Studies Associations, Social Values in Higher Education. Author: *Congo Crisis: The Role of the New States* (1961); *U.D.I.: The International Politics of the Rhodesian Rebellion* (1973). Co-author: *Alliance Policy in the Cold War* (1959); *Neutralism and Non-alignment: The New States in World Affairs* (1962); *The Mission of the Christian Church in the Modern World* (1962); *Foreign Policy in the Sixties: Issues and Instrumentalities* (1965). Co-editor: *Reinhold Niebuhr on Politics* (1960).

Charles Vernon Hamilton Professor of Political Science, Columbia University, since 1969. Received Ph.D. University of Chicago, 1964. Faculty member, Albany State College, 1957-58, Tuskegee Institute, 1958-60, Rutgers University, 1963-64, Lincoln University (Pa.), 1964-67; professor and chairman, Department of Political Science, Roosevelt University (Chicago), 1967-69. Served with U.S. Army, 1948-49. Charles Merriam fellow, University of Chicago, 1961-62; John Hay Whitney fellow, 1962-63; recipient, Lindback Distinguished Teaching Award, Lincoln University, 1965; alumni awards, University of Chicago, 1970. Member, American Political Science Association, NAACP. Author: *Minority Politics in Black Belt Alabama* (1962); (with Stokley Carmichael) *Black Power: The Politics of Liberation in America* (1967); *The Black Preacher in America* (1972); *The Bench and the Ballot* (1973); *The Black Experience in American Politics* (1973).

Ruth Simms Hamilton Professor of sociology and racial and ethnic studies, and associate director, African Studies Center, Michigan State University. Received Ph.D. Northwestern University, 1966. Current research: Return Rural Migration in Ghana; Women in Economic Development in Ghana; Theory and Research Publication on the African Diaspora. Author: *Racial Conflict, Discrimination and Power: Historical and Contemporary Studies* (1976). Editor: *African Urban Studies.*

Alexander Heard Chancellor and professor of political science, Vanderbilt University, since 1963. Received Ph.D. Columbia University, 1951. U.S. government service in departments of interior, war, and state, 1939-43; research associate, Bureau of Public Administration, University of Alabama, 1946-49; research associate/professor, Institute of Research in Social Science, University of North Carolina, 1950-58, associate professor/ professor of political science, 1950-63, dean, graduate school, 1958-63. Director, Time, Inc., 1968. Chairman, President's Commission on Campaign Costs, 1961-62; special adviser to the president on campus affairs, 1970. Delegate, county and state Democratic conventions, 1952-62; member, State Democratic Congressional District Executive Committee, 1954-56. President, board of directors, Citizen's Research Foundation, 1958-71; member, U.S. Advisory Commission on Intergovernmental Relations, 1967-69. Trustee, Ford Foundation, 1967-, chairman, 1972-; trustee, Robert A. Taft Institute of Government, 1973-76; public trustee, Nutrition Foundation, 1976-; council member, Rockefeller University, 1977-. Served to lieutenant, U.S. Naval Reserve, 1943-46. Member, International, American, and Southern Political Science Associations, American Association of University Professors, Association of American Universities, American Academy of Arts and Sciences. Author: (assistant to V. O. Key, Jr.) *Southern Politics in State and Nation* (1949); (with Donald S. Strong)

Southern Primaries and Elections (1950); *A Two Party South?* (1952); *The Costs of Democracy* (1960).

Aileen Clarke Hernandez   Urban consultant, San Francisco. Received M.A. Los Angeles State College, 1961. Co-chair, National Urban Coalition; trustee, the Urban Institute; chair, California Council for the Humanities in Public Policy; chair, advisory committee on the Rights and Responsibilities of Women to the Secretary of HEW; member, Equal Employment Opportunity Commission, 1965-66; national president, NOW, 1970-71; member, California Commission for Federal Judiciary Appointments, 1977-78; board member, Ms. Foundation for Women, Inc. 1975-; ACLU National Advisory Council. Recipient, Charter Day Award for Alumni Postgraduate Achievement, Howard University; Honorary Doctorate of Humane Letters, Southern Vermont College, 1979; a *San Francisco Examiner* Bay Area Distinguished Woman, 1968; State Department Labor Specialist in Latin America, 1961; Konrad Adenauer Foundation guest lecturer, Bonn, Germany, 1975; Women's Rights Tour, People's Republic of China, 1978.

Constance Bernette Hilliard   International director, Booker T. Washington Foundation, 1979-. Received Ph.D Harvard University, 1977. Visiting fellow, Princeton University, 1975. Executive director, African-American Scholars Council, Inc. (Washington, D.C.), 1976-79. Scholar in Islamic studies, fluency in Arabic and French. Member, African Studies Association.

Charles Peter McColough   Chairman and chief executive officer, Xerox Corporation, since 1971. Received LL.B. Dalhousie University, 1947; M.B.A. Harvard, 1949. Vice-president of sales, Lehigh Coal Navigation Company (Philadelphia), 1951-54; joined Xerox Corporation in 1954; director, Rank Xerox Ltd. (London), Fuji-Xerox Company Ltd., Citicorp N.Y., Citibank N.A. Member, steering committee, National Committee on Full Employment. Trustee, Committee for Economic Development, University of Rochester; chairman, executive committee, International Executive Service Corps; board of directors, Council for Financial Aid to Education, Rehabilitation International, U.S.A., Overseas Development Council, Joint U.S.-USSR Trade and Economic Council; vice-chairman, United Way of America; chairman, United Way of Tri-State Industries; advisory committee, Advertising Council; advisory member, overseers committee, Harvard Graduate School of Business Administration; member, advisory board, Yale University. Member, International Chamber of Commerce, Council on Foreign Relations, Business Council, Business Committee for Arts, Business Roundtable.

J. Irwin Miller   Chairman, Executive and Finance Committee, Cummins Engine Company (Columbus, Indiana), since 1951. Received B.A. Yale   **493**

University, 1931; M.A. Oxford University (England), 1933. Joined Cummins Engine Company in 1934; president, Irwin-Union Bank & Trust Company, 1947-54, chairman, 1954-75; director, American Telephone & Telegraph Company; member, Commission on Money and Credit, Business Council, Conference Board, President's Committee on Postal Reorganization (1968), President's Committee on Urban Housing (1968); chairman, President's Commission on Trade Relations with Soviet Union and Eastern European Nations, 1965; chairman, National Advisory Commission on Health Manpower, 1966; vice-chairman, UN Commission on Multinational Corporations, 1974; advisory council, U.S. Department of Commerce, 1976. President, National Council of Churches of Christ in the U.S.A., 1960-63; member, central and executive committees, World Council of Churches, 1967-68. Trustee, Ford Foundation, Yale University, 1959-77, Urban Institute, 1966-76. Assistant fellow, Branford College. Recipient, Rosenberger Award, University of Chicago, 1977. Served to lieutenant, U.S. Naval Reserve, 1942-44.

Alan Pifer   President, Carnegie Corporation of New York, since 1967. Received B.A. Harvard College, 1947. Executive secretary, U.S. Educational Commission in United Kingdom (London), 1948-53; joined Carnegie Corporation in 1953; vice-president to president, Carnegie Foundation for Advancement of Teaching, 1963-. Director, McGraw-Hill, Inc. Member, Management Committee, U.S.-South Africa Leadership Exchange Program, 1957-; chairman, Mayor's Advisory Commission, Board of Higher Education, N.Y.C., 1966-69; chairman, President's Task Force on Education, 1968-69; member, advisory council, Columbia School of Social Work, 1963-69; director, N.Y. Urban Coalition, 1967-71; National Assembly Social Policy and Development, 1967-71; member, Senior Executives Council Conference Board, 1973-74; member, Commission on Private Philanthropy and Public Needs, 1973-75. Trustee, Foundation Library Center, 1967-70, chairman, 1968-70; trustee, African-American Institute, 1957-72, University of Bridgeport (Conn.), 1973-, American Ditchley Foundation, 1973-; board of directors, Council on Foundations, 1970-76; board of overseers, Harvard University, 1969-75; member, President's Commission on White House Fellowships, 1975-77. Served to captain, U.S. Army, 1942-46. Fellow, American Academy of Arts and Sciences; member, Council on Foreign Relations.

Howard David Samuel   President, Industrial Union Department, AFL-CIO. Received B.A. Dartmouth College, 1948. Various positions, Amalgamated Clothing and Textile Workers, 1949-60, assistant to the president, 1960-64, vice-president, 1966-77; departmental undersecretary, Bureau of International Labor Affairs, Department of Labor, 1977-79; vice-president, New School for Social Research, 1964-65; executive director, Sidney Hillman Foundation, 1951-77; vice-chairman, New York Urban Coalition,

1969-74; member, governing body, Common Cause, 1971-77; secretary, National Commission on Full Employment, 1975-77. Member, National Manpower Advisory Committee, 1969-74; Commission on Population Growth and the American Future, 1970-72; National Democratic Charter Revision Committee, 1972-73. Executive director, National Labor Committee, McGovern-Shriver, 1972; delegate, Democratic Convention, 1976; trustee, Carnegie Corporation, 1971-77; trustee, Joint Council Economic Education, 1971-77; board of directors, American Civil Liberties Union, 1966-68. Served with U.S. Army, 1943-46. Author: (with Stephen K. Bailey) *Congress at Work* (1952), *Government in America* (1957). Editor: *Toward a Better America* (1968).

Franklin Augustine Thomas President, Ford Foundation. Received B.A. Columbia College, 1956; LL.B. Columbia University, 1963. Attorney, Federal Housing and Home Finance Agency (N.Y.C.), 1963-64; assistant U.S. attorney for Southern District, New York, 1964-65; deputy police commissioner in charge of legal matters, N.Y.C., 1965-67; president and chief executive officer, Bedford Stuyvesant Restoration Corporation (Brooklyn), 1967-77. Director/trustee, various business and charitable organizations, including Citicorp/Citibank, CBS, Inc., Alcoa, Cummins Engine Company, J.H. Whitney Foundation, Columbia University (1969-75), Ford Foundation. Navigator, U.S. Air Force, Strategic Air Command, 1956-60. LBJ Foundation Award for contribution to betterment of urban life, 1974, Medal of Excellence, Columbia University, 1976.

STAFF

John de St. Jorre Senior writer. B.A. history, Oxford University, 1959. Commissioned in the British Army, fought in Malaya in the mid-1950s. Served in the British Foreign Service in the Congo, Kenya, Somalia, Burundi, and Togo, 1959-65. Appointed *London Observer* correspondent for Africa, 1966-68; for Paris, 1969; for the Middle East, 1973. Joined Carnegie Endowment for International Peace, 1975. Currently on leave from the *London Observer*. Author: *The Brothers' War: Biafra and Nigeria* (1972); *A House Divided: South Africa's Uncertain Future* (1977). Articles, essays, and reviews for *Foreign Affairs, Foreign Policy,* the *New York Times Magazine,* the *Washington Post,* et al.

Marc Fasteau Staff director and general counsel. B.A. cum laude Harvard College, 1963; M.A. American history, Georgetown University, 1966; J.D. magna cum laude Harvard Law School, 1969. Editor, *Harvard Law Review.* Served on professional staffs of House of Representatives Banking and Currency Committee; Joint Economic Committee of Congress; and Senator Mike Mansfield, 1963-66. Research fellow in law and social policy, John F. Kennedy Institute of Politics, Harvard University, 1969-70. Prior to joining the Study Commission was in the private practice of law in New York City.

Milfred C. Fierce   Research director. B.A. and M.S. Wagner College (Staten Island, New York); M.A., M.Phil., Ph.D. U.S. History, Columbia University. Taught at Vassar and Hunter colleges. Prior to joining staff of Study Commission, served as executive director of the Association of Black Foundation Executives, Inc. Currently on leave from Hunter College (CUNY).

Paul Lancaster   Senior writer. B.A. DePauw University, 1952; M.A. University of Wisconsin, 1955. National reporter, the *Wall Street Journal,* 1955-60; front-page features staff, 1960-67; features reporter on South Africa, Rhodesia, Kenya, Uganda, 1966; front-page features editor, 1967-70; features editor, 1970-71. Free-lance writer, 1971-; articles for the *Wall Street Journal,* the *New York Times, Fortune, American Heritage,* et al. Returned to South Africa in 1972 to write an article on General Motors. Writer and editor for McKinsey and Company, Consultants, 1972; editor and publisher, *Nantucket* magazine, 1974-75; member, *Fortune* task force, 1977; writer, researcher, *American Heritage,* 1977-80.

Linda Potter   Assistant to the chair. B.S., School of Foreign Service, Georgetown University, 1977. Prior to joining staff of Study Commission, served as consultant for the Rockefeller Foundation; intern with *Foreign Policy* magazine, the Supreme Court Historical Society, and Senator Edward M. Kennedy.

Index

503

J

Jacobs, Professor Gideon, on lack of skilled workers, 144

Japan
investment in South Africa by, 302, 306–307
policy toward apartheid of, 301–302
South Africa and, 301, 306–307
South African trade with, 137, 302, 306–307
strategic minerals stoppage vulnerability of, 320–321

Jessup, Phillip, 349

Johannesburg, 103, 109, 123
contrasted with Soweto, 101–102

Johannesburg *Star,* 220

Johannesburg Stock Exchange, 174

Jonathan, Chief Leabua, 294

Johnson administration, 413–414

Johnson, Lyndon, South Africa and, 349–350

Johnson, R. W., on Russian submarines' blockage of Cape sea routes, 330

K

Kane-Berman, John
on Soweto, 101
on Soweto uprising, 168

Karis, Thomas G., on Soweto uprising, 168

Kaunda, Kenneth, xiii, 296, 325, 335, 354
on South African change, xxi

Kellogg, 98

Kennedy, John, South Africa and, 347–349

Khoikhoi, 26
Dutch East India Company and, 33
early colonists and, 33
Protestant missionaries and, 34
Khomeini, Ayatollah, Iran's oil exports to South Africa stopped by, 140

Kissinger, Henry, xiv
on Rhodesia, 354
South Africa and, 350–351, 353–355
on South African racial discrimination, 393

Knowles, John, xiv

Koornhof, Pieter, 106–107, 191, 195, 204, 212, 218
as leftist Nationalist, 208
on petty apartheid, 61
sports events permits and, 65–66

Kotze, Reverend Theo, on economic sanctions, 187–188

Kruger, James, on un-South Africanism, 183

Kruger, Paul, Boer War and, 30

L

Labor bureaus, 82–83

Latin America, South Africa and, 308–309

League of Nations, 30

Legal Resources Center, 440

Lesotho, 288, 290–292, 294
transport through South Africa and, 289

Lesotho Communist party, 326

Lever, Henry, on South African public opinion, 224

Levin, Bernard, on Steve Biko, 183

Lewis, Anthony
on civil liberties, 67
on "ideological symmetry" in human rights policy, 393

Liberal party, 56, 173, 175

Liberation Committee (OAU), 298

Liberia, 341, 349
South Africa and, 295

Libya, xvii
West German oil imports from, 304

Liquor Act, 64–65

Little, Arthur D., and Company, 97

Lombard Plan, 164

Lurgi, 304

Luthuli, Chief Albert, 176

M

Machel, Samora, 334, 355

Madagascar, South Africa and, 295

Malan, Daniel Francois, 40–41, 171
NATO and, 343–344

Malan, Magnus, 211–212, 214, 218, 235–236
business sector and, 216
on SADF, 244

Malawi, 288, 291, 295

East Germany and, 334–335
Guerrilla presence in, 237
transport through South Africa and, 289–290
USSR and, 324, 326, 328
Mozambique Resistance Movement, 138
Mphephu, Chief Patrick, 155, 160
MPLA, *see* Popular Front for the Liberation of Angola
Mugabe, Robert, 331, 335, 355, 445
on South Africa, 288
USSR and, 325
Zimbabwe and, 191
Muhammed, General Murtala, 298
Mulder, Connie, 78*n*, 212, 214, 218, 352
Muzorewa, Bishop Abel, Zimbabwe and, 191
Myers III, Desaix, on U.S. firms in South Africa, 96

N

Namibia, xvii, xix, 241–246, 290–292, 295–296, 298–299, 324–325, 328, 332, 334, 336–337, 340, 350, 352, 357–358, 400, 423
France and, 304
United Kingdom and, 304
United States and, 363–365
West Germany and, 304
Nasionale Pers chain, 221
Natal
Great Trek to, 27, 29
reserves in early, 34–35
Natal Chamber of Commerce, on skilled labor shortage, 144
Natal Native Affairs Commission, 343
National Aeronautics and Space Administration (U.S.), 347
National African Federated Chambers of Commerce, 198
National Front for the Liberation of Angola (FNLA), 326, 331, 353
China and, 336
National Materials and Minerals Policy Research and Development Act, 452
National News, 41
National party, xx, 40, 171, 185, 190, 201, 343, 357, 359, 395–398
African education and, 114–118
apartheid and, 48–66

apartheid as slogan of, 40
Chief Buthelezi and, 194–195
economic relations with black African states and, 294
efforts to devolve political power to homeland governments, 153–157
employment and, 82, 84, 86, 93
housing and, 102–104
leadership of, 207–208
majority in Parliament won by, 41
organization of, 207
political system and, 54–56
on separate development, 149–150, 166
white rule and, 207–208
National Security Study Memorandum 39, 350–352
National Supplies Procurement Act, 143
National Union for the Total Independence of Angola (UNITA), 241, 331, 353
China and, 336
National Union of Clothing Workers, 88
National Union of South African Students, 43, 73, 176
Native Lands Act, 103, 148
Native Laws Amendment Act, 82
Native Military Corps, 245
Native Trust and Land Act, 148
Native Urban Areas Act, 82, 102–104, 105
Natives' Representative Council, 39, 41, 170
NATO, *see* North Atlantic Treaty Organization
Nattrass, Jill, 133
Naude, Beyers, 183, 187, 231
New Republic party, 209
New Statesman, 302
Newson, David, 352
Newspapers, white rule and, 220–221
Nigeria, xvii, 353–354, 357
British trade with, 303
French purchases of uranium from, 306
French trade with, 304
leadership among African nations of, 298–300
West German oil imports from, 304
Nixon administration, South Africa and, 350–353

to assist economic development of other states in southern Africa, xxvii, xxix, 389, 410, 444–445

to make clear opposition of United States to apartheid, xxv–xxvi, xxviii, 388, 410–412

to promote genuine power sharing in South Africa, xxvi, xxviii, 388, 410, 432–433

to reduce impact of stoppages of key minerals from South Africa, xxvii, xxix, 389, 410, 449–450

U.S.S. *Franklin Delano Roosevelt* affair, 350

U.S.-South African Leader Exchange Program, 443

U.S. State Department, on Sharpeville shootings, 174

U.S. Trade and Development Program (TDP), 448–449

University of Stellenbosch Bureau for Economic Research, 136

Unlawful Organizations Act, 73, 173

Urban Bantu Councils, 55, 185, 191

Urban Foundation, 96–98, 106–107, 112, 217, 396, 399, 440

Urban Foundation standards, 96–98

V

van den Bergh, General Hendrik, 214

van Zyl Slabbert, Frederik, on role of Progressive Federal party, 210

Vanadium, 310–312, 316–317

U.S. potential self-sufficiency in, 311, 316

U.S. stockpiles of, 316, 319

Vance, Cyrus, xiv, 356

on influencing nations to adopt democratic values, 392

Verkramptes, 227–232, 395, 397–398

as ideological hard-liners, 229

Verligtes, 227–232, 395, 397–398

as "pragmatic centrists," 228–229

Verligte "reform," versus genuine reform, 231–232

Verwoerd, Hendrik, xx,172, 176, 294,348

assassination of, 211

on black education, 117

and homelands
"independence," 211
policy, 50
spending, 161–162

National party power structure and, 207

on separate development, 149

Viljoen, Gerritt, 120, 212

Volkswagen, 304

strikes at, 87

Vorster, John, 50, 78*n*, 89, 218, 295, 354–355, 357–360, 363

bureaucracy and, 213–214

business sector and, 216

delegation of authority by, 211–212

Desmond Tutu and, 181

homelands spending and, 162

W

Waldheim, Kurt, 364

Waring, Frank, 209

Washington, Booker T., 170

Watson, Cheeky, 65

Wells, L. G.

on correlation between poverty and poor health, 125

on government resources for curative services, 126

West Germany

on apartheid, 301

education of blacks in South Africa and, 123

as employer in South Africa, 96

investment in South Africa by, 133–134, 301, 304–305

Libyan oil exports to, 304

Namibia and, 304

Nigerian oil exports to, 304

South Africa and, 303–305

South African trade with, 137, 301, 304

UN arms embargo and, 301

Western Contact Group, 363–364

Western Europe

investment in South Africa by, 301

South Africa and, 301–306

White electorate

Afrikaner-English opinion among, 222–224

policy implications of opinions of, 224–227